I0129144

Anonymus

Illustrated Boston

The metropolis of New England

Anonymus

Illustrated Boston
The metropolis of New England

ISBN/EAN: 9783741166600

Manufactured in Europe, USA, Canada, Australia, Japa

Cover: Foto ©Thomas Meinert / pixelio.de

Manufactured and distributed by brebook publishing software
(www.brebook.com)

Anonymus

Illustrated Boston

ILLUSTRATED BOSTON

THE METROPOLIS OF NEW ENGLAND

CONTAINING ALSO

REVIEWS OF ITS PRINCIPAL ENVIRONS

SECOND EDITION

PUBLISHED BY
AMERICAN PUBLISHING AND ENGRAVING CO.
102 CHAMBERS STREET
NEW YORK

INTRODUCTORY.

NATION'S growth is centred in the freedom of its institutions, the multiplication and expansion of its workshops and factories, and the increase of its commercial establishments and facilities. Herein lie the attractions to the sons and daughters of other nations where freedom is restrained, despotism paramount, and commerce crippled, to come and abide with us and help us to build up this grand Republic into the greatest and most powerful nation the world has known.

Upon the historian rests the responsibility of chronicling the progress and achievements of communities from age to age, and of conveying to present and oncoming generations a faithful representation of the times in which he lives. The publishers of this volume have been actuated by a desire to place before the readers of these pages, not merely an account of Boston as it was in the past, but as it exists to-day—with its vast emporiums of commerce; its thousands of industrial establishments; its hundreds of wharves, to and from which the merchantmen belonging to all the countries of the world come and go; its half a million of people, representing every nation and tongue; its halls of learning; its institutions for the cultivation of the arts and dissemination of the sciences; its charitable associations and religious edifices; its beautiful parks and drives; its memorials of by-gone heroes by flood and field; its improvements over the past, in buildings and thoroughfares; its civic government; and its attainment to the distinction of the manufacturing and commercial metropolis of New England.

To every American citizen, some knowledge of the history of his country, and of its leading cities, is indispensable; and in the compiling of this work, telling of the origin of the second city founded on American soil, of its subsequent growth and present status, the publishers believe that they have not been uselessly employed, and that the reader will rise from the perusal of its pages with an increased knowledge of Boston and its progressive people. This book is intended for the average American; for the manufacturer and merchant, who have neither time nor disposition to plod through ten or twenty volumes of elaborate historical dissertations; for the practical man of the shop, the counter, and the plough. The story of the coming of the first settlers to the pear-shaped peninsula on which they began the building up of the present giant city of Boston is briefly but interesting.y told; the great work of converting that which was but a narrow neck connecting the city to the mainland, into what is now the broadest part of the municipality, is adequately described; the valiant deeds of the forefathers, who sounded the tocsin and fired the first guns of the Revolution; have been concisely but faithfully related, and old landmarks pointed out. But the ambition of the authors has been to give a pen-picture, with beautiful new illustrations, of the city as it is in this year of grace 1889; to tell of the character of its multifarious manufactures, and of its miscellaneous commerce; and to make the reader acquainted with its representative business men, who have won fame for themselves and made the name of Boston known and honored in all the corners of the earth.

The data given touching the various business enterprises have been drawn from the most authentic sources, have been carefully collated and intelligently revised; and the utmost care has been exercised in order that the

with regard to a community so useful and progressive in trade and manufactures as Boston is should be as widely diffused as possible. While it is not claimed that the work is free from imperfections and shortcomings, it is confidently asserted that no previous publication of a like character has contained so much new and valuable points for reference. The preparation of the work has needed much labor, patience, and perseverance; but, great as the task has been, the drudgery of compilation has been shorn of unpleasantness by the universal courtesy extended to us, and the cheerful manner in which information has been afforded wherever it was applied for. Without such help, this work could not have been issued in the form in which it now is. To so many are our thanks due, that it would be impossible to tender them individually; and though we do so collectively, our sincerity of appreciation of favors received is none the less.

Designed for distribution among persons residing in other localities, as well as among the citizens of Boston, and especially among those who are unacquainted with the real magnitude of the city and its extraordinary manufacturing and mercantile facilities, we are assured that this work will perform a mission of the highest utility. It is dedicated to the manufacturer, the merchant, the household, and to the libraries of the rich and of the poor. It is inscribed to the business man, to the father, the mother, the son, and the daughter of the American family. If the man of business, the father, mother, son, and daughter shall be more proud of their ancient city, the "Athens of the New World," and love it and their country better, if they shall understand more clearly and appreciate more fully the founding, progress, and growth of liberty in the New World, and be brought to a more perfect knowledge of the giant strides that are being made in manufactures and commerce in the capital of the Old Bay State, the publishers will be abundantly repaid.

THE PUBLISHERS.

GENERAL INDEX.

v

ILLUSTRATED

UNIV. OF CALIFORNIA

BOSTON

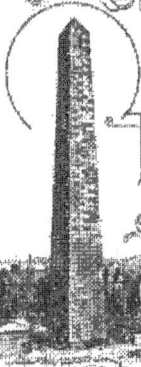

THE METROPOLIS OF NEW ENGLAND.

BOSTON, from whatever point of the compass approached,— whether by any of the eight railway lines which radiate from it as a centre; or by the numerous broad, well-kept highways that cleave the fragrant gardens and verdant pastures of its vicinage on the land sides; or by the ocean, whose shimmering waves dash and spend their force against the numerous wooden wharves which skirt the shore,— presents one object—a golden one, flashing in the rays of the hot summer sun, or dully glimmering under the fleecy winter sky—that arrests the attention of the traveller. It is a gilded dome, towering above all the thousands of buildings that cluster around it. It is the pivot of industrial, cultured, and fashionable Boston: in the characteristic language of Dr. Oliver Wendell Holmes, it is "the hub of the solar system,"—whence Boston's *sobriquet*, "The Hub." While from every side of the city this gold-leaf-covered cupola is seen to stand out prominently like a tall monarch overlooking ambitious minions compactly crowded on gentle slopes, its interior, which is open to visitors at certain seasons of the year, commands a view of unsurpassed grandeur. It is a vantage-ground from which the

eye can encompass the outlay and form of the city; the deep blue sea, dotted with innumerable islands and sailing craft of every kind, and stretching out to the level eastern horizon, whence tho sun meets the sky; tho picturesque Blue Hills of Milton and tho rocky heights of Essex; tho scores of white villages, towns, and hamlets, strewn, as it were, at random, and interlineated with tortuous rivers, like so many silvery belts; and the dark, wide-spreading forests which form the background of a beautiful landscape stretching to the westward sky line.

This "hub of the solar system" is tho dome of Massachusetts' capitol, which stands on Boston's highest ground, tho breezy crest of Beacon Hill, whereon for more than fourscore years "the wise men and foolish, noble men and petty," constituted by tho suffrages of the people "The Great and General Court," have managed and mismanaged the public affairs of the State, and influenced more or less the greater and more important national councils.

BEACON HILL

and its immediate surroundings are rich in historic associations. Historians tell of a time when there was only one solitary log but nestling on the breast of this far-famed hill, and of this being the only habitation on the whole of Boston's domain. It was the abode of an eccentric gospel minister, the Rev. William Blackstone, who, after fleeing from the haunts of men in old England, sought seclusion here. He it was who first purchased from the Indians the entire peninsula on which Boston now stands. At this time there were three hills on the peninsula, and these had given to them the name of Treamount, while the whole peninsula was designated Trimountaine, instead of Mushanwomuk, as called by the Indians, and since abbreviated to Shawmut. Mushauwomuk is variously assumed to have signified in the Indian tongue "living fountains," "free land," and "land unclaimed." These hills came to be separately known as Beacon, Copp's, and Fort Hills. Beacon Hill, however, had three peaks, and some writers claim that the name Treamount was derived from this fact. In 1633, Wood, the voyager, wrote of Beacon Hill as "three little hills on top of a high mountain." Blackstone's hut was situated near Pinckney and West Cedar Streets. East of the hut was the clergyman's garden; and a spring, from which he drew his water supply, and which proved to be the earliest inducement to the founders of New England's metropolis to come and settle here, was not far from the centre of the grass plat in the present enclosure of Louisburg Square.

A number of people from Dorchester, England, had in 1628 purchased the territory now known as the Massachusetts Bay State Colony. They were one of two parties of dissenters — Puritans and Separatists — from the Episcopal Church of England, and the laws of Britain made it a crime to worship God in any other form than that prescribed by this church, by law established. The religious dissenters, who came to the old Bay State for conscience' sake, were Puritans, who lamented the evils in the church, and hoped to reform it from within. The pilgrims who settled in the neighboring colony of Plymouth, about thirty miles from Boston, in 1620, were Separatists, who, believing Episcopalianism utterly corrupt, came off from it. The Puritans were a strait-laced sect, and came to the new colony accompanied by John Winthrop as their Governor, and by Thomas Dudley as lieutenant-governor. The colonists settled at Charlestown, which for a long time was a distinct municipality, but is now a part of the city of Boston. Experiencing at Charlestown a lack of wholesome water, a number of the colonists crossed the stream in a boat to Blackstone's peninsula to search for some. Here they found it in abundance, and this discovery led to overtures between Blackstone and the colonists. The negotiations resulted in Blackstone and many of the Puritans becoming close neighbors. Winthrop had at this time built himself a house at Charlestown, and there the headquarters of the colonists was located. Though a few houses rapidly grouped around that of Blackstone's, no thought had yet been entertained of establishing here a city which should one day be the most noted one in the Republic, and which should play an important part in the creation of the great United States. It is true the governor and his lieutenant had decided upon looking up a tract of country more suited for the seat of government than Charlestown was believed to be; but Boston had not been considered—if indeed any place had been thought of—as eligible for the distinction. Accordingly, one day in 1630 the governor and his lieutenant mounted their horses and started out to explore the plains and swamps and forests lying to the westward, and find a suitable site for a capital. The spot they finally picked out, with the help of some assistant magnates, lay about three miles west of Charlestown, on the banks of the tortuous little river since sung of by poets, and already named the Charles by Captain John Smith, who never saw it. The location seemed to Winthrop "a fit place for a beautiful town;" and accordingly, on the 29th of December, a goodly number of persons bound themselves with Governor Winthrop to build houses there in the following spring. The village they named Newtown, and this has since developed into the present Cambridge. The town was laid out regularly in squares, and early in 1631 houses began to arise. Governor Winthrop set up the frame of his dwelling on the very spot where he had first pitched his tent. But the people who had gone over from Charlestown to Boston had been promised by Winthrop that he would never move away anywhere unless they accompanied him, and of this

Scollay Square

promise they now reminded him in pretty strenuous terms. Bound by two solemn agreements, and under the necessity of breaking one of them, Winthrop found himself in a "fix;" but his conscience yielded to the promise he had first made. So, in the fall of 1631, he disappointed his Newtown friends by taking down the frame of his unfinished dwelling and by setting it up in Boston, near Beacon Hill. Dudley had completed his house and installed his family into it; and he and the rest of the Newtown colonists refused to accompany Winthrop. This led to an open quarrel between Winthrop and Dudley, and a coolness existed between them for years. Winthrop's excuse for quitting Newtown was somewhat strengthened in his own mind by the fact that Chickatabut, the chief of the neighboring Indians, had promised to be friendly, so that the necessity of having a fortified settlement in the colony, three miles west, was somewhat less urgent. The commercial

ters justified the lieutenant-governor by ordering Winthrop to get a clergyman for Newtown, failing in which he should pay Dudley £20. This sum Winthrop had to render, but the pacified Dudley was magnanimous in his triumph, and returned it with a polite note, in which he courteously intimated that he would rather lose £100 than Winthrop's friendship. Their difficulties settled, the two magnates lived on friendly terms thereafter, and

BOSTON BECAME THE COLONIAL CAPITAL.

Of the new State no one could become a citizen unless he was a member of the Puritan Church. Under a stern, theocratic discipline, the town and colony grew steadily and surely, and sanguinary edicts were issued

Post Office.

against the Baptists, Episcopalians, and Quakers who came to reside here. Rigid sumptuary laws were enforced. A high official was reprimanded by the governor for indulging in the luxury of a wainscot in his house; a clergyman was reproved for the vanity of painting his house on the outside. Fast riding, ball-playing in the streets, absence from church, speaking disrespectfully of the clergy, using tobacco publicly, charging high prices, denying the Scriptures, a man kissing his wife on the street or on a Sunday, and sheltering Quakers or Baptists, were all crimes in the sight of the lawmakers. Watchmen patrolled the streets by night, and walked "two by two together, a youth joined with an elder and more sober person." Their instructions

set forth: "If after ten o'clock they see lights, to inquire if there be warrantable cause; and if they hear any noise or disorder, wisely to demand the reason. If they find young men and maidens, not of known fidelity, walking after ten o'clock, wisely to demand the cause; and if they appear ill minded, to watch them narrowly, command them to go to their lodgings, and if they refuse, then to secure them till morning." The people were warned by the ringing of public bells when to go to bed, when to rise in the morning, and when to eat and drink. The ringing of the Boston town bells, at nine o'clock in the evening, was instituted in 1649, and was doubtless originated from the curfew, a custom introduced in England before the Norman conquest to command the people to put out their fires. The ringing of the nine o'clock bell remained a custom in the city within living memory, and the practice is still kept up in some New England villages. Josselyn, describing the town as it was between 1660 and 1670, says: "On the south there is a small but pleasant common, where the Gallants a little before sunset walk with their marmalet madams, as we do in Moorfields, etc., until the nine o'clock bell rings them home to their respective habitations, when presently the Constables walk their rounds to see good order is kept, and to take up loose people." The "morning bell," in those days of early rising was rung "half an hour after four." In 1664 an "eleven o'clock bell" was ordered "for the more convenient and expeditious dispatch of merchants' affairs." In course of time this bell became the recognized signal for the worthy tradesmen to adjourn from their places of business to the nearest tavern, there to take a "nip" of rum, Holland or Cognac (whiskey was not a beverage in those times). This ringing of the town bells at 11 o'clock continued until 1835, when the hour was changed to 1 P.M., or, as it was said, "from the hour of drinking to the hour of dining." Various bills in the city clerk's files, however, show that different hours were chosen in the different neighborhoods. In 1718, £3 were voted "to pay a Bell Ringer at the New South Meeting House for a year," he to officiate at five in the morning and nine at night, "as other Bell Ringers did."

The religious bigotry and civic intolerance on the part of his neighbors proved too much for minister Blackstone, the proprietor of the peninsula, for, said he, "I came from England because I did not like the

Lord Bishops, but I cannot join with you, because I would not be under the Lord's Brethren." Accordingly, about four years after the removal of the colonists to the peninsula, and being ill at ease among them, he agreed to sell to them the whole of the peninsula, except six acres where his house stood on Beacon Hill, for £30 ($150), and the money was raised by a rate, each householder paying six shillings (about $1.50). Compared with the price paid for Manhattan Island, the site of the commercial metropolis of the country, that paid for the peninsula on which New England's leading city stands was six times greater; but the former was bought from the Indians and the latter from an Englishman, and a parson at that. With the money received from the sale, Blackstone bought cows and other things, and travelled farther into the wilderness, establishing a new home, which he called "Study Hill," not far from Providence, R. I., on the banks of the picturesque river, which is now known as the Blackstone.

Since Blackstone shook the dust of Boston off his shoes forever, and looked for the last time upon the first house his own hands had reared on the site of the now prosperous city, Beacon Hill, with its three peaks, has undergone great transformations. The peaks have long since disappeared. One was located behind where the State House now stands, near Mount Vernon, Temple and Hancock Streets (where the beacon stood), and was for a time designated Centry Hill; another, situated farther west, was named Copley's Hill, and subsequently Mount Vernon, from which the present Mount Vernon Street derived its name; and the third, located to the east of Centry Hill, was first known as Cotton's Hill, and then as Pemberton's Hill, from which the present Pemberton Square took its name. The original Tremount stretched from the bend of the present Hanover Street on the east to near the present Charles Street on the west, and near West Cedar Street was a high bluff known as West Hill. From Cambridge Street on the north, the hill extended to the Common on the south, and its highest point was 138 feet above sea level.

The beacon—a fiery alarm to the surrounding country of invasion or other danger—was fixed on the summit of the hill, just below the present Mount Vernon and Temple Streets, in 1634, by order of the General Court, and thenceforward the eminence became known as Beacon Hill. The beacon consisted of an iron

Lief Ericsson—Commonwealth Avenue.

skillet, filled with combustibles always ready for use, and was suspended from a crane of iron at the top of a tall mast, into which were driven tree-nails that served the purposes of a ladder. The times in which this beacon was erected were troublous, and the beacon had often to render important service to the struggling and harassed colonists, of whom twenty thousand came to the colony in the first ten years after the settlement of Boston. When the beacon was raised on the hill, a rude castle arose on an island before the town, and war vessels were commissioned, because at various times the port was menaced with attacks from Dutch, Spanish, and French fleets. In 1639 a thousand well-armed men mustered on the Common, and powerful contingents went out from Boston to aid the British expeditions against Louisburg, Quebec, Acadia and Havana; and the colonists, marching side by side with the best troops in the world, became veteran and skilful soldiers. One of the earliest colonists wrote to his folks in the old country that the new land was "a hideous wilderness, possessed by barbarous Indians, very cold, sickly, rocky, barren, unfit for culture, and like to keep the people miserable."

The first beacon that was erected fell, through some unknown cause, and a new one was erected in 1768. In the dark days of the Revolution the British troops tore down the beacon and erected a small square fort in its stead; but as soon as the English left the town in 1776 the inhabitants again placed the beacon in position. During a gale in 1789 it was blown down. On its site, in 1790–91 was erected a monument of brick to commemorate the heroic deeds of those patriots who fell in the sanguinary struggle on Bunker Hill. The monument, which was sixty feet high and four wide, had a tablet on each of its four sides, and it was surmounted by a gilded eagle with outstretched wings. The inscription on the east-side tablet read: "Americans: While from this eminence, scenes of luxuriant fertility, of flourishing commerce, and the abodes of social happiness meet your view, forget not those who have by their exertions secured to you these blessings." That on the south side: "To commemorate that train of events which led to the American Revolution and finally secured liberty and independence to the United States, this column is erected by the voluntary contributions of the citizens of Boston. MDCCXC." The west and north-side tablets contained lists of the principal events connected with the War of the Revolution.

This hill formed a part of the public lands, and in 1811 the town sold off many of these, including the hill, to raise money to reduce its debts, which were pressing heavily upon it. Following the sale, a spirit of improvement set in, and the various eminences of Trimount were removed, much of the soil being used to raise the low land in the neighborhood of Charles Street, and to reclaim from the waters of the ocean the whole of the land now lying west of that thoroughfare. The tablets of the monument were placed in Doric Hall in the State House, and the gilded eagle occupies a place over the speaker's chair in the House of Representatives. The work of improvement lasted for about a dozen years, and the whole aspect of Beacon Hill was changed.

That side of the hill, overlooking the Common and the Public Garden, has for a hundred and fifty years been occupied by the most aristocratic houses in the city. Indeed, Beacon Street has been famed as the patrician street of New England, and as corresponding with Fifth Avenue in New York, though much less splendid than that grand thoroughfare, being lined with tall, sombre, brown stone structures, with no rich architectural grandeur in church edifices to relieve the monotony as in the avenue. Beacon Street runs in a straight line from Tremont Street over the crest of the hill, and has been extended by recent improvements to the aristocratic suburb of Longwood, running for a considerable distance close to and parallel with the river Charles. Along it and beyond it are the finest driveways in the country. On the hilly section of the street are the most fashionable and select clubs of the city, and here are or were several houses of interest to literary men. One of these—now rebuilt—was for twoscore years the abode of the late George Ticknor, the bosom friend of Hawthorne, the fast friend of Southey and Scott, and the historian of Spanish literature. Another was the residence of the famous blind scholar, W. H. Prescott, the historian of the Spanish Conquests of Mexico and Peru, etc. Among other residences may be pointed out that of C. C. Perkins, whose works on Tuscan sculptors and Italian art have had a world-wide circulation; that of one of the best poets of a past generation, Richard H. Dana; and that of Charles Sumner, the famous leader of the anti-slavery movement, also many others too numerous to particularize in this work.

Louisburg Square, situated on the western slope of the hill, and between Mount Vernon and Pinckney Streets, is an historic spot. Here was Blackstone's garden and spring. It is now private property, and in 1834 was enclosed and given its present name to commemorate the victory at Louisburg, upon which the French had spent twenty years and 30,000,000 livres in fortifying, as a menace to New England. In 1745 an army of 4000 undisciplined Yankee farmers and artisans left Boston and, joining a powerful British squadron, overthrew the fortress. The enclosure has many fine, noble trees, and two fine Italian statues of Aristides and Columbus.

In late years, even on the patrician Beacon Street, trade has planted its vigorous foot, and the aristocracy, as it has multiplied its members, has moved in a westerly direction, but under the shadow of the time-honored Beacon Hill. The sturdier rank and file of humanity and the representatives of commerce have taken possession of the other slopes of the hill, and among the changes of recent years, a massive, gloomy structure of granite on Derne Street, built in 1849 for a distributing reservoir, has been removed, and the heavy stone work has gone to form the Charles River embankment, and to aid in constructing a wilderness into a beautiful park in the Back Bay district, thereby adding much to the beauty of that section.

THE STATE HOUSE,

Whose gilded dome is, as we have already said, the first object that strikes the eye of the stranger approaching Boston in any direction by land or sea, stands majestically on the highest point of Beacon Hill, a fitting position for the capitol of the State. Its foundations are more than one hundred feet above water level. Its dome, which rises to an altitude of one hundred and ten feet, has, ever since it was reared, been a well-known land-mark in every direction; and since it was covered with gold leaf, in 1874, it has been an object prominent above all its surroundings, and an ornament to the city. Near to the State House stood the old Hancock House, the residence of Governor Hancock of Revolutionary fame, and it was one of the noblest private mansions of the colonial period. It was razed in 1863, and private residences now

Washington Street, Looking North.

occupy its site. The site of the State House was Governor Hancock's pasture, and over ninety years has slipped by since the town of Boston purchased it and presented it to the State. On July 4, 1795, there was a pompous display of Puritan burghers, the Freemasons marching to the strains of bands of music to lay the corner stone of the State House, under Grand Master Paul Revere, and Governor Samuel Adams, not long before exiled for liberty's sake, giving the speech of dedication. The stone itself was drawn up the steep slope of Beacon Hill by fifteen white horses, representing the number of States forming the Union. The edifice was erected under the direction of Charles Bulfinch, and in January, 1798, the members of the Legislature marched in solemn procession from the Old State House, at the head of State Street, and took possession of the new capitol, which is a plain enough brick building, constructed massively, but at small cost, and seeking ornament only in a dark colonnade of Corinthian pillars and its shining Byzantine dome. Lofty flights of stone steps .ead from the street to the main entrance, and the high terraces are kept enlivened by masses of brilliant flowers, in the midst of which stand bronze statues of the great orator, Daniel Webster, and of the famous educator, Horace Mann. The steps lead into a large hall, known as Doric Hall, where, in the recesses, protected by plates of glass, are shown the tattered remnants of several scores of flags carried by the Massachusetts regiments through the fierce struggles of the war for the Union. Here are also statues of Washington and Governor Andrew; busts of Samuel Adams, Charles Sumner, Henry Wilson, and Abraham Lincoln; fac similes of the tombstones of the ancestors of Washington, from England; the tablets from the Beacon monument, and many rare remembrances of ancient days in the Old Bay State. The Hall of Representatives has accommodation for five hundred legislators. Over the speaker's chair is the gilded spread eagle which once did duty on the summit of Beacon monument; and opposite hangs suspended from the ceiling the ancient wooden codfish brought from the Old State House, and typical of one of the foremost industries of the State. The Senate Chamber, where the Upper House meets, is adorned with notable trophies, and portraits of ancient worthies of Massachusetts; and near it is the State library, where more than forty thousand volumes are kept. Younger States—States that have sprung into being since this old edifice was built—have reared, where a few years ago were wildernesses, capitols with marble walls, fretted with sculpture and carving; but no State can be prouder of its capitol than that of Massachusetts, whose State House is typical of that simplicity and solidity which characterized the founders of the government. Plans have been prepared for enlarging the capitol and providing increased accommodation therein. On the slope and at the base of the hill, overlooked by the capitol, is

THE COMMON,

probably the most famous lot of land on the American Continent. It is an undulating natural park of forty-eight acres, surrounded by an iron fence over a mile long, crossed by five walks, shaded by a thousand ancient and graceful elms. It is located in the heart of the city, is surrounded on all sides by line upon line of busy and populous streets, and is the admiration not only of our own citizens, but of every visitor to the city, American and foreigner. When the early settlers purchased, more than two and a half centuries ago, the whole peninsula from Blackstone, they laid out this place for a "training field," and "for the feeding of cattle." Until 1830 cattle continued to be grazed on the Common, which is still sometimes used as a training field. Originally the Common extended in one direction as far as Tremont House, and in another to Mason Street, bordering westerly on the Back Bay, then a marshy tract, the waters of the ocean then flowing up to Charles Street and to the foot of the Roxbury Hills. Where Park Street now is an almshouse, a bridewell, and a granary stood, and was called Sentry Field. Forty-three and three fourths of the Common was enclosed in 1835 at a cost of $80,000, and later the remainder was enclosed. The Common is now surrounded on its four sides by Tremont, Boylston, Beacon and Park Streets, and it is one of the most beautiful and attractive parks in the country, rich in its greensward, its thousands of trees with umbrageous boughs, its ponds, monuments, and lovely walks.

The Common is not valued by Bostonians alone for its beauties and for the opportunities for out-door recreation it affords, but for its historic associations. In the old granary referred to were made the sails of the frigate "Constitution," or "Old Ironsides," concerning the threatened destruction of which Boston's favorite citizen, Dr. Oliver Wendell Holmes, wrote in pencil, in his attic room in Cambridge, in 1829, and when he was but twenty years old:

"And one who listened to the tale of shame,
Whose heart still answered to that sacred name,
Whose eye still followed o'er his country's tides
Thy glorious flag, our brave Old Ironsides!
From yon lone attic, on a summer's morn,
Thus mocked the spoilers with his school-boy scorn,"

The troops who captured Louisburg, the troops enlisted by Amherst, and who conquered Quebec, and the soldiers whose fights brought about the American Revolution, mustered here. Boston, as more copious histories will tell the reader, handled the torch that set aflame the Revolution. It had resisted the imposition of taxes by England time after time, and given the mother country to understand it was prepared to conduct business on its own account, if let alone. Its sons had boarded vessels in the harbor and thrown taxed tea into the sea rather than bear it. They had resented the Stamp Act and other imposts, and made themselves so obnoxious to the English government that the latter declared the former rebels, and ordered the army of soldiers quartered on the town to send them to England for trial. Between the soldiery and the citizens there was, of course, no kindly feeling, and the dislike was intensified by an event known as

THE "BOSTON MASSACRE,"

which, it is not too much to say, was one of the most important events which united the interests and feelings of the colonists, and brought on the revolutionary war. After the elapse of more than a century the event has been commemorated by the recent raising on the Common of a monument, known as the Attucks Memorial, which stands on the greensward near the Tremont Street Mall. The massacre occurred toward evening, on Monday, March 5, 1770, in the very centre of the business part of the town, in the rear of the State

Boylston Street, from Copley Square.

House, on King Street—known since, for nearly a hundred years, by the more appropriate name of State Street. Of the five victims of the massacre, four of them, namely, Samuel Gray, Samuel Maverick, James Caldwell and Crispus Attucks, where buried on the Thursday following, March 8, in what is still known as the old Granary burying ground, on the present Tremont Street. On the occasion of the funeral the bells of the town were rung, places of business were closed, and vast numbers of all persons of citizens were in attendance. Various accounts have been written and published of the Boston massacre, not differing, however, much in their essential particulars, and all appear to agree in condemning the outrage as a natural result from the quartering of troops in the town. The soldiers belonged to the 14th and 29th Regiments, and it has been well said that it was a more highly criminal to quarter troops in such a town as Boston then was. The people hated the soldiers, and this feeling was reciprocated by the latter with interest. The inhabitants could not go about their ordinary avocations without being challenged at every corner by sentinels, and often insulted and assaulted. Some outrage, it is said, was complained of every day; and if soldiers in all cases of misconduct and violence were not the offending parties, their presence induced them, and they generally had the credit of them. "From the time the troops arrived in September, 1768," says one account, "until they left the town, there were complaints against them and trouble with them." On the afternoon before the massacre the soldiers posted the following in writing as a warning to the people:—"Boston, March ye 5, 1770. This is to inform ye Rebellious People in Boston that the soldiers in ye 14th and 29th Regiments are determined to Joine together and defend themselves against all who Oppose them. Signed, Ye Soldiers of ye 14th and 29th Regiments."

"The evening of the 5th came on. . . . Parties of soldiers were driving about the streets, making a parade of valor, challenging resistance, and striking the inhabitants indiscriminately with sticks or sheathed cutlasses. A band poured out from Murray's barracks, in Brattle Street, armed with clubs, cutlasses and bayonets, provoked resistance, and a fray ensued. One soldier after another levelled a firelock and threatened to make a lane through a crowd. At about nine o'clock, a party of soldiers issued violently from the main guard, in King Street, their arms glittering in the moonlight, hallooing. 'Where are they! Where are they! Let them come on!' Presently twelve or fifteen more, uttering the same cries, rushed from the south-side into King Street, and so by way of Cornhill (Washington Street) toward Murray's barracks. They knocked a small boy down, and abused and insulted several persons at their doors and in the street, while their outcries of fire caused the bells to be rung. A body of soldiers came up Royal Exchange lane, crying, 'Where are the cowards?' and, brandishing their arms, passed through King Street, a crowd of boys following them. A parley occurred with the sentinel, who had previously knocked one of the boys down, and loaded his gun and threatened to shoot them. 'Stand off!' said the sentry. 'They are killing the sentinel,' reported a servant, running to the main guard. 'Turn out! why don't you turn out!' cried Preston, captain of the guard. A party of six, two of whom, Kilroi and Montgomery, had been previously worsted in a fight at the ropewalk, formed with a corporal in front and Preston following. With bayonets fixed they rushed through the people upon the trot, earning them and pushing them as they went along. They found about ten persons round the sentry, while about fifty or sixty came down with them. 'For God's sake,' said Henry Knox, who was passing by, holding Preston by the coat, 'take your men back again; if they fire your life must answer for the consequences.' 'I know what I am about,' said he, hastily and much agitated. None pressed on them or provoked them till they began bawling, when a party of about twelve in number, with sticks in their hands, moved from the middle of the street, where they had been standing, gave three cheers, and passed along in front of the soldiers, whose muskets some of them struck as they went by. 'You are cowardly rascals, they said, 'for bringing arms against naked men. Lay aside your guns and we are ready for you!' . . . Just then Montgomery received a blow from a stick which had hit his musket, and the word 'fire!' being given by Preston, he stepped a little on one side and shot Attucks, who at the time was quietly leaning on a long stick.

Statue of Gen. John Glover.

The people immediately began to move off. 'Don't fire,' said Longford, the watchman, to Kilroi, looking him full in the face; but yet he did so, and Samuel Gray, who was standing next to Longford, with his hands in his bosom, fell lifeless. The rest fired slowly and in succession on the people who were dispersing. . . . Three persons were killed, eight were wounded, two of them mortally. Of all the eleven, not more than one had any share in the disturbance. So infuriated were the soldiers that when the men returned to take up the dead they prepared to fire again, but were checked by Preston, while the 29th regiment appeared under arms in King Street. 'This is our time,' cried the soldiers of the 14th, and dogs were never seen more greedy for their prey.

"The bells in all the churches were rung, and the cry of the people was 'To arms! To arms!' 'Our hearts,' said Warren, 'beat to arms, almost resolved by one stroke to avenge the death of our slaughtered brethren.' The people would not be satisfied or retire till the regiment was confined to the guard room and the barracks, and Governor Hutchinson gave the assurance that instant inquiries should be made by the county magistrates.

Such, as we have described, was the Boston massacre and some of the attending circumstances. It was a rude and brutal and unnecessary murdering of the people, in support of unjust and wrongful claims and pretensions of the British ministry, Parliament and the King. It was the first blood spilled by British soldiers upon American soil, and, in fact, the initiation of the war which followed between the colonies and the mother country. From this time forward there was no longer agreement or concord of action between the government (king, ministry and Parliament) and the people of the American colonies.

On the morning following the massacre, the Sons of Liberty gathered in great numbers in Faneuil Hall, and resolved that the people and soldiers could no longer live together in safety. In the afternoon over three thousand persons assembled at the Old South Church and appointed a committee to wait upon the governor and Colonel Dalrymple, the commander of the forces, and to demand that the soldiers should be removed from the town if the peace of the province was to be preserved. The governor and his council and

Clarendon Street.

Colonel Dalrymple were in a dilemma, but seeing that the people meant business unless their demand was complied with, took the responsibility upon themselves of ordering the soldiers to remove to Castle Island, in the Harbor.

Captain Preston and eight of his men were put on trial for murder. The court, on a pretence of its inability to determine whether it was Preston or some one else who gave the order to fire, acquitted him. Two of the soldiers, who declared that they had simply done their duty in obeying orders to fire, were found guilty of manslaughter and sentenced to be branded in the hand in open court. For a long time the anniversary of the massacre was annually celebrated by Bostonians, but it was not until Wednesday, November 14, 1888, that a permanent memorial of the event was completed and unveiled on the Common with much ceremony, to immortalize Crispus Attucks and his fellow victims. Attucks was a negro, and the monument is named after him. By publicly immortalizing the name of a negro who, it is presumed, was a patriot, race distinction in this country has received a blow that should be fatal. By inference a man is now declared a man, be he white, black, rich or poor. This is undoubtedly the highest thought suggested by the dedication ceremonies, though they were confined chiefly to eulogy of the victims of the massacre by Professor Fiske and other orators on the occasion. The monument, while an ornament to the Common, stands as a silent encouragement to the valor of future generations. It is the work of Mr. Robert Kraus. It bears in bas-relief, a representation of the event as it occurred in King (State) Street. The soldiers are in the act of firing upon the people, at the command of their captain, while the victims are seen falling among the crowd of people which surrounds them. The work is very vivid, life-like, and a very excellent representation of the scene. The sentiments which have been inscribed upon the monument, with the names of the authors, indicate the public estimation of the event at the present time almost as emphatically as compelling the troops to leave the town did more than a hundred years ago. These sentiments are the following: "From that moment we may date the severance of the British empire."—DANIEL WEBSTER. "On that night the foundation of American independence was laid."—JOHN ADAMS.

After the massacre England continued to tighten the screws of exaction and oppression, while the Bostonians grew more obstinate. In March, 1774, the English Parliament ordered the closing of Boston port, and in the following September instructed the newly appointed governor of Massachusetts, General Gage, to reduce the colonists by force. A fleet and an army of ten thousand soldiers were sent to aid in the work of subjugation. Boston Neck was seized and fortified by the governor's orders; the military stores in the arsenals at Cambridge and Charlestown were conveyed to Boston; and the General Assembly was ordered to disband.

The Common became the fortified camp. Earthworks were thrown up on several of its eminences, of which all traces have long since disappeared. The British artillery was stationed upon Flagstaff, or Powder-house Hill, where there were intrenchments and a powder house. A battery was located on Fox Hill, which stood near the present Charles Street. On the Boylston Street side, opposite the present Carver Street, was a strong fortification. The marines were located near the Tremont Street side of the Common, and the infantry were scattered over the old "trayning field." Deep trenches were cut near the present Charles Street Mall, within a short distance of which was then the water front. Here during the winter of 1775-76 over 1700 British warriors waited in expectation of being attacked by Washington, for the whole town was in a state of siege.

When it became apparent what General Gage's instructions were, the Bostonians, concealing their guns and ammunition in cartloads of rubbish, conveyed them to Concord, sixteen miles away. Gage discovered the movement, and on the 18th of April, 1775, dispatched a regiment of 800 men to destroy the stores. Another purpose was to capture John Hancock and Samuel Adams, who were supposed to be hidden at Lexington or Concord. The fact was that they were not hidden anywhere, but were abroad encouraging the people. The plan of the British general was made with great secrecy; but the patriots were on the alert, and discovered the movement, and when the regiment, under the command of Colonel Smith and Major Pitcairn left the foot of the Common at Boston about midnight for Concord, under Gage's orders, the people of Boston, Charlestown and Cambridge were roused by the ringing of bells and the firing of cannons by the patriots. Two hours before, William Dawes and Paul Revere had started off on horseback to spread the alarm through the country, and at two o'clock in the morning a company of one hundred and thirty armed patriots had assembled on the Common at Lexington, with guns loaded. At five o'clock the English regiment hove in sight, and Pitcairn rode up and shouted: "Disperse, ye villains! Throw down your arms, ye rebels, and disperse!" The minute men stood still; Pitcairn discharged his pistol at them and cried "Fire!" The first volley of the Revolution whistled through the air, and sixteen of the patriots fell dead or wounded. The rest fired a few random shots and then dispersed. But the end was not yet. The British pushed on to Concord, but the inhabitants had removed the greater part of the stores to a place of safety, and there was but little destruction. Two cannons were spiked, some artillery carriages were destroyed, and a small quantity of ammunition thrown into a mill pond. While the English were pillaging the town the minute men gathered from all quarters, and came in contact with a company of soldiers guarding the North Bridge, over Concord River. For the first time the Americans fired under the orders of their officers and two English soldiers were killed. The bridge was taken by the patriots and the enemy began a retreat, first into the town and then through the town on the road to Lexington. Then the minute men attacked the enemy from every side, and kept up a terrible fire from behind rocks, trees, fences and barns. Nothing but good discipline and reinforcements which, under the command of Lord Percy, met the fugitives just below Lexington, saved the English from total rout and destruction. The fight continued to the precincts of Charlestown, the patriots becoming more and more audacious in their onslaughts. At one time it seemed that the whole

British force would be obliged to surrender. Such a result was prevented only by the fear that the English fleet would burn Boston. The American loss in this, the first battle of the war, was forty-nine killed, thirty-four wounded and five missing; that of the enemy was two hundred and seventy-three—a greater loss than the English army sustained on the Plains of Abraham.

The battle of Lexington inspired the patriots everywhere, and within a few days an army of twenty thousand men had gathered in the vicinity of Boston. A line of intrenchments encompassing the city was drawn from Roxbury to Chelsea, and the talk of the camp was to drive Gage and his army into the sea. On the 25th of May, Generals Howe, Clinton and Burgoyne arrived with more men, and the British army at Boston was increased to 10,000 strong. Gage issued a proclamation styling all in arms as rebels, and offering pardon to all who would submit to the King's authority except two, Samuel Adams and John Hancock, who were to be put to death, if caught, as traitors. A well-founded rumor was set on foot that the English intended to sally out of Boston and burn the neighboring towns and devastate the country. The Americans with a view to preventing this, seized and fortified Bunker Hill, but afterwards removed to a neighboring height, subsequently called Breed's

Park Street Church.

Hill, which was within easy cannon range of Boston. On the 17th of June the British advanced against the

bayonet. It was, however, a costly victory for the English, who lost 1054 men in killed and wounded while the American loss was 115 killed, 305 wounded and 32 prisoners.

The Bunker Hill fight showed that the British army was not invincible, and it was followed by increased enthusiasm among the Americans everywhere; and in all parts George the Third's authority was set at nought. Fifteen days after the Bunker Hill engagement General Washington arrived at Cambridge and took command of the patriotic army, while General Howe succeeded General Gage in command of the British troops in Boston. Washington besieged the city all winter, and by the middle of February the American army had increased to 14,000 men. Washington was frequently urged to force a fight with the enemy, but until the spring be contented himself with narrowing his lines, strengthening his works, and waiting his opportunity. On the north, Boston was commanded by the peninsula of Charlestown, and on the south by Dorchester Heights. Since the battle at Bunker Hill the former position had been held by the British; the latter was, as

Boston Museum of Fine Arts, Art Square and Dartmouth Street.

yet, unoccupied. Washington resolved to take advantage, by a strategic movement, of the enemy's oversight, to seize the Heights and drive Howe out of Boston. To distract the attention of the British, heavy cannonading was kept up from the American batteries for two days, and during the night of the 4th of March a detachment of Americans ascended the Heights and established a line of formidable intrenchments and cannon frowning upon the city. Howe was astonished next morning when he saw how he had been out-generaled, and that he must either drive the Americans from the Heights or abandon the city. He directed Lord Percy to place himself at the head of 2400 men and storm the redoubts before nightfall. It was the anniversary of the "Boston Massacre," and the patriots were eager for vengeance. Percy got as far as Castle Island, when a violent storm arose and rendered the harbor impassable all day, so that the attack could not be made. The Americans continued to strengthen their position until Howe found himself in the extremity of giving up the capital of New England to the rebels. By an informal agreement between Washington and Howe, the latter was allowed to retire from the city unmolested, on condition that he did not burn the place. On the 17th of March, Howe and his army and some 1500 loyalist citizens left, and from that date the contending hosts transferred their struggles to other parts of the country. On the 20th, Washington rode triumphantly into the city, and the ten months' siege had ended. The whole country was exultant, and Congress ordered a gold medal to be struck in honor of Washington, who went in pursuit of the enemy to Long Island, but not before he had strengthened the defences of Boston.

The Common not only played an important part in the Revolutionary era, but in the days of the Rebellion it was the mustering and encamping ground of the Massachusetts regiments which were sent to do battle with the armed hosts of the Southern Confederacy. The Common is yet the place on which military bodies muster on anniversary days and public events, and it has been the scene of celebrations of many military and naval victories. In ante-Revolutionary times, on this historic ground frequent executions occurred under the ancient trees, especially in 1676, when the Narragansett Indians had been subjugated in a fierce battle among the swamps of Rhode Island, and when many a valiant red-skinned warrior was brought hither in chains and suspended from the boughs of the wide-spreading elms. Thirty Indians were thus put to death in a single day. Here, too, Whitfield preached and Quakers were hanged for conscience' sake. The famous old Common has been swept by shot and shell by night and by day, and nobles, generals, and statesmen have plotted and planned, under the leafy shades, the fate of dynasties and empires; and, within its cool retreats, lovers have for ages held their trystings, built airy castles, and whispered "sweet nothings," Orators have fretted and fumed on the greensward over real and fancied public wrongs; youngsters have, year after year, made the air ring with their merry shouts and laughter as they have swiftly glided on the winter ice on the hill-slopes; musicians have filled, and do fill in the summer months, the balmy air with pleasant sounds; and on festival days the old Common is a scene of jollity, presenting many of the sights of a country fair.

The glories of statesmen, warriors, and scholars are commemorated on the Common by monuments and statues. On the highest point of the Common, long known as Flagstaff Hill, or Monument Hill, as it is now called, is the Army and Navy Monument, which is worthy of a city that gave to the cause of the Union in the War of the Rebellion 24,434 soldiers and 885 officers. This magnificent specimen of the sculptor's art was the work of the late Mr. Martin Milmore, and cost $75,000. The corner-stone was laid September 18, 1871, and at its dedication, September 17, 1877, militia, veterans, and civic societies, numbering 25,000 men, marched in procession. This monument bears this record: "To the men of Boston, who died for their country on land and sea in the war which kept the Union whole, destroyed slavery, and maintained the constitution, the grateful city has built this monument, that their example may speak to coming generations." The base is cruciform, three steps rising to a pedestal which is fired with large bronze reliefs, representing the departure of the State troops, battle scenes in which the army and navy were engaged, the work of the hospitals in the field, and the return of the volunteers to the city. Between and above these stand four heroic bronze statues: The Soldier, fully equipped, with his musket and bayonet fixed; the Sailor, facing seaward, with drawn cutlass; History, a female figure, laurel-wreathed, clad in Greek costume, and about to write on a tablet; and Peace, another classic female figure, seated and holding an olive-branch toward the South. Above these rises a tall Roman Doric Shaft of white Maine granite, with allegorical figures representing the North, South, East, and West at its base and four marble eagles at the top. The summit of the monument, seventy feet high, is a colossal bronze statue of the Genius of America, crowned with thirteen stars, holding a bare sword and two laurel wreaths in one hand, and a banner staff in the other, and with her face bowed towards the south. Of this great and imposing memorial we give a fine illustration in these pages.

At the foot of the hill, within an iron inclosure, stood an old tree, known as the "Old Elm," until the winter of 1876, when it was destroyed in a gale. It was believed to have been there even before Blackstone set foot on the peninsula, and was regarded as the oldest of its kind in Boston. It was decrepit even in 1775, and was tenderly cared for for more than a hundred years. It had been the scene of many stirring events. Witches, Quakers, murderers, pirates, and others had been hanged from its branches; the "Sons of Liberty" had illuminated it with lanterns in Revolutionary days; duels had been fought under its shadow; and it had been a tryst for generation after generation of Bostonians. A foot above the ground, its circumference was 22½ feet, and it rose to a height of over 72 feet. A shoot off the "Old Elm" is now thriving on the spot where the old monarch of the forest stood.

THE PUBLIC GARDEN

lies just to the westward of the Common, with which it forms one of the handsomest parks in the country. The Garden, which is only separated from the Common by Charles Street, is in form varying little from a parallelogram, and contains over twenty-four acres. The site of the Garden was formerly a dreary expanse of marshy flats, overflowed by high tides, and was known as Round Marsh, or "the marsh at the bottom of the Common." After a great fire among some rope-walks in the present Congress Street in 1794, the city, in a fit of generosity, gave the marsh to the burned-out ropemakers. In 1819 their rope-walks on the marsh were burned out, but, as the land round about had increased much in value, they determined that it would pay them better to sell the marsh for building purposes than to reconstruct their rope-walks. The citizens were indignant, but the ropemakers were determined, and finally, in 1824, the city fathers concluded to buy back their gift of thirty years before, for $54,000 to make a public garden out of the marsh. In this they have succeeded admirably. In the centre is an artificial lake, with fountains, swan-houses, pleasure-boats, etc. The Garden is intersected with fine, graveled, sinuous walks, the velvety lawns are kept in splendid order, and the floral displays are the finest in America. The Garden contains many fine statues, among them being a colossal equestrian one of General Washington, bronze statues of Charles Sumner and Edward Everett, and a granite and red marble monument to commemorate the discovery in Boston of ether as an anæsthetic. By night the Garden is illuminated by electric lights, and the place is a popular resort for persons of all conditions.

ORIGINAL AND PRESENT AREAS OF BOSTON.

In the preceding pages frequent reference has been made to the first settlement of Bostonians being on a peninsula. When Blackstone was here "lord of all he surveyed," his landed possessions formed a pear-shaped peninsula, and up to the beginning of the last half century the territorial area of the city was limited to the land owned by him. Its extreme length was less than two miles, and its greatest breadth a little more than one. The peninsula "hung to the mainland, at Roxbury," says one writer, "by a slender stem, or neck of a mile in length, so low and narrow between tide-washed flats that it was often submerged. Now the original 783 acres of solid land have become 1839. The broad, oozy salt-marshes, the estuaries, coverts, and bays once stretching wide on its northern and southern bounds have been reclaimed; and where then the area was the narrowest, it is now the widest. The hills have been cut down—one, Fort Hill, entirely removed; the whole surface of the original ground has been levelled and graded, and every square inch turned over and over; new territory has been added by annexing adjoining suburban cities and towns, until now the area of the city, with all its districts, is 23,661 acres (36½ square miles)—more than thirty times as great as the original area. The areas of the districts are as follows: South Boston, 1002 acres; East Boston, 836; Roxbury, 2700; Dorchester, 5614; West Roxbury, 7846; Brighton, 2277; Charlestown, 586; Breed's Island, 785; Deer Island, 184.

The following islands in the harbor of Boston belong to the city, viz.: Deer Island, containing 184 acres upland, and 80 acres flats, conveyed to the inhabitants of Boston, March 4, 1634–35; Thompson's Island, annexed to Boston by act of March 15, 1834; Great Brewster Island, containing 16 acres, purchased in 1848 for $4000; Gallop's Island, containing 18 acres, purchased in 1860 for $6800; Apple Island, containing 9½ acres, purchased 1867 for $3780; Rainsford Island, containing 11 acres, purchased, together with all hospital buildings and dwellings thereon, in 1871, for $40,000. Male paupers whose settlement is established in this city are now located in the large hospital building upon this island. Moon Island, containing about 30 acres, was taken by right of eminent domain from the heirs of James Hnckins and others in 1879, and constitutes the point of discharge of the great sewer of the city of Boston. The city has within it 123,268,852 feet of marsh-land flats; and the measurement of the city from north to south is eleven miles, and from east to west nine miles. The principal business section of the city, lying between the harbor and Charles River, is a mile and a quarter across.

The various annexations that have been made to the city have necessitated the building of many bridges over the water-ways that separate the city proper from the districts annexed. These bridges are: Broadway Bridge, over Fort Point Channel to South Boston; Cambridge Bridge; Western Avenue and North Harvard Street bridges, from Brighton to Cambridge; Canal, or Craigie's Bridge, Leverett Street to East Cambridge; Charles River Bridge, Charlestown Street to Charlestown; Chelsea bridges (North and South), Charlestown to Chelsea; Chelsea Street Bridge, East Boston to Chelsea; Commercial Point Bridge; Congress Street Bridge, over Fort Point Channel; Dover Street Bridge, to South Boston; Essex Street Bridge, Brighton to Cambridge; Federal Street Bridge, to South Boston; Granite Bridge, Dorchester to Milton; Malden Bridge, Charlestown to Everett; Meridian Street Bridge, East Boston to Chelsea; Mount Washington Avenue Bridge, to South Boston; Neponset Bridge, Dorchester to Quincy; North Beacon Street Bridge, Brighton to Watertown; Prison Point Bridge, Charlestown to East Cambridge; Warren Bridge, Beverly Street to Charlestown; West Boston Bridge, Cambridge Street to Cambridgeport; Western Avenue Bridge, to Watertown; Winthrop Bridge, Breed's Island to Winthrop.   A new bridge is now in course of construction from the Back Bay lands across the Charles River to Cambridgeport, and will be of vast service to the people located in these thriving sections.

CREATED LAND.

Proudly as she sits by the sea, majestic as she appears in her thrift and grandeur as the metropolis of New England, Boston has not acquired her present domain, her pre-eminence among the cities of the New

Post Office Square.

World, and her prosperity as a great manufacturing and commercial centre on the Atlantic seaboard, without a patient and prolonged struggle with natural obstacles and manifold adversities in varied forms. From statistics, given in a previous page, it will be seen that what are now the most valuable sections of the city have been stolen, as it were, by engineering skill from the boundless and restless ocean. Much of the original peninsula was rocky, and what is now the Common was liberally strewn with boulders deposited there ages ago. The first settlers found the peninsula abounding in abrupt and gradual elevations; large inlets of sea-water, that nearly divided it; broad fringes of ooze, and mud, and extensive marshes; an inner bay and with but a slender neck connecting it with the mainland. The greatest breadth of the Neck was at Beach Street, and its narrowest at Dover Street. From the latter point, says Drake, "it increased gradually in width to the neighborhood of Dedham Street, thence expanding in greater proportion to the line at the present car-stables, nearly opposite Metropolitan Place." In Revolutionary times the Neck was known as that part lying south of Dover Street, and at high tides the road was in some places covered with water which reached to the knees of horses passing through it. A sea-wall was built on the west side and a dyke on the east. A little south of the present Dover Street a fortification was built, and here were gates which were closed at night and which prevented any one from coming into or leaving the town on that side after a certain hour at night.

Since that time the city has been enlarging its area on every hand by making inroads upon the domain of Old Neptune, and this at fabulous cost, for the materials with which to do this have had to be carried from a distance. Trees were not found numerous on the peninsula by the first customers, though bushes were abundant; and to what extent the trees growing on the site served for house-building, the records are silent. But, when it was found necessary to construct piers or wharves, or to form solid borders to the territory over marshlands, or to push out to deep water, piles and timber had to be brought chiefly from the islands in the harbor. For a long time cargoes for sea going vessels had to be carried in small boats between the shore and the ships. It would be a curious calculation, were it possible, to estimate the number of forest trees which, from the earliest days to the present, have been driven into the marginal or alluvial soil of Boston, as solid land has been made over the water-frontage. These trees, covered with granite from the blowing up of local quarries and from Cape Ann, and with sand and gravel from hills a score of miles inland, illustrate the conditions by which a foothold has been secured on the peninsula. It is interesting, however briefly done, to inquire what has been achieved in this direction in the various

SECTIONAL DIVISIONS OF THE CITY

In the early days the "Old Canal," or Mill Creek, which ran on the line of the present Boston & Maine Railroad, from Causeway Street to Haymarket Square, thence through Blackstone Street and North to the old town

Odd-Fellows Monument.

dock, where North Market Street now is, divided the city into the North and South Ends. At the beginning of the present century the whole of what is now Haymarket Square—the termination of Union, Washington, Sudbury, Cross, Merrimack, Canal, Haverhill, Charlestown, and Blackstone Streets—was a pool, known as Mill Cove and Mill Pond, and this was spanned by a bridge. This waterway was known as the Middlesex Canal, by which canal-boats came down from the up-country, along the Merrimack, to the East-Side wharves of Boston. The Canal was filled up and Blackstone Street opened as a thoroughfare in 1834. At this time, and for some years afterwards, Commercial Street, from the Old Battery, or Battery Wharf, to Long Wharf, was a water-front; and, until Broad Street was laid out, in 1808, Battery-march, to its junction with Kilby Street, marked the water-line. Where Dock Square now is, was formerly the Town Dock, which ran along the foot of the Market Place, about where Faneuil Hall now stands; and near the junction of North and Union Streets was the "Watch-house." Near the latter was a reservoir of water, raised in the centre and sloping at the sides, and was called the "Conduit." It was about twelve feet square, and the top was utilized as a meat-market on Saturdays. At the foot of Merchant's Row was a swing-bridge over the dock. What is now Atlantic Avenue was at one time the site of an ancient harbor defence known as the Barricado, but sometimes called the "Sea Wall" or "Out-Wharves." It connected the South Battery, which was on the spot where Rowe's Wharf now is, with the North Battery, which was at the North End, opposite Charlestown. It formed a line of about 2200 feet in length, about 15 feet in height, and 20 feet in breadth at the top. It was erected in 1673, and was provided with openings to allow shipping to pass within its line, while it was calculated to mount heavy guns en barbette. It was of little use, fell into decay, and finally gave way to improvements. It will be seen that all the present water-front extending to a line with Commercial Street, and, in places beyond it, is made land, and the most valuable in the city. Atlantic Avenue, extending from the junction of Commercial Street and Eastern Avenue to Federal Street, was constructed by the city at a cost of $2,404,078, and is 100 feet in width. Here are immense wharves, huge warehouses, and immense traffic, which is facilitated by the railroad cars running along the line of docks. It was at one of these wharves—the Liverpool (formerly Griffin's) Wharf—where the famous "Boston Tea Party" took place, and to which we shall revert hereafter.

The term "North End" is usually applied to that section of the city lying towards Charlestown, between the Boston & Maine Station and Faneuil Hall. This was the first settled part of the town, and it is historic ground, and once the residential quarter for Boston's aristocracy, and now the abode of thousands of the

State House.

humbler classes. North Square, the small triangular inclosure between North and Moon Streets, was, in the early days, the heart of the "court end" of the town. In the immediate neighborhood the first families dwelt. For years the "Old North," the "Church of the Mothers," occupied one side of the Square, near where the Mariner's House now is. This church was torn down by the British during the siege of the city, and was used by them for firewood. In 1734 one of the three town markets was located in the Square, in which was located the residence of the Revolutionary hero, Paul Revere. Near the Square, on corner of North and Richmond Streets, was the famous hostelry, the Red Lion Inn, kept by a Quaker, one Nicholas Upsall, who, in the days of religious persecution, was put to death because of his Quakerism. In time this section became a "dangerous" quarter, the habitation of the immoral and vicious, but street improvements and electric lights have done much to take away from the locality a large measure of its unsavoriness. Till within a comparatively few years the North End retained the quaint, old-fashioned look of the town as it was a hundred and more years ago. Many of the ancient houses still remained, with "gambrel roofs and overhanging stories, standing close upon the narrow, crooked and winding streets that characterize the older portion of most old cities." But the hand of improvement has been busy here, as elsewhere; for streets have been straightened and widened, and the old houses sliced off, set back, torn down, or decorated with new fronts. The most marked improvement is in Hanover Street, stretching from Court Street, on the slope of the Pemberton Hill,—one of the peaks of the ancient Treamount,—to the water-front on Atlantic Avenue. This thoroughfare was opened out about a quarter of a century ago, since which time many old store edifices have given place to fine business blocks of spacious character, and Hanover Street is to-day one of the best-known business avenues of the city. Salem Street (which runs off obliquely from Hanover Street, and then runs nearly parallel with it), and the streets which cross it, offer to the lover of the antique and curious much to interest him. Modern innovations in the building art are here and there apparent, but on Salem and the intersecting streets there are still many good examples of the colonial style of building yet extant, with the second story projecting over the first. Salem, Cross and adjacent streets are to-day chiefly occupied by Jews, and their stores are the centres for trade in second-hand clothing, jewelry, and "odds and ends" of every description. From the left of Salem Street, through Baldwin Place, is the Home for Little Wanderers, where poor children, many of them orphans, are received and cared for, and ultimately given permanent homes in the country and in Western States on farms. Farther down Salem Street, opposite Sheafe Street, is the Industrial Home, where poor children and adults are instructed to become useful workpeople. The most interesting part of Salem Street is below Prince Street. The picturesque features are the old Christ Church, which fronts on Hull Street, and the ancient Copp's Hill Burying-ground near by. Christ Church is associated with the outbreak of the Revolutionary War. It was

> "Here the patriot hung his light
> Which shone through all that anxious night
> To eager eyes of Paul Revere."

An inscribed stone in the front of the steeple declares, in spite of some writers who have found time to argue to the contrary: "The signal lanterns of Paul Revere displayed in the steeple of this church April 18, 1775, warned the country of the march of the British troops to Lexington and Concord." Here, too, is the oldest chime of bells in America. The inscriptions on them tell their history. On the first is, "This peal of eight bells is the gift of a number of generous persons to Christ Church in Boston, New England, anno 1744, A. R.;" on the second, "This church was founded in the year 1723, Timothy Cutler, doctor in divinity, the first rector, A. R. 1744;" the third, "We are the first ring of bells cast for the British empire in North America, A. R. 1744;" the fourth, "God preserve the church of England, 1744;" the fifth, "William Shirley, Esq., Governor of the Massachusetts Bay in N. E., anno 1744;" the sixth, "The subscription for these bells was begun by John Hammock, Robert Temple, Robert Jenkins, and Ino Gould, church wardens, 1744;" the seventh, "Since generosity has opened our mouths, our tongues shall ring aloud its praise, 1744;" the eighth, "Abel Rudhall, of Gloucester, cast us all, anno 1744." The aggregate weight of the eight bells is 7272 pounds; they cost £560; the freight by ship from England was given by John Rowe, and the charges for wheels and hanging were £03.

These bells relate their own story so concisely that one wishes they could chronicle with equal clearness the events which have occurred around them since they rang their opening peal. What an interesting tale it would be! But they have had their share in making history, and their voices have often been lifted in behalf of liberty and humanity, as well as for the sacred cause of religion. The belfry in which the bells now are is not, however, the same that first received them. That was blown down by a tempest early in the present century, and the present erection, though old as things go in America, is modern compared with the main edifice. In the times that tried men's souls to the uttermost, the bells here tolled when danger for the colonists was at hand; they called meetings of patriots, and rang merrily when the independence of the United States was declared.

Near by the church is the ancient burial-ground of Copp's Hill, once the site of the homestead of William Copp, an industrial cobbler. The hill was originally much higher than it is now, but, notwithstanding changes affected in its surroundings, the old graveyard, where the bones of many noted old Bostonians have been laid at rest, has been carefully preserved, and is a place of great attraction to all who find interest in old-time associations. At one time a small mill stood on the summit of the hill, which in 1800 was laid out for a graveyard, and this for a long time was known as the Old North Burying-ground. In the siege of Boston the British established a redoubt on this hill, and from the battery here they fired upon the American earthworks on Breed's Hill in the battle of Bunker Hill. From here, too, the English poured hot shot into Charlestown, and destroyed the village. It is said that the British, while here, made targets of the gravestones of the burying-ground. When the English evacuated Boston, on March 17, 1776, three of the heaviest guns of the battery here were found to be spiked and clogged so as to prevent their immediate use.

In late years the whole of the North End has undergone great transformations. New churches have arisen, streets have been straightened and widened, and large warehouses, and factories, and work-shops have taken the place of what were once habitations of the humblest and least favored of the population. Haymarket Square, once a pond with a bridge over it, is now one of the busiest centres in the

The New Old South Church.

city, with streets branching off from it to all points of the compass. The Boston & Maine Railroad Station also fronting on the Square, and all the ground in the rear of it is made land, and now of enormous value. When the projected new Union Railroad Depot shall have been erected on Causeway Street and on the water's edge, the whole of the space now occupied by the railroad between Causeway Street and Haymarket Square will be thrown open for improvement and new buildings, and as important a change will be effected as was achieved in 1873-4 by the opening up of Washington Street from Dock Square to Haymarket Square at a cost of $1,500,000. But let us for a moment turn from the North End (which is the designation of that part of

THE SOUTH END.

This appellation now applies to that part of the city lying to the south of Dover Street and extending to the Roxbury district. All this area is largely made land, and the newer portion, towards the West, joins the New West End, or Back Bay distriet; but in the early days the canal which ran through Causeway Street, Haymarket Square, and Blackstone Street to the old town dock, where North Market Street now is, divided the city into the North and South Ends. The Old South Church, on the corner of Washington and Milk Streets, was, when erected, out at the South End; hence its name. For many years the South End contained the principal shops, the finest mansion houses, and the Common. What is now known as the South End was then the Neck Field. At a later date the present Winter Street formed the down-town boundary. Then the boundary was extended to Boylston Street, and next to Dover Street, which is now recognized as the line between the Central portion of the city and the South End.

For over thirty years subsequent to the settlement of Boston all that part of the South End embraced in the territory included between Kneeland and Eliot Streets north, and Castle Street south, was one unbroken field, the property of Deacon William Colbron. The "highway to Roxberrie," as it was termed, leading from North End, made a detour at Kneeland Street eastwardly, following thence the margin of the Old South Bay to Castle Street, whence a return was made to the road leading over the Neck, which, a short distance beyond the present Dover Street, had a gate across it to keep out marauding animals, and as a sort of protection against the incursions of Indians. In 1803, however, a straighter line was made for the highway by an opening through the Colbron field. When Washington Street—now a continuous thoroughfare from Haymarket Square, through the heart of the city, to the Highlands—existed under several titles, that portion of it southward from the intersection of Essex Street bore the name of Orange Street, and at this point the Neck of former days actually commenced. The tide came up to within a stone's throw of old Orange Street on the easterly side and to Pleasant Street on the westerly margin. From Essex Street the width gradually diminished, until there was a mere thread of land, which was often overflowed by the high tides. This part of the territory of Boston, a century back, was practically in the "country." There were not more than seventy-five families on the whole of it, extending from Essex Street to the Roxbury line and including all adjoining territory, and these families were distributed widely apart in the manner common with outlying precincts of villages. Each householder had and cultivated more or less of a garden for the growth of fruits and vegetables. Some of these residences were the abodes of persons of affluence who had retired from the active channels of trade. The district, too, was noted for several prominent distilleries a century ago. Following this period the town had a healthy growth, on the recovery from the depression consequent upon the Revolution, and there was excited and exploring spirit for new habitations. This led many seekers to the Neck district, and to the filling up of the vacant places with residences. Streets were opened intersectingly; and those openings which had previously been simple places or courts leading to single houses were rearranged for the purposes of thoroughfares.

In 1809 the Boylston Market was erected on the corner of Washington and Boylston Street, and its site was then on the outer margin of the town. This building (removed during the last three years) was named in honor of Ward Nicholas Boylston, a great benefactor of Harvard College. He it was who presented the clock that for so long a period did faithful duty in the tower of the quaint-looking old market, which contained three floors and basement. The land upon which the building was erected cost 75 cents per foot and the building itself $20,000. In 1859 the building was extended 40 feet, and in 1870 was bodily removed back from the street 11 feet. The lower floor served as the market, and the Boylston Hall, above it, was used for church services, musical, theatrical, and miscellaneous entertainments, drillroom, armory, etc. A new, elegant structure of larger dimensions, covering about 15,000 square feet and costing about $250,000 to build, has just been erected on its site. The lower floor is a clothing store, and the upper floors are divided into offices. In its day the old Boylston Market was a great factor in promoting good living, and it drew its patronage from the élite of the city. Its erection led to the building in its vicinity of other public edifices of considerable note, among these being Mellish Motte's Unitarian Church, Dr. Phelp's Congregational Church, the Franklin Schoolhouse, etc.

ever,—in 1844,—Harrison Avenue had been laid out, and in 1832 Tremont Street, on the west side of the
Neck, had been extended to the Roxbury line. When in 1856 the street-railroad system was introduced,—
the first line of the Metropolitan Company running from the old Granary Burying-ground, on Tremont Street,
to Roxbury—the South End at once became the favorite residence portion, and building was extensively
begun. Until the building up of the Back Bay district, the South End was the best residence section, and
large portions of it still contain fine estates occupied by the most substantial citizens of the city. Legrange
Street, once known as Legrange Place, was formerly one of the most charming spots in town, having nice
houses, in a secluded position, handy to business. For some unexplained reason, however, the tenants were
restless, and made frequent changes, but for many years tenants were drawn from the better class of citizens
engaged in mercantile life. In time "boarding-places" were opened, and later Langrange Place had become

Liberty Square, showing Mason Building and Kilby Street.

a centre for residences of inimical people. Since the place was opened out as a thoroughfare from Washington
Street to Tremont Street, it has been a headquarters for the sporting fraternity, besides being the locale of
one of the most lively police stations in the city. In former days the atmosphere of the South End was per-
meated with an aromatic and pungent odor derived from various distilleries. There were two distilleries in
the vicinity of Harvard Street, one of which was quite extensive, and was owned by W. C. Fay. Another,
kept by Gardner Brewer, was situated on the corner of Washington Street and the present Indiana Street
(then known as Distill house Street). Luther and Artemas Felton each prosecuted the distillery business a little

While three score years ago the air was redolent with the flavor of hops and the odor of new rum, there were three churches in this region exerting a "powerful influence in exhibiting the religious tendencies of the inhabitants. They were all flourishing to their utmost. Dr. John Pierpont's society, in Hollis Street, represented the most rigid Unitarians, and embraced in its congregation several who, like Francis Jackson, held advanced views upon moral questions, in common with their pastor. He was talented, and his independence often took an offensive form. On the corner of the present Motte Street stands a relic of what was one of the most fashionable Unitarian churches in town. Here Rev. Mellish Motte preached, and here Charlotte Cushman (before her theatrical days) sang in the choir, along with several members of the Handel and Haydn Society, including John O. Roberts, before alluded to. The immediate neighborhood of this church had then recently been improved and occupied by the residences of a number of its members. Orange Street then was a charming place, and its houses were eagerly sought for when erected. The houses are there now, but the street has a forbidding appearance. In placing the railroad bridge near by, it was made necessary to raise the grade, and the corners of Orange Street were demolished. On the lower corner the building contained an elegant hall, where fashionable parties and dances were held. Across the street, at its entrance, was sprung a tasty iron arch, holding a handsome lantern in the centre, which threw its rays down the street, giving a cheerful aspect after nightfall. The other church in allusion was known as the Pine Street Church. The old shell of this edifice still remains. The society held a first-class position under the ministration of Rev. Amos A. Phelps, and is perpetuated to-day by the church corner of Berkeley and Appleton Streets, as Mr. Motte's society is by that known as Edward E. Hale's." The site of the Hollis Street Church, which was built in 1819, is now occupied by the Hollis Street Theatre, and the congregation of the old church have now comfortable quarters in a fine new edifice on the corner of Exeter and Newbury Streets.

The avenues and streets of the South End section of the city are wide and handsome. It needs but little discernment for one familiar with the territory and its properties lying between Washington and Tremont

Young Men's Christian Association New Building.

Streets, and extending from School to Dover Streets, to divine the purpose of enterprising citizens in 1868 of laying out a new thoroughfare to the South End, midway between the then and now main arteries of the city. Shawmut Avenue did not then exist except as Suffolk Street, and that had not then been extended and widened to intersect with Tremont Street. Washington Street was narrow and crowded with traffic and stores, and Tremont Street was just beginning to develop into a business property. The improvements made, of what had been rear property, valuable front building lots, and new residences and stores soon lined the avenue. Shawmut Avenue and Tremont Street are of generous width, as also is Washington Street and likewise Columbus Avenue on the west, while on the east side the chief thoroughfares are Albany Street and Harrison Avenue. These are the main thoroughfares running from north to south, and all, with the exception of a small strip on Washington Street, are on made land. The streets crossing these are very numerous, several of them containing many beautiful residences, and the most of them lined with comfortable dwellings. The principal cross streets include Canton, Brookline, Union Park, Newton, Rutland, Concord, Worcester, Springfield, and Chesterpark Streets. The "through" streets are spoken of as East or West, taking Washington Street as the dividing line. Scattered all through the South End are many large public and private buildings, a number of noted church edifices, numerous large manufactories, and some of the finest apartment houses in the city and country.

The leading streets and avenues stretching from north to south extend for miles, and are lined with richly equipped marts of trade and attractive residences, sanctuaries, hospitals, halls, and educational Institutions. Building operations have been actively prosecuted in late years, the entire region of the South End has been changed in its aspect, and real estate has increased immensely in value. The whole district is intersected with horse railroads, and an old-time Bostonian can find much here to interest him in comparing the present with the past. Let him take a horse-car on Tremont Street, and as the vehicle sweeps round the corner of the Common into Boylston Street he espies on the opposite corner the Hotel Pelham, the first building of the "French flats," or "family hotel" class in Boston. The edifice was erected a little over a quarter of a century ago by Dr. John Dix, and has always been regarded as the finest and most popular of its kind. The building is valued at $120,000 ; the whole is assessed at $194,300, and the tax paid by the proprietor, Mr. J. L. Little, is $31,500. Some years ago, when Tremont Street was not so wide at this point as it is to-day, this hotel was raised up bodily and moved about twenty feet down Boylston Street, without disturbing the occupants, or in the least disarranging the interior. This was the greatest engineering feat of the age, being the first instance of the moving of such a large mass of masonry; and it not only excited the wonder of people at home but of those in Europe, where the newspapers published full descriptions of the work of removal. On the opposite corner is the Hotel Boylston, originally erected as an apartment house, with the kitchens in the upper story. It belongs to the estate of Charles Francis Adams. The total valuation of this house is $419,000, the building being assessed at $180,300, and the tax paid by the trustees amounting to $30,000. Adjoining the Pelham Hotel is one of the most useful and most appreciated institutions in the city—the Public Library. As the car sweeps along Boylston Street, the traveller notices many changes that have been made and that are being made in the buildings fronting on the deer park and the old burying-ground at the foot of the Common. A few years ago these buildings were occupied as residences by noted wealthy Bostonians; now they are being utilised for business purposes. Turning into Park Square, one notices here many improvements which did not exist a few years ago. A prominent feature in the Square is the "Emancipation Group" monument, representing Lincoln with the figure of a slave kneeling at his feet in gratitude for the Emancipation Proclamation, the broken fetters falling from his limbs. This group is of bronze, designed by Thomas Ball. It was presented to the city by Hon. Moses Kimball, proprietor of the Boston Museum. On one side of the Square is the station of the Providence Division of the Old Colony Railroad, built at immense cost, and forming one of the handsomest and best-equipped railroad stations in the world. The property in this Square and in the streets branching off from it has increased phenomenally within the past few years, and vast improvements are distinguishable on every hand. This increase between the Square and Church Street may be said to be greater than in any other section of the city. Ten years ago this property was held at a very low valuation, and some of it could hardly be given away, so to speak—that is, could not find a purchaser. Now some of it is immensely valuable, and all of it is very desirable, and with a great future before it. The corner building on the Square was erected by William J. Rotch of New Bedford, at a cost of $75,000. This estate is so valuable that it is assessed at about $40 a foot for tax purposes. The Hollander Building, adjoining, another fine business structure, cost $100,000 to build. The Hotel Thorndike, on Church Street, extending from Boylston to Providence Street, cost about $75,000. It is owned by the heirs of the late Dr. Thorndike. Many of the buildings between the hotel and the Square have been altered over for business purposes, and command high rents.

Let the voyager continue his ride, or his walk along Columbus Avenue ; in fact, explore the whole of the South End, and he will be amazed to witness the transformations that have been effected within a lifetime. Where the sea water once rolled unhindered in majestic waves there are beautiful, wide, well-shaded streets, lined with buildings varying from the plainest to the most splendid in architecture. On two corners of Columbus Avenue and Berkeley Street stand the handsome People's Church (Methodist Episcopal) and the equally attractive First Presbyterian Church, while to the right and to the left are costly apartment houses and mansions betokening affluence on the part of the occupants. Passing over the railroad bridge one sees on the corner of Clarendon Street the fine Columbus Avenue Universalist Church, the pastor of which is the Rev. Dr. A. A. Miner. Farther on, and located on the corner of the avenue and West Rutland Square, is a picturesque structure with ivy-covered walls. This is the Union Church (Congregational Trinitarian). The visitor may

vary his journeylngs as he pleases and find something to interest him at every turn in noting the improvements
effected and the air of refinement which characterizes this residential section.   If at Columbus Square he
turns down Warren Avenue to reach the far-stretching Tremont Street, his attention will be arrested by the
Church of the Disciples standing out prominently on the corner of Warren Avenue and West Brookline Street,
where the late Rev. Dr. James Freeman Clarke was for a long period the pastor.   Beyond, on the corner of

Paine Memorial Building, Appleton Street.

West Canton Street, is the Warren Avenue Baptist Church, and on the corner of Warren Avenue and Dartmouth Street stands one of the most noteworthy structures of its kind in the country—the building of the
Latin and English High Schools, containing seventy-eight rooms and halls, drill hall, gymnasium, etc., standing on an area of 423x220 feet.   Beyond the avenue a little, and to the left on Dartmouth Street, is the old

Army and Navy Monument, Boston Common.

lot adjoining the site of the Latin and English High School, and forming the corner of Montgomery and Clarendon Streets, stands the Clarendon Street Baptist Church, of which the Rev. Dr. A. J. Gordon is the pastor.

Continuing the walk along Warren Avenue until Berkeley Street is reached, there, standing on the corner, at the left, is the handsome Berkeley Street Congregational Trinitarian Church, and on the opposite corner, to the right, the handsome Odd Fellows' Hall building, with its marble front. Near the latter, on Berkeley Street, is the famous Parker Memorial Building, with the Parker Memorial and Summer Halls; while alongside of this edifice is the Paine Memorial Building, with its Paine and Investigator Halls. In the same vicinity are two notable circular buildings, with fortress-like entrances,—the Cyclorama of Gettysburg and the Cyclorama of the Battle of Bunker Hill, both of which are worth visiting.

Turning into Tremont Street, and proceeding up it, the Clarendon Hotel and the St. Cloud Hotel are reached, and opposite the latter is Union Park Street, with a trim, neat parkway in the centre. Through this a view is gained of what was once Edward Everett Hale's South Congregational (Unitarian) Church, but now a Hebrew synagogue. Farther along Tremont Street, and at the corner of West Brookline Street, the Shawmut Congregational Church (Congregational Trinitarian) stands; and when the corner of Pembroke Street is reached we get a glimpse, on looking down the latter street, of the imposing school building occupied by the Girl's Latin and the Girl's High School. Journeying farther up Tremont Street the corner of West Concord Street is reached, and here stands one of the most handsome churches of the Methodist denomination in the city. On Springfield Street, to the left of Tremont Street, is the Home for Aged Men, a most popular and well-managed institution.

Reaching Chester Square, a pleasant little park is seen, intersected with walks; and taking the centre path we reach Washington Street, where, on the left, between Springfield and Worcester Streets, looms up the large marble front building, the Commonwealth Hotel, recently remodelled at a cost of $100,000. Near it, standing in the midst of ample grounds on the corner of West Concord Street, is the building long occupied as the State Normal School for the training of teachers of drawing in the public schools of the State. The school is now located on Newbury Street.

While here it is worth while to turn into East Concord Street, then into Harrison Avenue, and inspect the City Hospital buildings, covering the entire block on this avenue, between East Concord and Springfield Streets. Near these buildings, on East Concord Street, are seen the Homœopathic Hospital and the Massachusetts Medical School. In the immediate neighborhood is the Church of the Immaculate Conception, possessing one of the richest and most impressive interiors of the Roman Catholic Churches in the city. Attached to it is the Boston College of the Roman Catholic body.

Passing into East Newton Street the New England Conservatory of Music—once the St. James Hotel, and now one of the largest and most useful educational institutions in the country—presents itself for inspection. This, started as a music school, is now a general college, with and without boarding conveniences. It is proposed to enlarge the building by making a large music hall, into which is to be placed the "Great Organ," long a noteworthy feature of the Boston Music Hall on Winter Street. In the rear of the Conservatory, and occupying the lot fronting on Washington Street, is the Old South Burying-ground, laid out in 1810. Here are two small, but much appreciated parks, lying on either side of Washington Street, and extending from Newton to Brookline Streets. That on the east side of Washington Street is Franklin Park, and that on the west side Blackstone Park.

Walking along Washington Street in the direction of Boylston Street, one recognizes vast changes in store and other buildings lining this magnificent thoroughfare that have been effected in recent years. Old buildings, of diminutive size, have given place to high, towering structures that are now busy, prosperous marts of trade. One of the most noteworthy edifices on this thoroughfare is the great Cathedral of the Holy Cross, located on the corner of Union Park Street. It is the largest and finest Roman Catholic edifice in the city. It covers more than an acre of ground and its style is of the early English Gothic, cruciform, with nave, transept, aisle and clerestory, the latter supported by two rows of clustered metal pillars. The total length of the building is 364 feet; width at the transept, 170 feet; width of nave and aisles, 90 feet; height to the ridgepole, 120 feet. The entire interior is clear space, broken only by two rows of columns, extending along the nave, and supporting the central roof. The arch separating the spacious front vestibule from the church is of bricks, taken from the ruins of the Ursuline Convent on Mt. Benedict in Somerville, which was burned by a mob on the night of August 11, 1834. The interior is very rich in decoration, and has pew accommodations for 3,000 persons. There are two main towers in front, and a turret, all of unequal height, and all to be eventually surmounted by spires, that on the southwest corner to the height of 300 feet, and that on the opposite corner to 200 feet. At the rear of the Cathedral, on the corner of Union Park Street and Harrison Avenue, is the residence of the Archbishop.

Another notable edifice, erected in 1887, is the Grand Opera House, a building of great size on Washington Street, just above Dover Street. At the corner of Washington and Dover Streets is the Grand Museum, opened in 1888. This was formerly the Windsor Theatre, and was the first "up-town" theatre in the city proper. It was at about this spot that the old fortifications at the "Neck," we have already spoken of, were located. On reaching Hollis Street it is well worth while paying a visit to the handsome theatre which has been erected on the site of the old Unitarian Church, and by the time Boylston Street—the starting point for the tour through the South End—has been reached, a most comprehensive idea of the wonders which have been wrought, and of the vast wealth now centred in the South End will have been gained.

THE BUSINESS DISTRICT.

The region between the North End and South End, the Common and the Harbor, is occupied by the "Business District," where the chief wholesale and retail shops are grouped, the theatres, the city and national buildings, and the older hotels. It is a region bristling with old time associations, is full of historic spots hallowed by the tread and blood of bygone heroes, and was the battle-ground where the forefathers dared to risk limbs and lives in resisting foreign oppression, to throw before them warlike shields, and, à la Macbeth, call to their political taskmaster to "Lay on, Macduff; and damn'd be him that first cries, 'Hold, enough.'" It is a region where the "Cradle of Liberty" has vigilantly rocked, where justice has been gagged and unbound, where fortunes have been won and lost, where statesmen have harangued and poets sung, where fire swept off buildings of generations and men's indomitable pluck and busy hands reared edifices more majestic and beautiful than those which went before, and where modern Bostonians love to point with pardonable pride to past achievements. Here are "items of interest" that would fill volumes, but the limits of these pages necessarily enforce conciseness.

Let us, however, take a hasty run through some of the principal avenues of this renowned, busy centre, and notice in brief some of the relics that have been preserved and link the past with the present, and jot down such chief improvements and alterations in latter days that catch the eye during the journey. Let our starting point be Scollay Square, through which Court Street passes, and from which Tremont Street at the south, and Cornhill at the north, begin. Here is a puzzle for a stranger to start with, for the Court Street which runs through the Square, and off which Brattle, and Hanover and Sudbury Streets shoot, is only a one-sided street, the other side of the thoroughfare—a busy shopping quarter—being designated Tremont Row, the why and wherefore of which it is difficult to discover. Scollay Square, now a great street railroad centre, takes its name from Scollay's Building, which for a long period stood in the middle of the Square, and had a streetway on each side of it. Scollay's Building was the last of a row of buildings, of wedge shape, that extended from the line between Tremont Street and Cornhill to Hanover Street. It was owned by William Scollay, an apothecary, hence its name. It was removed in 1871, and the site was then officially given the name Scollay Square, where, since September 17, 1880, a fine bronze statue of Governor Winthrop has stood.

Crawford House.

The two main streets of the city are Tremont and Washington. As we turn into the former from the

Square, we notice on the left corner that one of Boston's old landmarks has vanished. This was an old-time mansion, where Washington lodged on the occasion of his visit to Boston in 1789, but for a long period prior to its demolition in 1883 was devoted to business. It was originally a three-story building, and another story was added when it ceased to be used as a residence. On the Court Street front of the building, between the second and third stories, was a stone tablet, bearing the inscription, "Occupied by Washington, October, 1789." For half a century the lower story was occupied by S. S. Pierce & Co., grocers, and in the upper rooms Daniel Webster, Harrison Gray Otis, Judge R. I. Burbank and other notabilities had their offices. On its site now stands a high, towering brick structure of many stories, named the Hemenway Building, erected at a cost of $320,000. The old grocery firm are the occupants of the lower part of the building, the upper floors of which are used for offices. On the opposite side of the street, on the corner of Tremont Street and Pemberton Square, a number of old buildings, crowded with lawyers' offices, have within the past two or three years given place to a most imposing brick edifice of many floors, built at a cost of $75,000 by the heirs of Ebenezer Chadwick, and named the Chadwick Building. Here, as of old, the lawyers still "do most congregate." Adjoining the Hemenway Building is the Boston Museum, erected in 1846 at a cost of a quarter of a million of dollars. It is the oldest of the existing theatres in the city, and on its stage have appeared the most celebrated actors and artists of the time. The granite building next beyond, at Nos. 30 and 32, extends backward into Court Square. It is jointly occupied by the Suffolk County Probate Office and the Massachusetts Historical Society, which possesses a valuable library, a lot of rare relics, paintings, busts and unique curiosities.

Adjoining this building is the King's Chapel Burial Ground and the Old King's Chapel itself, occupying the corner of Tremont and School Streets. These are among the most cherished landmarks in the city, and the chapel still preserves in its name the memory of the ancient time when Boston was loyal to England's King. Now a Unitarian church, it was the first Episcopal church erected in New England. In the year 1646 a few Episcopalian citizens timidly craved the Puritan authorities to allow them to worship with the Book of Common Prayer "till inconveniences hereby be found prejudicial to the churches and colony;" but the stern old Roundheads would have none of it. The chaplain of Charles Second's Commission, however, introduced the Episcopal ritual by royal order twenty years later, and in twenty years more a church was erected. On the same site the present King's Chapel was built, in 1749-54, a small and massive structure of blackish stone, whose lower windows, deep set and square, gave point to Matthew Byles's pun, that he had heard of the cannons of the church, but had never seen the port-holes before. The interior, with its high, old-fashioned pews, its tall pulpit and sounding-board, its massive pillars, stained glass window, mural tablets and monuments, is remarkably attractive, and the organ, selected by Handel, the great composer, and sent hither from England in 1756, still serves the church. When the English army evacuated Boston in 1775, the rector left also, and carried with him the vestments and registers and the communion service, a gift of the King, and amounting to 2800 ounces of silver. In 1787 this parish, under the lead of its rector, exchanged Episcopalianism for Unitarianism, and King's Chapel became the first Unitarian Church on the American continent. The old burial ground is rich in coats-of-arms and quaint epitaphs on its monuments, and headstones, and here lie the remains of Winthrop, Shirley and others of the colonial governors, several of the early Puritan clergy, Isaac Johnson and other founders of Boston. Johnson's wife was Lady Arabella, daughter of the Earl of Lincoln, and the climate of New England proved too severe for both of them, for three months after her arrival she died at Salem, and a month later her husband was buried in the King's Chapel Burial Ground. In 1878 the city discussed a proposal to utilize the sites of the chapel and burial ground for a new court-house, but old landmarks were permitted to remain untouched.

In the rear of the chapel, and fronting on School Street, is the handsome City Hall, a costly white granite structure, in the Renaissance style of architecture, built in 1862-65. The city government, on its organization in 1822, was located in Faneuil Hall. Later the Old State House, at the head of State Street, was used as the City Hall, and in 1840, the old Court-House, which occupied the site of the present City Hall, became the seat of the civic government. When the present edifice was erected it was thought to be on a large scale, and sufficient for the needs of the city for many years; but it became overcrowded and for a long time past quite a number of departments have been located in other buildings in the immediate neighborhood. The building, which cost over half a million of dollars to erect, contains five floors and an attic, above which is a high louvre dome, surmounted by a balcony, from which rises a flag-staff 200 feet high. The attic and the dome are utilized as the centre of the fire-alarm telegraph system which spreads all over the city, and the rest of the building is utilized for the offices of the municipality. The structure is handsome and substantial, and is elegant in its appointments throughout. In front of the building is a neatly kept lawn, and this is adorned on one side with a statue of Benjamin Franklin, and on the other with one of Josiah Quincy, the second mayor of the city (in 1823). Probably when the new Court-House, now being erected in Pemberton Square, has been completed, the present Court-House, on Court Square, in the rear of the City Hall, will be utilized for the enlargement of the latter.

School Street (so called because of the old Latin school having been located here) is famous for its ancient corner bookstore. It has stores of a varied character, and lawyers' offices in considerable number, and is noted as the *locale* of the famous Parker House, which, before its costly enlargement, Dickens called the best hotel in America. Originally, it was a spacious six-story marble structure, and during the past four or five years it has been extended on to the corner of Tremont Street, the front of the addition being also of marble and towering higher than the older part of the building. The addition cost to construct over $100,000, and it forms one of the most imposing attractions on Tremont Street.

Revere House.

Opposite King's Chapel, and on the corner of Tremont and Beacon Street, Messrs. Houghton & Dutton have, within the past three years, erected, as an addition to their extensive store, a nine-story, fire proof structure at a cost of $190,000. On the opposite corner is the famous old Tremont House with heavy, dark granite walls, where Henry Clay, Andrew Jackson, the Prince of Wales, Charles Dickens and other notables have sojourned. Dickens wrote of it—"It has more galleries, colonnades, piazzas, and passages than I can remember, or the reader would believe." It has been recently considerably modernized. The heavy portico and flight of granite steps in front have been removed, and the office, reading-room, etc., brought down to the street level. It is said that Mr. Fred. L. Ames has acquired this property and purposes building upon its site a monster hotel in the near future. Adjoining the present building is the famous Old Granary Burying Ground, once a part of the Common. The title of the Old Granary Burying Ground was given to it because of its proximity to the old town granary, which stood where the Park Street Church now stands. More distinguished persons have been buried here than in any other place in the city. Here are entombed the remains of nine governors of Massachusetts, two signers of the Declaration of Independence, six famous divines, the victims of the Boston Massacre, John Hancock, Samuel Adams, Peter Faneuil, Paul Revere, Samuel Sewall, the parents of Benjamin Franklin, and many other notable Americans. Until about sixteen years ago, the crowded sidewalk in front of the burying ground was partly occupied by a line of noble elms, which were imported from England in 1672. To meet the demand of the street railways they were cut down at night, for the civic authorities feared the opposition of the people, who were indignant. Admission to the burying ground is by permit, obtained at the City Hall. On the side of this "God's Acre," is the Park Street Church, built in 1809. It was the first Congregational Trinitarian Church established after Unitarianism had won over from orthodox ranks its principal members. With such persistent earnestness was Calvinism con-

tended for from its pulpit that the "ungodly" of the other sects nick-named the locality "Brimstone Corner." It has now a large and wealthy congregation.

Opposite the Tremont House is a notable building, the Tremont Temple, sandwiched between marts of trade. Its site was formerly occupied by the Tremont Theatre, in which Charlotte Cushman, the famous actress made her *début* on April 8, 1835. In 1843 the Baptists bought the building and erected in its stead a Temple, which was destroyed by fire, as was also its successor, the present structure having

. Hotel Brunswick, Boylston Street cor. Clarendon.

been erected in 1870. It is the place of worship of the Union Temple Free Church, the headquarters of the New England Baptists, and a popular place for public meetings. The main hall is one of the finest in the country, and contains an organ of great power and singular beauty. The hall is 66 feet high and 122 x 72 feet in dimensions and has two galleries. There is seating accommodation for 2,600 persons. Beneath this hall is a smaller one, called Meionaon Hall, with a seating capacity of nearly one thousand. Farther along the street, and facing the Old Granary Burying Ground is the Horticultural Hall, a handsome granite edifice, standing between Montgomery Place and Bromfield Street. This is the headquarters of the Massachusetts Horticultural Society. It contains offices and large, handsome halls for meetings, exhibitions, etc. During a fire which occurred on December 29, 1888, many valuable paintings of past presidents of the society were ruined.

Bromfield Street is one of the many cross streets which connect Tremont and Washington Streets. It contains several publishing houses, offices, varied business stores, and a largely attended Methodist Episcopal Church, of which the Rev. G. A. Crawford is pastor. Some of the buildings adjoining the church have recently undergone extensive alterations and effected a marked improvement in the business aspect of the street. At the corner of Bromfield and Tremont Street is a handsome edifice, the Studio Building, devoted to offices, etc. It has quite recently been reconstructed to a considerable extent internally. Side by side with this building are art and other stores fronting on Tremont Street, and extending to the corner of Hamilton Place, whence Tremont Street is built up only on one side as far as where it is crossed by Boylston Street, the other side of the thoroughfare being occupied by the Common. This length, during shopping hours, presents at all times an animated aspect, the broad sidewalk being at all times crowded with persons good-naturedly elbowing their way through the moving throng.

At the corner of Hamilton Place and in the "place" itself two magnificent buildings have been lately erected at a cost of about $225,000 by the heirs of Jonathan Phillips, and on the opposite side of the "place" most of the old buildings have been rebuilt. In the "place" is one of the entrances to the great Music Hall, another entrance being on Winter Street. It was built in 1852, and is almost entirely concealed by surrounding buildings and is devoid of architectural pretensions, it contains two halls, one seating 2600 and the other 800 persons. The main hall used to contain the largest and finest organ in the world, and it is said it will soon be introduced into the New England Conservatory of Music on East Newton Street. The Music Hall seems to have outlived its usefulness as the home of musicians, and of late years it has been occupied for all sorts of purposes, including fairs, public meetings, balls, cat and dog shows, foot races, walking and wrestling matches, beer garden, etc. More than once the idea has been entertained of demolishing the building to make way for business improvements and to extend Hamilton Place straight through to Washington Street.

Near the corner of Winter Street and fronting on Tremont Street and the Common, is St. Paul's, a church of the Episcopal Communion, erected in 1819–20, and built of dark granite, with a fine Ionic portico and colonnade of sandstone. The ceiling is panelled and cylindrical, and the chancel contains modern frescos and a brilliant stained window. Winter Street, like Temple Place and West Street, is a fashionable retail shopping centre, filled with elegant stores, many of which have been improved and enlarged in recent years. On the corner of Temple Place used to stand the Masonic Temple, always an attractive feature from the time of its erection in 1832 owing to its peculiar formation. It was five stories high and was built of rough Quincy granite. The entrance was a low, broad Norman doorway, and the various floors were lighted by long arched windows. The building was surmounted by battlements and pinnacles and had two towers, each sixteen feet square and ninety-five feet high. The Masonic body held their lodges here until they erected their new Temple on the corner of Boylston Street, and then it was for years occupied as the United States Circuit Court. Three or four years ago the property was purchased by R. H. Stearns & Co., and the building was raised bodily and two stories built under it, while its outward aspect as well as its interior arrangements was entirely changed. It is now devoted to the dry-goods business.

From West Street to Boylston Street high, imposing buildings have been erected on the sites of old houses, and this quarter is now chiefly occupied by the Boston Conservatory of Music, and by so many piano manufacturing concerns as to have earned the name of "Piano Row." The new Masonic Temple, on the corner of Tremont and Boylston Street, built in 1867, is seven stories high, with octagonal towers rising 120

Brick Squares

fact. It contains three magnificent halls for meetings, one being furnished with splendor in the Corinthian style, another in the Egyptian, and the third in the Gothic.

We now turn into Washington Street, and retrace our steps northward along this busy thoroughfare, filled at all hours of the day with a seething mass of human beings. As we turn from Boylston Street (anciently called Frog Lane) into Washington Street, a tablet, with a representation of a spreading tree, will be observed on the front of the building on the east side of Washington Street, corner of Essex. Here stood the "Liberty Tree" under which the "Sons of Liberty" were organized in 1765, and under which meetings were held to give expression of opposition to the revenue oppressions of the English government. When a meeting was intended to be held the signal was given by placing a flag in the branches of the tree, and the flag is still preserved in the Old South Church. In the siege of Boston the tree was purposely destroyed by the British, to the grief of the people.

The present Washington Street has always been the chief artery of the town, though it has not always been known by the name it now bears nor was it formerly so far-stretching in its length. The name Washington was given in honor of General Washington on the occasion of his visit to the town in 1789. At first the present Washington Street was a series of streets from down-town to the Roxbury line, known as Cornhill, Marlborough, Newbury, Orange and Washington; and it was not until 1824 that the old names were dropped, and the entire thoroughfare named as now. Until 1873-4, the down-town end of Washington Street was at the present Cornhill and Old Dock Square, in that year, as noted elsewhere, the street was extended through to Haymarket Square, from which point it now stretches through the city and the Roxbury district to the Dedham boundary. A few doors north of Boylston Street corner we enter the theatre district, where are the Park, Globe, Boston and Bijou theatres, the neighborhood of which presents a very brilliant appearance at evening or just after matinees. In the bend of the street, near the Boston Theatre, is the Adams House, a splendid hotel built in 1883 on the site of the old Adams House, which itself long stood on the site of the Lamb Tavern, whence the first stage to Providence started before the days of railroads. Recently the proprietors of this house have acquired, on a lease for fifteen years at a rental of $30,000 a year, two estates on which they have erected an extension of the hotel. In this immediate neighborhood are the great retail dry-goods houses of the city, notably those of R. H. White & Co, and Jordan, Marsh & Co, with their acres of floorage space. Congregated about these are stores where every variety of merchandise is to be obtained; and the sidewalks are filled from morning till night with an ever-moving throng, while the carriage-way is frequently choked with vehicular traffic. Much of the property here was destroyed in the great fire of 1872, of which more anon. Most of the buildings lining this thoroughfare have, during the past sixteen or eighteen years been greatly altered or entirely rebuilt upon an expensive and ornamental scale; but the street is too narrow for these improvements to be seen to advantage and also for the accommodation of great traffic constantly found here.

Further on we come to the corner of Milk Street, where stands the famous old South Church, that relic of revolutionary times, that tells on a tablet in its tower that the church was erected, first, in 1669, rebuilt in 1729, and that it was "desecrated by the British in 1775," by using it as a riding school and liquor saloon. In these troublous times, however, neither the British nor the colonists hesitated to use the churches for the exigencies of war, for of the latter it is said that they took away the lead pipes from the then church at Cambridge and converted them into bullets with which to kill the armed hosts of England. The site of the old church was originally occupied by the house of Governor Winthrop, who lived and died here. The property was bequeathed by Mrs. Mary Norton (wife of Rev. John Norton) for the erection of a meeting-house. In the days immediately prior to the Revolution, meetings of citizens were held here to discuss their grievances, and such meetings British officers sought to repress. One such meeting was held here when the famous Boston Tea Party, which culminated in the Revolution, occurred on December 16, 1773. Paul Revere, Samuel Adams and about twenty other kindred patriots had been concocting a plan for some time to rid the port of some hateful tea chests that were at the wharves, or soon to arrive there—hateful because of the obnoxious tax of the British government, imposed upon it after the repeal of the "odious Stamp Act." It is said that Sam Adams had contrived this meeting to draw off the attention of the English officers from the scheme to destroy the tea brought over by the ships Dartmouth and Eleanor and the brig Beaver, then at Griffin's (now Liverpool Wharf). When the meeting opened, British officers, with wonted effrontery, crowded the pulpit, so that Dr. Warren, the pastor and the orator on the occasion, had to climb through a rear window to get into the pulpit, which he did. During the proceedings, John Rowe asked, "Who knows how tea will mingle with salt water?" a question which was greeted with shouts of laughter. About sunset an Indian yell was heard outside the church, and a band of men, disguised as Mohawk Indians filled the street. The meeting at once broke up; and the Indians in disguise marched down to the ships, whence they threw into the harbor 342 chests of tea. After the war, the church was used for divine service until the society erected the New Old South Church in the Back Bay district. The old edifice just missed falling a prey to the great fire in 1872, and was then for a time used as a post-office. It is now used for the exhibition of historic relics, lectures, etc., and the basement is occupied as an old bookstore. In the vicinity of the church on the opposite side of the street, formerly stood the Old Province House, of whose quaintness Hawthorne wrote so charmingly. It was built in 1679, and became the vice-regal residence of Shute, Burnet, Shirley, Pownall, Sir William Howe, and a long line of British governors, when the court ceremonies of the province were conducted within its halls, and the royal proclamations were read from its high balcony. The present Province Court was the way to the stables. From its high estate the vice-regal residence descended to the level of a shabby gin-mill and concert hall, and finally to that of a cheap lodging-house, while it became hidden almost from view to pedestrians on Washington Street by the tall buildings erected about it. Now, a handsome six-story hotel, to be named the Boston Tavern, is being erected on its site. In the same vicinity, too, is the great publishing centre, and the oldest bookstore in the city. Book houses are plentiful, and the leading newspaper offices are crowded into this locality. Opposite the church, in Milk Street, is the *Post* building, occupying the site of the house in which Benjamin Franklin was born. Near too, on Washington Street, is the *Transcript* building, and farther north, crowded near each other, are the offices of the *Herald, Journal, Globe, Advertiser,* and *Record,* all occupying tall, costly, well-appointed buildings, the *Globe* building being the latest accession and which is a fitting monument to its enterprise. The *Globe* Newspaper Company is comprised of some of Boston's most highly esteemed and public-spirited citizens, with Mr. Ed. Prescott as president and cashier, and Colonel Charles H. Taylor as manager. This represen-

Globe Building.

tative and progressive Newspaper Company are proprietors of the daily, Sunday, and weekly *Globe,* which are the recognized leading newspapers of New England. The *Globe* Newspaper Company was duly incorporated in 1872 under the laws of Massachusetts. It was reorganized in 1878, with a paid-up capital of $125,000, and now its daily and Sunday issues of the *Globe* have a larger circulation than any other Boston newspaper. The first editor of the *Globe* was Maturin M. Ballou, and the first paper, issued March 4, 1872, contained eight pages of seven columns, the price being four cents. He was succeeded, in August, 1873, by Colonel Chas. H. Taylor, who has been the editor and manager of the *Globe* from that time until the present. The success achieved has been due to his enterprise and industry. The building is one of the finest and largest in Boston, and was built expressly for the *Globe.* The building is admirably equipped with all modern appliances, including elevators, electric lights, etc., and so pains or expense have been spared to make this establishment complete in every detail. In the printing-rooms are three splendid single and two double Hoe presses, which are able to print 1400 papers in a minute. The machinery is driven by two superior 125 horse-power steam-engines, and the total number of persons employed in the various departments is about 300. There are likewise two elevator and electric-light engines on the premises, of the latest type. Eight editions of the *Globe* are turned out daily, which consume fifteen tons of paper. The daily, Sunday, and weekly *Globe* are got up in the highest style of the typographical art. An able and superior staff of editorial writers, reporters, and correspondents is employed. It has regular letters from its own correspondents abroad, and carefully covers all political, local, and foreign news; while at the same time it gives ample descriptions of races, base-ball, and all kinds of manly sports and pastimes. Its editorials are able, crisp, direct to the point, and treat all matters of interest in an impartial and fearless manner. The circulation of the Sunday *Globe* in November was 127,023, and the daily *Globe* 148,710. Its advantages as a splendid advertising medium have been recognized very generally by all classes of the community; and in this line it conducts the largest and most lucrative business in Boston. In consequence of its large size and vast amount of original and able reading-matter, it is not only the cheapest, but unquestionably the best, paper in the city. Colonel Chas. H. Taylor, the manager, was born in Charlestown, Mass., and during the civil war was a private in the 38th Mass. Vol. Infantry. He served one year, and was seriously wounded at the battle of Port Hudson, Miss., and eventually retired from the service, for disability. He was private secretary to Governor Claflin, and was also clerk of the House of Representatives. Colonel Taylor is a popular member of the Press, Temple, Central, and Algonquin Clubs, etc., and is one of Boston's highly esteemed and public-spirited citizens. The circulation of the *Globe* is steadily increasing, not only in Boston, but in all sections of New England, and its present prosperous status augurs well for the future. In "Printing House Square"—and Dock Square, are many old-time buildings, relieved by but few new edifices, prominent among which are Rogers' and Sears' Buildings, magnificent structures at the head of State Street. The whole of the buildings, except a few on the east side that line the remaining length of Washington Street from Dock Square to Haymarket Square, have been built or rebuilt since this section of the street was opened, and no city in the country can show a finer range of business blocks than those to be seen here. Dock Square, on the site of the old Town Dock, which was spanned by a swing bridge at the foot of Merchants' Row, is now a busy centre, and standing in the middle of it is a statue of Samuel Adams erected in 1880. From here is seen the front of Faneuil Hall, and off Washington Street, at this point, Cornhill and Brattle Street swing round to Scollay Square. The famous hostelry, Quincy House, stands on the corner of Brattle Street and Brattle Square; and in this square stood formerly a church which the British turned into a barrack during the siege of Boston. Cornhill, renowned for its old bookstores and up which we must now press once more to Scollay Square, was so named in 1828, having previously been called Market Street, because it lead to the market, the original Cornhill being at the foot of Washington Street before its extension. Having returned to Scollay Square, we must now prepare for a journey, through the principal sections of the great

Bunker Hill Monument.

FINANCIAL AND WHOLESALE BUSINESS CENTRES

of the city. These centres are confined between the harbor on the one hand, and the streets of Essex, Washington, and Hanover, on the other, and lie chiefly south of Blackstone Street. A large portion of this area is frequently spoken of as the "Burnt District," laid waste by the "Great Fire" in 1873. At 7.15 P.M. on November 9th in that year a fire broke out in a building on the corner of Summer and Kingston Streets, and spread with terrible speed, in spite of all the efforts that could be brought from far and near to suppress it, and, before the conflagration was quenched, it had spread over sixty-five acres, and destroyed about eighty million dollars' worth of property and many lives, leaving the entire district bounded by Summer, Washington, Milk, and Broad Streets a smoking chaos of ruins. This was a terrible blow to Boston, but the city soon recovered from it, and the "Burnt District" is to-day a section of imposing and substantial warehouses, its appearance greatly improved, and the wealth and convenience of this part of the city thereby increased. The financial centre is circumscribed by Washington, State, Broad, and Milk Streets. The great dry-goods and clothing quarter covers a large area. The wholesale trade is chiefly centred in Devonshire, between Milk and Franklin Streets, Franklin and its lateral streets, Winthrop Square and Otis Street, Summer and its lateral streets. The great woolhouses are located principally on Federal, Pearl, and High Streets; the boot, shoe, and leather, and hardware trades on Pearl, High, Purchase, lower part of Summer, South, Bedford, and parts of Lincoln and contiguous streets; the paper trade, on Federal Street and vicinity; crockery, on Federal and Franklin Streets; drugs, on Milk Street and vicinity; grocery trade in neighborhood of Broad, Commercial India streets; fish, on Commercial Street and Atlantic Avenue; flour and grain, on Commercial Street, near the principal wharves; fruit and produce, Merchants' Row, Chatham and South Market, Commercial, Commerce, and Clinton Streets; and provisions, on streets about Faneuil Hall Market and the new meat market on Mercantile Wharf.

As we start from Scollay Square, in the direction of State Street, the County Court-house, on Court Street (called Queen Street in pre-Revolution days), claims attention. It is a ponderous, gloomy granite building, with a heavy Doric portico in front, and formerly had a similar portico at the rear end of the building, facing the City Hall. Here numerous courts are held, and, as a consequence of its inadequacy to meet the demands upon it, the new court-house on Pemberton Square is being erected. On the old court-house, which was erected in 1836, an intense excitement centred many years ago, when the fugitive slave cases were under trial; and the citizens of Boston, indignant that men should be carried from their free soil into a terrible and degrading servitude, came near rebelling against the United States and rescuing the doomed negroes by force of arms. In the vicinity of this seat of justice are the Tudor Buildings, on the site of the home of Colonel William Tudor, a statesman and jurist of many years ago. In this neighborhood, also, Smibert, the canny Scot, painted "Landscapes," more than a century and a half ago; and Franklin printed his pioneer newspaper; and Captain Kidd, the famous pirate, was jailed; and Sir John Leverett, the friend and veteran of Cromwell, resided. Standing near the Court-house is the famous Young's Hotel, adjoining which is the splendid Sears' Building, occupying the corner of Court and Washington Streets.

Directly opposite this, occupying the head of State (once King) Street, is the old State-house, occupying the site of what was originally the old village market-place. A town-house was first erected here in 1658, and in 1748 a new building arose on the same ground, which was used for the Provincial Council, and also at different times for an exchange, a post-office, an engine-house, barracks for British troops, and a capitol in which the State Legislature met for fifteen years. Here, according to John Adams, "Independence was born;" here the death of George II. and the accession to the throne, of George III. were proclaimed; here Generals Howe, Clinton and Gage held a council of war before the battle of Bunker Hill; and a year later the Declaration of Independence was read from the balcony to the rejoicing soldiers and people below; and the constitution of Massachusetts was planned; and Governor Hancock gave a grand reception to the Count d'Estaing; and Washington reviewed the militia and was welcomed by the people. The quaint old steeple lost part of its height and the lion and unicorn disappeared from the angles of the roof after the Revolution and were burned; but otherwise the building maintained its original aspect. Some six or seven years ago the building was completely restored, to preserve its historic features, even to the fixing of the lion and unicorn on the west front, a fact which raised the ire of Irish citizens, who could recognize nothing even that was good out of the land of the hated Anglo-Saxon. Attempts were made to destroy these emblems in secret, but too strict a watch was kept on the toothless lion and blind unicorn, and they were permitted to remain; still the grumblers declined to be quiet until something of a counteracting character was put on the Washington Street end of the building, to balance it, to hold it down, or something of that kind. A gorgeous gilt eagle was accordingly spread on the outer wall, accompanied with the State's motto in gold characters on a broad ribbon—"Ense Petit Placidam Sub Libertate Quietem." And it did "quiet 'em;" so the old lion and unicorn are now at peace. It was near here—on the corner of State and Exchange Streets, where the Custom-house then stood—that the Boston Massacre, described elsewhere, occurred. On the building now on the corner the Bostonian Society, in 1888 placed a tablet bearing this inscription: "Opposite this spot was shed the first blood of the American Revolution, March 5, 1770." On the opposite side of the street, near the Old State-house, the first church was built in Boston. Brazer's Building now occupies the site, and near this is the office of the *Traveller* newspaper.

On State Street are numerous banks and insurance offices, and the headquarters of many mining and manufacturing companies and railways, shipping-offices, etc. The Merchants' Exchange, the Board of Trade, and the Stock Exchange are in the building No. 53, opposite 'Change Avenue. Great changes are projected here. The entire lot of buildings extending from the Tremont Bank Building to Kilby Street will soon be torn down to make room for a new Stock Exchange, to be erected at a cost of millions of dollars. Messrs. Peabody & Stearns have for some time been engaged in making designs, and the plans, sections, and elevations are completed. Builders will soon be at work, and the building they will raise will be the largest of its kind in the city. It will be ten stories high above the basement, and in parts eleven stories high. From the sidewalk on the State Street front to the cornice there will be a height of about 160 feet. It will have a frontage of 171 feet on State Street from the Tremont Bank Building (which is five stories high) to Kilby Street, about the same on Kilby Street, and 52 feet on Exchange Place and Post-office Avenue, the last named leading from

Massachusetts Horticultural Society Building

Congress Street, just in the rear of the Tremont Bank building. Stone will be the material for the two lower stories, the rest being of brick, with stone trimmings. The interior finish will be plain but very serviceable, in marble, natural woods, and plastered walls suitably tinted. Steam heat, open fireplaces, electric lights, and all the modern conveniences, together with six fast-running elevators, will make the building desirable in every way for the purposes to which it is to be put. The main entrance will be on State Street. A broad corridor, finished in marble, will lead direct to the entrance of the Stock Exchange Hall, and another corridor, at right angles to it, will lead from the Kilby Street entrance to an entrance at Post-office Avenue, a short alley leading from Congress Street. Near the junction of these corridors will be the large main staircase. In the basement, at the right of the main entrance on State Street, will be rooms and vaults for a safe-deposit company. In front is the large banking-room, 50 by 60 feet, and in the rear the vaults for about 10,000 boxes of varying sizes, as well as "coupon-rooms" for the patrons of the company. A novelty here is a number of coupon-rooms, eight feet square. At the left of the main entrance, and along the Kilby Street front, are half a dozen offices of varying size, the largest being the one on the corner, and this has a separate entrance at the intersection of the streets. In the wing of the building extending to Exchange Place are a couple of desirable offices fronting on that street, and several smaller ones. The Boston Stock Exchange, as already stated, will occupy a hall in the first story under a twenty years' lease. This hall will have an area of about 5000 feet, and will be in the Exchange Place wing. Here also are three large rooms for "puts" and "calls," and the bond and telephone rooms. The Stock Exchange will have a private entrance on Exchange Place. The main portion of this floor, with frontage on State and Kilby Streets, will be devoted to banking and insurance offices, which will be subdivided to suit tenants. The arrangement of the second story is very similar to the first, the Exchange Place wing being taken up by the Stock Exchange Hall, which is two stories in height, and the State and Kilby Street fronts being divided up into banking and insurance offices. Upon this story begins the light-well, 116x38 feet, situated west of the central stairway and over the safe-deposit vaults, which, as well as the rear of the offices on the first story, are lighted by it. This well extends from the Tremont Bank Building, parallel with State Street, and is nearly as broad as Kilby Street. By means of it, an additional row of well-lighted offices is obtained in the upper stories. Above the second story the arrangement of the floors will be substantially alike, as represented in the third-floor plan. The floors will be devoted to offices, ranging in size from 12x20 to 20x30 feet, which are reached by broad corridors following the several frontages of the building. The central stairway stops at the second story, and from thence upward there are flights of stairs in front and rear, directly opposite the elevator-wells. The third and the stories above have toilet-rooms over those in the basement, thus concentrating the plumbing as far as possible. There are 350 offices in the building. Changes in the floor plans will be freely made to suit tenants. In the interior finish, no elaborate effects will be sought, and the exterior convenience has nowhere been sacrificed for architectural effect. Nevertheless,

Commonwealth Avenue, showing Hotel Vendome.

the building will be an exceedingly handsome addition to the business blocks of Boston. It will be a year and a half before the building will be completed; and the cost of building and land will probably be upwards of $3,000,000.

On the north side of State Street the Hospital-Life Building has just been completed at a cost of $800,000, and opposite Merchants' Row there is now nearing completion a nine-story building erected by Mr. J. N. Fiske at a cost of half a million of dollars. State Street is, in fact, becoming a region of tall, costly buildings, and has changed much of its aspect of a dozen years or so ago.

Proceeding through Merchants' Row, the historic Faneuil Hall, the "Cradle of Liberty," and the New Faneuil Hall, or Quincy Market, are reached. The latter, built in 1825-26, is a granite structure two stories high, and covers 27,000 feet of land. The centre part rises to a height of 77 feet, and is ornamented by a graceful dome. The height of the wings on either side of the central part is thirty feet. The market is on the lower floor, the stalls are well arranged, and the place is always a busy one and worthy of a visit. The upper floor is used for offices, and a large hall under the dome is occupied by the Boston Chamber of Commerce, for whom it is proposed to erect at an early date, a separate building. Faneuil Hall was built in 1742, and presented to the town by Peter Faneuil, a prosperous Huguenot merchant, as a market and public hall; and the present city charter contains a provision forbidding its sale or lease. The lower floor is occupied as the market, and the upper floor as a hall, which contains no seats, and which gives standing room to thousands of people. In the galleries, however, there are settees. The platform is spacious, the walls are adorned with copies of large and valuable historic oil-paintings, the originals being deposited in the Art Museum for safe keeping; and the quaint and antiquated architecture is very interesting. When any great popular question takes definite form, the people say, "Let's go down and rock the cradle," and assemble in the hall, to be addressed by their favorite orators and leaders. It was so before the Revolution; it has been so since. It has, in fact, during its history, been used for all sorts of purposes. The coronation of George III. was celebrated in it, pirates and robbers have been tried in it, and the Earl of Elgin was feasted there. "Every political party in the country has had its use at one time or another. Anarchists, Socialists, Fenians, and Land-leaguers have spoken there. The Chinese have been told to go, and the poor Indian pitied by large audiences. The Constitution of U. S. has been styled 'a covenant with death and a league with hell' in this hall." In June, 1887, the British Charitable Society obtained the consent of the Mayor and Board of Aldermen for its use on the occasion of a banquet on the 21st of that month to celebrate the jubilee of Queen Victoria. It provoked a howl among the Irish residents against such a "desecration" of the hall, the use of which they themselves secured to protest against the "desecration" and to say hard things against Britisher, generally. The Aldermen reconsidered their resolution granting the use of the hall, but without change, and the Britishers held their banquet, and that a lively one, for a mob of about 15,000 persons gathered about the hall ready to turn the "cradle" over. The whole police force, of over 800 men, were called out, armed with revolvers, and 400 were stationed around the hall. Several of the military companies were under arms, and Gatling guns were placed in position to rake the mob if necessity required. Several persons were seriously injured, and during the night an attempt was made to pull, with ropes, the lion and unicorn from off the Old State-house. The occasion served as a lesson to the English, who had generally been indifferent to naturalization; they formed the British-American Association, with branches all over the country, the object of which was to encourage Englishmen to become American citizens and to vote against class rule.

North Market and South Market Streets, Chatham, Clinton, and Commerce Streets, running parallel with Faneuil Hall and Quincy Markets, and Blackstone, Fulton, and Commercial, and other neighboring streets are great centres for the wholesale trade in all kinds of food products. The conversion of the so-called Mercantile Wharf property, at the foot of Clinton Street and on Atlantic Avenue, into a country market, as well as a wholesale meat market, has attracted provision-dealers and grocerymen to that section of the city, and naturally the wholesale grocers in that vicinity, and especially on Commercial Street, have pushed their trade. Below this market, on Atlantic Avenue, is the Fish Market, another attraction to dealers. Property between Richmond Street and Faneuil Hall Market has improved recently in value, in keeping with the improved surrounding conditions. On Fulton Street the wholesale fruit trade is advancing, and tall warehouses have been and are being erected. To meet the exigencies of the shipping trade, costly warehouses have been erected along Atlantic Avenue, from near the corner of which, and extending almost close up to the Custom-house, on State Street, a magnificent, extensive granite block of spacious warehouses of pleasing exterior has been put up.

The Custom-house was built between 1837 and 1849, at a cost of over one million dollars, and rests on ground reclaimed from the sea, the foundation being composed of a deep bed of granite masonry, laid in hydraulic cement on the heads of three thousand piles. It is a massive granite structure, built to stand for generations. It is Doric in style, cruciform in shape, and fire-proof in construction, with thirty-two fluted monolithic columns, weighing forty-two tons each, fronting its stately porticoes and extending around the sides, surmounted by classic cornices and pediments, and sustaining a roof and dome of granite slabs. Under the dome is a handsome rotunda, surrounded by twelve tall Corinthian columns of white marble. This building is one of the principal attractions on State Street, which maintains its old-time supremacy as the financial centre, though in some of its off streets, notably Devonshire, Congress, and Kilby Streets, banks and brokers' and insurance offices are to be found in great numbers. These are located in buildings of large size and of great architectural beauty. Congress, Devonshire, Milk, and Water Streets, at their crossings, form Post-office Square, wherein stands the Government Building, an immense but very ornamental pile of Cape Ann granite. The erection of the building was begun in 1871 and some fourteen or fifteen years elapsed before it was entirely completed, the cost being upwards of six millions of dollars.

Fronting on Post-office Square are several fine specimens of the modern business structure, designed both for architectural effect and utility. On the south side of the square is a magnificent white marble building, with a majestic clock-tower. This is by some considered the handsomest block in New England and it cost $900,000 to build. It is owned and occupied by the Mutual Life Insurance Company of New York. The tower is surmounted by gilded crests and an iron flag-staff, and the height from the street to the top of the flag staff is 234 feet. At a height of 198 feet from the sidewalk is a balcony on the tower; and from this balcony a charming view of the city and harbor is to be obtained. Adjoining, and occupying the corner of Congress Street, is the handsome building of the New England Mutual Life Company, erected at a cost of $1,000,000. In the basement of the building are the extensive fire and burglar-proof vaults and the superb reading-room of the Security Safe Vaults Co. From the roof of this building a fine view is to be obtained. A few yards away, occupying the corner of Devonshire and Milk Street, is the splendid building of the Equitable

Boylston Street and Copley Square.

Life Assurance Society of New York, built in 1873 at a cost of between one and two millions of dollars. In 1885-86 the building was extended, and its Milk-street façade altered, at an immense outlay of capital. It stands on the site of the house of Robert Trent Paine, one of the signers of the Declaration of Independence. Within about a stone-throw from here, and bounded by Milk Street and Kilby Street, is Liberty Square, whereon stands an immense, imposing, solidly built business structure, presenting a roundling front on Kilby Street, and possessing a peculiar, dome-like roof. This is the Mason Building, occupied by banks and offices. Contiguous thereto are the great wholesale trade thoroughfares of Broad Street (opened in 1806 and originally called Flounder Lane) and India Street (opened in the following year for the East India trade).

Nearly opposite the Milk-street end of Mason Building, we enter Oliver Street and the "Burnt District," and by way of this street attain Fort Hill Square, where used to stand Fort Hill, one of the three noted hills of "Tremont." Half a century ago this was an aristocratic residential quarter. The hill has been carried away; and the work of doing this was started in 1868, and continued for years. A park occupied the summit of the hill, on which at one time were fortifications. Within the fort here Sir Edmund Andros, in 1689, sought shelter from, and was subsequently surrendered to, the enraged colonists, whose rights he had usurped. A neat circular grass-plat occupies the centre of Fort Hill Square, now the highest point of the hill. From here the entire area, stretching to Essex and Washington Streets on the one hand, and from Atlantic Avenue to Milk Street on the other, is occupied by Oliver, Pearl, Franklin, Purchase, Congress, Devonshire, Summer, Bedford, Kingston, Arch, Chauncey, and Hawley Streets and Winthrop Square; and here are control the great wool, boot, shoe and leather, hides, fur, oil, dry-goods, paper, hardware, and crockery jobbing-houses. This was the area swept and laid waste by the great fire of 1872. Here are now to be found some of the finest specimens of modern architecture; and no business section of any of our American cities presents more solid and attractive features than this one does. The buildings are painted in character, and new structures are continually rising and others being altered and extended. From the corner of Congress Street down to the property of the New York & New England Railroad, adjoining its passenger station, there is a row of six magnificent blocks of business buildings of recent erection the equal of which it would be difficult to match in the country. Five of them are occupied by extensive wool firm, and the sixth for other kinds of business. They are all six stories in height, of enough difference in façade to break up the monotony of equality in other respects. They are of solid and substantial construction, and have passageways on the sides and rens for receiving and shipping, which preclude the necessity of blocking sidewalks and stopping travel, as is too frequently the case in all cities. These buildings cost $411,000 to erect. On one corner of Purchase and Pearl Streets formerly stood a Protestant Church, which subsequently became a Catholic Church, and now it has been replaced, at a cost of $80,000, by a handsome six-story business building. On the opposite corner stand the remains of an old building that escaped the fire. This lot and one on the corner of Oliver and Purchase Street, are the only two which remain unimproved in the "Burnt District." The prospectus of the year 1889 indicates a large increase in building operations within the city proper, as well as the outlying districts. Plans now matured and presented, but for which permits have not yet been issued, are for some of the most palatial business structures, which will rival, if not surpass, any now erected in the Union.

THE BRIGHTON DISTRICT

constitutes the 25th ward of the city, and was annexed to Boston in 1873, and increased the city's dimensions by 2277 acres. The situation is one of the finest in the vicinity of Boston. The neighborhood generally is one of high lands, possessing fine facilities for drainage, and abounding in the finest locations for dwelling purposes to be found anywhere. A great feature of the Brighton District is Chestnut Hill Reservoir and the parkways about it. The construction of the reservoir was begun in 1865, and the city of Boston became possessed of 212½ acres of land, the work costing about $120,000 before it was finished. It is, in fact, a double reservoir, divided by a water-tight dam into two basins of irregular shape. Their capacity is 730,000,000 gallons, and the water-surface is 123½ acres. A magnificent driveway, varying from 60 to 80 feet in width, surrounds the entire work. In some parts, the road runs quite close to the embankment, separated from it by only a smooth, gravelled walk.

The splendid driveway around the reservoir is reached from Boston by the Brighton Road, which is a continuation of Beacon Street, and a noted trotting and driving course that at almost all seasons in the year is, especially on afternoons, crowded with gay equipages, worth coming from afar to see. Brighton can also be reached by the Boston & Albany Railroad, and by horse and electric cars.

Originally, Brighton formed a part of Cambridge, and was known as Little Cambridge. It became a separate town in 1807, and remained so until it was absorbed by Boston, in 1873. The elevated lands of Brighton afford charming views, and the streets are pleasant and shady. Brighton has long been noted for its extensive abbatoirs; and persons who know little about the place have pictured its streets as being crowded with cattle and hogs, and as being ill-smelling. The abbatoirs, however, are situated near the line of the Boston & Albany Railroad; and while thousands of cattle, sheep, and pigs are slaughtered here weekly, so retired are the slaughter-houses that the most refined inhabitant of Brighton may abide here in happy ignorance of their presence.

Brighton contains many beautiful mansions. Within the last few years, building operations have been active, land has increased in value, the population has multiplied; and it is predicted that the range of hills in this District, running southwest from Covey Hill, and including the latter, will in time be the "court end" of Boston. The opening up of Commonwealth Avenue, from Arlington Street to Chestnut Hill Reservoir —four and three quarters miles in length,—and also of Beacon Street, thus offering the finest facilities for travel, brought much low-priced farm lands into the market for building purposes. The route from the city proper to this section is a magnificent series of parks; and in the District itself are several fine parks, in the improvement of which considerable expense has been incurred. On Brighton Square is a splendid branch of the Boston Public Library. This branch was originally founded in 1864 as the Holton Library, by the town of Brighton; and on the annexation of the town the library became a branch of the now main library of Boston. The building is a very convenient one and well-stocked with books. Brighton was one of the first places in the State to erect a monument to the soldiers and sailors who fell in the War of the Rebellion. The monument, a very handsome one, stands in Evergreen Cemetery, and was dedicated July 26, 1866. It is 30 feet high and of Quincy granite. Brighton is assured a progressive and prosperous future.

SOUTH BOSTON

was set off from Dorchester and joined to Boston in 1804. The district extends about two miles along the south side of the harbor, an arm of which, known as Fort Point Channel, separates it from the city proper. This channel has been much narrowed by filling up, and the " made " land is chiefly occupied by the railroads. The channel is crossed by bridges. When South Boston was added to Boston, the city acquired 1002 additional acres of land; but at that time there were only ten families on the territory. The annexation, it is said, was the outcome of a real-estate speculation; and the most active promoters of it were actuated by a belief that in the near future this district would become a very populous and fashionable one. But their expectations were not as rapidly realized as they predicted. Soon after the annexation, a bridge was built across the channel at the " Neck," at Dover Street, and was opened in March, 1804, with a military display and great civic " pomp and circumstance." It was 1550 feet long, and cost $50,000 to construct it. In recent years there has been substituted a fine, substantial iron bridge. In 1828, a second South Boston Bridge was built, from the foot of Federal Street; and now in the matter of bridges the city proper and South Boston are adequately connected, the latest important addition in this respect being the magnificent iron bridge extending from Broadway to Harrison Avenue. The building of the earliest bridges led to an increase of the population of South Boston; and though the district failed to become, as had been predicted, the " court end " of the city, many fine residences were reared upon the sightly bluffs towards the South Boston Neck. South Boston experienced its most rapid growth after the street-railway system had been established, in 1854. Then it was that building operations multiplied. Dwellings arose on every hand, and several important and notable public institutions were erected here, while factories, foundries,

Bond Street.

street system of South Boston is very regular, which is more than can be said for the city proper, especially in its most ancient parts. Broadway is the principal thoroughfare, and runs through the centre from Albany Street, in the city proper, to City Point, at the extreme end of South Boston. The parallel streets on either side are generally numbered, and the cross-streets lettered. Broadway, on which are located many fine business blocks, splendid church edifices, and neat-looking mansions, is divided into West and East, that portion from Albany Street to Dorchester Street being designated as West Broadway, and that from Dorchester Street to City Point, East Broadway. A walk or ride up Broadway is interesting, particularly so beyond Dorchester Street. City Point is the common terminus for the horse-car lines, and is one of the two chief places of interest for the mere spectator, the other being Dorchester Heights. The Point is a favorite resort in the summer season, when the place presents a lively appearance, visitors finding all necessary facilities for fun and frolic and everything that can contribute to their enjoyment. The Point commands a magnificent harbor views, and yachting sights innumerable. Indeed, this is the greatest rendezvous on the Eastern Massachusetts coast for yachts, as respects numbers; for there are other places where yachts of larger tonnage than those which anchor here are more numerous. Southerly, a fine view is obtained of Dorchester, the Blue Hills, and parts of Quincy. The Point abounds in seaside hotels and cafés. Here, too, is the new Marine Park, with its long promenade pier extending nearly to Fort Independence (the old Castle Island) in the harbor.

In the immediate neighborhood is the School for Idiotic and Feeble-minded Children, at No. 783 East Eighth Street; also the City Asylum for the Insane, and the Suffolk House of Correction on First Street. Standing on a high elevation on the corner of Broadway and Emerson Street, and commanding charming views over land and water, is the building of the world-renowned charity, the Perkins Institution for the Blind, over which the late learned Dr. S. G. Howe presided successfully for many years. Near by are the historic Dorchester Heights, famous in Revolutionary lore. These heights were included in the territory annexed to Boston in 1804, and are sometimes spoken of as Telegraph Hill (though it is many years since it was used for marine telegraphing purposes) and also as Mount Washington. As mentioned elsewhere in this work, Washington, during the siege of Boston, by a strategic movement, seized upon these heights and fortified them, to the astonishment of the British, who were in possession of the city. All other points of vantage were in the hands of the English; and Washington, seeing they had neglected to hold the heights, determined, in March, 1776, to seize them and throw up formidable works with despatch. The ground was frozen and the weather bad, and his army was scattered over East Cambridge and Roxbury. When night set in, he caused a heavy cannonading to begin from both East Cambridge and Roxbury that should claim the attention of the English soldiery and prevent the work going on on the heights from being heard. To still further deaden the noise of the carts passing over the frozen ground, their wheels were bound with whisps of straw, and straw was strewn over the roads through which they passed. When daylight dawned on the morning of the 4th of March, the British were not only surprised, but alarmed, by the fortifications they saw on the heights. Howe, the English commander, determined to storm the fortifications on the following night, and to this end sent three thousand men to Castle Island (now Fort Independence), to make an attack from that side. A storm, however, arose, that prevented the carrying out of the design; and meanwhile the Americans kept on vigilantly strengthening their works until the British recognized they were too formidable to overthrow, and decided to evacuate the town. This they did on the 17th; and Washington, to the great delight of the citizens and the whole country, then marched with his soldiers into Boston, where he was hailed as a deliverer. This is regarded as one of the greatest military achievements of the "Father of the Country."

On the slope of hill on Old Harbor Street is Carney Hospital, a public institution of great excellence, conducted by the Sisters of Charity, and its usefulness is extended to both Catholics and Protestants alike.

A vast area of land has been reclaimed and is being reclaimed from the Bay at South Boston, and the place is renowned for its numerous and varied foundries, sugar-refineries, breweries, and other noteworthy industries. These are for the most part located along the water-sides of the district and afford employment to vast numbers of workpeople. Among the most noted works here are those of the South Boston Iron Company, on Foundry Street. The concern covers nearly seven acres, and is the largest of its kind in the country. It was founded by Cyrus Alger, the famous metallurgist and inventor, who constructed the first perfect bronze cannon for the national and State governments. Here have been produced the largest cannon ever made in America.

Handsome as South Boston is as a residential section, noted as it is for its cottages, and populous as it is, it has never been very attractive to the aristocratic citizens as a place of residence; and a peculiarity attached to it is the falling in value of property in what were once the most select sections and the growth in value of building-lots in others. The old-timers who owned the fine hill residences have been attracted to more fashionable sections of the city, or made homes in the suburbs; and, on putting their property into the market, have found that they could sell only at from thirty to fifty per cent below the cost of building. The consequence is that there has been considerable falling off in the valuation of property in this section of South Boston; but it has been more than made up by the advances realized elsewhere through the erection of tenement-houses and moderate-priced dwellings. Since 1883, about 600 houses (chiefly of the tenement class) have been erected in the district, most of them in the territory east of Dorchester Street and well toward the Point. These are occupied mostly by mechanics. Many single houses, too, have been erected, costing from $3000 to $4000. In Ward 13, there is a large co-operative tenement building on Second Street, corner of Athens, near Dorchester Avenue. It is a four-story building, and contains about thirty tenements, ranging from three rooms and upward each. There have been many improvements made at and near the Boston wharf property. Among others is the establishment at this place of the Chace Confectionery Works. To show how, on the other hand, land has varied in value, it may be stated that the local gas company, some ten or fifteen years ago, paid $2 a foot for a piece of land on the corner of B and Third Streets, for which a dollar a foot can now be hardly realized. There has been an offer of 75 cents a foot for it. Another peculiarity of land values is that, while vacant land on the south of Broadway is taxed at from 40 to 50 cents a foot, on the north side of that thoroughfare, it is taxed at only from 20 to 25 cents per foot. The valuation of the three wards, 13, 14 and 15, comprised in South Boston has increased in the last five years $2,939,100, and the population, according to the number of polls, about 7000.

EAST BOSTON.

This now populous and busy centre little more than half a century ago was a wilderness, and was occupied by only one family, while to-day it has upon it more than forty thousand people; is crossed and recrossed with streets lined with stores, factories, foundries, workshops, dwellings, churches, schools, etc., by the thousands; its thoroughfares are kept lively with the eternal jingle of the bells of railroad-car horses and the din of the wheels of traffic; from its piers ferry-boats flit hither and thither by day and by night; and to and from its extensive wharves ocean steamers come and go at will burdened with merchandise and human freight; while its shipyards turn into the deep vessels that plow the billows from coast to coast. And all this is the achievement of half a century!

East Boston is an island situated at the confluence of the Mystic and Charles Rivers, and is connected with the city proper by ferry, and with the mainland at Chelsea and Winthrop by bridges. Its original name was Noddle Island, and it received this appellation on account of having been occupied by one William Noddle, who, by old writers, was designated "an honest man from Salem." Its "settlement"—if such a term can be legitimately used—dates back to the earliest accounts of Massachusetts Bay, and its history includes many interesting incidents, both of a local and general character. From the time of its discovery it became, owing to its close proximity to Boston, a favorite pasture-ground. In this way both it and the other islands in the harbor yielded considerable revenue, and at the time of the Revolution all the islands were well-stocked with domestic animals. Noddle Island was also a favorite fishing-ground.

On November 3, 1620, King James I. granted the territory hereabouts to the council of Plymouth, who, on December, 13, 1622, gave to Robert Gorges, youngest son of Ferdinando Gorges (who had expended £20,000 in fruitless attempts to make settlements in various parts of Massachusetts) various lands. This gift included Noddle Island. Robert died, and his brother John, who succeeded him as proprietor in January, 1628, conveyed the island and other lands to Sir William Brereton, of Handforth, Co. Chester, England, who sent over servants to improve the lands and make hay; but neither the Plymouth council nor his own own government seem to have recognized his authority, and he does not appear to have ever come to the country himself. But be that as it may, it seems that according to the colony records, the General Court, on April 1, 1633, granted the island to Samuel Maverick, and this under the title of Noddle Island. This fact demonstrates that William Noddle, who is believed to have been one of Sir W. Brereton's colonists, and who was made a freeman in 1631, occupied the island previously. Prior to Maverick coming into possession the General Court seems to have exercised a care over the island, for in 1631 it passed an order restraining persons from "putting on Cattell, felling wood or raising slate" on this island. Like all the islands in the harbor, there appeared to be forests growing upon Noddle's Island in former times, and apparently a similar fate befel them all to be bereft of this growth. In 1632 the following order was passed: "Noe p'son wt'soever shall shoot att fowle upon Pullen Poynte or Noddle's Island, but the sd places shallbe reserved for John Perkins, to take fowle with netts." The following is a copy of the orders passed in favor of Mr. Maverick, who acquired all John Per-kin's privileges:

"Noddle's Island is granted to Mr. Sam'l Mavack to enjoy to to him and his heires for ever. Yielding and & payeing yearly att ye Generall Court, to ye Gov'n'r for the time being, either a fatt wether, a fatt hogg, or Xs in money, & shalle give leave to Boston and Charles Towne to fetch woode contynually, as theire needs requires, from ye southerne p'te of sd island." It appears that the "needs" of Boston and Charlestown re-

Museum of Fine Arts, St. James Avenue.

quired all the wood growing, and these two enterprising towns appear to have used it pretty freely, for by 1833 they had removed all the timber on the island except two trees!

Noddle's Island was "layd to Boston," as it was termed, in 1636. It originally contained about 660 acres, together with the contiguous flats to low-water mark. Before any alterations in topography had been made the island was fancifully stated to resemble a great bear, described as follows: "The bear's head, an elevated tract of land, was known as the 'middle farm,' with Hog Island marsh at its northeast. The small, round pond in this part called Eye pond in consequence of the loss there of the eye of a noted gunner helps out the fancied figure. The bear's back, fronting the mouth of Mystic River, was the most elevated part of the island, and was known as Eagle Hill, and its abrupt termination at the confluence of Mystic River and Chelsea Creek as West Head, and more recently as Eagle Point. The two fore feet of the assumed bear were called Eastern and Western Wood Islands, being isolated from the Great Marsh, which also isolated Camp Hill and its marsh, the two hinder paws from the same. The heel of the hinder leg was called Smith's Hill, the site of the old buildings which anciently stood on the island, and was separated from Camp Hill by Great Creek, since the canal of the water-power company, lying between the present Bainbridge and Decatur Streets. The old houses on Smith's Hill were destroyed in 1775, during the seige of Boston, and were rebuilt soon after the British evacuated the town from materials taken from the old barracks used by Washington's army in Cambridge. In 1776 a fort was erected on Camp Hill. This or Smith's Hill may have been the site of Mr. Maverick's fort of four guns erected in 1630." In 1814 another more substantial fort was placed on Camp Hill, called Fort Strong, in compliment to the governor then. This was long ago removed, and Belmont Square now occupies its site.

Samuel Maverick, who was the son of the Rev. John Maverick of Dorchester mentioned in the foregoing pages, was born in 1602. He was evidently in his day a man of considerable importance, and exercised great hospitality at his island home, where he was frequently visited by Governor Winthrop and other notabilities. When Mt. Wollaston in Quincy belonged to Boston, Maverick was there granted the use of five hundred acres for the pasturing of his cattle. In 1645 he made a loan to the town toward fortifying Castle Island, which the town guaranteed should be refunded "in case said garrison be defeated or demolished, except by adversary power, within three years." From the earliest settlement of Boston religious persecutions characterized the colonists, though they had fled from their native land on account of similar intolerance. Maverick was a devout Episcopalian and because of the persecutions to which he was subjected he gave up his residence, and, conjointly with his wife and son, Nathaniel, sold his property to Captain George Briggs of Barbadoes, who, in the same year (1650) conveyed it to Nathaniel, and the latter on October 28, 1650, conveyed it to Colonel John Burch of Barbadoes. In 1656

Thomas Boughton purchased the island through Richard Lewder, his attorney, who took the deed in his own name and that of Richard Newbold. On account of financial embarrassment Boughton, on April 19, 1658, conveyed the island and other property to Henry Shrimpton and Richard Cooke of Boston, and Walter Price of Salem, in trust for his creditors. Shrimpton declined this trust, as full pos-

Boylston Street.

session of Noddle Island had been previously given to Walter Price. In 1661 Sir Thomas Temple purchased Cooke's interest, and in 1687 Newbold's interest (as creditors of Boughton) in the island and became sole owner. In 1670 Temple sold out to Samuel Shrimpton, who, in 1682, by the payment of £30 to the State, cleared the island of all the conditions in the grant to Maverick, and thus became the first person who held it in his own right in fee-simple. The property descended to his widow, Elizabeth, who became the wife of Richard Stoddard, and by her will, dated April 11, 1713, she devised the island to her granddaughter, the daughter of her son, Samuel Shrimpton, Jr. This granddaughter married into the Stoddard and Yeamans families, and her three daughters married into the Chauncy, Greenleaf and Hyslop families, one of the Hyslops and a descendant of Shrimpton, also becoming the wife of Governor Increase Sumner. The representatives of these families came to have interests in the island, and finally death carried off some of the owners and the island came to be owned by David Stoddard, who held, in fee, three-sixths of the island; David Hyslop, who held one sixth: and Elizabeth (Hyslop) Sumner, who held two sixths. General W. H. Sumner, son and successor of the latter, purchased the others' interests, and in 1833 formed the East Boston Company, to accomplish the great object of his life—to make Noddle Island a valuable addition to the metropolis of New England.

One of the early arrangements made for travel to and from Noddle Island appears in the following order, passed October 30, 1637, authorizing Edward Bendall to "keepe a sufficient ferrie-boat to carry to Noddle's Island and to the Shipps riding before the Towne, taking for a single p'son ijd. and for two 3d." Prior to 1833, the island shores were resorted to by pleasure-parties, to cook their fish and to have a jollification, to which end they were aided by the hospitality of the one resident, Mr. Thomas Williams, as long as he lived. This gentleman and his father, Mr. Henry Howell Williams, held the lease of Noddle Island for seventy years; and as a consequence the place came to be frequently spoken of as Williams' Island. In the war of the Revolution, the island was occupied by the British, who carried off Williams' flocks and herds and made a bonfire of his farm dwelling. After the British evacuated Boston, General Washington gave, as a recompense, the building which had been used as barracks at Cambridge, to Williams, who removed the structure to the island.

After the East Boston Company was incorporated, on March 25, 1833, the island property, according to the survey of 1801, consisted of 663 acres of upland and marsh, surrounded by several hundred acres of flats, which were declared, by an act of the legislature, "to belong to the ordinary core water marks." The island was separated from Boston by a distance of 132 rods, which distance was afterwards diminished by the extension of the wharves. The island and the city of Boston, to which it was annexed in 1830, were originally reputed to be of about equal size, each being supposed to contain about a thousand acres, some three hundred acres of the island having been washed or worn away by the action of the sea.

Shares in the company were rapidly taken up, lands reclaimed and mapped out into streets, and building-lots set off and sold. In street nomenclature, the plan was of a judicious nature. The selection of names of American towns, commemorative of their services in connection with struggles for liberty, was not only thoughtful, but comprehensive. The names of Bennington, Lexington, Saratoga, Princeton, Eutaw, Monmouth, and Trenton were out of commonplace, and of a sterling character. Maverick, the early owner of the island, was not forgotten; nor were those patriots, Sumner, Webster, and Everett. These all made good names for streets. There can be little objection, also, to the names of Paris, London, Liverpool, and Havre, which constitute the other principal street names.

A census was made in 1833, but the numbering of the people was an easy task, for there were only eight persons—three males and five females—on the island, and these comprised three families. From 1833, to 1835, however, great progress was made, and the tax valuation rose from $60,000 to $406,000. In 1836, the Eastern Railroad Company was organized to construct a line of railway from East Boston to Salem, and at East Boston the company's depot was located until 1854, when it was removed to Boston. In 1839, the Cunard line of ocean steamships made East Boston their entrepot, and the construction of railway and wharves and the establishment here of a sugar-refinery gave an impetus to the settlement in that locality, of mechanics and others engaged about the wharves, depot, and in building operations. Portions of the land were laid out in sections, comprising those known as sections 1, 2, and 3; lots were then apportioned and sold off at auction. In a short time, as if by magic, a handsome edifice appeared upon the highest summit of the southerly portion, near the remains of an old fort which occupied that eminence in former days. This mansion was for the use of one of Boston's affluent citizens, Benjamin Lamson; and a more delightful situation could not be found in the vicinity, as it commanded a fine panoramic view of the city and harbor. This was the pioneer settler in that section of the island. Soon, however, others came in his train. Elegant mansions and more terraced gardens followed, until the whole southern slope, with Webster Street for a foreground, became a blooming paradise. Mr. Lamson also built a block of nine five-storied, swelled-front brick houses near his residence; and these had gardens in the rear. Beyond this block, and directly overlooking the fort, James Cunningham erected a princely mansion. The view from this house was the most extensive of any on the island, it being more lofty than others. Advancing to the extreme southerly point, passing several pretty cottages, there was seen at the terminus, like a bird's nest overhanging the water, the unique and romantic residence of Dr. Jeffries. This point is still known as "Jeffries' Point," in perpetuation of the doctor.

The only wharves at East Boston forty years back were those known as Cunard's (where the British steamers stopped); Locke's, on Marginal Street; Miller's, foot of Maverick Street; and Tuttle's, foot of London Street. It remained for after-developments to form a fringe of piers all along the harbor front. In the early

40's, there was considerable of a flow of population to East Boston, and by 1857 the residents numbered 16,618. There were 1679 dwellings, 11 churches, 10 schoolhouses, 24 manufactories and mills, 76 warehouses and stores, 109 mechanics' shops, several hotels, 5 fire-engine houses, 12 counting-rooms, and 77 stables; while 17 miles of streets had been laid out. The story of the building of bridges, the construction and operation of ferries, the creation of manufacturing enterprises, the growth of the ship-building interest, and other features would fill a volume. There are two ferries now—known as North and South—connecting East Boston with the city proper; and these are owned by the city. A ferry, owned by the Boston, Revere Beach & Lynn Railroad (whose depot is at East Boston) is run between the island and Atlantic Avenue.

East Boston and the other harbor islands comprise the first and second wards of the city, the "harbor islands" being included in the second ward. It is to-day one of the most populous sections of Boston; where the well-to-do people of industrial callings principally have homes. It is indeed a district of homes, and has not within its limits a modern apartment-house, though there are many blocks where two or more tenements

Public Garden, showing Commonwealth Avenue and Arlington Street.

for family housekeeping exist. It has abundant school and church accommodations. Its population is now computed at forty thousand. Its valuation has grown to $17,961,700, the increase since 1883 having been $1,883,900.

The building improvements in East Boston during the year 1888 have been far in advance of those made within the past twenty years. Many of the unsightly vacant lots on Chelsea, Paris, Havre, Bennington, and other adjoining streets have been brought up to the street grade, and fine tenement-house structures erected thereon. In the first section the most notable improvements have been made at the foot of Everett Street, where a long line of houses have been put up. On Maverick Street, east of Chelsea Street, it is intended shortly to make many improvements in the neighborhood of the dump, in anticipation of laying out new streets and

is the handsomest machine-shop in East Boston. The New England Cooperage Company recently vacated its extensive building on Sumner Street, to take up new quarters on Chelsea Street, and is employing a larger number of hands than ever. In the third section the most noticeable building is that of the new Trinity Baptist Church. It is an imposing structure and an ornament to the hill upon which it stands. The most extensive of recent improvements is that of the construction of the machine-works of the Boston Tow-boat Company, on Border Street. They cover several acres. In the fourth section over twenty houses and tenement blocks have been built. At Orient Heights and Winthrop Junction a number of new dwellings have been erected.

Among the improvements now making in the district are those of the East Boston Company. This company own about 110,000 square feet of land, bounded by Meridian, West Eagle, and Falcon Streets, which is from 25 to 30 feet above grade. The company also own about 36 acres of high marsh land, bounded by the city parkway, the Boston, Revere Beach & Lynn Railroad, Prescott Street, and the track of the Boston & Albany Road. The material from the high lands is being carted on to the marsh property, on which the street and cellar grades will be brought up to the city standard, viz.: 12 feet for cellars and 18 feet for streets. This is one of the choicest locations in East Boston, being on the harbor front and near the new city park. Some of the best houses recently built in East Boston was located in this neighborhood.

CHARLESTOWN.

The Charlestown District, an old-fashioned, quaint place, once a distinct city of itself, has formed an important section of Boston since its annexation in 1873. It now comprises the third, fourth, and fifth wards of Boston. It has an interesting history, dating from the very earliest settlement of the colony, for it was here that Governor Winthrop and his associates landed from their ship and established their abodes. Before they came the Indians were here, and the place was called Mishawum. Then it took unto itself the name of Charlestown, and as a town it embraced the areas of what are now the town of Burlington and the cities of Woburn, Malden, and Somerville, as well as parts of Reading, Medford, Cambridge and West Cambridge (now Arlington). Charlestown was a difficult place to get to from Boston until after the Revolution, for such ferries as existed between the two places were of a very primitive character, and wagons from the North End had to travel roundabout by way of Roxbury, over the "Neck," to reach Charlestown or Cambridge.

Charlestown, for all that, was a flourishing place in colonial times. It was founded in 1629, and in the following year many hundreds of English were trying to live in huts and tents on or around the Town Hill, at the foot of which was the great house, sheltering the Governor and his chief officers. A part of the inhabitants went across the water to keep minister Blackstone company and to found the city of Boston. Charlestown, however, continued to grow, if slowly, and when the revolutionary era arrived, there were some three hundred dwellings and from 150 to 200 other buildings in the place. There is nothing to be found now to tell us what the little settlement was like then, but whatever there was of it was wiped out by fire started by the British forces then located in Boston. General Gage had repeatedly warned the people that he would burn their town if they allowed it to be used as a basis of hostilities against his army, and he kept his word, for he wrote home to his government on June 26th, 1775, that the town "was set on fire during the engagement, and most part of it consumed." The engagement referred to the Bunker Hill fight, for this is the home of the far-famed Bunker Hill.

After the outbreak of the war at Lexington, armed colonists to the number of twenty thousand, formed an encampment around Boston from Roxbury to the Mystic River, and General Gage received powerful reinforcements, accompanied by Generals Howe, Clinton, and Burgoyne from England. Gage had the idea that the Americans wanted to drive him into the sea, and the colonists suspected that Gage and his troops intended to sally out into the country and burn up and destroy everything they could. The Americans determined to anticipate this movement by seizing and fortifying Bunker Hill, a height which commanded the whole peninsular of Charlestown. Orders were accordingly issued on the 16th of June, 1775, to Colonel Prescott, father of the historian of the same name, to proceed with a thousand men to occupy and entrench the Hill; but by some mistake, or designedly, as some assert, Breed's Hill was marked out instead of Bunker Hill, seven hundred yards distant. Bunker Hill was higher, but Breed's Hill was near Boston, and within common range of the city. Under cover of darkness, Prescott and his men reached the hill without being observed, and on the summit the men labored from midnight to dawn in building a redoubt, which the British viewed with considerable astonishment as soon as daylight appeared, for Prescott's cannon commanded the city. "We must carry those works immediately," said General Gage to his officers, and soon the ships in the harbor began to cannonade the new fortifications. The British battery on Copp's Hill also opened a heavy fire. But little damage was done in this way, and the Americans returned but few shots, as their supply of ammunition was very limited. Soon after noon, three thousand English, commanded by Generals Howe and Pigot, landed at Morton's Point to carry the hill by assault. The Americans numbered only one half of the British, and were wearied with their night's work and hungry as well; but they had a big stock of courage. When the cannonading was at its hottest, Prescott climbed out of the defences and walked leisurely around the parapet in full view of the British officers. Generals Putnam and Warren volunteered as privates and entered the trenches. At three o'clock in the afternoon Howe ordered his column to advance, and at the same time every gun in the fleet and batteries was turned upon the American redoubt. Then it was that Charlestown was set on fire and destroyed. The people mounted the house-tops in Boston to behold the engagement. On came the British with steady march, and not until they were within a hundred and fifty feet of them did the Americans show any signs of their presence. "Fire!" cried Prescott, and instantly from breastwork and redoubt every gun was fired, and the front rank of the British melted away. There was a recoil, and fifteen minutes afterwards a precipitate retreat. When beyond musket range, Howe rallied his men and led them to the second charge. Again the American fire was withheld until the enemy was but a few rods distant. Then, with steady aim, volley after volley was poured upon the charging column until it was broken and a second time driven to flight. The British officers grew desperate, and the vessels of the fleet changed position until the guns were brought to bear upon the interior of the American works. Then for the third time the assaulting column was put in motion, and the men came on with fixed bayonets up the hillside where were strewn the dead and dying. The Americans had but three or four rounds of ammunition left, and these were fired into the advancing enemy. Then there was a lull. The British climbed over the ramparts, and after a fierce struggle drove the patriots out. Prescott lived through the fight, but Warren was numbered among the slain. In this terrible engagement the English paid dearly for their victory, for they lost 1054 men in killed and wounded. The American loss was 115 killed, 305 wounded, and 32 prisoners. Prescott and Putnam conducted the retreat to Prospect Hill, where a new line of entrenchments was formed, and which still commanded the entrance to Boston. The fight showed that the British soldiers were not invincible, and the Americans were proud of their achievement, though defeated. The event is yearly celebrated at Charlestown on June 17th, by a holiday, processions, etc.

The event, too, has been commemorated by the building on the site of the redoubt a great granite obelisk, rising to a height of 221½ feet. It has a base 30 feet square and the column tapers gradually to 15½ feet at the apex. Inside the shaft is a hollow cone, surrounding which is a spiral flight of 295 stone steps, ascending to a chamber 11 feet square and 17 feet high, whence a beautiful view is obtained from the four windows. The capstone of the apex, above this observatory, is in one piece, and weighs 2½ tons. The room contains two small cannons, the inscriptions upon which tell their story. The corner-stone was laid June 17th, 1825, by General Lafayette, and it was dedicated June 17th, 1843. The orator on both occasions was Daniel Webster. The monument cost over $150,000, and at the foot of it is a building containing a marble statue of General Warren and various memorials of the battle. The surroundings of the monument are handsomely laid out, and in the main path of the grounds, on the spot where he is supposed to have stood encouraging his men, is a bronze statue of General Prescott, erected in 1881. The celebration of the centennial of the battle on June 17th, 1775, was an event which drew together military representatives and others from all sections of the country. The real Bunker Hill is crowned by a Catholic Church.

In 1777 the people began to rebuild their town, and by the end of 1785 there were 279 buildings and 909 inhabitants. In 1786 the Charles River bridge to Charlestown was built at a cost of $50,000. It was then considered one of the grandest enterprises ever undertaken in the country. It was 1503 feet long, and 42 feet wide, with a 30 foot draw. It was opened amid great rejoicings on the anniversary of the battle of Bunker Hill. In the following year (1787), a bridge was opened between Charlestown and Malden, another to Chelsea in 1803, and one to East Cambridge in 1820. These established communications of immeasurable benefit, and in 1793, when the work of constructing the Middlesex Canal was begun, it was of immense advantage to the town. It was one of the earliest undertakings of the kind in the country, and was to connect tidewater with the upper Merrimack. The canal was completed in 1803, but was never very profitable. The railroads came and took away the traffic. The charter was forfeited in 1860 and the canal destroyed.

Charlestown is adequately supplied with railroad and other transportation facilities. Formerly the Fitchburg passenger and freight stations were located here, but in 1848 were removed to Boston. The district has many objects of interest to visitors. The "Neck," over which the Bunker Hill warriors went to give battle, and over which they retreated when worsted, connects Charlestown with the mainland of Somerville beyond. It was washed by the tides in the early days, but has been entirely changed by the filling up of the marshes and flats on its borders. The Neck properly begins near the foot of Bunker Hill and ends at the boundary line over the Maine & Eastern Railroad Bridge, between the Charlestown district and Somerville. The Navy Yard stands on what was once Moulton's Point, at the confluence of the Charles and Mystic Rivers, and was founded in 1800. The Yard and buildings cover an extensive area, and as they are daily open to visitors, an inspection is to be commended. Another object of interest is the handsome Soldiers and Sailors' Monument

Public Garden, showing the Lake

in Winthrop Square, once the military training-field. On Main Street is Edes House, the birthplace of S. F. B. Morse (the inventor of the electric telegraph), and the oldest house in the district. On the same thoroughfare is the oldest burying-ground, where a granite monument surmounts the grave of John Harvard, the founder of Harvard College; and near by is the tomb of Thomas Beecher, ancestor of the Charles and Mystic family in America. The district also contains the old state prison, a free dispensary and hospital, several other charitable institutions, public free library, and schools, churches of all denominations, and many fine mansions and neat cottages. The streets are wide and well kept, and illumination is supplied by gas and electric lights, while the water supply is abundant in quantity and excellent in quality.

While Charlestown has not been what is called a manufacturing place, it has numerous industrial establishments of a varied and extensive character, and these are constantly being multiplied. The principal thoroughfare, Main Street, is lined with stores, in which every conceivable class of merchandise is to be secured.

Charlestown never had a theatre or concert-room, yet it has occasionally been favored by visits of a circus. Plays and concerts, however, have been given in the old Town Hall (where the public library now is), and in

stanced by the following statistics: In 1785 the population was 909; in 1800, 2751; in 1805, 2600; in 1810, 4756; in 1834, 10,000; in 1840, 10,872; in 1850 13,933; in 1855, 21,742; in 1865, 26,398; in 1870, 28,-323; in 1885, 37,073; and now it is computed to be over 40,000. Values of property, however, have been but little increased during the past few years by the erection of new buildings. As in the case of South Boston, noted elsewhere,—though in a greater degree,—much of the former high-cost property in residences has largely depreciated in value, owing to the desire on the part of owners to move into more fashionable quarters, and other causes that would induce vacation and sacrifice of property. Houses worth $10,000 and upward have shrunk in value, while lower-priced buildings hold their own. There have been some dwellings and a few apartment-houses erected in Charlestown in the past five years, but the decrease in residential property on the hill—where the wealthy people of the district mostly resided—has so largely off-set the increase of real-estate values thus acquired that in that period the gain in real-estate valuation has been only $1,717,300. The gain in population has not been large, as would naturally be expected from the fact that the district is pretty thickly built over, the only vacant land, and that limited in extent, being on the Neck.

THE NEW WEST END, OR BACK BAY DISTRICT.

The reader has seen, in the perusal of the foregoing pages, how the original boundaries of Boston have been extended, not merely by the annexation of out-lying districts, but by the reclamation of thousands of acres, of now valuable lands, from the ocean. He has, however, yet to be told of the greatest achievement of creating building land, and that the most attractive and valuable in the city. It comprises the whole region of the now showy and fashionable "New West End" or "Back Bay District," the "Court End" of the city.

When the present century was ushered in, the appearance of Back Bay was like unto that of Dorchester Bay to-day. At that time the waters of the bay flowed up to the present Washington Street at the "Neck," and swept over the present Public Garden and now forming Charles Street. At flood tide the bay was a beautiful sheet of water spreading out far and wide, with the Brookline Hills in the distance, much as the Blue Hills are observed from South Boston, with no bridge, dam, or causeway intercepting the view of rustic Cambridge lying amid forest surroundings at the foot of Mount Auburn, between the West Boston and Brighton Bridges. In 1814, the Boston & Roxbury Corporation was organized to utilize the water-power of the great basin by dams thrown across it, and to use these dams as causeways for communication between Boston and Roxbury and the western suburbs. The "Mill-dam," now lower Beacon Street; the "Cross-dam," now Parker Street; and the causeway, now known as Brookline Avenue, were made to divide the waters. The Mill Dam was completed in 1821, and three years later the business of the corporation was divided, the Boston Water-power Company being then chartered to use the water-power of the mill company, which retained the roads and the lands north of the dam, while the new company became possessed of the mills and water-power. In 1831, the Boston & Worcester and the Boston & Providence Railroad Companies were given authority to construct lines across the Back Bay, and the riparian owners power to fill up their flats—concessions which so interfered with the water-power as to lead to the Boston Water-power Company converting itself into a land company. Much of the sewage of the city was thrown into the basin, until it became a nuisance and the filling up of the bay an absolutely necessary sanitary act. Below the line of riparian ownership the State had the right to the flats, and in 1849 the State appointed a commission to deal with the subject of creating new land here. A comprehensive plan was reported in 1852, and it was arranged that the mill corporation should fill up the area north of the Mill Dam; that the State should attend to that north of an east-and-west line drawn from near the present Boston & Providence Railroad Station; and that the water-power company should see to all south of that line. The contractor for filling in and making marketable the whole of this section (in which work millions of piles were used) was Norman C. Munson, who received as payment for his first work $60,000 square feet out of upwards of a million square feet of land reclaimed. By continuous contracts, the work extended over twenty years, and finally Munson received about seven million dollars as reward for his enterprise. The work was planned by the famous architect Arthur Gilman.

The State filled in its section at a cost of $1,750,000, and it has since sold land for $4,625,000 and has yet 250,-000 feet unsold. The water-power company found the work alike profitable. The city, too, has for years been engaged in filling up swamps, levelling lands, constructing avenues driveways, and parks, and ornamenting the whole of this region, which for beauty and residential magnificence has no counterpart in either the New or Old World. Let the reader spread before him a map of the city as it exists to-day and strike a line through Charles,

Boylston, and Essex Streets, running crookedly from Charles River on the west to the Port Channel dividing the city proper from South Boston. All the area represented below this line up to the foot of the Highlands is "created" land, save where Washington Street runs, and this thoroughfare is over the Neck, which was itself frequently lapped by the waters of the ocean. All the land lying to the south of the Boston & Providence Railroad, including Columbus Avenue, is now territorially identified with the "South End," already referred to in these pages. The "Back Bay District" includes all the "made" land on the other side of the railroad.

In this district, running from Arlington Street (the western border of the Public Garden), and parallel with Beacon Street, are Commonwealth Avenue, Newbury, Marlborough, and Boylston Streets, with Huntington Avenue branching off the latter street at the junction of Clarendon Street. Parallel with Arlington Street are Berkeley, Clarendon, Dartmouth, Exeter, Fairfield, Gloucester, and Hereford Streets, West Chester Park, etc. As we have said, vast improvements are now in progress in this district, the most prominent of which is the opening up of Boylston Street to public travel in its entire length. This street, which skirts the Common on its southern end, as Beacon Street does on the northern side, is in every way a more available and convenient avenue from the business section of Boston to the Back Bay; but, owing to the fact that it crossed the tracks of the Boston & Albany Railroad near its junction with West Chester Park, and the difficulty and expense of bridging the railway, its completion was delayed, to the great inconvenience of the public, as well as to the stagnation of values of property on the unfinished line of the street. This condition is now in active process of being remedied. Boylston Street had been completed to Exeter. From this point down to where the line crossed the railway, the grade had to be raised, the filling in some places, viz., from Gloucester to Hereford Street, being from 15 to 18 feet. The work of filling in this section of street, as well as the portions west of the bridge and beyond to the Back Bay Park, was begun in the fall of 1887, and completed in February, 1888. The north abutment of the bridge, just beyond Hereford Street, was first built to enable the filling in of this section of the street to be accomplished, and to render available the use of the new police station and engine house which had been erected at the corner of Hereford and Boylston Streets. The work of grading and macadamizing is, at this writing, in active operation on the section of street in question, in conjunction with the construction of double street-railway tracks by the West End Railway Company. The railway tracks, it may be said, are now completed up to Hereford Street, and the street department is now macadamizing the driveways on each side in the most substantial manner. Every part and detail of this work is done thoroughly, and, when the street is opened, it will present one of the best driveways on the Back Bay. From the corner of Hereford Street to the bridge, the roadway will be paved, for the purpose of providing against the wear and tear of running in and out of the engine-house the fire apparatus; and the city will join with the railway company in this work. Beyond West Chester Park to the new Back Bay Park, the roadway of Boylston Street is completed, and now forms one of the entrance driveways to that attractive place. When this latter improvement was undertaken, it was found that, in order to conform to the grade established by the park commissioners and that already existing on West Chester Park, it would be necessary to raise the grade of Boylston Street about five feet near and at the point where Parker Street leads out from it. A block of new brick buildings on the south side of Boylston Street at the junction of Parker had to be raised in consequence of this elevation of the roadway, at an expense of over $30,000 to the owner, the city allowing but $5,000 toward the work. The cost to the city of the construction of the roadway of Boylston Street from Exeter Street to the park, not including filling in, of course, will be about $25,000.

The bridge over the tracks of the Boston & Albany Railroad is, owing to the acute angle at which the street crosses it, a structure of peculiar form and details. The width of the railway road-bed under the street is only 60 feet, yet on the line of the street there is a distance of about 210 feet between abutments. The north abutment has a length of 185 feet, with flanking walls or abutments of 100 feet in length on the north side of the street and 124 feet on the south side. The south abutment is 174 feet in length, with a southern flank of 36 feet and a northern one of 105 feet. The piles for the foundation are driven to concrete to the depth of 3½ and 4 feet is filled in, on which rubble masonry is laid. Then succeed granite blocks on the railway fronts. The height of the roadway above the track of the railroad is 20 feet, the distance from track to under side of bridge being but 14 feet. The length of the truss-spans of this bridge is each 210 feet, being the longest of any bridge-truss span in the city. The total weight of the bridge—that is, of the structure of iron and steel composing it—is about 400 tons. The total width of the bridge is 80 feet, which is the full width of the street. The width of the roadway inside the trusses is 44 feet. The construction was by the

Boston Bridge Works, of Cambridgeport. The bridge cost about $50,000, and is one of the best, as well as the most unique, of its kind in the city. The cost of the abutments of this bridge was about $80,000, which, added to that of the bridge superstructure, would make the total cost of the bridge $230,000. This is a costly improvement, to be sure, but one of great utility and public importance. With the completion of the bridge, the tracks of the West End Railway will be quickly pushed forward and united to those on West Chester Park; and a direct line of communication, not only to the Back Bay residences south of Commonwealth Avenue established, but to the Back Bay Park, which can thus be readily and quickly reached, and the round-about way through Marlboro Street avoided. Altogether this work of completing Boylston Street is one that

Statue of Washington—Public Garden.

adds another to the many great improvements that the city government is making on the Back Bay district of Boston.

In addition to these public improvements the whole of the Charles River embankment, beginning at Leverett Street near Craigie's Bridge, and extending to Cottage Farms Bridge, is being enlarged, fronted with a sea wall and laid out as a park, 200 feet in width, and will connect with a park at Brighton. Near West Chester Park a bridge—to be known as Harvard Bridge—is in course of construction across the Charles River to Cambridge, and will, when completed, be a great boon to residents on both sides of the river. West Chester Park is not a park but a street ninety feet wide. It crosses Commonwealth Avenue, about five blocks west of the Hotel Vendome, and beginning at Charles River, and varying its direction at Falmouth Street, runs across the city. Between Tremont and Shawmut Avenue it broadens into Chester Square, a modest park of 1¼ acres. East of Washington Street, it is called East Chester Park.

the waters of the Stony Brook, promenades, driveways, etc., connecting with Beacon, Parker, and Boylston Streets, and also with Commonwealth, Westland, Longwood, Huntington, and Brookline Avenues. The work is a costly one, but when the park is completed it will, in addition to its own attractions, have a surrounding of beautiful scenery, and will be a connecting link in a long splendid parkway stretching from the Common and Public Garden, through Commonwealth Avenue, along the Muddy River Improvement, Jamaica Pond, the Arnold Arboretum and ending in the spacious and picturesque Franklin Park. The Charles River embankment will be separated from the Back Bay Parkway, only by Beacon Street, which is itself a popular driveway, extending along the Mill Dam, the surrounding of Chestnut Hill Reservoir and the shady, rustic lanes of Brighton.

Back Bay is the richest section in the city, and it takes the lead in expensive dwellings and in the constant advance in the value of real estate. That portion of the district which is bounded by Charles River, Arlington Street, the Boston & Providence railway tracks and West Chester Park, in 1883 had a total valuation as follows: Land, $26,182,800; buildings, $22,315,200. In 1888, land in this section had increased to $34,036,500, and buildings to $30,504,500, a total increase of rising of $16,000,000. But Back Bay has, in fact, two districts. One is the ultra-fashionable and aristocratic section, and extends west from Arlington Street to West Chester Park, and is bounded on the south by the line of the Boston & Albany Railroad, and thence northward to Charles River. South of the railroad line, out to the Back Bay Park at least, the section is less aristocratic, and land is not much, if any, over one half the price that it is on the other side. No very costly residences are erected. On Huntington Avenue and on the back streets large apartment houses are being put up. West Chester Park, south of the Boston & Albany Railway track, besides family hotels, buildings with stores on the street level are being occupied; and, with the completion of the bridge at this point over the Charles River, this street promises to become an important thoroughfare.

But what shall be said of the Back Bay District as a whole? Volumes might be written descriptive of its magnificent thoroughfares, its architectural splendor, its palatial mansions and hostelries, its public institutions, and its creation from out of the sea into one of the most attractive and beautiful habited spots the world can show; but we are compelled to dismiss the whole in a page or two.

Commonwealth Avenue is undoubtedly the chief attraction in this charming section. It is, in reality, two streets in one, with a fine park in the centre, containing rows of ornamental trees, neatly kept paths, benches, and several statues. The width of the thoroughfare, from house to house, is 250 feet, and from curb to curb 175 feet. It extends through the new Back Bay Park to Brookline Avenue, and is lined with costly and beautiful residences, in the erection of which architects have had no limit to the exercise of their talents, nor had their plans marred by lack of capital. Commonwealth Avenue, from Arlington Street to West Chester Park, may be said to be practically built up.

The cost of Mr. Fred L. Ames' residence, on the corner of Dartmouth Street and the avenue, was very great. The residence of Governor Ames, corner of West Chester Park, is said to have cost $180,000, exclusive of the land. Mr. Nathaniel Thayer's house, on the corner of Fairfield Street cost about $135,000 to build; and on the corner of Gloucester Street and the avenue, Mr. Eugene V. R. Thayer recently completed a residence which cost $138,000. This is about as sightly a dwelling as there is on the avenue. On the corner opposite, Mr. Charles Francis Adams has erected a very fine dwelling which cost about $80,000. The residence of Congressman John F. Andrew, on the corner of Hereford Street, cost about $100,000 to build. One of the handsomest residences on the avenue is that of Mrs. William Powell Mason, located between Dartmouth and Exeter Streets, and built at a cost of $61,000. It is of the coming-into-fashion colonial style, and maintains the dignity of its ancestry even amid the more modern and artistic structures which are in its vicinity. Between Exeter and Fairfield Streets Mr. Alexander Cochran has an elegant residence, which cost in the neighborhood of $100,000 to build. The above are all on the north side of Commonwealth Avenue. On the south side of the avenue there are also many fine and costly residences of recent erection, ranging all the way from $30,000 to $50,000.

Beacon Street (from the corner of Arlington Street) has in recent years shown more activity in the erection of mansions than any other thoroughfare in this section. This is the most noticeable in the vicinity of and beyond West Chester Park. It contains some of the finest residences to be found in this section of palatial homes. General Whittier has put up a magnificent building at a cost of $145,000, and a number of other dwellings have been erected at a cost varying from $20,000 to $125,000. Beacon Street during the past two years, has shown a marked advance in building improvements, and real estate quotations have consequently been increased.

Boylston Street, in that section overlooking the Common and the Public Garden—once a fashionable residential quarter—is rapidly being given up to business, but beyond the Public Garden, there are many handsome residences and the opening out of the street in the region of West Chester Park, will lead to more buildings being put up. The Boston & Albany Railroad owns the land on the south side of this thoroughfare, west of Exeter Street, and may build a passenger station there. Owing to these conditions and other contingencies, the north side of the street has not been built upon, with two solitary exceptions, west of Exeter Street. That section of Boylston Street, between the Old South parsonage and Exeter Street, north side, has been built up mostly within the last five years, with a good class of dwellings, costing on an average about $20,000 each. The Hotel Kensington, one of those fashionable family hotels, is located on the corner of Boylston and Exeter Streets. It was erected by Mr. Henry B.

Williams, at a cost of about $200,000. Land prices have all along this street increased amazingly within the last few years, and in many places building lots command from $12 to $15 per square foot.

West Chester Park will soon be a busy scene of operations among builders, for the opening up of Boylston Street and the erection of the Harvard Bridge has brought this district into the market, and as both the thoroughfares just named are the only Back Bay Streets on which there are no restrictions as to business structures, it is likely that both will, ere long, become great centres of trade.

Almost everywhere in this section of the city new buildings are arising. In this region are some of the finest hotels in the country, chief among which are the marble Vendome, the imposing Brunswick, and the Victoria (the new " Delmonico "). Then there are numerous first-class apartment houses, the Hotel Berkeley being the first erected in the district. On Boylston Street is the handsome building of the Young Men's Christian Association, also the Natural History Society Building, the famous Institute of Technology, Trinity

The Chauncy Hall School, Boylston Street.

Church (Rev. Dr. Phillips Brooks, pastor), one of the finest and most impressive church edifices in the country ; and the Second Church (Congregational Unitarian) with chapel adjoining (Rev. E. A. Horton, pastor). The society worshipping here once occupied the Old North Church, on North Square, torn down and used for firewood by British soldiers during the siege of Boston. At one time Ralph Waldo Emerson was the pastor of the present church. Near this church is the far-famed Chauncy School. Opposite to it, with entrance on St. James's Avenue, is the Museum of Fine Arts, and beyond, on the corner of Boylston and Exeter Streets, is the Harvard Medical School. Near by, on the corner of Exeter and Newbury Streets, is the Prince School building, the only public school in the district. The other corners of Exeter and Newbury Streets are occupied by the South Congregational Church (Unitarian) ; the First Spiritual Temple, a costly, curious edifice ; and the Massachusetts Normal School. Farther on, on the corner of Boylston and Hereford Streets, is a handsome, new Romanesque building, occupied by the Back Bay police and fire departments. On Dartmouth Street, nearly opposite Trinity Church, the immense new Public Library building is being erected and will take years to complete. On Exeter Street and St. James Avenue, on December 29th, 1888, was opened the new Athletic Association building (erected at a cost of nearly $300,000), the finest edifice of its kind in the world. The New Old South Church—one of the costliest church buildings in the city—stands on the Dartmouth Street side of Copley Square, on the corner of Boylston Street. The society worshipping here formerly occupied the historic Old South, on the corner of Washington and Milk Street. Near the New Old South, on Dartmouth Street is the handsome new building of the Art Club. Located on the corner of Commonwealth Avenue and

Clarendon Street is the massive stone edifice of the First Baptist Church (formerly the Brattle Square Congregational Unitarian). The First Church (Congregational Unitarian) is located on Marlborough Street and Berkeley Street. It is the direct descendant of the first church established in Boston. The church was first formed in Charlestown, and the members of it, on coming to Boston, built the first meeting house on State Street, near where the Brazer Building stands. The church was afterwards removed on to Washington Street near top of State Street, then to Chauncy Place, and, finally to its present location. The Protestant Episcopalians have a fine church, with a very rich interior, on Newbury Street, known as the Emmanuel Church.

Boston Common—Beacon Street Mall.

A short distance from it, on the corner of Newbury and Berkeley Streets is the handsome Central Church (Congregational Trinitarian), which possesses the tallest spire in the city, the height being 236 feet. On Berkeley Street is the Notre Dame Academy, and at the corner of Boylston and Arlington Streets is the widely known Arlington (Unitarian) Church, of which Rev. Hereford Brooke is pastor. Huntington Avenue has upon it the famous exhibition building of the charitable Mechanic Association, covering an area of 96,000 square feet, and erected in 1881. A short distance from it is the Children's Hospital, a useful and well-conducted institution. There are many other notable residences and buildings, but space will not allow us to treat of them separately.

ROXBURY.

The thoroughfares leading to it are four, namely, Harrison Avenue, Washington Street, Shawmut Avenue and Tremont Street. This is the order of their succession, viewed laterally, Tremont Street being the most westerly. Columbus Avenue, which lies more to the westward, will in the future be extended through to the Roxbury district. At present Washington Street, Shawmut Avenue, Tremont Street and Huntington Avenue are available throughout by horse-cars, but the Washington Street route is to be preferred by the stranger and sight-seer. The Roxbury district includes the old city of Roxbury, which was annexed to Boston in 1867. It comprises wards 19, 20, 21, and 22, the latter being bounded on the east by West Chester Park, and including, therefore, a portion of the Back Bay territory. When first settled it was called Rocksbury, or Rocksborough, and was recognized as a town on October 8, 1630. The town originally included the present West Roxbury district (set off in 1851) and annexed to Boston in 1873, Jamaica Plain, and the present town of Brookline, known in the early days as "Punch-bowl Village." William Wood, the first historian of New England, writing in 1633, says, after describing Dorchester:—"A mile from this Town (Dorchester) lyeth Roxberry, which is faire and handsome Country-towne: the inhabitants of it being all rich. The Towne lieth upon the Maine, so that it is well-wooded and watered: having a cleare and fresh Brooke running through the Towne; up which although there come no Alewives, yet there is great store of Smelts, and therefore it is called Smelt-brooke. A quarter of a mile to the North-side of the Towne is another River called Stoney-river, upon which is built a water-milne. Here is good ground for Corne and Meadow for Cattle. Up westward from the Towne it is something rocky, whence it has the name of Roxberry," etc. Another writer (1651) describes the town as "being filled with a very laborious people, whose labours the Lord hath so blest, that in the roome of dismall Swamps and tearing Bushes, they have very goodlie Fruit-trees, fruitfull Fields and Gardens, their Heard of Cowes, Oxen and other young Cattell of that kind about 350, and dwelling houses neere upon 120. Their streetes are large and some Fayre Houses."

If inquiries were made of a hundred persons resident in Boston as to where the dividing line existed between the domains of the two former municipalities, no doubt 99 would not pretend to guess at what the hundredth would be likely to miss, yet that line is distinctly marked to-day. One at all curious in this regard needs only to bestow his glances when enjoying a horse-car ride in the direction of the suburbs over Washington Street, upon a granite curbstone post of the horse-hitching kind, which stands on the sidewalk abutting the old car station at the extremity of the Neck, near Lenox Street, where it has stood so long that it may be considered a landmark. On one side of this stone, in deep-engraved work, is, "R., A.D. 1823." On the reverse is a similar inscription, save that B. takes the place of R. This indicates Roxbury and Boston. At present the top of this puny post shaft is black and greasy, looking as though it had received the caresses of many dirty hands, which has doubtless been the case during the last 66 years of its standing as a monitor.

What, in the parlance of the inhabitants of Roxbury of former days, was denoted as "the street," or "Roxbury Street" (now Washington Street), commenced at this line and terminated at Vernon Street. Here were concentrated the shops; and a considerable degree of business was performed in them, especially before omnibus days. There were several local inns on this street, stopping-places for stages plying to and from Providence, as well as for transient travel, and local imbibing and feasting, to which, if rumor is to be believed, the ancient "gudemen" were somewhat devoted. On this "street" in later days were stores that prosecuted a large business; and hereabouts reside many old-timers. The "street" of to-day has been considerably elongated, and includes a great number and variety of stores, presenting quite a metropolitan aspect, both for this reason and for the magnitude of business performed there. At no place in the city, save in the main shopping district, two miles distant, is there more life and activity noticed, especially on Saturday evenings, when the citizens of the neighborhood turn out en masse, seemingly to do their shopping, thereby crowding the large clothing, dry-goods, boot and shoe, and furniture stores, likewise the many food-providers, the variety shops, the several gayly illuminated tea-stores, etc., to repletion, and forming kaleidoscopic throngs surging along under the electric lights. There is "a sight" of difference in this respect, compared with the "fayre" street views of the forefathers.

The territory now lying between the Lenox Street horse-car stables and the Roxbury stables at the Providence Railroad crossing, and including the contiguous streets and places, was formerly called Grub Village; and the name is still sometimes applied to it. This is a picturesque and unique locality, especially that part lying towards Tremont Street; and the business signs contain, for the most part, Teutonic names. It is, in fact, the mercantile portion of Germantown which is concentrated in this vicinity in consequence of the number of breweries in Roxbury, Boylston Station and Jamaica Plain, with which hundreds of the inhabitants are connected. Where or when the sobriquet of "Grub Village" came to be applied is a profound mystery to the present generation. The oldest inhabitant of the region knows naught regarding the inception of such a queer name.

Sixty years ago this territory was flooded by the tides of the Back Bay, and its only inhabitants were fishes and birds. In 1832, the Tremont Road (now Tremont Street) had been filled in, laid out, and became open for travel from Pleasant Street, South End, to Roxbury. Both sides of this roadway were marshes covered with water when the tide was in. Other land was acquired in the vicinity by the process in which most of the present South End and all of Back Bay were secured. Lots were quickly taken, and houses sprung up like magic. The outflow from South End—then a contracted and crowded region—took this direction naturally. Practically, it amounted to an exodus from the city to suburban homes, for there existed no means of public conveyance; and this necessitated the keeping of horses or long walks with business men who located there. In many respects it proved to be a charming place for residence, and, in fact, that portion of the city has always borne a good reputation for healthfulness. Gardens were planted, fruit-trees were set out, and shortly the locality gained credit for its lovely show of flowers and the quality of its fruit. While it has lost much of its former aspect, Grab Village has assumed other peculiarities which make it a very lively part of the city. The Tremont Street portion, from end to end of its three-fourths-mile length, is a busy mart of traffic. Stores of many kinds line both sides of the street. In no other part of Boston, away from the shopping district, excepting perhaps on Broadway, South Boston, is such a condition to be found. Some of these stores, in extent and appearance, with their large plate-glass windows filled with nice dress goods, etc., rival downtown concerns, and no doubt their patronage is commensurate with their spirit of enterprise. Veritably, Grab Village is a city in itself, covering over portions of several wards, and numbering a population high up in double numbers of thousands. Despite its seemingly derisive title, it constitutes a portion of the city that bears a good reputation; and that is highly cherished by the residents.

But let us return to the old boundary line between Boston and Roxbury—at the Neck, near the horse-railway stables, beside Lenox Street, for this is a historic spot. It was here that the American troops who were engaged in the siege of Boston erected strong fortifications and planted heavy batteries, to resist any attempt of the British troops to get into the country from the city. A few rods beyond this point is one of Roxbury's old landmarks—the venerable burying-ground, corner of Eustis and Washington Streets, where the remains of the Apostle Eliot lie. This ground has been sadly neglected in the past, and bears marks of desecration at present. In its vaults were deposited many of the bodies of the notabilities in Roxbury of colonial times. A writer of the olden time describes Eliot as "a young man at his coming thither, of a cheerful spirit, walking unblameable, of a godly conversation; apt to teach, as by his indefatigable pains both with his own flock and the poor Indians doth appear; whose language he learned purposely to helpe them to the knowledge of God in Christ," etc. His body, together with those of five other pastors of the First Parish, rests in the "parish tomb," and near by it are the graves of Governor Thomas Dudley, Governor Joseph Dudley, and Chief Justice Paul Dudley.

Proceeding a little beyond this resting-place of the forefathers, and still continuing on Washington Street, we reach Eustis Street, where the travel is divided into three principal lines. To the right, Roxbury Street stretches to Eliot Square, better known as Norfolk House neighborhood, on account of the large hotel there. To the left, Warren Street sweeps away through what were recently rural pastures toward Central Dorchester by the way of Grove Hall. At these points of divergence the principal stores, banks, public institutions, post-office, public halls, etc., of Roxbury are located. Washington Street extends towards Jamaica Plain, sweeps past Forest Hill Station and the noted cemetery of that name; and along its course is beautiful scenery and several old-fashioned mansions, each with an interesting story of its own of the past. The old First Parish Church, on Eliot Square, is an object of great interest as a splendid specimen of Puritan church architecture. It stands on elevated land, which was fortified by General Washington to command the roads from Boston. About a quarter of a mile to the southwest were still stronger works, known as the Roxbury Fort, whereon is now located the standpipe of the Boston Water-works, which, as an architectural column, is an object of great beauty.

Roxbury, small as she was, had a conspicuous part in the events of the Revolution. It was the native place of the immortal Warren, Heath, and Greaton, and the residence and burial-place of Dearborn—all generals in the Continental Army. The old Roxburyites have shown in various ways that they have not forgotten the heroes of those trying times.

Here is the great public pleasure-ground of forests and fields, formerly known as Roxbury, and now as Franklin Park, to which thousands daily find their way in the summer from all parts of the city. Not alone is the park an object of beauty, but the whole region of Roxbury, which in late years has become a favorite residential quarter, and consequently has experienced a large growth in population.

As we have already observed, Roxbury comprises four wards of the city. These wards contain more than one sixth of the polls of the city of Boston, which is a good index of the extent of their population. The same thing will show their growth in population in the past five years. In 1883, the number of polls in them was, in round numbers, 19,000; in 1888, it was 23,000—an increase of 4000 in the five years. The valuation of these four wards will also show their advance in material wealth. In 1883, their total valuation was $59,324,900; in 1888, it was $74,394,800—an increase of $15,069,900 in five years, a most encouraging showing. This great advance in population is due, in the first place, to Roxbury, with its high lands, abounding in the finest sites for residence, and being so situated that Boston seems to naturally merge into it, and to

Boston Common—Tremont Street Mall.

form a part of the city itself in reality, while still retaining many rural features. Another important fact is that there are several parallel lines of horse-railway penetrating every section of the district, and these led to the more convenient localities being seized upon for dwellings, and to the building of apartment-houses in great numbers. But even these failed to provide for all who wanted homes, and the territory beyond was encroached upon. On one of the main avenues, Warren Street, as far as Grove Hall, the drift of population found a way, as well as on Washington Street on the west and Blue Hill Avenue on the east, which crosses Warren Street in its course at Grove Hall. These streets and their affluents furnished land for dwelling purposes, which was utilized from time to time, until to-day there is but little land, comparatively, left in the limits of old Roxbury to build on, the last of the considerable farm properties (the Horatio Harris estate) being now in process of arrangement to be put upon the market. Land has consequently appreciated in value; for lots which five years ago or less were bought for 15 to 20 cents a foot are now held at from 40 to 60 cents per square foot. Walnut Avenue, running in a southwesterly direction from Warren Street, and nearly parallel to Washington Street, up to Franklin Park, opened up a district for settlement, in which many fine and costly mansions have been constructed in the past fifteen years or more. In the territory northwest and southeast of this avenue, and especially in the latter sections, there have been built in the past five years a large number of very fine dwellings. This section is known as Elm Hill; and on Elm Hill Avenue, and between it and Walnut Avenue, some of the best houses are located. Many of these are veritable palaces, representing all styles of architecture and varying in cost from $12,000 to $60,000. Many of them are surrounded with trees, shrubbery, flower gardens, or grassy lawns, adding to the beauty and attraction of the streets and avenues as excellent driveways. Walnut Avenue, Humboldt Avenue, and Elm Hill Avenue all lead up to Franklin Park, and the two latter end at Seaver Street, which skirts its northern side. The park is of vast extent, and, as no residential buildings can be put upon it, the rush of settlement in that direction to some extent has been stopped, and the operations here in the future will be the filling up of the gaps now existing, with the result in a few years of a compactly built district, though, compared with that north of it, owing to the nature of its settlement, it will be a great many years before houses in it are crowded so closely together. In other sections of the district, dwellings are rising rapidly. On nearly every street, from Dudley Street to Grove Hall, new houses have been erected in the past five years, either by those who had them built for their own use or to let or for sale; but there have been but few erections for business purposes in the district in the same period.

On the northwest side of the Roxbury district is Parker Hill, a splendid location, overlooking the city, and on which is located the Parker Hill Reservoir. Its high and favorable location places it in the line of future occupation.

THE DORCHESTER DISTRICT

which forms the twenty-fourth ward of the city, is delightfully situated on Dorchester Bay, an arm of Boston Harbor, and is a healthy, attractive and picturesque region. It is to-day one of the most interesting of the outlying districts of the city, and is a favorite place of suburban residence. It is, too, an historic place, and was established as a town on the same date as Boston itself. On the 20th of March, 1629-30, "that great ship of 400 tons," the Mary and John, set sail from Plymouth, England, for the New World, and during the ten weeks of the voyage the party on board, including two clergyman, Revs. Maverick and Warham, spent every day "in preaching or expounding the word of God." The ship, which was commanded by Captain Squeb, landed on May 30, 1630, at Nantasket (now Hull), where the captain turned his passengers adrift into the "forlorn wilderness," though his contract bound him to carry them to the Charles River. They found their way to Dorchester, then called Mattapan by the Indians, by whom they were well received. They at once changed the name to Dorchester, after the town of the same name in England. Dorchester has its quaint old town-hall; its ancient meeting-house and magnificent soldiers' monument on Meeting-House Hill; at Upham's Corner the graves of several eminent public men of the Colonial and Provincial periods; and Jones's Hill affords from its summit one of the finest and most extensive views in the neighborhood of Boston. Northward is seen the old city and the famous Dorchester Heights. Westward is presented an amphitheatre of hills and villages. Southward is a wide and deep intervale, the famous Blue Hills of Milton showing up on the horizon. Near at hand in this direction is observed Meeting-House Hill, capped by the First Parish Church and by the Soldiers' Monument of red Gloucester granite, rising to a height of 31 feet, and erected in 1867. Looking eastward the eye embraces within the range of vision nearly all the islands of the harbor, the harbor itself and its shipping, and the ocean in the extreme distance, while near at hand is Savin Hill, rich in rustic beauty and commanding charming views. An object of special interest and one meriting inspection is the Lyman Fountain, which is located on Eaton Square, a sightly and beautiful spot, well chosen for its situation. The fountain occupies the sight of a famous old tavern—the Eaton Tavern, kept by a once equally famous Captain Eaton.

Of this handsome fountain we give a fine illustration in these pages. It was erected in memory of one of Boston's noblest and revered sons, the late Theodore Lyman, Jr., who was mayor of the city in 1834-35. Mr. Lyman was a descendant from one of the pilgrim fathers who came from England to the Old Bay State in 1631 in the same ship that brought John Eliot. Mr. Lyman was born in Boston on February 20, 1792, and his father was one of the city's merchant princes. He received his early education at Phillips Academy, Exeter, N. H., and graduated at Harvard College in 1810. He afterwards became a student in the famous University of Edinburgh, Scotland, and then travelled extensively throughout Europe. In 1820 he published a work of much merit entitled "The Political State of Italy," and in the same year delivered the Fourth of

July oration before the town authorities of Boston. In 1826 he published an important work, "The Diplomacy of the United States." From 1820 to 1823 he was aide-de-camp to Governor Brooks, and from 1823 to 1827 was commander of the Boston Brigade. From 1820 to 1823 he was a member of the Massachusetts Legislature, occupying a seat in the Senate in 1824. In 1834 and 1835 he was mayor of Boston, and gave the city a dignified, fearless, and able administration, during a period that called for unusual qualities in her chief magistrate. He was a large hearted, generous man, and many noble public institutions had their usefulness developed by his munificence. One of his most intimate friends spoke of him as "a pure, loving, devoted man, of unusual grace of bearing and manly beauty," who "used the gifts of God as His steward, and not for his own indulgence." He died on July 18, 1849, but he continued to live in the memories of his friends, who, thirty-six years after his demise, determined to erect some tangible memorial of him. The leader in this movement was the Honorable Nahum Capen, and the erection of a water fountain was decided upon. A sum of two thousand dollars was quickly subscribed, and an application was made for an allowance from the Phillips Fund, the munificent gift of Jonathan Phillips, who gave by his will to the city of Boston, in 1860, the sum of $20,000, as a trust fund, the income of which shall be annually expended to adorn and embellish

Erected In Memory of Theo. Lyman, Jr., In Eaton Square, Dorchester.

the streets and public places in the city. The authorities voted from this fund towards the cost of the fountain $4050, and a further sum of $175 for incidentals.

The site for the fountain in Eaton Square was selected by Mr. William Doogue, the city forester, and the commission to design and construct the fountain was entrusted to Mr. M. D. Jones, of the firm of M. D. Jones & Co., No. 76 Washington Street. The design is original. The structure is of fine proportions, rich in ornamentation, and is believed to be the highest and handsomest fountain in the New England States. It rises to an altitude of 26 feet. The basin is of Monson granite, and 33 feet in diameter. The first pan is 12 feet and 8 inches in diameter; the second pan 6 feet and 8 inches. The surmounting groups of figures represent Venus, Cupid and swan, while the figures about the pedestals stand for the four seasons. The supply of water is from three pipes attached to a 3-inch main, a sixty-pound pressure providing ample force. One of these pipes discharges through the swan's mouth and through four dragons on the first pedestal and four griffins, between the first and second pans. Another furnishes a supply for one hundred and forty-four jets in the rim of the first pan, and eighty in the second, while the third pipe feeds the four cascades at the base of the pedestal. The water from the jets does not overflow the pan, but discharges through four gargoyle heads. The fountain proper is of bronzed iron and zinc. The whole reflects the highest credit upon Mr. Jones. His experience as a designer and builder of fountains in various parts of New England has been extensive, but this is one of his most ambitious undertakings as well as one of his most successful achievements. The basin was constructed by Mr. John Kelly, a Boston contractor. The fountain, in its playing power, has realized all expectations. Cut in the granite basin is this legend:—"In memory of Theodore Lyman, Jr., mayor of Boston in 1834-35;" and upon a bronze plate attached to the basin is this inscription.—"This fountain as a memorial was originated by Nahum Capen, designed and constructed by M. D. Jones, Boston, located by William Doogue, city forester, accepted and dedicated by Hugh O'Brien, Mayor, October 24, 1885."

The occasion of the dedication service was a red letter day in the annals of Dorchester. Around the fountain a large and interested company of prominent persons gathered, the Germania Band was in attendance, the fountain was accepted by Mayor O'Brien as a gift to the city, and speeches were delivered appropriate to the occasion by Honorable Marshall P. Wilder, Honorable C. Winthrop, Rev. Peter Ronan, Honorable Leverett Saltonstall, and Honorable Nahum Capen.

Dorchester, which was annexed to Boston, June 22, 1869, has, since it was accorded good railway and horse-car accommodation, enjoyed a large and steady growth in population and in popularity as a residential section. Hotels, apartment-houses and costly dwellings are more numerous than they were a few years ago. Farm lands are being constantly cut up into streets and offered to those who desire to build, and as a result there is a steady increase in the value of property. Since 1883, it is safe to say that there have been built in the Dorchester district from 700 to 1000 houses of various styles and grades of cost, the great majority of them being single dwellings. In that year the real estate valuation of Dorchester was $17,797,600. In 1888, it was $22,913,300, being gain of 85,113,700 or at the rate of over $1,000,000 of gain in this item of valuation per year. The number of polls in 1883 was 4981, and in 1888 it was 6803, or nearly 2000 gain. The gain in population has been a substantial one, and is due quite largely to the good railway accommodation afforded, as well as to the horse-railway lines and low fares.

STREETS AND AVENUES.

Boston is the most like an English city of any place on the American continent both, in the peculiarity of its ancient buildings and in the tortuous windings of its oldest streets. The crookedness of the streets, formed on the lines of old cow-paths, makes an unceasing puzzle to strangers to find their way about, and yet these twists and turns afford good opportunity for the display of architectural qualities of buildings, and add much to the picturesque appearance of the city. Millions of dollars have been expended in straightening old thoroughfares and in effecting improvements, but there are curves and bendings that will ever remain unless another conflagration like that of 1872 should involve the old parts of the city in ruins and provide an opportunity for remapping the section in "square cuts." The modern wards of the city, however, are laid out in Babylonian rectangularity, with streets that are broad and straight, and vistas ending on hills in the suburbs. Streets and avenues are being increased in number or length year by year, for there are thirty-two more miles of streets now, in 1889, than there were four years ago, the total number now being 412. The streets are most efficiently sewered, for Boston has the most perfect sewerage system of any city in the country; and this has been attained at immense cost. The thoroughfares are sufficiently illuminated. At this writing there are within the city limits the following street lamps in use: Gas, 10,104; oil, 2994; electric, 704; large gas-lamps, 74; naptha lamps, 49; total, 13,925.

The streets are divided up into twenty-five wards, and there are 262 miles of street-railway tracks. Formerly there were some six street-railroad companies in Boston, and some opposition in consequence but a year or two ago these corporations amalgamated, or formed a "trust," so that one huge corporation now controls the whole street-railroad system, not only in the city, but the suburbs also. The company have in use 1912 cars, and are now introducing electric cars through the Back Bay district, Brighton, Brookline, etc. and ere long it is likely these cars will come into general use. One need not be a prophet, however, to foresee the time when the elevated railroad will be one of the institutions of Boston. The Meigs plan of elevated railroad, now being introduced into Chicago, has been proposed, and a short experimental line built in Cambridge. By this plan the use of a ponderous, smoke-producing locomotive is entirely done away with, and in its stead is used the most improved form of the electric motor, the power of which is transmitted through a third rail and applied to every third car by a simple device hidden in the bottom of the vehicle, and which is under the immediate and perfect control of an attendant. The weight and size of the supporting posts are reduced to the minimum compatible with safety ; and, as all the structure is of iron and steel, the obstruction to light and traffic is almost inconsiderable. Every precaution has been taken in regard to safety, and the speed that can be acquired is one of the especial feature of the system. The expense at which the road can be constructed is marvellously small, and its operating expenses will also be much less than those of any other road—facts which will result immediately to the public benefit by allowing the fares to be placed at a very low point.

Of the architectural changes to be noticed in a walk through Boston's streets, the following, written recently by Mr. A. W. Barrett, is apropos :

"In place of the old buildings destroyed by the devouring element, have sprung up huge edifices imposing in their size and extent, and in some cases of architectural beauty. It is a fact easily proven that the architectural styles of Boston have closely followed the prevailing ones of the same period in Europe. Early in the century there was a Greek revival, the principal monuments of which are the Court and Custom houses, the Tremont House, Quincy Market and St. Paul's Church. In 1838 began the Gothic period, an example of which is found in Old Trinity Church. Then followed the 'French-roof' style. The Deacon, House on Washington, Concord, and Worcester Streets, was probably the first building of this style in the country. With the increase of popular travel, the influence of foreign models became more strongly felt in a great variety of styles. Northern and Southern Gothic, Romanesque and Renaissance, French Renaissance, became extremely popular and are the styles of many business and public buildings, including the City Hall and Post-office. Gothic has remained the favorite for churches. A peculiarity of Boston architecture is the richness and variety of the building-material. The prevailing material is red brick, but there is an abundance of light, dark, and red granite , brown, yellow, and buff sand-stones ; a variety of marble, Roxbury pudding-stone, and other material. When a 'big building' is mentioned, one naturally thinks of a huge edifice conspicuous for its size, and standing alone like a giant pine above the scrubby undergrowth. Examples of this kind of buildings are not uncommon in Boston ; and yet it must be borne in mind that there are hundreds of 'big buildings,' side by side for blocks and blocks that are worthy of the title, though they do not strike a spectator so forcibly as a building like the Mason Building, which stands by itself."

TRANSPORTATION FACILITIES AND COMMERCE.

At the close of the war of the Revolution, Boston was the most influential community in America, but now there are two cities of greater importance and four larger in population. Then she took the lead in commerce, now, although her trade is immense, she occupies a second-rate position. Her shipping interests are, however, multiplying, and she is growing in popularity as the western port of several lines of British steamships, doing an immense and increasing freight business, and favored by the depth and security of the harbor and by the marginal railways, which allow freight vans to be run directly out upon the docks. The distance from Boston to Liverpool is shorter than from Philadelphia to Liverpool by 370 miles, New York to Southampton, by 260 miles, and New York to Liverpool by 160 miles. The harbor of Boston is the most picturesque on the coast, is of ample dimensions, and of sufficient depth to accommodate the largest vessels afloat. Her wharves are extensive, and upon them are built large warehouses. The city, too, is the starting-point for eight extensive railway lines, and the headquarters for numerous railroad corporations. Her transportation facilities are therefore of the most extensive and complete character. The Inman Steamship Company, it is reported, intends to establish a line of steamers between Boston and Europe to compete with the Cunard and other lines already located here. The tendency of recent railroad construction in the Northwest, and the developments in trade that are promised in that quarter, all have the outlook of largely increasing the merits of Boston as a point of shipment for the export and import trade of this country. The old combinations made by the trunk lines have given in the past certain advantages in rates to New York and Philadelphia ; but it is questionable whether these can be maintained in the future. Then, beside having a large advantage, so far as ocean distance is concerned, over Philadelphia, and a considerable gain over New York, Boston has hitherto enjoyed the merit, when compared with the latter place, of lower port charges for the vessels which come here. Boston may perhaps never hope to compete with New York as the great centre of the export and import trade of this country ; but, as this trade is constantly increasing, there is no reason why it should not maintain its relative position ; and there are some reasons for thinking that it may in the next few years have a larger proportionate share of this business than it has enjoyed in the past. As an indication of the extent of the foreign shipping trade now done, it may be here stated that the receipts for duties at the Custom-house amounted in 1888 to $91,166,213.31.

Boston is the great centre, too, for internal traffic, especially in food products, shoes, leather, machinery, rubber, dry goods, etc.; and in all these great commodities there is an increase year by year, the record for last year being largely in excess of that of previous years. The city has its Shoe and Leather Exchange, Boston

Faneuil Hall Square, showing Faneuil Hall and Quincy Markets

Commercial Exchange, Produce Exchange, Chamber of Commerce, New England Furniture Exchange, Fish Bureau, Board of Trade, Firemen's Exchange, Boston Board of Marine Underwriters, Boston Board of Trade, Boston Fire Underwriter's Union, Boston Grocers' Association, Boston Merchants' Association, Master Builders' Association, National Association Wool Manufacturers, New England Cotton Manufacturers' Association, New England Retail Grocers' Association, New England Saddlery Hardware Association, Mechanics' Exchange, Merchants' Exchange and Reading-room, etc.

Financial facilities are afforded by sixty national and several private banks, seven trust companies, and thirteen savings banks; and numerous home and foreign insurance companies afford protection against losses by fire to buildings, merchandise, and other property.

SCHOOLS AND CHURCHES

Boston has always occupied a prominent position among the American cities in respect to literary and scientific culture. She has been liberal in her provision of public libraries and schools, which are renowned all over the country for their number, affluence, and efficiency. The public schools are under the direction of a school committee, elected by the popular vote, a superintendent, and several supervisors. There are 530 regular schools with 1253 teachers and over 56,000 pupils, and 21 special schools with 151 teachers and 4086 pupils,

In addition to these, there are evening schools, attended by about 1900 pupils. On June 12, 1888, the school board discontinued Swinton's "Outlines of History" from the textbooks of the English High-school, at Rev. Theodore A. Metcalf's instigation, for a harmless paragraph about the sale of indulgences while Leo X. was pope. This would not have created any great amount of popular feeling, perhaps, but, on the 19th of June, the school board accepted a report transferring Mr. C. B. Travis from his post as teacher of history in the English High-school, to another duty. This action of the board created much public indignation, which was expressed in various ways. A tremendous meeting was held at Faneuil Hall on the evening of July 11th, and an overflow meeting at Tremont Temple, to protest against the displacement of Swinton's "Outlines" from the textbooks of the English High-school and transferring Mr. Travis from the historical department of that school. This was one of the most memorable meetings held in Faneuil Hall during recent years. It took the

New England Conservatory of Music.

initial steps towards forming a committee of one hundred that wielded a marked influence upon the city election. Women were enlisted in the movement to reconstruct the school board so that it might be freed from mischievous ecclesiastical control, and several associations were formed to promote the assessment and registration of women to vote for school committee. The Loyal Women of American Liberty, Independent Women Voters of Boston, School Suffrage Association, Bunker Hill Educational Association, and Women's Christian Temperance Union took an active part in this work. The assessment of women elicited a spirited trial of strength between Protestants and Catholics. The Republican city convention to nominate mayor and school committee assembled on the evening of Nov. 10th, and on the first ballot nominated Thomas N. Hart for mayor. A committee was selected to nominate eleven members of the school board. Subsequently the Republicans nominated a ticket for school committee, which was indorsed by the committee of one hundred and the women's associations affiliating with them. A vigorous canvass was made in its behalf by the committee of one hundred and the women's organizations acting with them. This ticket had no Catholics upon it, but a women's ticket was sent to every woman registered, having upon it the names of Messrs. Williamson, Dunn, and Canning, then members of the school board, who voted to reject Swinton's "Outlines" and transfer Mr. Travis. Besides this, there was a regular Democratic woman's ticket. Mr. Hart accepted the Republican nomination on a non-partisan platform entirely. A citizens' movement, into which the British element threw all its influence and zeal, was started in his favor, and subsequently put a school committee ticket in the field, embracing, among others, the names of Caroline E. Hastings, Messrs. Williamson, Dunn, Canning, and Collins of the present school board. The Republican canvass for the city government was made on the issue of reform and the necessity of an entire change in methods at City Hall. The appeal was made to all parties, but a potent factor was the determination of the women to rebuke the school board for submitting to priestly control. Mr. Hart was elected mayor on the 11th of December by a plurality of 2021. The Republicans elected two-thirds of the aldermen, and gained in the Common Council. It was a rout of the City Hall ring. The people emphatically condemned the school board by electing the entire Republican ticket for school committee, which has been indorsed by the Committee of One Hundred. The city voted for license by a majority of 17,851, against 8493 last year. An enormous vote was polled, considering the heavy, penetrating rain which prevailed. The total for mayor fell short of the presidential vote only 1550. Of the twenty-one thousand woman registered, seventeen thousand voted under the most disagreeable circumstances as regards the weather. But this did not appear to daunt them in the least. They labored zealously and effectively from the opening to the closing of the polls, were everywhere treated with consideration, and had the satisfaction of having contributed very materially to the election of the Republican school committee ticket, made up wholly of Protestants. The school committee, as elected, consists of: Caroline Hastings (one year), W. A. Mowry (two years), Leliah B. Pingree, W. S. Allen, R. C. Humphreys, T. J. Emery, S. B. Capen, Dr. W. C. Green, Solomon Schindler, J. P. G. Winship, Dr. Liberty Packard.

There are over 320 churches in the city, representing all sects of religionists, and some of these and their pastors have won fame both at home and abroad.

THE CITY GOVERNMENT.

Boston received its city charter in 1822; and the government comprises a mayor, a board of 12 aldermen and a common council consisting of 73 representatives of the 25 wards. The executive power was formerly vested in the mayor and aldermen, but the law of 1885 (Stat. 1885, ch. 266), amending the charter of Boston, vests all executive power in the mayor, but retains, with very few exceptions, all the boards, commissions, trustees, and separate departments or offices existing at that time or since established. The number of those separate bodies exceeds 50, some of whom are not even required to publish regular reports. The election takes place annually on the Tuesday after the second Monday in December. From what has already been stated in connection with the election of the school committee (conducted at the same time) that of the mayor, aldermen and councilmen was, in December, 1888, an excitable one, and resulted in arresting the executive power so long held by the Democrats, by the Republicans, with the aid of the women and the British citizens.

The police force, numbering 800 men, some three years ago was taken from under the control of the civic authorities and placed under that of the State. Not including druggists, 1561 places were in 1888 licensed in the city for the sale of intoxicating drink, or one to every 263 persons, the population of the city on January 1, 1889, being computed at 410,666. The law of 1888 (chapter 340) demands the reduction of these licenses to 781, or exactly one half. The fire department is one of the most efficient in the country, and the water-supply is of a most adequate and excellent character.

THE CLIMATE AND HEALTH.

The climate of Boston is severe, especially in winter and spring; but the intense heats of summer are tempered by refreshing east winds, which fill the streets with the salty smell of the adjacent ocean. The death-rate in 1888 was 24.57 for each 1000 inhabitants, against 25.18 per 1000 in 1887.

THE SUBURBS.

No city has more attractive and picturesque suburbs than Boston, and it would take volumes to consider the traits and beauties of those outlying districts.

Many popular summer resorts are by the sea, and the most charming and most visited of these are Nantasket Beach, Revere Beach, and Point of Pines. A sail down the beautiful harbor is one of the special delights of Bostonians, and a pleasure which no visitor should forego.

ILLUSTRATED BOSTON.

THE pages that follow contain many of the representative houses of this metropolis, and in connection with the illustrated portion of the work will be found profitable and interesting.

W. L. MINOR, Architect, No. 4 Pemberton Square.—No feature of a great city is so prominently brought to public attention as that of its architectural display, and no profession is of greater or more lasting importance to every member of the community than that of the architect. Prominent among the leading architects of Boston is Mr. W. L. Minor, whose offices are situated at No. 4 Pemberton Square. Mr. Minor had also a branch office in Brockton, Mass. Mr. Minor is a native of Louisiana, and early in life devoted himself to the study of his profession, with zeal and success. In 1873 he commenced practising as an architect in Charleston, S. C., and he has also carried on business in Topeka, Kansas; Cincinnati, O.; and Cadettsburg, Ky. He built up the greater part of Cadettsburg after the great fire. Eventually Mr. Minor came to New Bedford, and then to Brockton and Boston. Proofs of Mr. Minor's skill and ability are numerous in the various cities where he has resided in the many substantial and splendid edifices he has erected in the past 15 years, which are much admired for stability, design, and elegance, while the elaboration of detail and care bestowed on every department of his work, reflect the utmost credit on his able and business-like methods. Mr. Minor was architect and superintend the construction the following buildings, viz.: Home Bank, Brockton, Mass., $100,000; Bixby Building, Brockton, Mass., $45,000; F. E. White's Building, Brockton, Mass., $40,000; F. R. Washburn's Building, Brockton, $50,000; G. J. Kingman's Residence, Brockton, $25,000; High School, Middleborough, $30,000; J. W. Minor's residence, Plymouth, $40,000; High School, Everett, Mass., $40,000, and many others. He is at all times prepared to furnish estimates, plans and specifications, and can always be implicitly relied on to spare neither time nor pains to fulfil the expectations and requirements of patrons. Personally, he is greatly respected by the community for his just methods and ability, and is thoroughly conversant with the wants and growth of Boston, and is fully competent to carry to successful completion all work pertaining to his profession.

POTTER LOVELL COMPANY, Dealers in Commercial Paper, No. 49 Federal Street, Corner Franklin Street.—A most important and duly appreciated financial factor in promoting the commercial and industrial prosperity of the New England and Middle States, is the Potter Lovell Company, the widely and favorably known dealers in commercial paper. This concern is one of ample resources, thorough responsibility, and the highest standing. It is a duly incorporated organization, having been put forward under the laws of Massachusetts in the year 1884, with a cash capital of $400,000, devoted to the discounting of prime commercial paper of all kinds. The company has, under its able executive guidance, made rapid progress and is the leading representative of its kind in the United States. The officers are as follows: President, Mr. Walter Potter, long and favorably known as an enterprising capitalist and sound financier; treasurer, Mr. W. D. Lovell, likewise a capitalist and banker of the greatest ability and sound judgment; secretary, Mr. George W. Terrill, who is widely and favorably known throughout the community. The company has made a prominent specialty of the

paper of dry goods and grocery houses and boot and shoe manufacturers; likewise of other staple industries, as well as city and town loans, and offers to capitalists and investors excellent and absolutely safe opportunities for investment in sound, legitimate commercial paper. It has numerous customers in New York, having an office at No. 40 Wall Street, and is the leading representative in its line. The best-known houses negotiate their paper through this honorable, responsible concern, which has achieved a most enviable reputation throughout the business world. The officers are gentlemen of integrity, and are recognized to be vigorous exponents of the soundest principles governing banking and finance.

THE ASHTON VALVE COMPANY, Manufacturers of the Ashton Safeties, Locomotive Safety-valves, etc.; Office and Works, No. 271 Franklin Street; C. J. Bishop, President; H. G. Ashton, Vice-President and General Manager.—We are constantly reading in our newspapers of terrible boiler-explosions, and the records for the last few years in the United States show that ten thousand persons were killed or injured by them. A large number of these explosions may be directly traced to false economy, which is satisfied with the cheapest instead of the best safety appliances. In connection with these remarks, we desire to make special reference in this commercial review of Boston to the reliable and representative Ashton Valve Company, manufacturers of the famous Ashton Safety-valves and Appliances, whose office and works are located at 271 Franklin Street. This progressive company was duly incorporated in 1877 under the laws of Massachusetts, with a paid-up capital of $150,000, for the manufacture of everything in their line. The works are admirably equipped with special tools and machinery, and they manufacture extensively the following first-class safety appliances, etc., viz.: The Ashton Noiseless Locomotive Blow-back Safety-valve, Locomotive Safety-valve and Muffler, Locomotive Open "Pop" Safety-valve, Locomotive Safety-valve and Muffler, Locomotive Open "Pop" Safety-valve for stationary, portable, and farm engines; Cut-beater "Pop" Valves, Gas or Air Valves, the Ashton Water Relief-valve, Hydraulic Valves, Cylinder Relief-valves, Locomotive Steam-chest Relief-valves, Bailing-valves, the Ashton Marine "Pop" Safety-valve, Noiseless Marine Blow-back Valves for steamships, steamboats, and pleasure yachts. They likewise have a specialty department, which enables them to design and furnish, on application, special valves for special needs, which often occur in steam or hydraulic engineering. All the safety-valves and appliances manufactured by this responsible company are absolutely unrivalled for quality of material, efficiency, utility, safety, economy, and general excellence, and are unequalled in America or Europe, while the prices quoted for all goods are exceedingly moderate. We know of no explosion where the Ashton valves have been in service on a boiler. The following gentlemen are the executive officers: C. J. Bishop, President; H. H. Ashton, Vice-President and General Manager; Wm. Howell Reed, Treasurer. The company's branch office in Chicago is at 118 Lake Street, and in New York at 96 Liberty Street.

PARKER HOUSE, Beckman & Punchard, Proprietors, School Street, corner of Tremont.—The history of the Parker House is one of a most gratifying character to the people of Boston and New England. Like the Fifth Avenue Hotel, at New York, or Willard's, at Washington, the Parker House has always been the popular hotel for public and political movements, and is one of the points where public opinion takes shape and through the pen of the reporter is made known to a national constituency. This famous hotel was established thirty-three years ago by Mr. Harvey D. Parker, who was succeeded in the proprietorship thirteen years ago by Mr. Joseph H. Beckman and Mr. Edward O. Punchard, gentlemen of vast practical experience in the most advanced circles of hotel life, and who are, in fact, thorough masters of the difficult art of modern hotel-keeping. ...

FERA, Confectioner, No. 181 Tremont Street.—The business of a caterer is one requiring a peculiar tact, as well as a high order of intelligence, and he who adopts this vocation and makes the development of a life-study must carry in his mind the countless combinations which enter into the great variety of confections and the different kinds of luxuries and delicacies that are necessary to meet the demands of the modern social public, and be prepared to cater to every taste and satisfy every fancy. ...

E. B. HAMLIN & CO., Hard and Soft Coal and Wood; Wharves, Nos. 834 and 836 Federal Street.—An industry of such importance as that conducted by Messrs. E. B. Hamlin & Co., the well-known dealers in hard and soft coal and wood, whose wharves are situated at Nos. 834 and 836 Federal Street, has so important a bearing upon the commerce and manufacture of this city, and is so directly conducive to the general prosperity, as to demand more than ordinary consideration at our hands. ...

E. T. COWDREY CO., Preservers and Importers of Table Delicacies, Nos. 78, 80, and 82 Broad Street — An important adjunct to the canned goods trade of New England is the old established and representative house of E. T. Cowdrey Co., whose office and warehouse in Boston are located at Nos. 78-82 Broad Street. This widely known and reliable house was established in 1865 by Mr. E. T. Cowdrey, who continued the canning and preserving business and importation of foreign table delicacies until within a few years, when

of the company now extends not only throughout the entire United States and Canada, but also abroad. The E. T. Cowdrey Co. preserve and can fruits, vegetables, meats, fish, poultry, soups, preserves, jellies, jams, pickles, etc. All of their food products are prepared with scrupulous care and cleanliness, and are warranted to be exactly as represented; while the prices quoted for all goods are as low as those of any other first-class house in the trade. Their factories are slightly located at the best centres of supply, and are furnished

he retired from active life, after a successful and honorable career. In 1893, the business was duly incorporated, under the laws of Massachusetts, under the style and title of the E. T. Cowdrey Co., the general manager and treasurer being Mr. Cromwell T. Schuhmacher, who for several years had been the managing partner of the old firm. The company's manufactories and canneries — admirably equipped with the latest improved apparatus and appliances — are situated at Boston, Littleton, and Dighton, Mass., and North Wayne, Me. Here 800 operatives are constantly employed, and the trade

with every facility for preserving the freshly gathered products of the farm. All the goods of the E. T. Cowdrey Co. are unsurpassed for quality and uniform excellence, and are everywhere recognized and appreciated by the trade as standard productions; the brands being general favorites with the trade and a critical public, always commanding a rapid sale. In conclusion, we would observe that the affairs of the E. T. Cowdrey Co. are placed in able and energetic hands, and is worthily maintains a leading position in this useful and valuable industry, reflecting the greatest credit upon all concerned.

BURLEY & USHER, Manufacturers of the Celebrated Granite State Ranges, Milton, N. H., Newburyport, Mass., and Springvale, Me.; Boston Office, No. 263 Devonshire Street.—One of the great representative firms of New England boot and shoe manufacturers is that of Messrs. Burley & Usher, of Milton, N. H., Springvale, Me., Newburyport and Boston, Mass. Mr. D. S. Burley and Mr. W. R. Usher formed the existing copartnership only seven years ago, and yet have outstripped all competition, and within the intervening period achieved a volume of trade and perfection of facilities attained by few houses in a lifetime. This is because of the push, energy, and ability of the partners, whose laudable ambition to excel has resulted in their trade-mark "Granite State Shoe" being in universal demand throughout the United States. Their large factory at Milton, N. H., proving too small for their requirements, the firm have now (January 1892) just finished building a splendid factory at Springvale, Me. It is four stories and basement in height, fitted up with the latest improved machinery and requirements, and having a capacity of one thousand five hundred pairs per day. Two hundred hands will be employed here in the manufacture of medium grade goat and kid shoes, and of a quality which will at once command the attention of the best class of trade. The firm's factory at Milton, N. H., is a four-story structure, 40 by 160 feet in dimensions, thoroughly equipped, and having a capacity of two thousand five hundred pairs per day, affording employment to two hundred and fifty hands. The finest line of goods shown is produced here, and the "Granite State" brand, every pair warranted, is a great staple seller all over the country. The firm have a third factory at Newburyport, five floors, 40 by 160 feet in dimensions, having a capacity of one thousand five hundred pairs per day, and affording employment to two hundred and fifty hands in the manufacture of the best grade of Goodyear Welts, and hand-turned goods, which have a heavy sale with the best city trade. The firm manufacture standard lines of women's, misses', and children's shoes, also slippers and wool-lined boots and shoes, all of the finest class, and sell direct to the retail dealers, to whom substantial inducements are offered. These enterprising manufacturers have about two hundred styles in stock, and the advantage of buying of one good, reliable brand over such a wide circle of the trade is shown by the fact that Messrs. Burley & Usher had over one thousand nine hundred customers on their books last year. Their Boston office and salesrooms are most conveniently located at No. 263 Devonshire Street, where full sample lines are carried. The firm require the services of fifteen travelers on the road, and are doing a business of commerce magnitude all over the west, south, and northwest, based strictly on the merit of their goods, which are noted for superiority of skins and leather, correct cut, fashionable styles of lasts, honest workmanship, elegant finish, and moderate price, and Messrs. Burley & Usher are to be congratulated upon the large measure of success attending their ably-directed efforts.

P. B. McCARGO & CO., Music Publishers, No. 32 Washington Street.—The name of P. B. McCargo has acquired an international celebrity as one who has practically revolutionized the music-publishing trade, and filled a long-felt want by providing a full and complete musical library at such prices as enable the poorest and humblest to possess themselves of it, and yet so finely executed in all details both of art and mechanism, and so exquisitely finished, that even the wealthy are proud to give it a place in their portfolio. Mr. McCargo was born in Virginia, and early in life became actively identified with the trade in which he has achieved such a marked success, and in which that peculiar enterprise has developed itself that has made him so great a benefactor of the people. He began his career in the music business in Philadelphia, and for a number of years conducted a flourishing and progressive business in that city, becoming noted for the wide variety and attractive character of his musical publications and developing a rare taste and marked tact in his selections—facts amply evidenced by their wide popularity. In 1886, Mr. McCargo became sole proprietor of all the Copyrights, Plates and Stock of the old music-publishing house of W. A. Evans & Bro. Soon after this, the firm of P. B. McCargo & Co. was formed; and then began that career of prosperity which has placed the firm on so strong a basis, and so much enlarged the sphere of its operations, and at the same time been so great a blessing to the people. Mr. McCargo at once greatly increased the facilities of the old concern, and, by his rare discrimination in selecting, added to the valuable catalogue to which he had accorded, in a short time made his house one of the foremost in the country in the variety of its music and the volume of its business. This house has forever put an end to the injustice of exhorbitant prices, and, with careful attention and good judgment, now publishes the largest and most desirable collection of the most popular and standard compositions of operatic, classical, sentimental, and religious music in this country, and is constantly adding to its catalogue the best of the latest compositions, vocal and instrumental, both original and reprints. In 1887, the firm moved into its present spacious warerooms, so advantageously situated at No. 34 Washington Street, where their trade has more than trebled during the past two years. The publications of the firm are sold all through the United States, and exported to every quarter of the civilized globe, including Russia, the far remote regions of Australia and South America. The firm is also agent for the publications of the National Music Company, which possesses a most desirable catalogue,—this list of publications, together with the large and extensive catalogue of P. B. McCargo & Co., covering the whole gamut of published music, should be in every dealer's hand. In addition to its vast business, the firm of P. B. McCargo & Co. makes a specialty of producing music for composers and dealers, and promptly fills all orders in the line of publishing or work. Personally, Mr. McCargo, the founder of the firm, is a genial, wholesouled gentleman, with a most agreeable and engaging presence, and is as much esteemed in private life for his many excellent social qualities as he is admired in business circles for his enterprise and fine ability.

JOHN CARTER & CO., Paper Warehouse Nos. 168 and 170 Congress Street.—The paper trade of Boston is one of much importance, and is a prime factor in the business development of the city. There are a number of first-class houses engaged in this line, but none which bear a better reputation or command a higher standing in commercial circles than that of Messrs. John Carter & Co., whose establishment is located at Nos. 168 and 170 Congress Street. The business of this firm was founded ten years ago by the active manager and proprietor, Mr. John Carter, who has been following the paper trade for more than a quarter of a century, and was formerly a member of the firms of Carter, Bros. & Co., and Carter, Pulsifer and Jordan. He is well known in the paper trade and is respected for the honorable principles which he exercises in all his transactions. For the purposes of the business an entire building is occupied, having six floors each 25x165 feet in dimensions, and appointed throughout with every convenience to facilitate the operations of trade. An extensive stock is carried of paper of every description, and a specialty is made of Byron's, Weston, and Crane & Co's papers for which the firm are agents. An active wholesale and jobbing trade is supplied, and the house has patrons in all parts of the New England States. Mr. Carter is a native Bostonian, has long been actively identified with the best interests of the city, and his ability and commendable methods have won him prominence in the mercantile world.

H. H. CARTER & CO., Paper and Paper-mill Supplies, No. 5 Beacon Street.—In the important line of paper and paper-mill supplies in Boston, a representative and prominent house is that of Messrs. H. H. Carter & Co., whose office and salesrooms are centrally located at No. 5 Beacon Street. The firm have also an extensive wholesale house in Boston, at No. 143 Pearl Street. This business was established twenty years ago by Mr. H. H. Carter, who conducted it till 1884, when Mr. James L. Carrick became a partner, and continued till January, 1889, when he retired on account of ill health. The premises occupied comprise a commodious store and basement, with salesrooms and warerooms in the adjoining building. These are admirably equipped with every convenience and facility, including cash carrier system, for the systematic and successful prosecution of this growing business. Here thirty efficient assistants are employed in the various departments, while several traveling salesmen represent the interests of the firm in all sections of New England and New York. Messrs. Carter & Co. keep constantly on hand an extensive stock of all kinds, qualities, and sizes of paper, cardboard and paper-mill supplies. They make a specialty of Christmas cards and folded papers; also of the finest note and letter papers. Only the best classes of paper, etc., are handled; and the prices quoted to all comers are as low as those of any other first-class house in the trade in Boston or elsewhere.

WALTER M. LOWREY, Manufacturer of Fine Confectionery. Nos. 97, 99, 101, and 105 Pearl Street.

L. C. CHASE & CO., Manufacturers of Horse-clothing, Carriage-robes, Mohair Plushes and Velours, Nos. 185-189 Washington Street.—No historical review of the representative houses of Boston would be complete without special reference to the firm of L. C. Chase & Co., manufacturers of horse-clothing, carriage-robes, mohair plushes and velours, whose office and salesrooms are located at Nos. 185-189 Washington Street. This extensive business was originally established, under the firm-name of L. C. Chase & Co., in 1847, by L. C. and H. F. Chase. Both brothers retired from the firm in 1863, and up to the time of their retirement they had taken no active part in the business for some years. Mr. L. C. Chase died in 1867, and Mr. H. F. Chase in 1869, after the completion of a successful and honorable career. They were succeeded by John Hopewell, Jr., O. F. Kendall, who were members of the old concern, and Frank Hopewell, and are now conducting the business under the firm-name of L. C. Chase & Co. The firm is interested in the Sanford Mills, of

which Mr. John Hopewell, Jr., is treasurer. These mills are the largest and best equipped of the kind in the world, and are located in Sanford, Maine. They are also interested in the Troy Mills, at Troy, N. H. There are employed in these mills and in their manufacturing department at Boston over a thousand operatives. The firm also have branch offices in New York and Chicago, and have every facility for rapid communication and prompt despatch of business with every portion of the United States, Canada, and Mexico in the wholesale trade. Their premises in Boston occupy four spacious floors, which are admirably equipped with every appliance and facility for the accommodation and display of the samples of the extensive and valuable stock which they manufacture. They make extensively all kinds of horse-clothing, and their carriage robes, robes and plushes are of recognized merit throughout the country, and are unrivalled in this country or Europe for quality and durability. The partners are Massachusetts men and residents of Cambridge. They are widely known as representative and honest business men and influential and public spirited citizens.

GEO. H. RICHARDS, JR., & CO., Diamonds, Watches, French Clocks, Jewelry, Silverware, Opera-glasses, fine Repairing and Engraving, No. 89 Washington Street, opposite Franklin Street.—For ages past, the diamond has been held in the highest estimation of those who love jewelry, while the splendor of the three stones has certainly justified the preference. A leading headquarters in this city for diamonds and first-class jewelry of all kinds is the establishment of Messrs. Geo. H. Richards, Jr., & Co., located at No. 89 Washington Street, opposite Franklin Street. This firm are widely prominent and popular as jobbers and retailers of diamonds, watches, French clocks, jewelry, silverware, opera-glasses, etc., and make a leading specialty of engraving and repairing. The business was originally established in 1875 by Mr. Geo. H. Richards, Jr., and in 1887 the present firm was organized by the admission of Mr. Charles E. Richards to partnership. The showrooms of the firm are spacious in size, elegantly fitted up with handsome wall cabinets and heavy plate-glass show cases for the display, and large safes for the storage of the choice and valuable stock, and perfect in completeness of arrangement for inspection and sale. Here will be found certain classes of articles of novelty, beauty, and merit, for decoration and personal adornment, to be obtained nowhere else in the city. In gold and silver watches, French clocks, rich jewelry and charms, solid silver and plated ware, opera glasses and optical specialties, the assortments are rarely equalled and never excelled by any contemporary establishment here. In gems and "stones of worth," the selections are among the largest and choicest on this side of the Atlantic. Here are diamonds of unequalled whiteness and clearness, and of absolute faultlessness, "gems of the purest ray serene," rivière solitaire, cluster, and pendant, panache and aigrette, necklace and bracelets, chains, earrings and chatelaines, are all fittingly represented. In the specialties of engraving and fine watch-repairing, this house is known to distance all competition, and to command the admiration and confidence of all who inspect its work in these important branches. A corps of fourteen skilled assistants contribute to the successful operations of the house; and the trade is at all times brisk and lively, at both wholesale and retail, inducements being constantly offered in reliability of goods and liberality of terms and prices which challenge competition. The Messrs. Richards are brothers, born in Keene, N. H., of large experience in the watch-making and jewelry industry, both as salesmen and principals, and highly esteemed in business and trade circles for their enterprise, reliability, and solid personal worth.

NICHOLS & FARNSWORTH, Importers and Dealers in Shoe-manufacturers' Goods, No. 96 Summer Street.—The prominent and prosperous house of Messrs. Nichols & Farnsworth, the well-known importers and dealers in shoe-manufacturers' goods, at No. 96 Summer Street, is one which, devoted to a given line of trade, thus receives all the advantages to be gained from undivided attention. The enterprise was inaugurated in 1864, by Messrs. N. Nichols and F. M. Farnsworth; and in 1867, Mr. Chas. C. Hoyt was admitted to partnership without change in firm name. The premises occupied for trade purposes are spacious in size, eligibly located in the heart of the great shoe and leather district of the city, and are at all times stocked to repletion with choice, desirable, and valuable specialties in this line, of both domestic and foreign production. No house in the country is better prepared to minister successfully and satisfactorily to the shoe trade, or stands higher in the esteem of shoe-manufacturers throughout all this great centre of the industry. The various goods represented in stock are of a thoroughly reliable and standard quality, and are selected with a trained and practical eye direct from the most reputable producing sources in this country and Europe. Their superiority is recognized by critical and discriminating buyers, and many of the largest shoe-manufacturers in Massachusetts make their purchases in this line at this establishment, being attracted by the honorable methods in force, the superior inducements offered, and the uniformly satisfactory manner in which their orders are fulfilled. Domestic goods are chiefly handled, while the firm import in large quantities such specialties as lastings, elastic webs, buttons, galloons, lacing hooks, etc. Their line of domestic goods is particularly worthy of attention in linings, stay webs, shoe lacings, threads, and other indispensables suited to the wants of manufacturers, while the liberal terms and prices which prevail are such as add materially to the popularity of the house among all classes of purchasers. The copartners are experienced in the needs and requirements of the trade, and are gentlemen in whose integrity the utmost confidence may be safely placed. Messrs. Nichols and Hoyt are Massachusetts men, while Mr. Farnsworth is a native of New Hampshire.

SHEPARD, NORWELL & CO., Importers and Jobbers of Dress Goods, Silks, and Velvets. Nos 46 to 48 Winter Street; New York Office, No. 873 Broadway.—A model American wholesale and retail dry goods house is that of Messrs. Shepard, Norwell & Co., which is to finance what that of Arnold, Constable & Co. is to New York at the present time, dealing only in the freshest, the choicest, and the best of reasonable offerings in high-grade imported and domestic silks, satins, velvets, dress fabrics, etc. The house has had a long and honorable career. The head of the concern and founder of the business, Mr. John Shepard, early in life entered upon a mercantile career, as clerk in a Hanover Street dry goods store. He early evinced those rare qualifications of executive capacity, sound judgment, and force of character which have proved such invaluable factors in his well-earned success, and when yet a youth embarked in business upon his own account, achieving well merited prosperity, and ever alert to progress, he in 1881 bought out the business of Messrs. Bell, Thing & Co. The location of a great retail business is an important matter, and Mr. Shepard, needing enlarged premises and looking to future growth, with sound discrimination, sought a location in Winter Street, at that juncture being given over to high-class mercantile establishments by the former fashionable residents. As the result of his negotiations with the dry-goods house of Wilcox, White & Forshek, already established in Winter Street, Mr. Shepard jointly with Mr. Henry Norwell, bought them out and entered into possession of their premises on January 1, 1883. Mr. Norwell was also a practical dry-goods merchant of vast experience, who had been engaged in business upon his own account in Nashua, N. H., previous to that time having been with the old house of Hogg, Brown & Taylor, achieving an enviable reputation throughout the trade. In 1878, after a steady enlargement of their trade, Mr. Robert Ferguson, who had held a departmental position of great responsibility in A. T. Stewart's mammoth dry goods store in New York, joined the firm, and subsequently Mr. Edward E. Cole, an able business man, was also admitted, rendering the house the strongest in ability as well as resources in its line, energy, capacity, and perfected facilities, building up what is recognized as one of the leading representative mercantile enterprises of Boston and of the United States at large. The rapid growth of their trade taxed the facilities of the firm to the utmost in their old premises, and in 1884 they inaugurated extensive enlargements and improvements. The structure was largely rebuilt, elevators put in, and in its modernized form, four stories and basement in height, fronting on Winter Street, it extended for a long distance on Winter Place, occupying the sites of the former mansions of Mr. Frederick Brown, Mr. Albert Fearing, and Mr. Henry Bardini, names long familiar in the world's commerce. Again in 1887 were further enlargements necessitated, the premises now comprising six floors and basement, with 150 feet in dimensions, most elaborately and elegantly decorated, equipped and furnished, and arranged in a manner as perfect in conception as admirably developed in detail. All the modern improvements have been introduced including safety passenger elevators, the automatic cash system, the electric light, steam heat etc. A thorough system of organization is enforced, and the various departments themselves distinct and separate, and for which the respective managers are responsible, form one grand homogeneous whole—a mammoth modern dry-goods emporium fully as large as the best in New York, and affording employment to about 600 clerks, salesmen, office staff, boys, and other assistants. The appearance of the interior of this immense concern is impressive and attractive. There is a large open space in the centre of the store, 80x60 feet in diameter, which extends entirely through to the roof, and where the staircases are built. This gives an unusually light and airy effect, while its breadth is seen in the splendid light at the alto, velvets, and dress goods counters, ladies being able to examine and compare colors and shades as well as at the doors. The firm are importers wholesalers and retailers of every description of dry-goods, and make specialties of the choicest fabrics whenever manufactured all over the world. The firm is one of the most active and extensive importing houses in these lines in the city and brings every possible facility to bear, fully qualified buyers representing it in the European markets, enabling it to be the first to secure choice novelties in the finest fabrics of the loom. The bulk of its business is in the finest imported goods; and buying on largely and possessing such extended facilities, they are universally noted for its splendid array of goods; and the lowness of its prices. Polite and intelligent salesmen are here to promptly wait upon customers, while the enormous stock contains everything desirable and seasonable in the lines of silks, satins, velvets, dress fabrics in all textures and shades, both imported and domestic; cloaks, seal plushes and chains; washable garments and other furs; housekeeping goods, flannels, blankets, linens; domestic cottons, white goods, etc. A vast stock of underwear, gloves, and hosiery is here; also full lines of fancy goods, laces, embroideries, ribbons, etc. The establishment is daily thronged with customers; the firm's announcements in the daily press are eagerly watched, and both as to prices and quality its assertions are ever accurate and truthful. The fame and high reputation of this house are so familiar to the general public that further comment upon our part would be superfluous. When the great New York dry goods house of J. C. Johnston & Co. failed recently, Messrs. Shepard, Norwell & Co. imported it, intending to buy it outright at a bargain if it suited them and their fine trade, but it is understood that that stock was not touched, being entirely unsuited to the refined requirements of the ladies of Boston. This shows the high place of excellence maintained by Messrs. Shepard, Norwell & Co. Mr. Shepard, during his lengthy and active business career, has won a measure of popularity, confidence, and respect in the mercantile circles of the country second to none. His majority the highest of reputations for enriching sound business principles, and is one of Boston's most enterprising as he is one of her most conservative and successful dry goods merchants and importers. He is a popular citizen, prominent in social circles, and one of the best judges of bonded horses in the country, his selections for his own use bespeaking his knowledge thereof. Mr. Norwell is an energetic business man, with a lengthy practical connection with the dry-goods trade, and possessing superior executive abilities, while his policy has ever been one of equity and honor. Messrs. Ferguson and Cole are valued and energetic coadjutors, prominent in the trade, and this great establishment reared by Messrs. Shepard, Norwell & Co. is a lasting source of credit to the city, and a monument to their own industry and enterprise.

JOSEPH T. BROWN & CO., Druggists and Chemists, No 504 Washington Street, Corner Bedford.—A time-honored and noteworthy Boston drug store is the elegant and well-ordered pharmacy of Joseph T. Brown & Co., druggists and chemists, which is one of the oldest and finest in this city, as well as the most reliable and popular; physicians' prescriptions and family recipes being here compounded in the most careful and accurate manner by thoroughly competent pharmacists, from absolutely pure and fresh ingredients; while the prices prevailing are maintained at bed-rock figures likewise. This handsome and flourishing pharmacy was established by Joseph T. Brown, who, after "serving time" with his eldest brother, opened his present store in 1891, who erected the present structure in 1851, and conducted the business alone up to 1888, when he admitted into partnership his son, Joseph T. Brown, Jr., and George F. Markoe, and, in 1878, Mr. Charles H. Bassett, who entered the store as a boy in 1864. Mr. Markoe retired some years ago, and in April, 1888, Mr. Brown died, leaving Mr. Bassett and Mr. Joseph T. Brown, Jr., as the surviving members of the firm. Mr. Brown retired on May 1st of this year, leaving Mr. Bassett sole proprietor, and who still continues business under the old firm name. The firm occupy two floors and basement of a fine 5-story and basement brick building, with spacious and very tastefully appointed store, a superb display being made, while nine experienced assistants are employed on the premises. An extensive and carefully selected stock is constantly kept on hand, including, besides pure and best quality drugs, medicines, and chemicals of every description, at wholesale prices, also all American, French, and English proprietary remedies of merit, at warehouse rates, and an A1 assortment of tooth, hair, and nail brushes direct from the manufacturers. The stock also embraces pure medicinal wines and liquors, mineral waters of all kinds, acids, extracts, flavors, essences, spirits, alcohol, pharmaceutical preparations in great variety, sanitary specialties, herbs, barks, roots, etc., and a first-class line of toilet articles, perfumery, fancy soaps, sponges, chamois, and everything comprehended under the general head of druggists' sundries; special attention being given to the prescription department; and, altogether, an exceedingly fine business is done. Mr. Bassett, who is a comparatively young man, is a gentleman of courteous manners and a skilful and reliable chemist.

R. W. KENDALL & CO., Manufacturers and Selling Agents, No. 99 Bedford Street.—Among Boston's staunch and representative business houses may be mentioned that of R. W. Kendall & Co., manufacturers of and commission dealers in cotton fabrics (Canton velvet draperies a specialty), whose capacious and well-ordered establishment is located at No. 99 Bedford Street, with branches at Nos. 64 and 66 Worth Street, New York, and No. 699 Chestnut Street, Philadelphia. No firm engaged in this important line of merchantile activity in the city maintains a higher standing in the trade, and few, if any at all, enjoy a larger measure of recognition, the total annual sales reaching a very handsome figure. This widely-known and responsible firm was established in 1872, and was originally located on Chauncy Street, whence the business was moved, a few years later, to Lincoln Street, and finally, in 1878, to the present elegant warehouse known as the Lee Building. The house is conducted on strict business principles, and its management characterized by sagacity, energy, and judicious enterprise, coupled with strict integrity; and all persons having dealings with the firm are certain to find the same of a very satisfactory character. They occupy the whole of the chambers of No. 99 and the third floor of No. 102, with spacious and elegant offices and sale-rooms, carrying always on hand an extensive and varied assortment of cotton fabrics in every pattern, variety, and grade, having special reference to their line of goods, in which they are pioneers. An efficient force of clerks and salesmen are employed, and the trade of the house, which extends all over the United States and the Canadas, is exceedingly large. Their goods are to be found in all the leading wholesale houses of the country, particularly in upholstery departments. The firm is composed of Messrs. R. W. Kendall and J. W. Allen, both gentlemen of middle age, and natives of this state. They are men of many years' experience in this line, thoroughly conversant with the trade, and enjoy an excellent reputation in mercantile life.

BLACKER & SHEPARD, Lumber, No. 250 Albany Street.—The rapid growth and development of the lumber trade in Boston has been largely brought about by the enterprise and ability of such houses as that of Messrs. Blacker & Shepard, who are located at No. 250 Albany Street. This firm have long been an important factor in supplying New England with lumber from the pineries and forests of the west and south. The business was established in 1875 by Messrs. James E. Blacker & H. B. Shepard, under the still existing firm name, the only change in the firm having been six years ago, when Mr. H. B. Shepard sold his interest in the concern to his brother, Mr. C. A. Shepard. From the inception of the business the house has carried on an extensive trade throughout the New England States, which has steadily increased, owing to the uniform excellence and reliability of all goods handled, and the prompt and honorable manner in which all their dealings are characterized. The yards are extensive, covering an area of over two acres, which is covered with sheds for the protection and storage of the large stock. The transportation facilities are unexcelled either by water or rail, the yards having a wharf frontage of 250 feet, also a frontage on Albany Street of 250 feet and running through 100 feet deep, affording ample space for handling and piling, and always contains over one hundred thousand dollars' worth of lumber of the choicest kind, specially adapted to the requirements of builders, manufacturers, and contractors. This includes quartered and all kinds of oak, walnut, cherry, pine, white spruce, white birch, and all kinds of building lumber, hard woods, etc., of which they sell $225,000 worth per annum. From twenty-five to thirty men are constantly employed, and seven single and three double teams are kept busy. The trade extends to all parts of the eastern states and the west, and the connections of the house with producers are influential. All orders are carefully and promptly filled at the lowest market prices. Messrs. Blacker & Shepard have had many years' experience in the lumber business, and no one has a more comprehensive knowledge of the wants of the trade, and can offer inducements in prices very difficult to be secured elsewhere in Boston.

D. M. HODGDON & CO., Manufacturers and Jobbers of Men's and Boys' Clothing, No. 98 Otis Street, and No. 114 Arch Street.—A representative wholesale clothing-house, and one of the most ably conducted in the whole United States, is that of Messrs. D. M. Hodgdon & Co., whose extensive factory and warerooms are at No. 98 Otis Street, extending entirely through the block to No. 114 Arch Street. The immense business conducted here was founded in 1882, by the firm of Knowles, Leland & Hodgdon. In 1886 the firm reorganized, and Mr. D. M. Hodgdon became sole proprietor, and has since carried on the business under the existing name and style. A native of the state of Maine, he came to Boston on May 1, 1865, and early in life became actively identified with the trade in which he has achieved such marked success. His business has grown at a rapid ratio, necessitating repeated enlargement of facilities, and his establishment now comprises four floors. This vast area is devoted to carrying the enormous stock, and to dealers', retailers', packers' and shippers' departments. Mr. Hodgdon selects his woolens and materials with the utmost care, and employs only the most skillful cutters. He strictly follows the latest fashions, and as regards quality, style, and workmanship, his clothing compares favorably with anything even or obtainable by the trade elsewhere. A large force of cutters and salesmen are employed here, while several hundred hands are employed outside in the work of manufacturing. This is Boston's leading industry in this line, and has grown at such a progressive ratio as to indicate how popular are these lines of men's and boys' clothing. The stock covers every grade, and Mr. Hodgdon sells to the jobbing and retail trade generally of New England, the middle states, and the west. Mr. Hodgdon is a merchant of integrity and great energy of character, and a worthy exponent of the staple branch of trade in which he has been so long and so successfully engaged.

GEO. R. TABER & CO., Law and Mercantile Collections, No. 21 Milk Street, Room 10, Brandeis Building.—There is no subject of more vital importance to the business community than that of a highly-perfected system for the proper collection of accounts. The more perfect the system the greater the protection; the more extended the territory embraced, the greater the number of people who can be benefited thereby. Among the few reliable organizations that have been established with this above object in view, there are none having a higher reputation than that known as the National Law Association, which has enjoyed an uninterrupted successful career since 1874, and has from that date had a vital influence in securing to the business community all the benefits which arise from comparative certainty in the prosecution of its various transactions. The association has correspondents in all the principal cities in the United States and the British Provinces, and offers unrivaled facilities for the faithful and quick collection of past-due claims through reliable attorneys, and is highly endorsed and recommended by merchants and business men generally. Prompt and vigorous attention is given to all business, and every possible remedy is applied in the interest of clients without leaving the issue uncertain, and no commissions are charged unless settlement is made. The operations are conducted under the immediate supervision of Messrs. Geo. R. Taber & Co., whose methods, immediate action, quick reports, prompt returns, and moderate rates have always insured the approval of patrons, and won for the association the unbounded confidence of all who have business with it. Mr. Geo. R. Taber, the head and founder of this association, has resided in Boston twenty-eight years, and is an old, esteemed business man. He has devoted with great energy many years to perfecting a system for the collection of accounts, and that he has been successful it is only necessary to look over the names and note the character and standing of those who are pleased to endorse the system, and the straightforward, liberal methods of conducting the business. References by permission: Hon. Edward R. Dunn (Dunn, Green & Co.), dealers in leather; No. 30 South Street, Boston; C. C. Griswold & Co., commission merchants, No. 43 Chauncy Street, Boston; George Dunbar, railroad supplies, No. 78 Pearl Street, Boston; Wm. P. Hunt, president and treasurer South Boston Iron Works, No. 37 Foundry Street, Boston; Hon. Jacob Sleeper, No. 61 Milk Street, Boston; Swain, Fuller & Co., boot and shoe machinery, No. 61 Lincoln Street; Wm. Reaves (Reaves, Whitney & Co.), bankers and brokers, No. 78 Devonshire Street, Boston; Boston Transcript Co.; Charles Baffum, shoe manufacturer, Lynn, Mass. Mr. Taber is well fitted to conduct this enterprise, inspiring at the same time the confidence, consideration, and regard of that public whose interests are so greatly enhanced by his labors. He is popularly known throughout this vicinity, and is held in high esteem by a wide circle of friends and acquaintances.

THE GLOBE GAS LIGHT COMPANY, Contractors for Street Lighting. Headquarters for Lamp posts, Lanterns and all Street-lighting Supplies, etc., Nos. 77 and 79 Union Street. —The Globe Gas light Company ably and energetically fills a most important and useful field, viz., the lighting of cities, towns and villages, in the most brilliant and economical manner, by their safe and reliable gasoline process. The company was duly incorporated about fifteen years ago, under the state laws, with a capital of $80,000; and during the intervening period, by wise and equitable management, as practical demonstration of the superiority of the "Globe" method of street-lighting, it has been contracted with by many of the leading cities and towns of New England to furnish light on their streets and avenues, which far exceeds coal-gas for brilliancy and economy in use. The company's officers are as follows: President, Mr. Francis W. Lawrence; Treasurer, Mr. Sumner Wheeler; Agent, Mr. D. W. Lee. They are able, practical business men, energetic and enterprising, and enforce a thorough

system of organization, promptly and faithfully carrying out all contracts entered upon. They are the leading manufacturers and dealers in New England of the famous and popular vapor-burners; likewise street lanterns and lamp posts, etc., of the most improved and substantial character. They are also refiners and manufacturers of the celebrated "Globe" naphtha, an absolutely pure, high fire-test and safe-burning fluid, in use all over Boston and New England; also throughout the west. The company is now under contract for and supplying lights, lamps, etc. throughout New England; and ably and faithfully carry out all undertakings in which they engage. First-class work at lowest prices is guaranteed, and town councils and committees on lighting should by all means investigate the superior inducements afforded by the Globe Gas light Company before placing contracts elsewhere or entering into the expensive and so often unsatisfactory coal gas or electric lighting. The officers are all natives of New England, popular and respected, and have become the leading authorities on and representatives of economical, efficient, and satisfactory municipal street-lighting on a scale of the greatest magnitude.

POTTER, WHITE & BAYLEY, Manufacturers of Boots, Shoes, and Brogans, Nos. 118 and 120 Summer Street; Factories Cochituate, Farmington, and North Abington.—One of the oldest-established and leading firms of boot and shoe manufacturers of New England is that of Messrs. Potter, White & Bayley, whose extensive salesrooms and warehouse are so centrally located at Nos. 118 and 120 Summer Street. The business was established in 1829 by Mr. Amasa Walker, succeeded in 1841 by the firm of Emerson, Harris & Potter. In 1847 it became that of Allen, Harris & Potter, succeeded by Potter, Elder & Note in 1855, and they, again, in 1866 by the firm of Potter, Note, White & Bayley. In 1868, Mr. Note retired, and Mr. John C. Potter, Mr. Franklin B. White, and Mr. James C. Bayley organized the well-known firm of Potter, White & Bayley, and who did so much to advance their quality of product, and introduce fine hand made and machine-sewed goods that are fully the equal of custom work. The decease of Mr. Bayley occurred in 1873, and of Mr. White in 1880; since which date Mr. Potter has actively conducted this immense business in copartnership with his son, Mr. F. C. Potter, a young man of great executive ability and sterling integrity, and Mr. H. M.

Stephens, a popular salesman. The honored old name and style, a veritable trade-mark, has been permanently retained, and the house maintains its lead in the van of progress, with perfected facilities and ample resources at command. Their factories are three in number, and situated respectively at Cochituate, Farmington, and North Abington. They are unusually extensive, substantial structures, fitted up with the latest improved machinery and appliances, and afford employment to upwards of fifteen hundred hands, engaged in the manufacture of the finest and medium grades of men's and youth's boots, shoes, and brogans. The proprietors exercise the closest personal supervision over their large concern, and are recognized authorities in their line, exercising the soundest judgment and the utmost care in the selection of leather and findings and being noted for the elegance of cut and perfection of finish, as well as the materials of strength and durability. These are the handsomest and most popular lines of men's fine and medium wear on the market today, and the firm's trade therein has attained proportions of great magnitude. They have three stores at Nos. 118 and 120 Summer Street, devoted to salesroom and carrying of a heavy stock. The importance of this to buyers is evident. These are not special sample lines, but the goods as will be shipped, every text subject to inspection, while, as regards price and quality, the firm challenge competition. Their goods are in growing demand throughout the entire United States, and the interests developed are of appreciated value in maintaining Boston's supremacy in this important branch of trade.

A. F. RICH & CO., Commission Merchants and Wholesale Dealers in Fresh Fish, No. 19 T Wharf.—Among the old-established and reliable wholesale fish commission houses of the city of Boston, a prominent one is that of Messrs. A. F. Rich & Co., whose office and salesrooms are situated at No. 19 T Wharf. This business was established nearly a quarter of a century ago by Mr. Rich, who, after having several partners, became sole proprietor in 1881. The premises occupied are commodious, and are fitted up with every appliance and convenience for the handling and storing of fish. Mr. Rich handles in large quantities all kinds of ocean and fresh-water fish, including mackerel, cod, herring, bad duck, salmon, trout, halibut, white-fish, lobsters, etc.; and the trade extends all over the United States. Only carefully selected stock is dealt in, and Mr. Rich is prepared to fill the largest orders at the lowest ruling market prices. He makes liberal advances on consignments of first-class fish, and his facilities and connections are such that quick sales are always secured, while his house has ever obtained an excellent reputation with shippers and the trade, for promptness in making returns. Mr. Rich is highly regarded in trade circles for his just methods and enterprise. He is a member of the T Wharf Fish Association, Massachusetts Fish Exchange, N. E. Halibut Company. Mr. Rich was one of the first to answer the call to arms for the defence of the Union in the war of the Rebellion; and served four years in the Navy during the hardest fighting, with honor to himself.

H. K. W. HALL, Paper, No. 145 Devonshire Street.—An old-established house engaged in extensive operations in the paper trade is that of Mr. Henry K. W. Hall, of No. 145 Devonshire Street.—Mr. Hall founded his enterprise in 1866, and had several partners up to 1872, when he was burned out in the great Boston fire of that year, since which time he has been alone in the management, and through his energy and equitable methods, he has kept since built up a large, permanent, and most desirable patronage, extending over all sections of the New England States. The spacious store occupied is 25x100 feet in area, and contains at all times a heavy stock of manilla and wrapping papers and twines of every variety; also sizing, chemicals, and mill supplies of all kinds for paper-manufacturers. Mr. Hall's long-established connections with the leading and most reliable sources of supply enable him to procure his goods at the lowest obtainable rates, and to sell the same at the same favorable terms. The complete stock carried allows all orders to be filled without delay, and goods are promptly shipped in every instance. Mr. Hall is a native of New Hampshire, and has been a resident of this city for the past thirty years, during which period he has become favorably known to mercantile circles. The growth and prosperity of his responsible house are only commensurate with the enterprise which has been displayed in its management, and in the satisfactory manner in which all the wants of the trade have been met.

STAR MANUFACTURING COMPANY, John W. Fletcher, Treasurer and Manager; Office, No. 2 Pemberton Square.—Prominent among the manufacturers of specialties peculiar to their respective establishments in Boston none is more widely known or deserving of more extended mention than the Star Manufacturing Company, whose office is situated at No. 2 Pemberton Square. This company enjoys a national reputation for introducing and manufacturing the Star clothes-horse, an invention of so useful and valuable character as to command universal attention and general patronage. The company was incorporated in 1887, under the

laws of the State of New Hampshire, and is represented by Mr. John W. Fletcher, as treasurer and manager. The clothes-horses are manufactured by contract, and are shipped in large quantities to all parts of the United States, being acknowledged, wherever introduced and tested, as the best thing ever offered for the purpose designed. All objections usually found in other clothes-horses are completely overcome in the Star. The material and workmanship are superior to anything ever seen in this line of goods. It is easily adjusted for use. After the clothes are properly aired and put away, it folds up in a neat, compact shape, and, when hung up, occupies no more space than a broom. They are sold at retail at $1 each. Both male and female agents are wanted in every city and town in the United States, to whom liberal terms and steady employment will be given. Mr. Fletcher is now introducing to the public an extension ladder of a new design, which is bound to revolutionize the manufacture and sale of this class of articles in this country, and which should be seen by all who are interested in the useful, utilitarian, and novel inventions of the day. Mr. Fletcher is a native of the State of Maine, a resident of Massachusetts for the past thirty years, and a prominent citizen of Chelsea. He was mayor of that city in 1871-2, represented his ward in the State Legislature in 1873-4, was president of the Chelsea Water Board for some years, and is honored and esteemed by his fellow-men in all the various walks of life as a staunch Republican, a public spirited citizen, and a thorough, reliable and clear headed man of business.

E. H. ROLLINS & SON, Bankers, No. 241 Washington Street, Globe Building and No. 25 Main Street, Concord, N. H. and No. 1016 Curtis Street, Denver, Col.—Boston is the recognized banking centre of the United States for the marketing of strictly A1 sound investment securities of all kinds. The New York is more of a speculative one, and for many years past the best classes of western bonds and stocks, have been sold in the New England States. The leading representative banking house in many respects, engaged in this branch of business, is unquestionably that of Messrs. E. H. Rollins & Son of Globe Building, No. 241 Washington Street, with branch houses in Concord, N. H., and Denver, Col. They are the largest firm of bankers in the state of New Hampshire, and have developed industrial connections of the most wide-spread character. They opened their Boston office about two years ago, and which is in charge of Mr. Louis G. Hoyt, a young man of wide practical experience in financial circles, and who has full charge of the bank stock department. The business was established in Concord in 1870 by Mr. E. H. Rollins, a recognized able authority in banking and finance. The persons attending him resulted in the formation of the present firm in 1886, his father, Hon. E. H. Rollins, ex-senator and ex-congressman of the United States coming in as senior partner. There is no need in this review to more than refer to Hon. Mr. Rollins' record of public service in the national halls. He was ever a steadfast and able exponent of a sound, political, and patriotic policy, one far removed above the clamor of faction, or the short-sighted aims of those views motives might not be disinterested. Mr. Rollins introduced many measures of practical value to the country, during his terms of service, and his sound financial views have had great weight and influence in shaping the government's fiscal policy. He is a capitalist of enterprise and sound judgment largely interested in New England industries, and is the able president of the Boston, Concord and Montreal M. R. The departments are active members of the Denver Stock Exchange, and are the principal stockholders in the Rollins' Investment Company incorporated under the laws of Colorado, with a paid-up capital of $100,000, being the successor of the long established firm of Rollins & Young, who for the past seventeen years have handled substantially the entire county and municipal issues of bonds and warrants in the state of Colorado. The firm do an enormous business in western municipal and county bonds of the soundest and most remunerative description. They last year sold upward of four million dollars worth, and leading capitalists corporations of New England are found among their permanent customers. They are also leading dealers in national bank stores and other desirable investments, and those seeking remunerative and absolutely safe uses for their capital, should investigate the reliable channels presented by this eminent honorable and responsible firm of bankers.

W. W. BENJAMIN, Fruits and Vegetables of all kinds, No. 14 Mercantile Street.—A successful and prominent house in Boston engaged in the wholesale commission trade in Cape Cod cranberries, Florida oranges, and fruits and vegetables of all kinds is that of Mr. W. W. Benjamin, whose office and salesrooms are located at No. 14 Mercantile Street. This business was established 15 years ago by Mr. Benjamin, who has since built up a liberal and permanent patronage in all sections of New England. The premises occupied are commodious and well kept, and a heavy and first-class assortment is constantly carried, including apples, oranges, onions, potatoes, tomatoes, squashes, melons, berries, nuts, and choice fruits and vegetables of every variety in their season. Dealers and retailers are supplied at the lowest ruling market prices. All orders are attended to in a prompt and satisfactory manner, and the trade, which is strictly wholesale, is prosperous and permanent. Mr. Benjamin makes liberal advances on consignments of first-class fruits and vegetables, and guarantees quick sales and immediate returns.

THE METROPOLIS OF NEW ENGLAND.

111

BAY STATE BOOT AND SHOE COMPANY. Manufacturers of all kinds of Ladies', Misses,' and Children's Fine Boots and Shoes, Factory, Mass.; Boston Salesroom, No. 108 Summer Street.—In reviewing the various enterprises that have made Boston a leading centre of business in this country, it is interesting and instructive to note the advances that have been made in each of the representative industries, and to ascertain as far as possible what has been achieved by energy and capital. In looking over the field, it is easy to see that the manufacture of boots and shoes has exercised a commanding influence upon the growth and prosperity of our commerce. Among the prominent representatives of this branch of industry should be named the Bay State Boot and Shoe Company, manufacturers of misses' and children's fine boots and shoes, whose factory is situated at Foxboro, Mass., with main office and salesrooms at No. 108 Summer Street, in this city. The foundation of this enterprise was laid in August, 1884, by the Bay State Boot and Shoe Company; and in October, 1886, the present company was organized, with the following board of officers, viz.: President, C. A. Parks; Vice-President, C. B. Rogers; Secretary, E. C. Siphney; Treasurer, E. B. Rogers. The president is a well-known business man of Kansas City, Mo., while the other officers are Massachusetts men long identified with the boot and shoe trade. The factory of this company furnishes steady employment to two hundred and fifty hands, and from twenty-five hundred to three thousand pairs of boots and shoes are produced daily. The misses' and children's fine shoes made by this house are unexcelled for beauty of design, superiority of finish, and artistic workmanship, and combine all the elements of durability with easy fit and attractive appearance. They are fast becoming popular with leading retailers throughout the United States, and a permanent and increasing demand is created wherever they are once introduced, on account of their great reliability and intrinsic merits. The Boston house carries a full and complete stock at all times, and is prepared to execute the largest orders in the promptest and most reliable manner, while terms and prices are placed upon the most liberal and equitable basis. The management of this company is intrusted to gentlemen of ample experience and sound practical judgment, who are very popular in mercantile and trade circles everywhere, and who have won for this company an influential position in the shoe trade by the exercise of intelligent enterprise strict commercial honor, and thoroughly reliable methods. The company's enormous business is one of legitimate growth, developing in response to the direct demands of the trade of a continent, and its financial standing is correspondingly solid. All sales are for cash, and the corporation seeks no credit; its ample resources enabling it to discount all its purchases of leather and materials in from ten to thirty days. The financial and commercial management is sound and conservative, and its guidance in the manufacturing departments of the most skilled character. Its goods are in ever-growing demand, because they give the best satisfaction to the public; and the company sells to the best trade—jobbing and wholesale—exclusively in large lots and often by the car-load at a time.

ROTCH & TILDEN, Architects, No. 85 Devonshire Street.—The rapid development of the material resources and wealth of Boston has created a demand for architectural talents of the highest order, and for the introduction of systems of construction that may be termed distinctively American. Prominent among the successful and reliable architects of this city is the popular firm of Messrs. Rotch & Tilden, whose offices are centrally located at No. 85 Devonshire Street. The partners, Messrs. Arthur Rotch and Geo. T. Tilden, are both thoroughly qualified and able architects, who, after years of foreign training, have evinced great skill and ability in the practice of their profession, not only in Boston, but also in the principal cities of the country. They have executed some important commissions, designing and superintending the construction of many prominent buildings in the city and elsewhere. Their many buildings are much admired by experts for their beauty and stability, while the elaboration of detail and care bestowed upon every department of their work reflect the utmost credit on the skill of this reliable firm. The firm transact a general business, including all branches of the profession, and cheerfully furnish plans, specifications, and estimates to meet the views of those intending to build. The partners are members of the Massachusetts Association of Architects. They are highly regarded by the community for their just methods, promptness, and energy; while they are personally conversant with the growth and wants of Boston, and possess every facility for the successful completion of all work pertaining to their profession.

FLOYD, PRATT & ROUNDS, Wholesale Watches and Jewelry, No. 408 Washington Street.—It is a pleasure to record the character and enterprise of those business-houses whose very existence is emphatic evidence of the honorable position they occupy, and the long course of just dealing which they have pursued. Such a house is that of Messrs. Floyd, Pratt & Rounds, the well-known wholesale dealers in watches and jewelry, located at No. 408 Washington Street. The business of this house was originally established in Providence, R. I., in 1878, by Messrs. H. F. Salisbury & Co., who were succeeded by the present firm in 1878. The business was removed to this city in May, 1885, and has here been developed to proportions of gratifying magnitude and importance. The salesrooms of the firm are spacious in size, attractive in all their appointments, and perfect in conveniences of arrangement for display, inspection, and sale. The firm are heavy importers of jewelry and watches from the leading capitals of Europe, and also handle extensively all kinds of American goods of the best makes in this line. The large experience and influential connections possessed by the proprietors give them advantages in obtaining their supplies that are not excelled by any of their contemporaries in the trade; while their activity in exacting tribute from every source that promises increased usefulness and popularity renders their establishment a desirable headquarters for dealers in quest of the latest novelties, and the most reliable goods. A corps of talented salesmen represent the interests of the house at the principal centres of trade throughout New England; and orders are filled in all cases with the utmost promptness and dispatch. The resort to inducements are constantly extended to the trade, as regards reliability and excellence of goods and liberality of terms and prices; and business relations once entered into with this firm are sure to prove both profitable and permanent. The copartners, Messrs. E. B. Floyd, W. H. Pratt, and A. W. Rounds, are all experienced jewelers and accomplished exponents of the trade. Mr. Floyd is a native of Hillsborough County, N. H., and was a member of the old firm of H. F. Salisbury & Co. Mr. Pratt was born in Norfolk, Mass., and is a member of the Jewelers' League, while Mr. Rounds is a native of Rehoboth, Mass., and all combine to form a firm of wide popularity and solid worth.

P. F. BURKE, Manufacturer of Patent Steel Tar-calks: Cold-iron Punching, Chain Links, Washers, etc., No. 880 Dorchester Avenue, South Boston.—Among the many and varied industrial enterprises that contribute to the sum of activity in South Boston, none is more worthy of notice in this review than the various concerns of P. F. Burke (successor to C. F. Dewick & Co.), manufacturer of patent steel tor-calks and horseshoer's supplies, No. 880 Dorchester Avenue, whose productions are in extensive and growing demand in the trade throughout the country, owing to their general excellence. The tar-calks manufactured by him (which received the premium and medal at the fourteenth exhibition of the Massachusetts Charitable Mechanic Association, held in 1881) are articles of exceptional merit, and for the purpose intended are unequalled by anything of the kind produced in the United States to-day. This flourishing enterprise was established in 1879 by Messrs. C. F. Dewick and P. F. Burke, and under the firm name of C. F. Dewick & Co., was conducted up to 1886, when Mr. Burke (who is the inventor of the tor-calk) assumed sole control, and has since continued the business alone with uninterrupted success. The factory occupies a commodious two-story structure with blacksmith shop, and is completely equipped with steam-power and all necessary facilities, including special machinery, while a dozen or more expert workmen are employed. Besides patent steel tor-calks, Mr. Burke also manufactures chain links, washers, and kindred devices, while cold-iron punching is attended to likewise,—all orders receiving immediate attention; and altogether a very large and constantly increasing business is done. Mr. Burke, who is a comparatively young man, spent his younger days in Worcester, Mass., where he learned the mechanic's art, and was a member of the Worcester County Mechanics Association.

JOHN D. & M. WILLIAMS, Importers of Wines, Spirits, Teas, and Cigars, Nos. 185 and 187 State Street.—No historic review of the rise and progress of the mercantile interests of Boston would be complete without special mention being made of the eminent house of Messrs. John D. and M. Williams, which, for upwards of 80 years has been prominent in the front rank of importers and wholesale dealers in fine wines, spirits, teas, and cigars. The business was founded in the year 1812 by Mr. J. D. Williams and Mr. M. Williams, brothers who had previously been in business for a number of years. They were at first engaged in the importation of sugar as well as wines and liquors, and continued to do a steadily enlarging business, and of the highest character. Mr. J. D. Williams, who was born in 1770, died in 1848, while Mr. M. Williams, whose birth was in 1778, actively continued the business for many years after the decease of the senior partner, his own death occurring in 1882. For many years before this his sons, Messrs. Moses B. Williams, and Thos. B. Williams, had been associated in partnership with him. They were business men of signal ability, enterprise, and push, and were accounted among Boston's foremost and most progressive merchants. In 1885 Mr. Otis K. Weld, a native Bostonian, was admitted to the firm. Mr. Barney Cory who was born in 1848 in New Bedford, Mass., and who had been first associated with the Messrs. Williams as a boy and then as a clerk was also afterward admitted as a partner, and he and Mr. Weld continued the business until Mr. Cory's death in 1896, when Mr. Weld succeeded to the sole control; since which date he has continued the enterprise with uninterrupted success. He has ever retained the old and honored firm name and style, which has become a veritable trade mark as regards the exceptional quality and purity of all goods dealt in. Mr. Weld's fine establishment is most advantageously located at Nos. 185 and 187 State Street, comprising five floors and basement, 80x115 feet in dimensions, and where he carries a very heavy stock of choice old wines and liquors of his own direct importation, including famous vintages of sherries, ports, Madeiras, Burgundies, clarets, etc. He is also the importer of the famous Roederer's and Schreider's champagnes, the most perfect brands on the market, and of a quality that commends them to all judges of champagne wines. Mr. Weld also deals in the most famous vintages of French brandies, in Scotch and Irish whiskies, gins, rums and liqueurs. He also deals in the choicest old and imported brands of rye and bourbon whiskies; while his stock of choice Havana cigars are grades far superior to what is termed the best of cheap here. To those seeking strictly the best and purest for table or medicinal use, the stock of this famous and honorable old house presents opportunities nowhere else duplicated, and the trade developed is of a correspondingly high character. Mr. Weld is a respected and influential merchant who has ever accorded a hearty support to all measures best calculated to advance the commercial interests of Boston. He is a member of the National Liquor Dealers' Association, and occupies various positions of trust as director of banks and insurance companies, and both socially and commercially is a prominent factor in Boston's progress.

H. C. JACKSON & CO., Wholesalers and Jobbers of Boston Rubber Shoe Company's Goods, No. 115 Federal Street.—The leading headquarters for retailers of rubber boots and shoes throughout New England is the establishment of Messrs. H. C. Jackson & Co., the well known wholesalers and jobbers of the Boston Rubber Shoe Company's Goods, located at No. 115 Federal Street in this city. The business of this house was originally established in 1850 by Messrs. Jackson & Durkee, who were succeeded by the present firm in 1897. The premises occupied for trade purposes are spacious in size, eligibly located, and perfect in convenience of arrangement for inspection and sale. The Boston Rubber Shoe Company are making a quality of goods that are rapidly winning their way to the favor of the trade and shoe trade of the country, and are widely preferred by dealers over all other makes on account of their great reliability and solid merits. They are now being made in such attractive styles and in so durable a manner that they are having an extensive sale in the rubber-using sections of the country, and are fast working their way into the south, where, until recently, rubbers have been practically tabooed. The industry carried on by this representative company is growing to great proportions in this country, and each year is gaining in volume, as the quality of the goods are improved. The specialties bearing the name of this corporation are strictly first-class, while the styles are novel and original. Notwithstanding the very extensive rubber interests at this point, the goods of the Boston Rubber Company occupy the foremost position, and the facilities possessed by Messrs. Jackson & Co. for supplying the great and growing demand of the trade are of the most complete and perfect character. Their stock is the largest and finest of its kind in the city, and the business of the firm has reached enormous and gratifying proportions throughout all the New England States. Inducements are offered to the trade, as regards both reliability of goods and liberality of terms and prices, which challenge comparison and defy successful competition. Mr. Jackson, the active member of the firm, is a Massachusetts man by birth and training, a well-known resident of West Medford, and a gentleman of large and intimate acquaintance with the trade, and a most worthy and capable representative of its growing interests in this busy metropolis.

ALLEN & KENWAY, Architects, No. 130 Devonshire Street.—The profession of an architect is one which is deservedly popular in Boston, and embraces within it many prominent names, among which that of the firm of Messrs. Allen & Kenway deserves special mention in this commercial review of the city. The firm's offices, which are fully supplied with every facility and convenience, are located at No. 130 Devonshire Street. The copartners, Messrs. Francis R. Allen and Herbert P. Kenway, are talented and capable architects, thoroughly accomplished in the arduous details of their profession, and at the same time have given many proofs of their skill and ability in the erection of a large number of handsome and substantial edifices, not only in Boston, but in other cities. The firm make a specialty of the designing and erection of fine private residences. They have built residences on Commonwealth Avenue for Alex. Moseley, Wm. H. Allen, Chas. A. Kidder, M. B. Mason, Henry C. Jackson, Charles L. Stratton, and J. J. French, and many other superior buildings on Beacon Street; notably C. C. Converse, R. D. Evans, and D. C. Kimarton, and many others in various parts of the city and elsewhere. The firm have also latterly erected St. Andrew's Church and parish chambers, Boston; extensive buildings in Kansas City; Public Library, Newton; Buzzard Hospital, East Concord Street, Boston; Brimley Hall, at Wellesley; The Library Building, Amherst College, etc. Their buildings are greatly admired by experts, for their stability and elegance of design, while the elaboration of detail and care bestowed upon every department of their work reflect the utmost credit on their able and honorable methods. Messrs. Allen & Kenway are assisted by a number of trained draughtsmen and are fully prepared to furnish plans and estimates for all classes of work, and spare neither time or pains to satisfy the requirements of patrons. Mr. Allen is a native of Boston, while Mr. Kenway was born in England. They are widely known as able business and professional men, fully meriting the influential patronage secured by their industry and energy.

PUFFER BROTHERS, Country Produce, No. 15 Concord Avenue and Nos. 16 and 18 Richmond Street.—Messrs. Puffer Brothers, wholesale dealers in and growers of country produce, and receivers of Long Island and Southern truck, are to be reckoned among the most noted and successful merchants in their line in Boston. The trade of this house has been one of steady growth, and it has increased every year since its beginning, till now it is, and has been for several years, one of the leading houses of its kind in the east. The individual members of the firm are Messrs. N. F. D. and Charles Puffer, aged respectively thirty-six, twenty-nine, and thirty-one years. They are natives of Arlington. They were born on a farm, which their father cultivates to this day, and they are all practical farmers of long experience, with a thorough knowledge of produce that well qualifies them for the important business in which they are engaged. They organized their partnership in 1880, and they have since built up a trade of great magnitude, that extends throughout the whole of the New England States. Their business premises are commodious, and are provided with every accommodation and convenience for carrying on trade on a large scale. In addition to the stocks drawn from their own farm at Arlington, they are in receipt of large consignments from the best producing sections of the country, and are in a position to fill the largest as well as the smallest orders with despatch and satisfaction. Their premises are connected by telephone, the call being 1470. The copartners are members of the Produce Exchange, and are energetic, reliable merchants.

E. HODGE & CO., Manufacturers of Marine and Stationary Boilers, Standpipes, Oil and Ship Tanks, etc., Liverpool Street, East Boston.—For variety first-class work in the line of boiler construction and plate-iron work, and for promptness and reliability in the execution of all orders, no house in the country enjoys a higher reputation than that of Messrs. E. Hodge & Co., whose works are situated on Liverpool Street, East Boston, and Boston office at No. 70 Kilby street, in this city. This firm possess an international reputation as manufacturers of marine and stationary

boilers, standpipes, oil and ship tanks, and all kinds of plate-iron work. The business was originally established in 1864, by Messrs. Ebenezer and James Hodge, the latter of whom died in 1879. The surviving partner continued the business as sole proprietor until 1891, when the present firm was organized by the admission of Mr. J. E. Lynch to partnership. The works, which were erected for the purpose by the original firm in 1881, were destroyed by fire in 1893, but were rebuilt the following year, and are ample and well equipped, every modern convenience and appliance being at hand tending to facilitate rapid and perfect production, while a suitable force of skilled and expert workmen contribute to the satisfactory operations of the house. Steam boilers of every size, style, and variety are constructed in the most expeditious manner and of a character for reliability, safety, and uniform excellence that commands universal admiration and wins the confidence and patronage of close and critical buyers. These boilers have given this house a prestige and a popularity both at home and abroad, which place it in the very front rank of enterprise and success, and of which the proprietors have every reason to be proud. The output is in heavy and influential demand, not only in this country, but throughout South America,

Cuba, and other foreign countries, and are preferred over all similar productions, wherever introduced and tested, by reason of their intrinsic merits and solid worth. They are pleased to customers and the trade at terms and prices which are safe from successful competition, while orders are always promptly and carefully filled. The co-partners are both practical, reliable, and accomplished manufacturers, combining ripe experience with youthful vigor to form a business firm of commanding ability and wide popularity.

WENTWORTH, HOWE & HARDEN, Pork, Lard, Hams, Side Meats, Sausages, Pigs' Feet, etc., Nos. 69 and 85 North Street, and Nos. 670 and 672 Harrison Avenue.—A representative and reliable house in Boston, actively engaged in the wholesale and retail provision trade is that of Messrs. Wentworth, Howe & Harden, whose office and salesrooms are located at Nos. 69 and 85 North Street, and packing house, etc., is Nos. 670 and 672 Harrison Avenue. This business was established thirty years ago by L. P. Wiggin & Co., who conducted it till 1885, when the present firm succeeded to the management. The copartners, Messrs. Thomas Wentworth, T. Horace Howe and Frank Harden, have had long experience in the packing and curing of provisions, and are fully conversant with every detail of this important business and the requirements of the trade and public. They deal largely, both at wholesale and retail, in pork, lard, hams, side meats, sausages, pigs' feet, bacon, tripe, sausage casings, bologna, etc. Only the best stock is handled, and the greatest care and attention are given to the meat in its various stages of packing, curing, smoking, etc. The firm's hams, provisions, etc., are unsurpassed for quality and flavor, and are everywhere recognized and appreciated by consumers as standard productions, while the prices in all cases are always regulated by the market. The trade of the house extends throughout New England, the south and west, and they likewise export large quantities of their famous hams and side meats to Liverpool, England, and Antwerp, Holland. Messrs. Wentworth and Harden are natives of New Hampshire, while Mr. Howe was born in Boxford, Mass. They are popular members of the Chamber of Commerce, where they are highly esteemed for their enterprise, energy, and integrity. This prominent provision-house gives every promise of a long and prosperous future, which a continuance of its present able management will certainly insure it.

KNIGHT & McINTIRE, Beef, Pork, Lard, Hams, Tallow, etc., No. 82 Chatham Street.—Not perhaps in any feature of progress has enterprise been more forcibly displayed of late years as in the construction and application of devices for preserving fresh meat. In this connection the attention of our readers is directed to the popular house of Messrs. Knight & McIntire, No. 82 Chatham Street. This flourishing enterprise was founded in 1886, and from its inception has proved a positive and permanent success; the general excellence and reliability of the stock handled and the energy and ability displayed in the management of the concern being the chief elements contributing to this gratifying result. The premises occupied for trade purposes are spacious in size, thoroughly equipped for the handling and perfect preservation of supplies, and every appurtenance and facility is at hand to expedite the business and render satisfaction to customers. Consignments are received from the west in refrigerator cars, also from the British provinces, and reliable producers and shippers in this and adjoining states; and a splendid stock is by this means constantly kept on hand, which recommends its own peculiar merits to the confidence and patronage of discriminating buyers and first-class dealers. The trade is exclusively wholesale, and is broadly distributed throughout all the New England States. The members of this firm, Messrs. Elbridge G. Knight and Joseph McIntire, are among the best-known merchants at "the Hub."

COMBINATION AUCTION AND SALES STABLES, Nos. 243 and 245 Friend Street, and No. 158 Canal Street. J. C. Richardson, Proprietor.—Prominent among the prosperous houses of the city of Boston in the stable business is that of Mr. J. C. Richardson, whose famous Combination Auction and Sales Stables are located at Nos. 243 and 245 Friend, and No. 158 Canal Streets. This extensive business was established fifteen years ago by Mr. Richardson, who has since built up a liberal and influential patronage in all sections of the United States and Canada. This establishment is recognized as the headquarters for the sale of horses in New England, and from this concern most of the finest horses seen in this section have been purchased. The Combination Auction and Sales Stables are among the most desirable buildings of the kind in the city near the Lowell, Eastern, and Fitchburg depots, and are fitted up with all modern conveniences and improvements. The building is a fine brick structure three stories high and 60x180 feet in dimensions, having accommodations for 400 horses. On the first floor to the left is located the office; back of this is a wide horse run, at which point begin the stalls. These extend on both sides the whole length of the building. They are large, double stalls, strong and well made of hard wood and iron. On the second floor on both sides, and down the centre, are rows of single stalls painted, like those below, a dark red. The third flat is devoted to hay, grain, etc., except a room in the front used for harnesses. The ventilation is perfect, while the constant work of the stable hands in cleaning obviates all disagreeable odors. In connection with this establishment, Mr. Richardson occupies the fine sales stable located at No. 50 Chardon Street, where he has a fine lot of horses and every convenience for carrying on this line of business. He can accommodate 200 horses here, making the capacity of both stables 600, to say nothing of his livery and boarding stable at Crescent Beach, Revere, Mass., where he has a number of very fine turnouts. His regular auction sales occur every Wednesday and Saturday at 10.30 A. M., while a large variety of horses are on hand at private sale. The sales stable at No. 50 Chardon Street has lately been entirely refitted, and is one of the finest in Boston. It comprises four floors, 40x100 feet in size, each floor accommodating 50 horses. Mr Richardson employs 20 buyers in the west, who are authorities on the value of horses, and understand the points that constitute a valuable animal. Horse palace cars are used by Mr. Richardson, which contain 20 horses, and are fitted up with every luxury for the comfort, convenience, and safe transportation of the animal. Last year Mr. Richardson sold 7,000 horses, and the business done amounted to $1,100,000. During the year 1888 he has sold to the Providence and Boston street railroads $150,000 worth of horses, and his trade is steadily increasing. Among the horse dealers he is known as "Big Rich," principally because he is a "son of Anak" in size, but also because he has a way of doing things on a big scale. When he first came to Boston to establish himself as a horse dealer, he put his "little all" entirely into a carload of horses, and determined to make the best of it, and it is presumably the boldness and persistence of his ventures which have given him the title of the "Horse Merchant" of Boston. Others have done well, and made fortunes, but this man in his line has become famous. Not a man in Chicago inquires for a reputable horse dealer in the east who is not referred to J. C. Richardson. He has the first chance among buyers, and has established such a reputation for taking ventures, and making them turn out well, that confidence is expressed in his judgment and in his capacity to an unusual degree. Mr. Richardson is eminently at home with a horse. It is seldom that he is seen without a whip in his hand, the tip of which rises above his soft felt hat, which is something more than six feet from the ground, and never did a man like to crack it in the air, or on something more substantial, if need be, better than he. It is worth a visit to his new and elegant stable, where 800 horses can be sheltered at one time, and where the appointments for the holding of auctions, and the exchange of horses are thoroughly first-class, to see this man in his element. Horsemen pay him deference as to a superior, but never, unless there is some sudden disturbance requiring the strong hand of authority, is his good nature ruffled. He is at once the inspiration and the "big boy" of the place. He is never alone. Horse buyers are always with him, and he is one who revels in the atmosphere from morning till night. The whole bearing of the man indicates his interest in his occupation. He is aided by employees, who are as able in their several lines as he is in the administration of his business as a whole. This man is full of rough, strong elements, and there is no more unique figure in all the horse marts of New England. Mr. Richardson is ably assisted in his extensive business by Mr. F. P. Bruce, the widely-known and reliable horse auctioneer, whose courteous manners put him in the front rank, and make him deservedly popular with all classes of horse-buyers. Mr. Bruce has a thorough knowledge of the business, and is considered one of the best judges of horses in America. Mr Richardson was born in Illinois, but has resided in Boston for the last twenty years, where he is highly esteemed by the community for his enterprise, sound business principles, and sterling integrity. He makes liberal advances when required on consignments of horses, guaranteeing always quick sales and prompt returns, and is making steady advancement with the ideas of the times.

LOUIS P. OBER, Restaurant Parisienne, Importer of Wines, Nos. 2 and 4 Winter Place.—The city of Boston has long been recognized as the centre where unlimited capital, vast practical experience, and boundless enterprise have combined to make its cafés and restaurants superior to any in the country. As the leading contributor to the reputation of the city in this regard, and as a model establishment of its kind, the Restaurant Parisienne, conducted by Mr. Louis P. Ober, at Nos. 2 and 4 Winter Place, stands pre-eminent. It was opened to the public in 1868 by its present proprietor, a native of sunny France, who came to this city twenty-five years ago, and who brought to bear a thorough knowledge of all the wants and requirements of the business, and quickly acquired a reputation and a patronage that placed his establishment in the foremost ranks of enterprise, popularity and success. Three spacious floors are occupied—the first as an elegant café and lunch-room for gentlemen, the second containing three public lunch-rooms, and the third for private supper-rooms, all arranged and appointed in the most appropriate and recherché style, reflecting the utmost credit upon the good taste and sound judgment of the proprietor, and insuring the convenience and comfort of all patrons. The cuisine is in charge of chefs of marked ability and national reputation. The management secures its table supplies from the most reputable and varied sources, all the important markets of the country paying tribute to its enterprise. All the delicacies that can possibly be obtained are served in liberal abundance, while the perfect manner in which the viands are served make a meal at Ober's a most agreeable experience. While there are larger restaurants in the country than Ober's, there are none which possess such well-founded claims upon public favor or enjoy a more deserved popularity. Any dish is cooked to order in the best manner, and at moderate prices, while the finest Bordeaux, Burgundy, Champagne, Rhine, and Moselle wines, sherry, port, Madeira, and claret, brandies and liquors, beers and ales, are served of the best quality and imported direct from the most celebrated sources by the proprietor. Attentive and courteous European waiters are in attendance, and the patronage is large, first-class, and influential at all seasons. Mr. Ober is a gentleman of tried ability as a caterer and restaurateur, and is held in universal esteem as an accomplished, reliable, and representative exponent of this important branch of mercantile activity.

WEINSTEIN & JONES, Architects, No. 41 Tremont Street.—Prominent among the talented architects of this city is the representative and reliable firm of Messrs. Louis Weinstein and W. H. Jones. Mr. Louis Weinstein commenced the practice of his profession in Boston 20 years ago, and eventually, in 1883, admitted Mr. W. H. Jones into partnership. They have executed many important architectural commissions, designing and superintending the construction of many prominent buildings, among which may be mentioned the following, viz., Dudley Street School, Boston Jewish Temple, Columbus Avenue, Adelphia, Comfort, and Dudley apartment-houses, Boston Highlands; Court-house, Jail, and Opera-house in Pittsfield, Mass.; Bowmier's Brewery and Store-houses and McCormick's Brewery, Boston; Hecht Bros. Wool-house on Federal Street; Morse Block, South Street; Prang's establishment and dwelling-house; and many other stores and residences. These buildings are much admired by experts for their stability, finish, and elegance, all details being carried out with thoroughness and accuracy. They employ several skilful draughtsmen, and all plans, specifications, and estimates are promptly and carefully furnished.

WRIGHT, BROWN & CROSSLEY, Solicitors of American and Foreign Patents, No. 91 Pemberton Square.—The firm of Wright, Brown & Crossley, solicitors of U. S. and foreign patents, at No. 91 Pemberton square, are the successors of Carroll D. Wright, the present Commissioner of Labor, whose name will ever bear an honored and prominent association with the mechanical and scientific development of the United States. Mr. Wright originally established himself in the practice of patent law in this city in 1865, subsequently forming a partnership with Mr. Charles F. Brown, a well-known mechanical expert, under the name and style of Carroll D. Wright & Brown. Mr. Wright retired from the business in 1878, and it was continued by Mr. Brown until November, 1885, when the present firm was organized by the admission of Mr. Arthur W. Crossley, late examiner in the United States Patent Office, to partnership. As thus constituted, the firm of Wright,

Brown & Crossley have established a national reputation as able, scientific, and successful solicitors, and experienced, clear-headed, and reliable counsellors in patent cases. Their practice comprises close and careful attention to the preparation and prosecution of applications for patents and the registration of trade-marks, including the making out of specifications, drawings, caveats, assignments, and all papers required for designs, reissues, trade marks, labels, and copyrights; the making of preliminary examinations as to the patentability of inventions, and also as to the scope and validity of patents; attending to cases in interferences, upon appeal and before the courts, and to every other item of service necessary to the complete success of the application, up to the time the patent is granted and issued by the office. No attorneys are better known at the Patent Office in Washington, and none can secure fairer treatment or more prompt consideration of their cases. Their papers filed in the interest of their clients are models of accuracy, wisdom, and perfect understanding of the cases in hand, while their facilities for securing both American and foreign patents are not surpassed, and rarely equalled by any practitioners in the country. Their clients come from all parts of the United States, Canada, Great Britain, and Europe, and bear testimony to the zeal and success that characterize all transactions of this firm. Fees are moderate and uniform, and the interests of every patron are skilfully guarded and intelligently promoted. A branch office has been opened by the firm in Washington, and another office is also operated at Manchester, N. H. Mr. Brown is a native of Maine, and resides in the neighboring town of Reading. His qualifications as a mechanical expert thoroughly fit him for successful practice in his chosen profession, and have served to place him in a position far beyond the requirements of any praise which these pages could bestow. Mr. Crossley is a Massachusetts man by birth and education, and during his connection with the administration of the Patent Office, as chief of the issue division and subsequently as a member of the examining corps, no officer in that bureau was more generally popular or more thorough and accurate in his work. They are developing a trade of wide extensions by reason of their honorable and just methods, and able and prompt manner in which they attend to all matters placed in their hands.

FRANCIS DANE & CO., Manufacturers of Grain, Kid, and Goat Boots and Shoes, No. 118 Summer Street.—The success of Messrs. Francis Dane & Co., as manufacturers of misses' and children's low-priced grain shoes, furnishes a strong illustration of what can be secured by straightforward and enterprising business methods. This business was established in Boston at No. 318 Summer Street, in 1886, by Mr. Francis Dane, who is sole proprietor. Mr. Dane's factories, which are fully supplied with the latest improved machinery and appliances furnish constant employment to 150 skilled operatives, and are situated at Salem and Marblehead. Mr. Dane manufactures extensively grain, kid, and goat boots and shoes, and makes a specialty of turning out misses' and children's low-priced grain shoes. He sells for cash only, and at the same time pays cash for all his manufactured stock. His boots and shoes, according to their grade, are unrivalled for quality, elegance, finish, fit, and workmanship, and have no superiors in this or any other market, while with regard to prices his goods defy competition. He keeps always a large stock in Boston, and his trade extends throughout the entire United States and Canada. All orders are promptly filled, and his goods are recognized by the trade as standards in the market. Mr. Dane is a native of Massachusetts, and a resident of Hamilton, Mass. He commenced life eight years ago in a small country store with his brother, working for fifty cents a day, and continued one and a half years, when he went to work for his uncle, J. F. Dane, in a large wholesale boot and shoe house, at a rate of salary of $400 for the first six months, and continued for five years, when he started in business for himself. Mr. Dane buys and sells for cash only, and during a period of several years has always conducted his business on a net cash basis. The daily transactions for leather and merchandise are settled every night, he being the only merchant in the shoe trade doing business in that way. Mr. Dane is a nephew of the late Francis Dane, who died in 1875, leaving a property of about one million dollars, the result of twenty-five years' work. His business has increased steadily for the last two years, and he has ever retained the confidence of the entire trade, and has achieved a record accorded only to those whose transactions are based on the strict principles of equity and just dealing.

C. T. SEAVERNS & CO., Importers of Precious Stones, No. 408 Washington Street.—The steady and substantial growth of material wealth in the United States during the past quarter of a century has, in the nature of things, developed a corresponding demand for rich and rare gems and the articles that beautify and adorn the person, as well as those that minister to the comforts and pleasures of mankind. The display made by a leading establishment in Boston devoted to the sale of precious stones to-day is truly magnificent. Notably is this the case at the salesrooms of Messrs. C. T. Seaverns & Co., located at No. 408 Washington Street. Mr. Seaverns, the active member of the firm, is a connoisseur and expert of celebrity, and, as an extensive importer of precious stones, is a recognized authority as to all the details and intricacies of the business. The house was originally established in 1865 by Messrs. Wyman & Seaverns, the present firm succeeding to the control in October, 1888. In gems and stones of worth, to which this house may be said to be second to none on this side the Atlantic, the selections are the largest and choicest to be found in the city. Diamond and emerald, ruby and beryl, opal and pearl, sard and peridot, jacinth and spinel, topaz and turquoise, sapphire and cameos, intaglios and sardonyx, agates and crocidolite, rock crystal and amethyst—all these and more. "Captain jewels in the carcanet" are fittingly represented. Here are displayed diamonds in all conceivable shapes and of unequalled whiteness, clearness, and absolute faultlessness, "gems of purest ray serene"; rivière collarets, cluster and pendant, panache and aigrette, necklace and bracelet, chains, earrings and chatelaines—in fact, every article esteemed for its genuineness and suitable for personal adornment here greets the eye and delights the senses. Only the finest and most reliable goods are handled, while the matching and cutting of stones find here the most expert and accomplished exemplars. The constant aim and ambition of Mr. Seaverns is the selection and purchase of articles of novelty, beauty, and merit; and his trade is very large and influential with the élite of this city, and with the matching and purchase of articles of novelty. Mr. Seaverns is a native Bostonian, an expert in gems, and a solid, reliable, and successful business man.

SINGER & CO., Manufacturers of Bicycles, Tricycles, and Multi-cycles, Coventry, Eng : United States Branch (W. L. Ross, Manager, Nos. 6 and 8 Berkeley Street.—The most noted and representative house, not only in England, but also in the United States extensively engaged in the manufacture and sale of bicycles, tricycles, and multicycles, is that of Messrs. Singer & Co., whose factories and headquarters are located in Coventry, Eng. The United States branch of the firm, which is under the able and careful management of Mr. W. L. Ross, is situated in Boston at Nos. 6 and 8 Berkeley Street. Messrs. Singer & Co., are now running three extensive and admirably equipped factories for the production of the celebrated "Singer" cycles. The patterns adopted by Singer & Co. have been selected by them after having been personally tested, and being satisfactory to the proprietors, they have great confidence that they will meet with the approval of those who require a comfortable, easy running, and thoroughly reliable mount which will always be a pleasure to ride upon. Messrs. Singer & Co. rely upon the intrinsic merits of their goods; they have no intention of manufacturing cycles merely to sell, and have never declined to sacrifice quality in order to secure imaginary cheapness. In fact, their cycles are absolutely unrivalled in America or Europe for quality, finish, comfort, and elegance of design, and are the embodiment of mechanical workmanship of the highest order of perfection, while the prices quoted for them in all cases are exceedingly moderate. The patterns offered by them are all thoroughly adapted to the requirements of the American roads, and the parts of these superior cycles are nearly all interchangeable. In bicycles, Singer & Co. have been able to make very little change, having practically perfected them last season. The "Challenge" and "Apollo" are really as good as can be produced, the former being a first-class bicycle at a low price, and the latter containing everything that the most exacting cyclist could require. In Safeties important improvements have been made, and the "Singer" Safety, of which thousands have been now made, is a thorough success. The firm also have the "Miniature" Safety, a perfect little cycle for youths. In tricycles a cheaper form of "S.S.H." and a new pattern, the "Special S.S.H.," are added, the latter a light roadster, with brakes to all three wheels, and other special points. A new " Ministers" has also been added. In tandems the " S.S.H." is considerably altered, and is greatly improved. Many special fittings are now offered, chief among which are luggage holders and bags, lamps, the "Singer" Gong (a really good thing), and other items. The tires on all these cycles are now fitted by patent spring wire, no nreure being used. Tires so fixed cannot accidentally come off. This principle was so perfectly successful during 1889 that the firm have adopted it for this season. Ball pedals of superior make are included in the price of nearly all cycles. Singer & Co. also manufacture war cycles fixing contractors to the English Government and other special designs, particulars of which may be obtained in the general catalogue. The "Singer" Safety for ladies is a fine machine, the construction of the framework insuring necessary strength, while it also assists in keeping the dress away from the chain, while it is light, strong, neat, and easy-running. Singer's "Straight Steerer" is capable of reduction in width from 38 in. to 22 in. in a few seconds. It is often a great inconvenience not to be able to pass a tricycle through the doorway of a house, and they have therefore designed an axle by means of which the width of the tricycle is reduced, not by telescoping, but by dividing the axle. The arrangement used is very simple, and the strength of the axle is not affected. The driving mechanism, brake, gear, etc., are contained in one part of the axle, and this part is not disturbed in the operation of division. The detachable part is separated from the other by removing one nut. By a simple mechanical operation a tapering spindle is then loosened, and the part is removed in a few seconds. The repair shop is fitted with machinery and appliances for all kinds of repairs to bicycles and tricycles, and they carry in stock a full line of parts of all their machines. They can procure at lowest market rates parts and fittings for all the several styles of machines, and they do the very best work in every instance, and guarantee satisfaction, the prices being as low as is possible for good material and good work. Every job is thoroughly inspected by the head mechanist, who has had years of experience with bicycle repairs. They also carry a large line of the leading sundries, both English and American, and will supply lamps, saddles, bags, etc., at lowest market prices; the "Invincible" head lamp for "Safeties" and tricycles being highly recommended. Messrs. Singer & Co., are

also sole agents in the United States for Arctic Liquid Enamel for bicycles, tricycles, stoves, furniture, etc., which imparts a rich, smooth, black surface of lasting brilliancy with a total absence of all smell or stickiness. They are also sole agents for the world-renowned Louden's Crescent, which is used by all the largest bicycle manufacturers in England and America. Many of their fine machines are being offered at a great reduction to effect a clearance, including the " Apollo," " Challenge," " Extraordinary," " British Challenge," " Safety," " Singer Straight Steerer," " Traveller," " Tandem, Tandem "Attachment," and Carrier bicycle. Mr. W. L. Ross keeps constantly on hand full supplies of Singer & Co.'s cycles and specialties, which are guaranteed to give entire satisfaction to patrons. The best proof of the merit of Singer & Co.'s cycles is the steadily increasing demand for them in all parts of the world. While no attempts have been made by the firm to gain a reputation by the employment of racing men, neither have they trusted to advertising their trade. The wide-spread reputation they have attained they expect to maintain, solely by continuing to supply cycles which will be satisfactory to the purchaser and a credit to themselves.

CHARLES F. RAND, Auctioneer, Appraiser, Insurance and Real-estate Agent; Boston Office, Rooms 40, No. 118 Devonshire Street; Newton Office, No. 417 Centre Street.—The real estate agent in Boston and its suburban towns has, at the present day, opened before him an ample field for enterprise and usefulness, and many of the most influential and energetic citizens are engaged in this important business. Prominent among the number thus referred to is Mr. Charles F. Rand, the well known auctioneer, appraiser, and real estate agent, who makes a specialty of Newton property, and whose Boston office is located at No. 118 Devonshire Street, Room 40, where he is to be found from 10 to 11.30 a.m. This gentleman has been established in the business since 1858, and by faithful, conscientious zeal for the best interest of his customers has long enjoyed the confidence of the community and secured a very superior clientele. He is familiar with both present and prospective values of realty in and around the city, and has always on his books many desirable bargains, including business, residential, and manufacturing sites, for sale, to let, or exchange. The large line of property in Newton which he handles is absolutely perfect as regards its title, and all really dealt in through him may be relied upon as a safe investment. Both Boston and suburban property is offered for cash or on instalments to suit the purchaser. Mr. Rand possesses unsurpassed facilities for the prompt negotiation of loans on bond or mortgage, and is, in this branch of his business, of the utmost service to both borrower and lender, securing to the one ample funds with which to extend his enterprise, and to the other a profitable and perfectly safe investment. His Newton office at No. 417 Centre Street, opposite the Public Library, is one of the finest in New England. It is supplied with all modern appliances for the prosecution of the business. The stock of shoes, boots, and rubbers is extensive and well selected, and this prison quoted necessarily attract the attention of close and prudent buyers. Mr. Henry holds auction sales every Tuesday at 10.00 a.m. All goods sold by him are guaranteed to be exactly as represented, and his patronage now extends throughout all sections of the United States. Mr. Henry is a native of Massachusetts, and a resident of Lynnfield. He is President of the Boston Merchants' Association, and president of the Boston Boot and Shoe Club, and is highly esteemed in trade circles for his enterprise, promptness, and just methods, and fully merits the liberal patronage secured in this important business.

JOHN J. HENRY & CO., Boots and Shoes, No. 82 Summer and No. 125 Devonshire Streets.—An old established and representative house in Boston, actively engaged in handling boots, shoes, and rubbers, is that of Messrs. John J. Henry & Co., whose offices and salesrooms are situated at No. 82 Summer and No. 125 Devonshire Streets. This business was established 30 years ago by Henry & Hatch, who were succeeded by John J. Henry & Co. Mr. Henry deals extensively in wholesale in boots, shoes, and rubbers, and controls the production of several factories at Haverhill, Lynn, Brockton, and Marblehead. The premises occupied in Boston comprise a spacious first floor and basement 30x110 feet in dimensions, fully equipped with every convenience for the successful prosecution of this growing business.

CYCLORAMA OF THE BATTLE OF BUNKER HILL. No. 401 Tremont Street.—The seventeenth day of June, 1775, was one of the most memorable days in the annals of the world, and especially in the history of the United States; and the Battle of Bunker Hill is one of the most important battles of all time. On that day a volunteer handful of farmers, without much organization or coherence, resisted to the death—and with considerable success—the repeated assaults of a large, well-organized, and perfectly disciplined army, bravely led, and determined to conquer or die. It is this wonderful battle which is illustrated in the Cyclorama now exhibited in a building erected for the purpose, and painted by the best living artists, who have made a life-long study of paintings of this character. The chief artists engaged in this work are Messrs. L. Kowalsky, G. Picard, Georges Bollanger, and V. Coppanolle. They are all graduates of the École des Beaux Arts in Paris. The canvas upon which this picture is painted is 400 feet in circumference and 50 feet in height, thus containing an area of 20,000 square feet, or nearly one half acre. Not only does this picture give the beholder a vivid and lifelike view of America's greatest battle, but also enables him to view the territory in and around Boston as it appeared 100 years ago. Boston when containing only 14,000 inhabitants; Fort Boston, or, as it was formerly called, Noddles Island; South Boston, formerly Dorchester Heights;

Chelsea, formerly Winnisimmet; Cambridge, Roxbury, Medford, Malden, and all the adjacent towns,—are represented in this immense picture. In connection with the Cyclorama is shown the Diorama of the "Boston Tea Party," which is as faithful a representation as one now is made of that startling episode. The vessels, as here shown, are copied from contemporaneous pictures, and are believed to give a correct idea of the style of ships in use a hundred years ago. It is needless to give any description — the pictures tell their own story. These pictures have been on exhibition for more than a year, and have now become a fixture, being daily visited by hundreds, and when you visit Boston do not fail to visit it. The building containing these pictures was built by the Bunker Hill Cyclorama Company for the express purpose; it covers an area of 20,000 square feet, and is situated at No. 401 Tremont Street, only a short distance from Boston Common.

ALFRED MUDGE & SON, Printers No. 24 Franklin Street.—The oldest established general printing-house in this city is that of Messrs. Alfred Mudge & Son, whose spacious premises are so centrally located in Franklin Street. The business was established in 1820 by Mr. Alfred Mudge, grandfather of the present proprietor. In 1858 his son, Mr. Alfred A. Mudge, came into copartnership under the now familiar name and style. The concern early achieved an enviable reputation for the superiority of its work, and its patronage has ever grown at a rapid ratio. In 1874, Mr. F. H. Mudge, became connected with the business, and in 1886 was admitted into copartnership and eventually succeeded to the sole proprietorship in 1878, permanently retaining the old firm name, a veritable trademark in its line. He is a recognized master of every detail of the business. His establishment has few its equal in the United States and is a model in all departments. They moved here five years ago, and occupy three floors each 50x125 feet in dimensions, completely equipped with presses, type and fixtures of the most modern style and best quality. There are here fully 20 presses of various sizes and for various

purposes, run by steam power. The composing-room is elaborately fitted up, and has one of the largest outfits of type, cuts, borders, and material in Boston. Mr. Mudge constantly adding new fonts of plain and fancy type specially adapted to his high class of typographical execution. From 150 to 175 compositors, printers, etc., are employed, and large quantities of fine book and magazine work are turned out here for leading publishers; also job work of all descriptions and in the highest style of the art. This is the best place in Boston to get fine printing done at moderate prices. Mr. Mudge was born in Boston and has here worthily succeeded his father and grandfather in the unbroken chain of continuing a business thoroughly representative year by year of typographic progress. Mr. Mudge is a member of the Master Printer's Club, of the National Printer's Association and of various social clubs and associations. He is universally popular and respected, and though young in years, is old in experience in his important branch of trade.

THOMAS C. PORTER & CO., Commission Merchants and Brokers in Dye-Stuffs, Chemicals and Tanners' Supplies, No. 165 Milk Street.—One of the oldest established and most responsible commission-houses in the city of Boston, extensively engaged in handling dye-stuffs, chemicals etc., is that of Messrs. Thomas C. Porter & Co., whose office and salesrooms are situated at No. 165 Milk Street. This business was established in 1865, by Cushing & Porter, who were succeeded by Cushing, Porter & Coden. Eventually in 1871 Mr. Thomas C. Porter became sole proprietor, and is now carrying on the business under the firm name of Thomas C. Porter & Co. Mr. Porter has been in the dye-stuff and chemical trade for the last 25 years, and is the oldest broker and commission merchant in this line in New England. He brings superior facilities consultation, and resources to bear, and is constantly receiving consignments of dye-stuffs, chemicals, and tanners' supplies from Great Britain, Germany, Norway, Sweden, etc., enabling him to offer advantages in quality of goods and prices, very difficult to be secured elsewhere. He occupies two spacious floors, each being 30x100 feet in area. These are fully stocked with a superior assortment of chemicals tanners' supplies, etc., which are guaranteed to be equal to any in the market. Mr. Porter was born in Maine, but has resided in Boston the greater part of his life and where he is highly regarded in trade circles for his enterprise, promptness and just methods. He is a popular member of the Dry Salters' Club. His trade extends throughout all sections of New England and New York, and is steadily increasing.

J. F. PAUL & CO., Lumber Dealers, Corner Albany and Dover Streets.—As a factor in the general sum of industrial and commercial activity in this city, the lumber interests are of surpassing importance, as it is needless to remark. Engaged in the line of business indicated, Boston contains, in the very nature of things, some notable concerns, among which may be named that of J. F. Paul & Co. (Bay State Mills), lumber and timber dealers, also manufacturers of mouldings, doors, veneers, etc., whose capacious establishment is situated at the corner of Albany and Dover Streets. This flourishing enterprise was established in 1857, by Paul & McNutt, who were succeeded by J. F. Paul & Sons, the style finally changing to J. F. Paul & Co. The mills occupy two floors, each 577x60 feet in area, and are supplied with ample steam-power and completely equipped throughout with all the latest improved machinery and appliances, including sawing, turning, and kindred devices, while employment is here furnished to from seventy to one hundred hands. A heavy and carefully assorted stock is constantly carried, comprising hard pine and spruce timber, walnut, ash, oak, butternut, chestnut, pine, cherry, etc., flooring, sheathing, base, etc., worked and kiln-dried; also rosewood and mahogany mouldings, doors, frames, veneers, shingles, posts, laths, and building materials generally. Ample and complete facilities are at hand for sawing the heaviest timber any desired dimensions and shape, and also for planing the same while jig-sawing, turning, etc., are done to order likewise in the most expeditious and excellent manner, and carpenter and building work also of all kinds is executed.

NICHOLS, DUPEE & CO., Wool Dealers, No. 180 Atlantic Avenue.—One of the most difficult branches of trade, and that requiring the highest qualifications of ability and experience, is that of the wool business. Few can achieve success and develop permanent widespread connections who cannot meet the most exacting requirements of manufacturers as to grades and qualities, and there is no house in the United States which has achieved such an enviable reputation in this direction as that of Messrs. Nichols, Dupee & Co. of Boston. The present business was established by Mr. George B. Nichols and Mr. William R. Dupee in 1882, under the existing name and style. Steady enlargement of business, perfected facilities, and influential connections have characterized their mercantile career, and repeated enlargements of premises have been necessitated. Two years ago they removed into their present building, No. 180 Atlantic Avenue, built purposely for the wool trade, and which

[illustration]

is a substantial structure, six stories and basement in height, 75 feet front by 180 feet in depth. Messrs. Nichols, Dupee & Co. are direct importers of assorted and grease wool from South Africa, Australia, Europe, Canada, etc., and are also leading dealers in all grades and qualities of domestic growths from California and Oregon eastward. The copartners exercise sound judgment and careful methods in sorting and grading, and all sales of wool sold by them can be relied on to tally with sample. This honorable old house supplies many of the leading mills in New England and elsewhere, and does a trade of extended proportions. Mr. Nichols is a native of Vermont, and has long been an influential and respected resident of Boston. He is a director of the Massachusetts National Bank of Boston, and a trustee of the city hospital, faithfully discharging every obligation devolving upon him. Mr. Dupee was born in Massachusetts, and has long been prominently identified with Boston's leading commercial and financial circles. He is the president of the National City Bank, which has been uniformly prosperous, while the same can be said of the Boston Five Cent Savings Bank, of which Mr. Dupee is a trustee.

JOHN BINGHAM, General Grain and Freight Broker and Forwarding Agent, No. 5 Chatham Row.—Under the vast and complex business system that prevails in the great department of trade and commerce in our chief centres of commercial activity the broker fills a niche of peculiar importance, as it goes without saying. And these remarks apply in especial manner to the grain trade, enormous quantities of cereals being purchased and shipped abroad through the agency referred to from this port annually. Among those engaged in this line in Boston there are few who are better known or enjoy a larger measure of favor and confidence than Mr. John Bingham, the well known and responsible general grain and freight broker and forwarding agent, whose office is located at No. 5 Chatham Row, with branch houses in Liverpool and New York. He is a native of England, but has resided in this country for quite some time, and is a man of the highest personal integrity, and thorough experience in all that appertains to the purchase and forwarding of grain, etc., and sustains an excellent reputation in commercial life. Mr. Bingham, is a well known member of the Boston Chamber of Commerce, and transacts a general grain and freight brokerage, attending also to the forwarding of general merchandise. He has been engaged in business in this city some eight years or more, and has built up a substantial and gratifying connection; all orders entrusted to this gentleman being executed in the most expeditious and reliable manner.

DR. WM. N. WELLS' Alleviation, No. 618 East Broadway, South Boston.—One of the most popular of the standard valuable proprietary preparations of merit on the market is that known as "Alleviation," which has attained so much celebrity all over the United States as a sure and immediate cure for rheumatism, neuralgia, pleurodynia, sciatica, lumbago, cramps in muscles of legs, back, sides, fingers, and bowels, also as a rmost safe and speedy cure of toothache and headache, as well as an indispensable palliative in throat and lung diseases. In consumption it also is highly recommended as it has been used in several thousand cases and has given universal satisfaction. This valuable compound has been before the public for over a quarter of a century, and thousands of testimonials have been received from physicians and citizens. Hundreds of shipmasters, also, appreciate its merits and request its use on shipboard as an indispensable requisite. Dr. William Nelson Wells was born on Long Island, New York, and was educated at New York's celebrated universities. He came to Boston, Mass., after an honorable and very active service throughout our Civil War, as is attested by many rankers, journalists, foreign and domestic, who are still doing his thrilling official reports. Dr. Wells has devoted many years of his life to perfecting and introducing to the world at large his celebrated "Alleviation;" and in offering his valuable remedy to the public he does so with perfect confidence, as it has and does accomplish all that he claims, and is a medicinal blessing to mankind. Druggists and the trade east of the Rocky Mountains are supplied from Boston, Mass., direct, and west of the Rocky Mountains, by special representatives. Dr. Wells, during his long and successful professional career has made his medicines highly popular; and it has attained a celebrity and reputation only equalled by the most sterling manufacturers of our country. The doctor is well known and is popular in professional circles.

WM. A. LOW & SON, Carpenters and Builders, No. 119 Harrison Avenue.—The inception of this extensive business dates back to the year 1845, Mr. W. A. Low, the founder, continuing the sole conductor until 1868, when his elder brother, S. O. Low, became a partner and continued so until 1871, when he retired from business. In 1873 W. A. took into copartnership his son C. A. Low, who had learned his trade and been identified with the house for some time previous. The premises at No. 119 Harrison Avenue consist of a shop and storeroom of spacious dimensions, the former equipped with all requisite tools, machinery etc., for getting out the material used in the building operations of the firm, while the latter contains a full stock of general supplies for the same purpose. Orders by mail receive prompt attention, estimates for all kinds of work are cheerfully furnished on application, and everything pertaining to this branch of skilled industry is executed in the highest degree of artistic and mechanical excellence. Messrs. Low & Son employ a large force of experienced and skilful artisans and are prepared to execute promptly all contracts for work in their line, satisfaction being guaranteed to every instance. The work done by the firm is invariably of the highest degree of artistic and mechanical excellence, much of the finest building work of the city and vicinity bearing evidence to the superior handicraft of the house.

A. O. VERY, Agent for the "Standard" Rotary Sewing Machine, No. 112 Tremont Street.—Mr. Very has been long identified with the trade in sewing machines, and is intimately conversant with all its details and requirements, and is eminently popular and successful in meeting its demands. He occupies spacious and desirable quarters, and is in a position to conduct the business under the most favorable conditions. The "Standard" Rotary Shuttle is the most wonderful invention in sewing-machines since the first. It is, in fact, acknowledged by all unprejudiced mechanics and sewing-machine experts to be superior to anything else in the world in its line, both for durability, power, speed, ease of operation, elegance of finish, and beauty. The "Standard" shuttle is wheel-shaped, and revolves upon its own centre. It does not cause its motion while the machine is in operation. The old style shuttles start and stop twice at every stitch. This causes great friction, strain, noise, and unsteadiness when rapidly run. The "Standard" runs as easy, smooth, and quiet at 1500 stitches per minute as most others do at 700. It is self-threading throughout except the needle, which is the shortest used in lockstitch machines, and is self-setting. No change of tension is required for different thicknesses of goods, nor for different lengths of stitch. The tension is entirely released when taking out the goods by a simple device peculiar to the "Standard." The manufacturing machine is constructed with special reference to the following points, viz.: great strength in the feed mechanism, the usual long levers being done away with; great speed; an easy movement by which friction is reduced to the minimum, and wear and strain proportionately reduced; great simplicity in construction. To sum up the matter, the "Standard" is the simplest, most easily operated, best made sewing-machine in the world. It is the perfection of mechanism for hemming, felling, trimming, binding, cording, smocking, braiding, embroidering, and other purposes too numerous to particularize, while the price is lower than is often demanded for inferior machines. Mr. Very is the inventor of a two-needle machine specially adapted to vamping and staying shoes; also a two-needle upper machine for shoes, gloves, suspender, and other work. These machines are in the "Standard" line and are made in two sizes called No. 9 and No. 10. They are meeting with a ready sale. Mr. Very is prepared to furnish the trade and the public throughout this important territory with the "Standard" promptly, and to grant patrons every advantage and benefit known to the trade. He employs a large number of agents, and is transacting an active and influential business.

E. G. TUTEIN, formerly Government Truckman, Port of Boston, and Forwarder of all kinds of Merchandise, No. 77 Central Street.—An important factor in the mercantile activity of Boston is the enterprise so successfully maintained by Mr. E. G. Tutein, as a truckman and forwarder of all kinds of merchandise, at No. 77 Central Street, opposite United States Appraisers'. This gentleman was for four years the government truckman for the port of Boston, and established his business here in 1878. He also operates an office in East Boston, at the corner of Webster and Lewis Streets. He purchased Cleary & Co.'s express in January, 1889, and is prepared to move and freight all kinds of merchandise, and for that purpose gives steady employment to twenty-five men and sixty horses. The express runs between Boston, Chelsea, Revere, Crescent Beach, and Beachmont. From the start Mr. Tutein developed a large and permanent patronage, and his horses quickly earned for itself the reputation of being thoroughly reliable and trustworthy in all its transactions. He enjoys a deserved popularity for handling all goods committed to his care with the utmost skill and circumspection, always makes it a rule to meet all engagements exactly on time, and places his charges at the lowest point of moderation. The offices in Boston for Chelsea are at No. 83 Court Square, No. 174 Washington Street, No. 15 Devonshire Street, No. 67 Franklin Street, No. 77 Central Street. Offices in Boston for Revere, Crescent Beach, and Beachmont, No. 83 Court Square, No. 67 Franklin Street, No. 77 Central Street. Office in Chelsea, No. 223 Broadway. Order boxes in Revere, Warren Frano's, Frank B. Patch's, S. E. Hardic's, Eastern R. R. Depot, McKay's store, and Beachmont Depot. Baggage is checked to all railroads and steamboats, and the telephone connection in Boston, 1817. Mr. Tutein was born in Boston in 1841, served in the navy five and one half years, and is a captain in the First Massachusetts Volunteer Militia, a member of the Loyal Legion and of the G. A. R., a Knight Templar.

T.HE ELITE MANUFACTURING COMPANY, Sole Manufacturers Warner's Newport Relish, No. 49 Oliver Street.—The manufacture of sauces and relishes of an appetizing nature for the table is an important department of industry. Competition in this line is of the keenest character, and genuine merit is a positively necessary agent in order that success may be achieved. A production of this kind which has been before the public for about a year and which has met with a high degree of popular favor is that known as Warner's Newport Relish, manufactured only by the Elite Manufacturing Company of this city, whose office and factory are located at No. 49 Oliver Street. This company was duly incorporated under the laws of New Hampshire in January, 1889, the capital being placed at $100,000. The officers of the organization are some of well-known reputation in business circles, and the energy and push brought to exercise in the management has resulted in placing their specialty prominently on the market, and secured for it a recognition from the most desirable class of trade. The factory has an area of 21,000 feet, and is equipped with all necessary conveniences for the prosecution of the industry. Warner's Newport Relish is designed for use with soups, fish, meats, game, etc., is made of the purest ingredients, has no equalled flavor, and as an appetizer has no superior. A large stock is carried to meet the demand, and dealers will do well to secure a supply, as it cannot fail to become popular among their customers. Warner's Newport relish is guaranteed to aid and strengthen digestion and cure dyspepsia.

G.EO. H. JACOBS & CO., Manufacturers of Ladies' Cloaks and Suits, No. 505 Washington Street.—One of the leading and most popular houses in the city of Boston engaged in this useful industry is that of Messrs. Geo. H. Jacobs & Co., whose office, salesrooms, etc., are situated at No. 505 Washington Street. This business was established in May, 1887, by Mr. Geo. H. Jacobs, who is sole proprietor. Mr. Jacobs has had great experience, and is fully conversant with every detail and feature of this useful business, and the requirements of jobbers and retailers in all sections of the country. The premises occupied comprise two spacious floors 25 x 110 feet in area, which are fully supplied with every appliance and facility for the successful prosecution of the growing business. In the workrooms 125 operatives are employed. Mr. Jacobs manufactures extensively ladies' cloaks and suits, which are manufactured from the most reliable imported and domestic fabrics, while every attention is paid to the latest and most fashionable styles and designs. A specialty is made of ladies' suits, which are general favorites with the trade and public wherever introduced. These superior goods find a ready sale in all sections of New England and New York, in rural sections being constantly on the road, while the local trade is always brisk and active. Mr. Jacobs was born in Boston. He is a just and able business man, and the extensive and influential patronage he has secured is but a fitting tribute to his enterprise.

C. H. THWING & CO., Tailors, No. 416 Washington Street.—This business was established in 1859 by the firm of Thwing & Collins, succeeded by Messrs. C. H. Thwing & Co. in 1872. The lamented decease of Mr. C. H. Thwing occurred in 1881, after a long and honored career in this branch of artistic industry. The important business existed, with its influential connections and celebrity, was continued by Mr. Orville A. Atkinson, who as proprietor and active director of every detail of the business, is one of the best and most favorably known members of the merchant-tailoring trade of Boston. He is a native of Laconia, New Hampshire, and from early boyhood has been actively identified with this branch of trade. His abilities and critical estimate of each separate figure recognizing costume, defects, and necessities are joined to remarkable skill and accuracy in cutting and fitting. All garments bearing his establishment are perfect examples of the tailor's art, both as regards materials, cut, workmanship, finish and the admirable manner in which they fit the form. Messrs. Thwing & Co. do a very large and growing trade, including among their permanent patrons many of the leading bankers, brokers, merchants, professional and social leaders of Boston and New England. No pains is spared to suit the most fastidious, and the reserve is in every way representative of the most advanced progress, and a credit to and valued factor in promoting Boston's mercantile supremacy. Mr. Atkinson is an active member of the Merchant Tailors' Exchange, and a deservedly popular and respected business man.

BOSTON BELTING COMPANY, Original Manufacturers and Dealers in Vulcanized Rubber Belting, Hose, Packing, and Mechanical Rubber Goods of Every Description, E. M. Converse, President; J. H. D. Smith, Treasurer, and James Bennett Forsyth, Manufacturing Agent and General Manager, Warerooms, Nos. 226 to 232 Devonshire Street, Boston; No. 100 Chambers Street, New York City; and agencies in all the principal cities in the United States and Europe. The Boston Belting Company, established in 1828, is the oldest company and has the largest works in the world devoted to the manufacture of rubber goods for manufacturing and mechanical purposes. It has a paid-up capital of

$700,000.00. The factory buildings covering two acres of ground with upwards of half a million feet of floor surface, are supplied with powerful engines and a boiler capacity of 1000 horse-power. The company employ 600 men, and consume daily ten tons of raw material.

Their great capacity is the patent stretched, smooth surface belting, which stands unrivalled throughout the world as a transmitter of power. Belts of any length and thickness up to six feet wide can be successfully made. The company annually turn out 4,000,000 feet of rubber hose for steam fire-engines, steam rock-drills, breweries, oil, water, and garden purposes; also large quantities of cotton and linen hose with or without rubber lining. Other specialties manufactured, are all kinds of packing, deckle straps for paper maker's use; baskets for bank, newspaper, lithograph, calico, enamel, and other printing; valves for steam-engines and pumps; gaskets and rings for steam, air, and water joints; springs, washers, tubing, and rubber-covered rollers for cotton, woolen and paper mills, print and dye works; leather-splitting, unhairing, and tobacco-cutting machines, and every variety of mechanical rubber goods. This company has received the highest diplomas and medals from the Massachusetts Charitable Mechanics' Association; the American Institute of New York; and the Cincinnati, St. Louis, and New Orleans Expositions. The salesrooms are located at No. 254 to 260 Devonshire Street, Boston, and No. 100 Chambers Street, New York, with agencies in all the principal cities of the United States and Europe.

WEEKS & POTTER, Importers and Jobbers of Drugs and Druggists' Sundries, Chemicals, Essential Oils, etc., No. 360 Washington Street.—The firm name of Messrs. Weeks & Potter, who has placed upon drugs, medicinal, pharmaceutical preparations, is a veritable trade-mark. For 40 years it has stood test for all that is excellent in the wholesale drug trade, and the results of their honorable and capable endeavors are seen today in a trade of enormous magnitude, and a reputation of the most enviable character. The firm are direct importers and wholesale buyers of all drugs, chemicals, essential oils, etc., known to the pharmacopœia, and have perfected facilities and most influential connections at command. Mr. A. G. Weeks was born in Portland, Me., and early in life came to Boston, where he became connected with the old drug-house of S. W. Fowle. Mr. W. B. Potter was born in New Bedford, and also has had a direct connection with this business from youth. They early achieved an enviable reputation for the superiority of their stock; and the growing demands of the trade necessitated repeated enlargements, resulting in their occupying their present premises twenty-eight years ago. These are most desirably located on Washington Street, 50x100 feet in dimensions, and fully equipped with every convenience. Here is carried the finest and most comprehensive stock in Boston, of drugs and druggists' sundries, foreign chemicals and essential oils, pharmaceutical preparations, extracts, etc.,— all of the highest standard of excellence, strength, and purity. The trade developed is national in extent and annually enlarging. Messrs. Weeks & Potter are prominent in the circles of their trade, being active members of the Massachusetts Wholesale Druggists' Association, and of the National Wholesale Druggists' Association. They are public-spirited citizens, and secure to Boston a most valued commercial factor. Mr. Potter is a director of the Home Savings Bank; also of the Central National Bank, and of the International Trust Company, faithfully and ably discharging the onerous duties thus devolving upon him. The firm is a representative exponent of the wholesale drug trade, and is progressive and enterprising, ever pursuing an enlightened, judicious policy, based on the principles of equity and integrity.

GEORGE M. COBURN, Manufacturer of Boots, Shoes, and Brogans, No. 68 High Street.—Prominent among the representative and most extensive houses successfully engaged in this trade is that of Mr. George M. Coburn, whose office and salesrooms are located at No. 68 High Street. This business was established in 1879 by Ames & Coburn, who conducted it till 1891, when Mr. Ames retired and Mr. George M. Coburn became sole proprietor. Eventually, in 1893, Mr. W. B. Lewis became a partner. The business, however, is still conducted under the old name of George M. Coburn. The factories of the house, which are fully supplied with the latest improved machinery, tools, etc., are situated at Alton, N. H.; West Medway, Abington, Reading, and Marblehead, Mass. Here 1000 skilled operatives are employed, and the trade of the house is by no means confined to the United States, but extends to Canada, Mexico, the Sandwich Islands, Central and South America. Mr. G. M. Coburn manufactures in vast quantities all kinds of men's and children's boots, shoes, and brogans. These goods are general favorites with jobbers, retailers, and the public wherever introduced, always commanding a ready sale, while at the same time they are unsurpassed, according to their grades, for quality, finish, durability, comfort and uniform excellence. The salesrooms of this enterprising and reliable house in Boston comprise two spacious floors, that are fully stocked with the firm's goods, which are offered to the trade at prices that necessarily attract the attention of close and careful buyers. Both Messrs. Coburn and Lewis are natives of Massachusetts and residents of Boston, and are highly esteemed in business circles.

S. G. CHICKERING & CO., Manufacturers of the "S. G. Chickering" Upright Pianos; Warerooms, No. 116 Tremont Street, Factory, No. 184 Hampden Street.—The S. G. Chickering upright pianos are recognized, by mechanical experts and the most eminent amateur and professional musicians, as the best embodiment of materials, workmanship, design, tone, power, and excellence of action, coupled with elegance of finish. Mr. S. G. Chickering, who is the proprietor of the manufacture of these deservedly famous instruments, was born in Massachusetts, and here, at an early age, began to learn the trade of a piano-maker. He early became proficient therein, and worked at the bench for fully 20 years before starting in business on his own account. [...]

MECHANICS' NATIONAL BANK OF BOSTON, No. 472 Washington Street; C. O. L. Dillaway, President; S. G. Morrill, Cashier.—Prominent among the principal fiscal corporations of the city is the Mechanics' National Bank, whose banking rooms are centrally located at 472 Washington Street. [...]

E. W. TYLER, Agent, Grand, Square, and Upright Pianofortes, No. 179 Tremont Street.—One of the leading representative dealers in pianos in Boston is Mr. E. W. Tyler, the agent of the famous Knabe pianos, which are the equal in every way of any instruments manufactured, and in many respects the superior. [...]

REPAUNO CHEMICAL COMPANY, Manufacturers of "Atlas Powder," and Blasting Apparatus, No. 16 Broad Street; B. B. Tuohy, Agent.—There is a despair among chroniclers as to how long explosive powder has been in use in the world, and there are some writers who aver that the knowledge of it appears to be coeval with the most distant historic events relating to China and India. It is not our purpose to endeavor to settle the dispute in these pages once and for all, nor to enter into a detailed description of the various ingredients in the composition of powder necessary to attain the greatest purity. Our purpose is to record things as we find them, and we find this: that the manufacture of powder has become one of the verily "great industries" of the United States, the business amounting to many millions of dollars a year. What is more, the powder, of whatever kind, made in America, whether it be of the blasting, mammoth, cannon-mortar, musket, diamond grain cage, musket, sporting, shipping, or fine description, is not excelled anywhere on the habitable globe. In blasting and mining powders, the Repauno Chemical Company, which has gained a world-wide reputation, have over and over again proved this. They are the manufacturers of the celebrated "Atlas Powder." Those whose occupation it is to quarry rocks and mines, know from experience that when the blasting apparatus and the "Atlas Powder" of the Repauno Chemical Company get their best work in, there is an effective displacement of something. It is because of their efficacy that they are so much in demand both at home and abroad, and that their sale has become enormous. The Company's works, which are very extensive, are located at Repauno, N. J.; their main office is at Wilmington, Del.; and they have branch offices at Boston, New York, Chicago, Atlanta, Denver, and other great commercial centres. The Boston office, located at No. 16 Broad Street, was founded ten years ago, and for the past four years it has been under the management of Mr. B. B. Tuohy, who is a native of New Jersey, and who has been connected with the powder business from his youth up. He has an extensive stock in his keeping and a fine, brisk trade throughout the whole of New England. In all his transactions, he is decisive, prompt, and reliable, and courteous to all.

C. A. CONANT, Eastern Agent for Millers and Grain-shippers, No. 5 Chatham Row.—The growth of the trade in flour, grain, feed, hay, etc., of New England's metropolis is one of the most important features of its commercial development, and gives evidence of the zeal, energy, and well directed efforts of the leading members of the trade. In this line the house of Mr. C. A. Conant has for the past seven years had an active and honored career, and now occupies a front-rank position in the trade. Mr. Conant who founded his enterprise in 1887 and brought to it a long experience and first-class business ability, is the eastern agent for numerous millers and shippers of grain, and a general commission agent for the finest grades of flour, feed, hay, and all kinds of cereals. The business was started at No. 141 State Street, on the corner of Chatham Row, and was subsequently removed to its present location, No. 5 Chatham Row, where Mr. Conant is in possession of suitable premises for the successful carrying on of his important and extensive trade. The business, which is essentially of a wholesale character, is a mammoth one, and extends to all parts of the United States. A specialty is made of cargo and car-load lots, and orders are shipped, when desired, direct from the sources of production. All transactions are characterized by promptitude, liberality, and honorable dealing, and the trade of the house shows a large annual increase. Mr. Conant is a native of Massachusetts. He is an active and popular member of the Boston Chamber of Commerce, and has taken a warm interest in its permanent welfare and prosperity. He stands high in the esteem of his fellow-members and the community generally.

WINCH BROTHERS, Manufacturers and Wholesale Dealers in Boots, Shoes, and Rubbers, Nos. 149, 151, and 153 Federal Street.—This representative and widely known firm commenced business in 1863 under the style and title of Sumner & Winch Brothers. Eventually, in 1870, Mr. Geo. L. Sumner retired, when Messrs. J. R. and J. F. Winch succeeded to the management. Last January, Geo. F. Winch and John R. Gibbs were admitted into partnership, the business, however, being still conducted under the firm name of "Winch Brothers." The firm are the largest wholesale dealers and jobbers of boots, shoes, and rubbers in this country, and control the production of four extensive factories in Massachusetts and one in Maine. They occupy three spacious connecting stores, having a frontage of 80 feet by a depth of 100 feet. The various departments are fully supplied with every appliance and facility for the successful prosecution of this steadily growing business. Messrs. Winch Brothers are the only firm in the United States that sell goods at the prices they pay for them. They always receive five per cent discount on all their purchases, and this forms their profit. During the past year their sales amounted to upwards of $3,000,000, and their trade extends not only throughout all sections of the United States and Canada, but also to Mexico and Central and South America. They deal in all grades of boots, shoes, and rubbers, and quote prices impossible to be duplicated elsewhere in this country. Messrs. Winch Brothers promptly and carefully fill orders for one or a thousand cases, and fully warrant all goods to be exactly as represented in every particular. They employ in their warehouses 60 clerks, assistants, etc., and six traveling salesmen on the road. The partners are all natives of Boston, where they are highly esteemed in trade circles for their enterprise, sound business principles, and integrity. The influence exercised by this responsible firm on the wholesale boot and shoe trade has been of the most useful character, and those interested in establishing a connection with this popular house may always depend upon receiving just and liberal treatment and marked advantage.

T. RESNICK & CO., Dealers in Cotton and Wool, etc., Nos. 496 to 500 Atlantic Avenue.—A leading representative house engaged in the cotton and wool trade is that of Messrs. T. Resnick & Co., with headquarters at Nos. 496 to 500 Atlantic Avenue. The business was established over 25 years ago by Mr. T. Resnick, a recognized authority in all branches of the trade in wool waste and cotton and wool stock generally. His early developed a business of great magnitude with important foreign connections. In 1884, Mr. A. Davidson and Mr. B. H. Davidson were admitted into copartnership, and bring to bear a wide range of practical experience and perfected facilities. The firm have moved into very commodious warehouses, Nos. 496 to 500 Atlantic Avenue, having two connecting buildings of four stories each, and 200-odd feet in dimensions. Here is a large area of floor space devoted to the storage of stock, and not enough to meet the growing requirements of the firm's business, as it has another four-story warehouse at No. 500 Atlantic Avenue. Here they deal in and carry the largest stock of cotton waste in Boston, an also full line of foreign and domestic wools, all of exceptional high quality and offered at lowest current market rates. The firm sell to consumers and manufacturers all over the United States, and are likewise heavy exporters of cotton waste to Germany and England, where it is deservedly popular on the best in these important markets. A prompt and equitable policy has ever characterized this honorable old house, and its operations are of direct value to Boston's commerce. Messrs. Resnick and Davidson are natives of Massachusetts, merchants of ability and integrity, and worthy of the large measure of success achieved.

AVALON GRAVES, Manufacturer of Shoes and Slippers, No. 161 High Street; Office, 110 Summer Street.—Mr. Avalon Graves, the widely celebrated manufacturer of fine and soft shoes, and full lines of slippers, began in business eighteen months ago, and has secured the favorable recognition of the trade of the country at large for his fine goods. His factory is situated at No. 161 High Street, comprising the four upper floors, each one having an area of 3000 square feet, giving him fully 12,000 square feet of floor space in all, and all needed to meet his growing requirements. He has put in the latest improved machinery and appliances, run by steam-power, and employs upwards of 60 hands in the manufacture of men's fancy slippers in all materials; mens', boys', and youths' canvas baby; men's fine soft low shoes; and ladies' congress and grain bals and buskins. Quality has ever been the first consideration with Mr. Graves, who adopts his aims, leather findings, etc., with the utmost care; his styles are the latest fashionable cuts, cut, workmanship, and finish are all perfect, and the prices quoted will be found difficult to duplicate elsewhere for similar grades of goods. Mr. Graves was born in New York State, and has long been identified with the branch of skilled industry in which he is achieving such success.

NEW ENGLAND MUTUAL ACCIDENT ASSOCIATION, No. 85 Water Street, Hon. A. P. Martin, President; B. F. Dyer, Secretary.—Having come to recognize the necessity of providing against loss of time by insuring against accident, we desire in this connection to make special reference to this commercial review of Boston to the progressive and reliable New England Mutual Accident Association, whose offices are centrally located at No. 85 Water Street. This association was organized under the laws of Massachusetts in 1884, since which period it has obtained a liberal and influential patronage. It has ever been the aim of the management to hold the cost of insurance in this association at a point as low as is consistent with the prompt and equitable adjustment and payment of all valid claims. The business of the "New Eng-

land" has steadily increased from date of organization. Certificates issued year ending Dec. 31, 1884, 1936; year ending Dec. 31, 1885, 2911; year ending Dec. 31, 1886, 5041; year ending Dec. 31, 1887, 7482; year ending Dec. 31, 1888, 7629. While the "New England" has upon its register a much larger number of what are generally known as preferred risks (those engaged in the least hazardous occupations) than of all other classifications combined, it does not confine itself to this class, but secures the additional strength which results from the extension of its benefits to all desirable risks, thus broadening the field which sustains the organization. Equity is secured to all, first by arranging the rating as nearly as possible to make the cost the same under each classification, and it is further provided, that payments required may be varied to equalize the apportionment. Each classification is thus made practically self-sustaining. The following gentlemen, who are greatly respected by the community for their honor-

able methods and executive ability are the officers, viz.: Hon. A. P. Martin, President; Chas. E. Carpenter, Vice-President; Benj. H. Tucker, Vice-president; Benj. F. Dyer, Secretary; A. S. Onta, Treasurer; John A. Follett, M.D., Medical Director; Wm. A. Robinson, Henry H. Earl, Wm. B. Gray, Directors. It is an admitted fact that one person out of seven receive fatal or total disabling injuries every year hence no person can feel secure; consequently, all prudent people should provide against such contingencies by securing a certificate in the "New England." Certificates provide the following benefits:

BENEFITS.	CLASSIFICATION OF RISKS.							
	A.	B.	C.	D.	E.	EF.	F.	FF. G.
Death by Accident								
Loss of Hand and Foot								
" Both Hands								
" Feet								
" One Hand								
" " Foot								
" Both Eyes								
" One Eye								
Permanent Total Disability								
Weekly Indemnity not exceeding 52 weeks								

ISAAC FENNO & CO., Men's and Boys' Clothing, No. 28 Summer Street, Boston has no industry that is of a more practically beneficial character both to her labor and her capital, than that of the wholesale manufacture of clothing, and in which line the great leading representative is the old established and nationally famous house of Messrs. Isaac Fenno & Co. It has had a long and honored career, one of marked enterprise and great success, based on the fundamental principles of equity and a progressive policy, ever on the alert to introduce ways and means to improve the quality of the clothing while reducing the cost. In all their enterprise no house has done so much for the public as that of Messrs. Isaac Fenno & Co. Mr. Isaac Fenno is one of Boston's self-made men, who early in life manifested those qualifications which have secured to his prosperous career a broad foundation and solid success. He comprehended the business of manufacturing clothing in first, next principled upon the well-defined policy of working to produce better made, better cut, and more durable clothing than his contemporaries were able to make. He was remarkably successful from the start, and repeatedly had to enlarge his facilities. In 1865 Mr. Charles M. Blake, a native of Vermont, came into copartnership, and in 1869 Mr. Adams K. Tolman, a Bostonian, was admitted; as also Mr. Henry G. Hartshorne, a native of Massachusetts. Four years ago, Mr. Chester H. Whitten, a native of Ohio, and Mr. William Smith, Jr., born in Massachusetts, were admitted, the firm thus having experienced partners at the head of the various departments, and ensuring the system of that thorough system of organization for which firm and establishment has become so justly celebrated. The premises comprise four entire floors with nearly 40,000 feet area, and fitted up in first-class style with all the modern improvements, including the Isaac Fenno Cloth Cutting Machine, the invention of the esteemed head of the house, and which does the work of a score of cutters, cutting from one to three thousand garments per day. Mr. Fenno and his copartners give the closest attention to the selection of their woolens and mixtures; all goods are most carefully examined for defects, and a slight imperfection, that the inexperienced eye would not notice, condemns a piece of goods at once. The firm employ none but the highest order of talent in their cutting-room, while they are leaders in the correct styles and employ several hundred of the most skilled tailors and operatives. In the making of the goods; only the best trimmings and fixings are used; all the latest seasonable shades, patterns and textures are found made up in this magnificent stock, the largest and finest at wholesale in Boston. The firm number among their customers the leading retail clothiers of Boston and New England; also in New York, where few manufacturers come up to this high standard of perfection. The firm also sell in the jobbers and retailers of the west and northwest, and the annual increase of trade indicates how superior and desirable is the firm's make of clothing. Mr. Fenno is the President of the Potomska Woolen Company, of Putnam, Conn., and also of the Calumet Woolen Company, of Uxbridge, Mass.

THE BOSTON DAILY GLOBE.—Boston, as a central point for distinguished journalistic enterprise and the development of high class newspapers, had long held a prominent position in the United States. In this connection we desire to direct special reference in this commercial review to the representative and progressive Globe Newspaper Company, proprietors of the daily, Sunday, and weekly Globe, which are the recognized leading newspapers of New England. The Globe Newspaper Company was duly incorporated in 1871 under the laws of Massachusetts. It was reorganized in 1878, with a paid-up capital of $115,000, and now its daily and Sunday issues of the Globe have a larger circulation than any other Boston newspaper. The first editor of the Globe was Maturin M. Ballou, and the first paper, issued March 4, 1872, contained eight pages of seven columns, the price being four cents. He was succeeded in August, 1872, by Colonel Chas. H. Taylor, who has been the editor and manager of the Globe from that time until the present, and the success achieved has been due to his enterprise and industry. The building is one of the finest and largest in Boston, and was built expressly for the Globe; is admirably equipped with all modern appliances, including elevators, electric lights, etc., and no pains or expense have been spared to make this establishment complete in every detail. In the printing-rooms are three splendid single and two double Hoe presses, which are able to print 1400 papers in a minute. The machinery is driven by two superior 165-horse power steam-engines, and the total number of persons employed in the various departments is about 300. There are likewise two elevators and electric-light engines on the premises, of the latest type. Eight editions of the Globe are turned out daily, which consume fifteen tons of paper. The daily, Sunday, and weekly Globe are got up in the highest style of the typographical art. An able and superior staff of editorial writers, reporters, and correspondents is employed. It has regular letters from its own correspondents abroad, and carefully covers all political, local, and foreign news, while at the same time it gives ample descriptions of races, base-ball, and all kinds of manly sports and pastimes. Its editorials are able, crisp, direct to the point, and treat all matters of interest in an impartial and fearless manner. The circulation of the Sunday Globe in November was 187,000, and the daily Globe 168,750. Its advantages as a splendid advertising medium have been recognized very generally by all classes of the community, and in this line it conducts the largest and most lucrative business in Boston. In consequence of its large size and vast amount of original and able reading matter, it is not only the cheapest but unquestionably the best paper in the city. Col. Chas. H. Taylor, the manager, was born in Charlestown, Mass., and during the civil war was a private in the 38th Mass. Vol. Infantry. He served one year and was seriously wounded at the battle of Fort Hudson, Miss., and eventually retired from the service for disability. He was private secretary to Governor Claflin, and was also clerk of the House of Representatives. Col. Taylor is a popular member of the Press, Temple, Central, and Algonquin Clubs, etc., and is one of Boston's highly esteemed and public-spirited citizens. The circulation of the Globe is steadily increasing not only in Boston, but in all sections of New England, and its present prosperous status augurs well for the future.

A. W. DOWNING & CO., Manufacturers of Morocco; Dongola, and Glaze-tanned Kid a specialty, No. 101 High and Nos. 919 and 921 Congress Streets.—In reviewing the numerous enterprises that have made Massachusetts one of the chief industrial centres in the United States, it is comparatively easy to see that the manufacture of, and trade in leather has exercised a great influence in promoting the general development and prosperity of the state. As old-established and prominent house engaged in this line is that of A. W. Downing & Co., of Nos. 101 High and 919-921 Congress streets. The active proprietor and manager of the house, Mr. Downing, as here established for the past twenty years, and is also a member of the firm of B. F. Thompson & Co., of No. 167 Summer Street, whose extensive factory is located at Philadelphia, Penn., where a large force of hands are employed. The house of Thompson dates its inception back to 1868, and is one of the oldest concerns in the leather trade in the United States. Its productions are so well known for their superior character, that extended comment upon them in this volume is rendered unnecessary. Mr. Downing occupies a spacious office and saleroom, the dimensions

being 35x100 feet, and every facility is possessed for promptly and satisfactorily meeting all orders. The trade extends to all parts of New England and the west, and is of a permanent and influential character. A heavy stock is carried of kid and goat skins, and a leading specialty is made of dongola and alum-tanned kid. All orders are given immediate consideration, and goods are shipped without delay. Mr. Downing, who is a native of New Hampshire, resides at Haverhill, is familiarly known in trade circles, and enjoys an excellent reputation both as a business man and citizen.

ISAAC McLEAN, Carpenter and Builder, No. 52 Lancaster Street.—Among those who have won a high reputation and an influential patronage by sheer force of merit in the building line is Mr. Isaac McLean, the well known carpenter and builder, and maker of mantels and interior woodwork, band-sawing and scrolling, whose establishment is located at No. 52 Lancaster Street. This gentleman originally established himself in business in 1865 at No. 19 North Anderson Street in Cambridge, removing to his present site in 1876. His career has been an successful as it has been honorable, reflecting the highest credit upon his practical skill and sound business principles. His workshop is spacious in size, equipped with the requisite machinery and ample steam power, and employment is constantly afforded to a force of eighteen skilled workmen. A leading specialty is made of the manufacture of store fixtures, in which branch of the business this house is widely recognized as excelling all its contemporaries. Orders and commissions are executed in the briefest time, in the most substantial manner, and give entire satisfaction to all concerned. Mr. McLean is a native of Prince Edward Island, a well known citizen of Cambridge, and noted in this city for his equitable methods and thorough salesmanship of his trade.

O. BOSFORD & CO., Dealers in Beef, Pork, Mutton and Poultry, Stall No. 9, Charles Market, Corner Beach and Lincoln Streets.—One of the pioneers of the Charles Market is O. Bosford, of the firm of O. Bosford & Co., provision dealers in that well known trading place. Mr. Bosford, who was a native of Vermont, came to Boston young, and at an early age connected himself with the business which he has since so successfully followed up. In 1882, with ample experience and sufficient capital, he established himself in the 9th Charles Market, and step by step rose to the esteem of the mercantile community for his enterprise, aptitude, and honorable record. He died on February 16, 1881, and his son has succeeded to the business. He occupies three stalls, Nos. 4, 5, and 11, which are provided with every convenience for the provision trade, and where five experienced salesmen are employed. A large business is transacted here in beef, pork, mutton, and poultry, which are received in the freshest condition daily and sold all the lowest market rates. Mr. Bosford is an active business man, attends to all the affairs of his establishment strictly and is justly held to be one of the leaders in his line in the city.

BARTON & CO., Manufacturers of the Belt Knife Leather Splitting Machine, Belt Knives, and Emery Wheels, No. 15 Chardon Street.—Like all the other branches of the mechanical arts, a high degree of excellence has been attained in the devices and tools that pertain to leather dressing; and in this connection it may not be amiss to direct attention here to the belt knife leather splitting machine, belt knives, and emery wheels manufactured by Barton & Co., of No. 15 Chardon Street, this city, which are articles of exceptional merit, and as a consequence are in wide and growing demand among curriers and tanners throughout the United States and Canada. This well-known and prosperous firm was established in 1877 and no better criterion of the superiority of the machines, knives, and wheels manufactured here could be offered than the unequivocal success that has attended the enterprise from its inception. The factory, which occupies a spacious fourth floor at No. 15 Chardon Street, is supplied with ample steam power and completely equipped with all necessary facilities, while some half a dozen skilled mechanics are employed, and all orders receive immediate attention, and the business of the firm, already extensive, is steadily increasing. Mr. D. O. Barton, who is the sole member, doing business under the style of Barton & Co., is a man in the prime of life, and a practical machinist of long experience in the exercise of his art, was born in the State of Maine but has resided in Boston for some thirty odd years.

PAGE BELTING COMPANY, New England Agents for the Gutta Percha and Rubber Manufacturing Company, Leather and Rubber Belting, and Hose, J. P. Jewell, Manager, No. 17 Federal Street.—A concern whose product has justly attained an international reputation is the Page Belting Company of Concord, N. H., and Boston. They have recently materially added to their facilities by assuming control of the New England Agency for the well-known Gutta Percha & Rubber Manufacturing Company of New York. The manufacture of various kinds of leather belting was begun at Concord, N. H., many years ago by the old house of Page Bros. In 1867 the important interests involved were duly capitalized, and owing to increasing growth of business the capital has been enlarged from time to time until now the paid-up capital stock is $200,000. Geo. F. Page, Esq., is president, and his brother, Chas. T. Page, is treasurer, and under their able executive management the company has had a career of marked prosperity. The works at Concord, N. H., are among the largest and best equipped of the kind in the world, the quality of the product having no superior. In November, 1886, they opened an office and salesroom in this city, most conveniently located at No. 17 Federal Street, under the experienced general management of Mr. J. P. Jewell, who has been connected with the company for seventeen years past. He also has the valued support of Mr. E. Daniel Downes, so long and so favorably known throughout this branch of trade, in charge of the rubber department. As a further important addition to facilities of the Boston concern, the Page Belting Company, in having secured the New England agency of the Gutta Percha & Rubber Manufacturing Company of New York, is here carrying a full and comprehensive stock of its Rubber Belting, Hose, Packing, and mechanical Rubber goods. These goods are of world-wide reputation, and there is an ever-increasing demand for them. Mr. Jewell guarantees factory prices, and has already developed a thriving business with excellent prospects for the future. Their stock also includes the Page Belting famous "Crown Extra" brand of leather belting, likewise all the staple and special grades of belting. The popular "Hercules Lacing," one of the very strongest and most durable on the market. "Hercules Raw Hide" belting, rubber and cotton hose and belting, cotton waste, packing of all kinds, corrugated matting, rubber tubing, and general mill supplies. An important feature is that of the most approved lines of fire hose, including the celebrated "Maltese Cross" rubber hose, also the "Maker Fabric" cotton rubber-lined hose, and the "Ajax" cotton mill hose, while in every department they offer substantial inducements both as to prices and quality. Their facilities are perfect, directly representing as they do two of the leading concerns of the kind in the world, and Boston is to be congratulated upon the opening of such an enterprising establishment within her midst.

MANHATTAN LIFE INSURANCE COMPANY OF NEW YORK—Boston Office, No. 40 Milk Street, Nathan Crowell, Manager.—Prominent among the substantial and reliable life corporations of the United States, is the Manhattan Life Insurance Company of New York, which was organized in 1850, and has now accumulated assets of upwards of $11,000,000, and a net surplus over all liabilities of $3,175,716. This old and reliable company now offers to the insuring public its new "Survivorship-Dividend Plan," which affords all the advantages of life insurance during the earlier years of life, and at the same time makes provision for old age, as the policy-holder can surrender his policy at the end of the survivorship-dividend period, and receive its full value in cash, thus combining investment and protection. Absolute security and prompt payment of all claims without litigation have secured the popularity of the Manhattan Life Insurance Company, whose patronage is steadily increasing in all sections of the United States. The following gentlemen who are greatly respected in business and financial circles for their prudence and just methods, are the board of directors and officers. Board of Directors:—James M. McLean, President Manhattan Life Insurance Company; Edward Schell, President Manhattan Savings Institution, 644 Broadway; John T. Terry (E. D. Morgan & Co.), 54 Exchange Place; Abram Du Bois, physician, 16 West Thirtieth Street; Henry Van Schaick, lawyer, 130 West Thirty-fourth Street; Ambrose C. Kingsland, merchant, 35 Broad Street; James Stokes, banker, 59 Liberty Street; Olin G. Walbridge (Calhoun, Robbins & Co.), 419 Broadway; D. H. McAlpin, tobacco, 673 Fifth Avenue; W. J. Valentine, Fordham, N. Y.; E. A. Walton, President Citizens' Insurance Company; George W. Quintard, Pier 27, North River; Leon Mann, merchant (L. & N. Blum), Galveston; C. Norwood, 122 West Forty-second Street; John W. Hunter, Treasurer Dime Savings Bank, Brooklyn; F. Van Zandt Lane (Blanchard Bros. & Lane), Newark, N. J.; Jacob Kayler, President National Bank, Philadelphia, Pa.; Edward King, President Union Trust Company, 73 Broadway; John H. Watson, President Columbia Bank, Fifth Avenue and Forty-second Street; James E. Yeatman, President Merchants' National Bank, St. Louis; N. K. Masten, banker, San Francisco; Spencer H. Smith, merchant, 681 Fifth Avenue; Henry B. Sloane, Insurance, 181 Broadway; George H. McLean, Vice-president, Citizens' Insurance Company, 156 Broadway; Philip Bissinger, diamonds, 47 John Street; Artemas H. Holmes, lawyer, Mills Building; James A. Garland, Vice-president, First National Bank, 98 Broadway; Frederick Billings, President, 279 Madison Avenue; Henry B. Peirce, Secretary of State of Massachusetts, Boston; Emil F. Del Bondio, merchant, New Orleans, La.; Wm. H. Oakley, President Citizens' Bank, New York; Robert A. Grove, Governor of the State of New Jersey; Jacob L. Rainey, Insurance, 181 Broadway; Arthur Leary, merchant, 73 William Street. Officers—James M. McLean, President; J. L. Rainey, 1st Vice-pres.; H. B. Stokes, 2d Vice-pres.; H. Y. Wemple, Secretary; B. N. Robbins, Actuary; A. Du Bois, M.D., Medical Examiner. The Boston office of the Manhattan is under the able and careful management of Mr. Nathan Crowell. Mr. Crowell was born in South Yarmouth, but has resided in Boston for the last fifty-one years.

N. Y. BRISTNALL & CO., Importers of Fine Wines, Cordials, Brandies, Gins, Scotch and Irish Whiskies, etc., Nos. 81 and 82 India Street.—Among the most reliable and progressive houses engaged in the importation and sale of fine goods in this line in Boston is that of N. Y. Bristnall & Co., located at Nos. 81 and 82 India Street. This house presents a striking instance of what can be accomplished by a steady application to business and a just and honorable course of dealing. Pure wines and liquors have become more than ever popular during late years, and those houses that keep these articles unadulterated, are the establishments most patronized by the trade and the public. Mr. Bristnall, who is sole proprietor, established this business here in 1874, since which period he has built an extensive and influential trade, both at wholesale and with private families, in this city and throughout the surrounding country, owing to the unrivalled quality, purity, and excellence of the goods handled. The business premises comprise a fine five-story building, admirably equipped with every modern convenience for the accommodation and preservation of the choice and valuable stock. This house is deservedly prominent and popular as a large importer of fine wines, cordials, brandies, gins, Scotch and Irish whiskies, St. Croix and Jamaica rums, also, as sole agent for the New England States, of the celebrated Ingleenoh vineyards, Napa County, Cal. The stock invariably includes all the different varieties natural, as well as old and reliable brands of bourbon and rye whiskies and the very choicest grades of New England and Medford rums; also, champagnes, ports, sherries, clarets, sauternes, Bordeaux and Burgundies, Rhine and Moselle wines; California and cognac brandies; fine bottled goods for family use, such as rock and rye whiskey, honey and horehound, bourbon, malt whiskey, Glenlivet Scotch whiskey; Bass' ale, Tennent's ale, Guinness' Dublin stout, and Tennent's porter; imported bay rum, apple-jack, brandied raisins, cherry-cordial, Vermouth, orange bitters, absynthe, etc. The rye and bourbon whiskies of this popular house are noted for their purity and evenness of quality, are entirely free from adulteration, and possess a natural flavor and fine tonic properties, while they are sold under a guaranty to give perfect satisfaction. The first great aim of this house has ever been to give to each and every customer full value for money expended, which is readily attained by the firm's large transactions, direct importations, influential connections, and low prices. A branch house is also operated at No. 90 Essex Street, devoted to the sale of fine wines, teas, coffees, cigars, and fancy groceries, and is immensely popular as a family wine store. In all his operations, Mr. Bristnall will be found prompt and liberal, always desirous of promoting the best interests of his patrons, and prepared to offer superior advantages and benefits in both goods and prices. He was born in Vermont, and came to Boston thirty years ago, where he is highly esteemed as an honorable and trustworthy citizen and a representative city merchant.

CHICKERING & SONS, Piano-forte Warerooms, No. 156 Tremont Street; Factory, No. 791 Tremont Street; New York, No. 130 Fifth Avenue (Chickering Hall). — The superiority of the piano-fortes manufactured by this world famous house of Chickering & Sons is so generally conceded, even by their imitators and competitors, that no argument on that score need be advanced. It will, however, be of interest to narrate a few facts concerning the rise and progress of this celebrated concern, the oldest and largest in the business in America. It was established in Boston by the late Mr. Jonas Chickering in 1823. He possessed the highest order of inventive and mechanical ability, coupled with a thorough knowledge of the laws of harmonics, and was soon able to disabuse the public mind that pianos the equal of, and in many respects superior to, any in Europe could not be produced here. To him is due the honor and credit of first producing the piano as it is generally made to-day, his improvements being generally known as "the American system" among piano manufacturers abroad, and were extensively copied and imitated. It need only be added that the Chickering piano has ever since remained the standard instrument of the world. Mr.

Chickering invented and introduced the entire iron frame for square pianos, and in 1845 invented the circular scale, to which two improvements are due all the excellences of the American square piano. They were never patented, Mr. Chickering generously giving the whole trade the benefit of these grand structural advances. In 1840 he brought out the first upright piano having full iron frame and overstrung bass. This has ever since remained the type of the upright. In grand pianos, the house was the first in the world to ever produce one with a full iron frame and with other radical improvements, and when these splendid instruments were exhibited at the World's Exhibition in London in 1851, they created a profound sensation, and were awarded a prize medal. Mr. Jonas Chickering thus saw the first fruits of his labor receive international recognition, and a big trade spring up prior to his decease in 1853, after a long, active, and honored career. He was succeeded by his sons, Messrs. T. E., C. F., and Geo. H. Chickering, under the familiar style of "Chickering & Sons." By 1858 the firm had received thirty-eight prize medals for the superiority of their manufacture, and had repeatedly enlarged their factory. In 1867 they exhibited their pianos at the Paris Exposition, where they received the highest award ever given to any piano manufacturer; a comprised the Supreme Recompense, the Cross of the Legion of Honor, and a gold medal. The progress of the house has been marked and rapid; numerous valuable improvements; have from time to time been introduced into its instruments, and the most unremitting personal care has been exercised in the management of the factory, which is the largest and finest in the world. It affords employment to upwards of 400 skilled hands, many of whom have been permanently with the house from boyhood. Up to date the house has manufactured over 75,000 pianos, and has a capacity of 60 per week. The materials used in their construction are the very choicest obtainable, all the methods and processes are the most accurate and perfect known, while every instrument is subjected to the severest tests prior to being shipped. In every respect the Chickering is the most perfect type of the modern piano-forte and affords the greatest satisfaction of any. They are undeniably the best and most durable, and thus the cheapest. The Chickering with its numerous improvements is refined and pure in tone, delightful in its singing qualities, and with great resonance and fulness of power. Of recent years the firm have brought out a beautiful series of uprights with new scales, the most perfect improvements of their class in the world; they stand in tune as well as the grand pianos, and have the new patent repeating action, new arrangement of the soft pedal, and new patent desks and fall. The actions are made with metallic rails and flanges, which thoroughly prevents the liability to become loose and require re-adjusting at various seasons of the year, as is the case with nearly all pianos made otherwise. The firm offer unrivalled facilities, among others making to order, grand square, and upright pianos to suit any style of furniture, and is highly commended upon. The firm's warerooms are situated most centrally at No. 156 Tremont Street, the 130 feet in dimensions elegantly fitted up and furnished, and where a large stock of their grands, squares, and uprights are carried. They make a magnificent display, the cases having solidity and strength, combined with beauty of outline and rich ornamentation, while their musical excellences are incomparable. Above the warerooms is Chickering Hall, so justly popular for the holding of concerts, soirées, etc. Upwards of thirty years ago the firm established their New York house, and which under the personal management of Mr. C. F. Chickering is the leading establishment of the kind in that city, and most desirably located in the premises No. 130 Fifth Avenue, owned by the firm and popularly known as Chickering Hall, by far the finest concert hall in America. Mr. George H. Chickering is the resident Boston partner, and a gentleman of the highest standing in financial and commercial circles. He has inherited his father's abilities, and under the wise guidance of himself and brother the house permanently maintains the leading position in the piano world. The Chickering piano has received the merited encomiums of the greatest pianists of the age, including the immortal Abbe Liszt, who declared the Chickering pianos "perfect, and perfectissima" impositively perfect. "There is no quality which is foreign to them. Your instruments possess, in the supreme degree, nobility and power of tone, elasticity and security of the touch, harmony, brilliancy, solidity, charm and prestige, and thus offer a harmonious ensemble of perfections, to the exclusion of all defects." Chevalier Boscovitz, the renowned Thalberg, the great composer Gounod, and the brilliant Goldschmidt, and many others of similar high standing render equally true and well-deserved homage to this the king of pianos, and which will ever shed a brilliant historic lustre round the name of Chickering. They are constantly widening and extending their business relations, and each year adds to the popularity of the firm, a fact proven by the annual increase of sales, each year surpassing the former.

OWEN BEARSE & SON, Mahogany and Hard-wood Lumber, No. 287 Albany Street.—Over fifty years of commercial prosperity arising from honorable dealing, industry, and reliability, and uniform excellence of the goods handled, coupled with industrial connections and perfected facilities, is the record in brief of the well-known and representative house of Messrs. Owen Bearse & Son, dealers in mahogany and hard-wood lumber, at No. 287 Albany Street and No. 17 Wareham Street. This old-established house is entitled to more than passing recognition in this review, as being not only conducting a trade of great magnitude, which extends from New Brunswick to Chicago, and in fact, has its ramifications in all parts of the United States. The business was established in 1837 by the senior member of the firm, Mr. Owen Bearse, who admitted his son, Mr. Horace L. Bearse, in 1873. The founder, Mr. Owen Bearse, died in 1888, after a long and honorable career leaving Mr. Horace L. Bearse as sole proprietor. The yards cover several acres and run from Nos. 2 to 50 Randolph Street, and from Nos. 625 to 649 Albany Street. Two large warerooms for the storage of lumber are occupied: one at No. 17 Wareham Street, which is 30x175 feet in size; and one at No. 287 Albany Street, 30x100 feet in size. These are fitted up with every facility for the handling, transportation, and kiln-drying of lumber, they making a specialty of the sale of kiln-dried, mahogany, and hard-wood lumber in their retail business. A large trade is done throughout the west in mahogany, and the trade, which extends throughout New England, is supplied with western lumber in oak, cherry, walnut, ash, maple, and white-wood, and also white birch and red birch from Canada and the west. They are also heavy dealers in southern cypress, which is largely used for interior house-finishing and furniture. They have recently begun to handle this in large quantities, the prices being about the same as for ash, while it is more expensive than white-wood. The trade is principally done among piano-manufacturers and car-builders, and they also sell lumber in the rough—kiln-dried lumber being made a specialty of. An immense stock is carried to meet the demands of the trade, and the sales amount to over 5,000,000 feet yearly. Fifteen horses and twenty-three men are kept constantly employed, and the trade is both wholesale and retail. Every convenience is at hand for promptly filling all orders, special inducements in terms and prices being given. All transactions are conducted on the most liberal basis, and the connections of the house with producers are of the most influential and favorable character, and all dealings with the house are sure to result profitably and pleasantly. The proprietor and energetic manager of this important enterprise is Mr. Horace L. Bearse, who for many years has been connected with the lumber trade; and no one possesses a more intimate knowledge of all the wants and requirements of the trade. He is a native of Barnstable, and is noted for his enterprise, business ability, and integrity, and possesses the confidence of the trade and public generally.

CREESY & NOYES, Contractors and Builders, Nos. 56 to 60 Wareham Street.—The contents of this work being designed to convey to the reader some idea of the business capabilities, industrial resources, and commercial relations of this city, it has been our aim to present to the public only such establishments as may be justly regarded as active and influential elements in advancing the general prosperity of Boston. It is therefore our privilege and pleasure to present a concern which is strength and enterprise is fully deserving of a warmest commendation. We refer to the house of Messrs. Creesy & Noyes, the well-known contractors and builders, located at Nos. 56 to 60 Wareham Street. The business of this house was originally established in 1853 by Messrs. Creesy & Cressy, who were succeeded by the present firm in 1871. The present proprietors are recognized as among the most prominent and responsible of the city's business men, and acknowledged leaders in their line of constructive enterprise. Their business premises comprise two floors and a basement, 60x80 feet each, with a yard of the same size for storing lumber, etc. The mills for sawing, planing, and general wood-working are abundantly provided with the newest and best machinery in use, operated by an engine of 110 horse-power, with three boilers of 100 horse-power each, and from two hundred to three hundred workmen are given constant employment. The range of manufacture embraces doors and an extended line of woodwork the character of which is familiar to those in interest, including, as it does, all the standard articles demanded by the contractor, carpenter, and builder in the erection of buildings. These are produced in great quantity and variety, the best-selected materials are utilized in all cases, and only reliable and first-class goods are turned out. As contractors for the erection of public buildings, business blocks, and private residences, this firm have long commanded the confidence of the general public and enjoyed a wide popularity. The character of the work with which they have been identified in this city and throughout the state serves as their best recommendation and their only needed indorsement. They erected the Danvers Insane-asylum, costing $400,000; the Union Depot at Worcester, costing $1,200,000; the new Boston & Albany Railway Depot in this city; and are now building the art museum for Wellesley Female-college, at Wellesley, Mass. There are but a few of the many prominent and important contracts which they have carried through to a successful completion, but they are sufficient to show how highly their ability and skill is appreciated; while this brief review of the record of their business may be justly regarded as an interesting chapter of the rise and progress of the building trade of Boston.

HECHT BROS. & CO., Wool, Nos. 207 to 219 Federal Street.—The leading house in the wool commission trade in this city, if not in the country, is that conducted by Messrs. Hecht Bros. & Co., at Nos. 207 to 219 Federal Street. This house has been in successful operation since 1873, and enjoys a reputation and a trade co-extensive with the country. Their new building, erected for their purpose in 1886, is the finest and best-equipped establishment of its kind in the country. It contains six stories and a basement 102x145 feet in dimensions, and is supplied with elevators and every modern convenience for the rapid handling and proper storage of supplies. This firm possesses unlimited capital and the highest credit with the trade, and is in constant receipt of heavy and important consignments of wool from all parts of the United States and the Territories, placing them in the best markets, which their large connection and valuable experience enables them to do with mutual and exceptional advantages. By strict adherence to one policy, handling entirely on consignment, and having correspondents in all parts of the world, this firm have established a prestige as leaders of the trade which gives purchasers every guaranty that all wool is as represented in quality and graded correctly. They have the credit of introducing the famous "Eberhards" and "Lagollet" pulled wools into this market, which rank among the very finest, and by their extensive business, have given a marked impetus to the wool trade and materially enhanced the qualities of wools handled, and greatly promoted the commerce of the city. The interests committed to their hands by shippers and consignors are always closely watched and intelligently guarded, and the firm are in just repute with wool-growers and the trade everywhere, for the honorable, efficient, and reliable manner in which all business is transacted.

BROWN & CLARK, Printers, No. 98 Federal Street.—Among the ablest and most popular exponents of the art typographical, as devoted to the needs of the mercantile world, is the well-known firm of Messrs. Brown & Clark, whose printing house is so centrally located at No. 98 Federal Street. Mr. L. R. Brown and Mr. J. C. Clark formed the existing copartnership and started in business in 1891. Though young men, they are old in practical experience and markedly skilled and accurate in the execution of all jobs, giving close personal attention to same. Their spirit of enterprise is manifested in their office, which is thoroughly organized, and fully stocked with the finest of new type, display bands, block letters, cuts, etc., of all kinds; also full lines of equipment, cases, racks, stands, stones, etc. The firm have four first-class presses run by electric power, enabling them to promptly turn out all classes of commercial printing in the finest style of the art. This is the best place in Boston to order your cards, bill heads, note-heads, circulars, statements, receipts, envelopes, etc., while checks, drafts, and fine blank work is a specialty. The firm are devoted to business, and every facility at command to promptly execute the largest orders at lowest prices, and in a style of elegance that elicits universal approval. Mr. Brown is a native of Boston, and Mr. Clark of Kingston, Ontario, both popular young business men, and worthy and able representatives of this art—that is so truly preservative of all arts.

EDUCATIONAL SUPPLY COMPANY, Publishers; Manufacturers and Importers of Microscopes, Chemical, and Physical Apparatus; Agents for the Papyrograph, No. 8 Hamilton Place. — To those of our readers throughout the country who are either dealers or users of microscopes, chemical or physical apparatus, the advantages and facilities possessed by the Educational Supply Company, will be of special interest. The resources and experience of this company in this difficult branch of trade are unrivalled by any other house in the country, and are the result of the consolidation of several houses in this line of trade, in 1880, and the incorporation of their interests under the present title, with Mr. George A. Smith as treasurer and general manager. Mr. Smith had been previously engaged in the business on Park Street, in this city, for some ten years, and was thoroughly versed in all the intricacies of the trade, and proved himself an able manager, and succeeded in meeting the demands of the patrons, and has placed the company upon a sound and permanent basis.

THE COLORADO FARM LOAN CO., Head Office, No. 35 Equitable Building, F. E. Orvell, President; W. H. Mitchell, Secretary and Treasurer. — The Colorado Farm Loan Co. was duly incorporated April 4, 1878, under the laws of Colorado, with a paid up capital of $100,000. Its main office is at No. 35 Equitable Building, Denver, Colo. The following gentlemen are the officers and directors: Officers: F. E. Orvell, President; W. H. Mitchell, Treasurer, Boston; F. G. Patterson, Manager, Denver. Trustees: Hon. George C. Wing, Auburn, Me.; William Bickford, M.D., Malden, Mass.; F. E. Orvell, Boston, Mass.; Pagwor Thomas, Esq., Boston, Mass.

BAKER, WITHERELL & CO. Wholesale and Commission Dealers in Fresh Fish, No. 10 T Wharf Fish market.—There is no branch of the commerce of Boston of more value, more highly creditable, or more flourishing than the wholesale fish trade, in which such immense capital is invested, and such market enterprise and ability manifested. The fisheries interests are looked of the first importance; and among the great leading representatives of this trade is the house of Messrs. Baker, Witherell & Co., of No. 10 T Wharf Fish market. This is without exception, one of the oldest established wholesale and commission dealers in fresh fish in New England, its inception dating away back to 1840. Bretton, Hill & Co. bring the original firm, subsequently becoming D. Hill & Co., and succeeded in 1884 by Messrs. Baker, Witherell & Co. The present proprietors, Mr. William B. Witherell and Mr. James E. Nason, bring to bear the widest range of practical experience, perfected facilities, and influential connections. Their trade is one not only of great magnitude, but has a widespread range, without question exceeded by none and equalled by few, for Messrs. Baker, Witherell & Co. fill large wholesale orders to the far-distant cities of the Mississippi Valley, north to St. Paul and Minneapolis, shipping in refrigerator cars. They have had to enlarge their facilities to meet the growing demand, and now occupy three floors, 50x60 feet each, in the T Wharf Fish market. They are here daily in receipt of cargoes of fresh fish direct from the most famous grounds, including all kinds of staple and fancy in season, including cod, halibut, herring, mackerel, weakfish, smelts, scallops and lake fish, lobsters, etc. They are interested in vessel property engaged in the coast, provincial, and banks fisheries; while here in Boston as brokers is better prepared to handle large commission consignments. Since Mr. Baker's retirement, in 1885, Mr. Witherell and Mr. Nason have been sole proprietors of this great concern, and devote themselves with marked ability and unflagging energy to meeting the most exacting requirements of the trade. Mr. Witherell was born in Wellfleet, and in early life followed the deep sea fisheries. He is thoroughly practical, having a personally acquired knowledge of every detail, and has resided in Boston for 30 years past. Mr. Nason was born in Boston, and has from his youth up been actively identified with the wholesale fish trade. The firm are prominent in all matters connected with the trade of commerce. They are active members of the T Wharf Fish Association, of the Massachusetts Fish Exchange, and of the New England Halibut Company, ever exerting a hearty support to all measures best calculated to advance the permanent welfare and prosperity of the trade, and basing all their numerous transactions on the strictest principles of equity and integrity.

THOMAS WHITE & CO., Manufacturers of Boots and Shoes, No. 69 High Street.—Though there are few boot and shoe factories actually operated in the city of Boston, Boston is the great market for all, and at the same time her capital is largely represented in the shoe factories of all the surrounding towns, the products of which are all sold here. Prominent among the representative and progressive houses extensively engaged in this growing industry is that of Messrs. Thomas White & Co., whose salesrooms in Boston are located at No. 69 High Street. The firm's factories which are among the best equipped in New England, are situated in Rohrook and Brockton, Mass., and Great Falls, N. H. Here 500 skilled operatives are employed, and the trade of the house now extends throughout all sections of the United States. Messrs. Thomas White & Co. manufacture largely men's, boy's and youth's calf and buff boots and shoes. They use only the best materials, and their goods are unsurpassed in this market for finish, style, durability, and comfort; and their flated graters are quite equal to superior custom work. The firm promptly fill orders at extremely low prices, and guarantee entire satisfaction to patrons. This business was established 30 years ago, in 1860, by Mr. Thos White the senior partner, who eventually, in 1888, admitted his sons, Messrs T. Edgar and H. M. White, into partnership. They occupy in Boston, for salesrooms, two spacious floors 25x80 feet each in dimensions, which are fully stocked with the firm's productions. All the partners are natives of Massachusetts. They are highly regarded in trade circles for their business ability, enterprise, and just methods, fully meriting the liberal and influential patronage secured in this growing and valuable industry.

A. H. POTTER & CO., Dealers in Diamonds, Watches, and Jewelry, No. 611 Washington Street.—One of the oldest established and leading representative firms of jewelers in Boston is that of Messrs A. H. Potter & Co., whose establishment is so centrally located at No. 611 Washington Street. Mr. A. H. Potter was born in New Hampshire, and early in life became identified with the trade in which he has achieved such success. He has had 30 years' practical experience as salesman and proprietor, and started in business in Boston in 1861. He early achieved an enviable reputation for the superiority of his stock and developed a trade of growing magnitude, resulting in his removal in 1886 to his present desirable location. This is an elegant store—in the finest section of Washington Street. This establishment attracts marked attention by reason of the excellent taste and sound judgment shown in decorations and furnishings. There is a marble tile floor and elegant cabinet and plate-glass show cases, setting off their magnificent stock to best advantage. Messrs. Potter & Co. deal in the highest grades of diamonds, watches, and jewelry, and there is no more generally recognized authority and expert on everything comprised in a stock of this kind than Mr. Potter. He selects his diamonds with the utmost care, giving attention to color, cutting, shape, perfection, and brilliancy; and always has on hand large parcels of desirable cut stones, also others mounted both white and perfect, and selling at remarkably moderate prices. This is the place to secure matched pairs, and fine gems for rings, studs, etc., in watches. Mr. Potter also takes the lead in the finest movements, including imported chronometers stop and split seconds, etc., in every variety of plain and fancy solid gold cases; also sterling silver watches at such a wide range of prices that every one can be suited. In jewelry, his magnificent stock compares favorably with any in Boston, and is notable for the richness and originality of styles, for the elaborate workmanship, and low prices. Here are sets, half sets, and single pieces in bewildering variety, and from which the most fastidious can readily be suited. Mr. Potter numbers among his customers the leading families of Boston and vicinity, and is a progressive business man, always the first with new styles, novelties, oddities, and ever pre-eminent for giving full value, handling the richest solid gold jewelry and the choicest gems. His policy has ever been one of equity and integrity; and this house is thoroughly representative of the best methods and finest work of the American jewelry trade.

ZENAS SEARS, Boot and Shoe Manufacturers' Goods, No. 25 High Street, Corner Federal.—One of the oldest and leading houses engaged in boot and shoe and shoe manufacturers' goods in this city is that of Mr. Zenas Sears, located at No. 25 High Street, corner of Federal. This house has been in successful operation for a period of thirty years, and enjoys a national reputation for the extent and superiority of its stock and the enterprise and reliability of its business management. The premises occupied for trade purposes are spacious and commodious; and the stock carried is one of the largest and most valuable of its kind to be found in the country. The proprietor is especially prominent in the trade as a large converter of a line of goods indispensable to the shoe-manufacturing sections of the east and west, and which are of a quality and character surpassing those of a similar kind manufactured in other cities. The articles handled include serges, elastic webbings, buttons, and other specialties pertaining to the dry goods part of a shoe. The goods are not only superior in make, but are sold in the trade by this house at prices which cannot be duplicated by other American houses. As a consequence, the business transacted is widespread and extends to all parts of the country. The proprietor is also agent for the Union Eyelet Company, manufacturers of eyelet and lacing work for Dunbar, McMaster & Co.'s Linen Thread, a full supply of which is always kept in stock. The intimate and influential connections enjoyed by this house with the best foreign manufacturers enable the proprietor to secure his supplies in vast quantities and at advantageous rates; and therefore he can guarantee the prompt and perfect fulfillment of all orders, and also offer such inducements to his patrons as render business relations with him of the most profitable nature. Mr. Sears is a Massachusetts man by birth and education, one of Boston's representative merchants and solid business men, a director of the Merchants National Bank, and prominently identified with the commercial growth and financial prosperity of the city.

G. A. KRERLE, Manufacturer of Clark's Linen Fire Hose, etc., Salesroom. No. 31 Hawley Street An old established and successful house in Boston engaged in the manufacture of linen fire hose, etc., is that of Mr. G. A. Kherle, whose factory, which is fully supplied with the latest improved appliances, is situated at Malden, Mass. This business was established in 1857 by Mr. John Clark, who conducted it till 1888, when Mr. G. A. Kherle succeeded to the management. Mr. Kherle manufactures Clark's famous linen fire-hose for mills, hotels, public buildings, steamboats, etc., also rubber lined linen-hose for fire departments, Clark's patent ring-screw couplings, hose pipes, etc. Clark's linen fire hose is made of

the best quality of Dutch flax prepared in a chemical solution to preserve it from mildew, and is recommended by all insurance companies as the best hose in the market. Its well-known reputation is sufficient evidence of its superiority, durability, and uniform excellence, while reference is made to many fire departments and leading manufactories throughout the country. The following are

some of the companies and fire departments which have been supplied with Clark's linen fire-hose, hose fittings, etc., viz.: Amoskeag Mfg. Co., Manchester, N. H.; Appleton Mfg. Co., Lowell, Mass.; Assabet Mfg. Co., Maynard, Mass.; Arnold Print Works, North Adams, Mass.; Arlington Woolen Mills, Lawrence, Mass.; Atlantic Cotton Co., Lawrence, Mass.; Augusta Fire Dept., Augusta, Me.; Bates Manufacturing Co., Lewiston, Me.; Berkeley Company, Ashton, R. I.; Blackstone Mfg. Co., Blackstone, Mass.; Boott Cotton Mills, Lowell, Mass.; Concord Fire Dept., Concord, N. H.; City Hall, Boston; China Mfg. Co., Suncook, N. H.; Cocheco Mfg. Co., Dover, N. H.; Chase Mills, Webster, Mass.; Cordis Mills, Millbury, Mass.; Framingham Fire Dept., Framingham, Mass.; Freeman Mfg Co., North Adams, Mass.; Great Falls Mfg. Co. Great Falls, N. H.; Graniteville Mfg. Co., Graniteville, S. C.; Grosvenor Dale Co., Grosvenor Dale, Conn.; Globe Woolen Co., Utica, N. Y.; Hinsdale Fire Dept. Hinsdale, N. H.; Holly Mfg. Co., Lockport, N. Y.; Hockett Mfg. Co., Hockett, N. H.; Hamilton Woolen Co., Amesbury and Southbridge, Mass.; Kearsarge Water P. Works, Warren, Mass; Lancaster Mills, Clinton, Mass.; Merrimack Mfg. Co., Lowell, Mass; Naumkeag Steam Cotton Co., Salem, Mass., New Adams House, Boston; Norway Plains Co., Rochester, N. H., Pemberton Mills, Lawrence, Mass.; Parker House, Boston; Renfrew Mills, Adams, Mass.; Rialto Building, Boston; Saxonville Mills, Saxonville, Mass., Simmons Building, Boston;

South Adams Fire Dept., South Adams; State House, Boston; Stevens Linen Works, Webster, Mass.; Williamsville Mfg. Co., Dayville, Conn.; Winthrop Mills, Winthrop, Me.; Willimantic Linen Co.; Willimantic, Conn.; Walworth Mfg. Co., Boston, Mass. Mr. Kherle promptly fills orders at extremely low prices and guarantees entire satisfaction to patrons. He is a native of Boston, and is highly regarded in business circles for his enterprise, promptness, and just methods. His trade now extends throughout all sections of New England, New York, and the adjacent states, and is steadily increasing, owing to the efficiency and superiority of his fire hose, fittings, etc. which are great favorites with users wherever introduced

J. D. MEAD & CO., Commission Dealers in Fruit and Vegetables, Southern Truck a Specialty, No. 23 North Market Street and No. 25 Clinton Street. Amid the great produce interests of New England's metropolis there is no firm more thoroughly reliable, or one more desirable with which to establish business relations than that of Messrs. J. D. Mead & Co., of No. 23 North Market Street and No. 25 Clinton Street. This is an old established and widely known concern, and it is as popular for its honorable business methods as it is known. It was founded under its present style in 1864 by the late Mr. J. D. Mead, who successfully conducted the enterprise for thirty years until his death in 1894. For some years he had associated with him in the business, as a partner, his son, Mr. George F. Mead, who has now for the past five years been the sole proprietor. This gentleman is a prominent member of the Fruit and Produce Exchange and of the Chamber of Commerce, and has the good will and esteem of his fellow members. He conducts a general commission trade in poultry, game, and eggs, and also fruit and vegetables. Consignments of these goods are received from all parts of the United States, and for these a quick and satisfactory sale is effected owing to the large distributing trade controlled by the house. Prompt and accurate returns with producers and shippers have always been the marked characteristics of this house. The premises occupied consist of a well-appointed store, 75x35 feet in dimensions, and this is suitably equipped with every convenience for facilitating the handling of stock and the filling of orders. From six to fifteen hands are employed, and prompt and courteous service is rendered. Mr. Mead is a native of Somerville, Mass., and his reliability as a business man is sufficiently attested to by the Traders' National Bank, Boston; Boston Produce Exchange; E. Roberts & Bro., Philadelphia, Pa.; Titus Bros., New York; R. B. Downer & Co., New York, and A. S. Makinas & Co., Chicago, Ill.

JOSEPH W. STONE, Provision Broker and Commission Merchant, No. 11 South Market Street. No one is better known or more highly respected in his line than Mr. Joseph W. Stone, provision broker and commission merchant, No. 11 South Market Street. Mr. Stone, so far back as 1858, half a century ago, established himself as a meat dealer in Faneuil Hall Market, and carried on the business there for a period of thirty years with great success. In 1888, he went into his present line as a provision-broker and commission merchant, and his great knowledge of the meat and produce trade enabled him to achieve a distinguished position in this branch of business. He alone deals largely in meat, produce, and provisions of all kinds, having the best facilities both in the purchase and sale of goods. His operations extend all over the west and south, while his trade in Boston has long been of the most extensive description. Customers of his house can always rely on getting prime goods at the lowest market rates, while the promptest attention is invariably paid in carrying out orders. Mr. Stone has long been a prominent member of the Chamber of Commerce. He was born in West Newton, Mass. For the half century that he has resided in this city he has occupied in mercantile circles a position of the first importance, and has always been held in the most honorable regard

CHUBB & SON, American Managers for Marine Insurance Company (Limited) of England; Boston Office, No. 55 Central Street; Wm. A. Comthouy, Agent.

NICHOLS, BELLAMY & CO., Builders' Hardware, No. 149 Devonshire and No. 56 Arch Streets.

E. P. SANDERSON CO., Iron, Steel, Heavy Hardware and Carriage Wood work, No. 60 Beverly Street.

CHAPMAN & BODEN, Manufacturers of Roofing Materials and Coal Tar Products, Nos. 114 and 116 Water Street.

J. H. LEWIS, Merchant Tailor, No. 417 Washington Street.—The history of prominent representatives of the tailor's art in Boston must start with the name of J. H. Lewis. He is the recognized leader of the trade in the city, and a tower of strength in advancing its mercantile interests. Mr. Lewis was born in North Carolina, came to New Hampshire at an early age, and learned the tailor's trade, and subsequently settled in Boston, where he perfected his knowledge of every detail of the business and established himself, in 1872, on Oak Street, in a comparatively small way. He early entered to the best class of custom, executing the finest and most artistic work, and by his industry, enterprise, and splendid acquirements in his profession he soon secured a fine, growing, first-class trade that ultimately gave him the pre-eminence which he now enjoys, and which he so honestly deserves. In 1888 he opened his present establishment at No. 417 Washington Street, between Bromfield and Winter Streets, which is justly regarded as the finest tailoring house in Boston. The furnishings and appointments of the spacious rooms are all in elegant taste, such as becomes the high character which the establishment enjoys, while every convenience is afforded for display, inspection, and sale. Here is exhibited the largest and finest stock of cloths and trimmings ever brought to Boston. It is complete in material, design, and novelty, and gives the limit of manufacture in high class goods. Many of the patterns are made exclusively for this house, while the very best sources of American and European production have contributed to the wealth of the display in the basement is located the cutting department, in which only the most skilled and expert artists and designers are employed. Mr. Lewis devotes his time and talents to the custom-work only, and the garments here made to measure are recognized by critics and connoisseurs everywhere as the perfection of style, fit, and artistic workmanship. He is the personification of activity in directing the affairs of his house, and every article made is forced to pass the crucial test of his examination. To be found among his prominent customers are very many of the best dressed citizens, collegians, and business men of Boston, gentlemen young and old, who understand the merits of a thoroughly first-class tailor, and who find in Mr. Lewis' establishment not only a line of goods that is at all times superior, but where the general make up, fit ... ? trimming of a garment is a matter of careful consideration and study. When it is learned that constant employment is given to a force of tailors running in number from one hundred and fifty to two hundred, and that the trade of the house demands their services, the immense business that is here transacted can be somewhat appreciated. Mr. Lewis is still in the prime of life, and a true type of a self-made man, who has risen by his own exertions to a prominence and popularity in his business of which he has every reason to be proud.

D. P. KENISON, Chiropodist, No. 10 Winter Street; Manicure, No. 10 Temple Place.—The prevailing tendency to conform to the demands of fashion by the younger people of the present day, by wearing ill-shaped boots and shoes much too small for the feet, and the blundering stupidity of those who make them, are the causes of so many deformed and painful feet at the present day, which call for the skill and practice of such skilled chiropodists as Dr. P. Kenison, who is located at No. 10 Winter Street. To acquire thorough skill and proficiency in this profession requires not only close application and study, but a thorough knowledge of the care of the many different bones, muscles, joints, etc., in the human foot. Therefore it is of the utmost importance to those suffering from corns, bunions, ingrowing nails, etc., to patronize only such practitioners of known reputation and skill in chiropody, and of such is Dr. Kenison of this city. The doctor is a native of New Hampshire, and has been actively engaged in this profession for a period extending over forty years, and is therefore not only one of the oldest, but the most skillful, in the United States. He removed into his present location in 1888, where he occupies spacious and commodious apartments, appropriately and luxuriously appointed, with private rooms and lady attendants for customers of the fairer sex. A corps of six assistants is constantly employed in the business, and the treatment of deformed feet, bunions, and corns is most successfully conducted at lowest prices. The painless extraction of corns is a specialty, and receives particular attention. In addition to this elegant establishment, the doctor conducts the manicure business at No. 10 Temple Place, where the beautifying of the hands, fingers, and

JOHN J. KEELEY, Apothecary, No. 22 Main Street, Charlestown.—In elegance, reliability, and extent of trade the drug establishment of Mr. John J. Keeley, No. 22 Main Street, occupies a leading position in Charlestown. Its business reputation is of the highest character, and the careful regard for the interests of the public which distinguishes its operations has gained for it a measure of popularity shared by few similar concerns in the community. It has been so successful in operation since 1875, and under its enterprising and reliable management the volume of its transactions has been constantly increasing. The store is handsomely fitted up for the reception of patrons, centrally and desirably situated for trade purposes, and replete with everything that can make a thoroughly first-class pharmacy. A very large stock is carried of pure drugs, chemicals, pharmaceutical preparations, essences and extracts, toilet and fancy goods, druggists' sundries, and other articles belonging to the trade. The proprietor makes his purchases from the most reputable sources, approaching first hands only—a fact which is daily appreciated by all who have their wants supplied by this house. The prescription department is carefully and efficiently directed, in charge of experienced compounders, and the limit of precision and safety is reached in every case. A specialty is made of cough syrup, prepared by the proprietor and highly prized for its curative properties by those who have tested its merits. Orders are filled with promptness and care in all cases, and popular prices prevail in all departments of the house. Mr. Keeley is a native of Boston, and known and honored in this community as an accomplished pharmacist and a gentleman of fine business talents and strict integrity. We cheerfully accord this house a conspicuous place in these pages, both on account of the reliability of its management and the importance of the industry represented to society at large.

H. CARRUTHERS & CO., Steam Fitters and Plumbers, Factory and Steamboat Work a Specialty, Nos. 1 to 5 Henry Street, East Boston.—There is not among the entire range of the mechanical arts any department or branch of activity in which such marked and gratifying progress has been made within recent years as in plumbing, steam-fitting, and kindred work, the advances made in this direction of late bring one of the notable features of the times. The leading steam-fitters and plumbers in East Boston are the firm of Messrs. H. Carruthers & Co., whose establishment is located at Nos. 1 to 5 Henry Street. The business of this reliable and responsible house was established in 1872 by Messrs. H. Carruthers and Henry Taylor, who continued it until 1888, when Mr. Taylor retired, since which date Mr. Carruthers has conducted the enterprise as sole proprietor under the original firm name. He occupies spacious and commodious premises, and carries constantly on hand a full and fine stock of plumber's materials and sanitary devices of all kinds. Factory and steamboat work is made a specialty, and plumbing, gas, and steam-fitting are executed in the most superior and expeditious manner, all work receiving the close personal supervision of the proprietor. Employment is furnished to a large force of skilled and expert workmen, and all orders receive immediate attention, no pains being spared to render the utmost satisfaction in every instance. The office is connected by telephone, and the wants of all classes of patrons are ministered to with promptness and satisfaction. Mr. Carruthers is a native of England, a resident of this country for the past thirty years, and known and esteemed in this city as an accomplished master of his trade, and a reliable, responsible business man.

H. N. LOCKWOOD, Watchmaker and Jeweler. No. 77 Bromfield Street.—The universal demand for watches and jewelry, especially of the better class, has of late years been one of the most marked indications of the higher civilization toward which we are rapidly progressing. Boston has long been noted as a leading centre of trade in this important line, and a young but flourishing house engaged therein is that of Mr. H. N. Lockwood. Mr. Lockwood was born in Norway, of American parents, learned his trade as a watchmaker and jeweler in that country, and came to Boston in 1862. For a number of years he had full charge of the watch and French-clock repairing department of the E. Howard Watch and Clock Co., who heartily indorse Mr. Lockwood as deserving the confidence of the trade, and in January, 1886, established business for himself at the above address. Here he occupies an elegant and attractive store, and in fact building up a large and permanent trade by force of merit as a talented master workman and a reliable, responsible dealer, and a very large and valuable stock is carried in every line. In watches, clocks, jewelry, charms, gold and silver ornaments, etc., the assortments are rarely excelled in the city. Precious stones of all kinds are extensively handled, including diamonds distinguished for purity, beauty, and perfect shape. Watches are demagnetized, and the repairing of all kinds is promptly attended to, and under Mr. Lockwood's personal supervision. The house is prepared to render the best satisfaction in all its operations, and is confident in its determination to furnish first-class goods and reliable work on the most advantageous terms that can be afforded. Samples of the new watch miniatures which have become so popular can be seen at this establishment; these miniatures are copied from a photograph of any size upon the inside case or cap of any watch, with soft pleasing effect, preserving all the delicacy of the original, and are guaranteed permanent.

H. HERBERT L. PERRY, Real Estate and Mortgages. No. 10 Milk Street.—Prominent among the representative real-estate agents in this city who make a specialty of handling business property and managing estates is Mr. Herbert L. Perry, who occupies eligible office quarters at No. 10 Milk Street. This gentleman has been established in business here for the past twenty years, and is a recognized authority on 'change in all matters relating to business property, and prominent in real-estate circles as an appraiser and expert. Merchants and trade representatives continue placing removal find him a reliable agent, who is sure to consult their best interests in securing for them desirable quarters; while landlords obtain through his agency responsible tenants. He controls the largest of several of the largest office buildings in the city, while many fine estates are placed entirely in his care while their owners go to enjoy travel and European life for years at a time. He has an intimate practical knowledge of everything desirable for rent or sale in the market, and investors and those in search of office or store room can rely upon his ability to meet promptly their respective wants. As a renting and collecting agent, he is implicitly trusted by owners of property, and can collect a fortune each month, disburse it in proper channels, and do everything, except selling, which the owner can do with his own. He is invariably prepared to render the public a service at once prompt, reliable, and faithful, and is naturally esteemed as a worthy exponent of a vitally essential branch of business effort. Mr. Perry is a native of Boston, a prominent citizen and representative business man of Boston.

J. R. CAREY & CO., Commission Merchant and Dealer in Flour, Produce and Provisions. Butter, Cheese, etc., No. 11 Merchants' Row.—Few firms engaged in this wholesale flour produce, and provisions trade in this city are more widely or honorably known, as few enjoy a better reputation in commercial life, than the popular and responsible firm whose name heads this sketch. It is, in fact, one of the most staunch and reliable concerns of the kind in Boston, and its business connection, which extends throughout the New England States, is of a highly gratifying character, growing and extending annually. This well and favorably known house was established in 1861 by Parker & Carey, who carried on the business up to 1878, when they were succeeded by Mr. Carey as sole member, who after removing to his present eligible location at that time has since continued the business under the style of J. R. Carey & Co. The business premises at No. 11 Merchants' Row, occupy a 35x75 front floor and basement, while a commodious warehouse is maintained

also at No. 35 India Street, and a number of salesmen and others are employed. The firm handles everything in the line of flour, provisions, lard, butter, cheese, eggs, etc., on commission, and carries on hand constantly a heavy and superior stock, doing a wholesale business exclusively. Consignments are received almost daily, and judiciously disposed of, a special feature being made of prompt returns for the same, and all orders are filled in the most expeditious and reliable manner. Mr. J. R. Carey, who is a gentleman in the prime of life, and a native of Stirling, Mass., is a man of entire probity in his dealings, as well as energy, capacity, and thorough knowledge of the trade, and stands high in the community both as a merchant and a citizen. He is one of the most respected members of the Boston Produce Exchange, on the charter-roll of which his name appears, and also enjoys the esteem of his associates in the Fruit and Produce Exchange.

W. M. A. CAMPBELL, Apothecary. No. 771 Meridian Street, Corner Princeton, East Boston.—One of the most popular and best appointed drug houses in East Boston is the one located on the corner of Meridian and Princeton Streets. This establishment was founded a quarter of a century ago by Mr. W. F. Pierce, who subsequently disposed of it to the Maverick Drug Company, to whose service Mr. William A. Campbell entered as clerk in 1884. In the early part of 1889 this gentleman purchased the business from the company. Since then he has fine sustained an enviable reputation for accuracy and reliability in compounding and dispensing prescriptions, and in the general exercise of his profession, of which he is a leading and most popular member, and enjoys the favor of many of the foremost physicians in this section of the city. Mr. Campbell, who is a young, pushing, energetic business man, and a native of Nova Scotia, is a registered druggist, and a skilful and expert pharmacist and chemist of considerable experience, and has developed the business of his house to large proportions. The store is a commodious one, and neatly fitted up and appointed. A carefully selected and choice stock is constantly carried, embracing pure and fresh drugs and medicines of every description, chemicals, extracts, acids, and pharmaceutical specialties in great variety, standard proprietary remedies and patent medicines of all kinds, spirits of alcohol, and medicinal liquors, mineral waters, flavors, perfumery, toilet articles, fancy goods, and druggists' sundries of all kinds. A handsome soda fountain, attractive show-cases, and tasteful surroundings render the place very inviting, while courteous and competent assistants are in attendance.

W. C. RICHARDS & CO., Stoves, Ranges, Furnaces, and Tinware, Table and Pocket Cutlery, Small Hardware, No. 161 Meridian Street, East Boston.—One of the oldest, best known, and most popular hardware, stove, and housefurnishing goods establishments in East Boston is that of Messrs. W. C. Richards & Co., located at No. 161 Meridian Street. This concern was founded over forty years ago by the senior member of the firm, Mr. W. C. Richards, who in 1878 admitted into partnership Mr. G. M. Porter. The premises occupied for the business comprise a fine, commodious store, with a frontage of 25 feet and a depth of 110 feet, giving ample accommodation for the prosecution of an active trade in all branches of the business. The stock is a large and comprehensive one, and embraces a line of stoves, ranges, and furnaces, embodying all the latest improvements in heating and cooking; lamps and lamp goods, tin and wooden ware of every description, kitchen furnishings in great variety, table and pocket cutlery, and small hardware in almost endless assortment. These goods are all supplied from manufacturers direct, and are the best and most desirable in the trade. In the sheet iron, and copper work this house is thoroughly equipped for rapid, successful, and satisfactory work, and every facility is afforded for the prompt and perfect fulfillment of all orders. A specialty is made of heavy sheet-iron work, and of the repair and setting up of stoves, ranges, and furnaces. Ten skilled and experienced hands are constantly employed, and no trouble is spared to afford the most complete satisfaction to patrons. The trade is large and influential in city and country, and under enterprising and progressive management is constantly increasing in volume and importance. Both members of the firm are natives of Maine, and both as business men and private citizens have an excellent record, and are widely esteemed.

JACKSON & CO., Hatters and Furriers, No. [illegible] Tremont Street, opposite Park Street Church.—In the eminent and ably conducted house of Messrs. Jackson & Co., Boston has a firm of hatters and furriers second to no other in the United States, and unrivalled in Boston and New England. The business was established in [illegible], and has had a rapid and permanent growth and development, early becoming the leading exponent in its line. In [illegible], in response to the demands of trade, the firm removed to their present centrally located and elegantly fitted-up premises at No. [illegible] Tremont Street, opposite the Park Street Church, and where is carried the most fashionable and comprehensive stock of hats, caps, and furs in season. The copartners, Mr. Joseph A. Jackson and Mr. Wm. H. Holloway, are Bostonians of the highest standing in social and commercial circles, and who have from their youth up been actively identified with this branch of trade, and are leading authorities therein, bringing to bear the widest range of practical experience, perfected facilities, and influential connections. They keep in stock all styles of high hats, derbys, etc., both of their own manufacture and including Dunlap's New York hats. These are the acme of perfection as regards style, materials, and workmanship; and Messrs. Jackson & Co., have long numbered among their customers the leading citizens of Boston and vicinity. The store is fitted up with rich quartered-oak fixtures and every modern convenience for handling and displaying the immense stock here carried, and in which a specialty is made of furs. This is the recognized headquarters for gentlemen's seal and other fur coats, gauntlets, and collars; for ladies' finest Alaska seal dolmans, sacques, Newmarkets, jackets, boas, tippets, muffs, and hats, all of elaborate perfection in design and workmanship; also all other fancy furs are kept in stock here and of the best quality obtainable, at prices remarkably moderate, the features of superiority considered. *Leading fashionable circles procure their furs here, and the firm lead in every essential.* They are also pioneers in affording the public special accommodation for the storage of furs, etc., having fitted up in their basement a numerous series of compartments alphabetically arranged, and in which furs and robes are stored through the summer and fall for patrons at a nominal charge, and insured against loss by fire by the firm's liberal policy. They are effectually preserved against the ravages of moths likewise, and this feature of the house commends itself to all who have furs, etc. System is maintained and customers' goods can be instantly proceeded to and taken out when wanted. Burglar alarms connect the storage department with the police station and the firm's residences. The premises are heated by steam to avoid all danger of fire, etc., and throughout Messrs. Jackson & Co.'s is the best equipped in town, and the model of its kind. Messrs. Jackson and Holloway are popular and respected merchants, who have ever retained the confidence of leading commercial circles, and are worthy representatives of their important branch of trade.

MORRILL BROTHERS & CO., Wholesale Dealers in Watches, Jewelry, Silverware, Canes, Opera-glasses, Diamonds, etc., No. [illegible] Washington Street.—The establishment of Messrs. Morrill Brothers & Co., the well-known wholesale dealers in watches, diamonds, jewelry, silverware, opera-glasses, canes, etc., at No. [illegible] Washington Street, is not only a splendid monument to the intelligent enterprise of its management, but it is also one of those houses whose great and honorable success reflects lustre upon the name of the city. As the leader in its line in Boston, it holds a commanding position among the mercantile institutions of prominence throughout the New England States. The business was originally established in [illegible] by Mr. C. F. Morrill, and in [illegible] Messrs. A. T. Morrill and O. A. Drinkwater were admitted to partnership, followed by the admission of Mr. Irving Smith in [illegible]. The neatly appointed salesrooms of this firm are fairly ablaze with the magnificent exhibition of valuable and beautiful goods. The stock includes the finest gold and silver watches from the most reliable makers in Europe and America, fine jewelry, rich gems, solid silver and plated wares, opera-glasses, and in fact everything that a general jewelry store needs. The department allotted to diamonds displays the genius of the jeweler in its highest form. The gems are purchased in Europe, are carefully selected for their flawless beauty, absolute purity, and perfect shape, and include rivière solitaire, cluster and pendant, panache and aigrette, necklace and bracelet, chains, earrings and chatelaines, while the setting and mounting is done by expert artists. Here will also be found certain classes of articles noted for their beauty and rarity, for decoration and personal adornment, which are not to be obtained elsewhere. The highest grade of goods only are handled, while inducements are offered to the trade, as regards terms and prices, which preclude successful competition. The Messrs. Morrill are natives of New Hampshire; Mr. Drinkwater was born in Maine; while Mr. Smith was born in New York City. All are experienced and accomplished masters of their art as watchmakers and jewelers, long identified with the business, of high standing in commercial, financial, and trade circles, and combine to form a firm of commanding influence, wide popularity, and solid worth.

C. M. LANDER, Newspaper Folding and Mailing, and Pamphlet Binding, No. [illegible] Broad Street.—The business represented by this house is one of those industries which have sprung into existence within the last few decades, and which are illustrative of the progress of modern ideas and of the extension of the division of labor. The establishment was founded by the present proprietor, Mr. C. M. Lander, in [illegible], at No. [illegible] Bromfield Street. He began upon a very limited capital, but, with a wealth of push, energy, and pluck, soon acquired the attention of the trade, and has since been enjoying a steadily increasing patronage as the fruits of his industry. In [illegible], he removed to his present spacious quarters, at No. [illegible] Broad Street, where he possesses unequalled facilities for meeting all demands that may be made upon his resources. Employing a force of twenty expert assistants, Mr. Lander carries on active operations as a pamphlet-binder. His leading specialty, however, is newspaper folding and mailing; and he does more work in this line than any contemporary concern in the city. His facilities enable him to execute all contracts in the most expeditious manner, and at prices that can safely admit of any comparison to which they may be submitted, while all work is done in the most careful and satisfactory way. Mr. Lander publishes *The Bostonian and Railroad Advertiser*, which is an eight-page paper devoted to instructive and spicy literature and correct time-tables with all the changes of the different railroads centring in Boston, and which makes a first-class advertising medium for business, theatres, etc. The circulation is large and has the advantage of being sent through the mails as second-class matter. The terms for this useful and instructive paper are one dollar per year, with the postage paid. Mr. Lander is a native of Boston, and is a resident of Somerville. He is favorably known in commercial circles, and conducts his business upon such fixed principles of equity that he has gained the entire confidence of all persons with whom he has had dealings.

THE BOSTON ELECTRIC PROTECTIVE ASSOCIATION, No. [illegible] Summer Street, Weston Lewis, President, G. W. Adams, General Manager.—At the present day, warehouses, mills, factories, hotels, etc., during the night are left solely in charge of watchmen, who have little chance, where the patent electric clocks of the Boston Electric Protective Association are utilized, to neglect their duties without being betrayed by these tell-tale time registers. This association was duly incorporated under the laws of Massachusetts in [illegible] with ample capital, since which period it has secured a liberal and influential patronage in all sections of New England. The following gentlemen, who are widely known in business circles for their enterprise, energy, and just methods are the officers: Weston Lewis, President; Benj. F. Dyer, Treasurer; G. W. Adams, General Manager. Directors: Henry W. Wellington, Benj. F. Dyer, Weston Lewis, G. W. Adams. The electric clocks of this popular association are the invention of Mr. Geo. W. Adams, the superintendent. They are absolutely unrivalled for efficiency, utility, and reliability, and also as burglar alarms are most effective. The association has now [illegible] of these electric clocks in use in the city of Boston, and if we add the large number put up in different sections of New England, it will be found that this successful company has a greater number of its clocks in use than all other competing concerns. The officers promptly furnish estimates for their clocks, and undertake the equipment of any building with them in all sections of the country. Wherever used, these clocks give entire satisfaction, and have no superiors in the United States or Europe. The association only leases their electric clocks. Architects, builders, bankers, etc., are requested to carefully examine these clocks, which are not only an absolute check upon watchmen, but also a complete protection by giving a necessary warning against the attacks of burglars.

BENJ. FRENCH & CO., Dealers, Importers and Manufacturers of Photographic Materials, Etc., No. 319 Washington street. —Boston as the recognized centre of mercantile activity in New England affords very favorable openings for well considered enterprises in every branch of trade. Prominent among these at the present day are the sale, importation and manufacture of photographic materials. A representative and the oldest established house in the city, and in fact in the United States actively engaged in this growing trade is that of Messrs. Benj. French & Co., whose office and salesrooms are located at No. 319 Washington Street, opposite the old South Church. Mr. Benj. French, who is sole proprietor, is a native of Lebanon, N. H. Mr. French was located at No. 140 Washington Street, for twenty years, and has been twenty-eight years at the present location. He is now sixty-nine years old, and came to Boston in 1841. Early learning the photographic art he engaged successfully in the business at an

operator, and in 1846 turned his attention to dealing in photographic supplies, and has kept fully up to the advancement and requirements of the times. The premises occupied comprise a spacious and well equipped store 240 feet in dimensions. The stock, which is the largest and best selected in Boston, includes cameras, lenses, dry plates, printing and toning outfits, tripods, lanterns pure chemicals and all kinds of photographic materials, which are offered to customers at extremely low prices. Mr. French makes a specialty of amateur photographic outfits. He is sole agent for the Voigtländer & son and Dariot lenses, and the Trapp & Munch Albumen Paper. The Voigtländer lenses have attained such world-wide fame, and continue to be universally recognized as the very finest lenses ever constructed, that it would be superfluous to dwell on their rapid growth, their unequalled powers, and the numerous high honors bestowed upon the makers—Messrs. Voigtländer & Son. The career of this celebrated firm is marked by an unbroken series of unqualified successes, as illustrated by their double portrait-objective—the first ever produced—their renowned Euryscope, and recently, their superb Portrait-Euryscopes. The Voigtländer lenses, in their present improved form, present the greatest perfection yet reached in photographic lenses, and there is no requirement in the wide range of photography to which they are not eminently suited, yielding results of appreciative excellence. Much of their phenomenal success is due to their uniform excellence. An inferior Voigtländer lens never having been produced. After a lens has been completed, it is subjected to a most thorough optical and practical test by Mr. Voigtländer himself, who permits no instrument to leave his establishment unless it is absolutely perfect in every detail, regardless of the time and material consumed in its construction. All Voigtländer lenses are composed of the choicest and most expensive optical glass, and occasional small bubbles, which are impossible to avoid in its production, are quite harmless, as they do not in the least affect the efficiency of the lens. Every genuine lens is en-

graved upon the barrel the number indicating its size, its designation, the manufacturers' number, and the makers' name—Voigtländer & Son. Mr. French also handles the famous Blair's Cameras, which possess a greater turning capacity than any others, three enabling the operator to use any make or style of lens without extension fronts. Professionals can always find at this establishment the best photographic apparatus and supplies in the market, while to amateurs he likewise offers substantial inducements and advantages. His patronage now extends throughout all sections of the United States and Canada, where he numbers his customers by hundreds. Mr. French publishes annually superior catalogues and price lists, which are forwarded promptly upon application.

THE ATLANTIC WORKS, Engineers and Builders of Steamships, Tow Boats, Steam Yachts and Launches, Etc., I. N. Lothrop, President, A. R. Cox, Treasurer, Nos. 60-76 Border Street, East Boston.—In compiling an account of the commerce and industries of Boston, we desire to particularly mention those classes of houses that are the best representatives of each special line of trade, and are contributing most to the city's fame and reputation. In this connection special reference is directed to the widely known Atlantic Works, engineers and builder of steamships, tow boats, steam yachts, launches, etc., whose yards etc., are eligibly located in East Boston, at Nos. 60-76 Border Street. This progressive and successful company was duly incorporated in 1853, under the laws of Massachusetts, with large capital, and since its organization has secured the greater portion of steamship building and repairing at this port. The yards are spacious and are equipped with all modern appliances and machinery, including marine railways, etc. Steamships of all kinds are docked and repaired by the company without delay at just prices, in the most workmanlike manner. From 200 to 500 skilled mechanics, shipwrights, etc., are employed in the various departments, and all necessary materials are kept constantly on hand. The company have already docked and repaired some hundreds of steam vessels of different descriptions, in addition to building a number of new ones. They likewise build in a very superior manner tow boats, steam yachts and launches, and also manufacture marine and stationary engines and boilers, tanks and general machinery, guaranteeing entire satisfaction in every particular to patrons. Only first class materials are utilized, and highly skilled workmen employed. Plans, specifications and estimates are promptly furnished for every description of engineering work, while no pains or time are spared, to fulfil the expectations of patrons. In conclusion we would observe, that the affairs of the Atlantic Works are placed in capable and honorable hands, and the company ably maintains the leading positions in Boston, in this growing and valuable industry, reflecting the greatest credit on all concerned.

KIDDER DRUG STORE, No. 65 Main Street, Charlestown.—In the name of this celebrated drug house is perpetuated the memory of its distinguished founder, Mr. Samuel Kidder, who in his lifetime gained great distinction as a pharmacist of first-class ability. Mr. S. Kidder started business at the present location, No. 65 Main Street, in 1836, and his successors were Messrs. D. F. White & Co., also were followed by Mr. John Stowell. In 1877 Mr. S. B. Bradford became the proprietor, and he has preserved the old familiar name for his establishment, the Kidder Drug Store. It is an elegant establishment in every way, being spacious in size, handsomely appointed, and under the most experienced and skilful management. A splendid line of goods is shown in every line of the business. The pure and superior assortment of drugs, medicines and pharmaceutical preparations are supplied from the most reputable sources, and are selected with special reference to strength and freshness. In the line of novelties in perfumery, toilet articles and fancy goods, the enterprise of this proprietor has placed within the reach of his patrons, the best articles that can be purchased. The house is perfectly equipped for his specialty of prescriptions, and absolute accuracy is assured in all cases, and it is also a popular store for purchasers of soda and mineral waters, etc., and in the holiday season it is extensively patronized by the old and young in search of useful and ornamental treasures for presents. Mr. Bradford is a native of Charlestown, an experienced pharmacist, and a useful, honorable citizen

A. R. & J. H. SHEDD, Real Estate and Insurance Agents, Conveyancers and Auctioneers, Commissioners for Maine and Vermont, Notary Public. No. 16 City Square, Charlestown District.—The real estate and insurance interests of Boston and its surroundings have attained proportions of such magnitude as to enlist the services of many of our most talented and enterprising business men. Prominent among the oldest established and most influential firms in this business in the Charlestown District is that of Messrs. A. R. & J. H. Shedd which is centrally located at No. 16 City Square. This firm bring vast practical experience to bear and an intimate knowledge of the value of real estate in every section of the city and its vicinity. This house was founded originally in 1854 by Mr. A. R. Shedd who is a native of Andover, Mass., and was conducted by him very successfully up to 1870 when his son J. H., who was born in Brookline, this state, was admitted into copartnership under the present firm title. They are recognized authority as to real estate values and transact every branch of the business, buying, selling, exchanging and renting property and possess ample facilities for conducting operations of any magnitude under the most favorable auspices, and are always enabled to offer investors a choice from a long list of eligible properties. They have brought to a successful issue many important transactions—several of great magnitude, and intending investors who rely upon their sound judgment and judicious advice in purchasing property will secure not only a steady income but likewise a prospective increase of value. Messrs. A. R. & J. H. Shedd make a specialty of the care and management of estates and have met with great success in this line. They secure responsible tenants, collect rents, pay taxes, and effect repairs in the most judicious manner and in every way maintain all properties placed in their hands at the highest standard of efficiency. The firm is very popular in insurance circles and are agents for the following financially sound and reputable companies, both foreign and domestic: City of London, England; Orient of Hartford, Conn.; Spring Garden of Philadelphia, Pa.; Traders' and Mechanics' of Lowell, Mass.; Dorchester Mutual of Dorchester, Mass.; Massachusetts Mutual Fire Insurance Company, and many others. They have developed an extensive patronage in this important line of business and are prepared to place risks with our best companies at lowest rates, and especially so in the case of well located residential property. They likewise attend to the auction sale of real estate and personal properties and faithfully serve the best interests of their customers. Conveyancing, and notary public business, etc., receive careful attention and they are the regularly appointed commissioners for the states of Maine and Vermont. Their office is on the first floor, of ample dimensions and supplied with every convenience for the transaction of business. They enjoy the highest confidence of our best commercial circles, and are recognized as honorable and reliable business men.

F. FIRST WARD NATIONAL BANK of Boston, Mass., Stephen H. Whidden, President, Geo. W. Moses, Cashier. Maverick Square.—Boston may with propriety be congratulated upon the conservative policy and marked prosperity and influence of her banks. No financial corporations in the state have a more enviable record than those of this city, and representative among the number is the First Ward National Bank, eligibly located on Maverick Square. This bank was duly organized in 1873 under the National Banking laws, and is to-day one of the most vigorous exponents of the sounded principles governing banking and finance. The paid up capital of the First Ward National Bank is $250,000, which has been further augmented by a surplus of $45,000. It is ably officered and its board of directors is composed of gentlemen more than usually prominent in financial and business circles. The list is as follows:—Stephen H. Whidden, President; Geo. W. Moses, Cashier; Frank F. Cook, Teller. Directors: Chas. A. Morss, Silvanus Smith, Stephen H. Whidden, E. H. Atwood, Samuel N. Mayo, Geo. W. Moses, Pembroke S. Hucknow, Wesley A. Gove, James N. Montgomery. The bank transacts a general business; its lines of discounts cover the best classes of commercial paper, its loans are judiciously made on approved collateral, and at the same time it gives close attention to collections, drafts, etc., having a chain of correspondents in all sections of the United States and Canada. The bank has always paid good dividends to stock holders without venturing upon hazardous business in order to realize profits. It likewise utilizes every modern system, which in any way tends to benefit or improve financial transactions, and extends to customers every possible facility and convenience. Mr. Whidden has held office as president since 1885. He is a thoroughly capable financier and is highly regarded by the community for his energy and integrity. Mr. G. W. Moses, the cashier, is an able and experienced bank officer, eminently qualified for his important position. He is also treasurer of the Chelsea Gas Company, and of the Winnisimmet Ferry Company, while at the same time he is one of the commissioners of the sinking Fund of Chelsea.

S. SANDERS & GIBBS, Plain and Decorative Paper Hangers Whitewars, and Dealers in Paper Hangings of all Varieties. No. 4 Meridian Street, East Boston.—This is an age of decoration, and as culture and refinement advance the demand for ornamental and tasteful home surroundings grows apace. The plain and often rugged, unshapely walls which satisfied the Puritan fathers are by no means pleasing to their descendants, who have discovered the means of combining the ornamental with the useful in all the affairs of life, and learned that the more the homes of the people are beautified the more attractive they are and the more the pleasures of the home circle are enhanced. In every branch of the decorative art great advances have been made and the production of paper hangings and other decorative materials gives ample evidence of this. Many of the hangings now made are veritable works of art, and numerous specimens of these are to be seen displayed in the establishment of Messrs. Sanders & Gibbs, No. 4 Meridian Street, East Boston. This firm are dealers in paper hangings of every description, plain and decorative paper hangers, whitewars, etc. They begin business in a small way in May, 1875, and by degrees have built up a very extensive trade connection. They occupy a neatly appointed store, with a capacity of 12,000 feet, and here carry a general line of all the various kinds of wall papers, dados, centre pieces, etc., representative of all the newest designs in beautiful figure and flower patterns, from the plainest to the most elaborate in beautiful tints and combinations of colors and gold. The firm give particular attention to interior decorations, and as paper hangers are highly endorsed and recommended for the skill and good taste they display in their work. Twelve hands are employed and all orders are promptly carried out to the entire satisfaction of customers. The co-partners are Messrs. A. J. Sanders and F. L. Gibbs. The former is a native of Quincy, N. H., and the latter of Framingham, Mass.

C. D. COBB & CO., Wholesale and Retail Grocers and Dealers in Fine Teas, No 1. Bunk Building, Bunker Hill District.—The wholesale and retail trade in fancy and staple groceries, is one of the most important branches of business carried on in any city. A reliable and representative house in the Bunker Hill District, successfully engaged in this important and growing trade is that of Messrs. C. D. Cobb & Co. This business was established twelve years ago by Messrs. J. H. Cobb & Co. who conducted it till 1883, when J. H. Cobb retired and C. D. Cobb and C. H. Cobb bought the interest of J. H. Cobb, and formed the firm of C. D. Cobb & Co. Mr. C. D. Cobb died in August, 1883. The surviving partners, Messrs. H. E. and C. H. Cobb, continued the business, which is now being carried on under the firm name of C. D. Cobb & Co. The store is spacious and commodious, and the stock of goods carried is comprehensive and well selected embracing everything in the way of fancy and staple groceries, teas, coffees, spices, canned goods, flour, fruits, The firm make a specialty of teas, and keep constantly on hand a superior assortment of fresh crop Oolongs, Japans, gunpowder, imperial young hyson, English breakfast and other standard teas, which are justly renowned for flavor and quality. The aim of this firm has always been to give to every customer full value for money expended, which is attained by the firm's large transactions, direct purchases and low prices. Courteous and prompt attention is given to all who patronize this store, and orders entrusted to Messrs. C. D. Cobb & Co. by mail receive the same careful attention as if given in person. The firm carry on an extensive trade throughout Everett, Charlestown and Somerville, which is steadily increasing. Mr. H. Cobb is senior partner of the extensive house of Cobb, Aldrich & Co., Washington Street, Boston, the noted grocers.

AUSTIN GOVE & SON, Dealers in Coal, Wood, Naval, Lime, Cement, Bricks, Etc., No. 314 Border Street, Central Square, East Boston.—One of the most important business enterprises in East Boston is that of Messrs. Austin Gove & Son, the widely and favorably known dealers in all the best brands of Anthracite and Bituminous coal, wood, and masons' and contractors' supplies. The business was founded in 1851 by the late Mr. Austin Gove, and who five years afterward admitted his son, Mr. Wesley A. Gove into copartnership under the existing firm name and style. The lamented decease of Mr. Austin Gove occurred in 1885, after a long and highly creditable mercantile career. Since then Mr. W. A. Gove has ably carried on the business upon the old basis of integrity and liberality and with every possible facility at command for the supply of his large and growing trade. His yards and office are most centrally located on Border Street at Central Square, and the area for storage is 30,000 feet in dimensions, with the best dock facilities in the harbor for steam craft to coal and water. Mr. Gove does the largest coal and coaling business in East Boston, and supplies the steamers, Pacific, etc...

JAMES A. COOK, Hardware, Paper Hangings, Cutlery, Carpenters' Tools, Window Glass, Paints, Oils, Drain Pipe, Etc., No. 207 Broadway, South Boston.—In reviewing the various mercantile enterprises which give this great business thorough...

EDWARD S. GILMORE & CO., Flour Dealers and Grocers, No. 29 Main Street, Charlestown District and Nos. 298 and 298 Broadway, South Boston.—Among Boston's successful and enterprising merchants is Mr. Edward S. Gilmore...

THOMAS DOANE, Civil Engineer and Surveyor, Consulting Engineer, No. 21 City Square, Charlestown.—Mr. Doane was born at Cape Cod, Mass., and after having received an excellent scientific education commenced the practice of his profession as a civil engineer, etc., in Boston in 1847...

JAMES G. ALLBE, Steam Job Printer, No. 18 Main Street, Thompson Square.—Prominent among the job printing establishments which has always maintained an excellent reputation for first-class work is that of Mr. James G. Allbe, of No. 18 Main Street, Thompson Square...

PARKER BROTHERS. Fans, Fancy Goods, Jewelry, Toys, Silver-plated Ware, Pocket-books and Albums, etc., No. 177 Tremont Street.—In tracing the rise and progress of the toy and fancy goods trade in Boston, it is noticeable how steadily, prominently and successfully the eminent house of Messrs. Parker Brothers, at No. 177 Tremont Street, directly opposite Park Street Church, has maintained the lead in the van of progress, and largely contributed to the development of the tastes of the public for the richest and most beautiful productions of the world in fancy-goods, jewelry, toys, fans, silver-plated ware, pocket-books, and kindred articles. The business was originally established in 1872, by Messrs. J. B. Parker & Co., who were succeeded by the present firm in 1875. . . .

E. C. WELCH, Merchant Tailor, Clothier, Gentlemen's Furnisher, etc., No. 1 Winthrop Block, East Boston. Merchant tailoring forms an important branch of industry in East Boston, and it is a line of trade which requires great skill and tact to win success in. . . .

A. McLAREN, Carpenter and Builder, Nos. 193 Border and 194 Liverpool Streets, East Boston.—Prominent among the most active members of the building trade in East Boston is Mr. A. McLaren. . . .

ASPINWALL & LINCOLN, Civil Engineers, No. 12 Pearl Street.—The firm of Aspinwall & Lincoln, at No. 12 Pearl Street, are deservedly prominent and popular as civil engineers of large experience and thorough training, who make a leading specialty of landscape engineering, water supply and drainage, development of real estate for building purposes, and general surveying. They established themselves in the practice of their profession in 1877, and are constantly engaged upon large and important commissions in this city and throughout New England. . . .

WESCOTT BROTHERS, Hardware, Cutlery and Tools, No. 159 Meridian Street, East Boston.—Another important branch of commercial enterprise, which is prosecuted with vigor and success in East Boston, is the trade in hardware, cutlery, and tools, and it is one in which many excellent concerns are prosperously engaged. Among the principal of these is that of Messrs. Wescott Brothers, whose establishment is centrally and eligibly located at No. 159 Meridian Street. . . .

S, G. BOWDLEAR & CO., Dealers in Flour, Small Grains and Fancy Breadstuffs, No. 194 State and No. 45, Commerce Streets.

CHARLES A. SMITH & CO., Importers of Fine Woolens, Merchant Tailors, Nos. 16 and 20 School Street.

THE BOSTON FRATERNAL ACCIDENT ASSOCIATION — George X. McKay, President; Henry A. Bates, Secretary and General Manager; Home Office, No. 165 Tremont Street.

PIERCE STEAM-HEATING COMPANY, Manufacturers of Steam and Water Heating Apparatus. Works and General Offices, Buffalo, N. Y.; Boston Office, No. 61 Oliver Street.—The most advanced, perfect, and economical methods of heating houses are those controlled by the famous Pierce Steam Heating Company, of Buffalo, N. Y., and which, in view of the growing demand in New England for its apparatus, opened a Boston office in February, 1891, at No. 61 Oliver Street, and also a warehouse 40x100 feet on Sharper Street, South Boston, and which under the able and enterprising management of Mr. J. A. Gendrich, an expert in the line, has become the centre of a large and growing trade. Mr. J. B. Pierce is the inventor of radical improvements in automatic steam heating

furnaces and the radiators for perfect diffusion of the heat. In fact, the greatest engineering experts have pronounced his "Peerless" direct steam radiator, his "Excelsior" indirect steam radiator, and the famous "Ideal" direct steam radiator (patents d on April 3, 1891), to be the best adaptation of the laws of steam engineering to secure the utmost radiation of heat with no trouble from condensation, while they occupy small space, and are of best materials tested up to 100 lbs. pressure. All sections being duplicates, any part can be readily replaced, while the connecting joints are all threaded, no packing or bolts being required. The company has introduced its radiators into the finest public and private buildings all over the United States, while its "Excelsior" self-feeding steam heater is equally popular. Its magazine is surrounded by water, and the heater combines all the principles required in a durable, efficient, and economical self-feeding boiler for steam-heating purposes. The company also make the J. B. Pierce Surface-burning Boiler, and the Direct-draft Boiler; also a line of the most perfect and efficient water-heating apparatus. Mr. Gendrich will be pleased to send his competitor's descriptive catalogue and long list of references to all jobbers, steam fitters, and private parties, who can thus secure an adequate idea of the importance of using the Excelsior heater and these improved radiators. The workmanship is of the very best character, while the prices are reasonable, and a favorable discount is allowed the trade. The Pierce Steam-Heating Company's works are the largest of the kind in the United States, fully two acres being under their roof, and thus forming one of Buffalo's most important industries. Mr. Gendrich is a popular and respected young business man, and in this cold climate has a certainty of developing a business of great and growing magnitude in the near future.

GEO. LOWNSBRO, Carriage Builder, No. 171 Border Street, East Boston.—This establishment was founded upwards of twenty years ago, Mr. Lownsbro succeeding to the business in 1878, associating with him Mr. A. Brearley under the firm style Lownsbro & Brearley. In 1889 the firm dissolved partnership since which time Mr. George Lownsbro has continued the business alone with that increasing success which has always been the characteristic of this concern from its inception. The manufactory comprises one floor, which has a capacity of 50x100 feet, and is equipped with the

best modern mechanical appliances known to the trade, while employment to two hands, skilled and experienced in their trade, are to put superior service. The manufacture consists of wagons, carriages, sleighs, and teams of every description, and finished in the highest style of the art of carriage-building. A special department is provided for repairing and repainting fine carriages, which is always done under the immediate supervision of the proprietor, satisfaction being always guaranteed. Mr. Lownsbro controls a large and growing trade. Mr. Lownsbro has spent the greater portion of his life in East Boston, and is a pushing, vigorous, upright man of business.

M. L. MANCE & CO., Commission Merchants, Dry Goods, Gloves, etc., No. 18 Kingston Street.—Among the most active and enterprising firms engaged in the commission trade in this city will be found Messrs. M. L. Mance & Co., commission dealers in dry and fancy goods, comprising foreign and domestic silks, velvets, ribbons, and kid gloves, etc., at No. 18 Kingston Street. Messrs. M. L. Mance and W. V. Judkins, comprising the firm, are vigorous young business men, of wide experience in, and possessing a thorough knowledge of, the commission dry-goods trade. They embarked in the present enterprise in 1892, January 1st, and by active and able management have already built up a large, prosperous, and fast-growing business. The attractive and conveniently arranged salesroom contains a full sample stock of the goods above enumerated, the assortment embracing the best productions in the several lines; and the trade, reaching throughout New England, including a large city patronage, is of most prosperous annual volume. Messrs. Mance and Judkins are highly respected in trade circles for their sterling business integrity, ability, and enterprise, and they are fast attaining a position in the front rank of merchants in their line.

MISS M. F. FISK, Glove Store, No. 54 West Street.—In 1874 the proprietor of this well-known and reliable glove establishment started in business for herself on Temple Place, where she carried on the enterprise until 1887, and in that year removed to her present eligibly located quarters on West Street. Miss Fisk is a wide-awake and energetic business woman of long experience, and her mercantile venture was a pronounced success from its inception. The premises occupied are 20x50 feet in dimensions, and not only well arranged, but elegantly fitted up for the comfort of patrons and the best possible display of the stock carried. A specialty is made of ladies', gentlemen's, and children's gloves of every style and size, and selections made from the assortment to be seen on counters and in show cases cannot fail to give satisfaction to the most critical taste. A large stock of the latest novelties is always on hand, and a force of six polite and experienced assistants is employed to receive and satisfy the orders of patrons. Miss Fisk is indisputably regarded as one of the leaders in this particular line of trade, and caters to the best families in the city. She is a native of Boston, and a highly respected member of the community.

BENJ. HADLEY & SONS, Milk Can Manufacturers and Dealers in Ranges, Stoves, etc., No. 361 Main Street, Charlestown.—In this sketch the attention of the reader is directed to the prominent establishment of Messrs. Benjamin Hadley & Sons, milk-can manufacturers, and dealers in ranges, stoves, etc. The premises consist of two floors, each 25x50 feet in dimensions, neatly fitted up and admirably arranged. Here is displayed a splendid assortment of milk-cans, sterled and stoppled, in all sizes; and ranges, stoves, and furnaces comprising all the most modern improvements. The premises are spacious and thoroughly equipped with all necessary machinery and tools for expeditious and rapid manufacture of tin and other sheet-metal ware. The firm makes a specialty of manufacturing milk-cans in all sizes, and these find a brisk and extensive sale all over the New England States. A competent staff of workmen find constant employment. This is the oldest house in this business, which was organized in 1856 by the senior member of the firm, Mr. Benjamin Hadley, who, in 1881, admitted into partnership his two sons, W. B. and G. F. Hadley. All the members of the firm are natives of East Lexington, and are well known in commercial circles as energetic and honorable business men. The telephone call is "No. 161-4."

THE S. S. WHITE DENTAL MANUFACTURING COMPANY, John F. Davis, Manager, No. 160 Tremont Street.—The progress in dental science is one of the most gratifying features of this progressive age, and the brilliant results achieved are largely due to the marked enterprise and energy of the famous S. S. White Dental Manufacturing Company, of Philadelphia, Boston, New York, and Chicago. This is the leading producer of full lines of dental goods, instruments, and equipment in the world, and has made such rapid, substantial progress as to far outstrip all other manufacturers, and practically leave it without a competitor. The business was founded at Philadelphia in 1844 by the late Dr. Samuel S. White. He was an inventor and originator of marked ability and enterprise, and, to all intents and purposes, revolutionized the trade in a large class of the appliances and materials of modern dentistry. During a long life and an active career, he continued to shape the policy and guide the operations of the great corporation that bears his name; and upon his decease, in 1879, the estate continued in active management until 1881, when the present company was organized with the following executive officers: Dr. James W. White, president; Mr. J. Clarence White, secretary; Mr. Henry M. Lewis, general manager, and Mr. Samuel T. Jones, treasurer. A more representative and experienced body of officers could not be brought together in this intricate branch of trade. The headquarters are in Philadelphia, where is located an immense factory, fitted up at enormous cost, with a complete equipment of special tools and machinery; a second large factory is situated on Staten Island, N. Y.; while the wholesale depots are located in New York, Philadelphia, Boston, and Chicago. It is also directly represented in London, England; Paris, France; St. Petersburg, Russia; Berlin, Germany, etc., etc. Boston has the honor of being the oldest centre of the business, the first store for the sale of the S. S. White dental goods having been opened here. It has had frequent enlargements, and eight years ago was removed to its present site, No. 160 Tremont Street. It is 30 feet by 125 feet in dimensions, and most elegantly fitted up, and carries a complete stock of the thousands of articles and specialties covered by the comprehensive catalogue of this enterprising company. Here are the most improved and richly upholstered dental chairs; electric motors of wonderful speed; all instruments for extraction, filling, cleaning, etc.; all tools and equipments for the manufacture of sets of teeth; artificial teeth of the most perfect character; gold, silver, and other materials, etc. This is headquarters for the dental profession of New England; and in this branch of surgery there are no members thereof who do not use more or less of the S. S. White Dental Manufacturing Company's goods. The company is by far the largest manufacturer of its kind, and sells fully seven eighths of the goods in use throughout the world. Mr. John F. Davis, the accomplished and experienced manager of the Boston establishment, was born in Boston, Mass., and has been permanently identified with the company for twenty years past. Progressive and enterprising, he is also thoroughly experienced, and is universally popular and respected, a worthy and successful representative of this grand American company, which controls the world's trade in dental appliances, covering Europe, Asia, Australia, America, and the civilized portions of Africa.

S. C. BIXBY, Agent for Choicest India Pale, Stock, and Cream Ales and Porter, in Hogsheads, Barrels, Halves, and Quarters, No. 114 Broad Street.—The leading agency for choicest India pale, stock, and cream ales and porter in this city is that so long and so successfully conducted by Mr. S. C. Bixby, of No. 114 Broad Street. This gentleman is deservedly prominent and popular as the New England Agent for the Highland Spring Ale Brewery, and the John R. Alley Ale Brewery of this city, which position he has filled in the trade for the past thirty years, and in 1871 he organized the National Sanitary Association, for the manufacture of Carbolic Disinfecting Powder, the best deodorizer known, and of which he is now sole proprietor. As agent for the finest grades and qualities of India pale, stock, and cream ales and porter, Mr. Bixby is in a position to supply dealers, families, and all classes of consumers throughout New England with these goods to the full extent of their wants, in hogsheads, barrels, halves, and quarters, as may be desired, rigid and special care being given to family trade. Every facility is possessed for the prompt fulfilment of orders of any size, and every article sold is guaranteed to be strictly pure, and free from all adulteration of any kind. The ales handled are pronounced by physicians to be highly beneficial for invalids or for persons with debilitated systems, who need building up. A trial is sufficient to prove their efficacy and excellence. The Carbolic Disinfecting Powder supplied by Mr. Bixby has become widely noted for its deodorizing qualities, and is in large and steadily increasing demand among jobbers, grocers, and druggists everywhere, practically supplanting all similar productions where once introduced and tested. It is a cheap and valuable article, and is in use by all who have investigated its merits, as being the very best deodorizer extant. Mr. Bixby, the talented proprietor of this enterprise, is a native Bostonian, and one of its best known citizens.

JOHN WALKER & CO., Manufacturers of and Dealers in Boot and Shoe Machinery, Duplicate Parts and Findings, Engines, Boilers, Shafting, Elevators, etc., No. 118 South Street.—In the manufacture of boots and shoe machinery the firm of John Walker & Co. occupy a position of prominence, and have become widely known throughout New England for the superiority of the various machines turned out. Mr. John Walker, the head of the firm, and upon whom devolves the general management of the business, has been identified with this special line of manufacture for some years, and from 1874 to 1880 was a member of the firm of Fifield, Walker & Co., and, the three following years, of Eddy, Walker & Co., and in 1883 organized the present firm, and has since continued the business on an extensive scale. The premises occupied, at No. 118 South Street, are commodious, and consist of two floors, each 25x75 feet in area, which are used as workshop, and office, and salesroom. Throughout the establishment is well equipped and complete in every respect, the special machinery and appliances being of the latest improved design, operated by steam power. On an average, from eight to ten expert workmen are employed, and every attention is given to the manufacture of all kinds of boot and shoe machinery, and also repairing, pegging, wax-thread, eyelet and crimping skiving machines, and boot and shoe machinery generally. In the salesrooms a great variety of this class of machinery is displayed, and also duplicate parts and findings, and a large business is also done in steam engines, boilers, shafting, elevators, etc. In every respect, this house may be regarded as a representative one, and is prompt, liberal, and enterprising to a marked degree. Mr. John Walker, its head and founder, is a gentleman about fifty-five years of age, a practical machinist of undoubted ability, and can always offer the best inducements to manufacturers and quote satisfactory prices.

CHAMBERLAIN BROS. & SON, Receivers of Chicago Dressed Beef, etc., Nos. 115 to 119 Clinton Street.—In no feature of business progress has enterprise been displayed to such purpose of late years as in the construction and application of appliances and devices for preserving fresh meat. At the present day, we have meat, killed and dressed, direct from the great western ranches, placed upon our markets, without having in the remotest degree lost its freshness, flavor or quality in transportation. Indeed, it possesses important advantages over home-killed stock, in that the cattle have not suffered from weeks of overcrowding and stifling in the cars during transit eastward. In this connection, special attention is directed, in this commercial review of Boston, to the old-established and reliable firm of Messrs. Chamberlain Bros. & Son. This business was established, a quarter of a century ago, by Messrs. N. and G. D. Chamberlain, who conducted it till 1871, when Mr. W. N. Chamberlain was admitted, the firm being known by the style and title of "Chamberlain Bros. & Co." The firm are large receivers of Nelson Morris & Co.'s Chicago dressed beef, rolls, loins, strips, shoulders, and tongues; also Brighton dressed mutton and lamb. The premises occupied are spacious, and are fitted up with every appliance and facility for the successful prosecution of this steadily growing business. The firm receive the beef in car-load lots, and carry on a strictly wholesale business, and their trade now extends throughout all sections of Boston and its vicinity. All orders are promptly filled at the lowest ruling market prices, and the quality of the beef handled is unrivalled for quality and excellence. Messrs. N. and G. D. Chamberlain are natives of Westboro, Mass., while Mr. W. N. Chamberlain was born in Framingham, Mass. In all transactions they will be found liberal and just, and those interested entering into business relations with them will obtain advantages very difficult to be secured elsewhere.

F. W. HUNT & CO., Importers and Wholesale Liquor Dealers, No. 5 India Street. —The consumption of wines and liquors in the United States is so vast, that the trade necessarily involves considerations of the greatest importance. Among the most reliable and best-known houses engaged in the wholesale branch of this trade in Boston is that of Messrs. F. W. Hunt & Co., located at No. 5 India Street, opposite the Custom House. This firm are widely prominent as extensive importers and wholesale liquor-dealers, making a leading specialty of fine goods, and have been established in the business here since 1867. Their success as merchants promote a striking illustration of what may be accomplished by a steady application to business, and a just and honorable course of dealing. The business premises comprise four floors 25 by 75 feet each, admirably equipped with every modern convenience and facility for the accommodation and preservation of the choice and valuable stock.

I. ISAAC T. CAMPBELL, Apothecary, No. 89 West Broadway, South Boston.—Considering the great number of mishaps that have taken place and are constantly occurring through carelessness, and want of experience in compounding prescriptions and medicines, too much care cannot be exercised in the selection of an apothecary whose high character of the management of his business renders such mistakes impossible. A house of that description is that of Mr. Isaac T. Campbell at No. 89 West Broadway, in South Boston, which is well known to the entire community, as it is the oldest of the kind in this portion of the city, and bears a reputation second to no other house in the same line of business throughout Boston.

D. O. ALDEN & CO., Trimmings and Small Wares, Laces, Buttons, Corsets, Hosiery, Yarns, Embroideries and Materials for Art Needle-work, Stamping and Designing, etc., No. 31 Winter Street. —Among the well-conducted mercantile establishments which buy this great trade avenue and can tribute to the commercial wealth and importance of the metropolis will be found the well-known house of Messrs. D. O. Alden & Co., dealers in trimmings, laces, corsets, hosiery, worsteds, yarns, embroideries, and small wares, at No. 31 Winter Street.

W. WILLIAM EDSON, Expert in Patent Causes, No. 19 Pearl Street. —One of the most expert and successful solicitors of patents, and counsellors in patent causes in Boston is Mr. William Edson. This gentleman has been established in the practice of his profession here for full thirty years, and enjoys a large and influential patronage, not only in all parts of the United States, but throughout Canada and Europe.

A. P. SMITH & CO., New England Agents for Bovinine, Hak-ka Cream, and Ouidiler. No. 149 Pearl Street. — Among the most valuable of the curative agents now prominently before the public, are the three articles mentioned in the caption to this sketch, viz., Hak-ka Cream, Bovinine, and Ouidiler. [...]

N. D. WHITNEY & CO, Importers and Wholesale and Retail Dealers in Berlin Zephyr and Knitting Worsteds, Threads, Yarns, Hosiery, Gloves, Hand-knit Goods, etc., No. 149 Tremont Street, Corner of Winter — Messrs. N. D. Whitney & Co. conduct one of the oldest-established businesses of its kind in the city of Boston, and one which has ever maintained the highest standard of excellence in all departments. [...]

FULLER & RENSE, Ladies' Custom Boots, No. 99 Winter Street, Room 2. — Perhaps in no article of male or female wear has there been noticed such marked improvement of late years in this country as in boots and shoes. [...]

A MOS E. HALL, Insurance Agent, No. 81 Milk Street, Room 4⁰. — Prominent among the leading representatives of fire insurance in this city stands Mr. A. E. Hall, whose office is eligibly located at No. 81 Milk Street. This gentleman is a well-known citizen and insurance agent, and besides the above office also has one at Nos. 618 and 646 Broadway, Chelsea, and another on Titsworth Street, Everett, and conducts an extensive business in Boston and vicinity. He has been established in business since 1869, and has met with marked success, representing solid and honorably managed companies that afford every safeguard to policy-holders and invariably meet promptly all claims. His business has grown to proportions of great magnitude and importance. No agent in Chelsea offers the choice of companies that he does, as he represents the following powerful and reliable corporations, viz.: the Niagara, the Commercial Union, the Rowary, and the Westchester, of New York; the Fireman's Fund, of California; the Citizens, of Pittsburg, Pa.; the Merchants', of Newark; the Lumbermen's, of Philadelphia; the Abington Mutual, of Abington, Mass.; the Fitchburg Mutual, of Fitchburg, Mass.; the Worcester Mutual, of Worcester, Mass.; and some fifteen more A1 companies, both stock and mutual. This is a list rarely equalled by any agency, and clearly demonstrates the high standing achieved by Mr. Hall in insurance circles. His facilities for conducting an insurance brokerage business in this city are such as can apply only to those who are prominent as underwriters and who enjoy the entire confidence both of insurance corporations and the general public. His policies are clear and explicit, his rates will be found the lowest for adequate security, and all losses are promptly paid as soon as adjusted. Mr. Hall controls the insuring of many of the finest lines of business and residential property in Boston and its suburban towns, as also large stocks of merchandise and much valuable personal property, and is doing an annually increasing business. He is widely recognized as an underwriter of commanding ability, influential faculties, and vast experience, having a thorough personal knowledge of all risks of any importance in this city, and is eminently popular with all classes of property-holders. Mr. Hall is a Vermonter by birth, a resident of Chelsea for twenty-two years, and a prominent member of the Chelsea Board of Underwriters (having been President of that Board since its organization); still in the prime of life, and highly esteemed in social, business, and financial circles.

M ASSACHUSETTS AUXILIARY FIRE-ALARM COMPANY, No. 175 Devonshire Street. Geo. E. Hitchcock, President; Jas. E. Leach, Treasurer; G. W. Daniels, General Manager. — This reliable and representative company was duly incorporated in 1887, under the laws of Maine, with a paid up capital of $200,000. It was organized for the purpose of introducing the Rogers System of Auxiliary Fire-alarm, which has received the approval of the Fire Department of the city of Boston and the Board of Underwriters. This auxiliary is the only system which has ever been allowed a direct connection with the fire alarm boxes, and is now in practical operation in Boston and many other cities. The company owns the patent rights for the state of Massachusetts, except the city of Boston, comprising upwards of 40 cities, which have now established a system of electric Fire-alarms, to which this is a very important auxiliary. This new system, which is very simple and comparatively inexpensive, where in no way interfering with the fire-alarm telegraph as now constructed, vastly increases its efficiency and value, by making each street-box now in use a central station, around which any number of buildings can be connected, so that from any of them the box can be instantly operated without going to it, by pressing an ordinary push-button, the latter being properly protected by glass which can be easily broken, or by weak or keys. Wherever the Rogers Auxiliary Alarm is in use, fifteen seconds only need elapse between the discovery of a fire and the departure of the engines from their houses to extinguish it. The Board of Underwriters has granted a reduction in the rates of insurance on buildings equipped with the Rogers Auxiliary System, which reduction is sufficient in many cases to defray its entire annual cost. The instruments system is installed, maintained, and inspected by the company at a very moderate annual rental. In public schools, hotels, theatres, etc., it is invaluable. Mr. Geo. E. Hitchcock, the president, has been City Treasurer of Malden, Mass., for the last seventeen years, and still occupies that position and is highly esteemed by all who have had business relations with him.

W GANZHORN, Dress and Cloak Maker, No. 179 Tremont Street. — In this progressive age the gentler sex have caught up with their brothers, at least in the fashioning of their apparel, and the term "ladies' tailor" is fast superseding the old-time "dress-maker." In this cultured and advanced city ladies' tailoring is extensively carried on, one of the popular exponents being Mr. W. Ganzhorn, whose fine establishment is eligibly located at No. 179 Tremont Street. Mr. Ganzhorn is a native of Germany, where he early learned and became an expert at the gentlemen's tailoring trade. Coming subsequently to Boston, he established in 1881 a business in this line at No. 21 West Street. In 1878 he sold out and spent the following two years in acquiring a thorough knowledge of ladies' tailoring. Having perfected himself in this modern art, he established in 1884 at the present site with a copartner, the firm being Ganzhorn & Bowire. In June, 1888, the copartnership was dissolved, and Mr. Ganzhorn has since been alone. The spacious premises are conveniently arranged, and fitted up in a style of modern elegance. In the salesroom is shown a superior line of fabrics, also patterns and models of costumes, wraps, etc., from which customers may choose, and in the workroom a competent force of experienced hands is kept busy in executing the many orders of the house. Mr. Ganzhorn has won an enviable reputation through the high artistic and mechanical excellence of his work, and among his many patrons representing the best city custom he is regarded as one of the most skilful city exponents of his art.

J B. CONANT & CO., Ship Brokers, No. 103 State Street. — A leading and energetic representative of the ship brokerage business is the old established house of Messrs. J. B. Conant & Co. The business was founded upwards of 20 years ago by Messrs. Kellam, Lord & Co., succeeded by Messrs. Conant & Fisteh. In 1876, Mr. Conant formed the present firm, and has largely developed the business upon the basis of equity, efficiency, and widespread, influential connections. Mr. Conant brings to bear a wide range of practical experience, and is a recognized authority in the maritime market, having a thorough knowledge of the wants of commerce, and affording the utmost facilities for the chartering of any amount of tonnage for every class of freight to any quarter of the globe. Messrs. Conant & Co. are ship owners as well as brokers, their interests being of a practical character, they offer every opportunity for charters, on the most favorable terms, of the best class of vessels, for long or short voyages, coastwise or "deep water." The firm number among their customers many of the most prominent commercial houses of Boston, vessel owners, consignees, etc., and are popular in mercantile and marine circles as honorable, responsible representatives of this most important branch of trade. Mr. Conant was born in Maine, and has from his first connection with active commercial life been connected with the ship-brokerage business. He is a popular member of the Vessel Owners' Association, and is materially contributing to Boston's prosperity.

R AND & STINEHART, Steam Job Printers, No. 5 Main Street, Charlestown. — A time-honored Charlestown printing establishment is the well known and popular concern conducted under the firm name of Rand & Stinehart, steam job-printers, at No. 5 Main Street, and which for nearly half a century has been in progressive operation. It is, in fact, one of the oldest and best-equipped establishments of the kind in the Bunker Hill District, and receives an excellent patronage. This thriving business was originally established in 1840 by Caleb Rand (deceased), who conducted the same alone up to some three years ago, when he admitted into partnership William H. Stinehart, who upon the death of the senior member, which occurred in September 1887, assumed sole control, but has still continued under the style of Rand & Stinehart. The quarters occupied for business purposes are ample and well ordered, a gas motor furnishing steam power, while several experienced workmen are regularly employed. Job printing in all its branches is executed in the most prompt and superior manner, special attention being given to fine commercial work, and altogether a very nice trade is done. Mr. Stinehart, who is a gentleman of forty-two, was born in New York State, but has resided in Charlestown since infancy. He is a thoroughly practical and expert printer, with long and varied experience in the exercise of his art, and prior to being admitted to the firm had worked for Mr. Rand since 1869.

M. STEINERT & SONS, Wholesale and Retail Representatives, in the New England States, for Steinway & Sons, Weber, Hardman & Peck, and Gabler & Bro. Pianos, Steinert Hall, No. 160 Tremont Street, Corner Boylston.—A widely known and reliable firm in Boston, successfully engaged in the wholesale and retail piano trade, is that of Messrs. M. Steinert & Sons, whose warerooms are centrally located at Steinert Hall, corner of Tremont and Boylston Streets. This business was originally established twenty years ago in New Haven, by Mr. M. Steinert, who eventually admitted six of his sons in the partnership, the firm being

known by the style and title of M. Steinert & Sons. The firm have, in addition to the Boston house, extensive establishments in Providence, R. I.; Newport, R. I.; New Haven, Conn.; and Cincinnati, O. They are wholesale and retail representatives, for the New England and western states, for the celebrated piano manufacturers Steinway & Sons, A. Weber, Hardman & Peck, and E. Gabler & Bro. The well known and world-wide reputation of the instruments manufactured by these firms has demonstrated beyond question that they are absolutely unsurpassed in America or Europe for tone, finish, style, and workmanship. M. Steinert & Sons carry a full assortment of the different styles of these pianos, making, in all, the largest variety of first-class pianos to be found anywhere in the world. All the members of this firm are practical piano makers and musicians, insuring their patrons thereby of the choicest selection to be found. Pianos in fancy woods are made a specialty. Mahogany, Oak, English Oak, French Walnut, Hungarian Ash, Bird's-eye and Curly Maple, Rosewood and Ebonized cases, are kept continually on hand. The characteristics which regulate the business policy of this responsible firm are such as to entitle it to every consideration, and the extent of its operations has made it a very prominent one in New England, while the inducements offered to purchasers are unsurpassed by those of any other similar establishment in this country.

BILLINGS, CLAPP & CO., Manufacturing Chemists, Nos. 165 and 167 High Street (Fort Hill Square).—One of the leading representative firms of manufacturing chemists in the United States is that of Messrs. Billings, Clapp & Co. It is also one of the oldest established, having been founded in 1857, and ever since has maintained the most enviable of reputations for the superiority of its products and ability and equity of its methods. Messrs. James R. Nichols & Co. carried on the business up to 1872, when the establishment, then at No. 130 Congress Street was destroyed in the great fire. Mr. Charles E. Billings and Mr. A. B. Clapp, who were his partners then, succeeded to the proprietorship, thus continuing until 1890, when Mr. H. S. Sears was admitted under the existing name and style of Billings, Clapp & Co. The house has achieved international celebrity for the accuracy, strength, and purity of its standard pharmaceutical preparations, fluid extracts, medicinal wines and syrups, etc., and they are prescribed generally by the medical profession. The proprietors are both, by reason of vast experience and their high order of professional attainments, thoroughly qualified for meeting the exacting requirements of the medical profession. They are excellent business men and are noted for the close care and scrutiny exercised in the selection of the drugs, roots, herbs, barks, chemicals, etc., entering into the vast list of the preparations they supply, and which covers every branch of the materia medica. The firm now occupy for their main office and warehouse in the city a fine four-story-and-basement building centrally located on High Street. It is admirably fitted up in every way for the purposes of the heavy trade transacted, and a thorough system of organization is enforced. Here are carried, and will always be found by the trade, the most comprehensive line of fluid extracts to be found in the United States, representing thousands of items, and constantly being added to; full line of elixirs added, as the profession demands, and put up in the most attractive and palatable manner, without sacrificing their remedial qualities to elegance of appearance and taste. All standard medicinal syrups, wines, and a lengthy list of specialties are obtainable here. Another important department is that devoted to chemicals, etc., both complete and of prices and quality that offer substantial inducements to the trade. The proprietors of this highly important concern, that ensures to Boston equal prominence to that of New York and Philadelphia in the pharmaceutical trade at wholesale, are universally respected, and have ever retained the confidence of leading commercial circles. They are types of the self-made, intelligent, and cultured New England business men, and are worthy of the marked appreciation manifested and material patronage accorded by the pharmacists and physicians of the United States and Canada.

RICHARDSON & DENNIE, Importers of Hides and Skins, Nos. 165 to 169 Congress Street.—Boston is the centre of the American trade in hides and skins of all kinds, and especially so for foreign importations. The house of Messrs. Richardson & Dennie has in this connection attained a leading representative position, and has manifested marked enterprise and energy. The business is very old-established, having been founded in 1826 by the old house of Messrs. Dennie & Boardman, succeeded by Messrs. Boardman & Co., and, in 1874, by the present firm, composed of Mr. Thomas O. Richardson and Mr. Edward M. Dennie. Both gentlemen bring to bear the widest range of practical experience, coupled with special facilities and influential connections. Mr. Richardson was born near Boston, and early in life became identified with this branch of commerce, and has been actively connected with this house for thirty-three years past, since 1861 being a copartner thereof. He is possessed of special qualifications, and is a recognized authority in regard to hides and skins. Mr. Edward M. Dennie was born in Boston, and is a nephew of the founder of the house, connected with the house for thirty-five years past, and a member of the firm since 1861. The firm's premises comprise three floors and basement 80x165 feet in dimensions, where is carried the most desirable and comprehensive stock in town. The firm are direct importers of hides and goat-skins from the East Indies, South America, etc., making a specialty of the finest India tanned skins, and doing a business of enormous magnitude, importing direct by the cargo, and selling to the trade of the United States to the annual value of from one to one and a half millions of dollars. The leading tanners and morocco manufacturers of New England and the Middle States are numbered among their customers, and the house is in every respect thoroughly representative of this branch of American commerce. Both partners are prominent in financial and social circles, and are worthy exponents of this branch of business, well know throughout New England for their sterling and honorable methods.

S. K. ABBOTT & CO., Pamphlet and School Book-binders, No. 18 Federal Street.—A leading representative of the American book-binding trade is the old established and famous house of Messrs. S. K. Abbott & Co., of No. 18 Federal Street. The business was founded over forty-two years ago by Mr. Jno. H. Abbott, brother of the present proprietor, who joined him thirty years ago, and succeeded him five years after. Mr. Abbott is a native of Massachusetts, and early in life learned thoroughly in detail the book-binder's art. The business as stated was originally started by Mr. John H. Abbott, and to show the progress and improvements made by the present enterprising proprietor, but heads are now employed, where the business was started with three girls, and one-half acre of ground is monopolized now by the house. The extent of the operations and facilities of this house are shown by the fact that an order has been recently delivered by this firm of 4,000,000 pamphlets, which shows what energy, enterprise, and honorable dealing can accomplish from the small beginning of forty years ago. Mr. Abbott early manifested a progressive policy after starting in business on his own account, and introduced numerous facilities and improvements in the departments of school book and pamphlet binding. His work was of such a superior order and accurate character, that he became celebrated as the leader in his line, and, devoting himself solely to these branches of book binding, has permanently maintained the supremacy therein. His facilities have repeatedly been taxed to the utmost, necessitating enlargements and introduction of new machinery, and his bindery is to-day one of the largest on the continent, comprising two large floors 60x100 in size, equipped in all respects to secure prompt despatch and the best work. Mr. Abbott devotes his special attention to pamphlet and school-book binding, his facilities being no equal for these branches of work elsewhere, while publishers duly appreciate the equitable reputation of this establishment for accuracy and promptness, and that the prices for good work cannot be duplicated by other concerns. Mr. Abbott does work for all the leading publishers and printers of Boston and New England, and employs an average force of 150 hands. He gives close personal attention to all orders, and his concern affords convincing evidence of the truth of Mr. Abbott's popular motto, that "industry must prosper." He is a popular and respected member of mercantile circles, and secures to Boston a business of exceptional value and importance.

L. LELAND, RICE & CO., Men's and Boys' Clothing, No. 101 Arch Street.—No industrial interest of the City of Boston is of more importance than that of the manufacture of clothing. Among the old established and representative houses actively engaged in this steadily growing trade, a prominent one is that of Messrs. Leland, Rice & Co, manufacturers of men's and boys' clothing, whose office and salesrooms are situated at No. 101 Arch Street. This business was established in 1848, by Gove, Stone & Co., Mr. J. D. Leland being the junior partner. In 1849, they were succeeded by John Gove & Co., Mr. Leland being still of the firm. Eventually in 1861 the present style and title of Leland, Rice & Co. was adopted, the copartners being Messrs. J. D. Leland and M. O. Rice. In 1878 Mr. W. G. Hayward became a member of the firm. The partners have had great experience, and manifest excellent judgment in the selection of all cloths and suitings entering their establishment, while at the same time they are always among the first to secure and make up all the new styles and textures of both domestic and foreign production. They give careful attention to all the details of manufacture, and employ outside and inside a strong force of skilled operatives. The secret of their success lies in their just methods and the superiority of their clothing, which is always maintained at the highest standard both as regards materials, cut, style, fit, and workmanship, while the prices quoted are so low, as those of any other first-class contemporary house in the trade. The premises occupied comprise five spacious floors, which are fitted with every appliance and facility, necessary for the systematic and successful conduct of the business. The trade of the house extends throughout all sections of the eastern states, New England and the middle and western states. Messrs. Leland & Rice are natives of Massachusetts, while Mr. Hayward was born in Maine. Mr. Leland has been a member of this house for the last 35 years, and Mr. Rice for 15 years. They are noted in business circles for their promptness and integrity, and those who enter into relations with this popular firm can rely upon securing advantages and inducements very difficult to be secured elsewhere.

W. R. THOMPSON & CO., Publishers, No. 33 Hawley Street.—Boston has long been a recognized head-quarters of the book-publishing trade, and a home of literature, a fact which has done incalculable work in bringing her prominently forward as one of the most intelligent communities on the globe. In the course of this review, special mention must needs be made to the leading houses engaged in the publishing, and among these must be numbered that of W. R. Thompson & Co., of No. 33 Hawley street. The proprietors of this establishment, which was founded in 1877, are Messrs. B. F. Whittemore, G. A. Kimball, and H. E. Russell, and are general New England agents for the most notable publishing houses of Hartford, New York, and Philadelphia. Some but standard works are offered to the public, and these are all in bound form, in a variety of styles. Among the most conspicuous of the publications handled have been the " Personal Memoirs of U. S. Grant" and " Personal Memoirs of P. H. Sheridan;" the latter is an intensely interesting work, which has met with very large sales and is still selling rapidly. The firm have sold Mark Twain's works, and also those of other famous writers. The books are sold for cash, this firm having never adopted the instalment plan. All orders or communications sent to this creditable house invariably receive immediate attention, and the advantages offered are of such a nature that they should not be neglected by the reading public. The members of the firm are representatives of three states in New England, Mr. Whittemore having been born in Massachusetts, Mr. Kimball in Rhode Island, and Mr. Russell in New Hampshire. All three are well known in business and social circles, and are held in general esteem for their ability and integrity.

A. ANDREWS & STEVENS, Tremont Market, No. 67 Brumfield Street.—An old established and leading meat and provision firm is that of Andrews & Stevens, whose well-ordered and deservedly popular stand, the "Tremont Market," is admirably located at No. 67 Brumfield Street. This is one of the oldest and foremost establishments of the kind in Boston, being in existence over forty-six years, and has a large, active, and influential patronage. This flourishing business was established in 1846 by Andrews & Ward, and under this style it was conducted up to 1866, when they were succeeded by Andrews & Stevens, who have since continued it at the present central location with uninterrupted success. They handle nothing but prime goods, and patrons can rely upon getting an A 1 article, all orders receiving immediate attention. The market is spacious, cleanly, neatly appointed, and completely equipped in every particular, every convenience and facility being at hand, while efficient assistants are in attendance; and a first-class stock is always kept on hand, comprising choice fresh beef, mutton, lamb, veal, and pork; fine poultry and game in season, also a carefully assorted line of fruits, vegetables, and table delicacies. They were the first to introduce Philadelphia butter into Boston market in 1846. Messrs. Alonzo Andrews and Chas. E. Stevens compose the firm. Mr. Andrews is a native of Hillsborough, N. H. Mr. Stevens is a Bostonian by birth. They are men of thorough practical experience in this line, as well as of entire probity in their dealings, and are well and favorably known alike to their business relations and in private life.

B. F. TENNEY, Stock Broker, No. 19 Congress Street.—There are few men better known or more generally esteemed in financial circles in Boston than Mr. B. F. Tenney, the popular stock broker, of No. 19 Congress Street. Mr. Tenney has been a prominent member of the Boston Stock Exchange for the past twenty-six years, and has also taken a deep interest and an active hand in all matters calculated to improve and strengthen this institution. Before engaging in the handling of stocks and bonds Mr. Tenney was for many years in the dry-goods trade. He was born in Boston, Mass., seventy-five years ago, and is still a hale, active, wide-awake business man, and his long experience in the arena of speculation and his high repute for square and honorable dealing are in themselves a sufficient assurance for faithful service to all who have financial dealings through him. Mr. Tenney buys and sells on commission bonds, stocks, and investment securities of every description, and no one is better able to form a sound judgment upon prospective values, while he has every facility for securing the earliest information of variations in quotations of value of securities on all the principal exchanges of the country. His clients are kept acquainted with all chances of values, and their instructions are faithfully carried out to the letter and prompt accountings made.

J. F. & W. N. FALVEY, Dry Goods, Small Wares, and Gents' Furnishing Goods, Corner Broadway and F Street, South Boston.

HADDOCK, SHONK & CO., Miners of Coal; Wm. C. Atwater, Sole Agent, No. 4 Liberty Square. Corner Kilby and Water Streets.

DANIEL LE BETTER, Storage Warehouse, Central Wharf.

J. W. HOBBS & CO., Importers of Foreign Manganese and Foreign Paints, No. 10 Central Wharf.

ELMER CHICKERING, Photographer, No. 21 West Street.—Not to speak of new processes and modes of manipulation almost constantly coming into vogue, the growth of the beautiful art of photography as a means of producing faithful, and at the same time most picturesque representations of natural objects, and especially of portraits and scenery, is deserving of particular notice. This is clearly shown at the popular art gallery of Mr. Elmer Chickering of No. 21 West Street. Mr. Chickering has been

identified with the photographic art nearly all his life. He started in business on his own account in 1870, and is admittedly the leader in his profession in the city. His premises are commodious and conveniently handsomely fitted up and appointed. Everything necessary for the production of the highest class of work is provided, and the very numerous and beautiful specimens with which the office and reception-rooms are ornamented testify to the high standard of excellence attained. Mr. Chickering shows a thorough mastery of a most difficult art. In all his details he reveals a perception of true artistic effect, and is careful to finish to withstand criticism. In oil, crayon, India ink, and pastel work Mr. Chickering is equally effective and successful, and he is assisted by a skilled and experienced staff of assistants. His patronage is drawn from the best classes of citizens and from the leading families in the suburbs, and the business done is of an extensive character. Mr. Chickering is a native of the city and personally very popular.

BENEDICT & BURNHAM MANUFACTURING COMPANY, Manufacturers of Rolled and Sheet Brass and German Silver, Brass, Copper, German Silver and Insulated Wire, Seamless Brass and Copper Tubes, etc., No. 84 Oliver Street; E. L. Ennis, Agent.—The largest brass and copper works in the world are those of the famous Benedict & Burnham Manufacturing Company, situated at Waterbury, Conn. They enjoy a national reputation as manufacturers of seamless brass and copper tubes, rolled and sheet brass and German silver, brass, copper, German silver and insulated wire, brazed tubing, brass burrs, copper rivets and burrs, drawer pulls, harness, lamp trimmings, etc., and have been established in the business for upwards of fifty years. The company operate an extensive salesroom at No. 84 Oliver Street, in this city, which is under the management of Mr. E. L. Ennis, and is a noted source of supply for the trade and consumers in this line throughout New England and Canada. The works at Waterbury cover a ground area of six acres, and give steady employment to a force of seven hundred workmen, while the output is one of great magnitude and variety. The Boston salesroom comprise two floors, 50x115 feet each, which are stocked to repletion at all times with a complete assortment of the productions of this representative company. The business here has been developed to large and important proportions, heavy sales being constantly made to leading manufacturers and consumers of

brass goods in this city and throughout New England, while indications are offered to patrons, as regards both reliability of goods and diversity of terms and prices. Branch houses are also operated in New York and Philadelphia, and the company persistently maintains the supremacy in its branch of industry in the country, having the advantages of large and ample capital, unequalled facilities for production, a complete understanding of all the needs and requirements of the trade in the different sections of the Union, and expert and loyal representatives to manage its interests in the leading commercial centres.

ALLEN, LANE & CO., Dry goods Commission Merchants, No. 80 Devonshire Street.—No branch of commerce in Boston is of greater importance than the dry goods trade. And it is safe to say that for the capital invested, enterprise and industry manifested, together with fair and honorable methods of dealing, those engaged in it, as a body, excel. In this connection it is our desire to mention to the readers of this volume one of the oldest firms, Allen, Lane & Co., who were at the outset 40 years ago dry-goods jobbers, but for a quarter of a century have been dry-goods commission merchants, and the selling agents of some of the best mills in New England. The firm at present is composed only of Frederick D. Allen and Jonathan A. Lane, with the parent house No. 80 Devonshire Street, and a branch at No. 49 Leonard Street, New York City. Mr. Lane has been in both branches of the legislature, on the Governor's Council, and at the present time is president of the Boston Merchants' Association. The mills for which this firm are the selling agents are all woolen mills, and their product is blankets, and woolen goods for the wear of both men and women. The principal of these mills and their production are as follows: Georges River Mills, Warren, R.I., which make the best cheviot and frieze of pure wool, and such as are not excelled by any goods of their class and kind made at home or abroad. Devonshire Mills, Manchester, N.H., make dry goods, cloakings, etc., also men's cassimeres. This property has recently passed into the hands of a new company, and has already made for itself an excellent reputation. Cordaville Mills, Cordaville, Mass., whose gray blankets are known for cheapness and excellence everywhere. Waushbie Mills, Northboro, Mass., whose Franklin blankets and robes are especially popular in all the southwest. Monadnock Blanket Mills, Harrisville, N.H., whose horse blankets of all descriptions are so acceptable to the saddlery and other trade that they are generally sold abroad. Rockfall Woolen Company, Middletown, Ct., whose horse covers are the best of their kind, and all of whose goods are superior for honest service. Designs Woolen Mills, Manchester, N.H., not a large concern, but new and enterprising; and their colored and white bed blankets are not excelled by any of the old establishments. All wholesale houses should not fail to know the above and scores other lines of woolens adapted to the trade of all portions of the United States.

O. J. FAXON & CO., Manufacturers of Piano-forte Hardware, Grand, Square and Upright Piano Plates, etc.; Office and Works, No. 5 Appleton Street.—A representative successful and old established house in the city of Boston extensively engaged in the manufacture of piano-forte hardware, machinery castings, etc., is that of Messrs. O. J. Faxon & Co., whose office and works are located at No. 5 Appleton Street. The firm's foundry, which is fully supplied with modern appliances and machinery, is situated at West Everett, Mass. This business was established in 1850 by O. J. Faxon and Edward Faxon, who conducted it till 1885, when they retired after a successful and honorable career. They were succeeded by Messrs. Edwin & George H. Faxon, who are now carrying on the enterprise under the old firm name of O. J. Faxon & Co. The partners give close personal attention to every detail of their extensive business, and manufacture carefully to specification all kinds of grand, square, and upright piano plates. Their name is a sufficient guarantee as to the excellence, finish, and thorough reliability of their piano-forte hardware all through the trade. They also drill, bronze, nickel, and arrafe piano plates, and turn out from their foundry all descriptions of machinery castings. The firm number among their permanent customers all the leading piano manufacturers of New England, and have in their possession numbers of unsolicited testimonials as to the unqualified satisfaction their piano plates invariably give. All orders are promptly filled at the lowest possible prices consistent with first class workmanship and materials.

JOSEPH HINTWELL & CO., Manufacturers and Constructors of Iron Work for Buildings, etc., No. 49 Broad Street. Joseph Hintwell, Boston Manager.—When the public becomes thoroughly acquainted with the advantages that iron possesses as a building material, it is considerably predicted that for superior edifices of all kinds, it will receive a general preference to granite, marble, or brick. In this connection we desire to make special reference in this Commercial Review of Boston to the old established and representative firm of Messrs. Joseph Hintwell & Co., manufacturers and constructors of all kinds of iron work for buildings, whose offices are located at No. 49 Broad Street. The works, which are very extensive and admirably equipped, are in Brighton. This business was established in Boston in 1859, and is under the able and careful management of Mr. Joseph Hintwell, who is a thoroughly practical engineer, fully conversant with every detail and feature of this industry and the requirements of patrons. Messrs. Hintwell & Co. have just completed an extensive contract for iron-work for the State Capitol, Austin, Texas, and have now on hand a large contract for the public library, Boston. The firm are constantly taking contracts for iron-work for the largest buildings, not only in Europe, but also in Canada and the United States, and guarantee entire satisfaction to patrons. Their work is unrivalled for strength, design, quality of materials, finish and workmanship, while the prices quoted in all cases are exceedingly moderate. They also contract for trestle work, viaducts, bridges, towers, etc. Among the prominent buildings erected by Mr. Hintwell since he established business here, five years ago, is the Texas State Capitol Building; Suffolk County Court-house; Tudor Building, Beacon Street, Boston; Massachusetts Hospital; Life Insurance Building, State Street; The Boston Tavern, which is a fire-proof building; Pearce Building, Tremont Street; Houghton & Dutton's Dry Goods Warehouse, Tremont Street; New England Mutual Life, Insurance Building, Kansas City, Mo.; Massachusetts Life Insurance Company Building, Kansas City, and many other public and private buildings. Mr. Joseph Hintwell, the Boston manager is highly regarded in trade circles for his skill as an engineer, prompt news, and integrity. It is with pleasure, therefore, that particular attention is called to this reliable house, being confident that those who establish relations with it will find their interests promoted and conserved in every judicious and available manner.

REDPATH BROTHERS, Manufacturers of Men's Boots and Shoes, No. 70 Pearl Street.—In the whole history of American industrial enterprise there is nothing more interesting or remarkable than the growth of the boot and shoe manufacture of the country. Within less than a quarter of a century a gigantic development of the industry has been accomplished, and the ultimate proportions cannot even as yet have been foreseen. Boston and her surrounding towns form the chief centre of the industry in this country, and here are employed many mill. Some of money and many thousands of skilled work-people. One of the leading houses engaged in this line is that of Messrs. Redpath Brothers, of No. 70 Pearl Street, where their office, salesrooms, and stock-rooms are comprised in a building having four floors, with the spacious dimensions of 25 by 150 feet. The business of this progressive concern was founded in 1875 by the present firm, who began as wholesale dealers, and who, in 1982, augmented their enterprise by beginning the manufacture of men's and boys' boots and shoes. Their record has been one of uninterrupted success from the outset, and the extensive trade that has been developed, reaches to all parts of the United States. The factory is situated in South Braintree, Mass., and is a building having four floors of spacious proportions. The place is equipped with the most improved steam-working shoe machinery, and employment is furnished a force of one hundred operatives in the several departments. The best of leather and findings enter into the production, medium and fine grades are made, and the goods turned out are unsurpassed for excellence of finish, style, variety, and for durability and comfort in wearing. Twelve travelers represent the house on the road, and the trade extends from the Atlantic to the Pacific coast. A heavy stock is kept at the Boston establishment to supply the demand, and orders are shipped without delay. The members of the firm, Messrs. E. W., L. H., and N. H. Redpath, are all natives of Pennsylvania, but have long resided in Boston. Mr. E. W. was formerly of the firm of Leonard, Redpath & Lamb, and L. H. Redpath of the house of Haydon, Gardiner & Co. Mr. E. W. Redpath has served creditably as a member of the city council. N. H. Redpath is the popular president of the Boot and Shoe Travelers' League of Boston, and all three gentlemen are held in favorable repute throughout the community, because of their enterprise, ability, and honorable business methods.

BIGELOW & DOWSE, Hardware Merchants, No. 229 Franklin Street.—The largest and leading representative hardware house of Boston is that of Messrs. Bigelow & Dowse, No. 229 Franklin Street. It is also one of the oldest established, having been founded in 1829 by Messrs. Horton & Curtis. The firm of Horton, Curtis & Co. was formed in 1843, succeeded by that of Horton, Hall & Co. in 1851. It then continued till 1864, when the firm of Bonner, Bishop & Co. succeeded. In 1865 Mr. Bigelow and Mr. Dowse both came in as partners, and the house had developed to be one of the strongest and leading in the line. In 1876 the firm of Macomber, Bigelow & Dowse was formed, and made rapid, substantial progress, outgrowing its old premises, so that in 1881 was completed specially for their purpose the magnificent building in Franklin Street now occupied by them. In 1894 Messrs. Bigelow & Dowse became sole proprietors of a business second to none in the United States in its line, and to which they have since made material addition. The premises occupied are exteriorly very handsome, and five stories and basement in height, 100x120 feet in dimensions, and equipped throughout with elegant fixtures and modern improvements. Here is accommodated the largest, finest, and most comprehensive stock of shelf and heavy hardware, cutlery, etc., in New England. A thorough system of organization is enforced by the enterprising proprietors, who bring to bear the widest range of practical experience, perfected forethought, and most influential connections. They are direct importers of fine Sheffield and German cutlery, and of lines of foreign hardware. In the catalogue of American hardware handled by this progressive and responsible house will be found the products of every firm or company of any celebrity. Specialty is made of fine builders' and cabinet hardware, tools, etc., in all styles, including solid bronze and silver and gold plated. The firm deal in full lines of carpenters, plumbers, blacksmiths, turners, and other tools, and the firm sell all over the United States. Messrs. Bigelow & Dowse have the highest standing in commercial circles, their scrupulous and honorable methods are duly appreciated.

THAXTER & BROTHER, Opticians, No. 9 Bromfield Street.—During the last half century steady advance has been made in the interesting and important branch of activity devoted to the construction of devices for aiding and extending the power of vision, and in the manufacture of optical instruments and kindred philosophical and scientific apparatus. The leading headquarters for this class of goods in this city is the establishment of Messrs. Thaxter & Brother, the well-known opticians, at No. 9 Bromfield Street. This is, by the way, the oldest house of its kind in the United States, having been founded by Thomas Penn some time in the eighteenth century. The next proprietor was John Pearse, who was succeeded by Messrs. Daniel and Joseph B. Thaxter. The senior brother died November 11, 1878, since which date the surviving partner has continued the business under the same firm name. Mr. Thaxter is a practical optician, manufacturing largely and dealing at retail in everything belonging to this trade. The instruments and optical goods manufactured by him have a national reputation, and are not surpassed, if equalled, in any feature of merit, in effectiveness, construction, design, finish, or durability, by the products of any contemporaneous establishment. His house has long been popularized and familiar throughout leading professional circles as the place above all others in this city where the best instruments and accessory apparatus can be purchased at the lowest prices. The stock here displayed is the most comprehensive and reliable in town, and comprises full lines of optical goods, telescopes, and microscopes of all standard powers, opera-glasses adapted to every want, and finished in all styles, spy-glasses, marine glasses, and field glasses, spectacles and eye-glasses of every conceivable power, with the best pebble and other lenses, and adapted to the most exacting requirements; also thermometers, barometers, and other measuring apparatus. All through this list the prices will be found the lowest quoted, while the house has acquired and permanently retains the patronage of leading surveyors, engineers, colleges, and seminaries of learning.

SPRINGER BROTHERS, Manufacturers of Fashionable Cloaks, Chauncy and Essex Streets and Harrison Avenue.—The fact that Boston permanently retains her supremacy as the metropolis of New England is due chiefly to her leading merchants and importers, who by their industry and thorough knowledge of the requirements of the public have enlarged their facilities, and increased their stocks, until they are quite equal to those of New York, Paris or London. The Boston manufacturers of fashion- able cloaks ...... Essex Streets and Harrison Avenue. The firm have likewise a large retail establishment at No. 509 Washington Street, corner Bedford Street, an extensive factory at the West End, where several hundred skilled operatives are employed, also a wholesale agency in San Francisco. This business was established in 1865 by Messrs. E. M and M. P. Springer, whose premises were entirely destroyed in 1872 by the great fire. Undaunted by their losses, they re-occupied the first building erected in the burnt district, and remained there till

this cloaks encountered from the start determined opposition from the New York houses. How well our Boston manufacturers have succeeded is shown by the fact that they now not only supply New England, but also have developed an extensive and increasing pa- 1886 when, in consequence of their rapidly increasing patronage, they removed to their present extensive establishment. Their principal store is one of the finest edifices in Boston. It is a very superior five-story harvested freestone building, having a frontage on Essex Street, and flanked by Chauncy Street and Harrison Avenue. The store is elegantly equipped, and a specialty of the establishment is a splendid ladies' cloak-room with cathedral windows. The stock is one of the finest in the United States, and includes every style of

tronage to New York, the middle and western states. In connec- tion with these remarks, we desire to make special reference in this commercial review of the city of the representative and enterprise- ing firm of Messrs. Springer Brothers, manufacturers of fashionable cloaks, whose office and salesrooms are located on Chauncy and fashionable cloaks, and also all kinds of cloaking materials, which are imported direct from the most celebrated European houses. Not only are Messrs. Springer Brothers' cloaks outwardly and appar- ently equal to the best, but the hidden material and the work are exactly what they purport to be. This has ever been the undeviaing rule of the firm, which has been the main secret of their success in every city where their stocks are brought into competition with those of other houses. In fact, the fine stocks of this popular firm are unrivalled for quality of materials, style, finish, and fashionable elegance, being equal in every respect to the best goods from London or Paris, while the prices quoted in all cases are exceedingly moderate. The trade of the house, which is both wholesale and retail, extends throughout all sections of the United States. The promptness, liberality, and just dealing with which all the operations of this establishment are conducted, are as commendable as they have become proverbial—a fact no doubt due to Messrs. Springer Brothers having always lived up to their rule of giving their customers a full equivalent for their money in the best and most artistic goods that can be produced.

CHARLES A. VINAL, Shoe Manufacturers' Goods, Glove and Calf Patent Leather, No. 85 High Street.—In reviewing the varied and vast interests comprehended in the general leather and shoe trades of New England's metropolis, more than passing mention should be given the widely and honorably known house of Mr. Charles A. Vinal, dealers in glove calf, patent leather and shoe manufacturers' supplies of all kinds. This gentleman was a member of the firm of Albert A. Pope & Co., who founded the business in 1870. In 1876 the firm was reorganized and its title changed to Vinal, Pope & Co. In January 1, 1881, Mr. Vinal started alone and assumed the sole direction and management of the enterprise, at No. 85 High Street, which from the beginning has enjoyed a large share of prosperity, the trade of the house extending over all parts of the United States and Canada and steadily increasing. The premises occupied for the business comprise two floors, each 25 x 60 feet in dimensions, of the building No. 85 High Street. Three are appropriately fitted up and arranged and provided with every convenience for the successful prosecution of the business. The stock of merchandise kept on hand represents every description of shoe manufacturers' requisites, a specialty being made of glove calf, grained and patent leather, and the finest quality of imitation leather manufactured. The last named article is made in white, black and colors, and being much cheaper than leather is destined to have a large and increasing sale. Mr. Vinal also controls the product of one of the largest manufacturers of hard and shoe lacings in the country, which he is enabled to sell at the lowest manufacturers' prices. He also carries in stock the largest line of colored and printed drills and ducks to be found in any house in the city. Mr. Vinal, who is a Massachusetts man by birth and a resident in Cambridge, is one of the most popular business men in this section.

ARTHUR H. TABER, Real Estate and Insurance, No. 610 Atlantic Avenue.—One of the most active, and successful real estate and insurance brokers in this city is Mr. Arthur H. Taber, who has been established in business here since the fall of 1887, and brings to bear that wide range of practical experience so essential to the best interests of the public at large. He has an intimate personal acquaintance with properties in various sections of the city, and is a recognized authority as to present and prospective values of realty in city and country. He is prepared to buy, sell, and lease property on commission, collect rents, negotiate loans, and place fire insurance risks in the best companies at the lowest rates of premium; while he is giving special attention to the management of the New Railway Building, located at No. 610 to 630 Atlantic Avenue, next to N. Y. and N. E. Railroad Depot, and one of the finest office buildings in the city. A few choice offices can still be let by applying to Mr. Taber at room 98. Mr. Taber also has several large new buildings for manufacturing and storage to let, while a safe in his office packed with powers of attorney tells the character of his clientage. So implicitly is he trusted, that by these powers of attorney he can collect a fortune each month, disburse it to proper channels, and do all, except selling, that any owner can do with his property. Houses of the largest estates in the city are placed entirely in his hands while the owners go to enjoy European travel and country life for years at a time. Almost every ward in the city is represented on Mr. Taber's books, as well as every class of property. He is popular as a general insurance broker, and is special agent of the Provident Life and Trust Company. Mr. Taber is a native of the State of Maine, a well-known citizen of Brookline, and deservedly honored and respected.

HENRY C. HUNT & CO., Manufacturers and Dealers in Oak-tanned Leather Belting, and Hose, Vulcanized Rubber Fabrics of Every Description; Office and Salesroom, No. 45 Arch Street; Factory, Nos. 85 and 86 Ulster Street.—Boston manufacturers and merchants enjoy a widespread reputation for the magnitude of their operations and the enterprise with which they are carried on—a reputation that has been acquired by a practical knowledge of the wants of the trade, and the energy and industry applied to the several undertakings. In its special department of industry the house of Henry C. Hunt & Co. is the foremost establishment in this section, and is of historical note because of its having been the first in this country to engage in the manufacture of leather belting for sale. The business was founded in 1847 by Mr. N. Hunt, and he was succeeded in 1865 by his son, the present proprietor, Mr. Henry C. Hunt, who has continued the enterprise with uninterrupted prosperity. The factory is located at Nos. 85 and 86 Ulster Street, the building occupied being four floors, each 30 by 120 feet in dimensions, and equipped throughout with the best steam-working machinery applicable to the industry, while steady employment is afforded a large force of expert workmen. The production of the house comprises Hunt's famous oak-tanned leather belting, Hunt's Indian tan lace, apron for cordage, covered and silk mills. The leading specialty is belting, which is manufactured of the best-selected slaughter hides, which are tanned expressly for this house, only oak bark being used in the tanning process. Believing that the interests of consumers are best served by the production of goods of reliable quality, and that the first cost of belting is less to be considered by them than the expense attendant upon the failure of belting of an inferior quality, Mr. Hunt would not attempt to compete with goods offered at such prices that the quality has to be materially reduced; for under no circumstances will the quality of his standard manufactures be impaired to lessen their cost. The trade supplied extends to all parts of the United States. At the salesroom, No. 45 Arch Street, a heavy stock is carried, and all orders are filled in the promptest and most satisfactory manner. Mr. Hunt is a native of Boston, is an active member of the Massachusetts Charitable Mechanics' Association, and he takes a most valued part in forwarding all the best interests of the city.

OLNEY BROTHERS, N. E. Agents for Binghamton Cylinder and Spindle Oils, and Dealers in Sperm, Lard, Illuminating, German Spindle, and Wool Oils, No. 140 Congress Street.—Messrs. Olney Brothers are deservedly prominent as New England agents for Binghamton cylinder and spindle oils, and dealers in sperm, lard, illuminating, and German spindle and wool oils. The main headquarters of the firm are at Providence, R. I., where they have been engaged in business since 1871, and in 1880 they opened their present house in this city. From the outset this firm have held a front-rank position in the oil business throughout New England. At the spacious salesrooms in this city is constantly carried a splendid selection of kerosene, white safety and signal oils, sperm, lard, and wool oils, gasoline, benzine, and naphtha, paraffine, cylinder, and spindle oils, engine, lubricating, and sewing machine oils, neatsfoot oil, tallow, and grease. The leading specialties are "German spindle oil," copyrighted by this firm; and "petrolina," manufactured by them from native petroleum, without the use of acids or alkalies, and recognized as one of the safest and most effective healing ointments made for burns, bruises, cuts, wounds, sprains, rheumatism, etc., and can be used internally for coughs, colds, and sore throats with the most beneficial results. These goods are sold by chemists and druggists all over the world, and have given this firm a national reputation in their business. The lubricating oils of this responsible house work splendidly on machinery, contain no acid or alkali to corrode, or grit to wear the metal, but are lasting and cleanly, promoting smooth running in the highest degree. This firm have built up a commanding position in the oil trade on perfectly pure and fine goods, has never desired to enter into competition with low-grade inferior oils, and is commended to the trade and the public as one every way worthy of confidence and trust. The copartners, Messrs. H. S. and A. H. Olney, are both natives and prominent citizens of the city of Providence, still in the prime of life, members of the Providence Board of Trade, and justly popular. Mr. H. S. Olney has the management of the Boston house, supplying the eastern section of New England.

134

BOSTON SUGAR-REFINING COMPANY. Office, No. 18 Central street.

HENRY K. BARNES, Manufacturer and Dealer in Oak-tanned Leather Belting, Lace Leather, Rubber Belting, Rubber, Linen, and Cotton Fire-hose, Nos. 119 and 121 Devonshire street, and No. 104 Franklin street.

C. A. NOYES & CO., Carpenters and Builders, etc., No. 8 Province Court.

A. GRIFFITHS, Manufacturer of Saws, etc., No. 40 Oliver street.

MR. N. J. GREGORY, Milliner and Dressmaker, No. 98 Washington street.

DANA, TUCKER & CO., Commission Merchants, Dry goods, Cotton Cloths, Woolens, etc., No. 40 Franklin street.

GEO. A. FERNALD & CO., Eastern and Western Investment Securities, No. 3 Sears Building.—The rapidly growing wealth of the American people is forcibly illustrated by the constant demand for reliable securities in which to invest surplus funds, and it is naturally to the great city of Boston that investors turn to seek the best terms and the most substantial classes of securities. In connection with these remarks, the attention of our readers and the public is directed to the representative and reliable firm of Messrs. Geo. A. Fernald & Co., dealers in eastern and western securities, whose offices are centrally located at No. 3 Sears building. This business was established in 1904 by Messrs. Geo. A. Fernald and Thos. S. Kruz, both of whom have had great experience ...

JAMES W. HARVEY, Machine Blacksmith, No. 696 Atlantic Avenue.—The leading representative of his special branch of industry in Boston is Mr. James W. Harvey, whose place of business, at No. 696 Atlantic Avenue, comprises two floors, 25x75 feet each, fully supplied with all the latest improved apparatus, appliances, and machinery known to the trade, and unequalled facilities are at hand tending to insure rapid and perfect production ...

H. D. HEDGER & CO., Makers Swiftsure Bicycles, Repairers, Nickel Platers, and Painters, No. 678 Tremont Street.—It is now but a little over six years since Messrs. H. D. Hedger, the well-known maker of the Swiftsure Bicycles, at No. 678 Tremont Street, first inaugurated his enterprise in this city; yet these few years have given the Swiftsure bicycle a name so familiar to city people and country folk as Shakespeare or Robinson Crusoe ...

MASON & HAMLIN ORGAN AND PIANO CO., Boston Office, No. 154 Tremont Street; Henry Mason, President and Treasurer; Henry Busford, Secretary.—The firm name of Mason & Hamlin will ever be justly honored in connection with the introduction of correct scientific principles into the manufacture of pianos and organs, coupled with a nicety of construction, and a perfection of workmanship that render them altogether unrivalled. This extensive business was originally established April, 1854, by ... rs. Henry Mason & Emmons Hamlin, who conducted it till 1860,

to be unequalled are not only a majority of the most eminent musicians of America, but also a host in Europe. The most famous organists of London, Paris, Vienna, Berlin, and St. Petersburg, with those of New York, Boston, Philadelphia, Chicago, and all the principal cities, and almost all states of the Union; composers whose fame is world-wide; most distinguished artists of the Italian and German operas; pianists of the greatest celebrity everywhere; musical critics of the European and American press; indrumentalists whose excellence has made them famous; conductors and directors of the

Mason & Hamlin's Grand Piano.

when it was incorporated under the laws of Massachusetts, with a paid-up capital of $500,000, and its patronage now extends to all parts of the civilized world. The manufactories of the Mason & Hamlin Organ and Piano Co., which are admirably equipped with the latest improved machinery and appliances, are situated at Cambridgeport, Mass. Here 500 skilled workmen are employed in the various departments. The Mason & Hamlin American cabinet or parlor organs have always maintained their supremacy as the best of this class of instruments in the world, greatly excelling all others in the more important qualities. Among those who declare these organs

principal orchestras, musical societies, and choirs; missionaries in the Indies, Africa, China (who have tested these organs in the most trying climates), and others testify by scores and hundreds. And the testimony is to the same effect; that the Mason & Hamlin cabinet organs excel all other instruments of their class in those qualities and characteristics which are most valuable. The Mason & Hamlin organs have carried off the highest medals and premiums, at all the Great World's exhibitions, since and including that of Paris, 1867. The distinguished enterprise and energy of this company has met with deserved success also in the kindred field of piano manufacturing. Pre

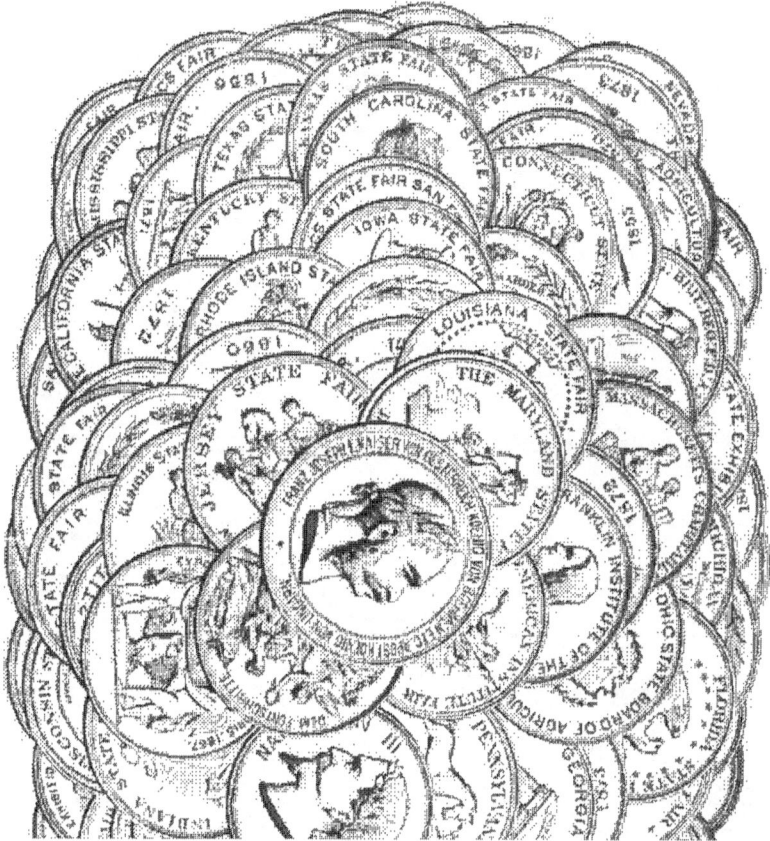

Mason & Hamlin improved method of stringing.

J. **FRANKLIN FULLER.** Civil Engineer and Surveyor, No. 12 Pearl Street, Rooms 16 and 17.—There is not, perhaps, within the entire domain of the arts and sciences, any feature of progress in which native genius and skill have been displayed to more advantage of late years in the United States than in civil engineering and landscape architecture. Among those who have won distinction in this line in Boston, none stand higher in public favor or deserve more honorable mention than Mr J Franklin Fuller, the well-known civil engineer and surveyor, whose offices are eligibly located at No. 11 Pearl Street. This gentleman has been engaged in the practice of his profession here since 1856, when he succeeded his father, Mr Stephen P. Fuller, who had been established therein since 1818. In 1872, the firm of Fuller & Whitney was organized, which was dissolved in 1897, Mr. Fuller continuing the business at the above address. Mr. Fuller makes a leading specialty of improvements on real estate, laying out lots, grading, developing, and general landscape work; and special attention is given to the development, improvement, and maintenance of public and private grounds, parks, cemeteries, rural, town and country residences, suburban building enterprises, recreation grounds for ball, tennis, etc., road construction of stone or gravel, etc., also to the ornamentation of public and private grounds, for city streets, suburban, and country roadways, railway depot grounds, and furnishes information and advice as to location, topographical resources, examinations, reports, surveys, preliminary studies, designs, working maps, estimates, specifications, and operative supervision. He occupies spacious office quarters, and has in his service a corps of experienced and capable assistants, devoting close personal supervision, however, over all work executed. Mr. Fuller has been for a period of twenty-eight years prominently identified with the notable improvements made on the Back Bay, making all surveys of the Back Bay improvements, and has been largely in the Fort Hill District, and is trustee for various valuable estates in the city and suburbs. His services and counsel are promptly and faithfully given, and his patronage is large, first class, and influential throughout all New England. Mr. Fuller is a native Bostonian, and an accomplished master of his art whose high repute and standing in professional and business circles places him far beyond the requirements of any praise which these pages could bestow.

F. **M. STEVENS & CO.**, Manufacturers of Rotary Trimmers and Arti-re, Trimmer Cutters and Irons, No. 19 High Street.— We have previously made numerous comments upon the character of those manufacturing enterprises which have done so much to promote the wealth and prosperity of this city. Taking up such industries in detail, special mention must be made of the house conducted by Messrs F. M. Stevens & Co. as manufacturers of rotary trimmers and cutters, trimmer cutters and irons, at No. 19 High Street. This enterprise was inaugurated in 1890 by the present enterprising proprietors, who have conducted all its branches with marked ability and built it up to proportions of gratifying magnitude and importance. The factory is thoroughly spacious in size, finely equipped with new and improved machinery, operated by steam power, and a force of fifteen skilled and expert assistants contribute to the satisfactory operations of the house. The machines and implements here manufactured for cutting and making edges and burs of bevels and shoes are made from original and ingenious designs, upon which patents have been secured, and they have met with great favor from the trade, as being the best, strongest, most simple, and easily operated machines of the kind on the market and have proved of invaluable benefit to shoe-manufacturers everywhere. Every implement is constructed with unusual care and accuracy, of the best and most durable materials, and the skill and patience applied by the firm to the completion of every article made by them has led to an extended demand for the products of the house, and besides being highly prized by the trade throughout the United States, they also find a ready and permanent sale in England, France, Germany, and other foreign countries. In all respects the house is adequate to any demands that may be made upon its resources, and those interested in the purchase of the products will find many advantages in opening business relations with the firm, which cannot be secured elsewhere. The individual members of the firm are Messrs. F. M. Stevens and H. Cunningham, the former a native of Maine, the latter of Bombay, India. Both are practical machinists and highly-esteemed citizens of Boston, and both devote their personal supervision to the business, insuring satisfaction to patrons and the steady growth of the house.

R. **B. CLARK.** Wool Broker, No. 100 High Street.—The whole sale and commission trade in foreign and domestic wool occupies a prosperous position among the diversified interests of the great city of Boston; and among the houses engaged therein that are worthy of honorable mention is that of Mr. R. B. Clark, located at No. 160 High Street. This gentleman is a well-known wool broker, commission merchant, and general wholesale dealer in both foreign and domestic wools, selling mostly by sample, and enjoys a widespread and influential connection both at home and abroad. The business thus so successfully conducted was originally established in 1860 by Mr. John Clark, who was succeeded at his death, in 1883, by the present proprietor. The business premises comprise three floors 60x100 feet each, and unsurpassed facilities are at hand for transacting business under the most favorable auspices and upon the largest scale. Bringing ample resources to bear, receiving supplies in vast quantities direct from the centres of growth, and controlling the products of many large wool-growers in the best sheep-raising regions of the country, the proprietor is enabled to meet promptly and satisfactorily every demand made upon him, and grant his patrons every possible advantage in both goods and prices. The trade of the house extends to all parts of the United States, and is repeatedly heavy and important throughout New England, annually increasing in magnitude and importance under enterprising and reliable management. Mr. Clark is a native of Massachusetts, a well-known citizen of Malden, and universally popular by reason of his energy, capacity, and integrity, and for the just and equitable manner in which he discharges his obligations to his patrons.

W. **C. & A. F. MENTZER.** Chicago Dressed Beef, No. 814, North Market Street.—A long established and well-known headquarters for the supply of Chicago dressed beef and provisions in this city is that well ordered and responsible concern conducted by W. C. & A. F. Mentzer, at No. 814, North Market Street. No firm engaged in this particular line in Boston sustains a higher reputation for excellent stock or reliable dealing, or few, if any, enjoy a larger share of public favor and confidence, while their business, which is at once large, prosperous and permanent, affords evidence of steady and very material increase. This enterprising and popular firm was established in 1872, and during the series of years since intervening its career has been a record of steady progress. They occupy for business purposes commodious and well-equipped quarters, every convenience and facility for the handling and storage of stock being at hand, while some half a dozen in help are employed. Messrs. Mentzer are agents for Armour & Co., Chicago, and receive fresh meat several times a week direct from Chicago and Kansas City by the carload, selling Armour's beef exclusively. A heavy and prime stock is constantly carried on hand, including, besides Chicago dressed beef, lean cuts, fancy brisket, salt meats and provisions, and the trade of the firm, which is of a wholesale character altogether, is principally located in and around Boston. Messrs. Mentzer, who are gentlemen of middle age, and natives of Somerville, Mass., are both men of ample experience in this line, as well as of energy and excellent business qualities, and are thoroughly conversant with the business.

W. **H. CHERMAN.** Receiver and Dealer in Potash, Pearlash, Caustic Soda, etc., No. 9 Central Street. An essentially representative house in Boston, largely identified with the potash and caustic soda trade, is that of Mr W H. Cherman, No. 9 Central Street. This business was established in 1857 by Mr. Cherman, who has since secured a liberal and permanent patronage from consumers and entire and various manufacturers in all sections of the United States. He is an extensive receiver and dealer of potash, pearlash, caustic soda, tallow and grease, which are noted for their quality and reliability, and have no superiors in the market. The premises occupied are central and convenient, fully stocked with the above-named products, which are offered to customers at the lowest ruling market prices. Mr. Cherman makes a specialty of potash, and offers inducements in quality and price very difficult to be secured elsewhere. All orders are promptly and faithfully filled, while all products are fully warranted to be exactly as represented. He was born in Maine, but has resided in Boston for the last forty years. He is a liberal, honorable, and able business man, who has obtained the entire confidence of his numerous customers in all sections of the country.

DAVIS SHOE COMPANY, Manufacturers of Ladies' and Misses' Boots and Shoes, Nos. 9 Summer Street, Boston, and 21 Exchange Street, Lynn.—Our boot and shoe manufacturers have attained a position in their art which is independent and representative. American boots and shoes have their own designs, their own style and their native qualities, making them distinctive and expressive, and meeting the approval of a critical public both at home and abroad. The leading manufacturers in their special branch of the trade are the Davis Shoe Company, manufacturers of ladies' and misses' boots and shoes, whose factories are located at Lynn, Mass.; Kennebunk, Me.; and Richmond, Va.; with office and salesrooms at No. 9 Summer Street, in this city. This company enjoy a national reputation as leading representatives of high-class goods in this country, and their products are sold to the very highest order of dealers throughout the United States. The foundation of this business was laid in 1884 by Messrs. Joseph Davis & Co., and in 1886 the present company was incorporated, with Mr. Joseph Davis as president, he occupying that position up to 1895, when Mr. Wm. H. Chase took his place. The present officers are Mr. Wm. H. Chase, president; Mr. Henry Kemp, vice-president; also, W. Williams, treasurer. The success of this company has been great, owing to the long years of study and attention given to the business by its officers and managers in the production of improved boots and shoes by new and better methods of manufacture. The combined product of their factories is six thousand pairs per day, and the demand for them is so great as to drive the three factories to their utmost capacity; while every effort is constantly being made by the enterprising managers to improve the quality and enhance the value of the output in all essential respects. The closest attention is given to the selection of materials, and other important details of the business; so that the product occupied by this company, at the head of the trade, has been honestly earned, and is well deserved. All goods of this house are noted for their superior workmanship, fine material, and elegance of finish, having all the elements of durability, with the added advantages of easy fit and attractive appearance. A specialty is made of "wool boots," manufactured expressly for severe winter weather, in which branch this company is acknowledged to excel all competition. Orders for these and other products of this house are promptly and carefully filled in all cases. The officers of the Davis Shoe Company are all Massachusetts men by birth and training, in the prime of life, of large and valuable experience in the shoe trade, and highly regarded in commercial, financial, and social circles for their business capacity, strict probity, and solid personal worth.

KOOPMAN & CO., Importers of Antique Furniture and Silverware, No. 17 Beacon Street.—The firm name of Koopman & Co. enjoys a national reputation as extensive importers of antique furniture and silverware, having establishments at No. 17 Beacon Street, in this city, and No. 88 Fifth Avenue, New York, and their main headquarters at Amsterdam, Leeds, Holland. They have been established in business here since 1860, and early acquired as enviable and wide-spread fame for dealing strictly in the most prized treasures of the Old World, largely purchased by them at the sales of famous collections in Europe. Their salesrooms in this city are spacious in size, elegantly situated in the most fashionable quarter of the town, and elegant and attractive in all their arrangements and appointments. Here is displayed the most extensive stock of rare and choice antiquities in furniture, bric-à-brac, china and brass goods in this city; including the most elegant drawing-room appointments in suites and old pieces, of rosewood, walnut, mahogany, and ebony, many being upholstered in fine silks and tapestries; ormolu-mounted buhl cabinets, Louis XIV. cabinets, old carved oak furniture and handsome sideboards, marqueterie centre and card tables, mantel ornaments in alabaster and onyx; Dresden china and porcelain vases, paintings, and brass novelties; while the stock of antique silverware here exhibited to duplicated elsewhere, much of it being of great value to those who appreciate the achievements in the silversmith's art. As direct importers, this firm is constantly receiving furniture and bric-à-brac of exceptional rarity, coming from the houses of various royal families and members of the aristocracy of Europe. They also manufacture furniture in antique designs, and conduct their immense business at both wholesale and retail. They number among their permanent customers the best classes of society, and are constantly on the alert to add articles of value to their varied and deeply interesting stock. The members of this popular firm are Julius Koopman, who resides in this city; H. Koopman, a resident of New York, and E. K. Koopman, who has personal charge of the interests of the firm in Holland.

HERSEY BROTHERS, Manufacturers and Designers of Special and Improved Machinery, Corner of Second and E Streets, South Boston.—A most important establishment, and one that secures to Boston the most advanced methods and most perfect facilities for the manufacture of special and improved machinery of all kinds, is that of Messrs. Hersey Brothers, of Second and E Streets, South Boston. The concern is the oldest, as well as leader, in its line. Messrs. Hersey & Hersey founded the business in 1863, Mr. Charles H. Hersey being the junior partner. In 1886, Messrs. Charles H. and Francis C. Hersey formed the existing copartnership, bringing to bear vast practical experience as skilled designers and mechanical engineers, perfected facilities, and industrial connections. Messrs. Hersey design and manufacture every description of special and improved machinery. Among full outfits obtainable here of the most perfect description, may be mentioned sugar house machinery; saltworks machinery; soap-works machinery; friction braiding machinery; grain and meal dryers; power and hand presses; power rotary pumps, etc. The works are extensive, being 60x150 feet in dimensions, equipped with a costly and elaborate outfit of machinery, including rolls, steam hammers, punches, planers, etc. An average of fifty-five hands are employed under the personal supervision of the proprietors, who maintain an enviable reputation for the perfection and durability of all mechanism leaving their establishment. They use only the best grade of iron and steel, and all workmanship is strictly first class. The firm have fitted up several of the great sugar-refineries, soap-works, factories, etc., of Boston, New England, and the west, and refer to these establishments as to the satisfactory character of their outfit. Those contemplating refitting or starting up new soap-works, salt works, sugar refineries, machine-shops, etc., should secure estimates from this able firm, which has coped with the most difficult problems in the progress of their business, and give customers the invaluable benefit of their wide range of practical experience. Mr. Charles H. Hersey is a prominent citizen of South Boston, and is vice-president of the South Boston Savings Bank, one of the most solid and prosperous financial institutions in the state; he has also been a member of the Board of Aldermen, faithfully discharging the duties devolving upon him, and ever pursuing a public-spirited, upright policy. Mr. Francis C. Hersey is also widely and favorably known throughout the community, and is a trustee of the South Boston Savings Bank, trustee of the Massachusetts Mechanics Association, an honored citizen, and an able business man, and Boston is to be congratulated upon the prominent possession of such a thoroughly representative and flourishing establishment as that of Messrs. Hersey Brothers.

PEOPLE'S DRUG STORE, Corner Havre and Decatur Streets, East Boston.—The "People's Drug Store," located on the corner of Havre and Decatur Streets, has been a noted and popular pharmacy for the past thirteen years. Since November, 1882, it has been under the direction and management of Mr. J. D. C. Pratt, who has fully maintained the high reputation the house has borne since its inception. Mr. Pratt is a graduate of the Massachusetts Pharmaceutical College, and is a young man of extended practical experience in the dispensing of drugs and chemicals. The location of the store is a most eligible one, and the store itself, which has a capacity of 20x50 feet, is most attractive in its arrangement and furnishings, which embraces artistic shelving and shelf ware, elegant soda water fountain, and plate glass show cases, etc. The stock is full and complete, and comprises fresh, pure drugs, chemicals, and the requisite proprietary medicines, together with toilet articles, perfumes, extracts, fancy goods, physicians' and surgeons' requisites, and druggists' sundries in great variety. Mr. Pratt gives his personal attention to the compounding of physicians' prescriptions and family recipes, employs only the best competent and duly qualified assistants, and uses only the freshest and purest drugs in the market. Prompt service and courteous and liberal treatment are accorded to all patrons, and satisfaction guaranteed. Mr. Pratt is a native of Boston, is a gentleman of fine scholarly attainments, enjoys the utmost confidence of all who know him, and is drawing from the people in the city a very large and lucrative business.

MINER, BEAL & CO., Men's and Boys' Clothing, Nos. 41 Summer and 6 Chauncy Streets.—Boston is to be congratulated upon having, in Messrs. Miner, Beal & Co., one of the great representative wholesale clothing-houses of the United States, and one whose policy, character, and magnitude of operations are abundantly indicative of the skill, experience, and superior executive abilities of the proprietors. The business is one of the oldest in its line, having been founded by Messrs. Merritt, Parkhurst & Co. in 1852. They originally located on Devonshire Street. In 1865, the firm was changed, becoming that of Messrs. Parkhurst, Miner & Beal. In 1870, the style of Messrs. Miner, Beal & Co. was adopted, the concern steadily enlarging its volume of trade. It had the misfortune to be burned out in the great fire of 1872, but, with characteristic energy and enterprise, were speedily in the field again

for the use of the house, and are of marble, five stories in height and 100 x 130 feet in dimensions. The interior arrangements and outfit are perfect, and a thorough system is enforced throughout the business establishment. All the modern conveniences are here, including safety passenger elevator in the centre of the building, steam heat, etc. The firm manufacture upon the most extensive scale, employing from two to three hundred hands, and selecting their woolens and cloths with the utmost care, introducing all the latest novelties in shades, patterns, and textures; while they employ the best talent in their cutting-department, and are justly celebrated throughout the trade for correct, fashionable styles, honest workmanship, and elegance and perfection of finish. The firm offer substantial inducements both as to price and quality, and carry an immense and fully assorted stock of seasonable goods, meeting the requirements of the best circles of the public. The firm sell to the trade all over the United States, and have a staff of 15 traveling salesmen constantly on the road. The house has achieved an enviable reputation as the leader in its line, and New York City can show no finer stock at more attractive prices than the one at all times carried by this old, honorable, and responsible house.

G. C. AIKEN, Wholesale Dealer in Confectionery, Cigars, Tobacco, and Cigarettes, No. 91 Union Street.—One of the most recently established houses in the wholesale confectionery, cigars, tobacco and cigarette line, is that of G. C. Aiken at No. 91 Union Street. Mr. Aiken opened his business at this address on the 1st of October 1890, after an experience of 10 years in running a confectionery town of his own to the towns around Boston. In this way he acquired a thorough knowledge of the business, and provided with ample capital was enabled to branch out on the large scale in which he is at present engaged. The store is a commodious one, 40 x 40 feet, and finely fitted up for the storage and handling of goods. Mr. Aiken has an excellent stock of the finest domestic and foreign confectionery, and in the line of cigars handles such well known and popular brands as "G. C. A.," a first-class ten cent cigar, "Yankee Star," "Howard and Acton" and "Young's Own" which are sold at five cents. In tobacco and cigarettes he also has a large wholesale trade, his customers being found all over New England. Mr. Aiken, who is a native of Vermont, has been twenty years in Boston, and bears an excellent name in business circles due to his honorable straightforward business methods.

In 1878, the firm of Miner, Beal & Hackett was formed, continuing until December, 1882, when the present copartnership was formed under the existing name and style, composed of Mr. George A. Miner, Mr. Leander Beal, Mr. William W. Bean, Mr. Charles B. Shaw, and Mr. S. Irwin Fowler. Messrs. Miner and Beal have been in the house ever since 1865, and recognized authorities in this branch of trade. Mr. Bean was admitted in 1878, and Messrs. Shaw and Fowler in 1882. The three last-named gentlemen had proved their abilities as commercial salesmen, and command, not only influential connections, but a personal acquaintance with the leading clothiers of the United States. The present magnificent premises were specially erected

ALEX WILLIAMS, Jr. & CO., Wool Commission Merchants, No. 161 Atlantic Avenue.—This business was established in 1885 by Messrs. Alex Williams, Jr. and Charles C. Williams, both of whom were previously with the widely-known house of Messrs. Walter Brown & Co. Both partners are possessed of a wide range of practical experience and are recognized as leading authorities in the wool market, while their connections are both influential and wide spread. They occupy a superior six-story building, 75 x 150 feet in area, fully equipped with every appliance and facility for the successful prosecution of their growing business. Both Messrs. Alex. and Charles C. Williams are natives and residents of Boston

HENRY J. PRESTON, Architect, No. 8 Exchange Place, Room 19.—

C. H. BANGS, Manufacturer of Druggists' Furniture, No. 347 Washington Street.—

GEORGE A. CLOUGH, Architect, No. 60 Tremont Street.—

FRANCK SHUTE & CO., Hardware, Iron and Blacksmiths' Supplies, No. 20 Pearl Street.—

LEWIS F. TENNEY, Boots and Shoes, No. 121 Summer Street.—

SAMUEL WHEELER, Dealer in Artists' and Painters' Supplies, No. 145 Milk Street.

NEAL, MORSE & CO., Woolens, New Boylston Building, Corner Boylston and Washington Streets.

DR. J. M. OSGOOD, Surgeon Dentist, No. 87 Tremont Street.

T. M. CLARK, Architect, No. 179 Devonshire Street.

A. A. BLAIR, Printer, No. 167 Devonshire Street.—A house which has kept full progress with the times in the "art preservative," and which can safely bear comparison with any similar concern in the city, is the printing establishment of A. A. Blair, located at No. 167 Devonshire Street. The industry was

inaugurated in 1872, under the style of Blair & Hallett. The firm was successful in acquiring a large, influential patronage, and an enviable reputation for excellence of work. The premises occupied consist of a spacious floor 30x100 feet in area, equipped with nine superior presses, operated by steam-power, every description of type, together with all the accessories belonging to the outfit of a first class printing establishment. A large force of skilled hands are employed, and printing in all its various branches is executed promptly and in the most workmanlike manner. The prices are invariably reasonable and satisfaction is assured all patrons. The present proprietor of the business, Mr. A. A. Blair, is a native Bostonian, and is held in high esteem among his contemporaries and all who have transactions with him. He is an active member of the Master Printers' Club, to which a cordial support is given, and is the equitable methods which are employed in the conduct of affairs the house is representative of the highest principles of business management.

MESSENGER BROS. & JONES, Tailors and Importers, No. 388 Washington Street.—A house in Boston which has done more than any other in the way of artistic elegance and excellence in custom made clothing is that of the representative and old established firm of Messrs. Messenger Bros. & Jones. This extensive business was established in 1847 by Messrs. Richardson & Messenger, who were succeeded by Messenger & Cabot. Eventually in 1875 the present firm was organized and assumed the management, the copartners being Messrs. Francis A., Charles A. and Winthrop Messenger, and W. E. Jones. The premises occupied

are handsome and commodious, and are fully supplied with appliances and facilities for the proper execution of the business, and the comfort and convenience of patrons. Messrs. Messenger Bros. & Jones make a specialty of London garments, ladies' habits, coats, ulsters, mantles, etc. One hundred skilful tailors are kept constantly at work, a number of whom are engaged in producing new and tasty designs, and are artists of no small reputation. All the members of this firm are accomplished tailors and cutters, and are quite capable of practically superintending every branch of this first-class business. Any riding-habit, mantle, or garment made by this popular and noted house is always indorsed by fastidious critics as superior to every respect and the great experience and skill of the firm make it the recognized authority and leader in this artistic business. The direct connections of the house with Parisian and London centres of fashion, and its facilities for arriving at reliable decision as to the prevailing modes for any season, have made Messrs. Messenger Bros. & Jones' patterns of tailor-made dresses, habits, and mantles as popular as they are eagerly sought after for artistic beauty, novelty, utility, economy, and fashionable elegance. Messrs. Messenger brothers are natives of Mass., while Mr. Jones was born in England.

THOMAS J. HIND, Slate, Tin and Copper, Composition and Gravel Roofing; Agent for Warren's Natural Asphalte, etc., Office, No. 101 Milk Street.—Although in business on his own account but a comparatively short period, Thomas J. Hind, slate, metal, composition and gravel roofer, also dealer in asphalte, roofing, and kindred materials, (Office No. 101 Milk Street, with wharf and storehouse located at East First, foot of First Street,) has already established a name and acquired a patronage second to few engaged in this line in Boston. For thoroughly first-class work, and for promptness and reliability in executing contracts and general jobbing, not one in the business in this city sustains a better reputation; among the more noteworthy jobs recently done by this gentleman being the roofing of the Thomson Electric Welding Works, at Lynn; the huge works of George W. Pope, and an extensive block of buildings on South Street. Mr. Hind, who is a native of Boston, is a practical and expert roofer, of long and varied experience in the execution of his art, and is thoroughly conversant with the business in all its branches, having formerly been superintendent of the roofing department of the Warren Chemical & Manufacturing Company. The office is connected by telephone (No.), and a heavy and complete stock is constantly carried on hand at the storehouse. Mr. Hind is agent for Warren's Natural Asphalte, gravel roofing, 1 and 3 ply ready roofing, collar scoriae, and general roofing materials, while sums (ready) in help are employed. Everything in the line of slate, tin, copper, composition, and gravel roofing is done in the most expeditious and excellent manner, and special attention is given to repairing and jobbing.

CURRY & HANNER, Hardware, Cutlery, Paints, Oils, Varnishes, etc., Nos. 1897-1898-1899 Washington Street.—This firm are extensive dealers in hardware, cutlery, paints, oils, and varnishes, and make a leading specialty of dogs' collars, and furnishings, builders' hardware, and mechanics' tools. The general stock carried is very elaborate and diversified. The assortments are kept full and complete, and embrace builders' hardware and shelf goods, carpenters', mechanics', and machinists' tools, locksmiths' and butchers' supplies, table and pocket cutlery, fire-arms, cartridges, and ammunition, Abbey & Imbrie's fishing tackle, Challenge Dog Food, dog-collars and furnishings, Little's "Soluble Phenyle," paints, oils, and varnishes, and general painters' supplies. All goods are received direct from the manufacturers, and special attention is given to the character and quality of the productions. Substantial advantages are extended to consumers in the matter of prices. Prompt clerks and three delivery wagons are kept busy, and the trade is brisk and lively at all times. The members of this firm, Messrs J. T. Curry and J. B. Hanner, received their training in the hardware store of Gardner & Chandler, and enter upon the responsibilities of mercantile life well-equipped, thoroughly informed, and keenly alive to all its needs and requirements. Mr. Curry was born in Tennessee, and Mr. Hanner is a Connecticut man by birth, and the firm are brimful of energy, pluck, and enterprise, and are accounted among that class of young business representatives in whose hands the continued development of the city rests.

W. H. DAVIS & CO., East India House, No. 51 Summer Street.—An important branch of commercial enterprise, and one deserving of special mention in a review of the leading business interests of Boston, is the importation of Oriental and Eastern fabrics and fancy goods as carried on by the representative East India House of W. H. Davis & Co., located at No. 51 Summer Street, with direct correspondents in China, India, and the Orient. This being the only house in its special line of trade in the United States, its business has naturally assumed large proportions, owing to the increasing demand for luxurious surroundings, of which this class of goods forms an inseparable basis. The firm established their business here in 1878, and speedily developed a trade of great and growing importance. The soft draping silks, cashmeres, velveteens, cottons, etc., in rare colors and exclusive designs, are particularly adapted for artistic costumes, and interior hangings and decorations. The stock includes genuine India and China silks, soft satins, gauzes, and muslins in superb colorings; the richest of embroideries, useful for various purposes; sixteenth century Portuguese embroideries, Canton crapes, seersuckers, pongees, grass linens, tiger-skins; bamboo lounges, chairs, and stools, Russian bowls and soaps, Bokhara dows, Madras handkerchiefs, Indian fans, pillows, bamboo verandah blinds, chutnees, curries, gingers, etc., and numberless articles suitable for furnishings of town and country houses. A new departure has recently been made, in the import to personal order, of gowns, hats, wraps, etc., for ladies and children, made in London, of these charming fabrics, in an artistic, graceful, and unconventional manner; and which have been much prized by ladies of refinement and correct taste. The stock embraces at all times many novelties in textures, patterns, styles, and shades that are not found elsewhere; while to the trade and consumers the display here presented offers features in completeness of assortment, quality, and desirability of goods that cannot be duplicated in the United States. Boston, the original seat of the East India trade in this country, is to be congratulated upon having permanently located in her midst such a representative house as that of W. H. Davis & Co., who are always pleased to furnish samples, estimates, and particulars. Mr. Davis, the active member of the firm, is a native and well known citizen of Boston, and one of its most enterprising and successful importers. With the advantages of several years' residence in India and yearly trips to the Oriental and European markets, he is thoroughly familiar with what can be had, and the demands of the trade in this country. The goods carried in stock are nearly all made to order, and personal selections. He is the authorized agent of Liberty & Co., of Regent Street, London, whose colors and fabrics are known and appreciated all over the world.

THE NATIONAL WEBSTER BANK, of Boston, Mass., Francis A. Peters, President; John C. Palfrey, Vice-president; Charles L. Riddle, Cashier.—A leading representative financial institution of Boston is the National Webster Bank, noted for the sound and conservative policy which has ever characterized its operations. The inception of this institution dates back to 1853, when it was organized under the state laws as the Webster Bank. In 1865 it was reorganized, under the National Banking Act, as the National Webster Bank with a capital of $1,500,000. It has continued thus, with ever-augmenting prosperity, its charter having been duly renewed in 1885. The National Webster Bank transacts a general banking business, the accounts of banks and other corporations, merchants, and individuals being received, and the usual financial facilities afforded. The bank has a very influential circle of customers and depositors, and it discounts much of the most desirable commercial paper offered in Boston. It has every facility for making collections, among its correspondents being the Importers & Traders National Bank and the American Exchange National Bank of New York. The directors are as follows: Messrs. Francis A. Peters, H. H. Hunnewell, Stephen W. Marston, Joseph A. Laforme, Samuel Johnson, Wm. S. Houghton, John C. Palfrey, Joseph G. Kendall, Henry Whitman, Thos. Motley, Jr., and Stanton Blake. A more representative body of active business men and capitalists could not have been gathered together, and their names are synonymous with equity, stability, and integrity. Mr. Francis A. Peters, the president, was elected in 1884; and his ability as one of Boston's most respected financiers is proverbial, being a vigorous exponent of the soundest principles governing banking and finance. Mr. John C. Palfrey, the vice-president, was also elected in 1884, and is an efficient and able financier, ever upholding a conservative, sound monetary policy. Mr. Charles L. Riddle, the cashier, has been with the bank since it first opened, thirty-five years ago. He has become thoroughly familiarized with its workings, and with every detail of a great business such as is transacted here, and since 1868 has most efficiently and faithfully discharged the duties of cashier. Loyal to this time-honored and solid old institution, its executive has a most creditable record as the result of its guidance, having now $2,344,230 of resources, of which no less than $701,000 00 are surplus and profits. These are figures speaking more eloquently than any words can, as to the wisdom of its management; and its deposits, verging closely on a million and a half, with loans and discounts of over two millions and a half, indicate how prosperous it is, and with what a degree of confidence the public select it as the channel of their monetary and commercial transactions.

EDWARD L. QUIGLEY, Insurance, Corner of City Square and Park Street, Charlestown, and No. 48 Congress Street, Boston.—The placing of risks on life and property constitutes, as it goes without saying a, sphere of usefulness of peculiar importance in every centre of industry, commerce, and trade; but it may be added that it is a branch of business that occupies the attention of some of the most staunch and sagacious citizens in every progressive community. Among those engaged in this line in Charlestown there is perhaps none who are better known or sustain a higher reputation for integrity and reliability, as few enjoy a larger measure of public confidence and favor, than Edward L. Quigley, whose office is located at the corner of City Square and Park Street, with headquarters with Charles W. Holden, at No. 48 Congress Street, Boston, Mass. Mr. Quigley, who resides in Charlestown, is a gentleman of entire probity in his business relations, as well as a man of energy and judicious enterprise, and is thoroughly conversant with every feature and detail pertaining to fire and life insurance. He has been engaged in an insurance office over seventeen years, giving personal attention to the management of both offices, and has built up a very fine connection. He conducts a general fire and life insurance business, placing all desirable risks with first-class companies, at the lowest rates consistent with absolute security, and is agent also for the following solid and substantial institutions: Rea. of London; Royal, of Liverpool; Merchants, of Newark; Washington Life Ins. Co., and others. Mr. Quigley makes a special feature of the prompt settlement of just claims.

COLEMAN COOK & CO., Auctioneers, Real-estate and Fire Insurance Agency, Nos. 9 and 10 Maverick Square, East Boston.—This business was originally established in 1868 by Mr. Coleman Cook, the present firm being organized in 1884 by the admission of Mr Andrew P. Fisher to partnership. Having the advantage of long experience in fire-insurance matters, and being thoroughly acquainted with every department from the framing of contracts to the adjustment of losses, these gentlemen are eminently fitted to serve their patrons with intelligence and ability, and deservedly enjoy a high reputation in insurance circles. They are agents here for the following well-known and reliable companies; viz., the Phœnix, the City of London, the Guardian, and the Norwich Union, of England; the Bowery and the Continental, of New York; the Franklin and the Spring Garden, of Philadelphia; the North American and the Dorchester Mutual, of Boston. Controlling the interests of these companies in East Boston, they are prepared to effect insurance in any or all of these companies in respect of all kinds of insurable property at the lowest possible rates consistent with security; and they promptly adjust and pay all losses that occur. In addition to their extensive insurance business, this firm are also prominent and popular as auctioneers and real estate agents, having an intimate knowledge of real estate in this section of the city and a wide acquaintance with capitalists, investors, and property-owners. Their services are promptly rendered, and are of great value to those who need reliable counsel and sound advice. Mr. Cook is a native of Provincetown, Mass., and has resided in East Boston since 1843. Mr. Fisher was born in Portsmouth, N. H., and came to this city in 1864.

JAMES TOWNSEND & SON, Insurance and Real-estate Agents, No. 216 Meridian Street, East Boston.—The best-known and most popular mediums through which to obtain fire-insurance policies in East Boston is the agency conducted by Messrs. James Townsend & Son, at No. 216 Meridian Street. [...]

A. H. ADAMS & CO., Rubbers Leather, Roundings, Shoulder-splits and Heel Stock, Calf and Kip Skiving, Specialties, No. 126 Summer Street.—This house was founded in 1846 by Mr. A. H. Adams [...]

EDWARD HARKINS & CO., Oiled Cowtree, No. 47 India Street, Corner of Milk.—In noting the many and varied business concerns that contribute to the general sum of industrial and commercial activity on India Street [...]

ELLIOTT PAPER BOX COMPANY, C. S. Crain, President and Treasurer, No. 121 Mill Street.—The Elliott Paper Box Company is widely and favorably known, being one of the leading concerns of this kind supplying the trade. [...]

E. O. THOMPSON, Tailor, Importer and Clothier, No. 344 Washington Street; also New York and Philadelphia.—For fine clothing having every feature of excellence in fashionable materials cut in the latest London styles [...]

DU PONT'S GUN POWDER. Sporting and Blasting, Shipping and Mining; George F. Smith & Co., Agents, No. 7 Central Wharf. —The Du Pont Gun Powder is the most justly celebrated of any in the world. It has upon its merits, in its various forms for sporting and military purposes, ever maintained its supremacy, and has been awarded the premium in the severest competition. In fact, the United States Government has, through its Ordnance Department, after the most exhaustive tests, pronounced this the best for the purpose of the army; and it now used for U. S. ammunition, besides being exported to foreign governments. It was in 1802 that Eleuthere Irenee Du Pont, a pupil of the famous chemist Lavoisier, and a native of France, founded on the banks of the Brandywine River, near Wilmington, Del., the works which have since grown to proportions of such magnitude, and whose product is so internationally celebrated. The works are the largest of the kind in the world, and annually consume over eight million pounds of saltpetre and nitrate of soda. Only the purest ingredients enter into these gunpowders, the reputation of the mills has stood unrivalled for 88 years—a just cause of pride to the successors of the honored founder of these internationally famous works. Boston has ever been a most important centre for the sale of Du Pont Powders, and it was 10 years ago that the late F. B. F. de Grand established the agency. About 1888 the late Mr Charles Smith succeeded him, and, upon his decease in 1888, was succeeded by Messrs. George R. Smith & Co. Mr George R. Smith is a nephew of Mr Charles Smith, and has been identified with the agency for over forty years past. He brings to bear the widest range of experience, and is the leading authority on gunpowder in New England. With offices at No. 7 Central Wharf, he has storage for a portion of his immense stock in the Harbor Stores, the bulk of it being in his large magazine at Quincy, Mass. He always has on hand, and is prepared to sell at wholesale, in any quantity, the celebrated Eagle Ducking, Eagle Rifle, and Diamond Grain powders in all numbers and of guaranteed superiority, also Cartridge, Mammoth, Cannon, Mortar, and Musket powders for Naval and Military use of U. S. Government standard; also the various grades of powder for sporting, shipping, mining, and blasting, also special grades for export. Mr. Smith was born in Boston, and is a popular and respected member of mercantile circles. He has developed a trade of great magnitude, and is the leading representative of the wholesale trade in powder in New England.

D. D. WHITE & CO., Manufacturer of Men's and Boys' Split, Veal Calf, Buff, and Calf Shoes of all kinds, Raynham Mass. At Boston Office, 134 Summer Street, Wednesdays and Saturdays —The manufacture of the various grades of calf shoes has steadily become a branch of industry of growing importance. The demands of the public are for a shoe of the highest standard of perfection, and a house which has achieved an enviable reputation, and which is thoroughly representative of the moral advanced methods in this line, is that of Messrs. D. D. White & Co., of No. 134 Summer Street. Mr. D. D White was born in New Hampshire, and early in life became actively identified with the branch of trade in which he has achieved such a substantial success. Twenty years ago he began manufacturing, and has ever been one of the most progressive and popular members of the trade, his goods invariably affording the utmost satisfaction, and proving permanent and ready sellers. On January 1, 1889, Mr. Harry T. White, his nephew, and a young business man of ability and energy, was admitted into copartnership under the existing name and style. The firm's factory is situated at Raynham, Mass., and is of large size and fully equipped with the latest improved machinery and appliances, affording employment to upwards of 60 hands in the manufacture of the finest and medium grades of men's and boys' split, veal calf, buff, dongola, kid, and calf shoes of all kinds. The firm bring to bear the widest range of practical experience, and exercise the utmost care in the selection of leather and findings. Nothing but the best quality is ever admitted into their factory, while their styles, cut, and workmanship are all of the most desirable and perfect character. The firm's laudable ambition to excel is generously recognized throughout the United States, and a trade of great magnitude is developing, of the greatest value to New England and to the highest degree creditable to the distinguished enterprise and energy of the popular proprietors.

W. M. SMITH & CO., Agents and Dealers in Real Estate, Mortgages Negotiated, Auctioneers and Appraisers, No. 27 Tremont Street. —The real estate broker's and auctioneer's calling is one of great importance in a large city like Boston, where property and business houses are continually changing hands. Prominent among the leading real estate men and auctioneers of this city is the firm of W. M. Smith & Co., whose office is located at No. 27 Tremont Street, opposite the Boston Museum. This firm are deservedly popular as agents and dealers in real estate, and as auctioneers and appraisers, making a leading speciality of auction sales of real estate, and have been established in the business here since 1875. Mr. Smith, the senior member of the firm, is a native of Boston, now a resident of Roxbury, and is a gentleman of ripe experience, possessing all the qualifications, aptitude, and enterprise of a first-class broker and dealer in real estate, and is also a justice of the peace. He handles every description of realty, both as agent and dealer, making a speciality of selling and exchanging farms throughout New England, and suburban estates, both large and small, near Boston; also dealing in all kinds of city property, either for sale, exchange, or to let; has business charges for sale; negotiates loans on bond and mortgage; places insurance to all the leading fire companies; and is always prepared to attend to auction sales in city or country for both real estate and personal property. Mr. J. E. Nevins, a resident of Boston, is the junior member of the firm, and is in charge of the office. This house is recognized as one of the most trustworthy in its line in the city; and patrons may rest assured that on placing their commissions with it, they will be effectively and faithfully carried out.

ANTHONY S HORNE. Hardware, Cutlery, and Tools, Brass Composition, and Galvanized Iron, Ship, Yacht, and Boat Blocks, Trimmings, etc, Galvanizing done to order, Nos. 210 and 212 Commercial Street. —The house so long and so successfully conducted by Mr. Anthony S Horne is a pioneer in the hardware trade of this city, enjoying a reputation that represents the results of forty four years of honorable and successful effort. The proprietor founded the business in 1844, and has steadily continued in the same groove. He deals in hardware, cutlery, tools, brass, composition, galvanized iron, ship, yacht, and boat supplies, —at both wholesale and retail. The business premises comprise four floors, 80x40 feet each, giving abundance of room for supplying the most extensive demand. The several departments are fitted with an elaborate and diversified stock, embracing builders' and general hardware; shelf goods and cabinet hardware; carpenters', mechanics', and machinists' tools; iron and steel, brass and composition goods; ship, yacht, and boat blocks and trimmings; table and pocket cutlery, and kindred supplies. These goods are purchased in vast quantities direct from the manufacturers. Significant advantages are extended to customers in the matter of prices. Both a wholesale and retail business is transacted, and in addition to a large local trade, a heavy demand is administered to, coming from all parts of the New England States. Mr. Horne is a native of Newburyport, Mass. and is honored and esteemed in this city as a reputable merchant.

OLIVER GREEN & CO., No. 184 Tremont Street. —The house of Oliver Green is doing much to foster and promote a love for the charming and indispensable accomplishment of music. This firm are agents for the Geo. Steck & Co., Decker & Son's, and Guild & Co.'s. Pianos, and as dealers in three celebrated instruments, and in other musical merchandise, possess a prestige rarely equalled by any contemporary house in the city. Mr. Green, the active member of the firm, is a prominent musician of this city, who was for eighteen years a tuner in Emerson's factory, and established his present business in 1878 at No. 175 Washington Street, where his own still operates a fine music-store. The Tremont street house was opened in October, 1888, and is finely arranged. His store is at all times stocked with a full line of the leading makes of pianos and organs, ranging in quality from the plain but substantial instrument to the most elaborate and costly. Prospective buyers will find here what is sure to be desired in musical instruments, and also have the valuable assistance of a reliable and trustworthy musical critic. Mr. Green is a native of Malden, Mass., of high repute and standing in the musical world, and universally popular with the host of friends and patrons.

IRWIN & CO., Fine Cigars, No. 180 Milk Street.—An enterprising, progressive, and representative house in the Boston (import) tobacco trade is that of Messrs. Irwin & Co. This firm are extensive importers of leaf tobaccos, and make a leading specialty of the manufacture and sale of all styles of Spanish and Cuban hand-made cigars, having their factory and general office at No. 180 Milk Street, with display and salesroom at [illegible] Hall, No. 349 Washington Street. Although established as late as January 1, [illegible] (in the manufacture of cigars), this house has quickly advanced to a leading position in the cigar and tobacco trade of this city and New England. Handling only fine, first-class goods, and making a specialty of supplying the wholesale drug trade, and other wholesale dealers, with special brands to order, the firm have built upon a foundation at once strong and permanent, and are steadily increasing their reputation with dealers and consumers wherever their goods are known. They have won a high prestige and deserved popularity as the makers of such celebrated brands of cigars as "La Henrietta," "The Irwin," "Los Doctores," "Boston Club," "[illegible]," "[illegible]," and others. "Los Doctores" is made especially for apothecaries' trade, is warranted free from artificial flavoring, and is unquestionably the [illegible] ten-cent cigar on the American market that can be sold by the [illegible] for twenty-five cents, or twelve for one dollar. It is manufactured from the finest kind of Havana tobacco (long filler), that is grown on the Island of Cuba, a grade (especially selected by them) which smokes rich and full without being strong and rank; it is mild and sweet, without being woody, dry and tasteless. It is like all cigars of this firm—handmade in a cleanly manner, by high-priced Spanish and Cuban workmen, under their own personal supervision, in their own factory—which makes its smoking qualities uniform and reliable. It is sold by druggists generally throughout the United States. The specialties handled by this firm have already attained an enormous consumption all over the globe, and are recognized as staples wherever once introduced. They are all noted for the splendid tobacco used, purity and care in manufacture, and are the most fragrant, agreeable, and reliable cigars in the market. They are handled by the best class of trade, and the business is rapidly increasing under enterprising and reliable management. Mr. J. A. Irwin, the esteemed proprietor, is a native of Boston, prompt, honorable, and responsible in his business dealings, and a man of high social and business standing.

MONTGOMERY & KELLOGG, Manufacturers' Agents, No. 630 Atlantic Avenue.—Standing prominently forward among the representative commercial houses of Boston is that conducted by Messrs. Montgomery & Kellogg, the well-known manufacturers' agents. This firm are general commission merchants in cotton yarns and warps, handling domestic products only, and are especially prominent as the New England agents for J. B. Montgomery & Co., manufacturers of novelty yarns, at Windsor Locks, Conn. They established their business here in 1887, and their wide and influential connections, coupled with their thorough knowledge of the wants and requirements of the trade, and the energy, business ability, and liberality that characterize all operations of their house, command for it a conspicuous and honored position among the mercantile concerns of New England. The business has been eminently prosperous and successful from the start, increasing steadily under energetic and enterprising management, until it now reaches to all parts of the United States. Their relations with leading manufacturers of yarns and warps are of that intimate and influential character that enable them to offer their customers advantages and inducements unsurpassed by any firm in the country. Orders by telephone or otherwise are promptly filled direct from the factory. There is no business establishment in the city better prepared to satisfy the requirements of its special line of trade or more really deserves its popularity and success. The individual members of the firm are Messrs. W. W. Montgomery, a native of Massachusetts, and C. A. Kellogg, a native of Connecticut, both reliable, responsible, and popular trade representatives.

FREEMAN & PEIRCE, Agents for the Standard Sewing Machine Company, No. 173 Tremont Street.—The "Standard" Rotary Shuttle Sewing-Machine is acknowledged to be the most wonderful invention in this direction, and is pronounced superior to any other in the world. The Standard shuttle is wheel-shaped, and revolves upon its own centre. It does not cease its motion while the machine is in operation. The old style shuttles start and stop twice at every stitch. This causes great friction, strain, noise, and unsteadiness when rapidly run. The Standard runs as easy, smooth, and quiet at 1500 stitches per minute as most others do at 700. The Standard is self-threading throughout, except the needle. The needle is the shortest used in lock-stitch machines. Finer needles, with the same sized thread or silk, can be used than in any old style shuttle machine. The needle is self-setting. No change of tension required for different thicknesses of goods. No necessity for holding the thread at the beginning of a seam to prevent it from being drawn down. No change of tension required for different lengths of stitch. The first stitch is perfect without holding the ends of thread. The tension is entirely released when taking out the goods by a simple device peculiar to the Standard. These unexcelled machines are made in several different styles for families, dress makers, and manufacturers. They are to be found on sale in all parts of the country and are highly endorsed. The agents in this city, Messrs. Freeman & Pierce, are both experienced men in this business, and have been the representatives of the Standard Company since 1887. A handsome store is occupied, in which a fine display is made of these machines. All the various attachments are furnished, which are made expressly for the Standard Sewing Machine Company, and are far in advance of any heretofore in use. The Standard is certainly the sewing machine needed in this progressive age, and is far ahead in every respect of those now on the market.

WARREN EMERSON, Importer and Jobber of Upholstery Goods, Furniture Coverings, Curtain Materials, Car Trimmings and Upholsterers' Supplies, No. 9 Arch Street, and No. 6 Hawley Street. The improvement in the culture and good taste of the people in the matter of interior decoration, has been most marked within recent years, especially in the line of upholstery goods, and there are some very superior productions in this branch of manufacture to be found in the market. A house which has for a third of a century held a representative position in the trade in this city, and has developed a trade which extends to all sections of the New England States, is that of Mr. Warren Emerson, located at No. 9 Arch Street, and No. 6 Hawley Street. This establishment was founded in 1855 by Mr. H. T. Champney and remained in his possession until eleven years ago, when Mr. Emerson succeeded to the control. The spacious warerooms, [illegible] feet in dimensions, is filled with an extensive assortment of foreign and domestic upholstery goods of every description, furniture-coverings, curtain materials, car-trimmings, and upholsterers' supplies in profuse variety. These goods are procured direct from the most reliable manufacturers, and are representative of the best creations in this line to be found in the market. Eight assistants are employed and an active trade is supplied, the facilities of the house enabling the proprietor to fill all orders at the shortest notice as well as on the most favorable terms. Mr. Emerson, who is a native of New Hampshire, has long resided in Boston, and is familiarly known in business and social circles. He is a member of the Boston Art Club, in which he takes a valued interest, and he enjoys the fullest confidence of the public, because of his sterling integrity, and thorough business enterprise.

BABB & STEPHENS, Printers, No. 124 Congress Street.—For some twenty-three years Babb & Stephens, the well known printers, have been steadily increasing their hold on public favor and patronage, owing to the excellence of their work, and their promptness and reliability in executing orders. The firm occupy one large floor, and have in service ample steam power, four fine presses, complete outfit of type, and every necessary facility, while ten or more expert hands are employed. Book and job work in all their branches are done in the most expeditious and excellent manner, at bottom prices, fine commercial printing being a leading specialty, while all work executed here is warranted to render satisfaction, the firm also filling orders for everything in the line of blank-books. The copartnership consists of Messrs. Walter Babb and George Stephens, both men of middle age, and natives respectively of Barrington, N. H., and Plymouth, Mass. They are practical and expert printers themselves, of long and varied experience in the exercise of their art.

172 ILLUSTRATED BOSTON.

W. B. CLARKE & CO., Importers, Booksellers, and Stationers, No. 340 Washington Street.—One of Boston's oldest business houses, surrounded by pleasant historic associations, is the book and stationery store of W. B. Clarke & Co. It was founded many years ago by W. H. Piper & Co., and was purchased by the present firm in 1874. Here rare and conspicuous is literature in their day—Longfellow, Lowell, Hawthorne, Holmes, Emerson, and others of wide fame in the world of American letters—were wont to gather for the interchange of good fellowship and art. Under the energetic auspices of the present management, this house has become one of the most complete retail book and stationery establishments in the country. The literary zone of Boston make it their chief rendezvous. The store is spacious in size, attractive in all its appointments, and stocked to overflowing with new and current literature, standard works of prose and poetry, fine stationery and fancy goods. It is a very popular shopping place for ladies, who largely patronize its church department for prayer-books, hymnals, and Bibles. It has a department for medical, scientific, and agricultural works; another for theological literature; another for guide-books; one for books in fine bindings, illustrated works, etc.; one for sporting and yachting books, and out-door literature generally; one for juvenile works, toys and games; and special counters for blank books, stationery, albums and fancy goods, and paper novels. This house is never without the best "new thing" in English or American literature. It also does a large importing business; purchases second-hand books, and offers subscriptions to leading periodicals at "club rates." All kinds of printing can here be conducted for; blank books are promptly made to order; and town libraries and clubs are supplied at short notice. A corps of twenty-four efficient clerks and salesmen contribute to the satisfactory operations of the establishment. Mr. Clarke, the enterprising proprietor, is a native of Northampton, Mass., a resident of Boston for twenty-four years, and one of its leading society leaders and business representatives, a lieutenant of the Boston Cadets, a member of various clubs, and eminently popular in literary circles.

PROVIDENT LIFE AND TRUST COMPANY of Philadelphia. Boston Office, No. 110 Devonshire Street; David N. Holway, General Agent.—One of those great representative and reliable institutions which are contributing so largely to Philadelphia's prosperity is the Provident Life and Trust Company. The Boston office of this famous corporation, under the able and efficient management of Mr. David N. Holway, is located at No. 110 Devonshire Street. This Company was duly incorporated under the laws of Pennsylvania in 1865, and is empowered to insure lives and grant annuities, to execute trusts, to act as executor or administrator, assignee and guardian of minors, and also in other fiduciary capacities. While organized originally with a view of promoting life insurance among the Society of Friends in the United States, it has never by any means confined itself to that field, but extends its benefits and advantages to all other persons of similar careful

habits. Its claims to public patronage are of the most forcible character, which are manifest to any one interested in the subject. The following gentlemen, who are all by any favorably known in financial and business circles for their prudence, executive ability, and integrity, are the officers and directors: Samuel R. Shipley, President; T. Wistar Brown, Vice-President; Asa S. Wing, Vice-President and Actuary; Joseph Ashbrook, Manager of Insurance Department; J. Roberts Foulke, Trust Officer; Dr. Thomas Wistar, Chief Medical Examiner; Jos. B. Townsend, Samuel Dickson, Legal Advisers; Directors—Samuel R. Shipley, T. Wistar Brown, Henry Haines, Richard Cadbury, Richard Wood, William Hacker, J. Morton Albertson, James T. Watson, Israel Morris, Chas. Hartshorne, William Gummere, Frederic Collins, Asa S. Wing, Philip C. Garrett, Justus C. Strawbridge. The condition of the company, January 1, 1890, was as follows: Assets at present value, $15,040,849 35; liabilities (Massachusetts Standard), $12,833,879.32; surplus to policy-holders, $4,207,050; 20,738 policies outstanding, insuring $41,001,974; $910 policies issued in 1889, insuring $11,122,675; amount paid

upon policies to date, $9,350,769.26; increased assets in 1889, $1,625,852.50; increased amount of outstanding insurance, $4,564,041. The relations of the two departments of the business are fixed by the provisions of the charter. The entire surplus in the Insurance Department accumulates for the benefit of the policy-holders. The only advantage, direct or indirect, which the stockholders of this company can at any time have from the union of the two features of their business results from the fact that the management of trusts, from which they derive their profits, is done for them without charge. The accounts of the insurance and trust departments are kept entirely distinct and separate. The Provident Life and Trust Company has never during its whole history contested a death claim, but has always conducted its business upon the enlarging basis of equity and just dealing. Its policies are models of simplicity and brevity, and include every feature of liberality and security to policy-holders. Its rates are exceedingly moderate, and those contemplating life insurance should send for his rate-book. Mr. David N. Holway, the general agent, has been twenty-two years with the company, and took charge of the Boston office in 1866, upon the death of Mr. G. C. Tieng. Previously he had acted as general agent in New York, and was for years at the home office in Philadelphia in the work of qualifying agents. He is now the oldest representative of the Provident in the United States. Mr. Holway is the author of "The Science of Life Assurance," "The Progress of Life Assurance," and a recent work entitled "Endowments." The two latter works are copyrighted and have an enormous circulation. Mr. Holway is First Vice-President of the Boston Life Underwriters' Association, which recently celebrated its sixth annual banquet. In both his departments of business the Provident Life and Trust Company has taken a leading position, not only provincial but national in its character and extent of operations, and is in every respect a permanent source of credit and honor to its officers and directors.

McKAY & BIGELOW HEELING MACHINE ASSOCIATION, No. 108 Summer Street.—In the intention of all kinds of labor-saving machinery American manufactures are greatly ahead of all the nations of the world. In this connection, we desire to make special reference in this serviceable review of Boston to the famous McKay & Bigelow Heeling Machine Association, whose offices are located at No. 108 Summer Street. This association was organized a quarter of a century ago, and its trade now is by no means confined to the United States and Canada, but extends to all parts of the civilized world. The company's factory is at Lawrence, Mass., and its principal offices are located in Boston. The heeling machinery of this company is abundantly unrivalled for efficiency, utility, economy, reliability, and general excellence, and has no superior in this country or Europe. The McKay Heeling Fastening Association are manufacturers and owners of the Standard Screw Machine, Cable Wire Tacker, and String Nail Tacker. These machines are general favorites with manufacturers wherever introduced, and are positively unequalled. The association issues a superior illustrated catalogue and price-list of spare parts, which is forwarded promptly upon application.

IRA A. BOWEN, Dry-goods Commission Merchant, No. 68 Summer Street.—This gentleman is especially prominent in the trade as agent for Henry Newman & Co., of New York, importers of British, French, and German goods for clothing and dry-goods trade, and converters of cotton goods; also agent for the City Mills Company's lambs' wool wadding. He established himself in business here in 1884, and by reason of his influential connections, ample resources, and strict attention to the wants of the trade, he has built up a large and prosperous business, which extends to all parts of the New England States. He sells entirely by sample, and is prepared to supply the trade with dry-goods, trimmings, and clothiers' supplies in quantities to suit, at the shortest possible notice, and at terms and prices which defy successful competition. His facilities for transacting business upon the largest scale are unusually complete. Its reputation for honorable and liberal dealing is firmly established beyond the requirements of praise. Mr. Bowen, the enterprising and popular agent, was born in New Hampshire, and came to Boston in 1865. He has a foundation understanding of all the needs and requirements of the dry-goods trade.

PENOBSCOT BAY LAND COMPANY, Brockton, Me.; Branch Office, No. 81 Milk Street.—This successful corporation was duly incorporated under the laws of Maine in 1884, with a paid up capital of $120,000. The property of the Penobscot Bay Land Company is situated on a bold headland known as Fort Point on Penobscot Bay, in the town of Stockton, Waldo County, Me.,—thirty miles from Bangor, and easily reached by both land and water. The property forms a peninsula, and has several miles of seashore on Penobscot Bay. The company own and control 800 acres of land, which are subdivided into 1000 lots. The following gentlemen are the officers: D. Lancey, President; A. H. Bodet, Secretary and Treasurer; Directors B. S. Grant, T. H. Dale, G. H. Burch, L. J. Moore, Wm. C. Clarke, ex-Governor of Massachusetts. The land for sale commands a magnificent view of ocean, island, mountain, and forest scenery; while in its immediate vicinity are charming inland views and delightful drives. The climate is perfection, mosquitoes and flies are unknown, while rowing, fishing, bathing, and canoeing can be enjoyed to perfection. Here can be secured a pleasant and healthful summer home, with almost every convenience for enjoyment, surrounded by pure air and charming scenery, and with the best of facilities for advent and departure either by Boston and Bangor steamers or Boston and Maine Central Railroad; and, with its many miles of seashore, commanding location and delightful climate, bids fair to become one of the finest summer resorts on the coast. The company also own the "Woodcliff," a large and elegant hotel, one of the finest on the coast, containing one hundred and twenty-five large and airy rooms fitted with all the modern conveniences and beautifully situated in an elevated position, commanding an unsurpassed view. For further particulars, plans, maps, etc., intending purchasers are referred to the office, No. 81 Milk Street. The company also own The Harvard Land Company, which is situated on Mt. Desert Island, at South West Harbor, and at Winter Harbor, on Frenchman's Bay, Maine; which is the largest and most fashionable summer resort on Mt. Desert Island, excepting Bar Harbor, comprising many large hotels and beautiful cottages, churches, schools, post office, and stores of all kinds, and is the landing place of all steamers running to and from Bar Harbor and the east. The company own here about two hundred acres of land, situated a short distance from South West Harbor proper, known as the "Sea Wall" property, beautifully located, with an unobstructed view of the ocean and surrounding mountains, and extending for two miles along the shore. They are the proprietors of the new Sea Wall Hotel, located about six hundred feet from the shore and facing the sea; with wide verandas, from which there is a most beautiful and varied view of all the loftiest peaks celebrated for their beauty, and the broad, rolling ocean, dotted here and there with picturesque islands. The company also own a tract of land situated at Lower Winter Harbor, less than one mile from Winter Harbor Village, on the eastern shore of Frenchman's Bay, Maine. It was formerly known as the "College Tract," having belonged to Harvard University—hence its present name. There are about two hundred acres of land, divided into eight hundred beautifully located building lots containing five thousand square feet each (after deducting thirty per cent for streets). And it has a continuous frontage extending for two miles along the shore, the land rising in gradual slopes from twenty to seventy feet above the water level. Thus this company offers special inducements to investors. The capital stock of the company is $350,000, divided into 70,000 shares; par value, $5 per share.

PROF. F. H. BAILEY, Astronomical Inventor, Author and Lecturer, No. 48 Federal Street.—The man who possesses the inventive faculty and can perfect his own inventions has a large field for the exercise of his talents on this continent. Such an one is Prof. F. H. Bailey, the celebrated astronomical inventor, author and lecturer, whose office is located at No. 48 Federal Street. As the inventor of Bailey's Cosmosphere and Bailey's Astral Lantern, this gentleman stands deservedly high in educational circles throughout the country. He is a Vermonter by birth, a graduate of Hillsdale College, Mich., and still in the early prime of life. He resides in Cambridge, and opened his office in this city in 1887. He is everywhere acknowledged to be without a rival in qualifications and equipment for the platform presentation of "The Queen of the Sciences." Being an easy extemporaneous speaker, and provided with the best illustrative apparatus ever invented, Prof. Bailey adapts himself readily to an audience of any class or grade, from one of primary school children to one of University students; and by the selection of common elemental subjects, and the treatment of them in an uncommon, but simple manner, a popular evidence of wide range is both interesting and instructed. No previous knowledge of astronomy is necessary for the complete comprehension of his popular lectures on "Phenomena and Poetry of the Heavens," illustrated with his mammoth globe eighteen feet and ten inches in circumference. He gave his lecture on "Phenomenal Astronomy" before a large audience in Cooper Institute, on December 6, 1888, and is prepared to lecture in any part of the country at the shortest notice. Bailey's Cosmosphere is the only one of its kind in existence, and the largest globe in America, as transparent as glass, and brilliantly illuminated; illustrates many celestial phenomena than any other instrument, shows the heavens as seen from any point on earth for every minute of the year, and the movements of sun, moon, and stars for any length of time, and presents to the eye clear and exact figures of the constellations with which the fancy of the ancients peopled the heavens. Astronomers agree that "the skill and accuracy with which it illustrates the precession of the equinoxes is a real triumph of inventive genius." The "Astral Lantern" is an illuminated panorama of the heavens, showing the position and movement of the stars for every minute of the year. It is admirably fitted to every latitude, but especially adapted for the North Temperate Zone, and it supplies a long felt need, enabling the student of the heavens, with the least possible labor, and without a teacher, to learn the names, positions, and movements of the stars and constellations. It provides a most interesting and instructive evening entertainment for old and young. It brings the knowledge of the stars within the reach of all and makes the study of astronomy both easy and fascinating. It has elicited unqualified praise from the best astronomers and most prominent educators in the country, many of whom have prophesied that it would not only revolutionize methods of teaching Uranography, but be the means of introducing the study of the heavens into thousands of schools and families. These inventions are manufactured by Messrs. F. H. Beal & Co. of No. 18 Federal Street, and are placed upon the market at prices which brings them within the reach of all institutions of learning. They are earnestly recommended to schools and colleges by prominent educators, as a most useful adjunct to lessons in astronomy and as superior to anything in use for the purpose intended.

B. EHRENRATH & CO., Manufacturers of Harness Dongola, No. 8 South Street; F. W. Forbush, Manager.—The history of the growth and progress of industrial activity in the United States presents few counterparts to the development of the tanning interests during the past quarter of a century. And it may be added, also, that the improvement made in the article produced within the period mentioned has fully kept pace with the growth of the industry. Especially is this true with regard to the upper leather known to the trade as "Dongola goat," to which a high degree of excellence has been attained by some of our leading tanners, notably by the widely-known and enterprising firm of B. Ehrenrath & Co., manufacturers of "Rardue" Dongola, whose capacious and well-equipped tanneries are located at Racine, Wis., and who are represented in this city by F. W. Forbush, with office and salesroom at No. 18 South Street. The productions of this firm in "Dongola," and are to extensive and growing demand throughout the entire country, particularly so among the New England shoe manufacturers, owing to the uniformly high standard of excellence at which this article is maintained. The Boston office of this concern was established in May, 1888, in order to meet the requirements of the large and rapidly increasing eastern business, and the unequivocal success that has attended the venture here from the first abundantly attests the wisdom that inspired the enterprise, as well as the energy and ability displayed in the management. A full and fine line of stock is constantly kept on hand, all orders being promptly and reliably filled and the trade which extends all over the New England States is very substantial and grows apace. Mr. Forbush, who is a gentleman of middle age and a Bostonian by birth is a man of ready yet practical experience, thoroughly conversant with the business, and prior to assuming charge here for B. D. Ehrenrath & Co. had been engaged in the leather trade in Chicago for eighteen years, and for some time subsequently also at Racine.

W. L. GARRISON & CO., Commercial Paper and Western Mortgages, No. 191 Federal Street.—The securities offered by western farm mortgages are becoming to be generally recognized as of a much more desirable character than those which are presented to capitalists in the eastern states, as they are constantly increasing in value, while real estate securities in the east have, as a rule, reached their highest point and their values in many cases are diminishing instead of increasing. A leading house engaged in handling western mortgages and commercial paper of various kinds in this city is that of Messrs. W. L. Garrison & Co., located at No. 191 Federal Street. The business here conducted was originally established by Mr. Wm. Lloyd Garrison in 1865, the present firm being organized January 1, 1885, by the admission of Mr. Percival B. Howe to partnership. This firm deal in Kansas farm and city mortgages, and in some Chicago and Minnesota property, and are making a leading specialty at the present time, of wood and electric light paper. Both gentlemen are able and experienced financiers, noted for their sound judgment and sterling integrity, and give their close personal attention to all the details of their business. Their office is one of the best managed mediums in this city through which to invest in western farm mortgages or in any commercial paper desired. Every guarantee and safeguard is secured, all loans are on first mortgage only, and on the farms of reputable and thoroughly responsible farmers. The security must be worth at least three times the amount of the mortgage, while the terms are strict and explicit. Loans are confined to the best sections of the most fertile States in the west, where farms are constantly rising in value, and where loans are used to improve the security and increase the productive capacity of the property. The electric light and other paper handled by this firm is thoroughly first-class and reliable, commending itself on its own merits to the consideration of careful and prudent investors, and as every transaction of the firm is placed upon a thoroughly substantial basis, their office is a favorite resort for capitalists. Mr. Garrison has been treasurer of the Edison Electric Illuminating Company, of Brockton, since its formation, and is esteemed in social and financial life. Mr. Howe is also a Massachusetts man by birth and education, and well known in the business circles of this city.

COHEN & SONS, Manufacturers of Hats and Caps. No. 94 Devonshire Street.—A noted establishment in the hat and cap manufacturing industry in Boston is that of Messrs. Cohen & Sons, located at No. 94 Devonshire Street. This house has been in successful operation for a period of twenty-five years, and has won a national reputation and a trade coextensive with the limits of the country. The firm are extensive manufacturers, importers, and jobbers of hats, caps, military hats, and uniform and variety head gear of all kinds, and carry one of the largest and finest stocks in this line ever brought to this city. They occupy very large and commodious premises for both manufacturing and sales purposes, and give steady employment to a force of fifty experienced hands. The hats and caps manufactured by this firm are of the very finest quality that are put upon the market, and are unexcelled for style, elegance, and artistic workmanship in this or any other country. They meet with ready appreciation and a permanent demand wherever introduced, and in many markets of the country are preferred by dealers over all other makes on account of their great reliability and uniform excellence. Patrons can rely upon securing the most desirable goods in this line, either of domestic or foreign production as they prefer, and can also depend upon terms and prices equally satisfactory. The house commands all the advantages naturally accumulated by long years of identification with a special branch of trade, while its ample resources, perfect facilities, widespread and influential connections both at home and abroad, enable it to grant its customers inducements that cannot readily be duplicated elsewhere, and also render it to the confidence and patronage of the trade everywhere. Although recently burned out and sustaining a heavy loss, this firm are now conducting their business upon the same broad and liberal scale as before, and are offering the rarest bargains to be found in their line of trade. They have just completed the purchase of one of the largest Scotch cap factories in the country, and will continue the manufacture of all kinds of Scotch caps and Scotch windows suitable for all classes of trade. Orders may be sent to the Hub Scotch Cap Co., No. 31 John Street, Utica, N. Y., or to Cohen & Sons, Boston.

THEOPHILE JOUVAL, Maison de Modes, No. 461 Washington Street.—In every branch of mercantile activity in Boston there is one house that is justly and popularly spoken of as the representative of its class. In the line of the finest imported millinery goods, the position of supremacy is held by Mr. Theophile Jouval, the popular proprietor of the Maison de Modes, at No. 461 Washington Street. This house was originally established in 1866 by Mr. H. Davidson, and after some changes, the present proprietor came into possession in 1877, as successor to J. Auguste Ross. Jouval is deservedly prominent as an extensive importer of fine artificial flowers, patterns for hats, and all kinds of Paris novelties; also, laces, lace, and coiffures from Paris, and which are also made to order; also a large assortment of perfumeries, and shell combs of every description, making a specialty of bridal veils, wreaths, and bride's hair-dressing. Laces are also repaired and done up, and special hair-work is manufactured for ladies and gentlemen, and hair dressed in the latest style. The stock here displayed is the largest and finest of its kind in the city, imported direct from the most famous Parisian houses, and offered to customers at extremely low prices. The assortments are replete with the richest novelties in flowers, feathers, ribbons, ornaments, trimmings, silks, and satins, while the hats and bonnets imported by this house are new every day, worn by the most fashionable members of Boston society. The house steadily maintains the lead against all competition, the result of sound judgment, correct taste, and the handling of only the choicest and latest importations in the line of millinery goods. Mons. Jouval was born in France, where he was engaged in business previous to emigrating to Boston in 1871. He entered this house as a clerk, was promoted to the position of manager, and finally succeeded to the sole control. He is still in the prime of life, alert and energetic in promoting the interests of his house, and commands the respect and esteem of the business community and the general public by reason of his promptness, courtesy, and thorough reliability.

MILTON A. KENT, Manufacturer and Wholesale Dealer in Gloves and Mittens, No. 81 Arch Street.—The leading representative of the wholesale trade in buck, kid, and castor gloves is Mr. Milton A. Kent. He was born in Berkshire County, Mass., and early in life became actively identified with this branch of trade. For a period of fifteen years he was one of the best known travelers in the glove trade in the United States, representing the most famous factories and offering the most substantial inducements. In 1882 he established the present business, and now does a trade of great magnitude. He is both manufacturer and wholesale dealer. His factories are situated at Gloversville, N. Y.; Bristol, N. H.; and Fonsburg Falls, Vt. At the latter establishments Mr. Kent manufactures the famous seamless wool gloves in all sizes and shades; also the finest quality of yarns, used for this class of goods. He manufactures buckskin and kid gloves at Gloversville and Bristol, and upon the most extensive and comprehensive scale. In his salesroom he covers the entire stock of gloves and variety of stock unequalled elsewhere. The general stock includes such specialties as genuine hand-sewed Plymouth, the popular glove of the day; full lines of buck gloves; Standard seamless, all wool felted gloves and mitts; also all-wool, seamless Scotch gloves, mittens of all grades, etc. Mr. Kent controls the best class of trade in New England, and quality is his first consideration. All goods of his manufacture are justly celebrated for their excellence of material, workmanship, and finish. Mr. Kent was burned out in 1872, at that time being located corner of Chauncy and Summer Streets.

F. W. BOYD, Wool, No. 116 Federal Street.—Among Boston's leading and most responsible wool brokers may be mentioned the name of F. W. Boyd. Mr. Boyd, who is a comparatively young man in the business by birth, but resides at Hyde Park. He is a gentleman of entire reliability in his dealings, as well as a man of energy and ample experience, and is thoroughly conversant with the trade. He has been in business on his own account about six years, and from the first he has steadily pushed his way to prominence and prosperity. Mr. Boyd is a general broker in foreign and domestic wool of all kinds, and has a chain of correspondents in the principal wool centres of the United States, buying largely in the east and southwest on orders for New England manufacturers, and is prepared to execute all orders for anything in this line in the most expeditious and satisfactory manner

SAMUEL CABOT, Inventor and Sole Manufacturer of Creosote Shingle Stains, No. 70 Kilby Street.—Progress is noticeable in every branch of the skilled industries of the age, and especially so in all that conduces to the perfection and beautifying of the modern building. In this connection, special mention should be made of the world-famous Creosote Stains, which were duly patented on April 23, 1884, and have since that date come into wide-spread use among architects and builders. The sole manufacturer of these stains is Mr. Samuel Cabot, with headquarters at No. 70 Kilby Street. For shingles, clap-boards, and other exterior woodwork, likewise for various styles of interior finish, these stains are unquestionably without a rival. Nowhere in the world is there anything approaching them for economy, preservation of the wood, the beautiful artistic effects, ease of application, and marked durability. These stains are admirable from every point of view, and, once introduced into a neighborhood, prove their own best advertisement. The use of creosote is a distinctive feature of these stains. This substance is a well known preservative of wood, and causes it to resist all changes from water or climatic changes; while it protects the wood from insects and notably that destructive pest, the white ant of the south. These stains are made by Mr. Cabot upon the most extensive scale and in every desirable shade and color at his large and splendidly equipped factory, situated at Chelsea. Twenty-six hands are there employed in the production of a vast variety of stains and other products. The stains are put up in barrels, half barrels, kegs, and one to ten gallon cans ready for use by the most inexperienced persons. Any one can dip the shingles in the liquid, while any boy can apply it with a brush. Mr. Cabot started the manufacture of coal-tar products in 1877, and after a series of experiments and tests, began the manufacture of Creosote Stains in 1883. He is a practically experienced and scientific chemist, a former student of the Institute of Technology, and he pursued his studies for some time at Zurich, Switzerland. He is a business man of marked executive ability, and has developed his industry systematically and upon a thorough basis of efficiency. His stains are now sold all over the United States, and Canada. These stains combine every feature that is desired for shingle roofs and clapboard houses. It preserves the wood from dry rot or decay through dampness. Mr. Cabot has tested its powers in the most practical manner, and finds it to be from one third to one seventh cheaper than paint. It is as durable as the best paint, the coloring effects are more beautiful and more clearly defined, while the creosote acts as a fire-protector—wood so treated burning with difficulty. These stains contain no water or benzine, and are the only exterior stains not adulterated with kerosene. Those interested and architects and builders everywhere should send for Mr. Cabot's samples, consisting of pieces of shingle cedar, colored with his Creosote Stains in about twenty shades of russet, brown, olive green, red, buff, yellow, etc. The public labor under heavy obligations to Mr. Cabot for the invention of these magnificent substitutes for paint for outside decoration and preservation; and he is well worthy of the large measure of success attending his ably directed efforts.

E. J. KNIGHT & CO., Stock brokers, No. 6 Court Street, Room 1.—Although a comparatively young firm, E. J. Knight & Co., the popular, responsible stock-brokers, with office at No. 6 Court Street, room 1, have attained a standing in financial circles both in New York and Boston, and have established a clientage vouchsafed to but few among the stock brokers firms that have come into prominence of recent years in this city. They occupy neat and well equipped quarters, having a direct wire with New York, and also a local wire, besides stock-indicator tickers and every appurtenance to a well-ordered office of the kind; and all orders are executed in the most judicious and reliable manner. The firm deal in stocks, grain, and provisions, selling on margin and commission in Boston and New York, and enjoy most favorable connections. All business intrusted to this house is transacted on sound and conservative methods, all their operations being characterized by security, energy, and ability, while strictly honorable principles govern every transaction, and altogether the firm have a flourishing patronage. They are gentlemen of entire probity in their dealings, as well as young men of ample experience, foresight, and judicious enterprise, and sustain an excellent reputation in financial circles. They have been established in business here something over one year, succeeding Nelson Tibbetts, who was successor to Mr. Irving; and from the first, their efforts have been attended with highly gratifying success.

FRANK WOOD, Steam Printer, No. 352 Washington Street.—The "art preservative of all arts" has a most able and enterprising representative in the person of Mr. Frank Wood, whose large steam printing house, so centrally and advantageously located at No. 352 Washington Street, is pronounced the best equipped in Boston or New England for all and every description of book, news, job, and fine commercial printing. He has been a resident Bostonian from childhood, and here thoroughly learned the art typographical in every minute detail. He brings to bear thirty-five years' practical experience, and started in business upon his own account about twenty years ago. In 1876 he removed to his present premises, 80x100 feet in dimensions, and where he has at all times maintained the finest possible improved equipment, with repeated additions of fast presses, etc.; their enlarged facilities enabling him to cope with the steady growth of trade. He now has fifteen presses in position, run by steam-power. His type and materials are all new and of the best description, and comprehensive of every style of fancy display and wood type adapted to fine job and commercial work; also full fonts of book and news type. He employs an average force of fifty hands, including the most skilled compositors, proof-readers, foremen, etc.; and over all gives his own close personal supervision. He served for seven years as an apprentice; for seven more foreman of a large office, in which he learned his trade, and acknowledged to be the best house in Boston in its day; for four years junior partner of the firm of Batchelder & Wood; and for sixteen years in business upon his own account. The finest class of work has ever been characteristic of his office, and he numbers among his customers many of the leading commercial houses of the city. Those who want any sort of printing done in an elegant, typographically perfect manner, with promptitude and despatch, we commend to this fine establishment, which has justly achieved such an enviable reputation throughout the community.

M. KILLILEA, Manufacturer of Marine and Stationary Boilers, Tuft's Wharf, Mill Street, East Boston.—A representative and progressive concern in East Boston is that of Mr. M. Killilea, whose works are conveniently located on Tuft's Wharf, Mill Street. This business was established seventeen years ago by Mr. Killilea, who is a thoroughly practical and expert boiler-maker. All the operations of his works are conducted under his personal supervision, thereby insuring to patrons only such productions as will withstand the most critical tests. His workshops are spacious, and are fully supplied with modern tools, appliances, and machinery. Here often 30 experienced mechanics and boiler makers are employed. Mr. Killilea manufactures, to order or otherwise, marine and stationary boilers, oil and ship tanks, stills, etc., a specialty being made of yacht boilers. All work turned out by this reliable house is unsurpassed for quality of materials, workmanship, and general excellence. Mr. Killilea has constantly on hand new and second-hand boilers, and likewise promptly and carefully attends to repairing, all work being executed in a first-class manner, at moderate rates. The trade of the house now extends throughout all sections of New England. Mr. Killilea was born in Ireland, but has resided in the United States for the last fifty-one years. He is a man of untiring industry and skill in his line, and is deservedly esteemed in trade circles.

MONUMENT NATIONAL BANK OF BOSTON, Thompson Square, Charlestown. The Monument National Bank of Boston, was incorporated in 1854, and eventually, in 1865, was reorganized under the national banking laws. It has a paid-up capital of $150,000, which is now further augmented by a surplus of $150,000. It transacts a regular banking business, such as the opening and care of current accounts, discounting first class commercial paper, making collections, and also advancing on good collateral security. The management of the Monument National Bank is judicious, prudent, and progressive, neglecting no point of efficiency demanded by modern commercial practice, and at the same time carefully guarding the interests of its depositors, and scrupulously protecting them against possibility of risk. Its officers and board of directors are men of experience, ability, and integrity. The list is as follows: James O. Curtis, president; Warren Sanger, cashier; John H. Gibbs, teller; Directors, James O. Curtis, Amos Stone, Henry C. Rand, Francis Hall, A. D. S. Bell, George B. Neal, Warren Sanger. Mr. James O. Curtis, the president, is now 84 years old. He is still hale and hearty, and a vigorous exponent of sound banking.

WM. P. SULLIVAN, Mill Wrappers, Manilla Paper, Twine and Paper Stock, Iron and Metals, No. 45 India Street. - For over thirty years the well known establishment of Wm. P. Sullivan, dealer in mill wrappers, manilla paper, twine, and paper stock, whose commodious warehouse is located at No. 45 India Street, in the oldest and most historic part of Boston, and in close proximity to the railroads and shipping, has been in prosperous existence. It is one of the oldest and most responsible concerns of the kind in Boston, in fact, the pioneer house in the business, and has a large active business connection. Its trade extending all over New England, and also to parts of New York State. The business was established in 1856 by J. O. Sullivan (deceased), who conducted the same up to about three years ago, when it passed into control of his son and successor, the gentleman whose name heads this sketch. The warehouse occupies four floors, and is well ordered and equipped throughout, while an efficient force of help is regularly employed. A heavy and carefully assorted stock is constantly carried on hand, comprising, besides mill wrappers, manilla paper, twine, and kindred articles; also paper stock, metals, iron, etc., consignments being received in any quantity and cash paid for old paper, and all orders for anything in this line are filled in the most prompt and reliable manner. Mr. Sullivan supplies the Boston Herald with wrappers in immense quantities, the average circulation of the daily Herald for the month of November, 1888, being 145,199, and the average circulation of the Sunday Herald for the same month bring 103,905 the circulation of the Wednesday edition of Nov. 7, 1888, after the Presidential election, being 444,785. Mr. Sullivan receives all the surplus paper from the daily papers of Boston, the public libraries, railroads, bank bindaries, and most of the large insurance and banking houses. When once the books and papers come into his hands, their contents never become matters of interest to any one else. Many firms are particular in this respect, and caring to have certain parties become conversant with their business methods through the medium of second-hand book collectors and dealers. Mr. Sullivan has in his possession a letter from a large banking house, acknowledging the receipt of $10,000 in worth of missing stock which he found in a lot of old papers it sold to him. He is a native of this city, is a young man of energy and judicious enterprise, strictly responsible in his dealings, and is thoroughly conversant with the business.

HIGGINS & THIBAUDEAU, Machinists, Die, Mould and Model Makers, No. 114 Pearl Street. - This business was established in 1887 on Lincoln and Essex Streets by the present proprietors and thence removed to the present location, where they occupy an entire floor, 25x100 feet in dimensions, and this is equipped with all modern facilities as regards machinery, tools, and the latest invented labor saving appliances. A staff of experienced and skilled mechanics are permanently employed in building all kinds of light machinery, making dies, moulds, and models, and in repairing engines, machinery, and small tools of all kinds. Messrs. Higgins & Thibaudeau are thoroughly practical mechanics. All the operations of their establishment are conducted under their personal supervision, thereby insuring to patrons only such productions as will withstand the most critical tests, both in regard to the materials used in the construction of the machinery and workmanship employed. They make a specialty of constructing experimental machinery, and of developing the crude plans of inventors, and also of dies, moulds, and models. The individual members of the partnership are Mr. James Higgins and Mr. Charles Thibaudeau. The former is a Massachusetts man by birth and resides in Boston, and the latter, who is a native of Canada, resides in Somerville. Both gentlemen are held in high regard by the community for their mechanical ability and integrity.

L. B. WILDER & CO., Mercantile Printers, Lithographers, Engravers, Blank Book Manufacturers, etc., Charles A. Patch, Sole Proprietor, No. 143 High Street. - This is in all respects one of the best equipped concerns in its line in the city, and it controls a trade fully commensurate with the capacity of the establishment. The business was organized in 1861 under the style of Locke & Wilder and from its very inception secured well deserved public favor and confidence. Subsequently Mr. Locke retired, and for a time the business was conducted under the sole management of Mr. L. B. Wilder who, in 1871 formed a partnership with Mr. Charles A. Patch. The style of the concern was then changed to L. B. Wilder

& Co., and this style is still perpetuated, although Mr. Wilder died in 1875, and Mr. Patch has ever since been the only proprietor. He is a thoroughly practical printer, an able, enterprising business man, and has developed a trade of great magnitude. The business embraces commodious, equipped with pressing and lithographic presses, cutting machines, steam-power, modern and antique types of every description, and all the necessary paraphernalia of a first class mercantile printing, engraving, and blank book manufacturing establishment. A full complement of operatives are employed in the several departments, and there is nothing in the whole realm of the printer's art which this concern is not able to execute. In the engraving and blank book manufacturing departments the governing rule is that of the highest perfection in everything executed.

CHAS. EMMEL, Wood-Carver, No. 55 Thayer Street. - The work to which Mr. Chas. Emmel, of No. 55 Thayer Street, devotes his time and talents has become an art requiring originality of conception, technical training, patient endeavor, assiduous and intelligent application, and the very acme of expert workmanship, to secure an artistic totality of a substantial and enduring quality. To fully meet these essential requisites has been Mr. Emmel's lifework. He was born in Germany, where he early learned the rudiments of the business of wood and stone-carving, and came to the United States in 1850. He was for some years in the employ of A. H. Davenport & Co., furniture dealers of this city, and established himself in the practice of his art in 1848. He manufactures the finest carved wood-work for interior decorations, also, the choicest and most expensive carved antique and modern furniture for the drawing rooms, library and dining room, including carved sideboards, tables, mantels and chairs. He is now making a specialty of stone-carving, decorating his patterns in plaster and then producing them on the stone trimming of fine residences and public buildings. He is at present engaged in the execution of carved designs on several of the handsomest buildings now in process of construction in this city. Many elaborate and artistic patterns are now worked on mantels and sideboards in paper mache, and the department of artistic endeavor also makes the attention of Mr. Emmel, and with the most brilliant results. All work proves as expensive, is guaranteed in every respect. The fullest extent of artistic possibility has signalized his many productions, which in themselves are his only merited endorsement. He is not only an artist-designer, but an artist-workman as well. He has done some of the finest work in the city, and first class furniture dealers desiring any costly or elaborate work in furniture-carving invariably depend upon Mr. Emmel, who employs a number of the most expert and skilled designers and workmen in the country at all times.

AMERICAN ELECTRIC REGISTER COMPANY., W. W. Montgomery, Manager, No. 85 Atlantic Avenue. - The electric fare register ought to attract the attention of every street railway manager in the country, since by its adoption on our lines thousands of dollars which are annually being misappropriated can be saved to railway companies. A recent telegram from Chicago affirms that a very serious "leakage" has been going on in the West Side Street Railway Company, of that city. A certain conductor interested in the scheme to beat the company has confessed, and implicated several of his confrères in the crime. One of these men, it seems, discovered how to set back the "fare registers," and managed in the course of a year to pay for a house and lot with his ill-gotten gains, and came to the conclusion that he could make a good thing by retailing the information among his fellow conductors. He fixed the price at twenty-five dollars a head, and found many customers, one of whom has now betrayed him. The fare registers in use in Chicago, as upon every other street railway line in the country, are purely mechanical in their operations, and differ very materially from the electric machines which are now being introduced by the American Electric Register Company of Boston. The unique character and the simple construction of this new apparatus will at once commend it, but better still, it cannot be altered, set back, or tampered with by human agency, to the detriment of the company owning it. It registers unfailingly every fare collected, both exteriorly and interiorly. If we are not greatly mistaken, it will come rapidly into use on all car lines. The electric railways of the country ought especially to investigate this new register, and if found right, adopt it.

J. A. MELVIN, Meats, Nos. 8 & 10 Lakeman Market. —The business corner of Mr J. Melvin embraces a period of thirty-five years, and in all that time he has given his attention to furnishing fresh meats to the citizens. He is one of the oldest dealers in Lakeman Market, where he has been since 1858, and became widely known, and established a first class, substantial wholesale and retail trade. The stall he occupies is numbered 8 to 10, and being large and commodious, affords every opportunity for making a fine display of the choicest beef, pork, and mutton, which he receives fresh daily, and supplies to the trade and his customers at the lowest prices. He is an energetic business man, and can always be depended on, and keeps only the very best and choicest meats to be found in the market. He was born in Charlestown, and has always been closely identified with the affairs of the city, and is well known and popular as a market man. About ten years ago Mr. Melvin discovered the valuable medicinal preparation known as the marketman's remedy for rheumatism and dyspepsia, which he prepares and has placed before

the public, and which has attained a celebrity throughout the Union as a certain speedy cure for dyspepsia, rheumatism, liver, kidney, and rheumatic diseases. This compound is purely vegetable, with no poisonous mineral ingredients of any kind, the spirits used in its preparation being only sufficient to preserve the medicine in any climate. It will purify and quicken the action, and remove any unnatural acrid or acid humor of the blood, relieving pain and preventing all irregularities of the system. Never before has there existed a remedy so unfailingly successful as this in its curative. It is invaluable in all diseases of the stomach, liver, kidneys, spleen, pancreas, heart, brain and lungs; and it removes like magic nervous, stiffness, and inflammation of the muscles and rheumatic affections, one bottle producing a cure in the most obstinate cases. This celebrated curative has been used by all classes of people, and that it will do all that is claimed for it is substantiated by testimonials from business men in Boston and vicinity, throughout New England, and in fact from all parts of the country. The price of the remedy is one dollar per bottle, and it is to be found on sale in all parts of the United States, and at wholesale by George C. Goodwin, Weeks & Potter, Carter & Hawley, Rust Bros. & Bird, Cutter Bros., Smith, Doolittle & Smith, Gilman Bros., Richardson, and Lawrence Pike, of this city. Circulars will be furnished and also testimonials, and all inquiries by mail or otherwise promptly answered, by addressing Mr. John A. Melvin, No. 67 Blackstone Street, Boston.

H. W. ROBY, Wholesale and Retail Dealer in Provisions, Nos. 14 and 16 Dock Square. —The establishment of Mr. H. W. Roby, at Nos. 14 and 16 Dock Square, is the head and centre of the most desirable class of patronage in the meat and provision trade of this city. The business of this popular house was originally established in 1861, by Messrs Partee & Roby, the present proprietor succeeding to the sole control in July, 1887. It has continued to extend its operations and enlarge its proportions on the solid basis of the choicest meats, fruits, vegetables, and game, fresh received each day and sold at reasonable prices. The proprietor is a merchant of large practical experience, through knowledge of the wants of the public, and all necessary facilities to meet the same. He is recognized as a leading representative of this branch of mercantile activity, and both at wholesale and retail he controls the most influential connections. His business premises are slightly isolated, spacious in size, and admirably equipped with refrigerators and all modern conveniences for handling and storing the rich and varied stock. In the choicest beef, pork, and mutton the stock here displayed is unrivaled In the season for poultry and game the proprietor handles many tons' weight; and having splendid cold storage accommodations, he is always ready to fill orders of any magnitude

promptly and satisfactorily. Fruits and early vegetables in their season are specialties with this house, and its trade is brisk and lively in this branch throughout the city and surrounding country. Our readers are recommended to secure their supplies in this line here, where both quality and extent of stock insure satisfaction. Mr. Roby is a native of New Hampshire, a resident of Boston for the past years, and of high repute and standing in business and trade circles.

A. & O. W. HEAD & CO., Produce and Provision Commission Merchants, No. 25 North Market Street and No. 25 Clinton Street. —In the wholesale commission trade in produce and provisions, there are no firms having a higher reputation in the city of Boston than Messrs. A. and O. W. Head & Co., whose office and salesrooms are situated at No. 25 North Market Street and No. 25 Clinton Street. This business was established upwards of forty years ago. The present copartners, Messrs. Adelbert, Oliver W. and Varnum B. Head have had great experience, and are recognized authorities in the produce and provision markets. Their facilities are perfect, and their connections influential, enabling them to promptly and satisfactorily handle the largest consignments of produce, effecting at all times quick sales and always making immediate returns. They deal extensively in butter, cheese, eggs, poultry, meats of all kinds, game, domestic fruits, and vegetables. Only the best stock is handled and the trade of the house now extends throughout the principal cities and towns of New England. All orders are promptly and carefully filled at the lowest ruling market prices, and the firm is number among their customers many of the leading grocers, dealers, and jobbers in Boston and its vicinity. The premises occupied comprise a commodious four-story and basement building, which is fully equipped with every appliance and facility for the successful prosecution of the business. The partners were all born in New England. They are prominent members of the Chamber of Commerce where they are highly regarded for their enterprise, promptness, and integrity, and it is to such responsible houses as this one, that Boston is indebted for her supremacy in the produce and provision commission trade of New England.

BAILEY & AYER, Commission Merchants for the Sale of Hides, Rough Leather, Calf and Sheep Skins, etc., Nos. 159 and 161 Purchase Street. —This firm are extensive commission merchants in hides, rough leather, calf and sheep skins, rough splits and finished card leather, handling domestic goods exclusively, and established their business here in May, 1865, succeeding the well known firm of Butler, Hayden & Co., in this branch of their business. They occupy spacious and commodious quarters, and carry at all times a large and valuable stock of tannages suited to the requirements of this market, including the finest grades of leather for articles being known to the trade. Consignments are received from all parts of the United States, and as extensive and rapidly increasing demand is supplied throughout the states of Massachusetts and New York. Shippers to this house have the advantage of getting their goods placed on orders direct, as the firm have established a superior connection with large buyers, and are on the ground where the principal consumers of the country are located. They are prepared to make liberal advances upon all consignments, and their quick returns, advantageous sales, strict probity, and careful management leave won for them the confidence of consignors and the respect and consideration of the trade in general.

KELTON & BRUCE, Manufacturers and Dealers in Mill Supplies, etc., No. 25 Lincoln Street. —A successful and progressive house in Boston, actively engaged in the manufacture and sale of "Indian tanned" face leather and mill supplies, is that of Messrs. Kelton & Bruce. The firm's factory, which furnishes constant employment to thirty skilled operatives, is situated in Salem, Mass. This business was established in 1884 by Mr. C. F. Kelton, who conducted it till 1888, when Mr. E. P. Bruce became a partner, the firm being known by the style and title of "Kelton & Bruce." The firm manufacture the "Indian tanned" face leather and deal largely in all kinds of mill supplies, mechanical combination packing, also engine and pump packings, leather, rubber, cotton and round belting, cotton waste, lace leather and belt hooks, cotton, flares, and rubber hose, sheet packing and gaskets. They also keep in stock tanners' rubber and canvas aprons of the best make, and the prices quoted in all cases are as low as the lowest.

GEO. W. BEARDSLEY, Agent for the Famous Höthner Piano, No. 178 Tremont Street.—In this age of well nigh universal musical education, when in every family of refinement a pianoforte is a necessity, it is a matter of general interest to secure some reliable advice as to the selection of the best instrument. There are good pianos of numerous American makes; but when we come to eliminate, investigate, and critically compare the merits of these all against those of the world-famous Höthner Piano, manufactured by Herr Julius Höthner, in Leipsic, Germany, we are constrained to admit that the latter are by far the best instruments in the world. So remarkable for their superiority indeed, as to receive the highest in demand from the eminent Liszt, Reinecke, Joseffy, and hundreds of other famous artists, musicians and composers. It is twenty-six years ago since the first Höthner piano was imported into the United States; and since that date they have become the popular favorites over and over board, and the sales are annually increasing in magnitude. In 1868, Messrs Harwood and Beardsley became sole American agents, and early developed an active demand and a thriving trade. In 1884, they were obliged to move into larger warerooms, at No. 178 Tremont Street, and where the business has since continued. The lamented decease of Mr. Harwood occurred in November, 189_, since which date Mr. George W. Beardsley has been sole proprietor. He is a leading expert authority on the pianoforte, bringing to bear vast practical experience, having been with the well-known house of Chickering & Co. for twenty years before embarking in business upon his own account. In his fine warerooms he carries a full line of the Höthner Uprights and Grands, all equally good and in a variety of styles. To meet diversified tastes, he also deals in S. G. Chickering, Kranich & Sons, and other popular American makes; and, while we mention this fact as giving the widest scope in selection, we would specially refer our readers to the splendid Höthner, with its inimitable singing quality of tone, its perfection of action, and elaborate finish. It is indeed a revelation to American pianists and connoisseurs alike, and embodies the greatest invention of the age, namely, the "Aliquot System," which may be briefly described, in the words of Herr Julius Höthner, as consisting of "a fourth string in the treble, which is suspended above the trichord, and tuned an octave above it. The hammers do not strike these fourth strings at all; but they emit a charming 'sympathetic overtone' vibration," caused by the blow of the hammer upon the trichords beneath. The tone of the treble is thus mellowed and beautified, and the sustained singing quality becomes marvelously pronounced. The most delicate shades of tone coloring can, by means of this wonderful invention, together with the careful use of the sensitive Höthner action, be developed to a remarkable degree. The Höthner is the court piano of the world, and over 35,000 are now in use. It wins the first grand prize wherever exhibited, and are copied by all the first makers in the United States, yet duplicated by none. Be sure to write to Mr. Beardsley for his interesting descriptive catalogue, and which quotes these beautiful instruments as low as $400 upwards. Since writing the above, we take pleasure in announcing that Mr. Beardsley has associated with himself Mr. Charles P. Cummings, a well-known business man in Boston, and the firm name will hereafter be known as Beardsley & Cummings, Nos. 178 Tremont and 27 Mason Streets.

WM. HODNETT & CO., Shipping-agents for the British Colonies, No. 178 Commercial Street.—The immense development of the import and export trade of the port of Boston during recent years has been greatly due to the enterprise of our ship and steamship brokers and merchants, as well as to the excellent facilities afforded to the largest classes of vessels to promptly secure outward bound cargoes and reliable crews. A leading and reliable firm of shipping-agents in the city, actively engaged in supplying crews for vessels engaged in both the coast service and foreign trade, is that of Messrs. William Hodnett & Co., whose office is located at No. 178 Commercial Street. The business of this agency was founded twenty-seven years ago by Messrs. Wherelock and Hodnett, and in 1891, on the retirement of Mr. Wherelock, the proprietorship became vested solely in Mr. Hodnett, who has since conducted the enterprise and is the style of William Hodnett & Co. Mr. Hodnett was born in Ireland fifty-six years ago, and for thirty-two years has been a resident of Boston. He has seen a good deal of sea service, both as a sailor and master, and knows just the kind of men that are needed on board ships. He holds the agency for the British Consulate, has every facility for transacting his extensive and steadily increasing business, and is enabled to promptly place at the service of masters of vessels the most desirable crews. Mr. Hodnett is widely known among ship-owners and brokers and masters of vessels, and can be fully relied upon to satisfactorily carry out all obligations into which he enters.

T. B. BAILEY & CO., Perfumers, No. 31 Hamilton Street.—As manufacturing perfumers, the firm of Messrs T. B. Bailey & Co. are widely prominent and popular. The business was founded in 1873 by Mr. T. B. Bailey, and in 1885 (the present firm was organized by the admission of Mr F. L. Bailey, the son of the founder, to partnership. The manufactory, laboratory, and salesrooms are perfectly equipped, and models of system, order, and good management; while twelve expert assistants contribute to the satisfactory operations of the house. The most delicious perfumes of every kind and variety are here manufactured and prepared for the trade. The business is conducted exclusively at wholesale, and the facilities of the firm for prompting and efficiently filling all orders are of the most complete character. The unique comprises a large number of fragrant and lasting perfumes for the toilet, distilled from flowers, including white heliotrope, white rose, lily of the valley, violet, musk, jasmine, white lilac, etc. All these goods are put up in bottles of different sizes for the trade, while the firm also prepare a superior article of toilet water, a variety of cologne, sachet powders, etc.; and druggists and dealers in fancy goods can find here everything they need in these lines, at such bottom prices. The trade is large, first-class, and influential throughout New England and New York. The Messrs. Bailey are Massachusetts men by birth and education, and are practical druggists and expert perfumers. The senior partner has been identified with the drug business for thirty years, and is a member of the Massachusetts Pharmaceutical Association.

CHAS. E. PERRY & CO., Paper Cutting, Nos. 65 Federal and 165 Congress Streets.—The leading exponent of paper-cutting, block and pad manufacturing, folding, etc., in this city is the house of Chas. E. Perry & Co., located at Nos. 65 Federal and 165 Congress Streets. The proprietor, Mr. Perry, started in business in 1879, with one paper-cutter, to supply the demands of printers and paper-dealers for work in this line; and the steady growth of his trade has been such that now nine machines are needed, and are in constant operation to meet the exigencies of the business, as well as a force of eleven expert assistants. His business premises are spacious in size, amply supplied with steam power; and business is brisk and lively from one day's end to another. Paper, card-board, label, picture, and cloth cutting is promptly, accurately, and satisfactorily executed, at the shortest possible notice and at minimum prices. Also, block and pad manufacturing and folding are given skilful attention, and the wants of all classes of patrons are maintained to with eminent success and conscientious care in all cases. Taking into consideration these facts concerning its facilities, management, and success, it may well be judged that this house is one with which it is a sure pleasure to form business relations, and that it has earned its success and popularity on the broad basis of supply and demand. Mr. Perry is a native Bostonian, and a young man thoroughly alive to the opportunity of making himself felt in the busy world, alert and active in making his way to popular favor, and merits the good will and confidence of the entire community.

J. G. BOWDEN, Manufacturers' Agent, Bindings, Tapes, Webbing, Braids, etc., No. 85 Kingston Street.—In the lines of bind ings, braids, webbings, etc., the leading agent for manufacturers is Mr. J. G. Bowden. The business was founded in 1870 by Mr J. W. Lynch, and succeeded in 1885 by Mr. Bowden, who represents the leading foreign and domestic manufacturers of Prussian and Petersham binding, slipper, blanket, and carpet binding; bed ties, tapes, webbing, galloons, cotton braid, worsted braid, shoe laces, etc. The stock is the heaviest in New England, occupying two entire floors, and is also the most comprehensive. Substantial inducements are offered both as to price and quality, and Mr. Bowden commands a trade of great magnitude, including not only New England, but every section of the United States. He is a resident of Melrose, for twenty years actively engaged in business in Boston, and is a worthy exponent of the most legitimate mercantile methods.

HOLMES & CO., Jersey-fitting Underwear, No. 17 Kingston Street.—This house occupies a niche in the commercial activity of this city peculiarly its own. It was founded in 1881 by John Holmes & Co., was burned out on Arch Street in the great fire of '72, and occupied its present site two years later. The firm style of Holmes & Co. was adopted in 1878, and the business has been steadily conducted throughout all these years under the personal management of Mr. John Holmes, one of Boston's oldest and best-known merchants, who, in his present specialty, has gained a national reputation and built up a trade co-extensive with the country. He occupies spacious and commodious quarters, and gives constant employment to thirty skilled and accomplished assistants. The special attention of our lady readers is called to the Jersey fitting Union Undergarments, manufactured and sold exclusively through this enterprising and reliable house. They were patented April 7, 1880, and this firm now hold the patent and trade-mark. They are made for ladies and children, in silk, wool, merino, cotton, and Dr. Jayne's imported all wool yarn, in winter, extra heavy, and summer weight, and are simply faultless in fit, while the peculiar elasticity of the fabric renders them delightfully agreeable. As a foundation to a close fitting dress or riding-habit, they appeal to the discernment of the most fastidious women. Each garment is made by hand in two separate pieces, from the neck to the ankle, with selvage edge, and formed, while being knit, so as to fit the body, and the weight of the garment is equally divided over every inch of the body. In a word, they are simply perfect in quality, workmanship, and price. They are sent to all parts of the United States, with rules for self measure, by this firm, and are warranted to give satisfaction. This firm are also extensive manufacturers of athletic and gymnasium goods, including Jersey-fitting shirts for bicycle riders, lawn-tennis players, yachting and rowing, base ball and foot-ball, gymnasium, etc., in league color, gray mixed, black, navy, or any color, plain or striped. Each garment bears the trade-mark of this firm, and are indorsed by the best manufacturers of bicycles, and by professional gymnasts. Mr. Holmes is a Massachusetts man by birth and training, and is reckoned among our solid business men.

THE LINCOLN NATIONAL BANK, Equitable Building, No. 180 Devonshire Street. Nathaniel J. Rust, President; Edmund C. Whitney, Cashier.—This is one of the strongest and most popular banks in the city of Boston. It was organized under the National Banking Laws in 1868, with a paid up capital of $500,000, which has now been further augmented by a surplus of $68,500 and undivided profits of $24,000. The management of the Lincoln National Bank is thoroughly conservative, and it has gained the confidence of the business community to the highest degree. A general banking business is carried on, collections being made on all points in the United States and Canada. The bank likewise makes telegraphic transfers of money, and receives on favorable terms the accounts of banks, bankers, corporations, manufacturers, merchants, and others. The investments of this responsible bank are made with care and judgment, and its ventures of capital are always well secured. The following gentlemen are the officers and directors: Nathaniel J. Rust, president; Edmund C. Whitney, cashier; Directors—Nathaniel J. Rust, Joseph Davis, William T Parker, John Shepard, Isaac P. T. Edmands, Irving O. Whitier, Horatio S. Burdett, Frank M. Ames, Henry J. Lewis, Edward E. Exeter, Benjamin W Currier, George W Williams. Mr. Rust and Mr. Whitney have held office since 1868. They are able and honorable bank officers, with every qualification for their responsible positions. The directors are influential citizens of Boston, and their connection with the Lincoln National Bank at once places it among the leading fiscal corporations of the state. The bank's New York correspondent is the National Bank of the Republic, No 33 Nassau Street.

GROUT, WARREN & BLANCHARD, Woolens, No. 77 Chauncy Street.—Few mercantile houses in Boston are so widely known as that of Messrs. Grout, Warren & Blanchard, wholesale dealers in woolens. The business was originally established in 1850, by Messrs. Richardson, Smith & Co., the present senior partner being a member of the firm, which was succeeded in 1873 by Mobbins, Grout & Co., and by the present firm in 1878. The business premises of the firm were destroyed in the great fire of '72, and the present site was soon after occupied. The establishment is four stories high, 60x100 feet in dimensions, and elegantly fitted up for the successful prosecution of the business. The house has continued to grow in strength, influence, and volume of trade, and now holds a commanding position among the principal mercantile institutions of this great metropolis. For variety, freshness, and completeness of assortment, the stock of woolens here displayed has few equals and no superiors. It is thoroughly complete in material, designs, and novelty, and the very best sources of European production have contributed to its wealth. The goods are purchased direct from the principal manufacturers of Europe, and the several styles and freshest novelties are obtained immediately as they are ready for the trade, while in regard to terms and prices, the long established reputation of the house is so well known as to guarantee the lowest quotation that the market affords. In a word the stock gives the limit of manufacture to high-class woolens. The trade is broadly distributed throughout the entire country, and in every important market the reputation of this house for promptness and reliability is unequalled The copartners, Messrs. Grout, Blanchard and Warren, are all prominent and popular Bostonians, long identified with this line of trade as salesmen and principals, members of the Boston Merchants Association, and business men of rare business tact.

CLEVELAND, BROWN & CO., Neckwear Manufacturers, No 11 Otis Street, Winthrop Square.—In the manufacture of neckwear of every description, the great representative house of Boston and New England is that of Messrs. Cleveland, Brown & Co., whose establishment is so advantageously located at No. 11 Otis Street, Winthrop Square. Mr. L. S. Cleveland and Mr. G. A. Brown formed the existing copartnership in 1882. From the start their product met the approbation of the trade by reason of its superiority, and the business has continued to develop at a rapid rate. The premises are very spacious, being 25x80 feet in dimensions, and well lighted. They are equipped in strictly first class style, and the manufacturing department affords employment to upwards of 140 hands. They select their silks, satins, ribbons, and other materials with the utmost care, and are the first to secure all the improved novelties in shades, patterns, and textures. The firm's ability and enterprise is shown in their frequent original designs, which "catch on" with the trade and the public, and receive the indorsement of the feeble institutions of competitors. In their show-rooms, buyers will find all the latest styles in the newest shapes, and no first class goods' furnisher can afford to be without them. The firm not only lead in all the fine grades of silk neckwear, but also in full lines of summer ties, including Kersages pique and lawn novelties. Their trade has deservedly attained proportions of great magnitude, and the copartners devote that close personal attention to the business that insures continued success. They sell to the trade of Boston and New England, likewise of the Provinces, while a growing demand exists in the west. Mr. Cleveland is a native of Maine, and Mr. Brown of Massachusetts, both of whom are popular young business men.

EDWARD JEWELL & CO., Commission Merchants in Hides and Leather, No. 873 Congress Street.—For the past thirteen years the house of Edward Jewell & Co., at No. 873 Congress Street, has been recognized as a prominent factor in promoting the commission trade in hides and leather in this city and throughout New England. Originated in 1873 by its present esteemed proprietor, the business has continued to enlarge from year to year, capital and facilities expanding together, until the house ranks equal with any of its contemporaries here or elsewhere. Handling hides and leather of every description on commission, this firm offers every advantage to both buyer and seller that is known to the trade. Consignments are solicited, promptly acknowledged, and carefully handled with profit to the shipper and satisfaction to the buyer in all cases. The demands upon the resources of the house are such that a very large and complete stock is constantly carried at all times, to the end that no delay may be experienced in the filling of orders. Every inducement is offered to the trade in both goods and prices that can be accorded in this market, and a business is annually transacted of great magnitude and value, which extends to all parts of New England, and is constantly increasing in volume and importance under enterprising, progressive, and reliable management. Mr. Edward Jewell, the active member of the firm, is a native of Massachusetts, and is well known and prominent citizen of Boston, whose high repute and standing is commercial, financial, and trade circles places him far beyond the requirements of any praise which these pages could bestow.

CHARLES H. MOULTON, Manufacturer of Boots and Shoes, No. 17 High Street.—...

LONDON AND LANCASHIRE INSURANCE COMPANY OF LIVERPOOL, Geo. W. Taylor, General Agent for New England, No. 19 Central Street.—...

JOHN F. SCANNELL, Sanitary Plumbing, No. 17 Milk Street.—...

HUGH CAREY, Tailor, No. 6 Hamilton Place.—...

JOHN R. NEAL & CO., Wholesale Fresh and Frozen Fish, No. 2 T Wharf.—...

GATES & CO., Printers, No. 117 Summer Street.—...

THOMAS O'GRADY, JR., Architect, No. 85 Devonshire Street.

ALLEN, NELSON & CO., Export Commission Merchants, Sole and Upper Leather, etc., Nos. 158 Summer and 141 Federal Streets.

WHITCHER & EMERY, Leather and Findings, Manufacturers of Sheepskins, No. 4 High Street.

SMITH, WHITING, CONNER & CO., Manufacturers and Jobbers of Clothing, No. 87 Summer Street.

W. D. BRACKETT & CO., Boots and Shoes, No. 111 Summer Street.

HALLET & DAVIS CO., Grand, Upright and Square Piano-Fortes, No. 179 Tremont Street; Factory, Harrison Avenue. —To those contemplating the purchase of a high class piano-forte, much of the bewilderment occasioned by conflicting claims of manufacturers may be avoided by following the unbiased opinions of the most eminent masters of this noble instrument. No instruments have received such emphatic and direct commendations of this character as those manufactured by the Hallet & Davis Company of this city. Here is what the world renowned composer and leader, Johann Strauss, has to say: Messrs. Hallet & Davis Gentlemen : Having heard your pianos at the World's Peace Jubilee, and also used them during my stay in Boston, I am free to say that I have never before seen pianos possessing such a combination of

truly wonderful quality and quantity of tone, meeting at once the wants of the largest concert-hall and the drawing-room. I consider them superior to any pianos that have come under my observation. Scores of other similar opinions, couched in language of the superlative degree, from the most eminent pianists, composers, leaders, etc., are printed in the company's handsomely illustrated descriptive catalogue procured on application at, or by sending to their elegant warerooms, No. 179 Tremont Street. The business was established fifty years ago by Messrs. Hallet & Davis; and who reared an imperishable record as skilled, practical, and honorable piano manufacturers. Though both members of the original firm are deceased, their establishment is in the hands of trusted and exceptionally able successors. Ten years ago the business was put into a stock company under Massachusetts laws, so the name and plant was of such value and importance that it demanded an incorporated existence, — which never dies, — and its vast interests are not depreciated by the death of any one member of the corporation. The company's factory is an immense six story structure, occupying an entire block on Harrison Avenue, equipped with the latest improved machinery and appliances, and af-

fording employment to over 200 skilled hands: the capacity being 50 pianos per week. The employees are, as a body, the most experienced and reliable in America. They turn out the best possible work in every minute detail; 100 of them have been employed by this house upwards of ten years; 30 for over fifteen years; 60 for twenty years; 35 for thirty-five years; and 14 for over forty years. Only pianos of the highest grade are produced here, embracing every modern improvement, including many exclusive to the company's instruments. Every part of their pianos is made under their own supervision in their own factory. This is one secret of the remarkable uniform excellence of all Hallet & Davis pianos. Their instruments have been awarded 25 first prizes, obtained in open competition with the best makers of Europe and America. Over 45,000 Hallet & Davis pianos have been made,

and are in use preferentially by the most advanced of the music-loving public. While it is needless to state that the very best of materials only enter into the construction of these splendid instruments, it may be added that some very important recent inventions have been introduced, including the Suspension Acrafix Bridge, the only infallible preservative of the natural rich tone of the piano for the entire lifetime of the instrument; the Grand Action, and the Movable Key Board, are appreciated improvements, while their uprights have their Patent Rolling Felt-Board and Music Desk. The Hallet & Davis pianos are rich and sweet in tone, perfect in their sharfp touch, beautiful in design, elaborate in finish, and of extraordinary durability. Through the finest pianos on the market to-day, the company, by reason of its splendid manufacturing facilities and large capital, sells them at moderate prices; and all interested should see and hear these magnificent pianos at the company's warerooms, comprising two entire floors 80x80 feet each. The company's trade covers the entire United States and Canada, with a heavy and growing export demand to Europe, and South America. The officers and managers are to be congratulated upon the success attending their efforts.

CODMAN & SHURTLEFF, Manufacturers, Importers, etc., of Surgical and Dental Instruments, Nos. 13 and 15 Tremont Street.—The firm name of "Codman & Shurtleff" has been so long and honorably identified with the trade in the finest classes of Surgical and Dental Instruments, trusses, etc., that it represents what a trade mark does to other branches of business. This extensive business was originally founded in 1826. In 1853, Messrs. B. S. Codman & Co. succeeded to the management, and 25 years ago Messrs. Benj. S. Codman and A. M. Shurtleff assumed control under the style and title of "Codman & Shurtleff." Mr. F. O. Whitney became a member of the firm in 1868. Messrs. Codman & Shurtleff are the largest and most noted importers, manufacturers, and wholesale and retail dealers in surgical and dental instruments in New England, and are manufacturers of all kinds of approved trusses, abdominal supporters, shoulder-braces, and spinal supporters, silk elastic hose for various veins, swelled limbs, ankles, and knees, silk elastic pregnancy supporters, London abdominal supporters, frames for correcting bow legs, knock knees, weak ankles, club-feet, and all kinds of deformities. They occupy in Boston a superior four-story and basement building, which is utilized for showrooms, etc., and where they have convenient application rooms with a lady attendant for ladies. The factory of the firm, which is admirably equipped with special machinery, tools, and appliances, and furnishes constant employment to 100 skilled mechanics and surgical instrument makers, is at No. 189 Columbus Avenue. The reputation achieved by this responsible firm of the highest character. All surgical and dental instruments, trusses, elastic hose, galvanic batteries, etc., sent out from their establishment are of superior finish, and are absolutely unrivalled in the United States or Europe. Messrs. Codman & Shurtleff were the first firm in America to manufacture steam and hand atomizers for employing atomized liquids in diseases of the throat and lungs, and have succeeded in producing a very simple, efficient, and satisfactory apparatus, which is now in large demand. All instruments bearing the name of "Codman & Shurtleff" are fully warranted. The firm's dental department is at No. 167 Tremont Street, and is conducted under the title of the Boston Dental Manufacturing Company. Benjamin L. Codman, M. D., graduated at the Harvard Medical School, 1845, and for the past 25 years has made surgical appliances his specialty, has been an active member of the Massachusetts Medical Society and Suffolk District Medical Society for more than forty years. Dr. Codman is a native of Boston, Mr. Shurtleff of New Hampshire, and Mr. Whitney of Massachusetts. Their patronage extends not only throughout all sections of the United States and Canada but also to the West Indies, South America, England, France, Germany, India, and Australia.

MASSACHUSETTS NATIONAL BANK OF BOSTON, No. 80 Milk Street. William A. French, President; Charles W. Perkins, Cashier.—Sixteen years before the dawning of the nineteenth century this substantial and reliable bank was founded, and its reputation, preserved for generations unsurpassed, has been well maintained by the successors of the founders. It was organized originally in 1784 as the "Massachusetts Bank," and eventually, in 1865, became a National Bank. The following is a statement of its capital from the inception of business, viz.: Capital; 1784, $300,000 Banians dollars; 1792, 100,000. Maximum dollars: 1791 $972,000 (American); 1792, $463,000; 1807, $800,000; 1808, $1,000,000; 1901, $800,000. At the present day the capital of the Massachusetts National Bank is $800,000, which has been further augmented by a surplus of $140,000. The administration of its affairs has always been characterized by prudence and honorable methods, and its officers and directors have ever been vigorous exponents of the soundest principles governing banking and finance. The list is as follows: William A. French, president; Charles W. Perkins, cashier; Directors: Henry A. Rice, Edward Whitney, Arthur T. Lyman, Nathaniel C. Chapin, Alexander H. Rice, Edward T. Russell, William A. French, George P. Gardner, George Hunnewell Kettell, Robert D. Evans. A general business is transacted, and every modern system which tends to benefit financial transactions is followed, while every convenience and facility are extended to customers. The bank receives upon favorable terms the accounts of banks, bankers, corporations, and individuals. It issues travelers' and commercial letters of credit, available in all parts of the United States, Canada, and Europe; makes collections, discounts first-class commercial paper, deals in government bonds and foreign exchange, and makes telegraphic transfers

of money, etc. The bank has always paid good dividends to stockholders, and no emergency has ever occurred in which its standing or strength could be questioned. The president, Mr. W. A. French, is a gentleman of marked business ability, as widely known for his conservative judgment as for the just manner in which he attends to the interests of the bank. Mr. C. W. Perkins, the cashier, has been with the bank for the last twenty years. He is an able and careful bank officer, eminently qualified for his responsible position.

F. P. BAKER MOULDING COMPANY. Manufacturers of White, Gold, Metal, Ornamented and Picture-rod Mouldings, No. 6 Hanover Street, Factory at Chelsea.—One of the representative industries of Boston is that so successfully conducted by the F. P. Baker Moulding Company, as manufacturers of white, gold, metal, ornamented, and picture-rod mouldings, with a factory at Chelsea, and salesrooms at No. 6 Hanover Street, in this city. This enterprise was inaugurated in 1876, and has been conducted with marked ability and steadily increasing success. The factory of the company, at the corner of Marple and Hawthorne Streets, Chelsea, is thoroughly equipped for systematic and successful production, the outfit of machinery including every late and valuable invention calculated to promote the interests of the business and enhance the value of its output. Employment is given here to some eighty skilled workmen. The finest material is used in every case, and the several stages of completion are guarded with scrupulous care and vigilance. The superiority in finish and workmanship of the specialties here produced has long been recognized by the market, and the company is firmly established in the favor of the building fraternity. The high quality of the mouldings here manufactured, and the great preference enjoyed by these goods, is shown in the influential and steadily increasing demand made for them in this city and throughout the New England States, and from Maine to Australia. A heavy stock is constantly carried, and the house is thus enabled to fill all orders promptly, while instruments are offered in terms and prices that cannot be afforded by smaller concerns. Mr. Baker, the moving spirit of this enterprise, is a native of Maine, of large and valuable experience in this branch of manufacture. Thoroughly original in designing and progressive in executing, and perfectly reliable and responsible in all his dealings.

EAST BOSTON SAVINGS BANK, Corner Maverick Square and Henry Street, East Boston; George T. Sampson, President; William B. Pigeon, Treasurer.—This savings bank was duly incorporated in 1848; and from its inception to the present time its officers and directors have included many of the ablest financiers in the city. The following are its officers and trustees for the year 1890: President, George T. Sampson; Vice-president, John Thompson; Treasurer, William B. Pigeon; Board of Investment, John Thompson, Nathaniel S. Jewett, Andrew M. Horton, William B. Pigeon, Directors: M. McPherson, George L. Thorndike, Rufus Cushman, Edward Brigham, Robert Crosbie; Trustees, Mark Gregian, Albert Bowker, Henry Pierce, Edward Brigham, Frederick Fross, George T. Sampson, Henry B. Hill, Nathaniel Hoover, John Thompson, Nathaniel S. Jewett, William L. Sturtevant, Rufus Cushman, Andrew M. Horton, William B. Pierce, William H. Grainger, Ebenezer M. McPherson, James Smith, George L. Thorndike, Robert Crosbie, Emory D. Leighton, Kendall J. Elder, James L. Welsh, Wesley A. Gove, William Waters, Jr., Joseph W. Robbins. The banking rooms of the institution are spacious and well appointed. The methods in vogue are practically the same as those of older great savings banks throughout the country. Its executive officers are gentlemen of financial ability and business experience, in whose hands the duties of their respective offices are wisely and honestly administered. Deposits of one dollar to one thousand are received; and interest allowed on deposits of $5 and upwards, and upon the interest accumulating thereon, until the principal with interest amounts to $1600. The bank is open for deposits and drafts from nine to two o'clock daily, and on Saturday evenings from 7 to 9. The following statement (to October 10, 1889, shown the affairs of the East Boston Savings Bank to be in a thoroughly sound and flourishing condition. Number and amount of deposits received during year ending Jan. 9, 1889, 11,883—$600,822.61; number and amount of withdrawals during year ending Jan. 9, 1889, 7385—$498,058.34; number of accounts opened during year ending Jan. 9, 1889, 1384; number of accounts closed during year ending Jan. 9, 1889, 1076. All securities at par.

C. H. ENGLISH, Importer, Agent and Contractor for Cotton, Woolen, Worsted, etc., Machinery, No. [illegible] Oliver Street. The prosperous house of Mr. C. H. English, at No. [illegible] Oliver Street, is one which, devoted to a given line of trade, thus receives all the advantages to be gained from undivided attention. Mr. English is an extensive importer of, agent and contractor for cotton, woolen, worsted, and other machinery, and a dealer in mill supplies of every description, making a leading specialty of card clothing, and established his business here in [illegible]. He enjoys a special prestige in the trade circles of this country as the sole representative in the United States and Canada of the "Walker & Hacking" cotton preparing and spinning machinery; Thorut & Brothers' woolen and worsted preparing and spinning machinery; George Whiteley's card clothing for cotton, woolen and worsted; and Henry Livesey, Limited, slasher sizing machines, etc. Handling such widely famous products, this house has become an important source of supply to manufacturers and mill-owners, and a great substantial success has been achieved during the comparatively short period of its operation. No house in Boston and elsewhere is better prepared to minister to the public want in its line, while Mr. English is a gentleman of vast practical experience and tried ability, in whose judgment and integrity the fullest confidence can be safely placed. He is thoroughly conversant with all the needs and requirements of cotton and woolen mills, while his unequalled connections with manufacturers of machinery enable him to promptly and satisfactorily meet every demand in this line. Many of the largest mill owners in New England make their purchases of mill machinery and supplies of Mr. English, being attracted by the honorable methods in force, the superior inducements offered, and the uniformly satisfactory manner in which their orders are fulfilled. The trade is rapidly extending to all parts of the United States and Canada, and the house is uniformly popular with its patrons everywhere. Mr. English was born in England, and trained to mill work from boyhood. He is still in the prime of life, active, alert, and enterprising in meeting the wants of his patrons, and thoroughly reliable and responsible in all his dealings.

J. MERRILL BROWN, Architect, No. 68 Devonshire Street.—Boston has proven a fruitful field for the exercise of the highest order of talent in the line of modern architecture, and on every hand are evidences of the skill, talent, and enterprise that have reared such permanent monuments of constructive effort. In reviewing the progress of architectural education in our midst, the name of Mr. J. Merrill Brown will at once suggest itself to many of our readers. This gentleman occupies eligible office quarters at No. 68 Devonshire Street, and is widely known as an accomplished master of his art in all its branches. He is a Massachusetts man by birth and training, and established himself here in the practice of his profession in 18[illegible]. At the present day he is recognized as a thoroughly representative builder of the distinctive American school of architecture, and has been eminently successful in solving the complex problem of how best to utilize the minimum of building area with the maximum of accommodation and architectural beauty of design. Proofs of Mr. Brown's skill and proficiency are numerous in this city and throughout all New England, as embodied in the many splendid edifices which he has designed and erected in the last few years, and which are greatly admired by experts for their stability and elegance. He has also executed a number of important commissions in New York and New Jersey, among them being the construction of Swift's Packing house at Jersey City. He is at all times prepared to give estimates and furnish plans to meet the views of those intending to build, and spares no pains to meet the expectations of his patrons, placing his terms at a just and equitable figure and guarding well the interests committed to his care. Mr. Brown is greatly respected by the community at large for his ability and probity, is a member of the Boston Society of Architects, and a young man of sufficient energy, zeal, and determination to win the highest laurels in his chosen field of labor.

WOODBURY & LEIGHTON, Building Contractors, No. 164 Devonshire Street.—Among the largest contractors and builders in the city are Messrs. Woodbury & Leighton. This firm established their business here in 18[illegible], and have achieved a reputation and acquired a patronage that place them in the front rank of popularity and success. Their business premises comprise a workshop containing one floor and basement, 185 by 30 feet each, together with a spacious lumber-yard, all equipped with derricks, hoisting engines, and other requisite appliances for conducting mason and carpenter work of every description, while steady employment is given to two hundred skilled and expert hands. The perfect facilities and ample resources appertaining to this house render the firm competent to offer inducements of the most desirable nature to patrons. Numerous proofs of their prominence and ability as builders are to be found in this city and elsewhere, and, as an example of their prowess, they are now engaged in building the new Public Library of Boston, which is to cover an entire block, measuring [illegible] by [illegible] feet, to be built of Milford pink granite from the Milford Pink Granite Co., of Milford, Mass., of which Messrs. Woodbury & Leighton are the practical owners, and to cost $1,300,000. The copartners, Messrs. I. F. Woodbury, who is a native of New Hampshire, and Geo. E. Leighton, of Maine, are acknowledged leaders in their line of industry. Mr. Woodbury is a practical mason, and Mr. Leighton is a trained carpenter. Their carpenter shop and mason yard is at No. 40 Thayer Street.

J. ALBA DAVIS & CO., Manufacturers and Dealers in Sheep and Goat Skin Stock, Nos. 73 and 75 High Street.—There is no house connected with the leather industry that is more widely and favorably known than that of J. Alba Davis & Co., of Nos. 73 and 75 High Street, this city, which has for the last quarter of a century been identified with, and actively promoting the interests of, this important branch of commerce and manufacture. The business was founded thirty years ago by Mr. Davis, success and prosperity have followed his intelligent and enterprising management. Mr. Davis carries on general operations as a wholesale dealer in sheep and goat skin stock, making a leading specialty of white linings and skivers. The factory whose product he controls is located at Peabody, Mass., and is thoroughly equipped for an extensive output of superior quality, the provision of machinery being as complete and perfect as it can be made, while the work is carried on in that systematic manner which insures the best results in every stage of manufacture through which the materials pass. At the salesrooms in this city a heavy stock is carried. The goods are recognized as standard in the trade, and command a decided preference throughout New England and the west, to all parts of which extensive shipments are made. The ample resources of the establishment enable it to offer better inducements than could be afforded by concerns less favorably situated, and orders are filled at terms which it would be difficult to duplicate. Mr. Davis was born in Maine, but has resided in Boston for the last forty years, and has seen it grow from a comparatively small city to the great metropolis it now is. He is know for his sterling integrity of character and sound business ability, and enjoys the respect of the entire community.

SIMONS, HATCH & WHITTEN, Importers and Manufacturers of Mens' Furnishing Goods, No. 1 Winthrop Square, and Nos. [illegible] to [illegible] Otis Street.—Boston is ably and prominently represented in the wholesale mens' furnishing-goods trade by the widely and favorably known house of Messrs. Simons, Hatch & Whitten. The business was founded upwards of twenty-five years ago by the firm of Simons Bros. & Co. They thus continued up to 18[illegible], when the present copartnership was formed. The firm is composed of Mr. Stephen B. Simons (the leading authority in his line), Mr. C. P. Hatch, and Mr. H. C. Whitten, who has also been identified with the trade for a quarter of a century past. The firm are direct importers of fine hosiery, gloves, underwear, handkerchiefs, etc., and are the leading manufacturers in New England of white muslin shirts, flannel shirts, neck-wear, etc. They have factories in operation at Watertown, Natick, and Provincetown, Mass. They employ upwards of [illegible] hands in the various departments, and manufacture fine white dress shirts as a specialty. These are goods that command the best class of trade, being cut from best muslins and linens, cut accurately and made up in the most thorough and careful manner. The firm's flannel shirts also maintain the lead for all purposes. At No. 1 Winthrop Square are the firm's magnificent salesrooms on the first floor, [illegible] feet in dimensions, and elegantly fitted for the display of this mammoth stock of men's furnishing goods of all medium and fine grades. The house has trade relations extending all over the United States. Messrs. Simons & Whitten have been actively identified with the men's furnishing goods trade for twenty-five years past. Mr. Hatch is also widely experienced, and a worthy exponent of the trade.

THE ASBESTOS PACKING COMPANY, Miners and Manufacturers of Asbestos, Patented; Asbestos Packings, Fire-proof Sheathings, Fibre, Threads, Cloth, Blotters, Roofing, Boiler Coverings, etc.; General Manufacturing Agents Hallenstadter Felting Company, etc.; Office, No. 169 Congress Street.—The natural Asbestos, instead of being, as formerly, merely a curiosity for the cabinet of the mineralogist, has, in the last few years, been utilized into manufactures of value and importance. It is a peculiar form assumed by the minerals hornblende, augite and serpentine, yet the origin of its fibrous forms so far, has not been explained, other than it is due to some process of decomposition. Mention is made, in the history of the 16th and 17th centuries, of cloth and handkerchiefs made of the material, but until a recent period it had no commercial importance or utilization, and beyond its well-known indestructibility by any degree of heat, none realized its other valuable qualities, or its adaptability for uses peculiarly its own. Asbestos is found almost everywhere in greater or smaller quantities, but principally in Italy, Russia, Germany, Australia, South America, United States and Canada. Previous to 1878, Italy furnished the only reliable source of supply, but since that time Canada has furnished the largest source of supply, and the finest fibre for practical purposes. The Asbestos Packing Company of Boston are the original Asbestos manufacturers of the United States, and to their enterprise may be attributed the extensive use which the material now enjoys. Previous to 1878, the only Asbestos for manufacture was imported from Italy, but in that year the company opened the celebrated Thetford Mines in the Province of Quebec, Canada, which produce fibre unequalled by any recent discoveries. The marked difference between the different qualities of Asbestos would hardly be realized by anyone not familiar with the different formations in different sections. While the Italian Asbestos possesses a strong fibre, it lacks the fineness and silky qualities of the Canadian, yet it excels the Asbestos found in the southern United States. At first Asbestos was utilized principally for piston and joint packings, for steam-work, non-conducting coverings, for steam-pipes, boilers, etc., until an increased knowledge of its adaptability for other uses, with the added information as to its manufacture, have extended the field, until now it has an extensive sale as a fire-proof paper for building purposes, between floors, under clapboards, shingles, etc., being a good non-conductor of sound, and heat, as well as a fire preventative. It is also made in different thicknesses like card board, for use wherever a fire-proof and indestructible material is desired. It is spun into threads, cords, and ropes, made into cloth for filtering purposes, theatre curtains, gloves, and other uses, and used as an indestructible fibre in cements, for various heat-resisting purposes, unexcelled for various uses for electrical purposes and its use is rapidly extending. The Asbestos Packing Company are constantly adding to their already large list of manufactured articles, demonstrating the value of Asbestos for new uses. They have lately made large additions to their manufacturing facilities at Baldwinsville, Mass., as demanded by their large and growing trade, not only in the United States, but all over Europe, South America and the Colonies. The principal office of the Asbestos Packing Company is at No. 169 Congress Street, Boston, with branches at New York, Philadelphia, Chicago, and London.

GEORGE W. CUSHMAN, Gents' Outfitter, No. 81 Cornhill, after October 1st will be at No. 17 Court Street (Adams Building).—The leading and most popular gents' outfitter in this city is Mr. George Cushman, located at No. 81 Cornhill, but after October 1st at No. 17 Court Street (Adams Building). This house was founded twenty-five years ago by Messrs. Henderson and Haywood, who were succeeded by Messrs. Briggs and Cushman, the present proprietor assuming sole control in 1885. He possesses facilities both as a retailer of gents' furnishing goods and as a custom shirt-maker, enjoyed by no other, while his aim and policy have ever been to attain a still higher standard of perfection in every article made or sold, to render his stock absolutely comprehensive of everything desirable both in foreign and domestic products, and as a designer and manufacturer, to make good his claim as a leader by originating exclusive new styles, accepted by the *élite* as *en règle*, and to which the homage of the trade is rendered by a close imitation. Mr. Cushman brings to bear large practical experience in catering to the wants of the fashionable public in this line, and when, with his experience and knowledge, are coupled with ample resources, perfected importing and manufacturing facilities, and unrivalled connections, it can be readily realized how he has outstripped all competitors. His store is a magnificent exhibit of modern taste and achievement in this line. The stock is displayed to the best advantage, from the three show windows, dressed as none others are to the lengthy array of shelving and show cases, where are carried everything stylish, novel, and valuable in hosiery, gloves, and underwear, white and colored shirts, scarfs, cravats and ties, dressing-gowns, slippers and smoking caps, umbrellas and walking-sticks, collars and cuffs, silk and cambric handkerchiefs, and other outfittings of the most desirable quality. Here also is headquarters for the finest shirts made. Gentlemen are measured in the store and there select their linens, which are promptly made up by skilled hands. In this branch Mr. Cushman safely defies competition, guaranteeing the latest mode and a perfect fit, and placing his prices at an eminently fair and equitable figure. Mr. Cushman is a Massachusetts man by birth and education, a resident of Cambridge, and a gentleman of fine taste and sound judgment who has won a brilliant mercantile success by intelligent enterprise and honest, honorable methods.

A. D. ROGERS, Commission-Merchant in Produce and Provisions, No. 46 North Market Street.—For a score of years or more, Mr. A. D. Rogers has been one of the best known, most successful, and popular commission-merchants doing business on North Market Street. He, as a member of the firm of Plummer, Rogers & Co., founded his enterprise in 1868, and this was the style of the house until 1873 when the firm was dissolved, and Mr. Rogers became the sole proprietor. He has since developed the trade to large proportions, and one which extends throughout Massachusetts and New Hampshire. Mr. Rogers conducts a general wholesale trade in beef, veal, lamb, poultry, and provisions and country produce of every description. His premises at No. 46 comprise a basement with an area of 30x80 feet, and this is provided with every convenience that can in any way facilitate the transaction of business. On the second floor of the building Mr. Rogers has a well appointed office. He was the first in Boston—and that was twenty years ago—to receive a load of Hammond's Chicago dressed beef that arrived here, and to begin the wholesale trade in this article which he still continues to handle in immense quantities. His stock in every department is always kept fresh, choice, and up to the highest standard of excellence. Consignments are received daily from the most reliable producers and shippers in the country, and as these find a ready sale through the medium of Mr. Rogers's establishment, this gentleman is enabled to make quick, accurate and satisfactory returns. Dealers find here the highest classes of goods in the market at the lowest prices, and courteous, liberal, and honorable treatment. The trade of the house requires the services of five assistants, and is annually growing in volume. Mr. Rogers is a native of Sudbury, Mass., and one of the most esteemed of our local merchants.

E. N. TAPPEN, Wholesale Dealer and Jobber in Chicago Dressed Beef, Nos. 44 North Market and 44 Clinton Streets.—The wholesale and commission trade in mutton, lamb, veal, and poultry has no more enterprising and successful exponent in this city than Mr. E. N. Tappen, who succeeded Thos. Hixon & Co. in March 1, 1882, and who was formerly associated with that firm for over two years. His establishment has been in existence for a period of six years, and has become a noted source of supply for dealers and large buyers of the above named products. The premises used for trade purposes are spacious in size and equipped with refrigerators and other modern facilities for preserving the choice and valuable stock. The management is in possession of the best possible facilities for procuring supplies from the most reputable producing sources, enabling it to offer customers fresh and first-class goods at prices which preclude successful competition. Only the best stock is handled, and the greatest skill and experience are brought to bear in selecting the requisite grade to supply the demands of an exacting and critical trade. Many of the largest and leading hotels, restaurants, public institutions, and dealers in this city are furnished with mutton, lamb, veal, and poultry from this house, which proves the esteem in which it is held by those who cater to the tastes of the public and are best able to judge of such commodities. The stock is kept steadily up to the highest standard of excellence by fresh and frequent invoices from the best producers and shippers in the country, and inducements are continually offered to the trade, in goods and prices which are rarely duplicated elsewhere.

A LBERT G. MEAD, Machinist, No. 76 Atlantic Avenue.—One of the most skillful and best known among Boston's machinists is Albert G. Mead, who enjoys an A1 reputation for skill and reliability. Mr. Mead was born in Berkshire, Mass., and has resided in Boston many years. He is a practical and expert machinist and die maker, of long and varied experience, and is a thorough master of his art in all its branches. He started in business in 1883, as partner in the firm of Mead & Addy,

whom he succeeded in 1892 as sole proprietor. The shop occupies a 30x75 feet floor with ample steam power and complete facilities, while several experienced hands are employed. Mr. Mead is prepared to execute all kinds of work in the line of light machinery construction and repairs, making a specialty, however, of glove fasteners and dies for the same, printing presses, stamping presses for stamping note paper, etc., while particular attention is given also to small mechanical devices, models and experimental work.

D R. W. A. POWER, Canine Specialist, No. 9 School Street.— The dog has an animal peculiarly susceptible to disease, which may be brought on by climatic changes, improper feeding, want of exercise and in many ways. As soon as the first symptoms appear the owner of a valuable animal should consult and follow the advice of the skilled canine specialist, and we know of no one having a larger experience or who is better qualified than Dr. W. A. Power of this city, with a branch office at Greenwood, Mass., where a well-equipped canine hospital and pharmacy, and also in administering to the ailments of his numerous patients. The Doctor has for many years made a special study of canine diseases and is familiar with the anatomy of dogs, and their complaints and knows how and when to apply the proper remedies, and is probably better equipped in this respect than any other in this city or in the country. Dogs are boarded while under treatment and every attention is given to their welfare. He is highly endorsed by prominent owners of hunting, watch and pet dogs, and is considered one of the most capable, efficient, experienced and successful canine specialists in the United States or Canada. Dr. Power is also the owner of the Greenwood Mastiff Kennels, located on Main street, Greenwood, Mass., in the Boston and Maine R. R., also miles from the city. These kennels have been established for years and have a world-wide reputation. Here he makes a specialty of breeding the English mastiff from the best imported, registered, pedigreed and prize winning strains in existence, thus securing not only strength, activity, beauty, intelligence, symmetry and courage, but the true type and characters. He also buys, sells and exchanges mastiffs, and always has fine specimens of this breed in the stud and has for sale stud dogs, brood bitches and puppies of both sexes at reasonable prices. The English mastiff stands pre-eminently the peer of all house and watch dogs and here in their headquarters and home. The spacious box stalls which these superb animals occupy are models of neatness and order, while the grounds surrounding the kennels with their wired exercise yards, and clean cut lawns form a picture not soon to be forgotten. The hospital and pharmacy could hardly be improved, cases containing the finest surgical instruments and appliances, also in hospital shop furniture bottles, well filled with the necessary drugs and medicines, and appliances for the compounding of pills, powders, ointments, tinctures and liniments meet the eye on all sides. Every care and attention is given to the feed of the animals and none but the best materials are used. Dr. Power is himself editor of our paper and correspondent in several others, a fact which enhances his judgment and opinion on matters pertaining to doggy affairs and interests. He has a large correspondence from all parts of the world. Polite and prompt attention is given to all inquiries and he is always pleased to furnish information in regard to English mastiffs, and dogs generally, also as a canine specialist.

J OTT GRANT, Manufacturer's Agent, Water Filters, No. 12 Doane Street.—An examination of the merits of the deservedly popular King Water Filter (reversible) of which Jott Grant, manufacturer's agent, is the patentee and proprietor, is in all respects the most effective, complete, reliable and altogether superior appliance for the purpose intended yet introduced. Convenient as it is to have water laid into our houses, it has become an admitted fact that the water often supplied is unfit for drinking purposes, and hence resource must be had to some system of filtration. In these days nothing need be said to enforce the desirability—nay, absolute necessity to health—of a supply of pure water. To insure this, it is of the utmost importance that the filter employed should be capable of being frequently and easily cleansed. The King water filter answers all these purposes. While removing from water all its dirt and atoms of mineral, animal and vegetable, it increases the volume of health-giving oxygen, and renders water markedly improved and sweeter to the taste. Mr. Grant is patentee of and agent for several other useful devices also, including napkin holders, trouser stretchers, and other patented novelties of merit, and has a large native trade throughout the United States; agents being wanted everywhere.

W ELCH & HALL, Blue Front Stable, Nos. 155 and 157 Portland street.—This firm have constantly on hand and for sale a fine assortment of Vermont, Canada and western horses, including draft, business, gents' driving and family horses, all of which are warranted as represented. They employ a corps of experienced buyers in various parts of the country, and are constantly in receipt of animals suited to the requirements of all classes of buyers and which recommend their own good qualities to the confidence and patronage of critical and discriminating customers. The members of the firm are expert horsemen, excellent judges of the noble animal, and are in a position to conduct the business with entire satisfaction to all concerned. They sell on the average from fifteen hundred to two thousand horses per year, and have built up a large and influential patronage throughout New England. All representations made by them concerning the stock can be relied upon implicitly. The copartners, Messrs. C. D. Welch and H. K. Hall, are both Vermonters by birth, and well and favorably known in this city and all through New England. Messrs. Welch & Hall established this business some twenty years ago, the present firm being organized in 1891, and altogether a creditable and steadily increasing custom has been developed.

A LDRICH & CO., Commission Merchants, Wholesale and Retail Dealers in Butter, Cheese, Eggs, Lard, Beans, Etc., Stall, No. 82 and Basement, No. 14 (North Side), Faneuil Hall Market.—One of the oldest among the well known produce commission houses in Boston is that of the firm of A. Aldrich & Co. It was established as far back as 1826 by Mr. A. Aldrich who conducted it until 1853 when he associated with him Mr. A. S. Morse who succeeded to the business in 1870 and has since continued it under the old firm name. The operations extend throughout New England where the house has extensive connections and is constantly receiving consignments of farm and dairy products. Every facility is provided for the reception of goods and a large widespread wholesale trade is done in creamery and dairy butter and cheese, and in eggs, lard, beans and farm produce generally. Mr. Morse is a native of New Hampshire. He has lived in Boston upwards of forty years and is thoroughly identified with the affairs of the city.

PARIS MANUFACTURING COMPANY, Manufacturers of Children's Sleds and Sleighs, Toboggans, Boys' Carts, etc.; Works, South Paris, Me.; A. H. Cushing, manager, No. 131 Congress Street.—One of the most enterprising and popular merchants of Boston is Mr. A. H. Cushing, the representative of the celebrated Paris Manufacturing Company, and sole proprietor of the Portsmouth Wrench Company. The Paris Manufacturing Company is a very old and prosperous concern, and is now one of Maine's leading industries. It was established over eighteen years ago, originally being known as the Paris Hill Manufacturing Company. In 1868 it was reorganized under the existing title, and is now, under the skilled and progressive guidance of Mr. George B. Crockett, treasurer of the company, the leading manufacturer of children's sleds and sleighs of all grades; the popular "Comet" toboggan; all sizes and styles of boys' carts and wagons, wheelbarrows, etc.; also of folding laundry benches, tables and chairs, step ladders, the Garfield cot bed, etc. Mr. Cushing became representative of the company in July, 1883, and early developed important connections and a rapidly growing demand for his goods. This is in fact the company's principal shipping depot in numerous points. Mr. Cushing is also proprietor of the Portsmouth Wrench Company, which manufactures that remarkably clever and useful invention, the "Always ready wrench." This wrench sells on sight; it is the best special article that either merchants or agents ever handled and yields good profits. This is the wrench of the age, and Mr. Cushing's sound judgment is manifest in his obtaining exclusive control. Mr. Cushing also has important commercial interests in Bridgeport, Conn., being senior partner of the widely and favorably known hardware house of Cushing, Morris & Co. He has been active in the hardware trade for 25 years past, and is a recognized leading authority therein. He bought the Wrench Company in December, 1888, and the same spirit of push and progress with which he guides its operations is devoted to the handling and sale of the goods of the Paris Manufacturing Company. Mr. Cushing has ever retained the confidence of leading financial and mercantile circles, and his ably and honorably directed policy is one of direct benefit and value to the great city of Boston.

D. H. TULLY & CO., General Importers; Sicily Produce a specialty; Office, No. 76 Kilby Street; Warehouse, No. 19 Central Wharf.—One of the great representative commercial establishments of Boston, and the oldest established in its line, is that of Messrs. D. H. Tully & Co., general importers and commission merchants. In Sicily products and merchandise from the Mediterranean the firm have long been justly celebrated, and are very important factors in promoting Boston's commercial prosperity. The business was founded a way back in 1819 by Frank Kortimann, the following being the changes in the firm: Stanton & Spofman; Stanton, Fisk & Nichols; Stanton, Nichols & Co.; Stanton, Nichols & Whitney; Nichols & Whitney; Hallett & Blake; John R. Blake; John R. Blake & Co., Mr. Tully being the junior partner. In 1879 Mr. Tully formed the firm of D. H. Tully & Co., developing a trade of great magnitude. His decease occurred in 1887, since which date the business has been conducted by Mr. E. A. Kinney, Jr., his nephew, and Mr. A. J. Maher. They are able, practical merchants, and have wisely retained the old and honored name and style. They are direct importers of fruits, nuts, briarstone, sumac, etc., and receive a notably high quality of these products. They are also the Boston agents for the famous warehouse Marsala wines, which are standards with the trade of New England and western and middle states. They are also heavy commission importers from England and France, and are the Boston agents for Palermo lead and sumac, the finest quality known to the dye stuffs trade. Their Bran warehouse is centrally located at No. 19 Central Wharf, and is five stories in height. Here the firm carry large stocks of Sicily produce, and are prepared to promptly fill the most extensive orders of a quality and at prices which cannot be duplicated elsewhere. The house of D. H. Tully & Co. has ever maintained the reputation of handling the best goods in its line, and of ever exercising most upright and enterprising methods.

H. O. STRATTON, Manufacturers' Agent, Hardware, Tools, etc., No. 109 Franklin Street.—Among the important and old-established mercantile houses of this city, is that of which Mr. H. O. Stratton, is the esteemed and enterprising proprietor. As manufacturers' agent he has for many years past represented several of the most famous producers of more, fine

HORACE DUTTON & CO., Paper Manufacturers' Supplies, Agents for Piqua Felts, Pearl Starch and Glens Falls Lime, No. 11 Federal Street.—The leading head-quarters in this city for paper manufacturers' supplies of various kinds is the establishment of Messrs. Horace Dutton & Co., located at No. 11 Federal Street. This firm are extensive dealers in rags, chemicals, sumac and old paper, and enjoy a high prestige in trade circles as the agents for a number of manufacturing concerns of national reputation and importance. The business was founded in 1866 by Mr. Horace Dutton, and on January 1, 1889, the present firm was organized by the admission of Messrs. D. T. French, F. H. Herrick and H. R. Smith to partnership. A specially made of handling imported goods, and the connections enjoyed with the best sources of supply abroad, enable the firm to secure their goods in vast quantities and at the most advantageous rates. This firm are also agents for the sale of Piqua felts, pearl starch, and Glens Falls lime, and have developed a large and influential trade with paper mills throughout the entire United States. It is apparent that the greatest care and enterprise research have been exercised to bring the specialties handled by this house to their present point of perfection; they are admirably adapted for the purposes to which they are applied, and have no superior in line or any other market. They are held in high favor by paper manufacturers all over the country, while numerous testimonials from content firms and corporations bear undoubted evidence with regard to their value and efficiency. The establishment of Messrs. Horace Dutton & Co. is a leading source of credit to the management, and to the city in which it is so permanently located. The copartners are all well-known Bostonians, expert and practical representatives of the trade which they so successfully represent, and of excellent standing in business, financial and social life.

W. B. HILL, Manufacturer of Electric Lamps, Dynamos, Fixtures, etc., No. 109 Oliver Street.—A reliable and progressive house in the city of Boston, successfully engaged in the manufacture of electric lamps, apparatus, etc., is that of Mr. W. B. Hill, whose office and factory are located at No. 109 Oliver Street. This business was established eight years ago by Mr. Hill, who is a thoroughly trained electrical engineer and expert, fully conversant with every detail of the manufacture of all kinds of electric appliances, and the requirements of patrons. His factory is fully supplied with special tools and machinery, and furnishes constant employment to thirty skilled and experienced workmen. Mr. Hill manufactures to order or otherwise, electric lamps, dynamos, fixtures, and other electrical apparatus, and makes a specialty of small dynamos, arc lights, and switches. All electrical goods and specialties turned out from his factory are unrivalled for reliability, utility, finish, and workmanship, and have no superior in this country, while his prices in all cases are extremely moderate. Being a thorough mechanic, all goods are manufactured under his immediate supervision, thus affording a guarantee to patrons that all work leaving this establishment shall be perfect in every respect, and those who use our Mr. Hill's electric apparatus and fixtures are enlisted in their support ever after. Mr. Hill is a native of Manchester, N. H. He is highly regarded in trade circles for his mechanical skill and just methods, and his prospects in the near future in this important industry are of the most favorable character.

H. B. SWAZEY & CO., Lumber Commission Merchants, No. 61 Doane Street.—The members of the firm of Messrs. H. B. Swazey & Co., the well-known lumber and general commission merchants, at No. 61 Doane Street, have been closely identified with the lumber trade of this city for many years, and their extensive experience, superior judgment, and influential connections enable them to enter most successfully to the demands of the trade. The business was founded in 1849 by Chas. Buck & Co. On Mr. Buck's decease, in 1853, the business was continued by Mr. Swazey. In 1864, Mr. Foster was associated with the firm, which continued for about fifteen years, when the present firm was formed in 1878, consisting of Henry B. and George H. Swazey. The senior partner was a member of the original firm, while the junior partner is his son, and the treasurer of the Boston Lumber Trade Association. They deal at wholesale by car and cargo lots, handling lumber exclusively on commission. They are selling agents for Wm. H. Dwight & Co., dealers in dressed pine and hard woods, of Detroit, and enjoy the most intimate relations with manufacturers in the principal lumber producing regions. They are recognized authority in the lumber market, and there are few of their fellow merchants so well informed in every detail of this important trade as are the Messrs. Swazey. They represent many of the leading manufacturers of the west and northwest, selling on commission; and their facilities for promptly filling all orders are of the most complete and satisfactory character. Shipments are made direct from the mills, and lumber is supplied in carload or cargo lots, either in the rough or dressed, and cut in any dimensions desired. Promptitude, liberality, and probity have been the characteristics of this house from the commencement, and the success achieved is due to a rigid adherence to these principles. Mr. H. B. Swazey was born in Maine, and came to Boston forty years ago. He is one of the best-known lumber men in this section of the country, and has contributed to the development of the trade with energy, discrimination, and great success. Mr. G. H. Swazey was born in Chelsea, and combines his enterprise and ability to form a firm of commanding influence, wide popularity, and solid worth.

JOHN ERLANDSON, Manufacturer of Modern and Antique Furniture, No. 41 Bristol Street.—There is perhaps not one among the industrial arts in which more steady and notable progress had been made of recent years than cabinet making and kindred branches. The improvement effected in fashionable furniture for the drawing-room, library, and office of late is one of the features of the times, while the variety and beauty of designs and exquisite workmanship in the articles indicated produced in a first-class shop in these days are especially worthy of note. Among those who have established a reputation for A1 work in this line in Boston may be mentioned the name of John Erlandson, manufacturer of modern and antique furniture, No. 41 Bristol Street, and than whom none in the business in this city excels for skill and originality. Mr. Erlandson, who is a gentleman of middle age, and a native of Sweden, is a practical and expert workman himself, of many years' experience, and is a thorough master of his art. He started in business on his own account here in 1865, and soon won his way to favor and recognition, owing to the superiority of his work, building up a large and flourishing trade. Mr. Erlandson occupies as shop the whole of a 30x60 foot floor, and has in service ample and complete facilities, while employment is furnished to from seven to twenty skilled hands. The productions include artistic furniture, both modern and antique, handsomely carved and superbly finished; elegant cabinets, beautiful bookcases, sideboards, wardrobes, desks, etc., while furniture is made to order likewise in new and original designs in the highest style of the art, at short notice; Mr. Erlandson doing a large amount of high class work for the leading furniture houses of Boston, and the principal cities of the United States.

THE TROTT MANUFACTURING COMPANY, Manufacturers of Horse Furnishings, No. 167 Pearl Street.—Among the leading houses engaged in the manufacture and sale of horse furnishings, in the city of Boston special mention should be made of The Trott Manufacturing Company, No. 167 Pearl Street, of which Messrs. J. Steinbacher and C. H. Hagley are the popular proprietors. This business was established 16 years ago by Mr. C. H. Trott who conducted it till 1868, when he was succeeded by the present company. The premises occupied comprise two spacious floors 35x70 feet in area,

fully supplied with every appliance and convenience for the successful conduct of this steadily growing business. The company manufactures largely harness, saddles, bridles, blankets, and a general line of horse-furnishing goods, which are fully equal in every respect to the best custom work. The Trott Manufacturing Company promptly fill orders at the lowest possible prices, and their trade, which is wholesale, now extends throughout all sections of New England, the middle and western states. Mr. Steinbacher was born in Germany, but has resided in the United States for the last 45 years, while his partner, Mr. Hagley, is a native of Boston. They are highly esteemed in trade circles as liberal and honorable business men, and guarantee entire satisfaction to customers in every particular.

GEORGE C. HOW, Manufacturer of Ladies' Fine Slippers. No. 905 Devonshire Street.—In no way can the advantages of a city be better portrayed than by a brief review of the extent and character of those establishments already located within its limits, and, in successful operation; and though their success is to a great extent the result of the individual ability of those who are managing them, it is also proof that advantages of location, shipping facilities, etc., must have contributed in no small degree to their subsequent success. An establishment that ranks among the most important of its kind in the city, is that of Mr. George C. How, of No. 905 Devonshire Street. Mr. How is a manufacturer of ladies' fine leather slippers, and has been established for the past ten years, during which time he has developed a large influential trade, having its ramifications throughout the entire Union, and his goods maintain an enviable reputation among first-class dealers. The spacious factory, which is located in Haverhill, is equipped with the most improved machinery, driven by steam-power, and steady employment is furnished a force of sixty expert operatives. The factory has a productive capacity of four hundred pairs of slippers per day, and the output is a heavy one. Mr. How, who resides in Haverhill, and personally directs his factory, manufactures ladies' fine leather slippers, using only the best of materials, and the goods turned out are admirable specimens of finished workmanship. A large stock is carried, favorable and advantageous terms are quoted, and all orders are filled without delay. Mr. How has had long experience in the trade, and possessing every advantage to be gained by extensive facilities, he will doubtless long retain that high commercial standing and business prosperity which he now enjoys.

EAGLE MANUFACTURING COMPANY, Makers of Improved Wire Hair Brushes, and Commission Merchants, Nos. 92 and 94 Broad Street.—The latest and most popular specialty in hair brushes is that introduced by the Eagle Manufacturing Company of Nos. 92 and 94 Broad Street, in this city, who have gained an international reputation as makers of improved wire hair brushes. These brushes are well-known and appreciated all over this continent, and are in steadily increasing demand throughout Great Britain and Europe. This company was incorporated January 1, 1886, under the laws of the state of Massachusetts, and its affairs are under the personal management of the treasurer, Mr. O. L. Herbert, who is also the principal owner, and who was the founder and manager of the Eagle Metallic Brush Company, which was in operation here for ten years, and were bought out by the present company in 1882. The Eagle Manufacturing Company are also agents for L. Letchner, of Berlin, manufacturers of grease, paints, and face powder. As manufacturers of improved wire hair brushes, this company possess every modern facility and appliance for the systematic and economical prosecution of the business, occupying spacious and commodious premises, employing a large force of skilled and expert hands, and making altogether sixteen patterns of hair brushes. These goods have merited the claim of being absolutely unrivalled for quality, durability, utility, and uniform excellence in this or any other market. They are widely preferred by dealers over all other makes on account of their great salability and solid qualities, while they are placed to customers at prices which defy successful competition. The company carries at all times a large and complete stock, thereby insuring the prompt execution of all orders, and their determination to yield their patrons entire satisfaction is steadily securing for them the most pleasant results. Mr. Herbert, the treasurer, is a native of Germany, a resident of this country for twelve years, and a gentleman rated high in the commercial world.

B. F. STACEY, Pharmacist, Bank Building, Thompson Square, Charlestown.

FROST & DEARBORN, Restaurant, No. 6 Pearl Street.

GEORGE COLEMAN, Blank Book Manufacturer, No. 61 Federal Street; Elevator, No. 170 Devonshire Street.

TOLMAN & BILLINGS, Merchant Tailors, No. 7 Park Street.

WILKINS & CO., Book, Law and Commercial Printers, and Blank Book Manufacturers, No. 187 Devonshire Street.

FRANCIS T. CHURCH & CO., Manufacturing Chemists and Apothecaries, Corner of Court and Howard Streets.

AMERICAN GOLD PAINT COMPANY, No. 16 Meridian Street, East Boston.

EMIL MEYERS, Kaiser Wilhelm Blacking, Universal Metal Pomade, Floral, Quickest, Cheapest, and easiest-working Metal Polish in the Market for any kind of metal.

ELIJAH REACH, Merchant Tailor, No. 303 Washington Street.

HERBERT F. RAY, Registered Pharmacist, No. 119 Main Street, Corner Thompson, Charlestown.

FREEMAN & GRAY, Men's Furnishing Goods, No. 134 Tremont Street, opposite Park Street Church.

THE STONY PATENT ADJUSTABLE COAT COLLAR SPRING Manufactured only by the Holbert Coat Collar Spring Company; B C Carleton, Sole Agent, No. 24 Court Square.—This is truly an inventive age, and almost daily inventors are productive to the world some new device for lessening the hardships of

SAVES THE WEAR ON BUTTON HOLES, WHICH DISFIGURES A COAT SO QUICKLY.

that in some way promoting the comforts and pleasures of the people and making life more enjoyable. The latest manifestation that there is still something "new under the sun" is the Stony Patent Adjustable Coat Collar Spring, which is manufactured by the Holbert

Coat Collar Spring Company, of this city, and for which Mr. E. G. Carleton, of No. 24 Court Square, is the sole agent. This is an invention that every man who desires to be decently attired will appreciate, and will find a convenience for one as soon as he sees it. We speak from experience, and as over a million have already been put upon the market and sold within the past twelve months, some idea of its popularity may be gained. By its use the coat collar and lappets always retain their shape, and never require pressing, thereby saving many times their cost in a short time. This spring is made from best oil-tempered steel formed to fit the coat under the collar, and hold it in place same as if buttoned, without any inconvenience to the wearer; also prevents the coat from opening when exposed to the wind. This is the only thing always sure to keep a coat in shape and prevent the front from breaking down. It saves the wear on button-holes, which disfigures a coat so quickly. For wearing with over coats, it is just the thing, as the coat can be worn unbuttoned, and

turn your coat collar up, place the spring around your neck, turn collar down, and you have the effect. Tailors and others can find no more salable article to keep in stock than this coat collar spring, and the most liberal terms are offered to the trade, who should communicate with the sole wholesale agent. His office at No. 24 Court Square is very centrally located and easy of access, being on the street floor. Mr. Carleton is one of those jolly good fellows with whom it is a pleasure to do business. He has agents throughout the civilized world, and the coat collar spring is bound to be a success wherever coats are worn and as long as gentlemen have any regard for their personal appearance. Have a heavy stock of springs is kept on hand to meet immediate orders, which are filled to the entire satisfaction of patrons.

GEO. C. LITTLEFIELD, Leather Broker, No. 1 High Street.— This gentleman has had an experience of forty years in this business, and established his present enterprise in 1871. He hence has since been recognized as a prominent factor in promoting the leather trade of this city and state. His connections have continued to expand from year to year, capital and facilities enlarging together, until his house ranks equal with any of its contemporaries here or elsewhere. Having a foundation understanding of all the details and requirements of the leather trade, Mr. Littlefield is a recognized authority as to quality and value in this market. The utmost trust and confidence can be safely placed upon all representations made by him, and large numbers of manufacturers in this city and throughout the state depend upon him for their supplies year after year. All interests committed to his keeping are closely watched and intelligently promoted, and he is prepared to offer advantages and benefits that are rarely, if ever, duplicated elsewhere. Mr. Littlefield is a native of Stoughton, Mass., a resident of Newton, and enjoys a wide acquaintance in trade circles and the respect and esteem of all in social, financial, and commercial life.

HARRISON & RENISON, Carriage Manufacturers, Nos. 657, 659, and 661 West Second Street, Near F Street, South Boston.— If long and faithful apprenticeship, supplemented by years of active experience in a mechanical industry directed by more than ordinary intelligence, is worth anything as an encouragement to public favor, then the firm of Messrs. Harrison and Renison, carriage manufacturers, may be most heartily commended. The individual members of the firm are Mr. Robert Harrison, about thirty-five years of age, who was born in England, but has been a resident of the United States since boyhood; and Mr. M. J. Renison, a son of Ireland, a trifle older than his partner, who has resided here also ever since he was a minor lad. Mr. Harrison established himself in business on his own account as a carriage painter in 1882, and Mr. Renison also started during the same year as a wood worker in carriages. They conducted their separate branches with more than usual success at their old stands, No. 661 F Street, corner of Third Street until January 1886, when they consolidated their interests under the present firm title and removed to their present location. The premises utilized comprise a two-story frame building fifty feet square in dimensions, in which will be found a full equipment of all the necessary tools, appliances, and in fact everything that can contribute to the production of the most efficient, stylish, and reliable work. None but skilled and perfectly competent workmen are employed. They manufacture for sale and to order all kinds of carriages, landaus, top and open buggies, road wagons, skeleton and buck board wagons, sulkies, sleighs, etc., all of which are put together in the best and most conscientious workmanship known to the trade, and in which only the very best and most thoroughly seasoned woods and best brands of steel and iron are used; while the upholstering, trimming, painting, and general finish cannot be surpassed by any rival concern in this city. They give special attention to all kinds of jobbing and repairing in

T. PARK BUCHER, Insurance, No. 6 Milk Street.—Probably no life-insurance company in the country has done more in recent years to establish firmly in the mind of the public the advantages of the life-insurance systems than has the Ohio Valley Life Company, of Washington, D. C., which is represented in this city by Mr. T. Park Bucher, state manager, at No. 6 Milk Street. This company was organized in July, 1876, for the sole purpose of granting pure life insurance, upon a sound, safe, and enduring basis. It has behind it the record of eleven years of successful business, in which it has paid all death-claims in full, and furnished trustworthy insurance at a lower cost than any other company has been able to show in the same period. Its plans are in harmony with the progress of the age, and within the reach of all eligible to membership. It commends itself to every one who will examine its leading features: First its plain, simple policy; second, its fixed and equitable rates; third, only six payments per year, and fixed dates when they are to be made; fourth, an incontestable policy; fifth, no restriction as to mode or place of travel; sixth, its reserve fund conserves—equity in the manner of its creation, and the purpose it serves in reducing the cost to the members by requiring to them at stated periods an equitable share of all accumulations in the reserve fund. The fact that large investments are constantly being made to its business, without resort to other than the most legitimate measures, is conclusive evidence of the high estimation in which this staunch and ably managed institution is regarded by the public, and proves that shrewd and prudent men are becoming more and more generally convinced when desiring insurance, that in a company doing what may be termed " pure insurance," like the Ohio Valley affords not only the safest, but one of the most profitable investments that can be made. This company has already run over seven million dollars, and is adding to this amount daily. Mr. Bucher, the agent, is one of the best known insurance men in Boston, having been established in the business here since 1878, and is deservedly prominent as a general insurance broker. He is prepared to place the largest risks in either life, fire, or accident insurance companies, quoting the lowest rates of premium, and promptly paying all losses as soon as adjusted. He has a large and influential patronage in this city and throughout the state, and is eminently popular in the business community. Mr. Bucher is a native of the state of Pennsylvania, a resident of Boston for the past twelve years, still in the active prime of life, a member of the Boston Board of Underwriters, a director of the Massachusetts Accident Insurance Association, and a thoroughly practical exponent of insurance.

CARPENTER, WOODWARD & MORTON, Paints and Varnishes, White-lead, Tinted Leads, Mixed Paints, and Painters' Supplies, No. 191 Milk Street.—The manufacture of paints, oils, and varnishes, like most of the other branches of trade, has experienced the march of progress until discovery, invention, and improvement have wrought a veritable revolution in the trade within a comparatively recent period. For example, the old way of mixing, by hand, color and lead is entirely superseded by the infinitely superior method of thoroughly grinding together by machinery; and so in innumerable other ways the great and steady advances made in this direction are apparent. An old-established and thoroughly representative house is that one in Boston is that of Messrs. Carpenter, Woodward & Morton, located at No. 191 Milk Street. This firm are extensive dealers in paints and varnishes, white-lead, tinted leads, mixed paints, and painters' supplies. The house was founded in 1849 by Mr. E. F. Pratt; and, after some changes, the present firm was organized, in 1884, by Messrs. Geo. O. Carpenter, E. T. Woodward and John D. Morton. The senior partner had been in the firm since 1862, while Mr. Morton was a partner in 1884. Mr. Frederic H. Newton was admitted in partnership in 1878; and in 1890, Mr. Edwin A. Rogers was also admitted to the firm. Mr. E. T. Woodward died in 1891, the remaining copartners continuing the business without change in the firm style. The business premises comprise three floors and basement, 100x100 feet each, all of which splendid floor space is utilized in the disposal of the immense stock of goods that is constantly carried. Through the superior quality of the goods handled, and the ability, business capacity, and enterprise displayed in the management, this house has spun forced its way to prominence and patronage, and to-day stands the foremost exponent of its branch of trade in New England. The business, which is chiefly wholesale and jobbing, is immense and influential in all parts of the New England States, and the stock carried is the largest and finest of its kind in the city, including many valuable specialties handled by no other house in this section of the country. Mr. John D. Morton, of this firm, is the New England manager for the St. Louis Lead & Oil Company, the reputation of whose products is so widely known and firmly established that they need no words of commendation in these pages. These and other important makes of goods bear such a high character for quality and usefulness as to claim universal attention and general patronage. Employing large and ample capital, and commanding advanced opportunities for procuring their supplies direct from the most reputable manufacturers, in large quantities and at advantageous rates, this firm are in a position to offer superior inducements to patrons in both reliability of goods and liberality of terms and prices. The members of this responsible firm are accounted among Boston's representative merchants and solid, substantial business men. Mr. George O. Carpenter is a native and prominent citizen of Boston, and a member of the Paint and Oil Club of New England. Mr. John D. Morton is a Massachusetts man by birth and training, still in the prime of life, a prominent member of the Paint and Oil Club of New England, and was its president for two years. Mr. F. H. Newton is a native of Massachusetts, and has been connected with the house since 1889, was secretary of the Paint and Oil Club of New England for two years, and resides in this city. Mr. E. A. Rogers has been in the house since 1878, and is also a Massachusetts man by birth. These gentlemen combine their energies, experience, and ability to form a business firm of commanding influence and sterling worth.

WM. A. THOMPSON, Manufacturing Jeweler, Diamonds and Precious Stones, No. 383 Washington Street.—Precious gems are always the most valuable of material presents, inasmuch as they always possess a comparatively unvarying intrinsic value, beside that which is associated with them as reminders of the donors; but the gift, to give the fullest measure of satisfaction to the recipient, should have an artistic setting, which to design should be particularly its own. To possess a necklace, brooch, ring, or tiara is indeed a pleasure; but when the possession is distinguished by a design that is its own, and of which there are no duplications, then it is naturally a greater source of pride and satisfaction. There are many dealers in this city, in precious stones; but there are very few who unite, to the distinction of carrying a rich and varied stock, the reputation for strikingly original and artistic designs—designs that will bring out the greatest beauty of combination, and outside of the attractive but stereotyped forms. Among the most artistic and accomplished of Boston jewelers, and the only one who makes a specialty of diamonds and rare and precious gems, is Mr. William A. Thompson, No. 383 Washington Street. In Mr. Thompson the patron finds more than the expert and business man—he finds an artist of acknowledged reminence in his line. As an expert and authority upon all matters pertaining to gems, he is without a superior; while as an artist-jeweler, it is doubtful if the city holds his peer. The ordinary wearer of diamonds has little idea of the skill necessary to mount, select, and best previous stones; but it is only necessary to place the work of Mr. Thompson's alongside the average cluster, to manifest the superiority of the artist to the mere artisan. In the arrangement of gems, the blending of different colors to produce the most exquisite harmony attainable by the skilled manipulators of many hues, is something few can do. Mr. Thompson brings to his work the taste and nice appreciation of color effects, twin gifts of the artist, and an expert eye of twenty-five years in the business. Besides being able to show specimens of any gems, in any color, he suggests an original design, and sketches the same for the customer. A practical mechanic, he is also an enthusiastic art student, who designs and paints to fine effect in water-colors. An inspection of the beautiful gems which Mr. Thompson can show is no less a treat to the connoisseur than to the novice; while a pearl and diamond necklace, a recent crowning triumph of his artistic skill and laborious search in securing the materials, is something the exquisite beauty of which must be seen to be appreciated. The prairie in this necklace are of many shades, and the blending of the colors in this arrangement is matchless and pendants in most exquisite. A visit should be made to his rooms by all who wish that their gifts shall take the highest form of value and beauty.

JOHN MEDINA, Importer and Manufacturer of Human Hair Goods, Paris Hair Store, No 613 Washington Street. — Mr. John Medina is the leading authority in Boston in every branch of the above business or rather artistic profession, and has developed a patronage of great magnitude, including among his customers the fashionable circles of society, and an influential connection throughout the United States. Mr. Medina was born in the Azores Islands, and early in childhood left his mid Atlantic birthplace for a home in the New World. The family settled in Lawrence, Mass., and there the subject of our sketch was raised and educated. Early in life he thoroughly learned the hair goods trade in its every detail, and in 1866 started in business on his own account in Lawrence. With steady growth of trade and need of enlarged facilities, Mr. Medina in 1886 permanently removed to Boston, and steadily developed a business that eventually became the leader in its line. In 1894 he removed to his present new central and desirable location. His establishment is known as the "Paris Hair Store," and an appropriate title it is, for nowhere, not even in Paris, could there be found a more complete, extensive, or desirable stock. The store is most richly fitted up, and contains full lines of hair goods, while in the rear are the hair dressing parlors, where cutting, curling, shampooing, singeing, etc., are attended to by the most expert attendants. Mr. Medina is nationally celebrated as the inventor and exclusive manufacturer of many popular and greatly superior waves, head-pieces, wigs, etc. Among his newest styles, and not duplicated anywhere else, are the lovely Sea Foam Wave, very popular for young and middle-aged ladies with this wave every lady becomes her own hair-dresser. The prices range, without back hair, from $5 to $8; and with back hair $6 to $16, and up. Medina's improved Lisbon Wave is recognized to be the prettiest, most youthful, becoming to the face, and the lightest of any wave made. It can be dressed in a variety of waves, and is made only from natural curly hair. It is the most stylish. The use of this wave avoids the wig like appearance common to all other waves, and greatly adds to the natural beauty of the features. His new Carina fringe is another deservedly popular style, having six points, and can be parted to suit the wearer. He also has full lines of other switches, and makes a specialty of ladies' wigs. Gentlemen's dress wigs of first quality are constantly on hand, and are made to order as desired. These hair goods are the best and most improved in the world. They won the silver medal and diploma at the Exhibition of the Massachusetts Charitable Mechanics' Association, and are spoken of in the highest terms. He is also an authority on the best methods of treating baldness, and is successful in inducing the hair or beard to grow again, to the great majority of cases. He does a heavy mail order trade, his customers residing in every state of the Union.

J. D. GILMAN, Ladies' and Gentlemen's Dining and Sample Rooms, Nos. 47 and 50 Summer Street, corner of Arch Street. — The city of Boston is widely recognized as the centre where unlimited capital thorough experience, and incomparable enterprise have combined to make its cafés and restaurants equal to any in the country. As a contributor to the reputation of the city in this regard, and as a model establishment of its kind, the dining-rooms for ladies and gentlemen conducted by Mr. J. D. Gilman at Nos 47 and 50 Summer Street, corner of Arch, stand pre-eminent as the midday lunching place of the city. It has been successfully operated for a period of twenty-five years, and is the daily resort for several hundred people, enjoying a first-class patronage from down town merchants, and is highly appreciated by the public generally. The dining rooms on the ground floor measure 82×100 feet, and their arrangements and appointments are of the best possible character, reflecting the utmost credit upon the taste and judgment of the proprietor, while the surroundings and comfort of patrons are perfectly insured. The bar, lunch, and oyster room are situated in the basement, and are ably managed. The cuisine is in charge of chefs of marked ability and national reputation. The proprietor secures his table supplies from the most varied sources, all the important markets of the country paying tribute to his enterprise. All the delicacies that can possibly be obtained are served in liberal abundance, while the perfect manner in which the viands are served make a meal at Gilman's a most agreeable experience. While there are larger cafés in the city, there are none which possess such well founded claims upon the public favor or enjoy a more deserved popularity. It is the one place above all others during the day where a first class meal is secured for a fair price. Twenty experienced and courteous assistants are in attendance, and the patronage is large, first-class, and permanent. Mr. Gilman, the moving spirit of this enterprise, is a New Hampshire man by birth and training, and honored and esteemed in this city as a gentleman of great executive ability and of strict business integrity, and as an accomplished exponent of the business in which he is engaged.

GREEN & CO., Produce Commission Merchants in Butter, Cheese, Eggs, Poultry, Game, etc., Nos. 30 and 32 South Market Street. — Among the widely known houses engaged in the produce commission business in this city is that of Messrs. Green & Co., who are extensive wholesale dealers in butter, cheese, eggs, poultry, game, etc., and carry on a general produce commission trade with all parts of the country. The business was originally established in 1873 by Messrs. Andrews, Green & Co., who were succeeded the following year by the firm as at present constituted. The premises occupied for trade purposes are spacious in size, and afford ample accommodation for the storage and preservation of the choice and valuable stock here carried. The facilities of this house are unsurpassed by any like concern in the city. Its relations with shippers and producers is the most direct and influential, and the choicest products of the farm, the orchard, and the dairy are daily received fresh from the hands of the producer, and are here to be found in stock at the lowest market prices. Liberal advances are made on consignments of produce when desired, while quick sales and prompt returns have always been a fixed rule with this popular firm. The trade is broadly distributed throughout all the New England States. The department, Messrs. R. T. and H. K. Green, are natives of Maine, members of the Chamber of Commerce and the Produce Exchange, fully conversant with every detail of the commission trade.

S. H. SANBORN, Bookbinder, No. 130 Congress Street. — This representative house was founded some thirty years ago by Messrs. Sanborn & Parker, and after several changes the present proprietor succeeded to the sole control in 1872. The business premises comprise two floors, 25×80 feet each, thoroughly equipped with the best machinery for the purpose, operated by steam-power, and steady employment is given to a large force of skilled and expert hands, ranging in number from twenty to thirty. The equipment of the folding, trimming, sewing, stamping, and other departments is thoroughly complete, and every appliance known to the craft is utilized in order to develop the best specimens of book binding. A specialty is made of cloth and rebound book binding for the trade, and publishers and printing establishments find it greatly to their advantage to forward their editions to this old established and justly famous house, stating style of binding required, or sending a volume that they have had previously bound as a sample. The resources and facilities of the house for edition binding are unrivalled, and rarely equalled by those of any other first-class house in the trade, while the prices quoted are as low as is consistent with first-class work. Mr. Sanborn, the worthy proprietor, is a native of Concord, N. H., a well-known resident of Cambridge, and a member of the Massachusetts Charitable Mechanics' Association.

L. E. COWLES & CO., Mercantile Printing. No 16 Arch Street. — This house was founded several years ago by Mr. L. E. Cowles, and was carried on alone by him until 1887, when Mr. A. T. Fasano was admitted to partnership. Both members of the firm have had a thorough and complete training in all the departments of their profession, and are therefore fully qualified to execute the most delicate work in an artistic manner. The spacious premises occupied, 25 by 100 feet in area, are equipped with seven superior printing presses, and a liberal and judicious selection of the most desirable type faces and ornaments, and all other accessories are utilized in producing everything in the line of fine mercantile printing. The brass ably sustains an excellent reputation for artistic work, and receives a liberal patronage from leading business houses of Boston and its vicinity. The volume of trade demands the constant employment of fifteen hands. The department, Messrs. Cowles and Fasano, the former a native of Connecticut, the latter of Abington, Mass., devote their entire attention to the direction of their affairs, and are prompt in the execution of all orders entrusted to their care.

FLAGG MANUFACTURING COMPANY, Manufacturers of Shoe Machinery. Union Dumpsters, Scalers, (Boiler Compound), etc., No. 110 Lincoln Street; Dr. G. H. F. Flagg, Manager.—
Prominent among the representative manufacturing enterprises of the city of Boston are those conducted by Dr. Flagg, at No. 110 Lincoln Street. These companies comprise the Globe Buffer Company, Union Edge Setter Company, Flagg Manufacturing Company, and the Boston Lasting Machine Company, all of which enjoy a national reputation, owing to their utility, efficiency, and reliability. The founder of these combinations of enterprise is Dr. Flagg, a dentist by profession, who established himself in dentistry in this city in 1882. Ten years later he became interested in this line of manufacture, and founded first the Union Edge Setter Company, then the Globe Buffer Company. In 1897 he consolidated the Champion Trimmer Company,

the bottoms of boots and shoes. By it the sand-paper is used in entirely a different form from that employed by all other machines, as endless belt of that paper being run over an idler and a flexible roll against which the shoe is held. It will do more than twice the work no-where used in the form of a sheet closely clasped around the old-fashioned roll. These machines are now in use in all parts of the

country, and practically supplant all similar productions wherever introduced. The Globe heel burnisher is a machine combining every advantage claimed for others. In addition also the improved wheel

Union Ink Company, and Columbian Manufacturing Company, under the care and rule of the Flagg Manufacturing Company. He makes a specialty of the production of the Union evenwater for distributing rubber cement, wherever it is used without a particle of waste, thus saving about 25 per cent of cement. This evenwater is for sale by authorized agents and dealers in shoe machinery and findings throughout all sections of the United States. The Union Edge Setter Company are noted as manufacturers of the Union Edge Setting machine, the only successful machine for the purpose yet invented, and of which there are upwards of 5200 now in use. The Columbian Manufacturing Company was established in 1893 for the manufacture of "Scalexor," a notable boiler compound. Thus consolidated, this enterprise has entered upon a thoroughly successful useful and prosperous career. The business premises consist of four spacious floors for the manufacture of the above named products, each being 3475 feet in area. The various departments are fully equipped with new and improved machinery operated by steam-power, and every convenience is at hand for insuring rapid and perfect production. Employment is furnished to a force of sixty skilled workmen, and the output is one of great importance. The "Globe Buffer" is the most successful machine yet invented for buffing or sand-papering

and device for stopping and locking the same while applying the paper avoids stopping the machine, and thereby saves much time. It is guaranteed to be the most thoroughly built and durable machine in the market. The wheels are made in three sizes, and are finished to fit all styles of heels, from straight to extreme French. For use on this machine and others also, Dr. Flagg manufactures a superior quality of sanded sand paper, "Ruby" and "New England," which he puts up in rolls of twenty-five yards each. Another valuable novelty of this reliable house is the "Globe [illegible]" an invention of great merit, which displaces the flexible leather now in use for insoles in shoes. It is guaranteed by hundreds of manufacturers who are using it as thoroughly reliable, and as a permanent substitute for leather being stronger than any leather of the same thickness; is preserved instead of destroyed by perspiration; the edges are smooth, which prevent them from cutting the stitches; shoes made with it will not squeak, and the proprietor claims it to be superior to the very best leather for this purpose. This company also manufactures the "Union Slip Insersole" the "Union Electric Insersole," [illegible] sheets, paper and numerous other specialties of great value to the shoe trade. These goods are used extensively in all parts of the United States and Canada, and a large export trade is also conducted with Great Britain, France, Germany, Switzerland, Australia, etc. The Flagg Manufacturing Company also manufactures the Boston lasting machine. This machine has advantages over all machines heretofore made in the following essential features: 1st. The shoe is lasted upon a jack, the upper being drawn over with pinchers in the hand of the operator, precisely as in hand-lasting; 2d. Any shoe whose upper can be drawn over by hand can be lasted upon this machine; 3d. A shorter tack is used than is practicable in hand-lasting; 4th. No tacks are wasted; 5th. Lasting upon this machine is far less fatiguing to the operator than hand-work; 6th. A laster can do twice as much work with the aid of this machine in a given time as by the ordinary hand method; 7th. The machine is very simple in construction. Royalty, one-half cent per pair; lease price, $150. Dr. Flagg is justly accounted among those progressive and successful American manufacturers who build up great enterprises in every avenue of industry, fully meriting the extensive and permanent patronage secured by his ability and energy.

IRA G. HERSEY, Contractor and Builder, formerly of Nos. 77 and 79 Wareham Street, Now Cambridgeport, Mass.—In carefully examining the industrial enterprises of this busy metropolis, it is a constant source of pleasure to note the advances that are constantly being made in many directions of usefulness, and the growth of industries that add so little to the wealth and prosperity of the city. A very popular and well-known contractor and builder is Mr. Ira G. Hersey, formerly of Nos. 77 and 79 Wareham Street, who moved to his present location, in Cambridgeport, about May 1st of this year. The business was originally established in 18[illegible] by Messrs. Mackenzie & Hersey, the present proprietor succeeding to the sole control in 18[illegible]. The premises are fully equipped with new and improved machinery and appliances and steady employment is given to from seventy-five to one hundred skilled hands. The proprietor is prepared to furnish pine and hard wood trimmings and interior finish, mantels, mirror-frames, hall-stands, hand-rails, newels, pine and hard-wood doors, and in fact every variety of builders' woodwork in oak, walnut, cherry, butternut, ash, whitewood, pine, etc., inside and outside blinds and house mouldings. Special attention is given to supplying ornamental woodwork from designs furnished and in any style desired. Only the most expert workmen are employed, and all orders are filled with despatch and at liberal rates. Estimates for all kinds of work in the wood-working line are cheerfully furnished, and contracts are entered into for the erection of buildings of every description. Mr. Hersey is known as one of the largest builders in the city, and has carried through to a successful completion many important and extensive commissions for the erection of public buildings, business blocks and private residences, all of which are specimens of mechanical genius and architectural skill of the highest order of perfection and serve to commend this house universally to public confidence and patronage. Mr Hersey is a native of Hingham, Mass., and is highly esteemed in this city as an accomplished master in his line of industry, and a solid, substantial, and responsible business man.

EATON & EUSTIS, Commission Merchants, and Dealers in Beans, Potatoes, Apples, Poultry, Butter, Cheese, Eggs, etc., No. 18 North Market Street.—The well known house of Messrs. Eaton & Eustis, commission-merchants and dealers in farm and dairy products and fruits, is one of the most reliable in the city. It was established by the firm in 18[illegible], and since that time a trade has been built up and connections made which have proved lucrative to the copartners and satisfactory to all who have had dealings with it. Spacious commodious premises [illegible] feet in area are occupied, and besides the firm two clerks are employed to facilitate transactions. As commission-merchants Messrs. Eaton & Eustis conduct extensive operations, and as dealers are doing a large wholesale business in beans, apples, potatoes, poultry and produce generally and also butter, cheese and eggs, and foreign and domestic fruits of all kinds. While the trade is principally local, an outside business with all parts of New England has been cultivated, the operations being conducted on quite an extensive scale. Mr J. C. Eaton and Mr C. L. Eustis are both natives of the state of Maine, and as merchants are very popular and prominent in this community. They are thoroughly upright and honorable, and correct and prompt in all business transactions, and consignors will find that they are faithful in the performance of all obligations.

N. E. HOLLIS, Produce and Provision Commission Merchant, Receiver of Swift's Chicago Dressed Beef, Nos. 50 and 51 North Market Street and No. 81 North Street.—In writing a detailed account of the industries of Boston, with some mention of those individual enterprises that have conduced so greatly to the benefit of the community, we must not overlook the fact that no little vitality has emanated from a trade in meat that appears to become more important annually. Among those who are well known in this city and have achieved prominence as general produce and provision commission merchants and receivers of Swift's choice Chicago dressed beef, is Mr. N. E. Hollis, whose establishment is centrally and conveniently located at Nos. 50 and 51 North Market Street and No. 81 North Street. This business was organized about twenty years ago by Messrs. Sawyer, Hollis & Co., who conducted it in partnership until 18[illegible], when Mr. N. E. Hollis purchased his associates' interests and assumed the proprietorship. The premises occupied comprise two commodious stores with basements, and these front on both North Market and North Streets. In addition, Mr Hollis also occupies, at No. [illegible] North Street, a store and basement as a packing-house. The business of this concern has attained very large proportions, and is still annually increasing in volume. Butter, poultry, eggs, and country produce of every description are handled at wholesale on commission, and a very heavy trade is done. The leading feature of the business is the trade in Swift's choice Chicago dressed beef; and as a plentiful supply of this indispensable commodity is always on hand, and as Mr. Hollis is always earnest in his endeavors to please, he has established a large business and enjoys a widespread custom. Indeed, he handles more beef than any other Boston house, and disposes of about twenty carloads per week in all his departments. The trade, which extends throughout New England, requires the constant services of thirty to forty hands, and it is constantly increasing.

BRIGHAM & SPOFFORD, Architects, No. 19 Milk Street.—Prominent among the reliable and leading architects of the city, is the widely known firm of Messrs. Brigham & Spofford. Mr. Charles Brigham, the senior partner, commenced the practice of his profession twenty-three years ago, as a member of the firm of Sturgis & Brigham, among their works being the Museum of Fine-arts, Y. M. C. A. Building, Boylston Street; Church of the Advent, Brimmer Street; private residences for Mr. Fred. L. Ames, John L. Gardner, E. Rollins Morse, Boston; the residence of H. H. Rogers, New York City; and he has had extensive experience in New York, Philadelphia, Baltimore and Washington. This partnership was dissolved in 18[illegible], and in February, 18[illegible], he entered into partnership with Mr J. C. Spofford, the firm being known by the style and title of Brigham & Spofford. Both partners are able and talented architects, fully conversant with every detail of the profession. Proofs of their skill are numerous throughout Boston and its vicinity, as embodied in the various splendid edifices they have erected in the last few years, which are much admired by experts, for their stability, elegance, and elaboration of detail. The following are a few of the buildings latterly erected by this popular firm: Boston & Providence R. R. Stations at Stoughton and Roxbury, Mass.; Massachusetts Hospital Life Insurance Company's Building, Episcopal Church, Melrose; Judge Macomber's House, Rochester, N. Y.; Y. M. C. A. Building, Everett, Mass.; School and Unitarian Chapel, Watertown, Mass.; the residence of the late Henry A. Whitney, Marlboro Street, Boston, and many others.

F. W. FOSTER & CO., Steam and Hot water Heating Apparatus, Specialties Public Buildings, Fine Residences, and Greenhouses, No. 51 Charlestown Street.—At the present time the value of steam and hot water for heating buildings has become so well understood and so common that it is unnecessary to enter into any argument to prove its superiority over all other methods of artificial warming. Its advantages have become so well known and approved that architects, scientists, physicians, and sanitary engineers have endorsed the system of steam and hot water as far more desirable than the use of stoves and hot-air furnaces. In connection with these remarks, special reference is made in this commercial review of Boston to the representative and successful house of F. W. Foster & Co., contractors for steam and hot-water apparatus, whose office and showrooms are located at No. 51 Charlestown Street. This business was established twelve years ago by F. W. Foster, upon his return from Ohio, where he was engaged for nearly two years passing

in and remodelling the heating outfits in public buildings, as at Akron and Columbus. The present firm are ever on the alert for the latest and best improvements; and among their line of specialties is the "Kasm Thermo-electric Regulator," a simple yet truly scientific attachment for hot-water outfits, and the only device now known that will positively control the circulating water, at any degree desired, in moderate as well as the most extreme weather. Foster & Co. make a specialty of heating and ventilating public buildings, fine residences, and greenhouses with steam or water, separately or combined; and make the best adapted for having the only apparatus that is equally well adapted for one or the other, and decidedly superior under any requirements of the three systems. This apparatus was adopted in 1876 by the directors of the new Hatch Experimental Station at the State Agricultural College, Amherst, Mass.; and their tabulated report just issued (April, 1888) shows a saving of 30 per cent in coal, and an average of nearly 8 per cent higher temperature in a comparative test between water and steam. There are two other remarkable facts in the history of the "Lydie" that are of general

record of over twelve years, with an increased annual sale in nearly every state in the Union, finds the market to-day without a single second hand boiler of this make to be found. Space is too short to give a detailed description of this boiler, and but one illustration—a general view as it appears set in brickwork. The interior is the most interesting, and all those contemplating any mode of heating should carefully examine the improved Lydie water tube, return-flue, cast-iron sectional safety boiler, for, by the special machinery now used in its manufacture, it can be offered at low cost, and with a positive assurance of highly satisfactory results as regards economy of fuel, capacity, ease, reliability, and durability—the latter believed to be at least three times that of the ordinary make. This firm also control the celebrated "Portable" hot-water boiler that is the best of its class. Interested parties can obtain full particulars by addressing F. W. Foster & Co., No. 51 Charlestown Street, Boston, Mass., U. S. A.

BEN. LEVY & CO., French Perfumers, No. 51 West Street.—Perfumery preparations have become a very important accessory to our present civilization and society, and so refined individuals of the present day consider their toilet complete without the use of some standard preparations in the shape of a perfume. The house of Ben. Levy & Co., No. 51 West Street, has gained a widespread and excellent reputation for manufacturing and dealing only in the purest and most lasting perfumes, their goods and specialties being in great demand in all sections of the United States and Canada. Mr. Ben. Levy, who is sole proprietor, established this business in 1871. He makes a specialty of manufacturing at his laboratory Levy's Parisian Cream, Levy's Perfine or Liquid Pearl, and Levy's French Cream. He makes a specialty of the La Blache face-powder, which has received the highest testimonials from the prominent celebrities of the stage both in America and Europe. Levy's French Cream is a scientific beautifier. It is the result of long observation, careful experiments, has had the aid of the best French chemist and of a skilful skin doctor of Paris. This is stated that the ladies may have no fear of bad results following the use, as in the case of cheap catchpenny preparations which have been forced upon the market. Levy's French Cream is not only harmless, but is positively beneficial. Mr. Levy has letters from Marie Rose Napierson, the celebrated vocalist, Sarah Bernhardt, and other prominent artistes of the lyric and dramatic professions, endorsing the claims for recognition in the warmest terms. They do not consider their toilet complete without this article. The price is only $1 per bottle, or three bottles for $3. Sent by express to any part of the country upon receipt of price. Levy's Parisian Cream (Creme Therapeutique) is a delightful preparation for purifying, refreshing, and renovating the complexion. Its capability of soothing irritation and removing all roughness of the skin renders it indispensable to every toilet. It is perfectly harmless, and can be used on the most delicate skin with the greatest safety. Jars, forty and seventy five cents. Levy's Perfine, or Liquid Pearl. A very fine preparation for imparting a delicate and youthful bloom to the complexion. White, pink, and cream tinted for brunettes. Price, only seventy five cents per bottle. Mr. Levy's store is elegantly equipped, and completely stocked with the finest extracts, colognes, soaps, lotions, cosmetics, powders, etc., which have been imported direct from the most celebrated Paris and

WHITTEMORE MANUFACTURING COMPANY, State Machinery. No 81 Haigh Street.—The Whittemore Manufacturing Company has made itself famous the world over by its ingenious boot and shoe machinery. This company is the outcome of the amalgamation, in 1872, of several individual concerns, engaged in the manufacture and sale of boot and shoe machinery into the State Machinery Manufacturing Company. The business of this company was purchased in 1875 by Mr. D. Whittemore, who, in the spring of 1884, was succeeded by his sons, Messrs. J. Q. A. and Charles Whittemore, who are continuing the enterprise under the style of the Whittemore Manufacturing Company. The works comprise a three-story building, 30x100 feet in dimensions. The lower floor is used as salesroom, and the machine-shops are on the upper floors. The mechanical equipments are of the most efficient description, and from ten to twelve hands are engaged here. Much of the machinery disposed of by this house is manufactured outside under contract, and a prominent feature of the business is the repairing of all kinds of shoe machinery. The concern is under the general management of Mr. Samuel F. Howard, who has been connected with it for the past twenty years. The company manufacture and deal in Bay State wax thread sewing machines; upside-down machines for stitching counters and straps; New Era, Champion, and Varney pegging machines; Star nail and upper leather splitters; vibrating rolls; McAndrew eyeletters; punching and eyeleting machines combined, for glove and cloth work; common foot-power and self-feeding punches; forepart edge setting and trimming machines, without royalty; foot and steam power strippers and rollers; side-welt machines; sandpapering machines, chan-shivers, counter shivers; heel breasting machines, sole moulding machines, rawhide mallets, screw press, burnishing machines; patent nail-drivers, lining shavers, cutting boards, brushes, machine awls, needles, casters; emery rubbers, crimpers, etc. The company, in addition to having a large trade with all parts of the United States, export goods to England, Germany, Australia, etc.

M. C. HOOD & CO., Perfumers, and Manufacturers of Hood's French Cologne, No. 28 Devonshire Street.—This concern had its origin about ten years or so ago, and was then founded by Messrs. M. C. & N. R. Hood, formerly natives of Vermont, but old residents in Boston. In 1885, Mr. N. C. Hood died, and since then the business has been perpetuated by the surviving brother under the original firm style. The third floor of the building is utilized as salesroom and manufacturing department, and this has an area of 25x80 feet. Perfumes of every description, and of a high quality, are produced here, and a specialty is made of a cologne that is widely known as Hood's French Cologne. These perfumes are put in various forms,—in artistic bottles, etc., and are a source of attraction wherever exhibited. The superior and uniform excellence of Hood's perfumes is universally conceded, and this recognition was indorsed in 1878 by the award of a diploma to Messrs. M. C. Hood & Co., at the Massachusetts Charitable Mechanic Association exhibition in that year. The business is exclusively of a wholesale character, and a vast trade is done through perfumers, druggists, dry goods houses, hair-dressers, fancy-goods dealers, etc., all over the country. Dealers find the produce of this concern most salable goods to keep in stock. Mr. M. C. Hood resides at Melrose.

J. H. POWER & CO., Steel and Stencil Letter Cutters, Die-sinkers, and Engravers, No. 84 High Street.—For thirty-five years or thereabout, the popular and well-known firm whose name heads this sketch has maintained a position in the forefront in its line in this city. For thoroughly fine work in the line of steel and stencil letter cutting, die-sinking, and engraving, or for promptness and reliability in executing all orders, small or large, no concern of the kind in Boston has a better name, and none deserves it, having been awarded medals at various periods by the Massachusetts Charitable Mechanic Association for meritorious productions. This prosperous enterprise was started in 1851 by the present senior member, who conducted it alone up to about ten years ago, when he admitted into partnership Thomas Ward. They occupy commodious and well-equipped quarters on the third floor of No. 84 High Street, ample and complete facilities being at hand, while four or more skilled assistants are employed. The firm are prepared to execute all work in the line of steel and stencil letter cutting, die-sinking, and engraving, in the highest style of the art, and in the most expeditious manner, at lowest consistent figures. Embossing presses and seals for bankers, merchants, notaries, and lodges are made to order likewise, and carried in stock; also rubber stamps, inks, pads, and kindred articles, fine steel letter cutting being a leading specialty. Altogether the firm has a large, active patronage throughout New England and portions of the west.

A. WILSON, Sailmaker, No. 416 Atlantic Avenue.—Among the leading sailmakers carrying on business in Boston to-day there is perhaps not one that enjoys a better reputation for fine work, or for promptness and reliability in executing orders in his line, than the gentleman whose name stands at the head of this sketch. Mr. Wilson is a comparatively young man, being about thirty-six years of age, and was born at Port Jefferson, N. Y., where his father had been engaged in the same line since 1868, and was succeeded by his two sons. He is a practical and expert sail-maker, of several years' experience in the exercise of his art. Coming to this city in 1888, he established himself in business here, starting out door to the present commodious quarters, which he has occupied since September last, and from the first his resume in Boston has been attended with uniform success. Mr. Wilson occupies an 25x80-foot loft, with ample and excellent facilities, and gives employment to from ten to twenty skilled hands; only first-class work being turned out here. Sails of every size, style, and variety are made to order in the most expeditious and excellent manner, yachts' sails being a specialty; while a fine assortment of new and second-hand sails may also be found on hand at all times.

W. F. SCHRAFFT, Manufacturing Confectioner, No. 11 Elm Street.—One of the best known and most popular manufacturing confectioners in this city is Mr. W. F. Schrafft. This gentleman is a native of Germany, who came to this country thirty-five years ago, and established his present business here in 1861. He occupies a building containing three floors and a basement, and possesses every modern facility for conducting the business under the most favorable conditions and upon the largest scale. Steady employment is given to a force of twenty hands, all skilled in the art of manufacture, and the output is one of great volume and variety. Both plain and fancy confections are produced, a leading specialty being made of fine chocolates and cream bonbons. Nothing whatever is utilized except the purest and the best, and no deleterious article of any kind is allowed for flavoring, color, or ingredient. The specialties in hard candies, gum work, chocolates, and bonbons have produced are widely preferred by both dealers and customers and are in demand throughout all the New England States. The business is annually increasing in volume and importance in consequence of the unsurpassed excellence of the goods. The proprietor justly merits the signal success he has achieved.

T. R. MARVIN & SON, Book and Job Printers, No. 48 Federal Street.—The oldest book and job printing office in the city of Boston, and one which has kept full progress with the improvements made in the printing art, is that of T. R. Marvin & Son. Although the house has been in existence for over sixty years, there has been but one change in the management, and that was caused by the death of the senior member of the firm. The business was founded in 1822 by Mr. T. R. Marvin, and was carried on under his sole direction until 1865, when his son, Mr. W. T. R. Marvin, was admitted to partnership. In 1874, the senior partner died. After a very long and honorable business career, Mr. W. T. R. Marvin has since been proprietor of the establishment, and is conducting it with the same success which attended the father's efforts. The premises occupied for the business are equipped with six steam presses and all the adjuncts of a modern printing establishment. Book, commercial, and general job printing are executed in all their various branches, a leading specialty being made of the animated church printing, and all work turned out of the establishment is notable for its general excellence of finish, while the prices charged are of the most reasonable character. Mr. Marvin, who is a native of Boston, is a resident of Brookline, and a member of the Brookline school board.

BUNTING & EMERY, Wholesale Dealers and Shippers of Fish, No. 5 T Wharf.—Prominent among the leading firms engaged in the handling of sea food in Boston is that of Bunting & Emery, wholesale dealers and shippers of all kinds of fresh fish. No concern devoted to this branch of commercial activity in the city maintains a better standing, as few receive a more substantial share of public favor, doing an extensive and flourishing business. This well and favorably known house was established in 1887, by Messrs. S. N. Bunting and Freeman Emery, and by three gentlemen it was conducted up to 1897, when Mr. Bunting was removed by death, and R. Franklin Blanchard admitted into partnership, the style of firm always remaining the same. They occupy three spacious floors, with ample office and ample and complete storage and shipping facilities, while eight or more to help are employed. A carefully assorted and big stock is constantly carried on hand, including fresh fish of every description, handling enormous quantities of mackerel and bluefish in their season, and the trade of the firm, which is of a wholesale nature altogether, is exceedingly heavy, extending throughout the New England States, while shipments are made also to New York City and State and to Philadelphia. Messrs. Emery and Blanchard, who are natives respectively of Charlestown and Cape Cod, Mass., are both gentlemen of push and enterprise, and are well known and highly regarded in the trade.

S. A. D. SHEPPARD & CO., Pharmacists, No. 1120 Washington, Corner Dover Street; and No. 1531 Washington, Corner Union Park Street.—In elegance, reliability and extent of trade, the two drug stores owned and operated by Messrs S. A. D. Sheppard & Co. occupy a leading position in the city. The spacious and elegantly appointed store at Washington and Dover Streets was opened March 4, 1888, and is undoubtedly the best-patronized pharmacy at the South End. The store at Washington and Union Park Streets was established in October, 1890. Both these establishments are under expert management. A very large stock is constantly carried of pure drugs, chemicals, and pharmaceutical preparations, essences, and cosmetics; wines and liquors for medicinal purposes; toilet and fancy goods; druggists' sundries; and, in fact everything kept in a first-class establishment devoted to this trade. The prescription department at each place is carefully and thoroughly directed, in charge of experienced compounders. The individual members of this responsible firm are Dr. S. A. D. Sheppard and Mr. Henry Thacher. Both are Massachusetts men by birth and education, graduates of the Massachusetts School of Pharmacy, and accomplished exponents of their profession. Dr. Sheppard has served as president of the Massachusetts School of Pharmacy, president of the Boston Druggists' Association, president of the Massachusetts State Pharmaceutical Association, first vice-president of the American Pharmaceutical Association, and is now treasurer of the latter association, and was the first registered pharmacist in Massachusetts. Largely through his efforts, the bill requiring owners or proprietors of drug stores to become registered was passed by the State Legislature in 1885, and signed by the Governor. Mr. Sheppard served for several years as a member of the State Board of Pharmacy. Mr. Thacher has been connected with Dr. Sheppard in the drug business for a period of thirteen years, and in 1894, combined his ability and practical knowledge to form this widely known and popular firm.

WILLIAM S. WHITE & CO., Commission Merchants in Leather, Oil, and Skins, Nos. 226 and 228 Purchase Street.— While our attention is directed to the various colonial industries of Boston to which the products of the tanner take so important a part, we should give cordial recognition to the enterprise so successfully conducted by Messrs. William S. White & Co. at Nos. 226 and 228 Purchase Street. This firm are widely prominent as extensive commission merchants in leather, oil, and skins, and also operate two tanneries, one at Cumberland, Md., and one at Hyndman, Pa., for the manufacture of sole and rough leather, having the capacity for utilizing one hundred hides per day, and furnishing employment to from seventy-five to one hundred hands. The business was originally established in 1877, at Cumberland, Md., by Messrs. C. B. and J. K. White. In September, 1888, the present headquarters of the firm were established in this city, and the father of the partners, Mr William S. White, was admitted to partnership under the present firm name. Here the firm occupy large and commodious premises for trade purposes. The Messrs White are all natives of Pennsylvania, Mr. C. B. White residing in Boston, while the other partners are residents of Hyndman, Pa. The position of the house in the trade has been honestly secured and is well deserved.

LEVISEUR BROS. & CO., Importer and Domestic Leather, No. 57 High Street.—Since its establishment here in 1877, the house of Messrs. Leviseur Bros. & Co., at No. 57 High Street, has been recognized as a prominent one in promoting the leather trade of Boston. The business, under able and enterprising direction, has continued to enlarge from year to year, capital and facilities expanding together, until the house ranks equal with any of its contemporaries here or elsewhere. The premises occupied for trade purposes are spacious in size, slightly located, and are stocked to repletion at all times with new, choice, and desirable goods. Jobbing in both domestic and foreign leather of all kinds, and making a specialty of kid, goat and sheep leather for ladies' fine shoes, this house is prepared to offer every inducement that can be accorded in this market, both as regards excellence of goods and economy of prices, and has built up a large and influential trade throughout all the New England States. The co-partners, Messrs. Louis Leviseur, Joseph Leviseur, and Chas. E. Conway, are experienced merchants and public-spirited, vigorous young business men. The Messrs. Leviseur are natives of Germany, while Mr Conway is a Massachusetts man, born and bred.

GEORGE E. CRAWLEY, Importer of European Novelties, Art Goods in Metal, and Household Goods in Brass, No. 177 Tremont Street.—This popular art-goods emporium is the leader in its line in the city, and has been in successful operation since 1892. The store is the most thoroughly attractive of any on this fashionable thoroughfare, and is the recognized headquarters for the unique and the useful, the curious and the beautiful, in metal and brass, and for the freshest novelties of the European markets. The name and fame of this house is redolent of the rare and precious in art; of the most skilful work of the designer; of gems of production in the line of brass and metal; of the finest achievements of the engraver, the carver, and the sculptor; and of the choicest exhibits of modern ware and of every clime in the rare, the novel, and the utilitarian. As a direct importer, Mr. Crawley is constantly receiving goods of exceptional rarity, which cannot be duplicated elsewhere. To meet the exacting demands of his trade he has representatives in all countries consistently on the alert for novelties, and his sound judgment and great liberality in securing the treasures of the world at any cost is meeting with the deserved appreciation of the critic, the connoisseur, and the lover of the beautiful in art in any form. The beauty of these goods and the magnificent display have made none be seen to be realized. Mr. Crawley is a Massachusetts man by birth and education, and has been prominent and popular in mercantile circles in this city for years.

LOUIS BASSILL, Brass Finisher, Dealer in Cutlery, Surgical Instruments, Trusses, etc., No. 15 Hawkins Street.—Attention is here directed to the reliable and well-equipped establishment of Mr. Louis Bassill, brass finisher, and dealer in cutlery, surgical instruments, trusses, and apparatus for deformities, etc., where can always be found an extensive and first-class assortment of everything in this line. Mr. Bassill, who founded his enterprise two years ago, has met with the most marked success. Until January, however, the business was conducted at No. 71 Sudbury Street, when it was moved to its present location. The premises occupied are spacious, and admirably adapted for the purpose to which they are devoted. The workshop is thoroughly equipped with the most improved and efficient machinery, which is operated by steam-power. Several skilled and experienced hands are employed, and every description of brass work is executed in a thorough workmanlike manner. Repairs are also neatly made, razors are concaved and scissors ground, and grinding and polishing are done satisfactorily. A fine stock of cutlery of all kinds, surgical instruments of every description, trusses and apparatus for deformities are always kept on hand, and in these lines Mr. Bassill is enabled to offer terms and advantages not readily procured elsewhere. He is a native of this city, and a gentleman of sterling qualities.

THE TRAVELERS INSURANCE COMPANY. Boston Office, Corner State and Kilby Streets; Hatch & Woodman, General Agents.—The old reliable Travelers Insurance Company has ever attained a large measure of popularity with the general public in the vast field of accident insurance, while in the business of life insurance proper its advantages and benefits are rarely equalled by any corporation extant. Its general agents for Boston and vicinity are Messrs. Hatch & Woodman. The Travelers' last semi-annual statement made July 1, 1888, shows the following facts and figures, viz.: ...

FRANK H. SKINNER, successor to Ford & Skinner, Bankers Paper, City and Town Loans, No. 110 Devonshire Street, Rooms 1.—Mr. Frank H. Skinner, the well known dealer in notes and commercial paper of a first-class character, has been prominently identified with the financial world for some years...

GEO. F. NEWELL, Manufacturer of Boot and Shoe Straps, No. 134 Atlantic Avenue.—This gentleman occupies spacious and commodious quarters at the address above indicated, and is recognized as the leading representative of this special line of industry in Boston...

B. C. BUDGE, Manager New England Agency, Barr Pumping Engine Company, No. 74 Federal Street.—The Barr Pumping Engine Company of Germantown Junction, Philadelphia, began operations in May, 1887, with a capital of $200,000, under the executive guidance of the following gentlemen: Mr. George Burnham, president; Mr. William M. Barr, vice president and manager; and Mr. George Burnham, Jr., secretary and treasurer...

CHARLES SCRIBNER'S SONS, Publishers, No. 62 Hawley Street.—Prominent among the leading publishing houses of the United States is that of Messrs. Charles Scribner's Sons. This house was founded many years ago by Mr. Charles Scribner, the firm afterward becoming Scribner, Armstrong & Co., the latter firm being succeeded by the present proprietors...

E. CLARK, Receiver of Spirits Turpentine, Rosin, Tar, etc., No. 3 Custom House Street.—This business was established in 1861 by the firm of Leonard & Clark, which continued up to 1864, when Mr. Clark assumed sole control, and has conducted the enterprise alone with uniform success...

A. MARTIN & SON, Cigar-manufacturer; Wholesale and Retail Dealer in Cigars, Tobacco, Smokers' Articles, etc.; No. 7 Lewis Street, East Boston.—This house was founded in 1859 by Mr. A. A. Martin, and in 1881 the present firm was organized by the admission of Mr. A. Martin to partnership. The firm are recognized as leading manufacturers and a reliable authority in the cigar trade. They have made a life-study of the business, and carry constantly in stock a varied and complete assortment of styles, sizes, and grades of domestic and imported cigars, smoking and chewing tobacco, and general smokers' goods, so as to be prepared to meet promptly every want of the public. The principal brands of cigars manufactured and sold by this popular firm are the "F. L. L." made from the finest Vuelta Abajo filler and Sumatra wrapper, the best ten-cent cigar in the market; "Lewis," "Waddle," and "Londres." They never deceive customers, always maintaining the full standard of all brands. All their goods are guaranteed, and their customers in the business are not allowed to keep goods unsatisfactory to their trade. In a word, Messrs. Martin & Son make their customers' interests their own, and dealers feel safe in buying from such an honorable, responsible house. The retail trade of this house is also large, first-class, and influential, a branch store being operated at the corner of Chelsea Avenue and Castle Street, Boston, and a fine growing business has been developed. A force of some fifteen workmen is employed, and unsurpassed facilities are at hand for guaranteeing prompt and perfect fulfilment of all orders. The senior partner was born in Spain and came to Boston thirty years ago. He is an expert cigar manufacturer of established reputation, while his son has been trained to the business, and now represents the interests of the house upon the road.

GEORGE HOLLISTER, Manufacturers' Agent for Dry and Kalsomine, and Fresco Paints, Ultramarine Blue, etc., No. 85 Federal Street.—Mr. Hollister is agent for Harrison's dry sized kalsomine, Harrison's mixed paints, and general dealer in ultramarine blues, fresco paints, dry colors of all kinds, brushes, etc. At his spacious, well appointed business premises, he carries of all things a very extensive and carefully selected stock, representing the finest products of manufacturers both at home and abroad. Mr. Hollister has had an extended experience in this line of trade, and the knowledge he brings to bear upon his enterprise is an advantage to those who wish to secure first-class, reliable goods in his line. He began business on his own account in 1885, and from the beginning has commanded a very liberal and substantial patronage. His stock is one of the most complete in the line in the city, and is sold at the manufacturers' lowest prices. The transactions of the house are of both a wholesale and retail character, and the trade extends over all parts of the New England States. Liberally, promptly, and straightforward dealing have ever been the leading principles upon which the business has been conducted. Mr. Hollister was born in Connecticut, and for over forty years has resided in Boston.

G. W. PEABODY, House Painter, Grainer, and Glazier, Mixed Paints, White Lead, Oils, Turpentine, Varnishes, Glass, and Putty, No. 347 Meridian Street, corner of Havre, East Boston.—The painter and decorator in this decorative age is one whose services are in great request, and particularly if he is as adept as his trade. This is precisely what Mr. G. W. Peabody is, and his ability is backed by long practical experience. He began business in 1875 on his own account at his present location, No. 347 Meridian Street, corner of Havre Street, and from the first has commanded a very liberal and substantial patronage. The store is neatly and orderly fitted up, and is fully stocked with decorative materials of all kinds. The stock consists of paints, oils, glass, putty, brushes, varnishes, white lead, oils, etc., the sales of which are made by wholesale and retail. House, sign and ornamental painting, graining, glazing, etc., are executed promptly and to the highest style of the art at short notice, and the fullest satisfaction is assured to patrons. The painting of signs is done in the most artistic manner, this part of the business being made a specialty. Specimens of the work executed by Mr. Peabody in all branches of his calling may be seen in all parts of East Boston, Chelsea, Cambridge, Winthrop, and Somerville. Mr. Peabody has the best of facilities for carrying out the orders of his patrons at reasonable charges. He employs from five to twenty five hands, averaging, as a rule, twelve. He is a native of

Boston, had an early training in his trade, and has been identified with it for the greater part of his life. He is a thorough master of his business, is an upright, energetic, reliable, and responsible tradesman, conscientious in the discharge of all his duties, and highly esteemed in the community.

W. C. ROGERS, Patented Novelties, No. 120 Pearl Street.—A house well deserving of more than passing notice is the popular and reliable concern of Mr. W. C. Rogers, dealer in patented novelties, small wares, etc., which has maintained from the start a standing of the highest commercial character among producers and purchasers of such commodities. Mr. Rogers is a native of Dover, N. H., but has been a resident of Boston for many years. Having had a long experience in this line of goods, and impressed with the necessity of providing a market and outlet for inventors of useful and small wares, he founded this establishment originally in 1877, and from the commencement he has met with uniform success. He occupies a spacious second floor, which is very conveniently arranged with special reference to his unique and interesting business, and is fully equipped with every facility for the receiving and shipping of goods which come and go. His stock comprises all those articles known under the general term of small wares, embracing rubber ware, goods of all kinds, needle cases, cutters of the latest and most approved styles, corset steels, clasps, dress shields, skirt and bone supporters, tidy and pillow shams, fasteners, clothes dryers, palms, carpet sweepers, rubber caps, bat and bonnet covers, belts, stationary packages, purse novelties, dolls and dolls' heads of every description, perfumery and toilet cases, patent household novelties, prize packages, patent key-rings, automatic savings banks for children, latest devices in collar and cuff buttons, button and scarf fasteners, coin holders and purses, in fact everything of the very latest and most useful invention. Mr. Rogers is prepared to negotiate with patentees and designers, also with manufacturers of such goods for the extensive control of their productions, upon the most liberal terms. He is a wide-awake, energetic man, and goods of this character placed in his control are sure to be placed prominently before the public.

GEO. B. YOUNG, Crockery, Glass, Cutlery, Tin, Plated, etc., No. 1088 Washington Street.—The neat and well kept emporium conducted by Geo. B. Young is a commodious and well-ordered establishment, in which can be found at all times a complete and first-class assortment of goods at exceedingly low prices. This thriving and prosperous business was established in March, 1885, by the present proprietor, and from its inception has proved a highly gratifying venture. It is the largest store per evidence for crockery, glass, and house keeping articles in this vicinity, and has a large, permanent, and growing patronage. This store, which is 25x80 feet in size, is attractively fitted up and excellently arranged,—a very tasteful display being made,—while an extensive and first-class stock is constantly carried, including everything in the line of crockery, earthenware, stone ware, tin, hotel and table glassware, cutlery and plated ware, superb lamps, shades, globes, and lamp fixtures, tin-ware, kitchen utensils, wooden and willow ware, novelties, fancy small wares, and a multifarious assortment of useful and ornamental articles. The store is kept open evenings for the convenience of patrons, and numerous polite assistants attend to the wants of customers.

W. C. BRAY, Freight Forwarder and General Trucking, Office North Side Central Wharf, Atlantic Avenue.—One of the most enterprising, go-ahead, wide-awake men in this community is Mr. W. C. Bray, proprietor of the general forwarding, trucking, and express business, whose office is on the north side of Central Wharf, Atlantic Avenue. Freight is received and receipted for, and shipped to any foreign port or point on the course or railroads in the United States, Canada, or the Maritime Provinces, or forwarded by express at regular rates. He is the owner of a number of teams, makes contracts and attends to orders for moving merchandise and heavy commodities, conducts the business upon a thoroughly organized system, and employs those who are experienced. A native of Gloucester, Mr. Bray has been identified with his present vocation 16 years. His facilities for the purposes of his business are complete and perfect, and he is highly commended by all who have occasion to require his services.

JOHN C. HAYNES & CO., Manufacturers of Bay State, Haynes Excelsior and Wm. B Tilton Guitars, etc., No. 35 Court Street and No. 453 to 463 Washington Street.—Americans are preeminent among the nations of the civilized world for their love of music, while every musical instrument known in Europe enjoys great popularity and sale in the United States. In this connection we desire to make special reference in this mercantile review of Boston, to the old established and representative house of Messrs. John C. Haynes & Co. This business was established sixty years ago, and is one of the oldest and best known in America. In 1881 the present copartners, Messrs. John C. Haynes, Oliver Ditson, and Charles H. Ditson succeeded to the management. The firm's main stores are located at Nos. 449 and 451 Washington Street, known as (Oliver Ditson & Co., and they have a branch establishment in New York City carried on under the firm name of Charles H. Ditson & Co., and another in Philadelphia as J. E. Ditson, & Co. The firm's factory, where guitars are made and where they constantly employ sixty skilled workmen, is in the building No. 33 Purchase Street. Messrs. John C. Haynes & Co., import and deal largely in musical instruments, strings, and merchandise of every description. Their guitars are absolutely unrivalled, and are general favorites with the trade and a critical public wherever introduced, while the prices quoted for them are extremely moderate. The business is chiefly wholesale and extends throughout the entire United States and Canada. During the last few weeks Messrs. John C. Haynes & Co. forwarded $11,000 worth of their select guitars to the west, and their trade is steadily increasing in all sections of the country, owing to the excellence of their instruments, which are guaranteed to give entire satisfaction. Mr. John C. Haynes, Oliver Ditson, and Charles H. Ditson are natives of Massachusetts. Mr. Haynes is the present manager in Boston, the New York branch is managed by Mr. Charles H. Ditson, and the Philadelphia store of J. E. Ditson & Co. by Mr. C. W. A. Trumpler. The partners are highly esteemed in trade circles as liberal and honorable business men, and the success achieved by them is only the just reward of their industry and energy. In consequence of the death of Mr. Oliver Ditson, and the desirability of making the business a permanency, it has been arranged to organize a corporation under the title of Oliver Ditson Company, including the two stores in Boston, New York and Philadelphia.

OLIVER DITSON COMPANY
AMERICAN AND FOREIGN MUSIC
449 & 451 WASHINGTON ST BOSTON

·BRANCH HOUSES·
C.H. DITSON & CO·   JOHN C. HAYNES & CO.   J E. DITSON & CO.
NEW YORK·   —BOSTON—   PHILA.

JR. PAYSE, Wood, Mantels, Cabinet, Case and Carpenter Work, Store and Office Fittings, Nos. 616 to 622 Harrison Avenue. Mr. Payse started in business on his own account in 1882, and soon established himself in public favor and patronage, building up in a short time a very fine trade. The building occupied is an old historic one owned by the city. The shop occupies an entire 50x100 foot floor, two stories high, and is completely equipped with all necessary facilities, including ample steam power and all the latest improved appliances, devices, and tools, while from ten to a dozen skilled mechanics are employed. Wood mantel and wood work of every description are made and put up to order in first-class style, and cabinet, case and carpenter work executed in the most expeditious manner; while jobbing of all kinds receives immediate attention.

HENRY GOULD & CO., Jewelers and Importers of Precious Stones, No. 431 Washington Street.—An old-established and thoroughly representative house is this city is that of Messrs. Henry Gould & Son, the manufacturing jewelers. This house was founded in 1845 by Mr. Henry Gould, the present firm being organized in 1866 by the admission of Mr. R. F. Gould to partnership. ...

THOMAS HILL & SONS, Hardware, Paper Hangings, Paints, Oils, Varnishes, etc., No. 169 Broadway, South Boston.—A firm known and leading general hardware and painters' supply store is the well ordered and largely patronized emporium of Thomas Hill & Sons, located at No. 169 Broadway, with branch stores also at Nos. 570 and 575 ...

HENRY HUBER & CO., Manufacturers of Sanitary Specialties, Brass Pumps, and Plumbers' Supplies. Eastern Branch, No. 825 Washington Street.—This is the Eastern Branch of the well-known New York house of the same name, and is under the management of Mr. J. L. Thurston. ...

HUNT & CO., Leather Boards, Shoe Counters, etc., No. 17 South Street.—Although, comparatively young firm, as such,—the business having been established in July, 1881,—Hunt & Co. have already built up a trade second to few concerns engaged in this particular branch of commercial activity in Boston. ...

M. BROWN, Ship-smith, Horseshoer, and General Jobber, No. 49 Atlantic Avenue and No. 211 Commercial Street.—One of the most practical and reliable men in his line in Boston is Mr. M. Brown, ship-smith, horseshoer, and general jobber, No. 49 Atlantic Avenue and No. 211 Commercial Street. Mr. Brown, who was born in Quebec, Canada, forty-five years ago, has been working at his trade some he was a boy. ...

CHARLES A PEARSON, Civil Engineer and Surveyor, No. 6 City Square, Charlestown.—Among the foremost and best equipped civil engineers and surveyors of Charlestown can be named Charles A. Pearson, than whom no member of the profession in the Bunker Hill District enjoys a better reputation for skill. Mr. Pearson, who is a gentleman of middle age and a native of Charlestown, is a man of entire probity as well as a thoroughly practical and expert civil engineer and surveyor, with ample experience in all branches of his profession, and was formerly assistant to Thomas Doane, Boston's leading civil engineer, for several years. ...

JOHN W. SPRAGUE, Furnishing Undertaker, and Practical Embalmer, No. 180 Meridian Street, East Boston.—Mr. John W. Sprague, the well known furnishing undertaker, has had an experience in the calling extending over many years, and has been established since 1877, and is pronounced one of the best funeral furnishers and directors in the city. His office and warerooms are at No. 180, and his residence at No. 182, Meridian Street, where he will always be found, and promptly attends to day or night calls. In the conduct of the business Mr. Sprague is careful and at the same time considerate, and has a tender regard for the feelings of bereaved families and friends, and so well are his duties performed, and the able, efficient manner he conducts affairs that his services are generally sought for. A native of Maine, Mr. Sprague, who was born in Bath, in that state, has been a citizen of East Boston for more than thirty-three years. He is well prepared in every respect to successfully embalm bodies, and furnish coffins and caskets, hearses and carriages and comfort funerals. Mr. Sprague is a war veteran and served his country for a period of three years as a member of the Twelfth Massachusetts Vol. Infy. He was in many important engagements and for six months was a prisoner at Belle Isle. He is a member of the U. A. M.

F. J. FENNO, Merchant Tailor, No. 198 Broadway, South Boston.—Mr. Fenno was born in the neighboring city of Fall River, but has been a resident here for over a score of years. Having learned the business in all its details in his uncle's employ, and after acquiring years of experience he succeeded to his relative's house and trade in 1878, which ever since the date of its inception has been the center of a first-class trade, with but few, if any, successful rivals in this part of Boston. The store, which is of ample dimensions, is elegantly fitted up and appointed, containing every convenience for the attractive display of goods. An extensive stock is kept constantly on hand, which includes the latest and most attractive styles and patterns in imported fabrics, seasonable woolens and worsteds, cloths, cassimeres, checks, serges, corkscrews, diagonals, tricots, plaids, tweeds, meltons, cheviots, stripes, casings and elegant settings in great variety. Mr. Fenno employs none but the most skillful and experienced workmen, whose operations are conducted under his immediate supervision. Being a skillful cutter himself, the fitting of all garments made here receive his personal attention; in fact every article produced by him is all in every feature, in cut, fit, finish and material. His trade is derived principally from among the most prominent and influential citizens, while his prices are very low.

B URNHAM & DURGAN, Groceries and Provisions, Meats, etc., Nos. 97 and 99 Meridian Street, East Boston.—The flourishing business established by Messrs. Burnham & Durgan, the well-known dealers in groceries and provisions, was established many years ago by Mr. Lewis Burnham, and carried on by him until 1886 when he was succeeded by the present firm, composed of Mr. Frank Burnham and Mr. Chas. Durgan, who have made many improvements in the store, and by the institution and ability have materially extended the operations and increased the trade. The store presents a double front of 30 feet with a depth of 40 feet and is fitted up with every modern convenience. The stock is always kept full and complete in every department, and the goods noted for their freshness, and will be found of the highest standard quality. All the details of the business are conducted under the immediate direction of the firm, who are assisted in their operations by three attentive clerks. Orders are filled and delivered promptly. Both members of the firm are natives of Massachusetts. Mr. Burnham was born in Essex and Mr. Durgan in East Boston. They are thorough, practical men.

H. W. DISMORE, Jobber and Retailer in Kitchen Furniture, No. 250 Main Street, Charlestown.—A leading and most reputable house in Charlestown is that of Mr. H. W. Dismore, which since its inauguration has attained a high prominence for kitchen furniture and other similar wares. Mr. Dismore was born in the neighboring suburb, Somerville, where he still resides, and has had a long experience in this line of merchandise. He founded this establishment originally in 1887, and although of recent origin he has had from the start a very large and sub-

stantial patronage. The premises occupied are spacious, and fitted up with special reference to the character of his business, and are provided with every convenience for the display of his large and A1 stock of goods. In his store will be found an assortment of all kinds of kitchen and housekeeping goods, embracing shelf and house hardware, cutlery, bedroom and other necessary wares calculated for the general comfort and assistance of the housewife, including fine china, queen's, crockery, earthen and glass ware, lamps and their fittings, all of the latest and most fashionable and unique designs, made by the most celebrated manufacturers in Europe and America; also stove fittings, hollow wares, cooking utensils, toilet articles, brooms, brass and bisque ornaments; and for use, laundry articles, tubs, clothes-wringers, flat and fluting irons, cutlery, silver and plated goods, wood and willow ware, step ladders, curtain poles and fixtures for shades. In fact, his supplies embrace almost everything classified under this term, house hardware. He also keeps a fine line of the latest novelties and specialties known as notions, toys, specialties, etc. Mr. Dismore is recognized as one of our most popular and enterprising merchants, who enjoys the esteem of all with whom he has any business transactions.

A. S. VOSE, Artistic Photographer, Maverick Square, Corner Lewis Street, East Boston.—One of the most prominent exponents of the photographic art in East Boston is Mr. A. S. Vose, who has been located in this section of the city since 1871. He employs several skilled assistants, all of whom are practical adepts in the business, and execute work in all branches of the art, the specialty being fine portraits which are perfect as likenesses, and superior in finish. Photographs direct are made as large as 16 x 20 inches, and particular attention is given to copying and enlarging pictures to life size. He is very successful with children, and out-door views, animals, and machinery, and in photographing merchandise, etc., and as an expert is unsurpassed in India ink, crayon, water and oil colors and pastile work, which is finished with that degree of elegance, and neatness, and beauty, only attained by the thorough skilled, photographic artist. The studio is tastefully furnished, the reception parlors being unexceptionally handsome, while the operating rooms are provided with the latest and best improved appliances required for executing all kinds of work pertaining to the art. Mr. Vose is a native of Montpelier, Vt.

C. P. FLYNN, Pharmacist, No. 506 Dorchester Avenue, South Boston.—An old established and representative retail pharmacy is that of Mr. C. P. Flynn. The business was originally established in 1871 by Mr. Wm. H. Flynn, a brother of the present proprietor, by whom he was succeeded in 1884, and from its inception the store has been liberally patronized by the best residents of the vicinity. The warerooms is a spacious apartment, 25 x 45 feet in dimensions, and with its plate glass front, tile floor, mahogany fixtures and large, well displayed stock, forms one of the attractive features of the avenue. The stock of drugs, chemicals, proprietary medicines, toilet and fancy articles etc., embraces all fresh and out-door views, animals and machinery, and in photo prescriptions, and several experienced clerks are required in supplying the wants of the large, liberal and highly desirable patronage. Mr. Flynn is a practical and skillful exponent of the business, with which for many years he has been prominently identified.

J COOPER, Plumber and Gas Fitter, No. 198 Harrison Avenue.—Among the well conducted and popular city enterprises engaged in this branch of skilled industry will be found that of Mr. J. Cooper, plumber and gas fitter. Mr. Cooper has been established in this city since 1871, beginning on Milk Street and reserving two years later to the present site, where he has built up a large trade and won an enviable reputation as a first-class workman. The premises occupied are commodious, well arranged and convenient, and a full stock of plumbers' and gas fitters' supplies is carried. A competent force of experienced mechanics is employed, and all kinds of plumbing and gas fitting work is done in the best manner and at the lowest rates commensurate with first-class service. Mr. Cooper was born in England, but has been for many years a respected citizen of Boston.

THE FOYE LETTER FILE, CABINET AND INDEX COMPANY.
Manufacturers of Cabinets, Letter Files, Indexes, and Filing Cases, No. 488 Washington Street, Boston. Fairbanks, Agent. The Boston office of the Foye Letter File, Cabinet, and Index Company, of Newark, N. J., is under the capable management of Mr Edson Fairbanks, a well-known business man of this city, as agent for the company. The ingenious devices here introduced are complete in every particular, simple in their construction, and are unequaled for utility and convenience by any similar inventions in the market, possessing, as they do, important features peculiar to themselves. The Foye Letter File can be so readily operated with the arm as with the hand, thus giving perfect freedom of both hands to turn over active rapidly the papers contained in the file, and enabling the user to withdraw or insert any letter, bill, or receipt, without displacing the remaining ones, as is the case in other files that do not contain the clip. The Foye file has a strong clip and automatic springs which give firm pressure, holding all papers, large or small, in their place without stopping to adjust any springs, as in other files, while there is no fear of spilling the papers upon the floor by careless handling. Another feature of the file is that you do not punch any holes in your letters, or papers, or deface one of your bills. They have the rovelled combination suitable for any number of files that may be desired. The Foye patent transfer cases are made of wood, and have two springs attached to the lid that hold the papers into their place when transferred from the file. They are neatly finished, and have the appearance of a book on the track. We cordially recommend the Foye inventions to merchants, manufacturers, and others wanting a simple and complete file at small cost. Mr. Fairbanks, the agent, is a native of New Hampshire, and has resided in Boston since 1844. He is deservedly prominent and popular as a real estate and business broker, handling all classes of realty on commission, and enjoys a large and influential clientage. To possessors unsurpassed facilities for the prompt negotiation of loans on hand and securities, takes entire management of estates, collects rents, and transacts a large and thriving trade in buying and selling business chances.

HUTLER'S Bonbons and Chocolates, No. 168 Tremont Street. In the sale of fine candies, bon bons, and chocolates, the name of Huyler's has a national reputation for the best and purest goods known to the trade. The Boston house of this name is very eligibly located at No. 168 Tremont Street. The headquarters of Huyler's is in New York, at No. 863 Broadway, while branch establishments of noteworthy importance are located in all the principal cities of the Union. The business premises in this city comprise a splendid salesroom on the ground floor and a well equipped basement for manufacturing purposes, thus giving ample accommodations for the systematic and successful prosecution of the business in all its departments. The output includes all kinds of bonbons, toffees, creams, caramels, chocolates, and their celebrated ice-cream soda and other toothsome confections too numerous to mention while the limits of this article. All these candies can be most indiscriminately as they are all warranted pure, and are universally regarded as the best of their kind over just upon the market. The stock on sale is probably the largest and finest in the city, and the house is a popular headquarters for everything in its line among the best classes of society. Orders of any magnitude are filled promptly and carefully. Mr. Deklyn, the manager, was formerly in charge of Huyler's house at Albany, N. Y., and has a foundation understanding of all the needs and requirements of the business.

JOSEPH E. BALLOU, Book and Job Printer, No. 191 High Street.—For excellent work in the typographical line, or for promptness and reliability in executing orders, not one in the business in this part of the city enjoys a better reputation than Joseph E. Ballou, book and job printer. Mr. Ballou is a native of Pharus, Mass., but long a resident of Boston. He is a practical and expert printer, of over a quarter of a century's experience at the case, and is a complete master of the art in all its branches. He started in business on his own account about six years ago, on Kneeland Street, whence he moved to Harrison Avenue three years later, and has occupied the present commodious quarters since September last. Mr. Ballou occupies here 20 by 50 feet of space on second floor, with thoroughly first-class equipment, while eight or more experienced hands are employed. Everything in the line of printing, from a business card and circular to a book and newspaper, is done in the most expeditious and superior manner at the very lowest current rates. All orders receive immediate attention, and all work is warranted to render satisfaction.

E. F. MAYNARD, Manufacturer and Dealer in Fine Harness, Bridle, Reins, Brushing and Trunk Leather, No. 168 Pearl Street.—The leather trade of Boston has connected with it no more popular and successful merchant than Mr. E. F. Maynard, who has spent in it the best years of a long life. Mr. Maynard is a Massachusetts man by birth, and no old resident in Boston. He engaged in business on his own account in 1870, and during this period has developed a trade of large magnitude. He is a manufacturer and dealer in fine harness, bridle, reins, brushing and trunk leather, and a specialty is made of heavy backs and welt leather. His premises are located at No. 168 Pearl Street, and he utilizes for the purposes of his business the third and fourth floors of the building, which is 30×50 feet in dimensions. These are provided with all necessary appliances and conveniences for the receipt, storage, and shipment of goods, and a large and complete stock is at all times carried. Mr. Maynard's long experience in the business qualifies him as an expert in leathers, and his patrons put the fullest reliance in his descriptions of his wares. His relations with the leading tanners and curriers in the country are of long standing and of such nature that enable him to secure the choicest grades of leather on such advantageous terms, that he is in a position to offer corresponding advantages to his customers, and his distributing trade extends throughout New England and the state of New York. Mr. Maynard, though past middle age, manifests a vigor, vigilance, and steady application to business that many young men might envy him of, and his home is in all respects a very desirable one with which to form commercial relations.

E. A. RUNNELLS, Manufacturers' Agent, No. 116 Pearl Street.—For the past five years Mr. E. A. Runnells has been known as one of the most active and successful of manufacturers' Agents in the city, and during that period he has built up a splendid trade connection extending throughout the whole of the New England States. Mr. Runnells has been located in his present quarters in No. 116 Pearl Street for three years past, and here he occupies the second floor, which has a capacity of 20×80 feet, and which is finely appointed and appropriately fitted up for the business. It contains an extensive and varied sample stock of useful salable goods of both foreign and domestic manufacture. Mr. Runnells is the trusted representative of the New York house of Mr. J. W. Leuterbach, importer of baskets and willow-ware; of Zen, Kling & Kramer of Philadelphia, importers of china; of the Triumph Wringer Company of Keene, N. H., manufacturers of wringers and iron toys; and is also general agent for toys, fireworks, Christmas cards, and novelties of all kinds. Orders are promptly shipped and billed direct from the factories, and in all instances Mr. Runnells guarantees the most complete satisfaction. Mr. Runnells has had long practical experience in this market, gives his close personal attention to all details of his trade, and is in every respect a popular and successful agent. He is a native of Massachusetts, and resides at Hyde Park.

J. L. McINTOSH, Numbering, Paging, Perforating, Nos. 54 and 56 Federal Street.—Mr. J. L. McIntosh has been established in business here since 1877, and has acquired a reputation and a trade that places him at the head of this branch of industry in this section of the country. His business premises comprise two floors, 15×70 feet each, splendidly fitted up for rapid, systematic and successful work, the equipment comprising eight numbering, five lettering, five perforating, four wiring, and two paper-cutting machines, while steady employment is given to eighteen skilled and expert hands. Much of the machinery in use is the invention of the proprietor. He is in a position to guarantee the quality of his work as well as entire satisfaction in all his operations, fulfilling all orders and commissions promptly and carefully. He has an extensive trade, enjoys special attention to calendars, numbers bound check-books, and devotes his time and talents to every description of eyeletting, round cornering, block and pad making and cutting, and to the manufacture of a most complete document holder. His prices are placed at the lowest point of moderation. Mr McIntosh is a native of Nova Scotia, a resident of Boston since 1861, in the prime of life, and respected as an accomplished master of his art.

206

ILLUSTRATED BOSTON.

CARTER, RICE & CO. (Incorporated), Manufacturers and Wholesale Dealers in Paper, No. 245 Devonshire Street.—Boston has rapidly developed national pre-eminence in the paper trade, among other great staples, and to-day one of the leading concerns in the country and by far the largest jobbing house in New England, that of the corporation of Carter, Rice & Co., finds its most congenial headquarters in Boston. The immense business radiating from the warehouse at No. 245 Devonshire Street was founded in 1871 by Messrs. James B. Carter and Frederick W. Rice, under whose able and energetic management it had such a rapid and permanent growth and development that in 1888 the important interests involved were duly capitalized and a company formed, with a capital of $800,000, to extend the trade throughout the United States. The company has not only ample resources, but every facility at command, and controls the products of many large mills. The company make a specialty of printing papers, book papers, cardboards, envelopes, manilla papers, twines, etc., and carries the largest and most comprehensively assorted stock of any house in New England. The premises occupied in Devonshire Street are of immense size, six stories and basement in height, and 60x100 in dimensions. A thorough system of organization is enforced throughout this magnificent establishment, and upwards of 150 hands are employed in the various departments. This is the best equipped paper warehouse in the United States, and its splendidly furnished offices on first floor are indicative of the correct taste and sound judgment of the proprietors. The decease of Mr. Frederick W. Rice occurred four years ago, and the executive now comprises Mr. J. B. Carter, Mr. E. H. Palmer, and Mr. George H. Lowe. Mr. Carter was born in Boston, and has long been actively identified with the wholesale paper trade; so has Mr. Lowe who is a native of Bridgewater. Mr. Palmer was born in New Bedford, and came to Boston to make a start in life only 16 years ago. With a capital of ability, industry, and integrity he has made rapid progress and is a valued member of the company, which has, by reason of its handling of such reliable qualities of paper, invariably up to sample and quoted at lowest prices, secured to itself the patronage of leading publishers, newspapers, and dealers throughout the United States, and Boston is to be congratulated upon having here made the headquarters of such a large and growing concern.

FRANK L. YOUNG, Manufacturer, Importer, and Dealer in Oil, Etc., No. 89 Oliver Street.—One of the most reliable and leading houses in Boston actively engaged in the manufacture, importation, and sale of oils, grease, etc., is that of Mr. Frank L. Young, whose office and salesrooms are situated at No. 89 Oliver Street. Mr. Young's factory and wharves are located at First and I Streets, South Boston. The factory is fully supplied with modern appliances, apparatus, and machinery, and is so situated that the goods are handled at the least possible expense of labor and freight. With ample wharf and storage facilities, this house possesses unsurpassed advantages for doing the business. Mr. Young is a large importer of pure cod-oil from the Newfoundland fisheries, and also receives quantities of domestic oil and is first hands on these goods. The concern also manufactures several specialties, including hard grease for staffing of leather, ultra sparm oil for spindles, and a fine line of lubricating and cylinder oils. Mr. Young is also selling agent for the celebrated "H. & H." brands of lubricating and leather-oils, made by the Meriam & Morgan Oil Company, so widely and favorably known. At the office and salesrooms a fine line of strictly reliable goods may always be found, at lowest market rates. All goods are guaranteed absolutely as represented, and probably no house in the trade has a more enviable reputation for square dealing. Buyers of oil who want prompt and careful attention to their orders will do well to correspond with this concern. They also have recently put upon the market the "Ultra Linseed Oil," which has stood the test of five years' practical experience, and is the best wearing oil for all outside painting, on the market. Dealers in distributing centres may obtain the selling agency of this oil by addressing the house, and exclusive territory is given.

A. S. PRATT, Manager of the Boston Office of Clark's Thread Works, No. 51 Kingston Street.—The Boston house of the internationally famous Clark Thread Works was first established in 1865, and has been permanently and most successfully conducted by Mr. Albert S. Pratt, a Boston business man of the highest standing in commercial, public, and social circles. Mr. Pratt has for twenty-eight years been actively identified with this branch of trade, and is the leading authority in his line throughout New England. His office and salesrooms were originally located at the junction of Summer and Lincoln Streets, but the premises were swept by the great fire of 1872, and Mr. Pratt eventually permanently located at his present central address. Mr. Pratt is a merchant of

ability and integrity, and is well known as a public spirited citizen. From 1867 to 1870, inclusive, he served as a member of the Boston Board of Aldermen, and supported all measures best calculated to advance the permanent welfare and prosperity of the city. His many sterling qualifications have permanently retained to him the confidence and respect of the commercial world, and he is a worthy representative of his important and staple branch of trade. The entire business of the great house of George A. Clark & Bro. in the United States is controlled, directed, and is the greater part owned by Mr. William Clark, of Newark, N. J., the only surviving partner of the original copartnership of Geo. A. Clark & Bro., of New York. The trade throughout the United States is supplied from the latter house, and from the branches in Philadelphia, San Francisco, and Boston. At the Boston agency a heavy stock is carried of all numbers and sizes of Clark's "O. N. T." spool cotton, and all sizes of the celebrated Kilward's Patent Helix twofire.

EASTERN FISH COMPANY, P. B. Wadsworth, Proprietor, No. 179 Tremont Street.—Among the leading representative houses in the city engaged in the wholesale and retail branches of this trade is that of the Eastern Fish Company, which started business in 1873 at No. 19 Kneeland Street, and removed therefrom in May, 1888, to the present premises. The premises occupied here comprise a finely appointed store, with a frontage of 85 feet and a depth of 80 feet, and fitted up with marble slabs, refrigerators, and all other accessories of a thoroughly equipped, first class establishment. The stock, which is supplied fresh daily from the fisheries, is maintained at the highest standard of excellence, and can always be relied upon for freshness and wholesomeness, while in the matter of prices the matters does not permit itself to be surpassed by those of any other house in the trade. The company handle every description of fish, oysters, lobsters, and other shell fish, and having in constant service three assistants, are prepared to fill all orders with despatch, and to insure to patrons the fullest satisfaction. Besides the large city and suburban trade done, extensive shipments are made to dealers in all parts of the New England States. The proprietor, Mr. P. B. Wadsworth, is a native of the city, has had long experience in, and is thoroughly acquainted with, every detail and feature of the fish trade.

H. O. LOTHROP & CO., Manufacturers of Patent Wire Ferrules, No. 312 Dorchester Avenue, South Boston.—In reviewing the noteworthy industrial interests of South Boston, and the concerns contributing thereto, more than passing notice should be given in this volume to the widely known establishment of H. O. Lothrop & Co., manufacturers of patent wire ferrules (for paint brushes), No. 312 Dorchester Avenue; and whose productions have been in wide and growing demand in the trade for some twenty-odd years owing to the superiority of the same. The ferrules manufactured by this firm are articles of exceptional merit, combining all desired features of strength, security, neatness, durability, and efficacy, and for general usefulness are unapproached, for the purpose intended, by anything of the kind yet placed upon the market. The Lothrop Patent Wire Ferrule, which is manufactured under letters patent, is fully protected, having been patented October 31, 1882, with a reissue June 20, 1871, and again patented March 7, 1882, and the Messrs. Lothrop are sole proprietors and manufacturers. This business enterprise was started in 1872. The factory is commodious, ample, and well equipped, being supplied with full steam power and the latest improved machinery, and all necessary facilities, while twelve or more hands are employed. They manufacture patent wire ferrules for paint-brushes, in all sizes and styles, the daily average production running above 15,000 ferrules, and the trade of the firm, which is large and active, extends all over the United States. Mr. Lothrop the elder, the patentee, is a gentleman in the prime of life, and a native of Cornish, N. H., coming to Boston from Milford, Mass., where he was for some time chairman of the board of selectmen. He also served with credit in the State Legislature during the sessions of 1881–1883.

ROBBINS & ROWELL, Tailors, No. 66 Winter Street.—Messrs. Robbins & Rowell, the popular and well known merchant tailors, are by general consent among the leading exponents of the tailoring art in Boston, and have a large and growing high class trade—receiving a fine college patronage. This business and prosperous firm was established in 1888, being located in the present desirable quarters since November, 1887; and from the first they have enjoyed a highly flattering share of recognition; the garments produced being first-class in every particular, alike as to cut, fit, finish and fabric. They are very commodious and easily appointed premises, conveniently located on the second floor, facing the Common, and carry constantly on hand an extensive and elegant assortment of imported woolens, worsted, and fashionable suitings in great variety, from which the most fastidious in dress may select. The stock embraces the newest styles and designs in overcoatings, cloths, cheviots, cassimeres, plaids, serges, tweeds, meltons, stripes and mixed goods, while an efficient corps of cutters and tailors are employed; every garment made in this establishment being subjected to close personal examination by the proprietors before being allowed to leave the place. Messrs. Luther O. Robbins and Charles A. Rowell, who compose the firm, are young men, and natives of this city. They are practical and expert cutters, and all around workmen themselves, of ample experience in the exercise of their art.

THE RICHWOOD HOTEL, Nos. 494, 496 and 498 Tremont Street.—The Richwood was first opened to the public in January, 1887, and has ever since been in charge of the present proprietor, Mr. A. B. Foster, who knows just how to meet the requirements of guests. The building is of brick, seven stories high, and thirty-five feet in dimensions, and is substantial in appearance and imposing in its architecture. The first floor is given up to the office, main dining room, dining room, etc., and the upper floors, utilized for parlors, sleeping apartments, bath rooms, etc., are reached by elevator and wide stair cases. The house is conducted on the American plan. No luxury afforded to attention, surroundings, and modern conveniences in any hotel is lacking at the Richwood. It is situated in one of the most healthiest and most convenient part of the city, within easy reach of railway depots and steamboat wharves, and is convenient alike to the permanent patron, the commercial tourist, and the transient guest. The house is lighted by electric lights and gas, heated by steam throughout, and provided with electric call-bells communicating with the office. The cuisine of the Richwood is especially worthy of commendation, being under the most expert management and kept up to the highest standard of excellence. All the necessities of modern hotel life are supplied by the enterprising proprietor for the comfort and convenience of his guests. The rates are two dollars per day. The service is prompt and courteous, and Mr. Foster is one of the most genial and obliging of hosts.

BETHUNE & HILL, Fancy Goods, etc., No. 8 West Street.—One of the most ably conducted and admirably equipped, general fancy-goods houses located in this section of the city is that which, since its inception in 1887, has been most successfully managed by its original proprietors, Messrs. Bethune and Hill, young ladies of pronounced ability, tact, energy, and enterprise. Previous to starting in business for themselves, they were employed by the well known firm of C. F. King & Co., and are practically versed in every detail of the trade engaged in. The premises occupied at No. 8 West Street comprise a neatly arranged and well appointed apartment, which is supplied with every modern facility and convenience, and contains, in the line of stock carried, a carefully selected and varied assortment of small wares, fancy goods, worsteds, yarns, embroidery materials, dress-linings, etc., all of which are both excellent and reliable in quality, as well as reasonable in price. A specialty is made of dressmakers' supplies, and fine stamping work is executed at short notice. A force of four competent and obliging assistants is employed to attend to the needs of a large and ever-increasing trade among the best classes in the community, and orders by mail receive prompt and satisfactory attention.

BRIGGS BROS., Stair builders, No. 73 Wareham Street.—Messrs. Briggs Bros., the well-known stair builders, enjoy a well merited reputation for skill and reliability, ranking among the foremost in their particular line in Boston. This popular and responsible firm was established in 1879, and, from its inception, has enjoyed an unbroken career of prosperity. The Messrs. Briggs, who are natives of Rehoboth, Mass., are practical and expert workmen of many years' experience. They are prepared to enter into contracts for all classes of work in the line indicated, furnishing posts, rails, balustrades, etc., both in plain and artistic designs, at short notice, and exercise close personal supervision over all work executed. They occupy a 40x40-foot floor as shop, and have in service ample and complete facilities; while from twenty to thirty skilled mechanics are employed.

RICHARD T. PURCELL, Wood Turning, Mortising, Moulding, Band and Jig Sawing, No. 73 Wareham Street.—Among Boston's most skilful wood turners and carvers may be mentioned the name of Richard T. Purcell. Mr. Purcell, who is a native of Halifax, N. S., but long in this city, is a practical and expert workman of many years' experience, and is a thorough master of his art in all its branches. He has been established in business for himself about fifteen years, and has a large patronage among builders. Mr. Purcell occupies the whole of a 37x100 foot floor, and has in service ample and complete facilities, while four to six expert hands are regularly employed. Wood turning, carving, and mortising of every description are all executed in the most expeditious and excellent manner, also moulding, band and jig-sawing, special attention being given to the production of fine rails, balustrades, posts, and kindred work, and all orders are promptly and reliably attended to.

E. GEHLBACH & CO., Importers of Artificial Alizarine, and Aniline Colors, No. 16 Hamilton Street. Main Home: No. 61 Cedar Street, New York; Branches, Philadelphia, Montreal, Toronto and Chicago.—One of the leading, representative firms identified with the important American trade in aniline colors is that of Messrs. Gehlbach & Co., of No. 61 Cedar street, New York, and who have branch houses in the principal cities of the United States and Canada. Here in Boston, Mr. Dawson Eldes has represented the firm, of which he is a partner, ever since the first opening of the branch here in 1871. ...

A. NDERSON & DICKEY, Architectural Wood-turning; Manufacturers of all kinds of Stair Posts, Balusters, and Rails, etc.; Nos. 87 to 41 Bristol Street. It is an agreeable task to describe, in this review of the industries and commerce of Boston, the resources and facilities of a house like that of Messrs. Anderson & Dickey, the well known architectural wood-turners and manufacturers of stair posts, balusters, and rails, wood mantels, office fixings, etc. ...

W. L. MONTGOMERY, Brokers and Manufacturers' Agents, No. 87 High Street.—A representative house. And one that for the last decade occupied a leading position in the particular branch of commercial activity in this city, is that conducted by W. L. Montgomery. ...

T. HOMPSON & NORRIS, Manufacturers of Paper Boxes, Cloth and Corrugated Goods. No. 43 Purchase Street.—The leading house in the United States devoted to the manufacture of fine grades of paper boxes, and of cork and corrugated goods for packing bottled merchandise and fragile articles, also for mailing purposes, is that of Messrs. Thompson & Norris. ...

G. EORGE M. STRONG, Dealer in Saddlery, Hardware, and Patented Saddlery Specialties, Nos. 180, 182, and 189 Beverly Street, East Boston. A reliable and old-established house in East Boston actively engaged in the manufacture of saddlery hardware and patented saddlery specialties is that of Mr. George M. Strong. ...

H. M. FORD, Real Estate and Mortgages, No. 21 School Street.—This gentleman has been established in the real estate business here for a period of thirty years, and has an intimate knowledge of the residential and business sections of the city and its suburbs. ...

G. H. GOODHUE & CO., Wool, Nos. 101 Federal and 138 Summer Streets.—Federal Street is noted as the busy centre of the great wool district of this city, and its commodious, but unpretentious line of stores handle almost the entire trade of the country in the staple article of wool. In the busy season millions of dollars in value change hands in this section with that rapidity that dreams and accompanies enterprising trade. Ranking among the leading and representative business firms in this line is that of G. H. Goodhue & Co., whose offices are located in the corner store fronting at Nos. 101 Federal and 138 Summer Streets. This firm are general dealers in both domestic and foreign wool, and established their business here in 1865. They have extensive storage quarters in the Prentice Building on Summer Street, and have unsurpassed facilities for the systematic and successful conduct of their business in all its branches. They have built up an extensive and influential trade in all the leading wool manufacturing districts in the United States and have secured their patronage upon the basis of reliability in goods, coupled with enterprising and responsible business management. They always carry full lines, and their samples never present a discrepancy between their quality and those of the stock. It is such vigorous and progressive business houses as that of Messrs. G. H. Goodhue & Co. that have been instrumental in making Boston a great wool empire. The members of this responsible firm are native and well-known citizens of Boston, deservedly popular in the business, financial, and trade circles, and their well-managed house is one to which the trade refer as an illustration of what energy, industry and honorable dealing can accomplish in the building up of business even when markets are sluggish and there is a general cry of hard times.

SEAVER & CO., Choice Family and Fancy Groceries, No. 14 Haverhill Square, East Boston.—An old established and well-patronized East Boston grocery store is the popular and excellent stand conducted by Seaver & Co., at No. 14 Haverhill Square, which for nearly half a century has been in prosperous existence. Here may always be found a complete and first-class assortment of everything in the line of family and fancy groceries, while patrons can rely upon getting prompt and polite attention, as well as a superior article and full weight, in every instance. The business was originally established in 1840, and after several changes in proprietors came into the control, something over three years ago, of the well and favorably known firm whose name heads this sketch, and under whose efficient management it has since been continued with uniform success. The store, which is centrally situated, is commodious and neatly arranged, and five competent assistants are in attendance. A heavy and finely assorted stock is constantly carried, comprising choice teas and coffees, pure and fresh spices, condiments, baking powders, sugars, syrups, dried fruit, prepared cereal food products, canned goods in great variety, sauces, pickles, preserves, olives and table delicacies, fine imported and domestic wines, liquors and bottled goods, fruits and everything for family and medicinal uses, prime dairy butter, cheese, eggs, best brands of western flour, oatmeal, rice, beans, peas, smoked meats, fish and general groceries; and the trade of the firm, which is large and active, gives evidence of steady increase. Mr. E. W. Seaver, who is the sole proprietor, the "Co." being nominal, was born in Newton, Mass., but has resided in this vicinity quite some time, and is well-known in the community. Mr. Nathaniel Seaver was the founder of the business and held it until three years ago, when he was succeeded by his nephew, the present proprietor.

BRADLEY & HUBBARD MFG. CO., Gas-Fixtures, Lamps, Andirons, Fire-Sets, Fenders, Broilers, Clocks, and Art Metal Work. No. 114 Franklin Street.—This company have the largest and best equipped manufactory of the kind in the United States, employing from one thousand to twelve hundred hands, and enjoy an international reputation and a trade that is practically world wide. They opened their house in this city in 1886, and placed it under the experienced management of Mr. E. H. Batchelder, who is intimately conversant with all the needs and requirements of the trade, and has proved himself eminently reliable, successful, and popular in meeting all its demands. The trade is conducted exclusively at wholesale, and is immense and influential throughout all the New England States. The sample stock here displayed includes a marvellous array of the finest work yet produced in brass, bronze, and artistic gas-fixtures and metal goods. The specialties in gas-fix-

tures for the drawing-room, hall, library and all parts of a private mansion are rarely equalled for beauty of design, fine finish, and artistic workmanship. The chandeliers and other fixtures shown here for churches, theatres, hotels, and public buildings are unsurpassed for elegance and durability, and are the embodiments of mechanical skill of the highest order of perfection. Another specialty for light made by this company is the celebrated and wonderful B & H central-draught burner, which is not excelled in any particular; being made with great care, giving a brilliant white flame, and mounted upon artistic, plain, banquet, and table lamps, as well as chandeliers, and it is without doubt the leader of all burners before. Its simplicity of construction is such that every one can easily understand how to use it. The other specialties besides lamps, are bronze figures and statuary, clocks, fire-sets, andirons, screens, cigar lighters, call-bells, and all kinds of metal goods manufactured by this company, command the admiration of critical and discriminating buyers at once. Mr. Batchelder, the manager, came to Boston a poor boy from the hills of New Hampshire, and after years of untiring labor and sacrifice, was placed in charge of the business of this company. He is a man of large experience, enterprising and untiring in his efforts to meet the tastes and requirements of all his patrons, and eminently popular with the trade.

MULLER & CO., Designers and Manufacturers of Wood Mantels, Nos. 10 to 14 Thayer Street, from No. 635 Harrison Avenue.—This firm stand deservedly high as designers and manufacturers of wood mantels, book-cases, sideboards, brackets, etc., and as regards artistic elegance, originality of design, elaboration of ornament, and perfection of workmanship, their productions rank with the greatest achievements of either American or European workers. The business of this house was originally established in 1868, by Messrs. Muller & Frese; and in 1888, Mr. E. Muller succeeded to the sole control, continuing the enterprise under the present firm name. This gentleman has been identified with the business for a period of twenty years, and during all this time he has stood to raise the standard of production. How well in has succeeded, is known to hundreds of our prominent architects, builders, and house-owners, and can be demonstrated to the satisfaction of the most critical and fastidious who will visit his establishment. His business premises are spacious in size and fully fitted up with the latest improved machinery and appliances, while a large force of skilled and expert workmen contribute to the satisfactory operations of the house. The public have again and again been agreeably surprised by Mr. Muller's fertility of design, and the beauty of the new styles offered by him in wood mantels. Many of his mantels are magnificently elaborate in finish and ornamentation, thoroughly adapted to the finest mansions, while the variety is such that the tastes and the means of all classes of patrons are readily suited. Elaborate and handsome book-cases are also made to order, to fit into the walls of dwellings; also side-boards, brackets, etc., suited to the varied requirements of the house-owner.

JOSEPH A. JACKSON, Fine Hats and Furs, No. 412 Washington Street.—The name of Joseph A. Jackson has long been honorably and prominently identified with the trade in fine hats and furs in this city and throughout all the New England States. Mr. Jackson has been established in the business for the past thirty years, and early developed a leading trade in his line. He is a merchant of the old school as regards reliability and integrity, but of the new as regards a progressive and enterprising business policy, and has long been a recognized authority in this city on all that appertains to furs, from their raw state until they are fashioned to adorn the fairest wearers. His business premises comprise a spacious and attractive salesroom on the ground floor and a well-arranged factory covering two upper floors, where employment is given to a force of twenty to thirty skilled hands. His real goods rarely need redyeing, because they do not fade. Here is displayed a most magnificent stock of hats, real caps, dolmans, ulsters, and small furs of all kinds, which are obtainable at very moderate prices. It is of vital importance to buy right, when the investment is in a line fur garment; and this is the place to patronize, as thousands of the best dressed people of Boston and other cities throughout New England know by personal experience. The assortments of caps, gloves, muffs, capes, collars, robes, rugs, etc., are comprehensive, carefully and skilfully made, beautifully trimmed, and offered at lowest prices. Mr. Jackson is a native of New Hampshire.

S. T. BIRMINGHAM, Native Botanic Physician, No. 14 Chambers Street.—From the very earliest ages the art of preparing from herbs, roots, and barks the compounds that alleviate and remove pain and heal the afflicted has justly been regarded as among the highest and noblest of human functions. Nor has the interest that attaches, by reason of their beneficent curative properties, to the effective remedies of the vegetable kingdom—nature's own laboratory—been without substantial results in the march of progress, as is amply attested by the steady and notable advance in botanic pharmacopœia and materia medica. And in connection with these observations, it may not be amiss to the readers of this volume to direct attention here to Dr. S. T. Birmingham, the widely known and skilful native botanic physician of this city, whose name has become famous for his unequalled success in the cure of disease, and has been long and favorably known as the native Indian physician of Boston, where he has for many years enjoyed the confidence of the public and accomplished many marvelous cures still continues at his office, No. 14 Chambers Street, Boston (formerly at No. 69 Cambridge Street), and is daily affording relief to many sufferers. His explanation and treatment of disease commend themselves to every intelligent and candid mind as the true and natural method by which the many ailments of the human body can be effectually and surely cured. It is perhaps needless to state (as his name is familiar in almost every household in New England), that during the thirty-eight years of his practice in Boston he has treated many thousands of persons, and his success has been unbounded. His fame has spread as a flame from one extremity of the continent to the other, and even across the broad ocean. This success and popularity are due to the following reasons; he, his ability of discerning at sight, where the patient comes before him (without asking questions), and from natural signs, the disease with which he (the patient) is afflicted; accurately and indisputably describing it and its location. 2d. His extensive knowledge of medicine, acquired by long and diligent research; by fifty years of active experience, as well as the knowledge of natural or Indian medicine derived from his ancestors in their native element. 3d. His absolute knowledge of the medicine which is suited to the disease and temperament of the man under consideration. 4th. His unbounded success in all cases where there is any hope, if his directions are strictly followed. His medicines contain no mineral or poisonous vegetable matter, but are compounded entirely from that portion of the botanic materia medica which cleanse, give tone, strength, and activity to the system. We fully believe that the great Creator intended as medicine for man the roots, herbs, barks, etc., which He has so kindly placed within easy reach, that they may be readily gathered for use. He is prepared to treat chronic dyspepsia, catarrh, cough, cancer of tumor, erysipelas, scrofula, salt rheum, ulcerations, sore leg, mercurial disease, syphiloid affection, skin disease, diabetes, difficulty in breathing, palpitation of heart, pain in the sides, breast, or limbs, kidney disease, dropsy, rheumatism, neuralgia, consumption, or any disease of the pulmonary organs, or in fact any disease arising from impurity of the blood; and his long experience and great success in the treatment of these diseases render his opinion of great importance to the afflicted, while the marvelous effect of his treatment in the many ills incidental to frames is indicated by the great number of ladies who have been cured, and many who have suffered long years from these complaints are now in the healthful enjoyment of life. Dr. Birmingham therefore invites all persons who are afflicted to call at his office and receive a thorough diagnosis of their disease, without asking questions, those who have been pronounced incurable by other physicians especially invited. He will tell you plainly whether and how you may be helped, and if desiring treatment, charges only for medicine given, no charge being made for advice. A large, varied, and carefully selected stock of pure and fresh herbs, barks, roots, and botanic medicines of every description is constantly kept on hand, while a competent assistant is in attendance. Dr. B. giving personal attention, however, in every instance, during the hours of 1 A.M. and 8 P.M. Tuesdays, Wednesdays, and Thursdays. Dr. Birmingham, who is a pleasant-mannered, active gentleman in the full prime of life, as well as a man of unquestionable skill and wide, practical experience in the laboratory and in his profession as a physician, was born in Delaware, whence he came to this city in 1860. He studied medicine with Dr. Dewees of the University of Pennsylvania, and, being an apt scholar, speedily secured an education which has placed him high among his fellow-men.

J. W. BRIGHAM & CO., Manufacturers of Boots and Shoes, No. 60 Pearl Street; Factory, Worcester, Mass.—The name of Brigham has long been honorably and prominently identified with boot and shoe manufacturing interests of New England. In fact, there are few if any gentlemen identified with the trade who have become such recognized authorities thereon as Mr. John W. Brigham. Born in Sutton, he at the early age of fifteen began to learn the shoemaker's trade; and, before attaining his majority, was an expert in the line. This practical knowledge has been utilized by him to secure to the public the best wearing brand of shoe now on the market. In 1869, Mr. Brigham began to job in shoes, and, in response to urgent demands, began to manufacture in 1880. His success was attended with great encouragement, and a lively demand at once grew up for his product, resulting in 1881 in his building a factory at Worcester, since repeatedly enlarged and improved. Mr. John W. Brigham, Jr., has been actively engaged in the business many years, and, though old in experience, is still a young man. He was admitted into copartnership in 1880, and takes active oversight in the carrying on of this enormous business with its vast interests. The factory at Worcester is a model concern and affords employment to from 150 to 200 in the manufacture of fine medium goods. The proprietors make quality their first consideration; they select their skins, leather, and findings with the utmost care, employ experienced cutters, using the most stylish and comfortable shaped lasts, while workmanship and finish command no argument. The result is, this brand of boots and shoes is much sought for by the trade of the United States, affording general satisfaction. The firm's warehouse, at No. 60 Pearl Street, is amply spacious, comprising five floors 30x100 feet in dimensions, where is carried full lines of boots and shoes for men, ladies, misses, boys, and children, and adapted to the needs of every section of the United States. The firm do a very widely extended trade. They employ 15 travelers on the road, and sell largely in the west, northwest, and southwest, with considerable middle states and export trade. Messrs. Brigham are honorable business men, who have ever retained the confidence of leading commercial and financial circles, and are worthy exponents of their important branch of trade. Mr. Brigham, Sr., is an active member of the Shoe and Leather Exchange, of the Boot and Shoe Club, etc., and is socially as well as commercially prominent in Boston.

FRANK HERMAN & CO., Manufacturers and Jobbers of Boots and Shoes, No. 107 Pearl Street, Corner of High; Factory, Medway, Mass.—One of the most progressive and popular houses devoted to the staple boot and shoe industry of New England is that of Messrs. Frank, Herman & Co., located at the corner of Pearl and High Streets. The proprietors, Mr. Joseph M. Herman and Mr. Abraham Frank, are still young men, yet old experienced in their line, and have achieved a substantial success since forming the existing copartnership in 1879. Their factory is located at Medway, and is of large size, fully equipped with the latest improved machinery run by steam-power, and affording employment to from 150 to 175 hands in the manufacture of medium and heavy boots and shoes. Men's goods have ever been a specialty, and their celebrated horseshoe brogan are the leader for all descriptions of rough and wearing work, proving the easiest and most durable shoe under all circumstances. The sales of their brogans have attained proportions of enormous magnitude, and every storekeeper throughout the mining regions requires them in stock. The firm's warehouse is five stories in height and 25x140 feet in dimensions. It is suitably fitted up to carry the heavy stock always found here of full lines and grades of men's and boys' shoes, including fine calf and the heavier grades for all purposes. Quality has ever been the first consideration, and Messrs. Frank & Herman handle no shoes not produced from the best materials, cut by experts, made up honestly, with good linings and findings, and finished equal to anything of the same grade in the United States. The firm's prices are notably low, and their sales are annually enlarging, air travelling men representing the house on the road. Mr. Herman has been in the shoe business for twenty-three years, and is a recognized authority thereon; as also is Mr. Frank, who has been identified with the trade for the past fifteen years, ten of which he has resided in Boston. Both gentlemen are members of the Boot and Shoe Club, and are worthy representatives of this important branch of trade, and have before them prospects of the most favorable character.

HILL'S CHAMPION COOKER, Formerly called Lewis's; Lewis & Co., General Agents, No. 149 Pearl Street.—As taverns in each had proved a boon to thousands of households, and which is regarded as an indispensable article everywhere it has been introduced, is that known as Hill's Champion Steam Cooker. This cooker is supplied by Hill, Whitney & Co. The firm have been conducting this enterprise for the past three years, and have developed a large, constantly-growing trade. The patent cooker supplied by them is the only perfect steamless and odorless one in the market. As it has an iron base there is no danger of warking or rusting out of bottom. It has a tube which takes all the surplus steam and odor arising from cooking, and carries it into the store and up the flue. It can be used as a steam or boiling cooker, or both at the same time, and its most remarkable feature is that any kind of meats, vegetables, and the most delicate puddings can be cooked at the same time with out the slightest intermingling of the flavors. Following are some of its advantages over all other cookers: 1st. The price is about one-half. 2d. It is more durable; no melting or rusting out of bottom, and is good for a lifetime. 3d. A greater intensity of heat, food is cooked

quicker, tough meats are made more tender, the nutritious elements are saved, and no loss by evaporation. 4th. It is warranted steam less and odorless; no steam or odor escaping into the house to soil furniture, pictures, etc., or fill it with odors, both disagreeable and unhealthy. 5th. More easily handled and kept in order. Will do the work of two or three common kettles, very easy to clean, requires but little attention while cooking, cooks food one-third quicker, will save one-third of fuel, and will pay for itself in a short time. It is one of the most practical and useful household inventions ever offered to the public. The cover having a water-joint, and the outlet tube being raised above the top of the cooker, the cover rests upon it and acts as a valve for the escape of steam. In this way the steam is kept in the cooker and greatly increases the heat. It has an adjustable dish which can be changed to three different positions to suit the space wanted for boiling and steaming. The cover and the tube together are so arranged as to make the former act as a valve and in this way get increased heat. The price of the cooker are $1.50, $2.75, and $3.25, according to size, this is a special feature as it is about one-half the cost of the cookers. It has only to be tried in order to be appreciated.

GREY, CLARK & ENGLE, Manufacturers of "Chicago" Calf, Veal, and Kip Skins, Glacé Calf, No. 109 South Street.—One of the principal points in the United States for the manufacture of calf, veal, and kip skins and glacé calf leather is Chicago where the firm of Grey, Clark & Engle conduct large operations and produce a line of goods of unrivalled excellence, which are staple and always in demand on the market. Their goods are eagerly inquired for in Boston and to meet the demand from the city and New England States, a branch house was established at No. 67 High Street, under the management of Mr. J. F. Reid, who built up a large substantial trade, and a year ago removed the business to the commodious premises now occupied at Nos. 167 and 169 South Street. The

building is a six-story structure 65x79 feet in size, and is complete in all its appointments for the purposes of the business, and contains a large stock of all the various kinds of leather manufactured by the firm. Mr. Reid who is a native of Saratoga County, New York, has been identified with the leather trade many years and previous to coming to Boston was in the Chicago house. He is popular in business circles in this city and stands high in the estimation of all who have dealings with him. He is a thorough business man and has built up a large and prosperous trade.

D. L. SMITH, Insurance Broker, Room 2, No. 41 Milk Street.—Of the many engaged in the business of placing risks on life in this city, there are but few who are better known or enjoy a higher reputation for reliability than D. L. Smith, the popular and responsible insurance broker. Mr. Smith who is a gentleman of middle age, and a native of Boston, is a man of energy, enterprise, and thorough experience in this line, as well as of entire probity in all his transactions and business relations, and has a complete knowledge of every detail appertaining thereto. He has been actively and successfully engaged in this special line for more than five years, and from the start he has steadily won his way to public confidence and recognition, building up an excellent business connection throughout the city and vicinity. Mr. Smith conducts a general life insurance business, placing all classes of desirable risks with any first class company desired, at the lowest rates consistent with absolute security, while special attention is paid to the prompt settlement of all just claims, and all persons having dealings with this gentleman are certain to find the same of an entirely satisfactory character.

CHAS. F. HOLLIS, No. 11 Custom House Street, between Broad and India Streets.—The old established and prosperous house of Mr. Chas. F. Hollis was founded in 1845 by Mr. H. J. Flint, who was succeeded by the present proprietor in 1859. The premises occupied for manufacturing and trade purposes comprise three floors, 25x60 feet each, thoroughly equipped in every respect with the most improved appliances, and furnishing steady employment for a large force of skilled and expert hands. A leading specialty is made of Hollis' Patent Swinging Oil Can, while the output comprises all kinds of cans, both round and square. From its inception this house has received a large measure of recognition from the trade throughout the entire New England States. A leading specialty is made in supplying the paint and oil trade of this and other New England cities, and in this direction its trade no house in New England is better prepared to meet every demand promptly and satisfactorily, while its terms and prices are as liberal as to add materially to the popularity of the house everywhere. Mr. Hollis is a native Bostonian, and a thoroughly practical and experienced manufacturer.

G. W. & F. SMITH IRON CO., Building Iron Work; Office, No. 611 Federal Street; Franklin Smith, President.—Special attention is directed to this commercial review of Boston to the old established and representative G. W. & F. Smith Iron Co., manufacturers of building and architectural iron work. The wrought iron works of the company are situated at No. 49 Federal Street, and the foundry at Farnham Street, Boston Highlands. This business was originally established in 1798 by G. W. Smith, who was succeeded in 1851 by the firm of G. W. & F. Smith. Eventually in 1880 the present company was organized with ample capital, and assumed the management, the executive officers at the present time being Franklin Smith, president and treasurer; Elmer F. Smith, secretary; Bryant G. Smith, general superintendent. The wrought iron works and foundry are fully equipped with the latest improved machinery and appliances, while employment is furnished in the various departments to 150 skilled workmen. The G. W. & F. Smith Iron Company produce extensively all kinds of cast and wrought iron work, structural work, girders, iron fronts, etc., which are unsurpassed for quality of material, finish and workmanship by those of any other first class house in the trade or in this country. The business of this responsible company extends throughout all sections of the United States. Mr. Franklin Smith, the president is one of the representative iron manufacturers of New England, and ably presides over the rapidly increasing business of his company.

L YMAN R. BROOKS, Designer and Engraver, No. 101 Franklin Street.—One of the styles of pocket checkbooks for which this house has become so widely noted is the smallest made, measuring, when closed, only 3x5¼ inches, but when opened showing a good-sized check...

J AMES M. HUDLEY, Manufacturer of Chamber Furniture, Nos. 157 to 161 Fulton Street.—Among the most enterprising, skillful, and leading representative manufacturers of chamber furniture in Boston and New England is Mr. James M. Hudley...

W M. H. VIALLE & CO., Graded Woolen and Cotton Rags and Wool Waste, Nos. 150 and 152 Fulton Street.—There is no more important centre in the United States for the wholesale trade in rags and waste than the city of Boston...

F RANCIS SPRAGUE & CO., General Auctioneers, Appraisers, and Commission Merchants; Real Estate and Mortgages, No. 79 Milk Street.—One of the most popular business houses in its special line in this city is that of Francis Sprague & Co....

H ILL & LANGTRY, Importers and Jobbers of Saddlery Hardware, Harness, etc., Nos. 10 Federal Street and 7 Leather Square.—This business was established eleven years ago by Messrs. W. P. Hill and J. H. Langtry, both of whom have had long experience...

LANE & HUBBARD, Woolen Drapers, No. 145 Tremont Street.—
The history of prominent representatives of the tailor's art in this city could be incomplete without the names of Lane & Hubbard, the well-known woolen drapers, at No. 145 Tremont Street. This house has long been recognized as a tower of strength in the mercantile activity of the city, and the enterprise and reliability of its management has served to build up a high reputation and a large first-class and influential trade. The business was originally established in 1884, by Messrs. Lane & Hubbard, and in 1889 Mr. Allen T. Hubbard succeeded to the sole control, continuing the enterprise under the original firm name. The business premises are very slightly situated in a fashionable quarter of the city, are spacious in size, elegantly appointed, and arranged for the reception of patrons, and contain one of the finest stocks of cloths and trimmings ever brought to the city. It is complete in material, design, and novelty, and the very best sources of European production have contributed to its wealth. Mr. Hubbard devotes his time and talents to fine custom clothing exclusively, and the garments made to order by him are recognized as simply perfect in style, fit, and artistic workmanship. To meet his services once is to be his patron always. To be found among his permanent customers are very many of the best-dressed citizens of Boston, gentlemen young and old, who understand the merits of a first-class tailor, and who find in Mr. Hubbard's establishment not only a line of business that are at all times superior, but also a place where the general make-up, fit, and trimming of a garment is a matter of careful consideration and study. A specialty is made in catering to the college trade, and the business in this branch has attained very flattering proportions. Mr. Hubbard is a Massachusetts man by birth and education, thoroughly liberal and experienced in all his dealings, and a reliable and responsible leader in his branch of trade with whom it is always pleasant and profitable to deal.

CONRAD EPPE, Die-sinker, Seal-engraver, and Letter cutter, No. 97 Oliver Street.—Mr. Conrad Eppe, since starting his business as a die-sinker, seal-engraver, and letter-cutter, in 1872, by the character of his work has won a host of patrons, and his business is continually showing signs of increase. This gentleman was born in Germany, and twenty-three years ago left his native land to make a home in the United States. He came to Boston, and on the eve of the great Boston fire in 1871 established himself in business on Province Court, to which place the fire, happily, did not extend. In August, 1887, he removed to his present quarters on Oliver Street, where he occupies two rooms on the second floor, and has equipped them with all the most modern mechanical appliances appertaining to his business. Everything in the line of die-sinking, seal-engraving, and letter-cutting is done in an absolutely first-class manner, Mr. Eppe's extensive practical experience enabling him to bring his art to a high plane of perfection. Steel dies and hubs for jewelry, silver-plated ware, medals, badges, etc.; steel rolls and dies for spoons, knives, forks, and fancy borders; embossing dies for paper leather, etc.; seals for lodges, societies, corporations, notaries, etc., and steel stamps for boot and shoe manufacturers, wooden-ware makers, etc., are made at his shortest notice. A specialty is made of the engraving of rolls for rubber shoes. A staff of competent artisans find constant employment, and all work is closely supervised by Mr. Eppe. The patronage of the house is drawn from all parts of the New England States.

CHARLES M. THACHER, Picture Frames and Mouldings, No. 10 Arch Street.—The picture-frame and moulding factory of Mr. Charles M. Thacher occupies a leading position in its line. Its salient has been one of steady progress since its establishment in 1888. The premises occupied for the business consist of three floors, each seventy-five feet square, and fitted up in all the departments with a complete mechanical outfit, the motor power for driving the same being supplied by electricity. Employment is furnished twenty experienced hands, and the operations of the establishment are conducted on a systematic and intelligent basis. Mr. Thacher, who is practically acquainted with all the details of his vocation, personally superintends the work of his assistants, and gives his attention to the production of picture frames and mouldings of every description. The trade is wholesale and retail, and extends to all sections of New England. A large stock is constantly carried on hand, and orders are carefully filled and shipped without loss of time.

H. C. HANSEN, Manufacturer of Printer's Materials. No. 45 Hawley Street.—Mr. H. C. Hansen, as a manufacturer and dealer in printers' materials of all kinds, controls one of the most enterprising and successful establishments in its line in the city. Mr. Hansen, who is a native of Norway and a practical machinist of great experience, came to reside in Boston twenty-two years ago. In his native land he had acquired a thorough knowledge of drawing, geometry, and mathematics, and served an apprenticeship to the trade of machinist. On the 11th of January, 1894, he was engaged by the Dickinson Type Company of this city, and was set to work to learn the business of brass rule-making, in which he soon became proficient, and took the position of leading workman in the brass rule department of the foundry. He effected many improvements to the mechanical appliances for manufacturing brass rules and leads, and in 1872 started business on his own account on Exchange Street, whence he removed on January 1, 1874, to his present commodious premises. Mr. Hansen occupies three floors of this spacious building as salesroom and manufacturing department. The latter is most efficiently equipped with the latest improved machinery and tools, most of which are of Mr. Hansen's own invention, and he has carried many of his own inventions and original designs into his manufactures. He has now the proud distinction of being at the head of the largest manufactory of brass rules and leads for printers in New England. Twelve hands are permanently employed. A heavy stock of rules in every size, shape, thickness, and design is to be found here in vast quantities, together with labor-saving metal furniture, ornamental brass dashes, steel composing-rules, brass composing-rules, circular brass corners, labor-saving slugs, spaces and quads for different fonts of type, type of all kinds, and machinery and presses of every description, and the best relations of the house extend to all parts of the New England States. Mr. Hansen is a member of the Massachusetts Charitable Mechanic Association.

E. WILLIAMS & CO., Commission and Shipping Merchants, No. 15 Central Wharf.—Messrs. E. Williams & Co., are extensive shipping merchants for the South American trade, taking out cargoes of merchandise of all kinds to that country, and importing the products of that clime to this city. They also charter, purchase, and sell vessels, and are owners and proprietors of two sailing vessels now upon the sea. The business was established in 1865 by Mr. E. Williams, and some years after he admitted Mr. P. F. Wells to partnership. In 1876 Mr. Williams died, and Mr. Wells has since continued the business, as sole proprietor, under the original firm-name. The premises occupied comprise three floors, 35x75 feet each, and unsurpassed advantages are possessed for conducting all branches of the business. The business penetrates the entire country of South America, extending to the West Indies, and is broadly distributed throughout all the United States. Mr. Wells is possessed not only of a thorough knowledge of the wants of the trade on both sides the ocean, but is in a position to supply them with ease and promptness in all cases. None but the purest and best productions are brought from the tropics, and the resources and connections of the house enable it to place all transactions on a solid and substantial basis. Mr. Wells is a Massachusetts man by birth and education, and recognized as a leading representative of his important branch of commerce in this city. He is a member of the Produce Exchange and of the Vessel Owners' Association, and a director of the India Mutual Insurance Company.

F. D. L. HICKMAN, Manufacturer of Platform Rockers, Lounges, Bed-lounges, etc., No. 43 Beverly Street.—This enterprise has been in successful operation since 1890, and its products have been maintained at such a high standard of excellence that they are as heavy and steadily increasing demand in all parts of the United States. The premises occupied for manufacturing purposes comprise two spacious floors, supplied with a complete equipment of the finest wood-working machinery and all the other appliances and facilities, including steam power, that can be used to advantage, while steady employment is provided for fourteen skilled and experienced hands. The range of manufacture comprises all grades of the above-named goods, and the output is recognized, wherever introduced, as absolutely unsurpassed for utility, elegance, and artistic workmanship. Mr. Hickman is a native of Cape Cod, Mass., and a reliable and successful business man.

J. D. POWELL, JR., Job Printing, Etc., No. 18 Cornhill.—Among the enterprising, popular, and successful business men of Boston is Mr. J. D. Powell, Jr., the proprietor of the fine job printing establishment at No. 18 Cornhill, and who is the able and talented managing editor of the *Boston Advocate*, the leading negro journal in the United States. Mr. Powell was born in Baltimore, and received his education and training as a skilled and practical job printer and publisher in Boston. Five years ago, in response to an urgent demand for a high toned, carefully edited organ to guide the thinking element of, and afford an organ of influence to the colored people of the country, he founded the *Advocate*, and also began the job printing business. He has achieved a deserved success. His office is fully equipped with the choicest of materials, type, etc. Careful compositors are employed, and job work in all its branches is turned out here, in the highest style of the art, with celerity and accuracy. The prices are remarkably low, and it is but natural that a very large and growing trade is centred here, where all orders receive immediate attention, from a business card to a pamphlet or book. A review of the *Advocate* shows it to be a large, four-page, seven-column paper, published weekly and commanding a desirable advertising patronage. Its editorials are clear, forcible, and fearless. They treat of the live questions of the day, political and social, and represent the just and prevalent views of the colored population not only of New England, but throughout the country at large. There are many columns of fresh original news, spicy personals, strictures, stories, etc., and in appearance, contents, and make up the *Advocate* is as highly creditable to its managing editor as it is widely circulated, over 11,000 copies now being issued weekly. Mr. Powell's assistants are Miss Lillian A. Lewis, society editor; and Mr. J. W. Powell, associate editor. They are a capable and hard working staff. Mr. J. D. Powell is also gifted as a public speaker, and his speeches during the recent political campaign were powerful and eloquent appeals to his fellow citizens on behalf of the principles of Republicanism.

W. SNELLING, Hardware and Mechanics' Tools, etc., No. 23 Maverick Square, East Boston.—The largest hardware establishment in East Boston is that of Mr. Washington Snelling, which enjoys a reputation and a trade that represents the results of thirty five years of honorable and successful effort. The proprietor also operates two branch stores, one at No. 353 Meridian Street, in East Boston, and the other in the neighboring town of Winthrop. The premises occupied on Maverick Square are spacious in size, and perfect in convenience of arrangement for display, inspection, and sale. The several departments are filled with an elaborate and diversified stock, embracing builders' and general hardware, shelf-goods and cabinet hardware, locksmiths' and butchers' supplies, carpenters', mechanics' and machinists' tools, table and pocket cutlery nails, glass, putty, paint, and bolting, ship and boat trimmings, and galvanized goods. The supplies are purchased in vast quantities direct from manufacturers, and special attention is given to the quality and character of the productions. Significant advantages are extended to customers in the matter of prices. Both a wholesale and retail business is transacted, and in addition to a large local trade, a heavy demand is ministered to, coming from all parts of New England. Employing ample capital, and commanding advanced opportunities for the procurement of goods, the house of Mr. Snelling may be justly considered as a tower of strength in the field of commerce. Mr. Snelling is a native Bostonian.

MULLIN & CO., Coal and Wood; Wharf, First Street, Foot of F Street, South Boston.—Among the leading and most active firms of wholesale and retail coal merchants of Boston and New England is that of Messrs. Mullin & Co. The business was established by Mr. P. J. Mullin in 1878, and who continued the same until 1880, when the firm of P. J. Mullin & Co. was formed. The decease of Mr. Mullin occurred in 1887, since which date Mr. Tigh has actively and successfully carried on the business under the old name and style, greatly enlarging the trade and offering substantial inducements to purchasers. He is a native of Boston, and long identified with the wholesale and retail coal trade. He has the finest facilities of any coal merchant in South Boston or the city proper, having a very commodious wharf, foot of F Street, and sheds that hold fully 10,000 tons. The premises extend from the main thoroughfare to the river and comprise several acres, affording proper accommodation for the immense stock of coal and wood always carried here, and for screening, weighing, delivering, etc. Mr. Tighe deals strictly in the choicest brands of anthracite and bituminous coal, received direct in cargo lots from tide-water shipping points. His contracts placed away ahead are at prices that enable him to offer substantial inducements to large consumers, etc., and he does a trade of enormous magnitude, requiring the services of from 16 to 20 men, and the use of from six to eight teams. The house of Mullin & Co. has become justly celebrated for the superior quality of the fuel dealt in. Only the best free burning coal is sold, and the wood is of best quality and thoroughly seasoned.

DR. HORACE HARDING, Dentist, No. 78 Main Street, Charlestown.—Prominent among the most successful and expert surgeon dentists of Charlestown is Dr. Horace Harding. This gentleman was born at Orleans, Mass., and his early training and education were directed to qualify him for the profession in which he has become a distinguished expert. He graduated with high honors at the Massachusetts Dental College. In 1882 he began business at his present location, and being devoted to his profession and acquainted with its every detail he soon took front rank in the line of his calling. His chambers are equipped with every modern appliance in use for the extracting and filling of teeth, etc. Dental work of all kinds is done scientifically and at the most reasonable charges. The disagreeable task of extracting and filling of teeth is rendered as pleasant as possible by prompt and skilful work and by the use of gas, when desired. Every care and attention is given to the making of artificial teeth, singly or in sets, and a correct and easy fit is guaranteed in every instance. Competent assistants are employed, and courteous service is rendered to all patrons; while the doctor has an excellent reputation throughout this section for superior work and reliability. Dr. Harding is a resident of Charlestown.

H. L. NORCROSS, Note-broker, No. 17 Pearl Street.—Mr. Norcross, although quite a young man, brings to bear a wide experience in this important line of business, and since he founded this establishment on his own responsibility, in 1887, he has developed a most influential connection, and includes among his permanent patrons many of our leading capitalists and financiers. He occupies a very neatly and comfortably furnished office, which is fully supplied with every convenience for the successful conduct of his business. Mr. Norcross is prepared to procure and negotiate loans for capitalists, to those desiring them, upon the most approved basis, and in the most satisfactory manner to both lender and borrower. He makes it a specialty of handling only "gilt-edged paper," and his supplies of funds are obtained from the most reputable and reliable sources. His line of business embraces loans on notes, secured by ample collateral on bonds or mortgages, ample indorsement, warehouse receipts, negotiable securities, etc., while his rates are always most liberal and free from any usurious calculations. He can be depended upon as conducting business of that nature in the most reliable and confidential manner.

DAVID A. McGRATH, Fine Boots and Shoes, No. 61 Bromfield Street.—Mr. McGrath has been a resident of this city since he was seven years of age, and learned his trade here, after which he added to his learning by several years of experience in some of the leading custom boot and shoe houses in the city, and finally decided to embark in the business on his own responsibility, and founded this house accordingly in 1871; and by close attention to the wants of his customers, handling and making only first-class goods, together with liberal treatment of customers, his establishment soon became the centre of a first-class trade. The premises occupied are commodious, and comprise a very attractive store, which is supplied with every convenience necessary for the display of his fine stock of goods. Connected with the store is a finely equipped and well-lighted workshop. In the store will be found at all times a full and general assortment of fine boots and shoes,—gentlemen's, youths', and boys',—and, in the line of articles for ladies, misses, and children, everything that is new, fashionable, and stylish, from the strong walking boot or school shoe to the exquisitely wrought kid or satin slipper. These goods have been selected by Mr. McGrath from among the best productions of the most eminent boot and shoe establishments in the country. He gives especial attention to making fine boots and shoes to order for ladies and gentlemen, in all the latest and most desirable styles, in the best manner, and from the very best materials to be found in the market.

COLTON DENTAL ASSOCIATION, Rooms No. 64, Beacon Street. - The Colton Dental Association has for over twenty-two years maintained a position in the forefront in this important and progressive profession. This well and favorably known Association was established in 1866 by Dr. Colton [for A. C. Varnum, and three years later came under the control of Levi Parker, who associated with him in partnership L. F. Jones and H. H. Parter, and with the exception of the death of Mr. Jones, which occurred in August last, the history of the enterprise has been a career of uninterrupted success. They are the originators of the use of nitrous oxide gas for extracting teeth without pain, and various other meritorious features of progress pertaining to dental practice. They occupy commodious and handsome quarters on the second floor of No. 64, Beacon Street, and have in service all the latest improved dental appliances, devices, and general appurtenances, while several competent assistants are in attendance. Dentistry in all its branches, both mechanical and scientific, is executed in the most thorough and skilful manner, at popular prices, teeth being extracted without pain, the Association administering their gas with absolute safety, while filling is attended to also, and plates inserted in the very best style of the art. Special attention is given to the treatment of the young also, and artificial work is promptly and reliably done likewise, in short, everything comprehended in modern dentistry is attended to in the most superior manner in every instance. The Messrs. Parter are practical and expert dentists, and have an extensive and influential practice, their patronage extending throughout a wide territory.

DEAN, CHASE & CO., Shoe Manufacturers' Goods, Nos. 135 to 165 Congress Street. - This house was founded some forty years ago, the present firm purchasing the business of Messrs. Stoddard, Lovering & Co. in January, 1878. They handle everything used in the manufacture of shoes save the leather, including goods of both domestic and foreign production, and carry one of the largest and most complete lines of merchandise of the kind naturally included in their business that can be found either in Boston or in any city in the country. Their trade is chiefly in the shoe manufacturing sections of New England and New York, and they operate a branch house at No. 6 Thomas Street, New York. Their intimate and influential connections with the best manufacturing sources in this country and Europe enable them to secure their supplies in vast quantities and at the most advantageous rates, and they are accordingly prepared to guarantee the prompt and perfect fulfilment of all orders, and to offer inducements to their patrons in the matter of terms and prices which cannot be duplicated elsewhere. The stock is thoroughly comprehensive of such indispensables as threads, buttons, elastic webs, stays, facings, and paper, etc., and is of a character and quality which speaks for itself. The individual members of this enterprising firm are Messrs. E. W. Dean, F. C. Chase, W. F. Skilton, and W. P. Edwards, all well-known Bostonians and standing deservedly high in mercantile and trade circles. Messrs. Dean and Chase were members of the firm of Stoddard, Lovering & Co., the former for forty years and the latter for nine years, while Messrs. Skilton and Edwards were connected with the house for several years, and became members of the new firm at its organization.

BURDITT & WILLIAMS, Builders' Hardware, Cutlery, etc., No. 20 Dock Square. - A house that has been established for upwards of a hundred years is that of Messrs. Burditt & Williams, dealers in all kinds of hardware, etc. Messrs. Chas. A. Burditt and Joseph Williams succeeded to the business in 1900, and conducted it till 1903, when Mr. James A. Monroe became a partner; the business, however, is still carried on under the old firm-name of Burditt & Williams. The firm have likewise a store at Washington, D.C., where they carry on an extensive retail and wholesale trade. The Boston warehouse is a spacious four-story and basement building, fully supplied with every appliance and convenience for the accommodation and display of the extensive and valuable stock. Messrs. Burditt & Williams deal largely in all kinds of builders' hard ware, carpenters' tools, cutlery and general hardware, and also keep in stock the largest assortment of bronze hardware in New England. The builders' and retail department is on the lower floor, while the jobbing department is located on the second floor. The firm have secured the most favorable arrangements with the leading American and European manufacturers, and offer advantages in goods and prices very difficult to be duplicated elsewhere in this country. Thirty assistants, clerks, salesmen, etc., are employed, and the trade of the house extends not only throughout all sections of New England and the eastern states, but likewise to Chicago, Kansas City and St. Louis. The firm make a specialty of builders' hardware. All the goods handled by this popular and trustworthy house are unrivalled for quality, reliability, and general excellence. Messrs. Burditt & Williams are natives of Boston, while Mr. Monroe was born in Cambridge, Mass.

WILHART & GREELEY, Fashionable Racines, No. 11 Franklin Avenue. Between Court Street and Cornhill. - An old and reputable firm in the hat trade is that of Wilhart & Greeley, No. 11 Franklin Avenue, between Court Street and Cornhill. The partners of this concern are Jas. H. Wilhart and Philip Greeley respectively, both of whom are practical in the trade, and have been identified with it for a period of nearly forty years. The business was established by them as far back as 1861, and they have occupied the same premises during the twenty-seven years that have since elapsed. Messrs. Wilhart & Greeley's principal line is in order and repair work. They are well-known fashionable hatters, having a large city trade in the best quality of silk hats, of which they keep a full stock constantly on hand. They also do an extensive business renovating silk and felt hats, making them in all respects equal to new. Two men are employed in the establishment, where customers can always rely on having their orders promptly filled. Mr. Wilhart, who is a native of Germany, has been in the United States for forty years. Mr. Greeley belongs to New Hampshire. Both gentlemen are good business men, and have a high standing in the hatter's trade.

NOVELTY WOOD-WORKS: John J. McNutt, Builder and Manufacturer Mouldings, Doors, Frames, etc., Junction Malden and Wareham Streets. - This business was established in 1844 on Tremont Street, and since 1887 has been permanently located at the junction of Malden and Wareham Streets. Mr. McNutt brings to bear the widest range of practical experience, coupled with matured skill and ability as a builder, contractor, and manufacturer generally of all descriptions of wood work, and builders' materials. His premises are unusually extensive and complete; yards and buildings cover an area of 60,000 square feet, the latter being three stories high, 50x50 feet in dimensions, and equipped throughout with the latest improved machinery and appliances. Two steam-engines, jointly of 120 horse power, supply the motive force, while there is an average force of 125 hands employed in the manufacture of wood mouldings, plain and fancy brackets, scrolls, doors, sash and blinds, counters, shelving, drawers, packing boxes, etc. All kinds of planing, sawing, fret-sawing, turning, etc., are done to order, also carving and pattern making. He is a builder of renown, whose methods, skill, and facilities place him in the front rank of the trade. He has built all kinds and sizes of warehouses, theatres, churches, factories, stores, private residences, etc., and has also made a prominent specialty of store fixtures, the fitting up of banks, counting-rooms, etc.

C. B. FOGG, Carpenter and Builder, Manufacturer of Hard and Soft Wood Doors, No. 35 Wareham Street. - This gentleman is prominent as a designer and manufacturer, of undoubted ability and skill, and has been established in the business here since 1879. His business premises are spacious in size, thoroughly equipped with new and improved machinery, and employment is afforded to twenty experienced hands. The range of manufacture includes all kinds of panel work, doors, window frames, counters and general store fittings, and the goods turned out are unrivalled for fine finish, originality and beauty of design, and artistic workmanship. The services of the house are constantly brought into requisition by our business men in the fitting up and furnishing of their places of business, and all orders and commissions meet with the promptest attention, while terms and prices are placed at the lowest point of moderation. By close application to the details of his business, and with an honest endeavor to excel therein, Mr. Fogg has built up a reputation that is bringing him a large, first class and constantly increasing patronage. Mr. Fogg is a native of the state of Maine, and has become well and popularly known as a most worthy business man.

THE F. W. ROSS CARPET CLEANING CO., Works, Nos. 54 and 56 Thayer Street. — Although a comparatively new enterprise, the positive and progressive success that has attended the F. W. Ross Carpet Cleaning Company, at Nos. 54 and 56 Thayer Street, ever since its inception, abundantly attests the wisdom that inspired the venture. Mr. F. W. Ross, the general manager, is an experienced master of the business in all its details, and has devoted much time and study to the invention of improved machinery for doing the work. The works of the company are among the largest of the kind in New England, but are hardly large enough for the increasing business transacted, and a larger factory will soon be erected. The capacity of the present works admits of the cleaning of 1000 yards of carpeting per day. The company devotes special atten-

[illustration of carpet cleaning machine]

tion to the interests of hotels and the trade, doing an immense and beneficial business in cleaning imported Turkish rugs for dealers. They have machinery for cleaning wool, cotton, and silk waste, buffalo robes and blankets, and have a separate department for their large family trade. No expense has been spared in fitting up the works with the latest improved machinery for doing the most thorough work quickly. They are not confined to any one process, as they have several distinct methods which they use, according to the requirements of the carpets or the wishes of their customers, viz.: steam tumbling, steam beating, surface cleaning, washing, naphthalizing, and dry steaming. Special attention is directed to their improved method for removing grease, tar, soot, and other stains from carpets by the use of carefully selected and prepared compounds, which brighten without blending the colors, or in any way injuring the texture or tints. No acids are used. Dust cannot be removed from carpets on the floor, but where they cannot be spared long enough to be taken up and thoroughly cleaned, the company will send experienced men to clean the surface, removing spots, brightening the colors, and making the carpet look fresh and new. The works are provided with five carpet cleaning machines, all of Mr. Ross's own invention, and the best and only scientific method of thoroughly cleaning carpets without the slightest injury to the fabric, color, or design, is in application here. Patrons are cordially invited to call and see the work executed and the machinery in operation. Carpets are called for and delivered free of charge, and arrangements are made whereby the teams of the company will call as often as the requirements of customers demand. Prices are furnished upon application at the office, and are made so low as is consistent with a service which will be satisfactory to all. All orders by telephone, mail, or otherwise, receive immediate attention, and prompt and thorough work is guaranteed in all cases. A specialty is made of packing for storage in moth proof, chemically prepared paper, and storage and insurance are furnished, when desired, at fair rates. The cleaning is all done under the personal supervision of Mr. Ross, the general manager, who has had an extensive practical experience and thoroughly understands the requirements of hotel and trade work. He also manufactures carpet cleaning machines to sell, which are of his own invention and are the embodiments of inventive genius and mechanical skill of the highest order of perfection. Both he and the treasurer, Mr. J. W. Merriam, are Massachusetts men by birth and training, and enjoy the confidence and esteem of leading commercial circles.

C. J. BAILEY & CO., Manufacturers of and First Hands for Patented Novelties, No. 102 Pearl Street. — This firm are manufacturers of and first hands for patented novelties, and their connections extend not only throughout this country and Canada, but also over all Europe. This business was inaugurated twelve years ago by Messrs. Clapp and Bailey, and in July, 1890, the firm became as at present constituted, the copartners being Messrs. C. J. Bailey and K. S. Lawrence. The former is in charge of the Boston establishment, the latter in charge of the London branch, under the firm style of C. J. Bailey & Co. The house has branches at No. 102 Main Street, Cincinnati, O., No. 372 373 Market Street, San Francisco; No. 50 Reade Street N. Y.; No. 141 Lake Street, Chicago, and St. Paul, Minn.; also at No. 50 Snow Hill, London, E. C., Eng.; and in Paris, France; while in Canada they are represented by Lyman, Sons & Co., St. Paul Street, Montreal, and in Berlin and Frankfort Germany, by Woods, Buchola & Co. Their factory is located in Akron, Ohio, and they are sole manufacturers and make specialties of the following articles: Bailey's patent rubber bath and flesh brush, Bailey's patent rubber tooth and toilet brushes, Bailey's elastic rubber brushes, Bailey's patent blacking daubers. These goods are wonderfully effective for the purposes to which they are adapted, and are unapproached by any articles of a similar nature in the market. A heavy stock is carried at each of the firm's houses and the wholesale trade is supplied on the most favorable terms, all orders being filled promptly and satisfactorily.

WESTGATE & JOHNSON, Insurance Agents and Brokers, No. 113 Water Street. There are but very few business men or owners of property to be found to-day who will answer in the negative to a proposal to effect an insurance against loss by fire, for fires are so frequent and losses thereby so far-reaching and injurious to their influence, that they meet with constant reminders that insurance companies stand between prosperity and ruin, and that it is best to be on the safe side and be protected against damages, for "no man knoweth what a day may bring forth." The facilities for effecting insurance at low rates are so great now-a-days that no man can offer a plausible excuse for not having his property insured. Insurance agents and brokers are numerous and ever ready to attend to the behests of a would-be insurer who means business. A noted firm of insurance agents is that of Messrs. Westgate & Johnson, of No. 113 Water Street. The firm have also an office in the Savings Bank, Town Hall, Melrose. The business was originally organized in 1880 by Mr. J. E. Westgate, who afterwards took into partnership his son, under the style of J. E. Westgate & Son. The son, Mr. H. H. Westgate, on the death of his father became sole proprietor, and in February, 1897, he formed a partnership with his nephew, Mr. H. E. Johnson. On the 23rd of October following, Mr. H. H. Westgate died, and the business is still being conducted by Mr. Johnson under the style of Westgate & Johnson. Mr. Johnson is a member of the Melrose Board of Underwriters, and is the representative of some of the most substantial foreign and home fire, life and accident insurance companies. He conducts a general brokerage business and makes a specialty of fire risks. To insurers he offers the most advantageous terms, and is prompt and reliable. Mr. Johnson is a native of Maine and for sixteen years has resided at Melrose.

D. P. BEDELL, Machine Twist, No. 37 High Street. — Mr. Bedell is the representative, for this state, of the celebrated Mayhew Silk Company, of Blackburne Falls, Mass., where their factory and headquarters are located. The business of this company was originally founded by Messrs. Streeter & Mayhew and was conducted under their joint control until three years ago, when Mr. Streeter's death occurred, and the present company was formed. The factory is equipped in the most approved fashion with first-class machinery, and ample steam-power; only expert operatives are employed and the most complete facilities are possessed for turning out a perfect production. Mr. Bedell carries a full stock of those goods which comprise woolen manufacturers' organzine, machine twist, floss, tram, and organzine silk of every variety. Orders are promptly filled and on the most advantageous terms. Mr. Bedell, who is a native of New York State, came to Boston fifteen years ago, and for the past nine years has been agent here for the Mayhew Silk Company. He has become well known in the leading business circles of the city, and is esteemed as a business man of push, ability, and industry, and a citizen of sterling integrity and worth.

THE BAY STATE CLEAN-TOWEL FURNISHING COMPANY, No. 84 Columbus Ave.—The Bay State Clean-towel Furnishing Company was founded in 1885 by the present proprietors, Messrs. A. Davidson and G. L. Goulding, and was originally located at No. 1 Hamilton Place. In the latter part of 1887, the present desirable site was secured, and here the firm have been constantly increasing the volume and prosperity of their business. The firm occupy a spacious and handsomely furnished office, with a well-appointed storage room in the rear, and have abundant outside facilities for the advantageous prosecution of their enterprise. The company furnishes to subscribers a neat dressing-case of ash, black walnut, or cherry, with mirror, and receptacle for towels and brushes, attached, and a toilet outfit comprising brush and comb, soap, blacking and brushes, and any number of clean towels per week, according to the requirements of the subscriber. The different articles are all first-class; the towels are pure linen, and plainly marked with the subscriber's name, thus insuring each one the return of his own; and all supplies are renewed when necessary. This outfit is furnished at a stated rate per month, the price being graded in accordance with the size of the outfit, special rates being made for large orders and roller-towels, so also for hotel, restaurant, and barber-shop work. The company has already secured a large and fast-increasing patronage. Messrs. Davidson and Goulding, it is scarcely necessary to state, are shrewd, enterprising business men.

SCHOELLKOPF, HARTFORD & MACLAGAN (Limited), Importers and Exporters of Drugs, Chemicals, etc.; General Commission Merchants; No. 108 Milk Street.—An important and reliable establishment in the New England States, engaged in the manufacture, importation, and exportation of drugs, chemicals, etc., is that of Messrs. Schoellkopf, Hartford & Maclagan (Limited), importers and exporters of drugs, chemicals, etc., also general commission merchants;—under the management of Messrs. Ellis and Mercer. These gentlemen are sole agents for the foregoing house, in New England, which has its headquarters at No. 8 Cedar Street, New York, with their works in Buffalo, N. Y., known as the Schoellkopf Aniline and Chemical Company. Mr. E. C. Ellis is well known in Boston and vicinity as the treasurer of the Republic Mills, of Lawrence, Mass., and Mr. G. R. H. Mercer, also of this city, has been known for many years as a practical cotton-man, having for various mills throughout this section of the country. The celebrated houses which they represent is one of the best and largest of the kind in the United States, and in their admirably appointed headquarters will be found a full and complete line of their products, together with importations of everything in the way of aniline colors, dye-stuffs; such as oil of vitriol; muriatic, nitric, and other acids; sulphates, nitrates, muriates, mineral dyes, ammoniates, chlorates, different-colored spirits, antimony, etc. These goods are pure and fresh, and are sold by samples; and all orders intrusted to Messrs. Ellis and Mercer will receive the most careful attention, and the goods will be shipped direct from either New York or Buffalo, saving thereby extra freight and drayage expenses. The agents of this establishment are well known to the leading cotton and woolen manufacturing houses throughout New England, and have always borne a most enviable reputation.

GEO. M. TUCK. Book and Job Printing, No. 69 Washington Street.—A deservedly popular exponent of the typographic art in this city is Mr. George M. Tuck who was brought up to the business, and has achieved a wide reputation for the neatness and elegance of his composition and press-work. He occupies desirable premises, being perfectly equipped and provided with the necessary presses and appurtenances for doing the very best book, job, and commercial work. Besides himself, he has three competent workmen, and orders are executed in a prompt, neat, and finished manner; while the prices charged are as low as desired. The business he is carrying on so successfully was established about three years ago by Bradmus & Tuck, and was afterwards continued by Ruff & Tuck, but since February, 1888, it has been under the sole proprietorship of Mr. Tuck, who has become well known in commercial circles and built up a large flourishing business by his enterprise, and executing the very highest class of typographic work. Born in Bangor, Me., he came to Boston several years ago, where he learned his trade. He is now living in Charlestown, and is very popular with all who have business dealings with him.

CARL SCHOENHOF, Foreign Book Seller and Importer, No. 144 Tremont Street.—Mr. Carl Schoenhof, importer and publisher of books, etc., in foreign languages, was born in Germany, and was specially educated for his present line of business. He has been a resident in Boston for about twenty-three years, and in 1869 founded his present enterprise, which has been conducted with marked skill and ability, and from the outset has commanded a very liberal and influential patronage. The store has a frontage of 25 feet and a depth of 70 feet, and is arranged and fitted up in the most satisfactory manner. Books of every description, in foreign languages, are to be found on the shelves and counters, and are offered at the most liberal prices. Mr. Schoenhof is the general agent for the United States for Hachette & Co.'s (London and Paris) publications for the study of foreign languages, for the use of English and American students and schools. A full stock of these publications is kept on hand, and supplied at the publishers' lowest prices. He is also the agent for Henry Holt & Co.'s (New York) publications, which are kept in large quantities in stock, and are sold at publishers' prices. Briger & Co.'s, Wm. R. Jenkins', Geo. R. Lockwood & Son's, Macmillan's, Appleton's, Barnes' publications in foreign languages are supplied at lowest rates. A general catalogue of school-books and miscellaneous books in foreign languages is supplied to all applicants. Any book desired, and not in stock, is immediately procured on order, and no effort is spared to meet the wishes of, and to afford the fullest satisfaction to, customers. The establishment is the leading one in its line in the city, and the proprietor has won a well deserved popularity.

WILLIAM MILLER, Importer and Publisher; Art Novelties, Reward, Birthday, Valentine, Easter, Christmas Cards, etc., No. 46 Arch Street.—The enterprise was founded originally by Mr. Miller, in 1880, in New York, and moved to Boston in 1888. Under Mr. Miller's care and supervision, the trade has increased to proportions of great magnitude, and is continually growing. Mr. Miller is a native of New York City, and although quite a young man yet, he is thoroughly educated to the business; and having great natural aptitude for it, he made it a close practical study, which conferred upon him that knowledge and comprehension of what kind of art novelties, etc., would meet with the tastes of the trade and the public, and provided accordingly. The premises utilized for saleroom and office are spacious and commodious, handsomely appointed and supplied with every facility for the advantageous display of the elegant stock of goods constantly on hand, which includes a superb line of reward-of-merit, birthday, valentine, easter, and Christmas cards, all of the most beautiful designs and artistic productions; also pastels, scrap, autograph, and marriage albums, easels, etc. These goods are of his own importation and publication, and are unsurpassed by any rival concern in the city. Mr. Miller has very extensive and intimate trade connections with the most celebrated publishing and manufacturing houses in this line of trade in Munich, Vienna, and Paris, from which he is constantly receiving the latest novelties. All goods handled by him are of the very best quality, and unsurpassed for elegance, finish, and uniform superiority, while the prices quoted are extremely moderate. His trade is of a wholesale character and extends throughout the United States and Canada.

C. W. BARCOM, Printer, No. 188 Federal Street.—Among the most reliable and popular printers in this quarter of the city may be mentioned the name of Chas. W. Barcom. He occupies here commodious and neatly appointed quarters, having in service ample electric motive power and a complete outfit of the latest improvements in presses, type, and printing materials. Both the job printing of every description is done here in the most prompt and excellent manner, special attention being given to the commercial work, while all orders receive immediate attention; and the work executed in this establishment is warranted first class in every instance. This thriving business was established about eight years ago by C. W. Symonds, who conducted the same up to February 1, 1892, when he was succeeded by the present proprietor, who has continued it with uniform success and doubled the capacity of the office. Mr. Barcom is a practical and expert printer himself of many years' experience, as well as a man of push and energy, and has a thorough knowledge of the business. He was previously well and favorably known in the business men of Boston, in the firm of Barcom & Crane, doing a printing business on Sudbury Street, from which firm he retired to take possession of his present establishment.

E. S. HUNT & CO., Commission Merchants in Finished Leather, Calf and Sheep Skins, No. 24 High Street.—Established in 1871, as commission merchants in finished leather, calf and sheep skins...

ELLENVILLE TANNING COMPANY, Manufacturers of Fine Wax Calfskins, No. 89 South Street; Works, Ellenville, Ulster County, N. Y.—The Ellenville Tanning Company was incorporated in 1874...

L. W. TYLER, Hand-sewed Shoes and Slippers, Boston Rubber Company's Boots, Shoes, and Arctics, No. 77 Bedford Street.—...

L. STEPHENSON & CO., Balance and Scale Manufacturers, No. 141 Broad Street.—The famous balance and scale manufacturing house of Messrs. L. Stephenson & Co...

J. & O. MURRAY, Curriers, No. 232 Pearl Street.—Among the active, energetic, and flourishing houses in this city engaged in currying and trading in leather...

S. B. DEARBORN & CO., Engravers and Printers; Wedding Cards, Invitations and Announcements, Visiting-cards, etc., No. 14 Bromfield Street.—...

C. H. DUNBAR & CO., Shoe Manufacturers' Goods, No. 73 High Street.—One of the largest and leading establishments in the United States devoted to dealing in shoe manufacturers' goods and findings, is that of which Messrs. C. H. Dunbam & Co. are the esteemed and enterprising proprietors. The business was founded in 1849 by Mr. C. H. Dunbam, who is a native of Connecticut and long actively identified with the commercial interests of Boston. From the start, Mr. Dunbam made quality the first consideration, and has always been noted for the exceptional quality of the goods he carried. The reputation of any brand of boots and shoes, rests so largely on the thread and other materials that no firm can afford to use an inferior findings, and it is on the basis of superior excellence that Messrs. Dunbam & Co. have built up and retained their large trade. Their warehouse and salesroom are centrally located at No. 73 High Street, where they carry a heavy and comprehensive stock, being the largest dealers in machine thread in Boston; they are agents for Hadley Bros.'s cotton shoe-threads; and also deal in linen thread; linings, white and colored drilling for gents's and ladies' shoes, canvas shoe goods, shoe-tops, etc. They also make a specialty of buttons, hooks, buckles, eye-eyelets, laces, braids, galloons, boot and shoe webs, etc. Mr. Dunbam offers substantial inducements of the most important character.

E. H. & F. A. KEITH, Importers and Manufacturers of India Tanned Sheep Skins, No. 98 High Street.—Messrs. E. H. & F. A. Keith, the widely and favorably known importers and manufacturers of India tanned sheep skins established their business here in 1878; which has had a rapid and permanent growth based upon the superior merits of their stock. The partners are brothers, natives of New Hampshire, and have been actively identified with the wholesale leather trade of Boston for the past thirty years. They are direct importers of sheepskins from the East Indies, and possess unusually excellent facilities for finishing these here in the most approved and perfect manner, their factory work being done at Peabody and Lynn. They carry an immense stock in their five warehouses, comprising two spacious floors 190 feet in depth. They here carry all grades of the choicest India tanned sheepskins, specially adapted to the needs and requirements of manufacturers of women's and misses' medium shoes. The demand is one of the most permanent staple character.

REINSTEIN BROS., Importers and Jobbers of Tailors' Trimmings, No. 65 Summer Street.—The house of Messrs. Reinstein Bros., the well-known importers and jobbers of tailors' trimmings, at No. 65 Summer Street, was founded in 1882, and has enjoyed a continuously successful and prosperous career, without change of ownership. The premises occupied for trade purposes are spacious in size, clearly located in the business heart of the city, and provided with all necessary conveniences for the handling of goods. The firm's importations embrace the productions of the leading manufacturers of England, France, and Germany, in cloths, cassimeres, vestings, trimmings and general tailors' supplies, and include all the latest patterns and freshest novelties in every line. The trade of the house reaches all portions of the New England States, and is annually increasing. Customers have the assurance that all their interests are closely guarded and intelligently promoted, and that all their orders will be promptly filled. The establishment is one of the most substantial, reliable, and responsible in the city, and its success has been achieved by the exercise of honest, honorable, and legitimate business methods. The members of the firm, Messrs. S. S and M. S Reinstein, are natives of Boston, of high repute and standing in business, financial, and trade circles.

BURRELL & DENNETT, Manufacturers of Square and Upright Piano Cases, Billiard Tables, and Cabinet Work in General, etc., Nos. 66 to 68 Harrison Avenue.—During the past twenty-two years the productions of the firm whose name heads this sketch have maintained an unbroken hold on favor, especially among piano manufacturers, owing to the superior excellence of the same. They manufacture square and upright piano cases, billiard tables, and cabinet articles in general, of a very superior character, the work turned out by these gentlemen being All in every feature of merit, in beauty of design, construction, exquisite carving, and superb fin-

ish; and their trade, which is of a most substantial character, grows apace with years. This flourishing enterprise was established in 1867, under the firm name of Burrell and Dennett. They occupy an factory premises at Nos. 66 to 68 Harrison Avenue, the whole of three floors, 40x60 feet in dimensions each, and have in service ample and complete facilities, including all the latest improved machinery devices and tools, while upward of fifty skilled hands are employed. Besides the manufacture of piano cases, billiard tables, piano trusses, and cabinets, the firm also are prepared to execute hand sawing and variety moulding of every description in the most expeditious and excellent manner, while the wood-turning and carving are done likewise in the highest style of the art at short notice, all orders receiving prompt attention, and satisfaction guaranteed in every instance. Messrs. R. O. Burrell and C H. Dennett, who comprise the firm, are gentlemen in the prime of life, and both are of thoroughly practical skill and experience, with a complete knowledge of every feature and detail of their business.

WHITALL, TATUM & CO., Manufacturers of Druggists', Chemists' and Perfumers' Glassware. Manufacturers and Jobbers of Druggists' Sundries, Nos. 41 and 48 Broad Street.—Foremost among the establishments devoted to the manufacture and sale of druggists', chemists', and perfumers' glassware in this country stands that of Messrs. Whitall, Tatum & Co., whose factories are located at Millville, N. J., with offices and salesrooms at New York, Philadelphia, and Boston. The head-quarters of the firm in this city are at Nos. 41 and 48 Broad Street, and were established in 1894 for the accommodation of the New England trade. The manager here is Mr. Joseph Amies, who has been connected with the house for many years, and is thoroughly conversant with all the needs and requirements of the trade. An immense and influential business is transacted with consumers of glassware, and also with dealers and jobbers in glassware and druggists' sundries, orders being filled direct from the works and also being made by sample. A complete sample stock is displayed at the salesrooms in this city, and patrons throughout New England are supplied at short notice. Samples are sent upon application, and liberal discounts made to the trade. They also have large and constantly increasing facilities for cutting and engraving their glassware. They have long made a specialty of stoppered ware, which they recommend with confidence as thoroughly reliable for corrosive and volatile fluids, or for packing with liquid contents. Founded in 1806, and pre-eminent in its special line of manufacture, the great house of Whitall. Tatum & Co. is in a position to name inducements to the trade in both goods and prices that cannot be duplicated elsewhere.

O. A. WIGGIN & CO., Fine Tailoring, No. 64 Washington Street, Room No. 4.—In the complexities of city life, the business of merchant-tailoring may be regarded as one of the greatest importance to the community; it is furnishing three evidences of refinement and taste that are represented in fashionable and well-fitting garments. As one of the houses in this line of business which is foremost in promoting the standard of elegance in dress, that of Messrs. O. A. Wiggin & Co., No. 64 Washington Street, room 4, has obtained an enviable reputation. Mr. O. A. Wiggin has had vast experience in the trade, and is a practical cutter and tailor of exceptional ability. For ten years he was in business at Lowell, Mass., and, in February, 1887, removed to Boston and opened his present retail business, which is neatly fitted up, and well arranged for the purpose to which it is devoted. Here is displayed a valuable and varied line of the finest European woolens and suitings, embracing the latest patterns in the market, and many colors of special designs not to be found elsewhere, as well as the standard goods generally sought after by those who are more conservative in the character of their dress. The long experience of Mr. Wiggin, coupled with an extensive knowledge of what constitutes symmetry and elegance of design in wearing apparel, has given him a proficiency attained by but few of his competitors; and the truth of this is exemplified in the high character which the garments of this house have obtained. The custom of the house is derived from the élite of the city and its vicinity, and is annually increasing in consequence of the unsurpassed quality, excellence, and workmanship of its productions. Mr. Wiggin is a native of Great Falls, N. H., and justly merits the success attained by his ability, energy, and perseverance.

BUFF & BERGER, Manufacturers of Surveying, Engineering, and Astronomical Instruments, No. 9 Province Court.—Boston is to be congratulated upon having permanently located in her midst a capable firm of scientific instrument makers, viz., Messrs. Buff & Berger. They manufacture and keep in stock full lines of their improved surveying, engineering, and astronomical instruments, which rank with the best produced abroad, and quoted at prices which cannot be duplicated elsewhere. Mr. G. L. Buff and Mr. C. L. Berger are natives of Germany, where early in life they thoroughly learned the trade in which they have become so prominent. Both were subsequently employed for several years in the finest shops in London, England; later on Mr. Buff was for a period of five years and a half engaged in the business in New York City, and Mr. Berger in Boston. Theirs is one of the largest and best equipped establishments of the kind in America, and is three stories in height, and 40 feet in dimensions. They have equipped their shops with the latest improved machinery and appliances, and have introduced many special machines and tools of their own improved invention, which secure greater accuracy and perfection of instruments. Their list of instruments is the most comprehensive of any manufacturer's in America, and all the leading civil-engineers, land-surveyors, city engineers, astronomers, etc., invariably prefer Messrs. Buff & Berger's instruments for difficult work and to secure the most correct results. They employ from eighteen to twenty instrument-makers of skill and experience. Messrs. Buff and Berger are remarkably enterprising, and have prepared and published at large cost an immense illustrated catalogue and manual of their improved engineer's field instruments. Limits of space prevent our referring to this book in detail, but we would earnestly recommend every seaside and profession reader to send for it, and then examine descriptions of the latest and most improved instruments. Messrs. Buff & Berger do a business extending all over the United States and Canada.

P. B. HOWARD, Commission Merchant, No. 60 Kingston Street.—Mr. P. B. Howard has throughout his long and honorable career become recognized as a leading authority on the foreign trade in high grade woolens and cloth trimmings, etc. The extensive business now conducted by him was in 1889 a representative of N. Noonan & Co., of New York, which house represented a trade of great magnitude. He has his offices and salesroom at No. 60 Summer Street, where he carries the finest line of samples in Boston—including, as is done, all the latest importations in novelties of shades, patterns, and textures. He is the direct representative of the famous English cloth manufacturers, Messrs. Briggs, Enta & Co. These goods are standards with leading retailers and high-class clothiers. In connection with these cloths, Mr. Howard is also the commission representative of Messrs. N. Erlanger & Co.'s fine tailor's trimmings. They are of the same high grade of excellence as the cloths and makings, and a fitting accompaniment. Mr. Howard does a very heavy and desirable local trade all over New England and westward. He is a native of Boston, ever a permanent resident, and is highly regarded by the community.

STAXTON & ANDERSON, Leaf Tobacco and Cigars, No. 41 India Street.—The firm-name of Staxton & Anderson is justly honored and esteemed in New England as that of leading exponents of the great wholesale trade in leaf tobacco and cigars. The business was originally established in 1887, by Messrs. Bosworth & Anderson, who were succeeded by the present firm on January 1, 1899. The business carried on includes the importation and sale of leaf tobacco, and the manufacture of cigars, a specialty being made of the production of special brands to order. In the latter department fifty skilled cigar-makers are employed, and a fine grade of goods only are manufactured. Sales are made principally to the wholesale grocery and jobbing trade, and under able and enterprising management, and in view of the rare inducements offered in liberal terms and prices, the trade created here is enlarging at a rapid pace. Dealers in this city and elsewhere will find it profitable to carry a full stock of the tobaccos and cigars offered by this house, as the goods command the patronage of the best classes of consumers. The individual members of this responsible firm are Messrs. H. C. Staxton and H. J. Anderson. Mr. Staxton is a native of Malden, Mass., and a practical cigar manufacturer of large and valuable experience. Mr. Anderson was born in Charlestown, Mass., and was raised in Cuba, where he became a tobacco planter and broker.

W. R. STORMS & CO., Manufacturers of Fine Shirts to Order, No. 384 Washington Street.—There is probably no article of male attire to which more attention is paid in these days than the shirt; and it may be added, in few garments, if indeed any, is it more difficult to render satisfaction to the wearer. To attain the desiderata in shirts and combine the elements of comfort, neatness, and durability at a minimum of cost calls for the exercise of a degree of skill and experience scarcely dreamed of by those not directly interested. And in connection with the foregoing remarks, special mention ought here be made of the productions of W. R. Storms & Co., manufacturers of fine shirts to order, No. 384 Washington Street, which are so compared in any feature of merit by any articles of the kind produced in Boston. They are in fact the ne plus ultra in dress shirts, being perfect in fit and of A1 make, finish and fabric, and, as a consequence, have secured an enduring hold on popular favor among the male portion of the community. This flourishing business was established in 1860 by Harlow & Mason, the style subsequently changing to F. W. Mason & Co., which continued up to August 1887, when they were succeeded by the enterprising and popular firm whose name heads this sketch, and who also purchased the patterns of W. F. Nichols and consolidated the business of both houses. The factory is commodious and well-equipped, ample steam power and complete facilities being in service, while a dozen or more expert hands are employed. Five custom shirts are the only goods produced, and the patronage, which extends all over the Union, is of a very substantial and influential character, while the trade grows apace. The firm is composed of Messrs. W. R. Storms, W. R. Hotchkiss, and Abner L. Baker, gentlemen widely and favorably known in business and social circles.

FRANK DUPEE, Wool Broker, No. 105 Summer Street.—An old established and popular house identified with the wool interests of the city is that of Mr. Frank Dupee, whose establishment is located on the corner of Summer and Federal Streets. He brings to bear upon his enterprise a wide range of experience, and is regarded in the trade as an expert and authority on the quality of wools. He was for a long period employed as a salesman before he engaged to business on his own account, and this he did in 1888. His business career has been an exemplary one, and from first to last has enjoyed the confidence of all with whom he has had dealings. He has a fine, well-lighted office, as unobstructed and direct light being furnished on all wool for sale. Mr. Dupee conducts a general brokerage business in foreign and domestic wools, and has a high reputation in the trade. He is a native of Boston.

SAMUEL J. SANGER, Currier, No. 187 Medford Street (Charlestown District).—Mr. Samuel J. Sanger is one of the leading curriers and manufacturers of fine glove and grain leather in the United States. He is a native of Massachusetts, and early in life thoroughly learned the currier's trade in every detail. In 1878 he started in business upon his own account, and has a large three story factory at No. 187 Medford Street, fully equipped with the latest improved machinery and appliances, and where an average force of 25 to 40 hands are employed in the production of the finest grades of glove and grain leather, in constantly growing demand throughout the trade. Quality is Mr. Sanger's first consideration, and the high finish of his leather is a strong recommendation for its use by leading manufacturers. Mr. Sanger exercises personal supervision over the processes of manufacture, ever maintaining the highest standard of excellence for his product.

THOS. KELLOUGH, Shipwright and Caulker, No. 43 Border Street, East Boston.—Mr. Thos. Kellough, shipwright and caulker, and fitter-up of steamers for cattle and grain, established this business ten years ago, and has since secured a liberal and permanent patronage from many of our leading merchants and shipowners. He promptly attends to all kinds of repairing and caulking of vessels, but makes a specialty of fitting steamers for cattle or grain, putting in stalls, shifting-boards, bulkheads, etc. Mr. Kellough does a large amount of work for the Allan line and other European steamers, giving entire satisfaction to owners, while his prices in all cases are extremely moderate. His business requires the services of 40 carpenters and shipwrights. Mr. Kellough was born in Nova Scotia, but has lived in Boston since boyhood.

THOMAS E. MOSELEY & CO., Dealers in Boots and Shoes, No. 469 Washington Street.—In no branch of trade is sounder judgment, wider experience, and greater care required than in that devoted to fine boots and shoes. It is also apparent that nowhere in the world so greatly as in Boston—the very heart and centre of the American boot and shoe interests—is the public educated up to such a high and critical standard; thus it reflects great credit on such a leading representative house as that of Messrs. Thomas E. Moseley & Co. to control a trade of such character and magnitude as it does. This business was founded by Mr. Moseley in 1847, and has permanently remained on Washington or Summer Streets, for the past forty-two years occupying the present desirable premises, No. 469 first in .... In 1884, Mr. George A. Merrill came into copartnership, and in 1880 Mr. Charles H. Spencer was likewise admitted. The house is the strongest, as it is the most ably managed, of any making a specialty of fine goods. The display made is magnificent; the store is most elaborately fitted up, and carries the most comprehensive stock of fine goods in town. There are in every way the equal of custom-made shoes, being manufactured from the choicest stock, cut by experts in the latest styles, made by careful, experienced workmen, and finished in the most perfect manner. Having full lines of widths and sizes always in stock, Messrs. Moseley & Co. are prepared to fit every body, guaranteeing elegant, durable, and comfortable boots and shoes at moderate prices. The first families in Boston and suburbs are regular patrons here, while the firm sell to numerous customers at far distant points, who, once gratified and getting a stylish, easy shoe, become permanent patrons. Quality is the firm's first consideration, it handles only the product of a few responsible manufacturers, who never lower quality but ever seek to raise it. It is true economy to wear the best grades of boots and shoes, and to make sure of doing so, go to Messrs. Moseley's, where a good fit and comfort at moderate price awaits you. Mr. Moseley is a popular and respected merchant, and so are his copartners; the policy of the house is equitable and honorable, and Boston has in it its leading representative in the retail boot and shoe trade.

J. J. ARAKELYAN, Printer, Nos. 164 and 180 Pearl Street, Boston.—Mr. J. J. Arakelyan, is a native of Armenia, and came to the United States twenty-two years ago, acquired a thorough knowledge of the English language, also a sound experience in the printing industry, and in 1883 he launched into the venture which has since met with such material prosperity under his management. The premises occupied for his purposes comprise a neatly furnished office on the first floor of the building mentioned, while the basement, which has an area of 440 square feet, is fitted up in the most approved manner as a press room, being equipped with first-class printing presses, operated by steam-power, and employment is afforded a force of experienced pressmen and assistants. A leading specialty is made of the press work of books and newspapers, work of this character being executed to order at the shortest notice and in the most workmanlike manner, while the charges will compare most favorably with those of other establishments. An extensive order executed for the great dry goods house of Jordan & Marsh by Mr. Arakelyan was a large illustrated catalogue, the number printed being 100,000. In regard to the manner this work was done Messrs. Jordan & Marsh wrote, "You printed our Fall and Winter catalogue in a very satisfactory manner. The quality as well as promptness of the work was better than we ever had before." Mr. Arakelyan also is a publisher of religious works, among the books that have appeared from his press being "The Romance of Missions in the Land of Ararat," by Maria A. West, missionary of the American Board in Turkey, and a number of other equally interesting and valuable works.

CHARLES R. JUDKINS, Insurance and Real Estate Agent, No. 388 Broadway, South Boston.—Few, if any, engaged in the placing of risks and the handling of realty in South Boston are more widely or honorably known than Charles R. Judkins, the popular and responsible insurance and real estate agent. Mr. Judkins, who is a native of the state of Maine, has long been a respected resident of this vicinity, and sustains an excellent reputation in the community. He has been identified with the insurance and real estate interests hereabouts for many years, and prior to embarking in business on his own account in 1874 had been a clerk in the same

line for quite some time. Mr. Judkins, who occupies a handsome office at No. 389 Broadway, and is assisted by two competent clerks, conducts a general insurance and real-estate business, placing all classes of desirable risks with first-class fire, life, marine, and accident companies; buying, selling, and exchanging city and suburban property, while money is loaned on mortgages, either in small or large amounts. Rents are collected, and estates judiciously managed likewise, while advances are made for the building of houses, the office hours being from 6 A.M. to 8 P.M. (and on Wednesday and Saturday evenings until 9 o'clock); and, altogether, Mr. Judkins does an excellent business, numbering among his extensive clientele many of South Boston's solid citizens.

J. W. WILDES & CO., Furniture, Upholstery Goods and Draperies, Nos. 84 and 86 Bromfield Street.—This business was established as far back as 1825, by Messrs. Lawton & Livingston, who in 1861 were succeeded by Messrs. Humphrey, and Livingston. In 1868 this firm was re-organized, and became Humphrey, Trott & Currier which in 1878 was changed to J. Humphrey & Co. In 1880, on the death of Mr. Humphrey, the management of the business devolved upon Mr. J. W. Wildes, who had been a partner in the business from 1873, and the title of the house was then changed to its present one of J. W. Wildes & Co. Mr. Humphrey's widow has an interest in the enterprise. Mr. Wildes is a thoroughly practical cabinet-maker and upholsterer, fully conversant with every detail of this important and artistic industry and the requirements of customers. The premises occupied comprise a capacious four story building and basement, the whole covering an area of 30,800 feet. The manufacturing department is in the upper part of the building, and is fully supplied with every facility and appliance necessary for the successful prosecution of the business, employment being given in the various departments to twenty skilled operatives. Much of the wood-work is turned and fashioned outside the premises, the finishing and upholstering being attended to principally here. The salesrooms are very elegant and attractive in their fittings and appointments, and here is displayed constantly an extensive assortment of all kinds of parlor, dining-room, chamber, hall and kitchen furniture and upholstery goods and draperies, which are unrivalled for quality of materials, style, finish, and workmanship, while the prices quoted in all cases are extremely moderate. The finest grained woods, and the richest fabrics in all shades are used, and the business is both extensive and influential. Mr. Wildes is a native of this city.

S. W. FULLER, Lumber Dealer, No. 387 Main Street (Charlestown District).—The importance of the wholesale lumber trade in Charlestown is forcibly demonstrated by a review of the leading establishments prominently located here. Representative among the number is that of which Mr. S. W. Fuller is the esteemed and enterprising proprietor. Mr. Fuller was born in Charlestown, and early in life became identified with the important branch of trade in which he is achieving such success. In 1865 he established in business upon his own account, and early developed a large and growing trade. He has a conveniently located wharf and yard at No. 387 Main Street, covering 16,000 feet in dimensions, and where he carries a heavy stock of choice seasoned spruce and pine. He is prepared to promptly fill the largest orders for the best grades of lumber for builders, architects, contractors, and manufacturers, and has developed influential connections, numbering among his customers many of the leading builders of Boston and vicinity. Mr. Fuller brings to bear every qualification for carrying on this branch of trade upon the most reliable basis.

GEORGE HARRINGTON, Wool Dealer, No. 136 Federal Street.—Mr. George Harrington has been established as a dealer in wool for the past fifteen years, and in that time has built up extensive connections with the manufacturers throughout New England and the state of New York, and is among the most prominent dealers and always in a position to fill orders for imported or American wool of fine or medium grades, and name the very lowest market quotations for any quantity that may be desired. As a practical expert judge of the various grades of wool, Mr. Harrington is popularly known in commercial circles, and is straightforward and prompt in his dealings, and controls a large first-class business. He was born in Alabama, and at the present time resides in Winchester.

STOCKTON MINERAL SPRING COMPANY, Stockton, Waldo Co., Me. Office, No. 81 Commercial Street.—The Stockton Mineral Spring Company was incorporated in 1878 under the laws of the state of Maine, for the purpose of supplying the public with the mineral-spring water which bubbles forth, at the rate of 850 gallons per day, from a well in the town of Stockton, Me. The Company has a capital stock of $400,000, and is officered as follows, viz.: President, E. H. Denslow, of New York; Treasurer, C. P. Lovell, of Boston; Directors—E. H. Denslow, New York; C. P. Lovell, Boston; E. F. Staples, Stockton, Me.; I. P. Pace, Stockton, Me.; Alexander Staples, Stockton, Me.; P. P. Nichols, Searsport, Me.; Ed. Pope, Boston. The Stockton Mineral spring water is becoming widely known and highly prized as a positive cure for Bright's disease of the kidneys, calculi or stone in the bladder, disease of the urinary passages, catarrh of the bladder, stricture, inflammation of the bladder, kidney complaints, chronic gout, rheumatic gout, rheumatism, dyspepsia, faintness, nausea, sickness of the stomach, nervous complaints, and blood diseases of all kinds. The action of the water thoroughly cleanses the system, is a very mild cathartic, but powerful in its action on the kidneys, removing all impurities. Being also a tonic, it maintains the strength of the patient, imparting renewed vigor and energy. All other liquids should be avoided while drinking the Stockton Mineral-spring water. The keeping properties of this water are such that it will remain sound for a long period of years, and its refreshing power is unaided by no other water in the world. As a table beverage, too, this water is unequalled. The company are doing a flourishing business as manufacturers of aerated waters, ginger ale, and tonics of which the Stockton water is the base, and their products are in extensive and rapidly increasing demand in this city and throughout the New England States, by hotels, restaurants, druggists, saloons, and sample rooms. Orders are filled at the shortest possible notice, and prices are placed at an universally fair and equitable figure.

E. W. TYLER, Agent for Grand, Square, and Upright Pianofortes, No. 178 Tremont Street.—Those in quest of a piano that will prove to be what it is represented would do well to consult as agent who has had experience in testing and handling different makers' instruments. Such a one is Mr. E. W. Tyler, one of the best known and most popular of the dealers in pianos in the city. He has been identified with the trade for the last fifteen years. In 1879, he took the agency of the celebrated piano manufactured by Wm. Knabe & Co., Baltimore, which, through his hands, have had extensive sale in this section of the country. Later, he accepted the agency for the famous pianos (New York), established 1799, and the oldest piano house in the United States, an instrument of superior quality of tone, beauty of construction, and durability in service. Until 1881, Mr. Tyler was located on Washington Street, and in that year removed to his present location, where he has a very commodious warerooms, extending back 100 feet and fronting on Boston Common, well stocked with these well known instruments, which are guaranteed to be precisely as represented. These pianos are sold at favorable rates for cash, or on the instalment plan at easy terms, or let out on hire. The house is in all respects a leading one in point of extent of stock, trade, and influential character of patronage. Mr. Tyler is a native of the Old Bay State.

ADAMS & ILSLEY, Manufacturers of Fine Harness, Saddlery, and Horse-clothing, Solid Sole-leather Trunks, Valises, and Bags, No. 150 Tremont Street.—One of the oldest and leading houses engaged in this trade is that of Messrs Adams & Ilsley, who are extensive manufacturers of fine harness, saddlery, and horse-clothing, solid sole-leather trunks, valises, and bags; and their goods are standard the country over. The business was founded in 1848 by Messrs J. B Baker & Co., who were succeeded in 1877 by Messrs. Hankes & Adams, and in 1880 the present firm was organized. The premises occupied for manufacturing and sales purposes are spacious and commodious, and every modern facility is at hand for insuring rapid and perfect production, and the prompt and satisfactory fulfilment of all orders. The output is one of great magnitude and value, and the goods possess a high reputation for utility, reliability, and excellence. The ample resources and fine facilities of the firm enable them to offer inducements to the trade, as regards liberality of terms and prices, which add materially to the popularity of the house. The copartners, Messrs Frank Adams and Daniel P.

Ilsley, are well-known Boston men, long identified with the best interests of the city.

F. A. HOLBROOK & CO., Manufacturers of Wood Mantels and Interior Finish, No. 41 Beverly Street.—This firm established their business here March 1, 1883, and quickly won a high reputation and a large and growing trade, owing to the superior excellence of their products and the enterprise and reliability of their business management. They occupy spacious and well-equipped premises, finely fitted up with new and improved machinery operated by steam-power, and steady employment is furnished to a large force of skilled and expert workmen. The productions in wood mantels and interior finish embrace both fine and medium grades of goods, and the specialties of the house bear such a character for beauty of design, practical utility, and artistic workmanship as to command universal admiration and general patronage. Private and public buildings are supplied with these superior articles of interior decoration, in a manner that reflects the utmost credit upon the skill, taste, and judgment of the management. Prices are placed at the lowest point of moderation. Mr. Holbrook is a native of the state of Maine, a resident of Boston since 1878, and eminently popular.

G. W. BARTLEY & SON, Riggers, Loft, etc., No. 22 Sumner Street, East Boston (Near North Ferry).—To conduct successfully any branch of business for the long period of thirty-five years is a fact which bears recognition in a work devoted to a description of the mercantile and industrial occupations in Boston and its surroundings. Such is the history of the establishment of Messrs G. W. Bartley & Son, the well-known experienced riggers, of No. 12 Sumner Street, near North Ferry, East Boston. This business was founded in 1852 by the senior member of the firm, Mr. G. W. Bartley, who is a native of New York City. In 1874, he admitted his son, Mr. A. B. Bartley, who was born in East Boston, into partnership. Since then the style of the firm has been that of G. W. Bartley & Son. The firm occupy the second floor of the building, and this has an area of 50x100 feet. It is well equipped with every appliance requisite for the prosecution of the business. The firm employ on an average about eight hands, and from fifteen to twenty persons in busy seasons. They attend promptly in order to the rigging of ships, the hoisting and moving of machinery, etc., and are very reasonable in their charges. They have a fine local patronage; and all interests committed to the care of this representative and responsible house will be faithfully guarded and protected.

A LVAH A. SMITH, Railroad and Municipal Bonds, No. 80 State Street, Room No. 77, Traveller Building.—Among those engaged in the purchase and sale of railroad and municipal bonds in the city, few are more widely or more honorably known than the gentleman whose name heads this sketch. Mr. Smith, who is a man in the prime of life, active and energetic, was born in New Hampshire, but has resided in Boston for many years. He is a gentleman of thorough experience as a stock broker, as well as of sagacity and integrity, and maintains an excellent reputation in financial circles. Mr. Smith has been engaged in business since 1870, and has from the first has enjoyed a very gratifying patronage, having now acquired a large, active, and permanent clientage. He buys and sells railroad and municipal bonds of every description, on commission; and all business intrusted to this gentleman is certain to be transacted in the most judicious and satisfactory manner to those interested.

T. M. BEAL & CO., Manufacturer of Tables, No. 14 Beverly Street.—Mr. Beal established this business about fifteen years ago. He was born in Dickson, Mass., and early in life thoroughly learned the furniture-manufacturing trade in all its details, and he has made his fame of plain and fancy tables the leaders in the market. The best houses in the trade handle his products, being only the choicest, seasoned materials, and employing none but skilful, experienced hands. He has excellent factory facilities, the machinery being run by steam power. Mr. Beal devotes close personal supervision to all the processes of manufacture; and his first consideration is quality, while he offers substantial inducements as to prices. His trade extends throughout New England and New York State; and if ladies in New England homes knew the care that was taken in the manufacture of the tables, they would never buy any but the Beal centre tables.

HAWKINS MACHINE CO., Manufacturers and Dealers in Boot and Shoe Machinery, Steam-engines, Boilers, and Elevators, Shafting, Hangers, and Pulleys, No. 110 Lincoln Street, Factory, East Cambridge.—The great demand for boot and shoe machinery of all kinds places the manufacture of such supplies in the very front rank of our national industries. A constant effort is being made to produce something which will do the greatest amount of work in a given space of time, and make durability with compactness and easy management. As manufacturers of and dealers in improved high-class machinery in this line, the Hawkins Machine Co., of No. 110 Lincoln Street in this city, long ago achieved a position in this community, and a celebrity throughout the United States, which is the travel test of the merit of its productions. The business was originally established in 1861 by Mr. L. D. Hawkins, and in 1880 the present Co. was formed by Messrs J. R. Hawkins, George C. Clay, and N. M. Seelye as proprietors. The factory of the Co. is located at East Cambridge, and is thoroughly equipped with new and improved machinery, operated by steam-power, while steady employment is given to twenty skilled and expert hands. The house possesses all the facilities for building boot and shoe machinery, and also manufactures steam-engines, boilers, and elevators [of which they make a specialty], shafting, hangers, and pulleys, and attends to repairing and machine work generally. The specialties of the house are rarely equalled and never excelled in this or any other market, for material, workmanship, and economy of operation; while they are furnished to customers at prices which are safe from successful competition. In its honest policy the Co. has an enviable reputation for promptness, reliability, and liberality; and it is with pleasure that we commend it to our readers using machinery, as worthy of every trust and confidence. Mr. Hawkins has personal management of the office in this city, and is a well-known Bostonian. Messrs. Clay and Seelye have charge of the Co.'s works at East Cambridge, are both native of Massachusetts, thoroughly practical, expert, and never picked as manufacturers, and reliable and responsible as business men.

A. & E. LANE, Tanners of Buff and Split Leather, No. 80 South Street.—Among the representative exponents of the leather industry in Boston, are the firm of Messrs. A. & E. Lane, the well-known tanners of buff and split leather, whose tannery is located in Albion, Oswego County, N. Y., with salesrooms at No. 80 South Street, in this city. This house was originally established, in 1869, by Messrs. Lane, Pierce & Co., who were succeeded by the present firm in July, 1882. The tannery at Albion consists of an extensive plant, in which provision has been made of all the machinery, appliances, and devices that can be advantageously employed, and employment is given to one hundred skilled hands. The salesrooms, in this city, are spacious in size, and are constantly filled with the choicest products known to the trade in the special lines of buff and split leather. The products of this firm are widely preferred by manufacturers for their thorough reliability and uniform excellence, being universally esteemed for utility and fine finish wherever introduced. The best possible facilities are possessed for the prompt and perfect fulfilment of all orders, of whatever magnitude, and the house will be found a desirable one with which to form business relations. Its goods go to all parts of the country, and its trade is annually increasing. The Messrs. Lane are Massachusetts men by birth and training, and of high, social and business standing in this city. Mr. A. Lane has been prominently identified with the leather trade for the past twenty-five years. Mr. E. Lane was major of the Forty-third Mass. Infantry during the war, and was subsequently in business in New Orleans for a period of fifteen years.

GOWING, SAWYER & CO., Commission Merchants, No. 78 Bedford Street.—This house has been in successful operation for a period of fifty years, the present firm succeeding to the control in 1888. A branch house is conducted in New York City, at No. 60 Leonard Street. The members of the firm, Messrs. H. A. Gowing, D. M. Sawyer, and C. N. Blake, are gentlemen of large experience in the trade. They handle scores cloths of every description suited for the manufacture of men's goods, and have obtained a large and influential patronage from jobbers, clothing manufacturers and retailers, throughout the United States. The goods handled comprise the best grades of hosiery, shirts, and drawers, cassimeres, suitings, vestings,

and overcoatings from American looms, which are received direct from the most famous mills, and which commend their own merits to the confidence and patronage of critical and discriminating buyers. As commission merchants in woolens, this firm commands every favorable opportunity of the market for the procurement of supplies, and to offer inducements to the trade in reliability of goods and liberality of terms and prices which challenge comparison. Mr. Gowing, the senior partner, is in charge of the interests of the firm in this city, and is a Massachusetts man by birth and training, and well known in this city as an enterprising and progressive merchant. Messrs Sawyer and Blake reside in New York.

CREESEY & NOYER, Grain and Feed, No. 107 State Street.—Among the influential and prominent houses in this city engaged in handling grain and feed on commission at wholesale, is that of Messrs. Creesey & Noyes. This house was founded, twenty years ago, by Messrs Aldrich & Creasey, who were succeeded by the present firm in October, 1888. This firm carry a stock of western grain and feed in elevators, and always have cars in transit to the principal points in New England. They receive as large an amount of grain on consignment as any house in this city, having intimate and influential connections with shippers in the best producing sections of the country. Liberal advances are made on consignments of grain and feed, while quick sales and prompt returns have ever been a leading feature with this house. The firm number among their customers many leading merchants, millers and exporters. By industry and sound business principles, they have won a name in the commercial world, and are recognized as authority in grain shipping circles. The individual members of the firm are Messrs. J. R. Creesey and F. A. Noyes. Mr. Creasey was born in Rowley, Mass., while Mr. Noyes is a native of Auburn, Me.

NATH'L R. LEMAN, Manufacturer of Organ and Piano Leather, One Morro Leather, Linings, Findings, etc., No. 70 High Street.—For forty-odd years and more the productions of Nath'l R. Leman, manufacturer of organ and piano leather, fine morro leather, linings, bindings, etc., have been in steady and growing demand in the trade. The goods produced by this gentleman are of a very superior quality, being noted for their durability, finish, and general merit, and are unsurpassed by anything of the kind today upon the market. Mr. Leman, who is a man of ideas nearly thirty-five, active and energetic, was born in this State, and has lived in Boston many years. He has been established in business in this city since 1845, and is widely and favorably known in the trade. The premises occupied [an office and factory] are commodious and well equipped, all necessary facilities being in service, while an efficient force of help is employed, the skins being tanned outside, and the finishing done here. A large and first-class stock is kept constantly on hand, and all orders are promptly and reliably attended to, while the business, which extends all over the United States, is quite substantial.

J. MORRISON, New England Agent for Glass manufacturers, No. 85 Franklin Street. Mr. J. Morrison has been in business in this city the past three years, and is carrying on an extensive operation as New England agent for a number of prominent glassware manufacturers. A native of New Hampshire, Mr. Morrison has been following his present line of business for the past thirty years, a good portion of the time being passed as a glassware agent in New York City. He has therefore had mature experience in his vocation. The concerns now represented by him are the North Wheeling Glass Company, of Wheeling, W. Va., manufacturers of flint-glass bottles; the Belaire Goblet Company, Belaire, Ohio; Columbia Glass Company, of Findlay, Ohio; and the Brilliant Glass Company, of Brilliant, Ohio, manufacturers of tableware and lamp goods. He is also agent for Beatty Bros. Belaire Company, manufacturers of lamp chimneys, and the Fredonia grey Glass Company, of Cowiston, Ky. A full sample line of the superior goods manufactured by these houses is carried, from which orders may be made, and shipments are made without delay in any section of the New England States. The terms on which orders are filled are sufficiently reasonable to attract the attention of the trade; and the amount of business received is steadily becoming augmented to greater proportions.

UNION BUTTON SEWING MACHINE COMPANY, Office and Manufactory, No. 164 High Street.—One of the most important labor-saving inventions of the age is the machine made by this company for sewing all kinds of buttons with eyes to any fabric. The company was duly incorporated in 1881 with a paid-up capital of $35,000 to acquire the patents included in this remarkably useful machine, and to engage in its manufacture and keep upon the most extensive scale. The company's officers are: President, Waldo F. Ward; treasurer, K. H. Murdock, and managing director, L. C. Wing. They are representative capitalists and business men, and under their able and honorable guidance the company has been uniformly prosperous. The office and factory are centrally located at No. 164 High Street, and where a full stock of these machines is kept for lease. They are especially adapted to clothing of all kinds, overalls, jumpers, knit goods, ladies' and children's underwear, gossamers, and every variety of rubber work. There are numerous, substantial reasons why manufacturers of the above lines of goods should fully test the utility and superiority of this excellent machine. It is fully warranted against any defect in material, workmanship, or performance; it is as easy to run as the ordinary sewing machine, and the operator cannot slight the work as it must put in the number of stitches for which it is set, all the way from two to forty-eight. It does the work of from three to six hand sewers, according to the expertness of the operator, and sews the buttons on much more strongly than by hand, each thread being fastened by the lock stitch. It is already largely in use all over the United States, and agents are located in all the principal cities of the Union. Messrs. Ward and Murdock have long been prominent in the dry goods commission trade. Mr. Wing is a popular and able business man, who has thoroughly organized the business of the company.

RICHARDSON, ROWE & LOVEJOY, Manufacturers of Ladies' Muslin (Cotton) Underwear, Wrappers, Aprons, etc., No. 48 Chauncy Street.—The manufacture of ladies' underwear, wrappers, aprons, etc., is carried on extensively by the firm of Richardson, Rowe & Lovejoy, whose establishment is one of the largest and most important in the business in the city. The foundation of the enterprise dates from January, 1878, when it was established by Richardson & Co., who conducted it until 1879, when the present firm was formed, and from that time the business has been prosecuted vigorously, and the facilities enlarged and the trade extended throughout the United States and portions of Canada. The premises utilized for manufacturing purposes are very spacious and commodious, and consist of four floors in a large building 80x100 feet in area, and two floors of the same dimension in the building adjoining, which are complete and perfect in every detail and provided with the necessary machines for executing the best class of work. From 200 to 275 operatives are kept constantly employed, besides a number of clerks and packers and shippers. The goods are in all the new styles, fashionable and desirable, and command the attention of the trade, and every attention is given to making and finishing the goods in the very best manner. Mr. Henry Richardson, Mr. Henry F. Rowe, and Mr. Herbert M. Lovejoy are all natives of the state, and are well known in commercial circles upon which their enterprise and remarkable success has conferred many advantages.

WM. HEXDEN, Printer, No. 61 Hawley Street.—This business was inaugurated originally by Messrs. Morse & Norden, in March, 1876, and was conducted very successfully under that firm title until the 1st of February, 1882, when Mr. Morse retired from it. The present proprietor, Mr. Norden, is a native of New York, but has been a highly respected resident of this city since 1870. He has devoted a number of years to acquiring a thorough knowledge and practical experience in the various branches of the art of printing, and brings a wide range of experience into the business, and since his assuming the sole proprietorship of his concern, a success was won from the start, while the patronage is steadily increasing to industrial proportions. The commodious premises, which were moved into in October, 1886, and used for the purposes of the business, are fitted up in an appropriate manner, and fully equipped in the most complete style, with all mechanical appliances requisite, including seven fine modern printing presses, cutting machines, plate and all the latest styles of modern types, borders, embellishments, furniture, etc., and employment is furnished constantly to

a full force of competent and proficient compositors and pressmen. The machinery and presses are operated by ample steam-power, and the range of work executed includes letter, note, bill, and statement of account headings, envelope and postal-card work, business and visiting cards, wedding, party, ball, reception and other invitations, programmes, circulars, society work, hotel and restaurant bills of fare, placards and announcement posters, festival and picnic work, catalogues, price lists, political campaign work, labels, shipping tags.—in fact, every kind of work pertaining to commercial job printing. Engraving work receives most careful and special attention; while his prices at all times are extremely reasonable.

N. E. FITZ & CO., Coal and Wood, Lime, Sand, and Cement; Office and Wharf, No. 545 Main Street, Charlestown.—No firm in this business in the Bunker Hill District maintains a better reputation for excellent stock or reliability, as few, if any enjoy, a larger measure of popular favor and confidence, than that of N. E. Fitz & Co., patrons being assured of getting a first-class article and full weight as well as prompt service in every instance here. The business was established in the year 1864, by Fitz & Todd, who conducted the same up to 1878, when Mr. Fitz assumed sole control, and, under the style that lends this sketch, has since continued it alone, with uninterrupted success. The yard or wharf is capacious and well equipped, every facility necessary thereto being at hand, and a heavy, first-class stock is constantly carried, including best qualities of anthracite, bituminous, and coastal coal, all thoroughly screened; fire and kindling wood of every description, in cord, sawed, and split, also lime, cement, and sand. An efficient force of help is regularly employed,—from three to fifteen, according to season,—while several teams are in steady service supplying customers, and the trade of the firm, which extends throughout Charlestown and Somerville, is at once large and active.

C. H. HOLM, French and American Paper-hangings, etc.; No. 6 Waverley Block, City Square, Charlestown.—Mr. C. H. Holm is an extensive dealer in French and American paper hangings, window shades, curtain fixtures, etc., and carries, at his establishment, one of the largest stocks of these goods to be found in the Charlestown District. Mr. Holm is one of the most experienced men in this line of industry in this section. He was born sixty-five years ago in Copenhagen, Denmark, and for forty years has resided in America. He has, from the time he founded his present enterprise, been noted for his discriminating selection of the most perfect types of material and pattern that human skill and taste have been able to devise in decorative materials. His stock of paper-hangings represent all grades from the plainest to the most artistic and costly, and abundant choice is afforded to patrons, who will also find here a splendid display of window shades, curtain fixtures, and kindred goods of the finest quality, and at prices which cannot be readily duplicated elsewhere. The store is 80x50 feet in dimensions, and is handsomely fitted up and conveniently arranged. Paper hanging is the special feature of the business; and all work undertaken is executed in the highest style of the art. Ten skilled and experienced workmen are employed. Estimates are furnished when desired.

H. KRIKORIAN, Manufacturer of Oriental and French Confectionery, No. 49 Thayer Street.—One of the most popular and successful manufacturers of confectionery in Boston is Mr. H. Krikorian. This gentleman established his business here in 1882, and has since built up an extensive and steadily increasing patronage with first-class retailers in this city and through out the surrounding country. He occupies spacious and commodious premises, and gives constant employment to thirty skilled and experienced hands. He gives particular attention to the production of Oriental and French confectionery, and makes a leading specialty of fig-paste, gum-drops, chocolates, creams, and French mixed candies. Purity is the main essential with these goods; and the advantage of dealing with a house whose reputation is so high for making none but the purest and best goods is at once manifest to all dealers who cater to a strictly first-class trade. As a result, the leading retailers depend upon this house for many kinds of their supplies. Orders of any size are filled at the shortest notice and prices are invariably placed at the lowest point of moderation. Mr. Krikorian is a native of Turkey, and well known for his business ability and personal worth.

A. B. CROCKER & CO., Fittings of Every Description, No. 147 Kingston Street.—Experienced business men do not need to be told that it is always one of the most encouraging "signs of the times" to see a great many prominent business houses moving into new premises, for the reason that in nearly all cases such removals are due to expanding trade, having made more room and better facilities absolutely necessary, and it is quite certain that never before in the history of this city were there so many notable removals in a corresponding period of time as there have been thus far during 1889. Among influential houses now to be found in new premises may be mentioned A. B. Crocker & Co., the

well-known manufacturers and commission dealers in feltings, heretofore located at Nos. 35 and 37 Avon Street, but who have removed to the new Kingston building recently erected by the Boston Real Estate & Trust Company, corner of Kingston and Essex streets, where they will occupy the entire first floor and basement of this spacious building. This building has a frontage on Kingston, Essex and Edinborough streets, giving a floor area of 5000 feet. Thus the rooms are lighted from three sides by large plate-glass windows extending from floor to ceiling, making it one of the best lighted show rooms in the city. For many years Crocker & Co. have been engaged in the handling of feltings, and have made for themselves the reputation of handling the productions of the best mills in the country, and as reliable as any to be found in the American market, and to-day they are recognized as leaders in the felting trade in this country. They are the selling agents of the City Mills Company and the Worcester Felting Company. They carry a large stock at all times for all purposes, and at their new location have unusually good facilities for displaying their goods, and can quote the lowest prices for even the finest and best goods. There is no doubt but their removal will greatly add to their already large business. The individual members of the firm are Mr. A. B. Crocker and Mr. Fred. I. Pratt, both of whom are well and favorably known. Both gentlemen are members of the Home Market Club. The New York office is at Nos. 92 and 94 Worth Street.

EASTERN MANUFACTURING AND ADVERTISING COMPANY, Owning and Controlling Advertising Mediums, No. 400 Atlantic Avenue.—In this age of progress the public more than ever before appreciates novelty, originality and fresh innovations in every branch of effort. Notably so in that of the advertiser, who seeks the utmost publicity at the least cost. The newspapers' charges are exorbitant. There are, however, numerous other channels for reaching the public, at nominal cost, yet permanent, sure and popular. The best of these methods are controlled by the Eastern Manufacturing and Advertising Company. The company was duly incorporated in 1888 with a paid up capital of $100,000, and owns the patents of and manufactures a number of absolutely perfect devices for the purpose of universal, permanent advertising. One of the attractions is a rotating, clear cutting and clear lighting machine which has in its front a large space for the display of advertisements. Every time the cutter is used a fresh advertisement turns to the public. It is the most popular advertising novelty of the day, and is eagerly demand in cigar stores and mercantile houses generally. The company puts it to free to the storekeeper and gets a revenue from the charge for advertising, which is very reasonable. It is a well-known fact that the wise and tobacco trade are among the most extensive advertisers. It is said that one firm alone in 1887 expended $100,000 in advertising. This firm have always led the van. The agent of this firm informs us that his house put out one device in the shape of a steel engraving that cost with frame complete upwards of thirty dollars each, and that they could not place much more than one-half the supply they had contracted for, owing to the fact that all the available space was occupied by the large number of elaborate designs in the drug and tobacco stores. There came to be such competition in this line of advertising that it has practically destroyed the effect, not only as regards satisfactory results, but from the amount of money expended to keep up with the competing houses in the same line of trade they do not give comparatively any adequate return for the money expended. The medium offered by this company furnishes a device which is essential to every place where cigars are kept on sale, from the fact that it is the best cigar cutter at any cost there is in the market, as it includes all the different styles of cutting in one machine and also furnishes the most elaborate design, which far exceeds anything ever designed for similar use. Its elaborateness and utility make it the very best advertising medium and its necessity and usefulness make it both permanent and desirable. Unlike all other methods it furnishes to the advertiser absolute means of knowing just what he gets for his money. There is no fictitious circulation and every dollar expended can be seen in its equivalent in actual space and operation and the returns for it easily computed. The company furnishes a list of the location of each cutter and figures so that the advertiser by referring to it can always inform himself as to what extent, where he is absolutely sure his advertisement is conspicuous. The company has also produced a most ingenious and amusing finger pull test for testing and comparing the strength of fingers. The machines work automatically. Some of the pulls are of large size. When a penny is dropped in the slot the tester can pull and register his strength, while at the same time as advertisement is displayed, and a metal check is dropped out containing the advertiser's card or other notice, which the customer pockets, and thus insures further reference and publicity. The machines are remarkably ingenious and are being manufactured in large numbers in order to meet the rapidly growing demand. The officers of the company are Mr. W. P. Reed, treasurer, and Mr. F. M. White, general manager. Both are able, enterprising and practical business men. The company controls the rights for operating in New York, Brooklyn, Philadelphia, Baltimore, St. Louis, Chicago, Detroit, Milwaukee, Cleveland, Washington, Boston, and many other important points.

FRED. POPE, Architect, No. 329 Washington Street.—A well-known and successful exponent of this useful and indispensable profession in Boston is Mr. Fred. Pope, whose offices are centrally located at No. 329 Washington Street. Mr. Pope was born in Boston and after having received an excellent scientific education commenced the practice of his profession in this city in 1885. He has built up a liberal and influential patronage, having prepared the designs for and superintended the erection of many of the finest and most elegant public and private edifices, residences, stores, office blocks, etc., not only of Boston but also in many cities and towns of New England. The lately erected Rogers building in Washington Street, its which and in the old Jay building formerly on the same site, Mr. Pope has had his offices for more than twenty years, is without exception one of the finest and most convenient office structures in the city. This was erected by Mr. Pope, whose plans, estimates and specifications are always complete in detail, and are based most on the practical and comprehensive knowledge of quantities and values. Under his careful supervision, expenses for the erection of buildings are kept to the lowest point commensurate with efficiency and stability, while his plans for interior arrangements are happily conceived, utilizing every square foot of space, and affording every accommodation. Personally, Mr. Pope is highly esteemed in the profession, and we know of no one whom we can more cordially recommend.

COBURN & WHITMAN, Manufacturers and Jobbers of Over-
Shirts, Overalls, Cardigan Jackets, Low Priced Pants, Boys'
Knee Pants, Nos. 71 & 73 Summer Street.—In their special
branches of manufacture the firm of Messrs. Coburn & Whit-
man, the oldest established house in the business, has secured an enviable success. They are extensive manufacturers and jobbers of over shirts, overalls, men's, boys', and youth's low priced pants, boys' knee pants, etc., and throughout all the New England States an immense consumption exists for their goods. The business was originally established in 1874, by Messrs. Tileon & Coburn, who were succeeded by the present firm in 1891. The premises occupied for manufacturing and sales purposes comprise a five-story building, 24.40 feet in dimensions, with basement, while much of the work is done outside, and steady employment is given to some three hundred skilled hands. In every minor detail the utmost vigilance and care are taken to secure superiority in the product, and as a result the goods are eagerly sought after by buyers, and where once sold they are sure to lead to a duplication and large increase of orders. The proprietors give their close personal supervision to each and every process of production. The firm is composed of Messrs. J. Alvin Coburn and Joseph E. Whitman, both of whom have been identified with this trade as salesmen and principals, and have a foundation understanding of all the details and requirements of the business. They are both active, energetic, and enterprising in all their business methods, and eminently popular.

H. A. PHINNEY, Commission Merchant and Dealer in Leather, etc., Nos. 220 and 222 Purchase St.—Established in November, 1867, the house of Mr. H. A. Phinney, has become deservedly popular with the leather trade of this state as a leading headquarters for scrap leather of every description, rough splits, skirting, roundings, and all kinds of sole, heel, and stiffening stock. The proprietor was formerly connected with the house of Henry R. Read & Co., three years as clerk and four years as partner, and brings to bear the widest range of practical experience, coupled with perfected facilities and influential connections, enabling him to conduct the business under the most favorable auspices, and by reason of which he is in a position to grant every advantage known to the trade to his patrons. He has speedily achieved a high reputation for the uniform reliability of all goods handled, while as a commission merchant he offers the most substantial inducements to both buyer and seller. His business premises comprise an entire four-story building, 25x60 feet in dimensions, with basement, while the demands upon the resources of the house are such that an immense and valuable stock is necessarily carried at all times. The trade of the house extends to all parts of Massachusetts, and is constantly increasing. Mr. Phinney is a native of Maine, a resident of Arlington, Mass., and has lived in business in this city for the past twelve years, where he is known and honored as a keen business man and a reliable and successful exponent of his special branch of commerce.

JOHNSON & SMITH, Nahant Fish Market, No. 48 Bromfield Street.—The business of supplying fresh fish to the people of Boston and other places throughout the state has long constituted one of the principal industries of this city, and the oldest and best-known exponent of the trade is the house known as the Nahant Fish Market, and so long and so successfully conducted by Messrs. Johnson & Smith. The business was founded in 1867, by Mr. Geo L. Johnson, who retired in 1868, and was succeeded by his brother in 1869. Mr. J. O. B. Smith came into the business in 1873, and thus formed the firm of Johnson & Smith. In October, 1888, Mr. Johnson retired, and Mr. Smith has since continued the business as sole proprietor under the same firm name. He has been identified with the fish industry since his boyhood, having been in the business with Mr. Geo. Johnson the founder of the house, for some years, and is widely known as an authority upon all matters pertaining thereto, and as the originator of the idea of supplying fish "fresh from the water" to patrons in Springfield, and other cities and towns in the state taken from the water in the morning and placed on the customer's supper table the same evening. His patronage in this special branch is probably the largest and most influential of any one in the business here. He deals in every description of ocean, lake, and river fish, as well as oysters, clams, and lobsters. The principal varieties of fish dealt in are salmon, cod, halibut, mackerel, trout, blue fish, white fish, haddock and pickled fish, green turtle and terrapin. The present

market has been occupied since 1869, and is a deservedly popular source of supply. Mr. Smith was born in Dover, N. H. has been in Boston since 1845, and has grown with the growth and prospered with its prosperity, gaining the confidence of the public and a prominence in his business of which he has every reason to be proud

WM. MATTHEWS, JR., Wholesale and Retail Dealer in Paper Hangings, Stock Selling off at Lowest Wholesale Prices, No. 16a Milk Street, Opposite Kenox Building.—The house of Wm. Matthews, Jr., is a recognized headquarters for paper hangings and the leader in low prices. The business was founded twenty-five years ago, by Mr. Wm. Matthews, who was succeeded at his death in 1885 by his son, the present proprietor. The salesrooms are spacious in size, intelligently and attractively arranged, and afford ample accommodations for the large and growing trade of the house. The paper hangings here handled are brought from the most noted manufactories of Europe and America, and the display is of the richest and most elegant character. All the most exquisite designs and patterns and the freshest and most popular novelties are shown in the greatest variety and abundance. Mr. Matthews has the advantage of ample capital, and has effected arrangements with producers for the purchase of supplies that justify him in offering very superior inducements to customers. Buyers sending their orders to this house can rely upon the promptest response and the lowest wholesale rates. The trade is brisk and lively, at both retail and wholesale, and extends to all parts of New England. Mr. Matthews is a native Bostonian, trained in this line of business from his youth up.

W. A. GREENOUGH & CO., Compilers and Publishers of Directories and Maps, No. 88 Otisv Street.—A leading house engaged in the publication of directories in New England is that of Messrs. W. A. Greenough & Co. The business of this concern was inaugurated in 1860 by Mr. W. A. Greenough and was conducted by him under the present firm style until 1882, when his death occurred, and he was succeeded by Messrs. Elmer Littlefield and James E. Huntress, who are continuing the enterprise under the old firm name. The directories that are regularly published by the firm are the following: Augusta, Hallowell and Gardiner; Bangor and Brewer; Bath, Brunswick and Richmond; Biddeford, Saco and Old Orchard; Boston Business Directory; Boston Street and Avenue; Brockton and Bridgewater; Brookline; Cambridge City; Concord; Haverhill and Bradford; Lewiston and Auburn; Malden, Melrose, Medford and Everett; Marlborough and Hudson; Massachusetts Business Directory; Merrimack River; Milford, Hopedale, Natick, Framingham, and Holliston; Nashua City; New Bedford City; Portland; Portsmouth City; Rockland, Belfast and Camden; Somerville; Waltham and Watertown; United States Iron, Hardware, and Metal Trades Directory; Woburn; Marlboro; and the American Railway Manual and Supply Directory. The prices of these are from $1.20 to $3.00 respectively, and are sent to any address on receipt of price. Price-lists are sent free on application. At the office of the firm, it may here be stated, directories of all the principal cities of the United States are kept on hand for reference. The printing department is at No. 29 Purchase Street, where a force of skilled hands are kept constantly employed. Messrs. Littlefield and Huntress are both natives of Massachusetts, and the former resides at Topsfield, the latter at Newton.

H. A. LAMB, Dry Goods Commission Merchant, No. 88 Chauncy Street.—A gentleman contributing materially to the sum of activity in this line in the city is H. A. Lamb, the well known and responsible dry-goods commission merchant, whose business connections extend throughout the New England States. The transactions along through the territory of the commission house in Boston annually represent an almost fabulous sum in cash figures, while the volume of trade grows steadily apace and is of a very substantial character. Mr. Lamb, who is a Bostonian by birth, well and favorably known in the mercantile circles of the city, is a gentleman of entire probity in his dealings, as well as a man of enterprise, energy, and excellent business qualities. He is the New England agent for Wm. Wood & Co., Wm. Ayres & Sons, R. D. Wood & Sons, W. J. Dickey & Sons, and other manufacturers; while his trade, which is large and active, affords evidence of constant and gratifying increase

T. PARKER STORY, Provisions, Poultry, Game, etc., No. 31 Central Square.—The grocery and provision store of Mr. T. Parker Story was founded in 1867, and at once bounded into popularity. The store has a frontage of 19 feet and a depth of 50 feet. In its style of fittings and fixtures it is elegant and attractive, is clean and orderly, and is well arranged. The establishment is a general family supply store, and, as such, has attained its widespread popularity. The stock is an extensive and comprehensive one, and embraces the finest teas and coffees, staple and fancy groceries of every description, canned goods, jellies, sauces, pickles, table delicacies of all kinds, flour, butter, cheese, fresh eggs, and a full line of grocers' sundries; also choice cuts of beef, mutton, lamb, veal, and pork; together with sausages, smoked hams, and provisions of every kind; poultry, game, vegetables, and fruits in season, etc. Polite and courteous assistants attend to the wants of customers, and orders are delivered by wagon at residence of patrons. Mr. Story has, from the beginning, sought to supply his customers with the best class of goods in the market, and at prices that no other house could excel and do an honest, legitimate business. In this he has succeeded. He devotes his entire attention to his business, is courteous and obliging to all who have dealings with him, and neither he nor his assistants spare any efforts to satisfy and please his patrons. Mr. Story is a native of Essex, and resident of East Boston for ten years.

I. JACOBS & Co., Manufacturers of Fine Havana Cigars, Park Square.—This business has only been established about a year, but by assiduous attention to the demands of the trade, and producing a line of goods first class in every respect, a large business has been built up. The firm manufacture a number of special brands of fine Havana cigars, and employ a staff of experienced hands, and can always guarantee the goods to be of a uniform quality. In addition to handling the fine goods of their own manufacture, the firm also do a large business in imported and domestic cigars, and also in smoking and chewing tobaccos, pipes, cigarettes, etc. The store and workshop on Park Square, opposite the Providence depot, is quite commodious, and is well stocked with a valuable line of goods. Mr. I. Jacobs, upon whom devolves the general management of the business, is a practical cigarmaker, a native of Boston, and a young man of push, vim, and enterprise. He has succeeded in establishing a large wholesale, retail, and box trade.

WILLIAM BRADFORD, Merchant Tailor, No. 611 Washington Street.—Among the skilful and popular exponents of the merchant-tailoring trade doing business in this city will be found Mr. William Bradford. Mr. Bradford is a native of New York but has resided in Boston for upwards of 20 years. He early served his apprenticeship and became an expert tailor, and subsequently was employed as cutter for some of the prominent city establishments. In 1881 he embarked for himself in the business, and by superior work and a generally active, able, and popular management has secured a large and highly desirable trade. The several premises, which have been occupied since 1870, consist of one attractive salesroom 80x40 feet in dimensions, containing a full line of imperial and domestic suitings, vestings, trouserings, overcoatings, etc., carefully selected from the newest novelties and most desirable patterns. The cutting is done by Mr. Bradford who also gives his personal supervision to all branches of the work. The garments turned out have a standard reputation in the trade, for superior artistic and mechanical excellence, and among his many and influential patrons, Mr. Bradford is regarded as one of the oldest city tailors.

WILLIAMS & MAGNUS, Riggers, No. 80 Sumner Street, East Boston.—In consideration of the great maritime interests centering in East Boston, and the vast transportation business that is done by water, the business conducted by Messrs. Williams & Magnus, the well-known riggers, is one of great and growing importance to the community. The business is so successfully conducted by them was originally established some fifty years ago, by Messrs. Miller & Starr, who were succeeded in 1878 by Messrs. Miller & Williams and in 1881 the present firm was organized. They occupy large and well-equipped premises, eligibly located between the ferries, and over H. Pigeon & Son's spar shop, and give employment to a force of skilled and expert hands, varying in number from ten to twenty-five. Machinery is handled with care, jobbing

of all kinds is promptly attended to and satisfaction guaranteed in all transactions. All work done by this firm is noted for its absolute accuracy, thorough durability, and excellence of finish; and orders by telephone No. 26-4, receive immediate attention. No house in this line stands better in shipping circles or is more fully prepared to render efficient and satisfactory service. The members of the firm are Messrs. D. F. Williams and Andrew Magnus. Mr. Williams is a native of East Boston, while Mr. Magnus was born in Germany and has resided here since 1870. Both are able and experienced riggers.

WADE'S DETECTIVE AGENCY, No. 17 Dunne Street.—Established in 1875 the above concern has succeeded in making a reputation for unveiling the closest mysteries, and foiling the most desperate and accomplished of criminals. Captain J. P. Wade has had vast practical experience in this line. He was born in Chautauqua County, New York State, and for four and a half years took an active part in the war of the Rebellion. He is a gentleman of middle age, and Boston has been his home since boyhood. He occupies a neatly appointed office in room 13, No. 17 Dunne Street, and takes the leading position in the local private detective agencies. He undertakes investigations relating to all kinds of crime, and also works up evidence in civil cases, such as disputed wills, railroad accidents, suits in connection with corporations, and any description of legitimate secret inquiries. He is assisted by a crew of skilful subordinates, all of whom are experienced, determined, and intelligent. Particular attention is given to the most intricate cases, and the fullest satisfaction given. Capt. Wade is in direct communication with competent detectives in all the cities of the United States, Canada, London, and Paris. No charge is made for consultation, and special contracts are made when desired. In concluding this brief sketch, we desire to recommend to business men this enterprising detective, and advise them that in cases of embezzlement, fraud, etc., their cheapest and wisest course is at once to seek an interview with him. It will be found to be the best and quickest means of arriving at results satisfactory to all concerned.

E. F. HUFF, Merchant Tailor, No. 6 Winter Street, corner Washington Street.—A prominent merchant tailor of the metropolis, who has enjoyed a successful career of twenty years, and caters to the better classes in the community, is Mr. E. F. Huff, who since 1866 has occupied his present eligibly located quarters, where he carries a large and comprehensive stock of imported cloths, cassimeres, and vestings, of new design and excellent quality, and which are manufactured into perfect-fitting and durable garments by expert workmen. The show-room and custom work department are ample and commodious in dimensions, and are not only well supplied with every needed convenience but possess all an approved facilities for displaying the stock to the best possible advantage. Mr. Huff gives his close attention to all work done by his tailors and permits none but the most satisfactory garments to leave his establishment. He is a native of Maine but has lived in Boston since 1845, and has had a life long experience in the merchant tailoring business.

S. P. FRENCH, Bananas, Lemons, Bonds, Spices, Roundings, and Hard Stock, Nos. 23½ Purchase and 25 High streets.—This house has been in successful operation under its present able management since 1879, and has gained a national reputation, and developed a trade that overleaps the limits of our own country, extending into Great Britain and other foreign countries. The store, fronting on two of the principal streets in the shoe and leather district of the city, is desirably situated for trade purposes; is spacious in size, measuring 80x100 feet. The demands upon the resources of the house are such that a very large and complete stock is incessantly carried to the end that no delay may be experienced in the filling of orders, while the proprietor commands every favorable opportunity of the market for the procurement of supplies in vast quantities and at the most advantageous rates, and is therefore prepared to fill all orders with the utmost dispatch and to place all transactions on a thoroughly substantial and satisfactory footing. The business is exclusively wholesale. Mr. French is a native and popular citizen of "The Hub," and is closely identified with its leading branch of commerce.

BOSTON LEATHER AND RUBBER REPAIR SHOP, No. 61 Elm Street.—This somewhat unique and thriving enterprise was started about fourteen years ago by the present proprietor, and from its inception has proved a positive and permanent success. From the first business has steadily improved, until now the patronage is quite extensive and gives evidence of continual increase. The work executed is of a very superior character, being not in fact surpassed, if indeed equalled, by anything in this line turned out in Boston, while the prices prevailing are exceedingly low, all things considered. Rubber boots and overshoes of all kinds are repaired in the most superior manner at short notice and rubber soles are applied to leather boots in the very best style of the art; the latter being a leading specialty. Boots and shoes of every description are made to measure also in first-class style, at bottom prices, none but expert hands being employed; while soling, heeling, etc., are promptly and reliably attended to likewise, all work being fully warranted, and the trade of the establishment extends throughout the city, suburbs, and the principal portion of the New England States. Mr. Drew, who is a native of New Hampshire, is in Boston since 1873, is a gentleman of strict integrity in his dealings, as well as of many years' practical experience and skill in his line, and fully merits the success that has attended his efforts.

BARBOUR & STOCKWELL, Improved Machinery for Bread and Cracker Baking, etc., No. 11 Charden Street.—Messrs. Barbour & Stockwell enjoy a national reputation as manufacturers of improved machinery for bread and cracker baking, including Rayney's patent reel ovens, shafting, pulleys, hangers, and other bakers' tools, and whose establishment is located at No. 11 Charden Street, with also a foundry in Cambridge with a capacity of 80 to 90 tons per day. This enterprise was inaugurated so far back as 1868, by Mr. Charles Roberts, and, after several changes, the present firm succeeded to the control in July, 1888. The machinery and technical equipment for the business are the most perfect of any in the country, including ample steam power, and a force of skilled and expert workmen, ranging in number from fifteen to thirty, is constantly employed. The bakers' machinery and tools here produced are unexcelled for ingenious construction, beauty of finish, and wonderful adaptation to the purposes for which they are intended, and are practically unsurpassed by all similar productions wherever introduced, being in steadily increasing demand not only in all parts of this country, but also in South America and other foreign countries. Orders are promptly and carefully filled in all cases, and inducements are offered, as regards both utility and reliability of goods and liberality of terms and prices which challenge comparison and defy successful competition. The members of this enterprising firm are Messrs. W. O. Barbour and F. P. Stockwell. Mr. Barbour was born in Saratoga, N. Y., and is a well-known citizen of Cambridge, while Mr. Stockwell is a native Bostonian and resides in Somerville.

M. H. MERRIAM, Manufacturer of Leather Shoe Binding, Leather and Textile Stays, etc., No. 82 High Street.—Mr. Merriam is a type of New England's self-made men, uniting education in the highest order of mechanical skill, coupled with marked executive capacity and energy of character. In 1857 he began the manufacture of leather shoe bindings, etc., in copartnership with Mr. E. L. Norton. The firm had a long, honorable, and careful career, building up the leading business of their kind, the partners continuing together until Mr. Norton's lamented decease in 1882 since then Mr. Merriam has remained sole proprietor of the concern. His factory is situated at Lexington and is the largest and best equipped of its kind in the United States affording steady employment to upwards of thirty hands in the manufacture of leather shoe bindings of every description, including leather and textile stays, piping, gusseted square and diamond snipped; also artificial leather and remgarded cloth leather, welting and fancy leather goods. This is recognized headquarters for the best qualities of strip or "ribbon" leather goods for all lines of manufacture, and under Mr. Merriam's able management the highest standard of excellence coupled with moderate prices prevail. The importance of this industry is forcibly illustrated by the fact that Mr. Merriam sells to the leading dealers in shoe findings, and boot and shoe manufacturers, of the United States; and also exports largely to England, Germany, Australia, etc. His Boston warehouse is centrally located at No. 82 High Street, whence his shipments are made. Mr. Merriam was born in New Hampshire, and has been a permanent resident of Massachusetts since 1849. He has led an active and useful career, his versatility being manifest in numerous ways. He learned the profession of mechanical engineer in its every detail, and had as partner a Mr. Crosby, under the name and style of "Merriam & Crosby." During the war Mr. Merriam was appointed superintendent of engines and machinery at the Charlestown Navy Yard, ably and faithfully discharging the onerous duties thus devolving upon him.

LEWIS JONES & SON, Undertakers, Nos. 67 and 69 La Grange Street.—This business was founded in 1849 by Mr. Lewis Jones, and in 1879 the present firm was organized by the admission of Mr. Lewis L. Jones to partnership. The building occupied for manufacturing and sales purposes is a four story brick with basement, 25x80 feet in dimensions, the ground-floor being finely fitted up for office and warerooms. The range of manufacture embraces every conceivable description of white-wood and black walnut coffins, rosewood, black walnut, metallic, and covered caskets, as well as everything used in connection with the burial of the dead. The best materials are invariably used, the methods of manufacture are peculiar to the house, and the principles involved in the construction such as are approved by sound judgment and long experience. In every pattern and style made, the variety of which is as wide as the possibilities of the industry will admit, the greatest taste and elegance obtain, the beauty and finish of the work standing unrivalled in the market and distancing competition. The facilities for production are of the most complete and perfect character, including a working force of twenty-two experienced hands, while all the machinery, tools, and devices have been employed that bear upon the character of the goods produced and which serve to insure rapid progress in the industry. A specialty is made of fine covered caskets, and care is exercised to keep the largest variety of the same to be found in the city constantly on hand. The firm also have the largest line of air tight caskets in New England, either cloth-covered, draped, solid bronze, or finished imitation rosewood, which are sold at lowest prices, either at wholesale or retail. The Messrs. Jones are well known and highly esteemed Bostonians, of excellent standing in business and social circles, and justly popular with their host of friends and patrons everywhere.

GRAND VIEW HOTEL, George A. Davis, Proprietor, No. 397 Atlantic Avenue, Corner India Street.—This well and favorably known house was formerly known as the "Atlantic Hotel," and was opened to the public six years ago by the present enterprising and genial proprietor, Mr. George A. Davis. Last winter it was entirely remodelled and renovated throughout, and furnished in the most comfortable and modern style. The premises occupied comprise a fine five-story building, containing sixty-five sleeping apartments parlor, halls, dining-room, etc., and a corps of experienced and polite assistants is employed in attending to the requirements of guests. The house is equipped in every department with all needed and improved facilities, and the table is supplied with the choicest food in the market, which is neatly and abundantly served, while the rates are eminently moderate. Mr. Davis, the experienced host, is active and earnest in his endeavors to make his guests' stay in his house satisfactory, in which his large patronage shows his success, and is very popular with all with whom he comes in contact.

W. D. WARNER, New England Agent for the Underwood Manufacturing Company, Sole Manufacturers of Patent Cotton Leather Belting, Dealers in Cotton Waste, Lace Leather, Belt Hooks and General Mill Supplies, etc., No. 131 Pearl Street.—Mr. Warner is a general manufacturers' agent and dealer in cotton waste, lace leather, belt hooks, and general mill supplies. He, in December, 1877, in partnership with Mr. H. E. Birds eye, and under the firm style of Warner & Birdseye, founded this enterprise, which has been marked by the most gratifying success. In December, 1888, the partnership was dissolved, and Mr. Warner assumed the sole management, for the purpose of which he occupies the first floor and basement of the building, which covers an area of three thousand feet, and here is displayed an extensive assortment of mill supplies of all kinds, the trade in which is of both a wholesale and retail character. Mr. Warner is the New England agent for the Underwood Manufacturing Company, of Tolland, Conn., manufacturers of patent cotton-leather belting, also sole agent for the Dodge "Independence" wood split pulleys, and dealer in cotton waste, lace leather, belt hooks, and mill supplies of every description. The stock is an extensive one, is of careful selection, and has no superior in the city, while the prices ruling are not easily duplicated here. The transactions of the house are of both a wholesale and retail character, and a brisk and large trade is done throughout the whole of the New England States. Five salesmen are employed, and prompt attention is given to the filling of all orders. Mr. Warner has also a branch office at No. 49 Exchange Place, Providence, R. I., in which city he resides. He is a native of Connecticut, and a merchant of strict probity, as well as push, enterprise, and ample experience.

J. S. BEERS, Auctioneer and Commission Merchant in Boots and Shoes, No. 149 Summer Street.—This gentleman has been established in business here since 1873, and commands the confidence and respect of all who have here brought into trade relations with him. His excellent standing with the trade in different parts of the country is best shown by the list of well known houses whose interests he represents in this market, viz : A. S. Richards & Co., auctioneers and commission merchants boots and shoes, Nos. 59 and 61 Reade Street, New York; Grotjan, Mitchell & Co., auctioneers, No. 17 Sharp Street, Baltimore, Md.; S. H. Penland & Co., auctioneers, Galveston, Tex. Consignments of boots and shoes are respectfully solicited, promptly acknowledged, and carefully handled, with profit to the shipper in all cases. Mr. Beers' extensive acquaintance with manufacturers and buyers makes his house eminently worthy of the attention of both, bring a bright, wide awake concern, always ready for business; while promptness, despatch, and fidelity to the best interests of patrons is the motto upon which the management is conducted. Mr. Beers is a native of Lynn, Mass., a well known resident of Charlestown District, energetic, industrious, and thoroughly enterprising.

WILSON G. HAMMOND, Wholesale Dealer in Southern Eastern, and Western Lumber, No. 11 Central Street.—One of the most successful and best known among the younger lumber merchants of Boston is Wilson G. Hammond, wholesale dealer in southern, eastern, and western lumber. Mr. Hammond, who is a native of the State of Maine, has been identified with the lumber interests in this city for quite some time, and resides at Quincy. He is a young man of energy, enterprise, and thorough experience in the trade, and sustains an excellent reputation. Mr. Hammond has been established in business on his own account close on six years, and has built up a very substantial and gratifying connection, his trade, which extends throughout New England, being very active. He handles southern, eastern, and eastern lumber of all kinds, and does a general commission and wholesale business in hard and soft lumber, door frames and kindred building supplies; shipping direct from the mills to dealers and large consumers. Sales are exclusively by cargo and carload lots, the total annual transactions reaching quite a handsome figure.

THE LACING STUD COMPANY, Manufacturers of Lacing Studs and Hooks, No. 55 Lincoln Street; W. C. Bray, Secretary and Treasurer.—This successful company was duly incorporated in 1879 with ample capital, and since its organization has secured a liberal and permanent patronage in all sections of the United States and Canada. The company's factory, which is admirably equipped with specially constructed machinery, is situated at Wollaston, Mass. The business is under the management of Mr. Mellen Bray, who brings great practical skill and experience to bear, coupled with an intimate knowledge of every detail of this unique and growing industry, and the requirements of patrons. The company's lacing studs and hooks and machines for applying are unrivalled for utility, durability, efficiency, and excellence, and have no superiors in this or any other market, while the prices quoted for all goods are extremely reasonable. The premises occupied in Boston comprise three commodious floors 35x80 feet in area, which are fully stocked with the company's goods and specialties. Mr. Bray, for many years a resident, is highly esteemed by the community for his enterprise, business ability, and just methods, fully meriting the large measure of success achieved by his energy and perseverance.

WM. O. HOWE, Stock Broker, Room 4, No. 18 Congress Street.—Mr. Howe established himself in his present line of business over thirty years ago, and his honorable methods have secured to him throughout his long career a most liberal patronage. Mr. Howe is prepared to buy and sell on commission stock, bonds, grain, provisions, and oil on margin or for cash, making a specialty of dealings in fractional lots. He has a private wire to the New York and Chicago exchanges, and parties desirous to speculate legitimately in these commodities have here every facility at their command, the same as if they were on the floor of the Stock Exchange in person. As all fluctuations in prices are reported here immediately, and the information furnished at once to customers are as soon as the facts are known, every facility is afforded of watching the market and taking advantage of movements and prices, and the firm are always prepared to render to customers every possible advantage. Orders by mail or telegraph receive immediate attention, and prompt response is made to investors desiring information or advice. Market letters and latest information are constantly received from perfectly reliable sources. Mr. Howe was born in Haverhill, Mass., is thoroughly experienced in stock matters.

DWIGHT SMITH, Dealer in all kinds of Wool Waste and Flocks Nos. 169 to 175 Purchase Street.—A house which is carrying on extensive transactions in handling all kinds of wool waste and flocks is that of Mr. Dwight Smith. The foundation of this business was laid some twenty five years ago by the present proprietor, in Athol, Mass., and was carried on there for several years, when a removal was made to Worcester, where the enterprise was prosecuted until five years ago, when Mr. Smith came to Boston. During the quarter of a century that he has been established he has developed extensive business connections, and a permanent, influential trade that extends to all sections of New England. The office and wareroom used for the business are of spacious dimensions, and a large stock is at all times carried to meet the active demand supplied. While Mr. Smith makes no ostentatious claim to any peculiar advantages in the conduct of his affairs, we can safely assure our readers that his facilities and thorough knowledge of all branches entitle him to at least equal consideration from the trade with those who are less modest in this respect. A native of Massachusetts, Mr. Smith resides in Worcester, and enjoys the confidence and respect of a large circle of business and social acquaintances, who esteem him for his business ability and strict personal integrity.

MAREWARD & CO., Upholsterers and Interior Decorators, No. 565 Washington Street.—Established in 1878, this enterprising and popular firm has from its inception steadily increased its hold on public favor and patronage. The work turned out here is of a very superior character, alike as to originality and beauty of design, workmanship, and finish, while the lowest prices consistent therewith also prevail. The business premises occupy two 25x70 foot floors, with ample and excellent facilities, and a number of expert hands are regularly employed. An A1 assortment of upholstered goods and general interior decorations is constantly carried in stock, including superb curtains, window shades, lambrequins, cornices, mirrors, and kindred articles, while upholstery, etc., are made to order likewise, and expertise attended to in the very best style of the art, at reasonable rates. Mr. Charles L. T. Mareward who is the sole supplier, was born in Germany, but has been in this country since 1867. He is a practical and expert upholsterer and decorator himself, of many years' experience.

E**VERETT PIANO COMPANY, Corner Albany and Wareham Streets; William Moore, Treasurer.** — An industry in which Boston holds a leading place is the United States is that devoted to the manufacture of pianos and the production of her manufacturers in this line have become famous the world over by the superiority of the instruments produced by them. Among the many concerns of the kind, none have advanced to the front so rapidly as the Everett Piano Company, whose headquarters are located at the corner of Albany and Wareham Streets. This company was organized in 18—, with ample capital, and such able executive officers at the head of the enterprise. The thorough experience and practical knowledge brought to bear in the management of

affairs soon resulted in bringing the attention of the public to this new claimant to their favor, and leading musicians and the musical world in general were not long in discovering that everything merit marked the pianos turned out by this company. The trade rapidly augmented, and in 18— the firm completed and took possession of the splendid factory which they have since occupied. This is one of the finest equipped piano factories in the world. The premises consist of a six-story brick building 7x——— feet in dimensions, appointed throughout with the latest and most approved machinery and mechanical appliances, and steam power is furnished by a one hundred horse-power engine and two large boilers. Employment is afforded to the various departments to one hundred skilled and expert artisans. The handsomely furnished office and salesrooms are located on the first floor, and a large stock is shown here. The company manufacture square and upright pianos in a large variety of styles. Every particle of the work of construction, from kiln drying and sawing of the wood to the final finishing touch, is all executed here, and the most delicate care is exercised to secure a perfect production. The artistic and mechanical properties of the instruments are manifest at once, for the tone is clear, pure, and sympathetic, while the touch is exceptionally easy and elastic. Orders received from anywhere are carefully filled, and instruments are safely packed and shipped without delay.

H**. M. KINPORTS, Watches, Clocks, Diamonds, Jewelry, Silverware, Bags, Carpets, Novelty Furniture, etc., No. 71 Cornhill and No. 16 Brattle Street.** — For excellent value in the line of watches, clocks, jewelry, rugs, carpets, and household specialties, or for low prices and easy terms of purchase, no establishment of the kind in Boston compares with that of R. M. Kinports, No. 71 Cornhill and No. 16 Brattle Street, with branch stores also at North Adams and Springfield, Mass. This flourishing business, which has its headquarters at No 71 Cornhill, was established something over two years ago, and from its inception has been conducted with eminent success, each of the four places proving highly gratifying ventures. Goods are sold either for cash or on easy payments by the week or month, liberal, and honorable terms prevailing in every instance, while the prices quoted are maintained at bed rock figures. A large and first-class assortment is constantly on hand, comprising fine gold and silver watches, French, Swiss, and American clocks, superb diamonds, elegant jewelry, solid silver and plated ware, exquisite designs in oriental rugs, mats and carpets, cabinet articles, novelty furniture, and hundred interior decorations in great variety, a large portion of the goods being sold through one or more of whom an efficient force are in regular service, and, altogether, a very prosperous business is done. Mr Kinports, who is a native of Philadelphia, and a resident of this city eight years, is a man of enterprise probity in his dealings, as well as of energy and enterprise, and fully merits the success that has attended his well directed efforts from the start.

H**. CARMICHAEL, Ph.D., Analytical and Consulting Chemist, Office and Laboratory, No. 7 Broad Street.** — There is no profession carrying with it weightier responsibilities or requiring higher and more comprehensive qualifications than that of the analytical and consulting chemist. A valued acquisition to Boston's representatives in this line was two years ago, when Mr. H. Carmichael, doctor of philosophy, and the well known ex-professor of chemistry in Bowdoin College, settled here and opened his office and laboratory at No. 7 Broad Street. Mr. Carmichael brings to bear special qualifications. A native of Brooklyn, N. Y., he early acquired a thorough collegiate training, graduating at Amherst College in 1867, and subsequently pursuing a full course of study at the famous University of Gottingen, Germany, receiving the degree of Ph.D., and upon his return being appointed professor of chemistry in Iowa College, and a year later was elected professor of chemistry in Bowdoin College and in the Maine medical school. For many years he also held the position of State Assayer of Maine. He has faithfully and ably discharged the important duties devolving upon him, and resigning from Bowdoin to enter the broad field of usefulness offered by the mining and manufacturing world. Dr. Carmichael attends to orders in all branches of his profession; he analyzes and reports upon waters, foods, chemicals, dyestuffs, etc., and also devotes much time to the analysis of the materials they use. He also tests and assays ores of the precious metals, iron, steel, etc., reporting every feature of commercial value and contributing to advanced knowledge of practical enlargement of knowledge in this branch of physics. Dr. Carmichael is an analyst and chemist of international celebrity; his tests are accurate, and his researches exhaustive and his clients can duly rely upon the reports submitted. As an expert and authority in his line he is frequently called upon, and no one is better qualified. His business is large and growing; his connections are most desirable and influential and he is a worthy representative in his line. Dr. Carmichael has given particular attention to the investigation of these ores, and his well known inventions in this field serve as a basis of one of the large industries of the country. It should be added that he is an active member of the Association for the Advancement of Science.

F**RED HARTLEY, Wool Broker and Importer, No. 153 Federal Street.** — The well-known broker and importer of wools, Mr. Fred Hartley of No. 153 Federal Street, enjoys a national reputation for handling foreign and domestic wools of all kinds, making a specialty of worsted wools; placing consignments in best markets, which his large connection and long experience enables him to do with unusual and exceptional advantages, and buying on orders for others in this country and all foreign markets. He established his business in this city in 18—, operating a large business also at Philadelphia, and acts as agent in this country for his brothers, L. Hartley & Co. of Bradford, England; and Walter Hartley, of Marsden, England; both of whom are extensive woolen manufacturers. He imports his foreign wools direct from the best producing sources, having correspondents in all parts of the world, and buys the entire consumption for some of the largest mills in New England. He has established a reputation as a most successful handler of wool, while his high personal character gives purchasers every guarantee that all wool is as represented in quality and graded correctly. His efforts to supply this market with the best worsted wools have given a new impetus to that important branch of the wool trade, and his imports of this grade are indorsed by buyers all over the country. So enterprising and progressive a house must necessarily have an influence in trade circles that is appreciated, and, as a result of his well directed labors, Mr. Hartley is in high repute among wool growers, consigners and buyers for his great dispatch of business, the successful placing of consignments, and honorable, reliable dealing. His importations include mohair and botany wools, and much of his stock is left in bond. A corps of two experienced salesmen is employed. Mr. Hartley was born in England, and came to this country ten years ago. He resides in this city, and has developed a reputation and a patronage in trade circles of which he has every reason to be proud, and one which is now reaping him good returns.

JUSTICE, BATEMAN & CO., Wool Commission Merchants. No. 101 Atlantic Avenue.

HARTFORD & CO., Wholesale and Retail Commission Dealers in Foreign and Domestic Fruits and Produce, No. 214 Concord Avenue and No. 107 Arlington Avenue, Mercantile Market.

EDWARD T. GAY, Fish and Oysters, No. 9 St. Charles Market, Corner Lincoln and Beach Streets.

D. T. ELLS, Boarding and Baking Stable, No. 97 Richmond Street.

M. BAKER, Apothecary, No. 170 Hanover Street, Corner Parmenter.

HASKELL & CO., Wholesale Dealers in Fresh Fish, etc., No. 195 Commerce Street.

J. M. READ, Manufacturer of Read's Patent Regulating Clock Dampers, etc., Nos. 61 and 63 Blackstone Street.

R. SMITH & SON, Wholesale and Retail Beef, Mutton, Lamb, Veal and Poultry, Stall Nos. 19 and 19 Central Market.

L. E. BOW, Outfitter, No. 41 Causeway Street.—The store of L. E. Bow is admirably arranged and handsomely fitted up and contains a well selected assortment of shirts of all kinds, underwear, gloves, hosiery and all the new ideas and designs in neckwear, collars and cuffs, umbrellas, canes and an almost endless variety of sundries belonging to the business. A specialty is made of fine grade custom shirts to order, which are cut upon scientific principles and warranted in every respect. They are made of Wamsutta muslin and No. 220 linen, with hand-made bosoms and linen neckbands and wristbands, initialed and made by experienced operators and sent by express to any address for the low price of six for $9 unlaundered, and will meet a sample shirt free if the goods are not perfectly satisfactory in every reasonable particular. Laundry work is also quickly done, pure spring water only being used for this purpose. Prices are fair and reasonable at this establishment and every attention is given to those who favor it with their patronage. Mr. L. E. Bow, the courteous proprietor, came to this country from Italy upwards of twenty years ago. He is very well known in this community in connection with his barber shop in the Boston and Lowell Depot, and No. 6 City Hall Avenue. He is doing a large business and maintains a high reputation in this community.

T. B. EVANS, Produce Dealer, Nos. 28 and 30 North Street.—One of the old established houses in the produce business is that of Mr. T. B. Evans, who succeeded the well-known firm of Sears & Evans, which was established twenty years ago, and continued till the year 1891. He does an extensive wholesale and retail business in butter, cheese, eggs, poultry, vegetables and farm produce generally, receiving fresh supplies daily from the surrounding country, and being in a position to fill the largest orders on the shortest notice. Mr. Evans carries on hand a large stock of produce at all times. His stall is one of the most attractive in the neighborhood, and the best attention is paid to customers, three clerks being employed in the place, while Mr. Evans pays the closest attention himself to all the details of the business. He is a native of Woburn, Mass., where his home still is, and where his reputation in social circles as in the commercial circles of Boston stands very high.

ZIMRI S. BARNES, Beef, Pork, Lard, Hams, etc., Stall, No. 6 St. Charles Market.—Mr. Zimri S. Barnes has been identified with the provision trade for over thirty years, and has been in business on his own account for a quarter of a century. He is the occupant of the commodious and well equipped No. 6 stall in front of St. Charles Market, on the Beach Street side, and opposite the United States Hotel. Here is to be found at all times the choicest quality of beef, pork, lard, hams, and other meat products, in which Mr. Barnes has a firm, substantial and influential trade in both this city and suburbs. His supplies are drawn from the most reliable sources, and handling none but first-class stock, we know of no house in the city where quality, quantity and prices can be obtained to surpass those of Mr. Barnes. His stall is among the most popular in the market. Mr. Barnes is a native of Stoneham, Mass., and a well-known sportsman. From boyhood, now over fifty years ago, he has been well acquainted with the leading sportsmen of Boston, and his reputation is that of a crack shot and expert angler. He has carried off many prizes at famous pigeon shooting contests. Even now, although upwards of sixty years of age, he frequently, during the shooting season, takes his gun and goes off to some of his old haunts in quest of quail, woodcocks, etc. He is also a noted bird and dog fancier, and has raised and broken some of the best hunting dogs in the state.

CHARLES H. ORDWAY, Wholesale Commission Dealer in Fruits and Produce of All Kinds, Country Produce a Specialty, Nos. 191 and 195 Arlington Avenue, Mercantile Vegetable Market.—Few engaged in the handling of fruits and produce in the Mercantile Vegetable Market are better known or enjoy a more liberal share of popular favor than Charles H. Ordway, wholesale commission dealer. Mr. Ordway, who is a native of New Hampshire and has been a resident of Boston seventeen years, enjoys an excellent reputation in the trade. He established himself in business here in February, 1878, and during eleven years since intervening he has maintained a career of unbroken prosperity. Conducting all his transactions on strict business principles, prompt and thoroughly reliable in his dealings, it is only in the nature of things that this gentleman should have attained success. Mr. Ordway occupies ample and commodious quarters, and carries constantly on hand a heavy and first-class stock of everything in the line of vegetables, fruits, berries and produce of all kinds, country produce being a specialty, while several efficient assistants are in attendance. An exclusive commission business is done, and the trade, which is of a wholesale character principally, is at once large, prosperous and permanent.

SUFFOLK KINDLING WOOD COMPANY, No. 285 East First Street, Near K Street, South Boston.—This is in all respects one of the leading and largest concerns of the kind in Boston, and has been in successful operation upward of a quarter of a century. This flourishing enterprise was established in 1864, and from its inception up to February, 1895, the manufacturing was done here on the premises, but owing to the plant being destroyed by fire at the period mentioned, the company have their wood sawed and split by steam-power, with improved machinery, at Bangor, Me., whence it is shipped by rail to their commodious yards and storehouse in South Boston. An exceedingly large and first-class stock is constantly carried on hand to meet the requirements of the steady and extensive demand, and so efficient force of help is here employed, while eight or more teams are in regular service supplying customers, all orders receiving immediate attention, and the business, which extends all over the city and suburbs, is of a most substantial character, and grows apace annually. Messrs. William H. Harvey and J. Banner Wright, the proprietors, are men of energy and enterprise.

COLTMAN, DUNHAM & CO. Manufacturers of Boots and Shoes, No. 19 High Street.—This firm are widely prominent as manufacturers of medium grades of men's, boys' sewed and standard fine foot wear which are manufactured in calf, and unlined hips, and which have no superiors in the market for fit, comfort, durability or style and which are in large demand by jobbers and dealers throughout the United States. The business was founded by the present firm in 1891 and have since that time developed a good trade throughout the United States, obtained by the uniform good quality of the products as the result of unremitting care and close personal attention on the part of the proprietors the purchase of the best raw material and sparing nothing in expense or labor to improve the quality and enhance the value and desirability of the goods in all essential respects. The spacious salesrooms are filled to repletion with the various specialties of the house and orders are filled of any magnitude with the utmost despatch. At the factories a force of upwards of 350 hands are employed. The firm offer substantial inducements to the trade both in prices and quality of goods which would be difficult to duplicate elsewhere, and we commend the house to our readers and the trade everywhere. Mr. E. S. Coltman is a native of Massachusetts, and Mr. E. F. Dunham of South Carolina.

A. H. HOLWAY, Real Estate and Insurance, No. 570 Washington Street, Boston, and No. 10 Fairmount Block, Everett Square, Hyde Park.—A gentleman who has for the past quarter of a century occupied a prominent position as an operative in the real estate and insurance business, is Mr. A. H. Holway. Mr. Holway has built up a patronage of a very extensive and influential character, numbering among his patrons many leading property owners and capitalists. He has always upon his books the best available bargains in lands, houses, stores, etc. Mr. Holway is also a heavy real estate owner himself, among his acquisitions being the elegant bank building on Everett Square and Fairmount Block in this town. He carries on a general business in buying, selling, building, leasing, exchanging, appraising, and renting property of all kinds, negotiates mortgages at reasonable rates, and insures risks in all reliable and substantial fire insurance companies. Mr. Holway's long experience in the real estate business enables him to meet all requirements in a prompt and satisfactory manner. His judgment may in every case be depended upon as being strictly reliable and sound.

R. A. PERKINS & CO., Wholesale Dealers and Packers of Beef, Pork, Lard, Hams, etc., Barrel Beef for Family Use a Specialty, Stalls No. 5 and 6 Central Market, No. 70 North Street.—The business of supplying beef and pork by whole-sale and retail has long been a prominent feature in the commercial activity of this city, and a leading house devoted to this special line of trade is that of R. A. Perkins & Co., occupying stalls Nos. 5 and 6 Central Market, No. 70 North Street. This firm are extensive whole-sale and retail dealers in beef and pork exclusively, and have been established in business here since January, 1878. The stalls are fitted up with special reference to the requirements of the business, and supplied with cold storage for the perfect preservation of perishable goods in hot weather, enabling the management to supply patrons at all times with the freshest and most reliable supplies at the lowest prices. This firm determined at the outset that everything leaving their hands to be served to customers should be of the very best that was reared and handled. They spare no pains or expense to procure the choicest of meats, and possess facilities for procuring the same not enjoyed by other concerns. Their goods are the best in the market for quality, flavor and excellence, while order and system prevail, and the entire place is a model of neatness, cleanliness and good management. Goods are freely shipped to all parts of Massachusetts and Maine, and the trade is steadily increasing in volume and importance. Mr. Perkins, the active member of the firm, is a native of the state of Maine, a resident of Boston for the past thirteen years, and a young man of high social and business standing, reliable and responsible in all his dealings, and eminently popular with his host of patrons.

W. R. OSWOOD, Mutton, Beef, Lamb, Veal, Wild Game and Poultry, English Cured Bacon, and the Famous Oxford Sausage, Nos. 1 and 8 St. Charles Market, Corner Beach and Lincoln Streets.—Among the enterprising young business men in the St. Charles Market, there are none more popular than Mr. W. R. Osgood, who occupies stalls Nos. 1 and 8 on the Beach Street side. Mr. Osgood has had quite an extended experience in the meat and provision trade, and for some time was with Mr. H. A. Pillsbury, whom he succeeded in August last, and has since con-tinued to do a large wholesale and retail business, which he is prose-cuting vigorously. He is ably assisted by three employees, and fills orders with that promptness their importance demands. Mr. Os-good makes a fine display of choice cuts of fresh beef, veal, lamb, pork, and also poultry and game, and numbers among his customers many of the leading hotels, restaurants and families. He is a na-tive of Maine, and has lived here twelve years, and during his busi-ness career he has always made it his aim to supply his patrons with the very best class of meats, poultry, etc., and the success he enjoys is as well merited as it is deserved. He is very popular in the mar-ket and among his customers, and is active, wide awake, thorough-going and reliable.

JAMES TRYON, Wholesale and Retail Dealer in Pork, Lard, Hams, Dressed Hogs, Tripe, Sausages, Pigs' Feet, etc., Nos. 1, 3 and 5 Lakeman Market, Corner Blackstone and North Streets.—Prominent among the solid and substantial provision merchants doing business in Lakeman Market is James Tryon, wholesale and retail dealer in pork, lard, hams, etc., who occupies stalls Nos. 1, 3 and 5. Now engaged in this line here-abouts is more widely or favorably known, as few, if any at all, enjoy a larger meas-ure of public favor and patronage, his trade, which extends all over the New England states, being of a most substantial character. Mr. Tryon, who is a gentleman of middle age, was born in the state of Maine, but has resided in Boston over twenty-eight years. He is a man of energy and judicious enterprise, thoroughly reliable in all his dealings, and is a popular and well-known member of the Boston Chamber of Commerce. Mr. Tryon occupies three commodious and excellently kept stalls with ample and complete facilities, every con-venience being at hand, while eight or more efficient salesmen are in attendance. A heavy and first-class stock is always kept on hand, including prime, salt, corned and pickled pork, smoked hams, bacon, lard, dressed hogs, tripe, sausages, pigs' feet, tongue, etc. Pork and hams are a specialty, and the trade, already large and active, grows apace annually. This prosperous business was established at the pres-ent location in 1871 by the gentleman whose name heads the sketch, and from its inception has been conducted with eminent success.

CROCKETT BROS. & SANBORN, Commission Merchants, Flour, Grain, Provisions, etc., No. 84 Commerce Street and No. 69 South Market Street.—This business was established in 1867 by Hathaway & Woods, who continued it till 1881, when the present firm succeeded them. The copartners, Messrs. Chas. B. Crockett and J. Walter Sanborn, have had great experience in the grain and provision trade, and are noted in business circles for their energy, promptness and thorough protection of their customers' best interests. They carry on an extensive commission business in flour, grain, provisions, hay and straw, and also export largely to Great Britain, France, Belgium, Holland, etc. They represent thirty famous mills in Illinois, Wisconsin, Minnesota, Ohio, Michigan, Indiana, Dakota and New York, and make a specialty of cargo and car load lots of grain, flour, etc. The firm promptly handles the largest consignments of grain, flour and provisions, advancing when required to any extent upon the same, and at all times giving their patrons the benefits of the most favorable quotations on 'Change. Mr. Crockett was formerly a member of the firm of Crockett Bros., and Mr. Sanborn was for seventeen years connected with Hathaway & Woods. Both gentlemen are members of the Chamber of Com-merce. Mr. Crockett was born in Boston, while Mr. Sanborn is a native of Somerville, near Boston.

A. HAYDEN & CO., Commission Merchants and Dealers in Fruits and Produce, Nos. 5, 6 and 7 Quincy Row (Between South Market and Clinton Streets).—This well and favorably known firm was established in 1878, and from the first has maintained an unbroken record of prosperity. Conducting the house on strict business principles, thoroughly reliable in their deal-ings, and being wished fully conversant with the trade, it is only in the nature of things that they should have attained success. The firm conducts a general wholesale business in fruits, nuts, berries, vegetables and country produce, handling everything in this line in season, and receive consignments fresh daily, making a special feature of prompt returns. They occupy spacious and ample quar-ters, and carry constantly on hand a large and excellent stock, while several efficient salesmen are in attendance, and the trade of the house, which is of very substantial proportions, extends through-out New England, New York State and the British Provinces. Mr. Hayden, who is the sole member, sustains an A1 reputation in com-mercial life.

ISAAC H. DYER, Wholesale Dealer in Mutton, Lamb, Veal, etc. Cellar, No. 8 Clinton Street.—One among the most active of the enterprising business men in this city engaged in the sale of fresh meats is Mr. Isaac H. Dyer, who has been established in the business since 1888, and for the past six years has occupied the basement at No. 8 Clinton Street, which is well equipped for business purposes and provided with a refrigerator of large capacity. He also has a wagon fitted up for the purpose, from which sales are made outside Faneuil Hall Market. Mr. Dyer is a reliable, careful business man, whose long, practical experience in this line of trade and whose business connections are such that he can fill orders to the entire satisfaction of customers, and supply the choicest mutton, lamb and veal at popular prices. He employs three assistants to aid him in his operations, and is doing an extensive wholesale and re-tail trade derived from the city and adjacent sections. He is a na-tive of Watertown in this state, and an old resident of Boston.

S. N. LOCKE, Produce Dealer, No. 108 Clinton Street.—One of the most popular and successful among the younger produce dealers doing business in the mercantile vegetable market is Mr. S. N. Locke. Mr. Locke, who is a native of Winchester, Mass., where he was brought up on his father's farm, is a young man of sterling qualities. After starting in business here he soon established himself in public favor and confidence, owing to his promptness, reliability and straightforward dealing. Mr. Locke occupies commodious quarters, and carries on hand at all times a fine stock, which includes potatoes, onions, apples, vegetables and country produce generally, while a reputable assistant is in attendance also. He handles goods on his own account altogether, receiving stock fresh daily, and does a wholesale business principally, while the trade, which extends throughout the city and suburbs, gives evi-dence of constant and gratifying increase.

AMERICAN DECORATIVE COMPANY, No. 116 Pearl Street.—This Company makes a specialty of embossed wall-papers made from pure wood fibre. They style their product lignomur (meaning a wall of wood), and the manufacture of the same is fully protected by United States patents. The goods are manufactured at Cumberland Mills, Maine, by a patent process; and by the use of their new and improved machinery, made especially for them, a surface is produced on the goods on which the most delicate tints and shades are easily produced, either in oil or water colors, in the greatest variety, such as satin effects, royal Worcester, old ivory and faience, cordova leathers, etc. The company has brought out many very beautiful designs in high relief in perfect imitation of the finest carved work, or the most expensive leathers, the finest and most delicate lines being reproduced, giving a most beautiful and artistic effect. Although the company has only been organized a short time, yet they have sold their goods to the most prominent dealers throughout the country from Boston to San Francisco, and decorators everywhere speak loudly in praise of the goods over all others. *Lignomur* is made in the white for decoration, and in various colors for direct application to walls and ceilings, and although the material is so beautiful and artistic, yet the price for the same is very moderate. The company is supplying a want long felt, and they are meeting with the success which they deserve. The office and warerooms are at No. 116 Pearl Street, Mr. Edward S. Sears being president, and Mr. Elijah Parker, treasurer.

KINGSTON KNITTING MILLS, No. 67 Kingston Street.—There is a growing interest and attention to physical culture now engaging the attention of many of the young and middle-aged men everywhere: in the gymnasium for in-door, and bicycle riding, boating, base-ball, lawn tennis, and other sports for out-door exercise. The dress and material for these athletes, are somewhat peculiar in their fabric and weaving, and especially in the style, elasticity, and fit of the garments required. There is no establishment more deservedly popular and more successful in meeting this need than the Kingston Knitting Company, whose office is at No. 67 Kingston Street. The proprietors, Messrs. J. A. Hatch & Co., are among the first to introduce polo worsted suits in the market, and every one is ready to concede that their knowledge of the wants of clubs and the trade in these goods, with their reputation for honorable dealing, inspires the confidence of every one doing business with them, consequently they are decidedly popular. In addition to almost every style of garment used by athletes and sportsmen, they are manufacturers of the celebrated Niantic worsted bicycle stocking, in light and heavy weights, which has no superior in the market. The varied styles and make-up of their suits for athletes, and their growing interest in their business in getting up the latest novelties, and best goods used we commend to every one interested in this popular exercise, either by correspondence or a visit to the Kingston Knitting Company, No. 67 Kingston Street.

J. G. McCARTER, Manufacturer of Piping, All Colors, Binding and Stay, Imitation Lace Fronts for Boots and Shoes, No. 103 Utica Street.—J. G. McCarter, manufacturer of piping in all colors, binding and stay; also dealer in all kinds of fancy stitch coat looping, which is in all respects, one of the leading and most responsible establishments of the kind in Boston. This flourishing business was established in 1881, and from the first the productions have been steadily growing in demand among shoe manufacturers throughout the whole of the United States. The goods turned out here are of exceptional merit, and for general superiority are unequalled by anything of the kind produced in the country. The factory occupies three commodious floors, and is supplied with ample steam-power and the latest improved machinery, while fifteen to twenty expert hands are employed. A large and first-class stock is always carried on hand, comprising piping in all colors, binding and stay of every description, imitation lace fronts for boots and shoes, fancy stitch coat looping and shoe manufacturers, supplies in great variety; and all orders by mail or otherwise are promptly and reliably attended to. Attention is particularly called to the patent edge welting for boot and shoe uppers, which he has lately placed upon the market, samples and prices of which are sent on application. Mr. McCarter is a native of Boston, and a man of energy, enterprise, and many years' experience.

THOMAS CHRISTIAN & CO., Importers and Jobbers of Laces, Handkerchiefs, Small Wares, and Hosiery, No. 71 to 75 Chauncy Street.—An old-established and noteworthy house is that of Thomas Christian & Co., importers and jobbers of laces, handkerchiefs, hosiery and small wares. It is one of the oldest and leading firms engaged in this particular branch of mercantile activity in Boston. This flourishing business was originally established in 1848, as a retail store, and as such was conducted on Washington Street, until 1860, when the firm moved to Arch Street, and embarked in a wholesale way. Here business continued to improve steadily up to 1872, when it was burned out by the great fire of that year. Subsequently the firm resumed business at Nos. 32 and 34 Chauncy Street, where they remained until November last, when they removed to the present commodious quarters. They occupy here as salesrooms a 50x150 foot floor and basement, handsomely fitted up and well ordered in every department, an exceedingly fine stock being constantly carried, while some twenty or so clerks and salesmen are employed; and the trade of the house, which is very large, extends all over the New England States. Mr. Thomas Christian in 1887 took his son, Mr. Thomas F. Christian, into partnership. The senior member of the business was born in Belfast, Ireland, but has resided in this city forty-five years.

DANIEL PRATT'S SON, Importer and Dealer in Foreign and American Clocks and Clock Materials, No. 53 Hawley Street.—This is the oldest concern in its line in the city or in New England. The business had its beginning at No. 49 Union Street in 1848, where it was founded by the late Mr. Daniel Pratt, who died in 1871, and was succeeded by his son and son-in-law, under the firm style of Daniel Pratt's Sons. This was dissolved in 1880, and Mr. D. F. Pratt continued in the same business. He has since conducted the business with increased success under the style of Daniel Pratt's Son. He has had a life-long experience in the business and there is no better judge of clocks in the country. He has located in his present convenient premises for the past four years and here he controls a very extensive wholesale and retail trade, shipping, as he does, goods to all parts of the country. Mr. Pratt carries at all times a very large and complete stock of foreign and American clocks, timepieces, and clock materials of every description.

W. F. RUISSEAU, Restaurateur, "The Woodcock," No. 1030 Washington Street.—The deservedly popular "Woodcock," presided over by W. F. Ruisseau, is a well-ordered, elegantly appointed, first-class place, and, by common consent, one of the very best restaurants in this quarter of the city. The steaks, chops, oysters, and other toothsome edibles served here are of the choicest and juiciest the market affords, while the cooking, etc., is of a kind to tickle the palate of an epicure. Delicious tea and coffee also may be had here at all times, besides cold meats, delicacies, cake, pastry, etc., popular prices too prevailing, while the proprietor exercises close personal supervision over the establishment. The dining-room, which has a private parlor for ladies on one side, is spacious, tastefully furnished, and inviting, several courteous and efficient waiters being in attendance likewise, and altogether, the "Woodcock" receives a large and influential patronage. Mr. Ruisseau, who is one of Boston's best-known caterers, is a gentleman of courteous manners and excellent business ability.

FRANK WOOD, Hairdresser, Nos. 9 and 10 Franklin Avenue, Opposite Young's Hotel.—A well-conducted barber-shop which has gained a widespread popularity and an influential patronage is that of Mr. Frank Wood. Mr. Wood is a native of Canada, and a practical barber of long experience. He has been in business in Boston for the past twenty-eight years, and during that time has won fame as an expert and secured a patronage second to that of none of his contemporaries. In 1873, he began business in his present shop. This has an area of 30x60 feet, is located on the first floor, and has two entrances. The furnishings are of the most handsome and attractive character, and 11 chairs, requiring the services of twelve assistants, are almost constantly occupied by the patrons of the establishment, who can always rely upon being courteously, promptly, and satisfactorily attended to. To be shaved at Frank Wood's is a luxury, for the keenest-edged cutlery is in use, and both Mr. Wood and his assistants know what to do to afford satisfaction to patrons, and do it.

BOSTON COMFORT CORSET CO., Manufacturers of Corsets and Waists, No. 18 Chauncy Street.—From a hygienic standpoint, ease and comfort are of paramount importance and the corset that combines, in all these features, durability, with perfect fit, beauty of design and durability, has manifestly attained the desideratum in corsets. And in this connection special mention should here be made of the favorite "Comfort" corset, manufactured by the Boston Comfort Corset Co., No. 18 Chauncy Street, which is an article of exceptional merit, alike for ladies, misses and children, and which is, in all respects, the most complete and effective article of the kind yet introduced. It is by general consent the ne plus ultra in corsets, and of this assertion no better proof could be desired than the large sales this really meritorious invention is meeting with throughout the country. This corset has a socket

adjustment for the shoulders, so nicely contrived and fixed that it cannot by any means slip up on the neck, or down on the arm. By this invention the whole burden of the clothes is transferred to that part of the shoulder best adapted to sustain their weight, supporting everything without the least inconvenience, and almost without the wearer's consciousness, realizing the name given in the garment —making it in very truth a comfort corset. It has no laces to break. In the place of these are inserted continuous rows of very soft cord, which give all the support of bones with the advantage of yielding to every movement of the form, and of being washed without disarranging the fabric of the garment. It has a variety of shapes sizes for each waist size, so as to meet the requirements of a tapering waist, as well as of a straight form. The principle of following the form, from a given waist measure is peculiar to this corset, and is one of the things secured by patent. No other corset has more than one size at the top for any one waist size, consequently the variety of forms cannot be so well fitted with any other corset. Stylish and long as a French corset, yet combining ease and comfort with elegance and shape, the "Comfort" corset has the unqualified approval of every physician that has seen it. For children the advent of this corset marks a new era in children's wants. No more need of the arms can displace the shoulder socket —stockings and skirts are always in position, and all is ease and comfort. Walking or running, sitting down or jumping rope, it is all the same. The ladies' corset fastens in front and laces at the sides; the child's waist buttons in the back, but it is a perfect little corset in its beauty of lines to the form. Each corset is stamped with two numbers signifying the two measurements; the first being the size in inches around the waist, and the second around the shoulders, and the variations are such that any lady or child can be easily fitted. The success that has attended the introduction of their ladies' corset has corroborated the Boston Comfort Co. in introducing to the public a line of misses' corsets, embracing the same general principles as their "Comfort" corset for ladies, and which have made the same so popular with those who have worn them. The misses' corset also is made of the best materials, and by the most thorough manner. It is adjustable at the shoulder and waist so that any form can be easily fitted. The Boston Comfort Corset Co. was established in 1875, and from its inception the enterprise has proved a signal success, the business growing apace all over the United States until it has become exceedingly large.

P. E. TESCHEMACHER, Solicitor of Patents, and Mechanical Expert, No. 38 Washington Street.—It is a well established fact that no inventor alone and unaided can secure the benefits arising from a patent. The assistance of experienced and honorable solicitors is necessary, and an experience of over a quarter of a century enables Mr. Teschemacher to offer the best possible facilities to all desiring to procure strong and valid letters patent in any country of the civilized world, or requiring any investigations of advice in connection therewith. Inventors can always obtain here an expert opinion in regard to the patentability of any device, free of charge. Applicants, by putting the main points of their invention clearly before Mr. Teschemacher, can expect a prompt answer, often by return mail. He transacts every description of patent office work, including the prosecution of appeals, renewal of forfeited applications, prevention of infringements, reissues, extensions, etc., and makes a leading specialty of foreign patents, having expert and reliable correspondents in the different foreign nations, who carry through to a successful issue the most important and complicated cases. His clients come from all parts of the New England States, and bear testimony to the real and marvellous characteristics all the transactions of this house. Fees are moderate and uniform, commissions are executed with care and dispatch, and the interests of every patron are skillfully guarded and intelligently promoted. Mr. Teschemacher is a native Bostonian, in the prime of life, widely noted for his legal ability and professional attainments, and perfectly reliable, responsible and trustworthy in every respect.

B. T. MILLS & CO., Wholesale and Retail Dealers in Beef, Pork, Mutton, Lamb, Veal, Poultry, etc., Stall No. 9 Union Market, No. 15 New Washington Street.—An unbroken career of prosperity extending over a period of forty-five years marks the history of the well and favorably known firm of B. T. Mills & Co., wholesale and retail dealers in meats and provisions, who occupy stall No. 9 Union Market (No. 15 New Washington Street). It is, in fact, one of the oldest concerns engaged in this line in Boston, and fully maintains to-day its old-time reputation for prime goods and upright dealing, while the trade is large, active and permanent, and gives evidence of steady increase. This popular and responsible firm was established in 1845 on Tremont and Pleasant streets, where the business was located up to 1876, when it was moved to Boylston Market, where it was conducted for eighteen years, occupying its present quarters since 1876. The stall here occupied is ample, cleanly and carefully kept, while a large and first class stock is always carried, including choice fresh beef, pork, mutton, lamb, veal, poultry and game in season, lard, corned, smoked and salt beef, meats of all kinds and provisions. Orders are called for, and goods delivered free in any part of the city, several assistants being in attendance, and customers can rely upon receiving prompt and satisfactory service, as well as getting a very fine article and full weight in every instance from this veteran and prosperous firm. Mr. Mills, who is the sole member, the "Co." being nominal, is a gentleman somewhat past the meridian of life, but active, energetic and devoted to his business, was born in New Hampshire, whence he came to Boston in early manhood, and is a respected resident of Medford.

H. W. WELLS, Produce Dealer, and Mercantile Vegetable Market, No. 98 Arlington Avenue and No. 16 Concord Avenue.—One of the most reliable and prosperous produce dealers doing business in the mercantile vegetable market is H. W. Wells. He has been actively engaged in this line here during the past eight years, and has built up a very fine patronage. Mr. Wells occupies commodious and well kept quarters at No. 98 Arlington Avenue and No. 16 Concord Avenue, and carries on hand at all times a large and carefully assorted stock, receiving supplies fresh every day, while a competent assistant also is in attendance. He handles everything in the line of country produce and domestic fruits and berries in season, including apples, onions, potatoes, cabbage and staple vegetables of all kinds, and his trade, which is both wholesale and retail, is quite extensive. Mr. Wells, who is a native of Georgetown, Mass., and a resident of Cambridge, is a man of strict integrity in his business relations, as well as push and experience, and is well and favorably known in the produce trade.

P. O'RIORDEN, Teamster and Contractor, Office, No. 53 Chelsea Street, Charlestown.—The subject of this sketch, Mr. P. O'Riorden, ranks among the most enterprising of the citizens of Boston. He was born in Ireland, and eventually when very young came to the United States. Mr. O'Riorden commenced business thirty years ago as a teamster and contractor, and has become one of the most industrial and wealthy men in New England. He undertakes all kinds of teaming, and contracting for foundations of buildings, the making of roads, streets, etc. Mr. O'Riorden owns 214 horses, and his extensive stables are all required for his own use. He constructed the new driveway around Boston, the boulevard, which is about seven miles long. On this work he employed 6,000 workmen and 90 to 200 horses. Ten years ago he hauled to Mt. Hope Cemetery a monument weighing sixty tons, and he also placed the Soldiers' Monument on Boston Common, in its present position. Formerly all the cannon for the Charlestown Navy Yard were hauled by him; he has also frequently transported locomotives, etc. He owns the largest wagon and teaming tackle in the United States. The rigging of which weighs ten and a half tons. Mr. O'Riorden has extensive stand pits at Concord, Lexington, Newburyport, Wilmington, Montreal and Winchester; also gravel pits at Chelsea, and a blue stone ledge at Somerville. He promptly fills the largest orders for sand, gravel and loam at extremely low prices, and also carefully attends to teaming and contracting. His order boxes are at No. 365 Mechanics Exchange (No. 81 Hawley Street); No. 164 Master Builders' Exchange (No. 164 Devonshire Street), Boston, while his office is at No. 53 Chelsea Street, Charlestown. The importance of Mr. O'Riorden's transactions as a teamster is exemplified by the fact that thirty-five horses were used in conveying Summer's Monument to Boston Common, and sixty-seven horses were used in conveying a monument to Mount Hope Cemetery. He hauled 100,000 tons of stone to the Boston Post Office when in process of construction, some of which weighed as high as twenty tons. As an executive Mr. O'Riorden's operations are in accordance with the above. He did all the excavations on the site of the new Post Office and dug the main sewer in Boston, which is sunk thirty-seven feet in the earth, and has just completed a large railroad at Lake Village, N. H., and is at present filling a large trestle at Marlboro, N. H. He employs his own carpenters, painters, wheelwrights, blacksmiths and harness makers and has shops adapted to the various branches, and is one of the largest real estate owners in Charlestown, owning property all through the State. The house is connected by telephone.

OTTO VON DER HEYDE, German Pharmacy, Chemist and Druggist, No. 187 Meridian Street, East Boston.—This gentleman was born and received his education and training for the pharmaceutical profession in Germany, and came from the fatherland to East Boston and established his present enterprise in 1871. His venture has been a most successful one, and his pharmacy is today one of the most popular and best patronized in this section of the city. The elegant arrangement of his compact store is offered by all who enter it, being handsomely fitted up with artistic counters and shelving, plate-glass show windows and cases, etc. The stock embraces a large and carefully selected assortment of fresh and pure drugs and chemicals of the highest standard, proprietary remedies of well-known merit and established reputation, toilet and fancy articles, perfumery, druggists' sundries, mineral waters, physicians' and surgeons' requisites, and, in fact, everything to be found in a first-class pharmacy can be obtained at this house. Mr. Von der Heyde is the manufacturer and proprietor of the noted and efficacious "McK Cough Balsam," which has obtained a widespread and extensive sale. A special feature is made of the compounding of physicians' prescriptions and family recipes, and every care is taken to secure accuracy. Three competent assistants are kept busy. Mr. Von der Heyde is a gentleman of culture and refinement and very popular in the community.

FRANK H. BLANEY, Insurance Agent and Broker, No. 3 Winthrop Block, East Boston.—Of those houses that have exerted considerable influence and obtained an enviable reputation in these departments of commerce, that of Mr. F. H. Blaney, real estate and insurance agent, is among the most popular. Mr. Blaney was born in this section of the city, where he still resides,

and it may be said that he was born and reared in the business, as his father, Mr. D. H. Blaney, is still one of our most prominent operators in the same line and occupies the same office. Mr. F. H. Blaney, desiring to establish himself in business on his own account, founded this enterprise originally in 1870 in the city of Worcester, Mass., after which he removed to Kansas, but preferring home surroundings he returned east and re-established himself in this city, and owing to his long experience and knowledge of all its details, he is thoroughly qualified to carry it on most efficiently. His office is on the first floor, and is very neatly furnished with all the necessary conveniences. The transactions of this concern include all the departments of a general real estate and insurance business, such as the buying, selling, renting, or management of estates, the collection of rents and other income, conveyancing, the negotiation of loans on bond and mortgage and the investment of funds. His long experience, coupled with his intimate knowledge of the values of residential and business property in all sections of the city, render his advice and judgment valuable to intending investors. Mr. Blaney likewise carries on an extensive insurance business, having connections with some of the most reliable and financially sound companies in the world, and pays all losses without litigation, always discharging the important trusts committed to him with great fidelity, and to the complete satisfaction of all concerned. Insurance risks are effected immediately, and policies written up to any amount on all classes of insurable property at the lowest rates compatible with safety. Mr. Blaney enjoys the fullest confidence of capitalists and land-owners, and is constantly handling large sums of money in mortgages, ground rents and other securities.

LEOPOLD BABO & CO., Apothecaries, No. 4 Columbus Avenue, Opposite Providence R. R. Depot.—Among the old established apothecaries in Boston is the firm of Leopold Babo & Co. The foundation of the establishment dates from 1855. It was carried on at No. 851 Tremont Street for five years, from which place it was removed to No. 85 Boylston Street, where the business was carried on for twenty-five years. About two years ago the premises now occupied were secured. The location, a very desirable one, is opposite the Providence railroad depot, and the store, which is quite commodious, forms one of the features of that busy section of the city. In all its appointments it is perfect and complete; the fixtures are of hardwood, and all the surroundings are in perfect keeping with the character of the business carried on. The assortment of drugs includes everything known in modern medica, also chemicals and proprietary medicines, of virtue and standard value, and also perfumes, extracts and everything required for the toilet. Mr. Leopold Babo, who has the general management of the business, was born in Germany and graduated at the University of Heidelberg. He has had fifty years' experience as an apothecary and came to the United States in 1865. He is an old esteemed resident of Boston and is very popular as a professional gentleman. He is one of the oldest apothecaries in the city and enjoys the confidence of all who have dealings with him. Two practical pharmacists assist him in conducting his business.

S. M. CARO, Gents' Furnishings, Hats and Gloves; also Agent for Troy Laundry, No. 157 Knowland Street.—The practical experience of many years amply qualifies Mr. Caro to carry on the enterprise which he established in 1888, and which has thus far met with a flattering degree of success from many of the best known residents of the community and suburbs of Boston. His handsomely appointed store is located at the above given address, and an elegant stock of men's furnishing goods, hats, gloves, hosiery, collars, neckties, scarfs, etc., etc., is always artistically displayed for the inspection of customers, and selections made therefrom cannot fail to please the most fastidious taste. The store being between the two depots, the Old Colony and the Boston and Albany, is necessarily the leading depot for all transient trade on those railroads. Two polite and efficient clerks are in constant attendance and the needs of patrons receive prompt and satisfactory attention. This store is only one of his numerous enterprises as Mr. Caro is also an agent for the Troy Steam Laundry, and all laundry work entrusted to him is done with efficiency and dispatch. Mr. Caro is a native of Germany, but has lived in Boston for thirty years. He is a popular and energetic young business man, and his patronage truly shows a steady increase each year.

S. PRENTISS HILL & CO., West India Goods, Grain and Meal, No. 1## Main Street, and No. 94 Warren Street, Charlestown District.—This firm are extensive retail dealers in West India goods, grain and meal, and their name is familiar to the public as representing all that is substantial, pure and reliable in the family groceries. The foundation of the business was laid some fifty years ago, by Mr. S. Prentiss Hill. In 18## Mr. Jonathan Hatch was admitted to partnership, and in 18##. Mr. J. P. Hill also became a partner in the firm. The founder of the business died in April, 18##, Mr. Jonathan Hatch deceased in 18##, and Mr. A. W. Hatch was admitted to the firm in March, 18##. The business premises comprise three floors and a basement, ## x 100 feet each, giving ample accommodations for supplying the local extensive demand. The establishment is recognized as headquarters for the choicest foreign and domestic groceries, table luxuries, teas, coffees and spices, family flour, sugars, syrups and molasses, and all the good things from every quarter of the globe. The proprietors will handle nothing but the purest and the best, and therefore cannot offer any doubtful goods for sale. Aside from the question of reputation, purity is with this trustworthy firm one of the standing principles which cannot be deviated from. Their spacious salesrooms are at all times stocked with an assortment of staple and fancy groceries which have no superior in this city, while the prices quoted are always regulated by the market. A corps of experienced salesmen give prompt and courteous attention to the wants of customers, and orders are filled with the utmost dispatch. The copartners, Messrs. J. P. Hill and A. W. Hatch, are both natives of Charlestown, and bring large practical experience to bear upon their business, coupled with an intimate knowledge of every detail and feature of the grocery trade.

JOHN READE, Funeral Director, and Furnishing Undertaker, No. 187 Main Street, Charlestown District.—The splendid record made by Mr. John Reade as a funeral director and furnishing undertaker, commends him peculiarly to the people of Charlestown and vicinity. He established himself originally as an undertaker in Milford, Mass., in 18##, and removed to this city in 18##. No similar establishment in the district is better prepared for furnishing or directing funerals. Every necessary article can be here obtained, while in maintaining the latest and best processes are employed. The utmost despatch is used in answering calls by day or night, and it has always been the policy of the proprietor to make his charges as reasonable as is consistent with first-class service. Mr. Reade is also prominent and popular in the community as an auctioneer and appraiser, also acting as an agent for the purchase and sale of real estate, and has unsurpassed facilities for the prompt negotiation of loans on bond and mortgage. He also owns and operates hack, boarding and livery stables, at the corner of Gray and Water Streets, and Hamilton Court, where he keeps a stock of twenty-five horses to let, and has ample accommodations for boarding. Orders for carriages and horses may be sent by telephone No. 119-3 or No. 179-2, and will receive prompt and careful attention at all times. Mr. Reade was born in Ireland, city of Kilkenny, and came to this country in 18##. He served three and one-half years as an officer in the Union army, enlisting as a first lieutenant and raising his own company. He was subsequently attached to the forty-eighth and fifty-seventh Massachusetts Regiments, and was invested a captain by order of President Johnson for meritorious service. He was captured at the battle of Petersburg, while engaged in blowing up a mine, and was kept a prisoner for seven months and ten days at Columbia, S. C. He was the only officer of the fifty-seventh Massachusetts, who was neither wounded or killed; is a prominent member of Post 11, G. A. R., and is highly esteemed by his fellow men.

JAMES WHITE, Merchant and Military Tailor, No. 8 Waverly Block, Charlestown District.—This gentleman came to America in 18##, and was for twenty-seven years engaged in this line of business by J. Earl, of Washington Street, and in 18## started business on his own account. For the past four years he has occupied his present eligible premises, which comprise a handsomely appointed store, ## x 50 feet in dimensions. The stock is large and complete and makes a tasteful and handsome display. It includes the finest fabrics from the best looms in America and Europe in suitings, cassimeres, diagonals, broadcloths, cheviots, beavers, vestings, etc., in their different varieties and qualities. Measures are taken and the best fitting garments, trimmed and made in the most desirable manner, and accurate in cut and fit, are furnished at short notice. Every suit that leaves the establishment is made from the best quality of material, and is beautifully finished and of the most stylish and fashionable patterns. A specialty is made of military costumes. A number of skilled and experienced tailors are constantly employed, and all work is executed under the supervision of Mr. White, whose long experience and fine taste and judgment combine to make him a connoisseur in this particular line. The patronage is drawn from the best classes of society, and the house is one of the most popular of its kind.

EDWARD L. ORCUBY, Watch and Clock Maker, No. 117 Meridian Street, East Boston.—Among the many establishments in this city devoted to the watch-making and jewelry trade, the oldest is that of Mr. Edward L. Orcuby. Mr. Orcuby was born in Portland, Maine, and has had over sixty years experience as a watchmaker and jeweler, and is pronounced one of the best representatives and most skilled and correct reliable workmen in Boston. He has been established in business in East Boston since 1844, and is well known to the trade and citizens generally as a watch and clock maker and repairer of superior ability. The store, which has a front of ## and a depth of 40 feet, contains handsome show cases and ornamental fixtures and a full and general assortment of everything in the line of rich, elegant jewelry, and also watches in gold and silver cases, optical goods and clocks of all kinds. Mr. Orcuby warrants all his goods and workmanship and will be found in every way reliable. One-half of the store is occupied by his daughter, Miss Susan E. F. Orcuby, who has a large and complete stock of toys and fancy goods of every description, which are being offered at remarkably low prices.

JOHN A. KELLY, Funeral Undertaker and Practical Embalmer. Warerooms and Residence, No. 11 Meridian Street, East Boston.—The old established, well-known, popular undertaker and practical embalmer of East Boston, Mr. John A. Kelly, has been engaged in the vocation for fourteen years. He is careful and considerate and can always be relied on with the fullest confidence. He gives his personal attention to the management of funerals, and furnishes everything required, coffins, caskets, robes, hearse and carriages, corpse preserved, and also secures burial plots in any of the cemeteries in this vicinity and attends promptly to all orders at all hours of the day or night. Mr. Kelly enjoys a wide reputation as an embalmer, and by new and improved processes achieves remarkable results in this direction and is pronounced one of the most expert and successful in the city. He also gives his personal attention to removing bodies, and in the performance of the duties connected with his calling exercises rare tact, skill and judgment. A native of Ireland, Mr. Kelly has lived in Boston and vicinity for more than forty years.

W. HUGHSON, Carpenter and Builder, No. 171 Eliot Street.—One of the most reliable and competent carpenters and builders in the city is Mr. Wm. Hughson, No. 171 Eliot Street. Mr. Hughson has been a resident of Boston for a period of twenty-one years, having come here where he had carried his twentieth year. He has been established in business for himself since 18##, and during the past six years has occupied his present commodious premises which are 40 x 40 feet in dimensions and have every facility for carpenter work of all kinds. Mr. Hughson employs from four to six men in his establishment and has an extensive business throughout the city as a builder, his work standing the best tests on all occasions. He makes a specialty of carpenter jobbing, which he executes in the promptest and most satisfactory manner and at extremely reasonable charge. In addition to his carpenter and building business, Mr. Hughson is engaged in the letting of houses and stores, collecting rents and taking care of real estate. He is a first-class business man, forty years of age, and possesses the highest confidence of all who have had business transactions with him.

MRS. M. W. COLE, French Millinery and Fancy Goods, Stamping, etc., No. 647 Main Street, Charlestown.—Mrs. M. W. Cole, dealer and manufacturer of French millinery and fancy goods, stamping, embroidering and painting, etc., is a resident of this city and having acquired a thoroughly practical knowledge of and experience in the art of millinery in all its branches by years of close application, she inaugurated her present enterprise at the present location in 1884, and the success which she has met with is indicative of what a lady can accomplish by strict attention to the wants of customers, handling only first-class articles, prompt and faithful execution of orders and liberal business methods. The premises utilized for business purposes comprise a spacious and commodious store, with workroom attached, and fitted up in a very attractive manner. In the store will be found at all times a splendid line of fine French millinery goods such as bonnets, bonnet frames, also English round hats, in fact all that may be included under the general term of ladies' head covering, all of the finest quality and most fashionable shapes. These are both trimmed and untrimmed, and patrons not suited with those in stock can have their wants supplied immediately under their own personal instruction when desired, by the most proficient milliners, whose services are in constant employment in the establishment. The millinery products of this house embrace all the latest and newest styles in comparable goods of the most recent production of Parisian modistes, which also receives regularly, simultaneous with their appearance in London, Paris or Vienna. Mrs. Cole also devotes particular attention to all orders for stamping and designing, enabling customers to have their wants filled while waiting for them, and she also keeps on hand a full line of elegant and artistic hand embroideries, and all kinds of materials for such work, such as crewels, silks, chenille, arrasene, plushes, satins, felts. Germantown wools, Saxony yarns, worsteds, etc., also perforated patterns, church, household and other designs, monograms, ornate letters, etc. Hand-painting and dress garnishing receive prompt attention, also the cleaning and dyeing of gloves, feathers curled and colored; besides she is the agent for the Troy Laundry and Chelsea Dye House. Mrs. Cole gives special attention to mountain goods orders, which are executed in the highest style of art, promptly, on the shortest notice.

S. A. FREEMAN, Apothecary, No. 349 Main Street, Charlestown District.—A thoroughly reliable and competent druggist is Mr. S. A. Freeman, whose fine store has been for many years a noted landmark in this section of the city. Being a thoroughly skilled and practical pharmacist, he founded this establishment on his own responsibility in 1877, and its success since that date is the best evidence of the manner in which it has been conducted, as its patronage is large and rapidly increasing. The premises occupied are spacious and commodious, neatly and appropriately furnished in the latest modern style. Having a very largely developed prescription and family recipe trade, and fully appreciating the great responsibility attending their preparation, he has provided a distinct department for that branch of the business, in which will be found all the latest improved appliances and devices to secure accuracy. In his stock will be found the freshest and purest of drugs, chemicals and pharmaceutical preparations, proprietary medicines of all known reputation for efficiency, fancy and toilet articles, perfumery, fine stationery, select brands of foreign and domestic cigars, physicians' and surgeons' requisites, druggists' sundries, foreign and domestic mineral waters, etc. In connection with his pharmacy he keeps constantly on hand all the latest publications of periodicals and weekly papers, and on his counter can be found all the latest and most prominent daily newspapers of Boston, New York, and other cities. Prescriptions are compounded in the most careful manner at all hours of the day or night. Mr. Freeman is a thorough pharmacist, fully posted in every branch of the profession.

FRANK J. WILLIAMS, Provisions, Fruits and Vegetables, No. 684 Broadway, South Boston.—One of the best conducted establishments of South Boston in its important branch of trade, is that of Mr. Frank J. Williams, dealer in provisions, fruits and vegetables, butter and eggs. The spacious and finely fitted up salesroom contains a full and complete stock of the staple commodities above enumerated, which are received fresh from the most reputable sources of supply, and no establishment is better prepared to cater successfully to all requirements of the trade in this connection. The house from its inception has been a popular purchasing depot for the surrounding trade, and the services of two experienced clerks are required in the transaction of the prosperous and growing business. Mr. Williams is a native of Boston, and a gentleman thoroughly conversant with the provision trade. He began business in the Highlands in 1890, and in October, 1893, removed to this city and established this enterprise.

THOS. H. RATIGAN, Plumber, No. 778 Tremont Street.—This business was originally established in 1802 by Thomas Ratigan, who conducted the same for sometime, when it passed into control of his son and successor, the gentleman whose name heads the sketch. Mr. Ratigan occupies commodious quarters as store and shop, and keeps always on hand a complete assortment of everything comprehended in plumbers' materials, including lead and water pipe, fittings, sheet lead, water closets, marble basins, sinks, pumps, faucets, sewer traps and sanitary devices, while half a dozen or more skilled workmen are employed. He is prepared to enter into contracts for all classes of work in the line of plumbing, giving special attention to house drainage and ventilation, while jobbing like this is done in the most prompt and excellent manner, all such being executed under the immediate supervision of the proprietor, and satisfaction guaranteed in every instance. Mr. Ratigan, who is a native of this city, is a practical and expert plumber himself, of ample experience in the exercise of his art, and is thoroughly conversant with every feature and detail of this business.

C. H. WACHTER, Manufacturer of Home-Made Candies and Ice-Cream, No. 197 Broadway, South Boston.—Among the popular business men in South Boston there are none more prominent than Mr. C. H. Wachter, manufacturer of home-made candies and ice-cream, whose handsome attractive store and neat and tastefully fitted up parlors are at No. 197 Broadway. Mr. Wachter has had a long experience in this business and about a year ago succeeded his brother, who had established it in 1870. Besides himself, four assistants are employed, and a large substantial business is being carried on. Choice home-made candies and fine confectionery of all kinds, and ice-creams of all flavors are made fresh every day, and a first-class family trade is supplied, and a splendid custom, including many of the best citizens of this section, visit the parlors to partake of the delicious ice cream and ices he prepares. He makes a leading specialty of furnishing parties and weddings, and can always be depended upon to fill orders in a satisfactory manner. In the manufacture of candies he uses only pure sugar and has won an enviable reputation. He was born in Germany thirty-three years ago, and came to Boston when a child and learned the trade of a confectioner in the city.

BOSTON PORK STORE, Nos. 816 and 818 Main Street, Charlestown; Frank Warner, Proprietor.—This establishment, which was founded in 1846 by Mr. Frank Warner, is one of the finest of its kind in this section, is conveniently arranged and conducted in the most systematic manner, and is liberally patronized by all the best classes of citizens. Mr. Warner has had a long experience in the meat trade, and thoroughly understanding the wants of the public knows how to meet them. The store, which is 48 x 60 feet in dimensions, is kept scrupulously clean, is well lighted, is provided with a refrigerator and with every facility for filling orders, and is made attractive and inviting by the excellent manner everything in the line of choice cuts of beef, real lamb, mutton, pork, etc., is displayed. Oysters and all kinds of fish form a special feature of the business, and the house has always the finest and freshest that come to the Boston markets. Mr. Warner has also a department for sausages of all kinds, lard, tame, head cheese, pickles, tomatoes, corn, horseradish, German mustard, yeast cakes, Bell's dressing, tomato catchup, duo table sauce, milk, etc. In fresh meats this establishment cannot be surpassed, either in quality or price, and the stock is renewed daily. Orders are promptly attended to, and goods are delivered free in any part of the city, five assistants and a delivery wagon being in constant service. Mr. Warner, who is a native of this state, is a gentleman of real worth and sound business standing.

GEO. F. JAMES, B-B Hanger, No. 41 Border Street, East Boston. —The introduction of electricity into the operations of so many branches of industry during the last quarter of a century, has had a tendency to make them more useful and to create a greater demand for their supplies. This is particularly noticeable in the business of the bell-hanger and his kindred occupations. A home with an established prestige in this special line of trade, in East Boston, and with a standing of the highest character among our tradesmen houses and ship owners, is that of Mr. George F. James, bell-hanger, at No. 41 Border Street, which has always borne an enviable name for the excellence of its work. Mr. James is a native of Medford, this state, and has been a resident of this part of Boston for many years, and being a thoroughly practical and experienced man in this line of intricate mechanics, he founded this establishment on his own account, originally in 1856, and by close attention to the wants of customers, executing first-class work and liberal dealing he soon obtained a prominent position in the front rank of his profession, and has continued to occupy the same ever since. The premises occupied are spacious and commodious, and comprise a store with workshop attached. In the latter will be found all the necessary tools and appliances required in the mechanical department of his business, and constant employment is furnished to skilled and competent workmen. The store is neatly and appropriately fitted up with every convenience for the display of goods and the successful transaction of business. The stock kept constantly on hand embraces everything pertaining to the line of bell hanging, such as bells and gongs of all sizes for house, hotel and steamship purposes, wires, swivels, pulls, knobs, buttons, electric batteries and annunciators. Mr. James being a practical man is prepared to execute all work in this line of business at the shortest notice and in the best possible manner. All kinds of ship work receive especial attention, all emergency calls receive prompt response. Annunciators are properly adjusted, and repairing of the same is done in the best style of workmanship known to the trade, and in fact all kinds of light house-outfitting is promptly done. Mr. James takes especial pride in doing first-class work, and as evidence of his skill he refers to any of his work to be found in and around this part of the city.

WILLIAM H. OAKES, Fancy and Family Groceries, a Complete Line of Imported Pickles, Sauces, Condiments, Preserves, etc., No. 311 Main Street, Charlestown. - This house was opened by the present proprietor in 1881, and has been conducted with marked ability. The premises occupied are very spacious in size, attractive in all their appointments, and perfect in convenience of arrangement for inspection and sale. The stock is large and completely assorted, covering every branch of fancy and staple groceries, all fresh and splendid goods, which are quoted at the lowest ruling market prices. As dealer in teas, coffees and spices no house is better prepared to quote bed-rock rates for the choicest grades. The house always carries a fine assortment of fresh crop Oolongs, Japans, Gunpowder, Imperial, Young Hyson, English breakfast and other standard teas that are renowned for flavor and quality, and are justly popular with the public. A specialty is also made of coffees. The extra Java, Ommus, and extra Rio here offered are absolutely unrivalled for purity, quality, flavor and excellence. The same high standard characterizes the selections of spices, both whole and ground, as well as the fine stock of imported pickles, sauces, condiments and preserves, which form so important a feature of the trade. In such staples as sugars, syrups and molasses, cereals, farinaceous goods and family flour, Mr. Oakes is prepared to offer substantial inducements in regard to both reliability of stock and economy of prices. Mr. Oakes was born in Cohasset, Mass., and is a prominent citizen of Charlestown District; he now serving his second term as Councilman of Ward 4, in Captain of the Charlestown Cadets, a member of the Odd Fellows and Masons.

WILLIAM P. HENRY, Provisions, Country Produce, etc., No. 17 Main Street, Bunker Hill District. —One of Charlestown's most popular and best known provision and produce stands is the well kept and excellent store of William P. Henry. It is a convenience, neat and first-class establishment, one of the very best of this kind in the Bunker Hill District, where can always be found a very fine assortment, while customers are assured of getting a superior article at the lowest prices consistent with choice goods and upright dealing at all times here. The stock, which is large and carefully assorted, includes choice meats, poultry and general provisions, prime lard, fine butter, cheese, eggs, fruits, vegetables and table delicacies, while three courteous assistants are in attendance, all orders by telephone (B-3) receiving immediate attention, and altogether, an excellent trade is done. This prosperous store is an established one twelve years ago by the present proprietor, and from the inception of the business Mr. Henry has enjoyed a large and active patronage. Mr. Henry is a gentleman of middle age, and a Vermonter by birth, but has resided in Charlestown since 1870. Mr. Henry served with credit during the late war, sharing the fortunes of the Sixteenth Vermont Volunteer Infantry and the Twentieth Vermont Cavalry for three years, enlisting as a private and rising to the rank of corporal, and is an active member of the G. A. R.

CHARLES M. BROMWICH, Manufacturer and Dealer in Stoves, Tinware, Crockery and Glassware, etc. Plumbing, Tin Plate, Sheet Iron, Brass and Copper Work, etc. Corner Broadway and I Street, City Point, South Boston. Among those engaged in business in South Boston is Mr. Charles M. Bromwich, manufacturer and dealer in stoves, tinware, crockery, glassware, kitchen furnishing goods, wooden-ware, etc. Mr. Bromwich was born in England, but has been a resident of the United States ever since he was a mere lad. After serving a long and faithful apprenticeship in the manufacture of tin, sheet iron, brass and copper wares, supplemented by years of service in some of our best houses devoted to that mechanical industry, he established this enterprise originally in 1878, and during its lengthy career of almost a third of a century it has always maintained the highest of reputations. The premises utilized for the business are of spacious dimensions, comprising a store having a frontage of twenty five feet with a depth extending almost three times that distance, to which is attached a spacious and well-lighted workshop, which is fully equipped with all the necessary tools and machinery for the manufacture of his products, at which a number of skilled and competent workmen are constantly employed. Here will be found at all times a full and complete assortment of parlor, office, and cooking stoves, ranges, heaters, furnaces, grates, also gas and oil stoves of the very latest approved patterns and styles, all of which have been carefully selected from among the productions of the most celebrated manufacturers in the United States; also a fine assortment of fine tin, sheet iron, brass and copper ware, all of his own superior make, in which none but the best material and workmanship are used. He keeps also a large and elegant assortment of fine foreign and domestic china, queen's, crockery and glassware of the best quality in full and broken sets, in all the latest, most fashionable and unique designs, also lamps and their trimmings, together with everything in the way of wooden, willow and general kitchen furnishing goods, etc. Mr. Bromwich is agent for the Globe ventilator and chimney cap, which is pronounced to be the best device of its kind that has been introduced to the public. A special feature of this business is sanitary plumbing, tin plate, sheet iron, brass and copper work done to order. Mr. Bromwich is a practical sanitary plumber, and is prepared to execute all work pertaining to it at the shortest notice in the most satisfactory manner.

CHARLES A. MOFFATT, Cigars and Tobacco, Pipes and Snuffs, No. 141 Hanover Street and No. 90 Kingston Street. —Among those prominently identified with the trade in cigars and tobacco there are some who have met with a more deserved success than Mr. Charles A. Moffatt. Everything in the line of cigars and tobacco is to be found in his well-kept store, including all the favorite brands of imported and domestic goods and the popular brands of cigarettes, chewing and smoking tobacco; also pipes, and all the various articles that belong to the business. Two assistants are employed by Mr. Moffatt, who has gained a large wholesale and retail patronage from those who appreciate a good cigar and the best quality smoking and chewing tobacco. He is from Sydney, Cape Breton, and has been a citizen of Boston many years.

E. R. CUTLER, Selling Agent, Woonsocket Rubber Company, Bedford and Kingston Streets.—At the present day the manufacture of India rubber goods is one of the most important of American industries. Not only are waterproof garments, boots, and shoes made of this valuable material, but by means of chemical processes may be made to assume any degree of hardness, and by the action of heat can be moulded into any desired shape. A representative and one of the most famous houses in the United States extensively engaged in the manufacture of all kinds of rubber boots and shoes, is that known as the Woonsocket Rubber Company, whose offices and salesrooms in Boston, under the able and careful management of Mr. E. R. Cutler, the selling agent, are located at the corner of Bedford and Kingston Streets. The works of the company, which are among the largest and best equipped in America, are situated at Woonsocket, R. I. The Boston salesrooms comprise a

spacious floor 130x100 feet in area, elegantly equipped and fully stocked with the company's rubber boots and shoes. These goods are unrivalled for quality, finish, durability, and excellence, and have no superior in the American or European markets, while the prices quoted are as low as the lowest. Special attention is given to the promises embodied in their manufacture, and all boots and shoes made by this popular company are fully warranted. A very high status has been given the Woonsocket Rubber Company's goods, the trade not only extending throughout all sections of the United States and Canada but also to South America, Europe, Australia, and New Zealand. Mr. Cutler has been connected with the company for the last twelve years. He has had great experience in the rubber trade, and his high standing is a sufficient assurance that all orders and commissions will receive faithful attention.

GRAY'S DYNAMO ELECTRIC MACHINE COMPANY, No. 15 Chardon Street.—Gray's Dynamo Electric Machine Company enjoys a national reputation as manufacturers of the celebrated Gray dynamo electric machine, and was incorporated in 1892 under the laws of the State of Maine, with a capital of $100,000, and is under the management of Mr. Wm. G. Lewis as president; S. B. Buckin, treasurer; Joshua Gray, general manager. The latter gentleman is the largest shareholder in the company, and the machines which bears his name is manufactured from his own patents and is the product of his inventive brain. He is widely prominent as a practical machinist and electrician, and is specially known to fame as the inventor of Gray's magazine rifle and breech-loading guns, used during the war, and of permanent value as a fire-arm of great power. He also invented a large part of Singer's sewing machine, and produced many other articles of value to humanity. Without entering into a comparison of the "Gray Dynamo Electric Machine" with others now in use, it is sufficient to call attention to the results exhibited, viz: That, with but a one and one-fourth inch belt, this company is enabled to light continuously two hundred incandescent lamps of sixteen candle-power. Facts are stubborn things, and so theories of scientists can not these aside. True science is but the illustration of the truths of nature, and in electrical machines, as in others, theory must yield to fact. The great reduction in power, as exhibited by this company, commends itself to all practical and economical minds, and to meet it appeals with confidence. Scrupulous business probity, keen intelligence, broad, liberal treatment, courteous cultivation of pleasant relations with others, and a rigid avoidance of speculative schemes have combined to make this house what it is. The president, Mr. Lewis, is a native of Boston, well known and highly esteemed in his business and financial circles, and resides at Mansfield, Mass. Mr. Buckin, the treasurer, was born in Providence, R. I., and is a prominent, public-spirited citizen of Boston. Mr. Gray, the general manager and moving spirit of the enterprise, is a native and leading citizen of Medford, Mass., while his position as an inventor and electrician places him far beyond the requirements of any praise or eulogy which these pages could bestow.

HENRY M. SOURNE, Architect, No. 5 Pemberton Square, Room 6.—One of the most competent and reliable among the younger architects of this city is Mr. Henry M. Sourne, who enjoys an excellent and merited reputation for skill in his profession. Mr. Sourne is a native of this city, and a thoroughly practical and expert draughtsman and all around architect, of ample experience. He has been established in his profession some three years or so, and from the first he has steadily won his way to public favor and recognition, owing to uniform satisfaction rendered in every instance to those engaging his professional services. Mr. Sourne is prepared to make plans for all classes of buildings, in the most reliable and excellent manner, designs, specifications, and estimates being promptly furnished, while construction is personally superintended also when desired; and altogether, this gentleman receives a very flattering city and suburban patronage.

MEADE, DODGE & CO., Importers and Dealers in Artists' Materials, and Art Novelties of all Kinds, No. 6 Park Street.—A prominent and reliable house engaged in importing and dealing in artists' materials, architects', engineers', and draughtsmen's supplies, etc., is that of Messrs. Meade, Dodge & Co. Mr. Meade, the senior member of the firm, was for many years with the "Prang" house. During his service there he opened to the public the finest appointed store for artists' materials to be found in the United States. After conducting this department for several years, the house desired to turn their attention in other directions. Upon this Mr. Meade withdrew, soon after forming the above firm, in 1887, and from the start they have been the recipients of a very large patronage. They occupy a spacious store, having a frontage of twenty feet, with a depth of three times that space, which is very elegantly fitted up with every convenience for the artistic display of their large and varied assortment of artists' materials, etc. They are direct importers from the European markets, and possess excellent facilities and the finest of connections among the most celebrated manufacturers in Europe; also of this country. In their stock will be found everything that an artist may wish, together with a choice assortment of art studies and decorative goods of all kinds. These goods are all of the very finest quality, and are offered at as leisurely low prices. Having every facility at their command, they are prepared to execute all kinds of framing for works of art, in any desirable style and material, promptly and in the best style of workmanship. Messrs. Meade, Dodge & Co. are very popular with the art profession and the general public.

J. A. HASTY, Architect, No. 13 Tremont Row, Room 8.—Prominent among the leading architects of this city is Mr. J. A. Hasty. Mr. Hasty commenced the practice of his profession five years ago, and has since secured a liberal and influential patronage. His work bears evidence of care and talent, coupled with a thorough knowledge of modern requirements. He has designed and superintended the erection of many substantial and handsome buildings in Boston and its vicinity, and spares neither time or pains to satisfy the wishes and requirements of patrons. Mr. Hasty has just erected the Cambridge Mutual Fire Insurance Building, Cambridge, costing $70,000; also the handsome residence of Mr. Wm. H. Wood, Cambridgeport, and that of Mr. Wm. Austin, proprietor of Austin's Nickelodeon, at Brookline. He promptly prepares plans, specifications, etc., for all classes of work. Mr. Hasty was born in Maine, and is now a resident of Cambridge. He is a thoroughly capable architect, and can always be implicitly relied on to satisfactorily execute all work pertaining to his profession.

ALEXANDER CAMPBELL, Gas Fitter, Plumber and Sanitary Engineer, No. 4 Main Street, Charlestown.—The imperious demands made upon the gas fitter and plumber of the present day are much more exacting in their nature than at any previous time in the history of his trade, and in order to successfully conduct the business, the very best mechanical skill and knowledge of sanitary engineering are required. A veteran popular and representative member of this character in Charlestown, is that of Mr. Alexander Campbell, gas fitter, plumber and sanitary engineer, at No. 4 Main Street, which is one of the most reliable houses of the kind in this section of the city. Mr. Campbell is a native of Scotland, who has been a resident of the United States for almost half a century, and the greater portion of the time of this city. Thoroughly practical and experienced in every branch of his business, he founded this house originally in 1858, and during the entire intervening period of thirty years, he has had a constant succession of prosperity, and his establishment is well and favorably known to the whole community, and distinguished for its general superiority, and its perfect adaptation to all the purposes to which it is devoted. The premises utilized are of spacious dimensions, and comprise an admirably fitted up store, supplied with all the conveniences for the accommodation of his splendid stock of goods, and in the rear is attached a workshop fully equipped with all the necessary tools, machinery and appliances of the most improved designs, and where a force of competent workmen are employed constantly. His assortment of goods embraces a full and complete line of chandeliers, candelabras, hall, wall and drop lights, shades, and other gas fixtures, also plumbers' supplies, such as bath and water closet fixtures, wash bowls, water-backs, reservoirs, bed, block tin, wrought and cast iron, and terra cotta service or drain pipes, etc. He will furnish a fine line of parlor, office and cooking stoves, ranges, grates, furnaces, heaters, oil and gas stoves, all of the latest improved designs, and selected from among the productions of the most reliable manufacturers in this country. He is also engaged in the manufacture of all kinds of tin, sheet-iron and copper ware, all of which is made from the best quality of materials in the best style of workmanship, an assortment of which is to be found in his store, together with everything else in the line of housekeeping hardware, and offered to the public at lowest prices. Mr. Campbell is prepared to do all kinds of gas and steam fitting, also plumbing in the most approved manner, and furnishes estimates, enters into contracts of any magnitude for all such work, also metal roofing, spouting, which are performed in the most satisfactory manner promptly and at lowest prices. He is a reliable and thorough tradesman and mechanic, and no evidence of his skill be in the particular attention to his fine line of manufactured goods, and the many specimens of his work to be found in some of our leading business houses and residences.

ALFRED W. TILTON, Apothecary, Corner Prince and Salem Streets.—The oldest drug store in Boston is an interesting one that which is now identified with the name of Alfred W. Tilton, corner of Prince and Salem streets, sign of the best Eucalyptus, which is made of camphor wood and was carved in Rome, and is one of the noted antique features of Boston, being over fifty years old. This well known establishment was founded in 1797, by Robert Fennelly, who died in 1808, and was succeeded by Reza Lincoln, who in turn was succeeded by Seth W. Fowle, and afterwards by Henry D. Fowle, who conducted it successfully for a period of forty years, and which has been carried on under successive management ever since, when the present proprietor, Mr. Tilton, assumed control of the business in July, 1888. He carries a fine line of the purest drugs and chemicals, proprietary medicines, etc., and does an extensive business in the thickly settled neighborhood, compounding the prescriptions of most of the physicians around, two experienced assistants being employed. Mr. Tilton conducts a strictly first class prescription drug store, no liquors being sold. One of Mr. Tilton's best known specialties is the "Black Bottle" formerly prescribed by the late Dr. Nyndman, one of Boston's most noted physicians, for coughs and lung troubles, which has been found an invaluable remedy in such cases, and is largely used throughout the city. Mr. Tilton is a Boston man, and an apothecary of the highest standing.

M. CARBEE & CO., Machinists, Brass Finishers and Pipe Fitters, Manufacturers of Steam-Engines, Brass and Iron Valves and Fittings, etc., No. 67 Haverhill Street, East Boston.—On the first day in the year 1886, Mr. Carbee, then, as now, a practical mechanic of esteemed experience, started business in a small way in the premises he now occupies, his principal capital consisting of a pair of brawny arms and an active brain. For a time he encountered many obstacles and reverses, for his facilities were very meagre, but orders were plentiful and his work first class, and his ability and high reputation brought him increased patronage. By degrees his facilities for manufacture were multiplied, and to-day he has under his dominion one of the best machine and engine shops in East Boston, and a trade at once substantial and influential. Mr. Carbee is a machinist, brass finisher, pipe fitter, and manufacturer of steam-engines, brass and iron valves and fittings, and dealer in wrought-iron and brass pipes for steam, gas and water. His leading specialty is that of steam fitting and piping. His machine shop comprises one floor, with a capacity of 30 x 80 feet, and is appropriately fitted up and equipped with every mechanical device, and appliances that can contribute to the successful and economical carrying on of the business, while from eight to ten skilled and experienced workmen are permanently employed. The trade comes from all parts of the city and its populous surroundings. Mr. Carbee was born in New Hampshire, and since 1886 has resided in East Boston.

EMBER COSTUME PARLORS, W. C. Montgomery, Proprietor. No. 40 Essex Street.—Mr. Montgomery succeeded to this old-established business in 1886. A native of Bradford, Mass., he came to Boston in 1876, and was successively in the confectionery and shoe business, in both of which he did well and remained for a number of years. Since he assumed the direction of his present enterprise, he has displayed high intelligence and business capacity, in meeting the requirements of the numerous patrons of the establishment. He occupies commodious premises, 25 x 60 feet in dimensions, and has always on hand a large variety of fancy costumes for all occasions, theatrical or otherwise, embracing the styles of the various historical periods, and made up in the most elaborate and costly style. Mr. Montgomery is also the inventor of the famous rat-trap which is meeting with such success throughout the country.

MISS ANNIE MORGAN, Millinery, No. 30 Beach Street.—A widely known and deservedly popular establishment is the millinery line is that of Miss Annie Morgan. Miss Morgan is a Bostonian, and in addition to being an expert milliner, brings to bear a rare degree of business tact and executive ability. She first began business in 1871 at the corner of Washington and Beach Streets, and since 1881 has been located at the present site. The premises are commodious and convenient in arrangement and the general appointments includes all the modern adjuncts of elegance and utility. In the business she shows a tasteful and by means of various ingenious interior devices is advantageously displayed a full line of fashionable hats, bonnets, and in short everything in the line of millinery goods, while in the shop in the rear a corps of experienced hands is employed in making up the artistic creations in this line for which the establishment is noted. Miss Morgan counts among her numerous patronage the best local custom.

DANIEL BUCKLEY, Registered Plumber, Office, No. 440 Broadway, South Boston.—One of the oldest and best known exponents of this important branch of skilled industry in the city is Mr. Daniel Buckley, plumber and general jobber in sheet iron work. Mr. Buckley was born in this city, and early learned and became a skillful exponent of the plumbers' trade. At far back as 1880 he began business for himself in the vicinity of the present site, and in the interval, by superior work and fair and equitable dealing, has reared a prosperous, general trade. The spacious and well-ordered premises, 25 x 60 feet in size, consist of an office and shop, the former fitted up in an attractive style, and the latter equipped with all modern facilities for the advantageous prosecution of the work. Mr. Buckley employs from six to ten experienced workmen, and does everything in the line of sanitary plumbing, special attention being given to drainage and ventilation.

W. L. ANDERSON & CO., Diamonds, Watches, Clocks, Jewelry, Silver and Plated Ware, Spectacles, etc., No. 91 Main Street, Bunker Hill District.—The great perfection which has been attained in this line can be seen by paying a visit to the old and reliable house of Messrs. W. L. Anderson & Co., dealers in diamonds, watches, clocks, jewelry, etc., where are shown the finest modern productions of these valuable and beautiful goods, all of which represent the highest artistic forms of mechanical skill and ingenuity. Mr. Anderson is a native of Charlestown where he still resides, and after serving a faithful apprenticeship for a number of years, supplemented by long experience in the industry, he determined to embark in the business on his own account, and inaugurated this establishment originally in Boston proper in 1861. He removed to his present address in 1878, which at once succeeded far beyond his expectations. His finely furnished store contains the most superb stock of pure and sparkling diamonds, rubies, sapphires and other precious gems to be found in Charlestown, also beautiful jewelry, such as crosses, bracelets, necklaces, watch chains and charms, lockets, plain and chased rings, chatelaines, studs, scarf and lace pins, collar and cuff buttons, pendants, etc., in profuse display, and all the leading makes and styles of American and European watches in both gold and silver. His assortment includes also a fine line of French, Swiss and American clocks in all the latest and most unique styles and designs, solid silver and plated wares, novelties and fancy goods, bric-a-brac, also gymnasiums, spectacles, opera-glasses, etc., in fact everything pertaining to a first-class jewelry house. A specialty is made of repairing fine watches, clocks and jewelry. They make a specialty of loose diamonds, ready for mounting, so that you can select the size and quality of diamond you wish and have them mounted in rings, ear jewels, studs or pins. By so doing you can suit your own taste and also know just what you are buying so imperfections are not easily detected after being mounted. We buy our diamonds direct from New York importers for cash and are satisfied with small profits.

J. A. OBERMEYER, Dealer in Groceries and Provisions, Nos. 29 and 31 Broadway, South Boston.—A house in this portion of Boston well worthy the attention of consumers and purchasers is that of Mr. J. A. Obermeyer, dealer in groceries and provisions. Mr. Obermeyer is a German by birth but has been in the United States for many years, having become a resident of Boston in 1869. Having acquired a thorough knowledge of this line of trade as a clerk for a long time, he founded this enterprise originally on his own responsibility on South Street, in 1878, where he met from the start a very large and influential trade, which increased to such an extent that he was compelled to seek larger and more commodious quarters and removed to his present location in 1882, where he occupies a very commodious and spacious store. It is very neatly and appropriately fitted up and supplied with every convenience. Here will be found at all times a full and general assortment of almost everything in the line of food products, embracing the purest and freshest teas from China, Japan and Formosa, coffees from Rio, Mocha, Java, Maracaibo and other countries, hermetically sealed goods in glass and tin, sugars, syrups, foreign and domestic green and dried fruits, flour and meals of all descriptions, spices, bakers' and laundry supplies, smoked and dried meats, provisions, etc., also potted and canned meats, table luxuries, vegetables, dairy and creamery butter and cheese, fresh eggs, and other products of the farm, garden and dairy. Purity and first-class quality is the essential requirement of all goods kept by Mr. Obermeyer, and customers dealing with him can always have the satisfaction of knowing that no inferior or adulterated goods will be offered to them. His connections with the trade are very extensive and enable him to secure first quality of goods, and at prices by which he can offer them at figures which defy successful competition, and orders are delivered at residences in this city free of charge.

GEO. O. AYER, Photo. Artist, No. 74 Meridian Street, East Boston.—Among the prominent representative photographers in this city there are probably none excelling a higher class or better finished work than Mr. Geo. O. Ayer, who has been identified with the art for many years and has kept pace with all the improvements and advances that have been made in it. Very handsomely furnished premises are occupied, the office and reception rooms being on the third floor and the operating rooms on the fourth floor. Mr. Ayer is particularly expert in fine portrait work and in groups, and in all his work is plainly discernible the marked hand of the thorough artist. Crayon work is also executed, and a special business made of finishing photographs in ink, oil, water colors or pastilie as may be desired, in the highest style of the art. Mr. Ayer's skill and artistic ability are highly appreciated in this community, and as evidence of his popularity as a photograph artist is only necessary to state that his patronage is not only derived from Boston but comes from all the adjoining cities and towns. Born in Maine Mr. Ayer commenced business operations as a photographic artist in Augusta in that state in 1855, where he is still doing a large business. He has been established in his present location in East Boston about three years and keeps in his employ six assistants.

CHARLES F. BYAM & CO., Jobbers and Retailers of Boots, Shoes and Rubbers, No. 857 Main Street, Bunker Hill District.—The old reliable house of Messrs. Charles F. Byam & Co., jobbers and retailers of boots, shoes and rubbers, has enjoyed a note-worthy popularity for a period extending over thirty years. This concern was founded originally in 1848 by the senior partner, Mr. Charles F. Byam, who is a native of South Charlestown, Mass., whose individual enterprise carried it so successfully down to 1881 when the above firm title was adopted by the admission into copartnership of Mr. M. Clarence Hall, a native and resident of Charlestown, and who, by long experience and sound business qualifications, is well adapted for the business. The trade of this house is both jobbing and retail, and extends throughout this city and the surrounding vicinity. The premises utilized for business purposes comprise a commodious store with basement, which are fully provided with all conveniences for the successful prosecution of their large and steadily increasing trade. This firm represents some of the most celebrated boot and shoe manufacturers in this portion of the country, and in their salesroom will be found a full and complete assortment of fine and medium grades of hand-made and machine-sewed boots, shoes, gaiters, slippers, etc., for men, youths and boys, also everything in the line of rational foot wear for ladies, misses and children, from the strong walking boot and school shoe to the most delicately made bid slipper. In addition to these will be found a complete line of rubber boots, arctics, overshoes, sandals and slips. These goods have all been carefully selected from among the productions of the best manufacturers, by both members of the firm, who are careful judges and experts in the materials and workmanship of boots and shoes. Polite and intelligent assistants serve customers promptly. Both members of the firm are gentlemen whose integrity and ability require no words of comment.

W. C. HALLETT, Watches, Clocks, Jewelry, Silverware, and Optical Goods, No. 4 Meridian Street, East Boston.—Among the young business men of East Boston who have made a success in their special field of enterprise Mr. W. C. Hallett, the widely and favorably known jeweler and watchmaker, merits special recognition. Before venturing into business on his own account, which he did 1884, he wisely determined to make of himself an expert in his chosen line of industry, and when he opened his store doors and invited the public to put their confidence in him as a seller of jewelry and as a maker of watches, he could satisfactorily point to the fact that his knowledge of the trade was backed by hard practical experience extending over eleven years. His fine, handsome store is elegant and attractive in its display and appointments, and it glistens with a splendid display of diamonds and other precious stones, rings, bracelets, charms, pins, bangles and jewelry ornaments of every description, unique and artistic in design; silver and gold watches of foreign and domestic makes, clocks of all sizes and forms; silverware, chaste and elegant in design and ornamentation, and optical goods to suit the necessities of all who require them. The prices are such that few houses can excel. In watch and jewelry repairing the work is perfect, and the business is growing. Mr. Hallett is a Massachusetts man by birth and an honor to his profession.

C. H. WHITING, Receiver and Jobber of Flour, No. 301 Broadway.—A prominent and long established house engaged in handling these products is that of Mr. C. H. Whiting, receiver and jobber in flour, etc. Mr. Whiting is a native of this part of the city of Boston and about forty-six years of age. He acquired a thorough, practical knowledge of and experience in this line of commercial industry as a clerk and assistant in this house, which was established originally by Messrs. Porter & Co., in 1861, the present proprietor assuming sole ownership and control of it in 1893. The premises utilized for business purposes comprise a large and spacious store appropriately fitted up with an office and other conveniences and a basement, all of which are supplied with every facility for the handling of goods pertaining to the trade. Mr. Whiting carries on a very extensive trade in receiving and jobbing all kinds of flour and mill products, and keeps constantly on hand a full assortment of choice family, shipping and bakers' flour, which are received direct from the best producers and millers in the United States, including the best spring wheat products from Minneapolis, Duluth and other portions of the great northwest; also the finest grades of winter wheat flour from Ohio, Indiana, Illinois and Missouri, together with pure bolted and unbolted corn, meal, Graham, rye and buckwheat flour, wheaten and oat grits, and all other cereal products for table consumption. The brands of these commodities are the very best to be obtained in the market. A specialty is made of the Hazall brand, the reputation of which is so well known to the community that no encomiums of ours upon its excellence are necessary. He is a close observer of the markets, their supply and demand, and his knowledge of the same will compare favorably with any others in the town.

DEXTER'S HARNESS SHOP, Harnesses to Order. Aims Dealer in Whips, Blankets, Robes and Horse Goods, No. 479 Main Street, Charlestown.—Ex-Charlestown as located enjoys a better reputation in this line than that of Dexter's harness shop, manufacturer of harnesses, and dealer in whips, blankets, horse goods, etc., which has always maintained the highest standard of excellence in the trade. Mr. Dexter is a native of Boston and a resident of Somerville, and although a young man yet, he has acquired a thorough proficiency in all branches of this industry by years of close application and practical experience as a saddle and harness maker. This house was established as a harness shop and factory over twenty-five years ago, and after many changes in proprietorship, Mr. Dexter went into it on his own account in 1886, and since that date has attracted his business. The premises occupied are spacious and appropriately fitted up, comprising a store and workshop. In the latter will be found a full complement of skilled and experienced workmen engaged in the manufacture of fine and medium grades of harness, while in the store will be found a full and complete assortment of saddles, harness, bridles, halters, etc., of his own superior production, which are made of the very best quality of leather and accompanying trimmings. He also carries a fine stock of blankets, fur and lap robes, whips, nets, sheet protectors, sunshades, feed bags, housings, collars, hames, halters, sheets, horse boots, brushes, sponges, combs, etc.; in fact everything in the horse-furnishing line. These goods are all of the very best materials, made to wear rather than to sell, and cannot fail to give satisfaction. A specialty of this house is the manufacture of light and heavy, single or double harness to order, and repairing is also executed in the most skilful manner and promptly. Many of our most prominent citizens and business firms are patrons of this reliable house.

I. J. WYZANSKI, Dry and Fancy Goods, Nos. 109 and 111 Meridian Street, East Boston. The leading headquarters for dry and fancy goods in East Boston, is the establishment of Mr. I. J. Wyzanski. The popular proprietor has resided in this country for the past twenty-one years. He established his business here in 1875, bringing to bear upon his enterprise a thorough knowledge of the wants of the public. The store is superior in size, attractive in all its appointments, and perfect in convenience of arrangement for inspection and sale. The stock is varied and comprehensive, and is representative of all that is choice, including the and novel in dress goods, shawls, silks, satins, velvets, linens, housekeeping goods, hosiery, gloves and underwear, corsets, hoopskirts

and hankies, laces, ribbons and embroidery, notions, fancy goods and small wares in almost endless variety. He makes a specialty of kid gloves, being the first to introduce them to the citizens of East Boston, and also makes a specialty of laces and embroideries. The proprietor makes it a special feature of his establishment to charge no fancy prices for goods, but to mark everything as low as can be done consistently with a living profit; hence it is that his counters are daily thronged with customers from all classes of society. A corps of experienced clerks and salesmen contribute to the satisfactory operations of the house, and the business here carried on is an important and growing factor in the mercantile activity of this community.

SHAWMUT FURNITURE COMPANY, House-Furnishing Goods of Every Description, No. 54 Shawmut Avenue, J. P. Atkinson, Manager.—In Boston no house takes a higher position in the general house-furnishing trade than that of the Shawmut Furniture Company, who are extensive dealers in fine furniture, carpets, oil-cloths, refrigerators, stoves, crockery, and in everything needed for the complete furnishing of the mansion or the cottage. The business of this concern was organized in 1871 under the style of R. A. Atkinson & Co., and in 1884 the concern became an incorporated company with the title of the Shawmut Furniture Company, at the head of which is the popular and widely-known great establishment house-furnisher, and the founder of the business Mr. R. A. Atkinson, while the enterprise is under the general management of his brother, Mr. J. P. Atkinson, an energetic, pushing young business man, who was reared in this line of trade. The premises occupied, comprise an entire building 25 x 80 feet in dimensions, and contains three floors and basement. The warerooms are elegantly appointed and attractive in appearance in every department with new, choice and valuable goods. The stock embraces everything that can be desired in parlor, chamber, dining-room, kitchen, office, hall and library furnishings, and the goods are of a class that rank superior, not only in the quality of material, but in the equally important matters of material design and artistic workmanship. The relations established by this concern with manufacturers of the highest repute, both at home and abroad, enable them to obtain the lowest prices and give to the trade advantages scarcely in this season. The business is conducted on the most liberal plan.

L. S. STEVENS, Boots and Shoes, No. 437 Broadway, South Boston.—Among the old time representative mercantile establishments of South Boston should be prominently mentioned that of Mr. L. S. Stevens, dealer in boots and shoes. This business was founded by the present proprietor as far back as 1855, and from its inception has been characterized by a degree of ever-increasing prosperity. The commodious store is fitted up in a style which is a happy combination of modern convenience and elegance, and with its entire plate glass front and handsome interior fixtures, constitutes one of the attractive features of this popular thoroughfare. Mr. Stevens possesses the happy faculty of selecting goods especially adapted to the requirements of the retail trade, and is the large, comprehensive and complete stock of men, women and children's high grade foot wear displayed in his salesrooms the most refined customer cannot fail to be suited. Mr. Stevens, the especially popular proprietor, was born in the town of Norwich, Conn. He early went to sea, beginning like all thorough seamen, on the forecastle—aye the quarter deck. Before he had reached his twenty-first year he had become a master, being brought about as follows. His ship in which he belonged reached the East, which islands en route to China after a hard voyage. The discomforts of the voyage being greatly augmented by the bad treatment which officers and crew had received at the hands of the captain. As soon as possible after making port, the officers deserted the ship and the captain dying soon after, the second just Mr. Stevens as master, although not yet of age. He completed the voyage and so pleased the owners by his fidelity and successful care of their interests that he was retained permanently as the captaincy. Mr. Stevens subsequently made many prosperous voyages, adding to all parts of the globe. He subsequently retired from the profession which for twenty-eight years he had successfully followed, and in 1855 came to Boston.

JOHN HALL, JR., Successor to John D. Dodge, Dealer in Provisions and Produce, No. [illegible] Broadway.—Mr. Hall is a native of Natick and has had many years of practical experience in this line of commerce, having first engaged in it on his own account on A Street in 187[illegible], and which house he still carries on at the present time in connection with the former mentioned concern, which was founded originally by Mr. John D. Dodge in 18[illegible] and has been ever since a popular house with the entire community in that portion of the city. Mr. Dodge was succeeded by the present popular proprietor in 188[illegible], who has augmented its trade very materially since that date, having been obliged to increase the capacity of his storerooms, which is of commodious dimensions. Mr. Hall keeps constantly on hand a very full and comprehensive stock of all kinds of provisions and country produce, which comprises the choicest and most popular brands of canvased and uncanvased smoked hams, shoulders, bacon, beef, corned beef and pork, also sausages, fresh and smoked, in all varieties, pickled and smoked tongues, also pigs' feet, tripe, pork and beef tenderloins, fresh country sausages, roasting pigs, fresh veal, mutton, lamb and pork, also choice poultry in season. These articles are all selected with the greatest care. Besides this immense stock Mr. Hall also keeps constantly on hand a full and general line of country produce, such as fresh selected eggs, choice dairy and creamery butter, pure leaf lard, potatoes, fruits, beans, peas, canned goods of every description, and in fact a general assortment of farm, garden and dairy products, all fresh and pure. Prompt attention is given to all customers' orders, while the very lowest prices always rule in this establishment.

S. B. SPARKLIN, Millinery and Fancy Goods, No. 115 Meridian Street, East Boston.—This gentleman inaugurated his enterprise here in 18[illegible], and has met constantly increasing success from the outset, building up a first-class line of patronage strictly on the merits of his goods. The store has an area of [illegible] x 50 feet, is excellently fitted up for the purposes of the business, is provided with a cash carrier system, and is admirably arranged for securing convenience to customers and an effective display of the large and varied stock. All the latest novelties in millinery and fancy goods of every kind, in hosiery and underwear, in gloves, corsets, ribbons, laces, neckwear, and every description of ladies' and gents' furnishing goods, in jewelry, notions, etc., are to be found displayed here in profusion, and temptingly offered at prices that cannot be surpassed elsewhere. The stock is kept abreast with the varying fashions of the hour, and customers can always rely upon obtaining here the latest representations of modern styles. Two assistants are in service, and patrons are accorded prompt attention. Mr. Sparklin is a native of Maryland, and has resided in East Boston for nearly twenty years.

C. A. DODGE, Mason and Builder, etc., No. [illegible] Devonshire Street, Wharf No. [illegible] Albany Street.—Among the comparative few who have by force of merit become noted for the success with which they have invariably accomplished every undertaking, is Mr. C. A. Dodge, the well-known mason and builder, and dealer in brick, lime, cement, sand and hair, whose offices are at the rooms of the master builders' association. The business of this house was originally established in 18[illegible] by Messrs. Vinal & Dodge, the present proprietor succeeding to the sole control in 188[illegible]. The business premises cover an area of [illegible] by [illegible] feet, and comprise spacious storehouses and sheds, and excellent wharfage facilities, giving ample accommodations for the convenient receipt and storage of supplies, while the stock of brick, cement and other building materials here carried is one of the most complete and comprehensive in this section. The connections of the proprietor with the best sources of supply are so intimate and influential that he is enabled to procure his materials in large quantities and at advantageous rates, and consequently to offer his patrons the rarest inducements in terms and prices. Mr. Dodge is a large contractor for building work of all kinds, and has carried to a successful completion many heavy and important commissions in this city and adjoining towns. He is in a position to undertake the erection of the most extensive and difficult works, and to guarantee the most entire satisfaction. Mr. Dodge is a native of this city, and a prominent member of the master builders' association.

B. P. SPEAR & SON, Practical Plumbers, and Dealers in Plumbers' Supplies, No. [illegible] Warren Street, Corner Thompson, Charlestown District.—Among those who have acquired a most enviable reputation in this important industry in the Charlestown district of the city, Messrs. B. P. Spear & Son, practical plumbers and dealers in plumbers' supplies, are deserving of especial recognition. The senior partner of this firm is a native of Vermont, but has been a resident of this state for many years, having resided in Chelsea, Mass., a long time, where his son and partner was born, and removed from there to this city. Both are practical and experienced plumbers and thoroughly proficient in all its branches. They founded this establishment under the present firm title originally in 18[illegible]. The premises occupied are eligibly located on a corner and comprise a finely fitted store with all conveniences for the accommodation of their fine stock of goods, to which is attached a large and commodious store, both covering an area of 1[illegible] feet. The shop is fully equipped with all the latest appliances and tools required in the mechanical department of the business, while the store contains an extensive and complete assortment of everything in the line of plumbers' supplies, embracing wrought iron and cast iron, block tin, lead and earthern pipes, bath tubs, faucets, automatic water closets and urinals in all styles, wash-bowls, showers, valves, traps, lift and force pumps, chandeliers, brackets, side and drop lights, gas jets, lava tips, boilers and water-backs for ranges, etc. These goods are all of the very best manufacture and of the latest and most desirable patterns, and are offered at the lowest prices. The firm is prepared to execute all kinds of work in the way of ventilating, lighting, sanitary plumbing, making sewer connections, etc., in which a full and competent force of skilled workmen are given constant employment. Both being practical workmen, no work is permitted to leave their hands that does not come up to the highest standard of excellence. They have telephone communication No. [illegible], and all orders received by that source receive prompt response. Repairing receives special attention.

JAMES P. STEWART & CO., Coal and Wood, Wharf, No. [illegible] Medford Street, Charlestown District, Boston Office, No. [illegible] Exchange Place.—The house of James P. Stewart & Co., dealers in coal and wood, was originally established twenty years ago, by Messrs. Winslow & Stewart, the present firm succeeding to the control in 187[illegible]. They deal extensively at retail in both hard and soft coal for domestic and steam purposes, and their wharf has a storage capacity for fifteen thousand tons, and every demand of the public is met with promptness and satisfaction. The most careful attention is given to the quality of the different varieties of coal and wood handled. The supplies are received from original sources, and the firm command the best opportunities for securing the choicest and most popular in large quantities and at advantageous rates. Orders, either large or small, receive immediate and careful attention, and a force of twenty workmen contribute to the satisfactory operations of the house. A branch office is operated at No. [illegible] Exchange Place, Boston, and telephone connections are provided at each office. Mr. Stewart, the active member of the firm, is a native of Vermont and a well known citizen of Everett, Mass.

JORDAN'S, Famous Candies and Ice-Cream, No. [illegible] Meridian Street, East Boston.—An establishment well known in East Boston and a great convenience to the citizens in that section is "Jordan's," which has become famous for pure candies and ice-creams. It was first opened by Mr. W. H. Jordan, in 18[illegible], and from that time, owing to the superiority of his delicious confectionery and rich ice-cream, which are unrivalled in purity and wholesomeness, he has established a large family hotel and restaurant custom, which is steadily growing yearly. A store and basement, each [illegible] x [illegible] feet in area, is occupied, and on an average from three to five candy makers and confectioners are kept steadily employed engaged in the manufacture of candies of all kinds, including caramels, chocolate creams and bon bons generally, which are made fresh every hour, also ice-cream of all flavors and sherbets and frozen puddings to order. Church fairs, parties, sociables, weddings, etc., are furnished, all orders receiving the prompt personal attention of Mr. Jordan, and are delivered to any part of the city without extra charge. The store is neatly fitted up, as is also the ice-cream parlor.

GEO. H. DUPEE, Dealer in Provisions, Fruit and Butter, Poultry and Game in their Seasons, No. 685 Tremont, Corner of Berkeley Street.—If a long honorable career entitles any enterprise to prominence and confidence, then certainly Mr. Geo. H. Dupee can make that claim. For more than thirty years he has been catering to the public, supplying substantials and delicacies for the table, and has become widely known, and is receiving a liberal patronage from the best class of citizens. During a period of fifteen years he was located on Tremont Street, and last year he

TRADE MARK.

occupied the premises at No. 685, on that thoroughfare at the corner of Berkeley Street, which have a front of 10 with a depth of 61 feet, and are attractively fitted up and thoroughly equipped, presenting at all times a neat, clean and orderly appearance. Mr. Dupee is a careful business man, and each day receives the choicest and best cuts of all kinds of fresh meats, sweet pure dairy and creamery butter, poultry produce, all kinds of game and dressed poultry when in season, also foreign and domestic fruits, and always has the best quality of smoked and salt meats to place before his customers. He is ably assisted in business operations by three courteous clerks, and orders are filled and delivered without unnecessary delay. Telephone connection—No. 4449-3 also materially facilitates operations and quick deliveries. Mr. Dupee deals in only the choicest and best food products, and can be depended on to supply the freshest at all times. He is a native of Brighton, about fifty years of age, and has been a permanent resident of Boston since he was a young man. Mr. Dupee established the "Newton City Market," Newton, Mass., where he did a large business in provisions, fruit and butter for ten years previous to his going to Dakota to look after his 1880 acre market.

LUTHER S. HANDY, Charlestown Stove Company, Nos. 515 and 517 Main Street, Charlestown.—Among the houses in Charlestown extensively engaged in dealing in stoves, furnaces, heaters, ranges, etc., may be named that of Mr. Luther S. Handy, who deals also in stoves, new and second-hand furniture, crockery, glass and wooden ware, and is also a plumber. Mr. Handy is a native of this state, and has been a resident of this district a number of years. Having a complete knowledge and many years of experience in this line of business, he founded this establishment about the year 1870, under the present firm title, and from the date of its inception has been the recipient of a very liberal and permanent patronage, which is continually increasing in proportions of great magnitude. The premises occupied are of spacious dimensions, having a double frontage of two street numbers, and 130 feet in depth with a workshop on the second floor. A full force of competent and reliable workmen are given constant employment, and in his stock will be found a complete and varied assortment of parlor, office and cooking stoves, ranges, heaters, furnaces, open grates, etc., all having been carefully selected from among the productions of the most famous manufacturers in the country, also a fine line of the latest improved gas and oil stoves. The stock of furniture embraces fine parlor, hall, library, chamber and dining-room suites, also sofas, lounges, rockers, upholstered goods, kitchen furniture,

extension and plain tables, carpets, oil-cloths, mattings, rugs, spring beds, mattresses of every kind, feathers, etc., new and second hand, the latter all in complete order. His assortment of crockery includes full and broken sets of china, queen's, granite, C. C., yellow and stone ware, also glass goods of every description, lamps and their fixtures, likewise cooking utensils, wooden ware, etc., in fact all kinds of household specialties, which are offered to the public at the lowest prices consistent with a living business. Mr. Handy is a practical plumber and sanitary engineer, and is prepared to execute all work in that line at the shortest notice, promptly, satisfactorily, and at moderate prices. He also sets, cleans and repairs stoves, heaters, ranges and furnaces in the best style of workmanship. For the benefit of those desiring any of his wares on easy terms, he has adopted for their benefit the installment plan.

GREENLEAF & CO., Wire Workers and Manufacturers of Wire Cloths, Foundry Riddles, No. 90 Union Street.—This first-class concern was established in Providence, R. I., in 1850, and in 1851 was removed to Boston. The premises occupied at No. 90 Union Street comprise a building of four floors, 45 x 60 feet in dimensions, equipped throughout with the latest appliances in wire working and in which eight experienced hands are employed. The firm manufacture all kinds of wire work for the general trade and to order, including wire cloths, foundry riddles, iron railings, window guards, window coal and sand screens, patent tinned oval slaters, spatter cloths, flour sieves, mosquito and poultry nettings, skylight screens, etc., which are all done by hand work exclusively. The trade is of the largest dimensions, covering the west as well as the whole of New England, the goods of the house being unsurpassed by any other in the line. Mr. Greenleaf, who is a Maine man, has a thorough, practical knowledge of the business.

C. CHAPMAN, Stoves, Furnaces, Ranges, etc., No. 676 Broadway, South Boston.—An old-time honored and representative South Boston establishment is the line is that of Mr. C. C. Chapman, plumber and general jobber, also dealer in stoves, ranges, furnaces, tins, britannia, iron and wooden ware, etc., etc. Mr. Chapman was born in the town of Dennis, Mass., and early learned the trade with which for nearly forty years he has been most prosperously identified. He established the present enterprise in 1885 and from the start has enjoyed a large business. The spacious store, 30 x 75 feet in dimensions, contains a large, comprehensive and complete stock, embracing the best improved makes of heating and cooking apparatus; also all kinds of kitchen furnishing goods, together with iron sinks, lead pipe and water fixtures. In the rear is a well equipped shop, where a corps of experienced workmen is employed, and all work in the plumbing and general jobbing line is executed in the most skillful manner. Mr. Chapman counts among his numerous patronage the best custom of the vicinity.

GEORGE BARNES, Family Bread, Cake and Pastry Baker, Nos. 434 and 778 Tremont Street.—Mr. George Barnes is a practical bread, cake and pastry baker, and has occupied the stores Nos. 434 and 778 Tremont Street about a year, succeeding Mr. J. B. Whitney who had established the business in 1865. Both stores are perfect, complete and very handsome in their appointments, and well adapted for meeting the demands of the public. The bakery is well equipped, and eight competent assistants, who are proficient in their respective departments, are kept constantly employed. The very best home-made family bread, rolls, etc., and plain and fancy cakes and pastry are made fresh every day, and hot baked beans on Wednesday and Saturday evenings, and every Sunday morning hot brown bread and baked beans, which are supplied to families, hotels, restaurants and boarding houses. Everything used in these establishments is of the best quality, and the premises will be found scrupulously neat and clean. Mr. Barnes also furnishes to order roast turkey, chicken, beef, boiled tongue and ham, giving his personal attention to orders, and is indefatigable in his endeavors to please his patrons. His business is large and steadily growing, the products of his bakeries being highly esteemed. Mr. Barnes' prices are very moderate, and all who desire sweet, nutritious, wholesome, home-made bread and rich pastry and properly cooked beans and brown bread should not fail to send him an order.

WILLIAM H. WALL & CO., Dealers in Provisions, Fruits and Vegetables, Fifth Street, Corner of D Street, Branch Store, No. 805 East Fourth Street, South Boston.—Mr. Wall, by long experience in this line of business, is thoroughly versed in all its details. He founded this enterprise originally in 1871, under the present firm title, and has occupied his present eligible location in East Fourth Street ever since 1873, and has established his other house in Fifth Street subsequent to that date, and by wise and able management he has developed a very large and rapidly increasing business. He handles none but the very choicest stall fed beef, veal, mutton, lamb, pork, fresh and salt water food, poultry and game in their season, while his cured meats, both foreign and domestic, are noted for their excellence, flavor, etc. The first poultry and game of the season are always to be found in his establishment, fresh and untainted, direct from the yard or the hunters' skill, while the most delicious fruits and berries and all continuous vegetables are secured by him to meet the demands of his customers. Tropical and southern state productions are received by him direct from producers, as is also all his California delicacies. A special feature of his establishment is the preparation of his meats and provisions in perfect order, dressed and cleaned ready for the range. His stores are spacious and commodious, elegantly fitted up in central wood fixtures, and have every modern convenience, including cold storage for the preservation of perishable articles in hot weather, which enables him to supply his patrons with the freshest and best during all seasons of the year at the most reasonable prices. Both stores are models of neatness and cleanliness. Mr. Wall is a native of this section of the city, and is popular with the community.

WILLIAM E. BROWN, Funeral Undertaker, No. 14 Bennington Street, East Boston.—One of the oldest undertaking establishments in this vicinity, is that now conducted by Mr. William E. Brown. It was established in 1816 by Mr. William H. Brown, his father, whom he succeeded in 1864. Mr. Brown was born and brought up in this community, and has had many years' practical experience as a funeral undertaker, and in the prosecution of his calling is very considerate, and having a natural adaptation to it, discharges the duties comprised therewith with a fine sense of delicacy and sympathy. He attends personally to all details of funerals, furnishing everything necessary, including hearse and carriages, and takes full charge of affairs from the house to the cemetery, and will always be found prompt, faithful, obliging and courteous.

ALFRED ROGERS, Dealer in Choice Groceries and Provisions, No. 781 East Broadway, near L Street, South Boston.—A well-known figure in South Boston whose operations in these articles are as creditable as they are extensive is that of Mr. Alfred Rogers, dealer in choice groceries and provisions. Mr. Rogers is a native of Marshfield, is forty-two years of age, and has been in this line of business for a great many years, having founded this establishment in 1873. In order to accommodate his steadily increasing trade he was obliged to seek more commodious quarters and removed to his present location in 1881, where he occupies a very spacious store and basement, having a frontage of twenty-five feet with a depth four times greater than that space. It is very handsomely and appropriately fitted up with every convenience and facility for the successful prosecution of the business and ease of patrons, and contains an unusually large and first-class assortment of fancy and staple groceries, including French, English, German and Italian delicacies, sauces, relishes, condiments, etc., hermetically sealed goods in glass and tin, foreign and domestic fruits, canned fish, potted meats, bakers' and laundry supplies, choice spring and winter wheat, family flour, rye flour, corn and oat meal, corn starch and other cereals, smoked and pickled meats of every variety, choice dairy and fancy creamery butter, foreign and domestic cheese, fresh eggs, vegetables and other farm, garden and dairy products. The great specialties of this house are its sugars, syrups and molasses, and particularly its fine grades of fresh and pure teas, coffees and spices. The prices asked for these articles are the same as paid for inferior grades in other places. Mr. Rogers is one of our most popular citizens and tradesmen, and highly respected.

BUNKER HILL FURNITURE COMPANY, Furniture and Carpet House, Nos. 244, 246, 248 Main Street, Charlestown District.—This enterprise was originally established in 1862, by Mr. Edward White, who was succeeded by the present proprietor, Mr. J. V. Steele, in 1882. The premises occupied comprise a three-story building, 40 by 80 feet in dimensions, arranged in the best manner for storage and exhibition, and the rapid and economical handling of goods. An immense stock is carried, embracing furniture, carpets, stoves, ranges and household goods generally. The furniture, which is carried in magnificent assortment, ranges in quality from the plainest to the most elegant and elaborate styles, and many beautiful specimens of mechanical skill and excellence are shown that arrest the attention and win the admiration of critical and judicious purchasers. The supply is of the most complete and comprehensive character, and is well calculated to meet the requirements of every taste and fancy. In the carpet department a fine display is made of goods representing the products of the most noted American and European manufacturers, and the stock contains the latest novelties and most exquisite designs known to the trade. The line of stoves and ranges includes the most valuable improvements made for both heating and cooking. The prices are placed at the lowest point of moderation, and a specialty is made of the popular installment plan, which brings the goods within the reach of all classes of patrons. The trade is at all times brisk and lively. Mr. Steele is a native and well-known citizen of Somerville. He also operates a plumbing and furnace workshop at No. 75 Blackstone Street, Boston, and is a gentleman of marked business ability.

JOHN McWEENY, Dry Goods, Millinery, Gents' Furnishing Goods, etc., Nos. 17 and 19 Meridian Street, East Boston.—The establishment of Mr. John McWeeny is the leading dry goods house in East Boston. He established himself in business in 1878, originally locating at No. 8 Meridian Street, and in 1885 removed the dry goods business to his present store, on the same street, retaining the old store for his gents' furnishing goods, hat and cap departments. His dry goods emporium comprises two floors and a basement, 40 by 90 feet each, the interior of which is fitted up and furnished to keeping with the correct taste and sound judgment of the proprietor. This store is the busiest in this line in this community, its counters being daily thronged with patrons from all classes of society. Each department is complete within itself, while the staff of employees, numbering fifteen in all, are noted for their courteous and obliging manners, and a faculty for anticipating the wants of customers, laying before them a full variety of fabrics, patterns and shades from which to choose. Customers can here find a complete outfit of dress goods, housekeeping goods, shawls, suits and cloaks, hosiery, gloves and underwear, corsets, hoop-skirts and bustles, laces, ribbons and embroideries, notions, fancy goods and small wares, all at prices which defy competition. The establishment at No. 8 is managed with equal success, and is stocked to repletion with choice stylish and reliable goods, including gentlemen's dress shirts, gloves and underwear, hosiery, handkerchiefs and general outfittings, as well as the latest styles of hats and caps. Mr. McWeeny is a native of Ireland, and justly accounted as one of East Boston's most able and progressive merchants.

EMERSON & FRYE, Country Produce, No. 8 C Street, South Boston.—Fish and Oysters, No. 9 C Street, South Boston.—Furnishing the citizens of South Boston with food supplies in a business of ever expanding dimensions, and is well represented by Messrs. Emerson & Frye, whose ably conducted store was first opened in 1881 by Mr. E. B. Emerson, who carried it on until January last when he was joined by Mr. W. A. Frye. They are both experienced men in the business and from long association with it fully understand the wants of the public. The store is size is 25 x 50 feet and in its appointments is admirably adapted for the purposes of the business. The firm has every advantage for procuring the finest and best country produce and fish and oysters, while important interments are held out in the matter of prices. Each day a fine display is made in the meal, clean premises and two assistants besides the firm are kept busy filling orders. Messrs. Emerson & Frye can always be depended on to furnish only the very best and choicest food supplies to be obtained in South Boston. They are both from the state of New Hampshire.

H ENRY J. ADDISON, Watches, Clocks and Jewelry, Eye-Glasses and Spectacles, No. 478 Main Street, Charlestown.— Among the noteworthy houses in Charlestown is that of Mr. Henry J. Addison, dealer in watches, clocks, jewelry, eye-glasses and spectacles, which is one of the most reliable concerns in this section of the city, and its goods are in extensive and steady demand, owing to the high reputation they sustain. Mr. Addison was born in England, but has been a resident of the United States ever since 1867, and after acquiring a thorough practical knowledge of his trade in years of practical experience, he inaugurated this enterprise in 1886, and the justice and permanent success that has attended his efforts, from the start, fully attests the general excellence of the goods handled and the honorable methods he employs in dealing with patrons. His store is spacious and commodious, and appropriately furnished for the attractive display of his large and valuable stock, which embraces a full and complete assortment of fine gold and silver watches of both American and European construction, in all varieties of styles, diamonds, rubies, emeralds, sapphires and other precious gems of dazzling brilliancy, set in the latest and most unique designs, plain and fancy gold rings, watch chains and charms, bracelets, necklaces, lace and scarf pins, chatelaines, collar, cuff and sleeve buttons, studs, etc. Also fine French, Swiss and American clocks, solid silver and plated wares, gold pens, pencils, eye-glasses, spectacles, opera and field glasses, together with other optical and scientific wares pertaining to this line of trade. These goods have all been selected with the greatest care, and cannot fail to supply every want as they are sold at the very lowest prices. Mr. Addison makes a specialty of Odd Fellows jewelry, also of other societies, and carries in this particular feature of his business. He devotes particular care and attention to the repairing of fine jewelry, watches, clocks and silverware and employs for that purpose only reliable workmen.

A. L. ADAMS, Apothecary, No. 296 Meridian Street, East Boston.—The oldest and best known pharmacy in East Boston is the well-ordered and neat drug store of A. L. Adams. Physicians' prescriptions and family recipes are here compounded in the most accurate and reliable manner in every instance, from absolutely pure and fresh ingredients, while best rock prices at all times prevail. The store, which is compact and ample, is neatly appointed and well equipped, and a large, carefully selected stock is constantly kept on hand, including drugs, medicines and chemicals of every description, extracts, acids, compeers, spirits, alcohol and pure medicinal liquors, wines and mineral waters, herbs, barks and roots, all the standard proprietary remedies, sanitary specialties, pharmaceutical preparations in great variety, and a fine line of toilet articles, perfumery, fancy soaps, sponges, chamois, medicated paper and everything in the line of druggists' sundries, while a competent assistant is in attendance likewise, the proprietor however exercising close personal supervision over the prescription counter. Mr. Adams, who is a gentleman somewhat past the middle age, but active and energetic, was born at Boston, Vt., where he established himself in business over thirty years ago, subsequently moving to Lodlow, same state, and has conducted the excellent pharmacy here in East Boston since 1886.

J. P. E. PARKER, Tobacco, Cigars and Smokers' Articles, No. 44 Howard Street.—The business house of Mr. J. P. E. Parker was established about two years ago, and under his able management a large, substantial trade has been built up. The store is complete in all its appointments, and neatly and tastefully fitted, and well stocked with a large and varied assortment of all the leading popular brands of imported and domestic cigars and smoking and chewing tobaccos, cigarettes, and all those articles required by consumers of tobacco in its many forms. Mr. Parker is agent for the sale of the celebrated cigars manufactured by the Eastern Cigar Company of Westfield, Mass., and is conducting a large wholesale trade, supplying a large demand from dealers in the city. He makes a specialty of the popular "Harvard" cigar, which are selling for the moderate price of 5 cents, and the N. H. cigar selling for 10 cents, three for 25 cents. He is a native of New Hampshire. Mr. Parker is also agent for the Troy laundry, and gives his prompt attention to orders and work left at his store.

E LLISON J. KINGTON, Apothecary, Cambridge and Kingston Streets, Charleston District.— Mr. Ellison J. Kingdom's handsome apothecary store has been known for many years as one of the safest drug houses in the city. Mr. Kingdom is a native of Vermont, but has been a resident of this city ever since 1870. The establishment which he conducts was founded originally in 1859, and after some changes of proprietorship he became sole owner of it in 1882, and under his administration since that date has greatly increased its patronage, clearly indicating what may be accomplished by close attention to the wants of customers, handling pure and fresh goods only, and liberal business methods. The premises occupied comprise an elegant corner store, which is neatly and appropriately fitted up in the most improved modern style, with handsome display windows, showcases, beautiful counters, also an elaborate cool water fountain. Fully appreciating the responsibility attending the compounding of physicians' prescriptions and family recipes, he has provided a separate department, devoted exclusively to this branch of the business, in which will be found all the latest appliances that tend to insure accuracy, and he devotes his personal attention to their proper dispensation. He keeps on hand constantly a full and complete stock of pure and fresh drugs, chemicals and pharmaceutical preparations, all of which are up to the highest standard demanded by the United States. Pharmacopoeia, botanic remedies, proprietary remedies of well-known efficiency and reputation, toilet and fancy articles, perfumery, foreign and domestic mineral waters, physicians' and surgeons' requisites, druggists' sundries, in fact, everything usually found in a well regulated pharmacy. Prescriptions are prepared at all hours of the day or night, and at most reasonable prices.

W. C. TOWNSEND, Groceries and Provisions, Fruits and Vegetables, No. 232 Sumner Street, East Boston.— This gentleman began business here six years ago, and has gained a widely extended reputation for the high character of his goods and the care he exercises in meeting the wants of his customers. His premises comprise a salesroom and basement, each with a capacity of 25 x 35 feet, and the salesroom is a model of neatness and order. The business is divided into two departments, one being devoted to groceries and the other to provisions. The stock carried is a large and comprehensive one, and includes the choicest teas from China and Japan, coffees from South America, Mocha and Java, the finest flour made in the country, creamery and dairy butter, canned goods in great variety, pickles, sauces, table delicacies of all kinds, grocers' sundries of every description, choice cuts of fresh beef, mutton, lamb and pork, sausages, smoked hams and tongues, salted meats of all kinds, fruits and vegetables in season, etc. The stock is frequently renewed and kept up to the highest standard of excellence, while the prices are kept at the lowest point consistent with a living business. Mr. Townsend is ever at this post of duty, exercising a close supervision over his affairs, and he and his three assistants are kept busy. A special feature of the business is the handling of ship stores and yacht supplies, and in this line the trade is brisk and growing. Mr. Townsend is a native of Cambridge and a resident of East Boston.

A. LEIGHTON, Merchant Tailor, No. 26 Meridian Street, East Boston.— A noteworthy and successful house deserving of special mention in this work is that of Mr. A. Leighton, who brings a wide range of practical experience to bear on his enterprise. He started business here in 1885, and at once secured a substantial and flattering patronage that has kept on increasing year by year. Mr. Leighton occupies a neat, well ordered store, 20 x 30 feet in dimensions, and here he carries constantly on hand an exceedingly fine assortment of imported and domestic suitings, elegant worsted and worsted suitings in the newest styles and most fashionable designs and patterns, cassimeres, cheviots, cloths, meltons, cheviots, stripes, venetians, etc. Measures are taken and garments trimmed and made in the most desirable manner, and accurate in cut and fit, and furnished at short notice. Every suit that leaves the establishment is made from the best quality of materials, and is beautifully finished and of the most stylish and fashionable patterns. Mr. Leighton makes a specialty of the finest work, is an experienced and first-class cutter, and has in service a competent staff of tailors. The patrons include the best classes in the city. Mr. Leighton is a native of Portland, Maine.

MRS. P. H. SPELMAN, French Millinery, No. [illegible] West Broadway, South Boston.—An old and long established house engaged in the millinery trade in this city is that of Mrs. P. H. Spelman. Mrs Spelman is a native of this city and has been in this line of industry for a period extending over a quarter of a century. Having a thorough and practical knowledge of it in all its intricate details, she established herself in business on her own account, originally in Boston proper in [illegible] and after ten years of unremitted prosperity there she removed to her present location in [illegible], bringing with her a large share of her old patronage, and rapidly acquiring a very liberal and permanent trade from among the leading and most refined families in this portion of the city. She occupies a handsome store of large proportions, which is elegantly fitted up in the most approved modern style and fully equipped with every convenience for the attractive display of her superb stock of seasonable goods. Here will be found at all times a full and general line of almost everything that adds to the personal appearance of the gentler sex in the way of head covering, embracing imported and domestic bonnets and hats, trimmed and untrimmed, of every variety, in the latest and most fashionable designs and patterns, trimmed to order in the newest and most correct styles, also superb plumes, feathers, stuffed birds of rare and gorgeous plumage, ostrich tips, French artificial flowers, fruits, etc., also beautiful trimmings, silks, satins, velvets, plushes, ribbons and in fact everything in French millinery. She also keeps constantly on hand a fine stock of crape goods, and especial prompt attention is given to all crape orders. Mrs Spelman enjoys unusual facilities with the largest and most reliable importers, which enables her to give her patrons special inducements which cannot be obtained elsewhere. She keeps a number of artistic and thoroughly experienced milliners constantly employed, and a specialty is made of rush orders or trimming while customers wait. Mrs. Spelman is greatly esteemed in social and mercantile life, and justly merits the success attained by her ability, enterprise and perseverance.

S. GOLDSBERG, Men's, Youths', Boys' and Children's Clothing, and Gents' Furnishing Goods, No. [illegible] Sumner Street, East Boston.—One of the well-known dealers in East Boston in clothing and furnishing goods is Mr. S. Goldsberg, who has been established in the business for the past eighteen years. The store is very neatly and tastefully fitted up and presents the ample area of [illegible] feet, and is well stocked with a large, valuable assortment of men's, youths', boys' and children's clothing in all the new fashionable styles, cut in the best manner, suitable for all seasons. The goods have been carefully selected and will bear the most critical examination and inspection, and are warranted by Mr. Goldsberg in every respect. He also makes a fine display of everything desirable in gentlemen's furnishing goods, and also new style fashionable hats and caps, and boots and shoes, slippers and rubbers of every kind, and trunks, satchels, etc. Mr. Goldsberg is a thorough, active, energetic business man, who can always be relied on and never makes misrepresentations to sell goods. His prices are low, and the stock will be found first class in every respect. He was born in Poland and came to this country over twenty years ago.

ORIN CURTIS & SON, Dealers in Choice Family Groceries, No. [illegible] Main Street, Charlestown.—A conspicuous establishment engaged extensively in this department of commerce, and deserving a marked high degree of popularity, is that which is so ably conducted by Messrs. Orin Curtis & Son, dealers in choice family groceries. The individual names of this firm are Orin and Frank L., the former being a native of Vermont, but a resident of Charlestown for [illegible] years where his son and partner was born. The business was founded originally by the senior member of the firm in January, [illegible], and owing to the rapid growth of its patronage, which required additional capital and enterprise, the present copartnership was formed in the following month of March, and since that date has been most successfully conducted under that firm title. In addition to his connection with this wide-awake concern, Mr. Frank L. Curtis is superintendent of the Waverly House, which duties he performs in the most satisfactory manner to all concerned. The store and basement occupied are of spacious dimensions, finely appointed throughout, and provided with every modern convenience to facilitate the operations of business, while the reputation of the house is first class, both for the quality of the goods handled and for the correct methods that are strictly observed in its management. They carry at all times a large and fresh stock of the finest, purest and freshest of teas, coffees and spices, of which specialties are made; also cocoa, chocolate, flour, corn and oatmeal, and other cereals, sugars, syrups, table delicacies, foreign and domestic green and dried fruits, canned goods, condiments, hermetically sealed goods in glass and tins, bakers' and laundry supplies, covered and uncovered hams, bacon, shoulders, salt, dried and smoked fish, vegetables, choice dairy and fancy creamery butter, full cream cheese, freshly laid eggs and other products of the farm, garden and dairy. The store is a model of neatness and cleanliness.

N. ERSKINE, Pictures and Frames, No. [illegible] Meridian Street, East Boston.—An old-established and popular art emporium is the well-known store of N. Erskine, where can always be found a complete and first-class assortment of pictures, frames and kindred art novelties, and which for more than thirty years has been in prosperous existence. It is about the oldest and leading establishment of the kind in East Boston, having been established in [illegible] by the gentleman whose name heads the sketch, and for the past twenty-seven years has been conducted at the present location. The store is commodious and well kept, with workshop in the rear, and three expert assistants are employed. A full and fine stock is constantly carried on hand, including beautiful oil paintings, engravings, etchings and elegant pictures in quite a variety; also superb picture frames, cornices, etc.; artistic gilt frames and genuine works of art being a specialty, while frames are made to order likewise and regilt in first-class style at short notice. Pictures are framed also, and old paintings, engravings, etc., renovated equal to new, at reasonable rates. Mr. Erskine was born in the state of Maine, but is an old and respected resident of East Boston.

LEVI W. DODGE'S Pharmacy, No. [illegible] Main Street, Charlestown.—Among the old-established business places in this section of the city, that familiarly known as Dodge's Pharmacy is one of the most prominent. It was founded about a quarter of a century ago by Mr. Levy O. Dodge, who was succeeded by his son, the present proprietor, Mr. Levi W. Dodge, in [illegible]. He has had many years practical experience, and was brought up to the business under the careful tuition of his father. In compounding physicians' prescriptions, Mr. Dodge exercises care and judgment, and in their preparation uses only the freshest and purest drugs, and combines accuracy with promptness. The store is [illegible] feet in area, and is handsomely fitted up in an elaborate style, and is well equipped in every respect for the purpose of compounding and dispensing medicines. The assortment of drugs and chemicals, and standard proprietary preparations, and pharmaceuticals, and toilet goods is perfect and fine and complete, and everything belonging to the business can always be obtained in this establishment. Of Mr. Dodge, the proprietor, who was born in Charlestown and has always lived here, it is only necessary to say of him personally that he stands high in professional circles.

DEMPSEY BROS., Wholesale and Retail Dealers in Beef, Pork, Mutton, Poultry, Vegetables, Butter, Lard, Eggs, etc., Nos. 74 and 76 Beach Street.—Among the best conducted and most popular city establishments in the provision trade should be mentioned that of Messrs. Dempsey Bros., wholesale and retail dealers in beef, pork, mutton, poultry, vegetables, butter, lard, eggs, etc. This well-known firm began business on the corner above in [illegible], and have been at the present site since [illegible]. The spacious and well arranged premises are handsomely fitted up with hardwood fixtures, marble slabs, etc., etc., and the general appointment embraces all the latest improved methods and appliances for the display and handling of stock. Here is at all times to be found a full line of the staple commodities above enumerated, carefully selected in each department from the best markets, and with due regard for the requirements of all classes of trade. A goodly corps of experienced assistants is kept busy in supplying the wants of the numerous patronage, and goods are delivered at Newton, Brookline, Longwood and Dorchester, besides delivering goods at Boston. Messrs. C. H. and C. S. Dempsey, composing the firm, are natives of Maine, and gentlemen of long experience in and possessing a thorough knowledge of the provision trade.

GEORGE W. BALL, Dealer in Coal and Wood, First street, between F and Dorchester Streets, South Boston.—In this portion of Boston we find the active and enterprising establishment of Mr. George W. Ball, coal and wood merchant, which ranks second to no other in South Boston, in its line. Mr. Ball is a gentleman of about middle age and is a Bostonian by birth, well and favorably known in commercial and social life. This business was founded originally in 1877 under the firm title of Messrs. Cushing and Ball, and was continued under that copartnership until 1882, when Mr. Ball became sole proprietor, and his operations were removed from the old stand foot of C street to the present location during the same year. The premises utilized for the business comprise a very neatly arranged office for the transaction of business, and a yard 80 x 100 feet in dimensions. This spacious and commodious plant is supplied with every appliance and convenience for the proper conduct of its trade, which includes shedding capacity for over 600 tons of coal, also proper protection for the large stock of wood constantly on hand, also a full force of teams and drivers, coal screens, power for sawing and splitting wood, standard scales properly and legally tested, in fact all appurtenances to a first-class coal and wood yard. Mr. Ball keeps at all times a full and complete assortment of hard and soft coal of all sizes and grades, and is prepared to execute orders of any magnitude for these articles promptly and in the most satisfactory manner, grade, quality and quantity being guaranteed in all cases. He has direct connections with producers and his anthracite varieties are from the most famous mines in the Lehigh, Lackawanna, Wyoming, Lykens and Schuylkill regions in Pennsylvania, as is also his wood and full bituminous varieties from west of the Alleghanies in that state. He also carries a fine line of cannel coal for grate consumption. His stock of wood embraces all the different varieties of hickory, oak, maple, birch, ash, walnut, also pitch and black pine, and hemlock. Mr. Ball can offer superior inducements to manufacturers and the general public. Mr. Ball was elected by the fellow-citizens to represent them in the state legislature and as such acquitted himself with the same satisfaction to them that has followed him in his long business career.

S. A. THORPE & CO., Beef, Mutton, Lamb, Veal and Poultry, No. 1025 Washington Street.—The establishment of Messrs. S. A. Thorpe & Co., at No. 1025 Washington Street, and known as the Chicago Cash Market, is a prominent and popular one in its line. They conduct an extensive trade as dealers in beef, mutton, lamb, veal and poultry, butter, eggs, fruit, vegetables, salt and pickled fish, making a specialty of supplying hotels, boarding houses and restaurants at special rates. The market is a model of cleanliness, order and good management, and here is to be found at all times the finest stock known to the trade in meats, fruits, vegetables, fish and country produce, offered at prices which are safe from unsuccessful competition. The meats handled by this firm are the choicest that can be secured from any section of the country, while the connections of the house with producers and shippers enable the firm to supply the trade and consumers with first-class goods in quantities to suit and to guarantee the prompt fulfillment of all orders. The reliability of the firm is too well known to require comment in this work. Mr. Thorpe, the active member of the firm, is a well-known Boston market man, who has been established in the business here since 1862 and is eminently popular.

AMOS T. WHITE & CO., Groceries and Provisions, No. 478 Broadway and 174 Dorchester Street, South Boston.—Attention is here directed to the spacious and finely appointed store of Amos T. White & Co., located at No. 478 Broadway (with branch store also at No. 174 Dorchester Street) where can be found at all times a complete and very fine line of everything comprehended under the general head of "groceries and provisions," and where purchasers can rely upon getting a first-class article, full weight and satisfactory treatment in every instance. The firm handles nothing but first quality goods, while the prices prevailing are the very lowest consistent therewith, and all orders receive immediate attention, from six to eight efficient and polite assistants attending to the wants of customers in the Broadway store. The premises here occupied comprise a handsome store, 30 x 100 feet, and basement of like area, while an extensive and A1 stock is constantly

DOWLEY & PROCTOR, Manufacturers and Dealers in Furniture, Carpets, Rugs, Lamps, etc., No. 651 Broadway, South Boston.—Among the large, well conducted business enterprises which line this popular thoroughfare will be found that of Messrs. Dowley & Proctor, manufacturers of and dealers in furniture, carpets, rugs, lamps, mirrors, clocks, musical instruments, etc., etc. The spacious and attractive salesroom, 30 x 60 feet in dimensions, is heavily stocked with the newest novelties and latest and most fashionable designs in the staple house furnishings above enumerated, which are sold to customers at the lowest rates, for cash or upon the installment plan, with easy weekly or monthly payments. The superior goods and fair and equitable dealing of the house have made it a favorite purchasing depot for the trade of the vicinity. Messrs. G. W. Dowley and W. W. Proctor are natives respectively of Vermont and Maine and practical, go-ahead business men. They embarked in the present enterprise in the spring of 1885, and have already reared a business which places them in the front rank of South Boston merchants.

C. RAUCKMAN, Dry and Fancy Goods, Corsets, Hosiery, Gloves, Buttons and Trimmings, No. 807 Washington Street.—Prominent among those of the dry goods stores on Washington Street that have gained a high reputation in the trade is Mr. C. Rauckman. His dress fabrics have been very carefully and judiciously selected, and all novelties in the latest designs either of staple or material will be found upon his shelves. Large purchases and close cash payments enable him to mark goods down to the lowest possible point. Mr. Rauckman has been in the dry and fancy goods trade since 1877, and he removed, in 1886, to his present store, which has an area of 20 x 60 feet. It is neatly and attractively fitted up, and contains a full assortment of all the latest novelties in dress goods of the most costly and cheapest fabrics, fancy goods in great variety, corsets, hosiery, gloves, buttons, trimmings, ladies' and gentlemen's underwear, etc. His notion department is one that gives him pre-eminence as a caterer to a variety of customers. Four assistants are in constant service. Mr. Rauckman is a native of Nova Scotia and is popular with all to whom he is known.

ROBERT J. RODDAT & CO., Furnaces, Ranges and Stoves, Manufacturers of Tin, Sheet-Iron, Zinc and Copper Ware, No. 398 Dorchester Avenue.—Among the well conducted and prosperous business enterprises in this section of the city should be mentioned that of Robert J. Roddat & Co., manufacturers of tin, copper and sheet iron ware, and dealers in stoves, ranges, furnaces, etc. The spacious and well arranged premises consist of a store 20 x 60 feet in dimensions, with a commodious shop in the rear, supplied with all requisite tools and appliances. The general stock of stoves, ranges, furnaces and kitchen ware carried, represents the finest productions in this line, and the work turned out in the shop has a standard reputation for general excellence. The house is liberally patronized by the best custom of the vicinity, and the general business is both large and lucrative. Mr. Roddat is a practical and skillful exponent of his trade, and brings to bear a wide experience in the conduct of his enterprise. He has here established since 1879, and in the interval has built up a business which distinguishes him as one of the leading local merchants in his line.

DALY & CO., Manufacturers of Fancy Saddlery, Etc., No. 40 Sudbury Street.—This enterprising and reliable house opened its doors to the business world in 1880, and from the first has been attended with remarkable success. Its motto has always been "Honest work and square dealing," and it has brought its reward to build up a large and permanent trade. The leading speciality of the house is the manufacture of women's hats and women's supplies, which have gained a widespread reputation, and the trade in which is rapidly increasing in volume. Shipments are made to all parts of the United States and Canada, to the British Provinces and the south also a very extensive, carefully selected and miscellaneous stock is continually kept on hand to meet the immediate demands of the trade. Born in Ireland in case of the United States citizen eight years ago, and is now a resident in business circles he has a high reputation for promptness and probity and stands high in all circles.

BOSTON CHAIR MANUFACTURING COMPANY, Chas. P. Hemenway, President; W. G. Wheildon, Treasurer, No. 92 Canal Street.—Extensively engaged in the manufacture of reed, cane and wood seat, bent-wood and other chairs, we find the representative and progressive Boston Chair Manufacturing Company, whose office and sale-rooms are centrally located at No. 92 Canal Street. This company was only incorporated under the laws of Massachusetts in 1880, since which period it has built up an extensive and influential patronage not only in all sections of the United States, but also in Mexico, the West Indies, Central and South America, Europe, Africa, Australia and New Zealand. The factories of the company, which are admirably equipped with the latest improved machinery and appliances, and furnish constant employment to 300 operatives are situated at Ashburnham, Mass. The company's reed, cane and wood seat chairs are unrivalled for strength, finish, quality, elegance and general excellence, and have no superiors in this or any other market, while the prices quoted in all cases necessarily attract the attention of close and prudent buyers. The factories are under the able and careful management of Mr. F. S. Coolidge, who is an expert in the manufacture of chairs. A large stock is constantly on hand in the Boston store, and all goods are fully guaranteed in every particular. The company have likewise a branch in New York at No. 99 Mott Street, and in London, England, at No. 16 Great Eastern Street.

J. B. PARKER, Hats, Caps, Gloves, Hammocks and Umbrellas, No. 278 Washington Street.—There are few articles of male outfit to which more attention is paid in these days of beautiful attire than hats and gloves, and in this connection it may be observed that very marked improvement has been effected in these articles of late years, as the excellent display made in a leading hat store to-day amply attests. Right here, attention is directed to the real and popular emporium of J. B. Parker, No. 278 Washington Street, where may always be found a complete and assortment of everything in this line, from the most fashionable silk tile to the hardest derby, from the foremost manufacturers only derbies goods being handled while exceedingly low prices prevail. The store is compact and tastefully appointed, while several efficient assistants are employed, hats being made to order, also, in the latest style at short notice. The assortment embraces besides hats and caps of every size style and variety, also an elegant line of gloves, furs, umbrellas, hammocks, etc., and altogether this reliable establishment has a large and substantial patronage. Mr. Parker, the proprietor, is a gentleman of middle age and long business experience, and was born at Hartford, Conn., but has lived in this city many years. He opened this present store here in 1870 and during upward of eighteen years since intervening, the business has been conducted with uniform success in every particular.

MANISON & CO., Real Estate, Etc., No. 194 Washington Street.—This reliable and well-ordered agency was established in 1881 by Fuller & Co., who were succeeded two years later by F. A. Manison (formerly junior member of the firm), and by this gentleman the business was conducted up to 1887, when he associated with him in partnership, Charles H. Hersey, thus constituting the firm, whose name heads this sketch. Mr. Hersey, retiring in the firm. They transact a general real estate business, buying, selling and exchanging all kinds of city and country property, including farms, houses, lots, etc.; also business chances of every description, such as stores, factories, mills, docks, express routes, hotels, boarding houses, restaurants, saloons, etc., special attention being given to the care of estates and the collection of rents. Loans are effected also, on real and personal property at low rates of interest and mortgages are negotiated while investments are desirably placed. In short, everything that appertains to the purchase, sale, transfer and management of real estate and kindred interests is attended to in the most judicious manner. Messrs. Manison & Co. are gentlemen of agreeable manners and strict probity, as well as men of energy and sagacity, with reference of the most flattering character, and all persons having business relations with them will find the same profitable.

GEO. W. BUSS & CO., Manufacturers of Wooden things, Ironing Tables, Boards and various other Kitchen Goods, No. 99 Beverly Street.—This thriving enterprise was started in 1877, and from its inception the venture has proved a positive and permanent success. The shop, which is located on the fifth floor, at No. 99 Beverly Street, is ample and well-equipped, full steam power and all necessary facilities being in service, while several skilled hands are employed. The firm manufacture wooden things of every description, also ironing tables, shirt boards, pastry boards and a variety of kitchen specialities, a complete assortment being kept on hand always, all orders for the trade receiving immediate attention, and the patronage of the concern which is chiefly located in and around Boston, is quite large. Mr. Geo. W. Buss, who is sole proprietor, is a native of New Hampshire, but has been a resident of this vicinity for over thirty years. He is a practical and skilful workman himself, of long and varied experience.

ATWOOD & RICH, Ship Brokers and Commission Merchants, No. 100 Commercial Street.—This prosperous and prosperous firm was established in 1876 and during the eleven years since intervening Messrs. Atwood & Rich have steadily increased their hold on public favor and confidence in the shipping circles of the city and surroundings, until their business has attained quite extensive proportions. They conduct a general ship-brokerage and commission business, chartering, freighting and sending out ships to all the principal American, Canadian, South American and European ports, while cargoes are insured likewise at the very lowest consistent rates. The firm are agents also for the steamer Longfellow, plying between Boston and Providence, and have an interest in a number of vessels, being part owners, and all business entrusted to these gentlemen is certain to be attended to in the most expeditious and satisfactory manner. Messrs. T. D. Atwood and Lyman B. Rich, who compose the firm, are both gentlemen and natives of Cape Cod. They are men of sound judgment, energy and long practical experience.

JAMES H. DUNNE & CO., Importers and Jobbers of Cutlery and Fancy Hardware, No. 57 Washington Street.—This enterprising and prosperous firm was established about three years ago, and its career from the first marks a record of steady and substantial progress. The office and salesroom, which are located on the second floor at No. 57 Washington Street, are compact and ample, and a large and superb assortment is constantly carried in stock, including the finest imported cutlery of every description (table and pocket), knives, fancy steel and metal novelties and hardware specialities in great variety, all orders for the trade being promptly and reliably filled, some half dozen clerks and salesmen are in attendance, while seven experienced representatives are maintained on the road, and the business of the firm, which is principally with jobbers throughout the United States, is all over large and flourishing, the total annual sales reaching a very big and some figure.

232   ILLUSTRATED BOSTON.

W M. B. HOWARD, Apothecary, No. 251 Hanover Street. — One of the oldest established houses in the drug trade in Boston is the well-known concern with which the name of Wm. B. Howard is now identified at No. 251 Hanover Street. This first-class business was founded in the year 1841 by Charles French, and was successfully conducted under his management up to 1872, when Wm. P. Howard succeeded to the concern and gave renewed impetus to the trade. He died in 1886, and Wm. B. Howard succeeded. Dr. French left the college of pharmacy here. He was a very noted man in a popular way, and held in much esteem. He was frequently urged to accept city offices but declined. Many of the earlier plans for municipal elections were prepared in the old store, which was a sort of headquarters for the politicians of his day. The store still contains the original fixtures, is commodious, being 15 x 35 feet deep. It contains a first-class stock of the purest and freshest drugs and chemicals, patent and proprietary medicines, and pure confectionery for a fine family trade. Mr. Howard makes a specialty besides of cough mixtures, sarsaparilla, Russian tooth paste, etc., which are in great popular demand. He also takes the greatest care in compounding physicians' prescriptions, employing two experienced clerks to attend to the trade. Mr. Howard is a native of Boston.

E T. PIGEON, dealer in Boots, Shoes and Rubbers, No. 147 Meridian Street, East Boston. — The boot and shoe industry has always occupied a foremost position in the commerce of every civilized community, and in this city it is one of the most prominent factors in its resources. A thoroughly representative house engaged in this line in East Boston, and popular with patrons, is that of Mr. E. T. Pigeon, dealer in boots, shoes, rubbers, etc., whose handsome establishment is located at No. 147 Meridian Street. Mr. Pigeon is a native of this portion of the city, where he still resides, and having acquired a thorough knowledge of this branch of mercantile life, inaugurated his present enterprise in 1871, and the grand success he has achieved since the commencement, is a striking illustration of what can be accomplished by attending closely to the wants of customers, handling only the best qualities of merchandise and straightforward business methods. His trade is derived principally from among our most intelligent and refined citizens, and in his dealings he not only endeavors to obtain new patrons, but to retain them. He occupies a spacious and commodious store, which is very neatly and appropriately equipped with every convenience for the accommodation of his extensive stock and the comfort of patrons while transacting business. He keeps constantly on hand a full and comprehensive assortment of everything in the line of fine and medium grades of boots, shoes, ties, gaiters and slippers for gentlemen, youths and boys, and in the line of extra and fine wear for ladies, misses and children, everything that is fashionable, novel and desirable, from the strong walking boot or school shoe to the delicate kid or satin bound slippers. In connection with this superb stock he also carries a complete line of rubber goods for foot wear, including rubber boots, overshoes, sandals, arctics, slips, etc. These articles have been most carefully selected from among the best productions of the most celebrated manufacturers in the country by Mr. Pigeon, whose long experience enables him to distinguish the best and most durable materials and workmanship, as well as the latest and most becoming styles, and all goods sold by him are guaranteed to be as represented in every particular, while his prices are extremely reasonable. Repairing receives special attention and is promptly executed. Polite and courteous assistants serve customers intelligently, and every effort is made by the proprietor to meet all requirements of the trade in his line of business.

G EORGE A. LAWS, Pianos, Organs, Musical Instruments of all Kinds, No. 341 Main Street, Charlestown. — Prominent among those engaged in the sale of musical goods in Charlestown is Mr. George A. Laws, dealer in all kinds of musical instruments. Mr. Laws is a native of this city, where he still resides, and has been in the music line a number of years, and established this industry some time ago. The premises utilized are of ample dimensions, neatly and appropriately fitted up, and supplied with every facility for the proper transaction of business. In his store are found an assortment of square and upright pianos, parlor, school

and church organs of the most celebrated makers; also automatical instruments to operate which requires no knowledge of music whatever; various string and reed instruments, such as violins, guitars, mandolins, zithers, harps, banjos, violoncellos, double bass, clarinets, piccolos, flutes, fifes, cornets, accordeons, harmonicas, etc. He also carries a fine stock of Italian violin, harp, cello, guitar and other strings, key-pads for wind instruments, clarinet reeds, etc. Mr. Laws keeps a complete assortment of all the latest productions in sheet music, including the scores and librettos of all the leading and latest operas and operettas, together with all the standard works of the old composers, besides new ballads, part songs, choruses, oratorios, galops, schottisches, polkas, waltzes, and in fact everything pertaining to the musical profession. Mr. Laws is a piano polisher by occupation, and is well qualified to make selections of these popular household instruments. He is the agent of the United Piano Makers of New York, instruments which are well known by all musical people to possess all the best qualities of the much lauded instruments of more pretentious makers. Orders for tuning pianos are received and given prompt attention.

H N. HATCH, Dealer in Hardware, Cutlery, Crockery Ware, etc., Plumbing, Tin and Sheet Iron Worker, etc., No. 120 Broadway, South Boston. — Among those houses engaged in this line of commercial industry in this section of Boston is that of Mr. H. N. Hatch, dealer in hardware, cutlery, etc., plumber, tin and sheet iron worker, etc. Mr. Hatch was born in Maine, but has been a resident of this city for the last quarter of a century. Having a thorough and practical knowledge of this business and its kindred industries he inaugurated this house in 1869 which from the start has been the center of a first-class trade. The premises are of ample dimensions, and comprise a store with workshop in the rear, the latter being spacious and well lighted, and thoroughly equipped with all the latest improved tools and devices necessary for the successful prosecution of the mechanical part of the business. The store is admirably fitted up, and the stock carried embraces all kinds of shelf and general hardware, cutlery, housefurnishing goods, mechanics' and machinists' tools, manufacturers' and builders' supplies, and numerous other articles that are in daily request by the housekeeper, builder, mechanic and manufacturer. He also carries a full and general assortment of china, queen's, crockery and glass ware, including lamps and their fittings, wooden and willow ware. His stock of stoves comprise parlor, office and cooking stoves, ranges, heaters, grates, furnaces; also gas and oil stoves, all of the very latest and most improved patterns which have been selected from among the best productions of the most famous manufacturers in the United States. In addition to these goods he keeps constantly on hand a full assortment of tin, copper and sheet-iron ware, all of his own superior manufacture, in which only the best materials are used, and the most skilled workmanship employed. He keeps a full force of skilled and experienced workmen constantly employed, and is prepared to execute all kinds of out-door work, such as roofing, spouting, etc., and he makes a particular specialty of plumbing in all its branches, which is executed upon true sanitary and scientific principles. He does all kinds of stove and other repairing in this line in the best manner possible. Mr. Hatch is a reliable, painstaking merchant.

C HARLES H. ORR, Meats, Poultry, etc., No. 214 South Street. — One of the most reliable and well-known meat and provision markets in this section of the community, is that which is located at No. 214 South Street, and was originally established in 1881 by the present proprietor, Mr. Charles H. Orr, a young man who has long been actively engaged in this particular line of business. The premises occupied are 22 x 60 feet in area, and are fitted up in hard wood, marble topped counters, the latest improved refrigerating facilities, etc., while several skilled assistants are employed to attend to the needs of customers, and all orders are promptly and satisfactorily executed. The stock of food products dealt in is selected with great care, and includes a full line of fresh, salt, and smoked meats, poultry and game in season, fruits and provisions in general. All of which are guaranteed to be pure, fresh and wholesome when offered for sale, and may be purchased at fair prices. Mr. Orr is a native of this state.

JOSEPH A. PETERS, Manufacturer of Havana and Domestic Cigars, Special Brands Made to Order, No. 39 City Square, Charlestown.—Mr. Joseph A. Peters, manufacturer of Havana and domestic cigars, is a native of one of the Azores, and although quite a young man has been a resident here for some time. Having a thorough, practical knowledge acquired by long experience as a cigar maker, and desirous of embarking in business on his own account, he founded this establishment originally in the autumn of 1888, and although of such recent origin the trade has become very large and permanent, which is a sufficient guarantee that its business is conducted upon strictly honorable and straightforward methods. The premises occupied are of spacious dimensions and complete in appointments with workshop connected in which his favorite brands are manufactured under his own immediate supervision, while his store is very neatly fitted up with special reference to the business, and with every accommodation for the display of his fine assortment of goods and the comfort of customers. From the start Mr. Peters decided that he would manufacture or handle only such goods as would meet the highest appreciation of expert judges. That he has succeeded in this is evidenced by the large trade he enjoys. His business is both wholesale and retail, and is rapidly extending. In his store will be found a choice and selected assortment of all his private brands, fine Havana and domestic cigars, conspicuous among them being his famous "J. A. P.," a ten-cent cigar honestly made from the best quality of material, but so inexcelled as to flavor, fragrance and smoking properties. Besides these he likewise carries a choice line of foreign and domestic cigarettes, smoking and chewing tobaccos, and snuffs, also meerschaum, wood and clay pipes, cigar and cigarette holders, amber mouthpieces, pipe stems, pouches, cases, etc., in fact everything in the line of smokers' articles, all of which are offered to the public at lowest prices. Mr. Peters is prepared to make to order all kinds of special brands and makes a specialty of this branch of the trade.

HALL'S BEE-HIVE, Dry Goods, No. 185 Washington Street.—Hall's Bee-Hive is a representative concern in the retail dry goods trade. Mr. Hall has been identified with this trade nearly all his life as a salesman and employee. He started business on his own account in 1887 at No. 542 Washington Street, and here he remained until August, 1888, when he removed to No. 185. This store has an area of 18 x 60 feet, and is eligibly and attractively fitted and equipped, with every convenience and appliances for facilitating the operations of the business. To speak of the stock in detail would fill more space than is at our command; suffice it to say that the house of every country in the world contributes to make up its variety. It embraces dress goods of every description, household linens, flannels, cottons, etc., ladies' and gentlemen's furnishing goods of every kind, notions and fancy goods in almost endless variety. Four assistants are kept busy to attend to the wants of customers, who are accorded courteous and liberal treatment. This house has a fine, substantial city and suburban trade. Mr. Hall is a native of Maine.

W. P. STEVENS, Merchant Tailor, No. 200 Main Street, Charlestown.—The merchant tailoring trade of Charlestown is well represented in the popular and firmly established house of Mr. W. P. Stevens. The business was established in 1870 by Mr. Stevens, and has grown up with the advancing demands of the times. The store is 18 x 26 feet in size, is handsomely and attractively appointed, and is provided with every convenience for the successful prosecution of the business. There is a fine display of fabrics, of the latest and most desirable designs, in cloths, cassimeres, meltons, stripes, checks, suitings, vestings, etc. Measures are taken and garments made promptly to order, in the highest style of the tailors' art. Mr. Stevens is a practical cutter of long experience, and has been identified with the trade from his youth up. He has in service an excellent corps of skilled and experienced tailors, and does all work done here exercises a close supervision, which enables him to guarantee to all his customers that every garment leaving his establishment shall be of the best material and workmanship, perfect in cut, style, fit and finish, and his prices compare favorably with those of any competing house. Mr. Stevens was born in Portland, Me., thirty-four years ago, and for upwards of twenty-one years has resided in Charlestown.

H. A. DERBY, Dealer in Horses, Carriages, Harness, Whips, Robes, Blankets, etc., Boarding and Sale Stables, Meridian Street, East Boston.—Among the leading sale and boarding stables and its kindred branches in East Boston, well worthy of the consideration of our patrons, is that which is conducted by Mr. H. A. Derby, dealer in horses, carriages, harness, etc., also boarding and sale stables. Mr. Derby is a native of Quincy, Mass., but has been a resident here for a number of years, and is a thoroughly practical man in all matters pertaining to the different branches of his industry. Devotedly attached to everything connected with the amelioration of the noble animals' condition, and desiring to embark in business, he inaugurated this establishment originally in 1873, with results of the most successful character. The premises occupied for business purposes are very spacious, embracing two floors each 50 x 100 feet in dimensions, which are divided into suitable departments in order to facilitate business transactions. The store contains a full and complete assortment of everything in the line of horse furnishing goods, such as heavy and light, single and double harness, bridles, reins, collars, saddles, halters, blankets, whips, horse covers and brushes, horse boots of every style, bridles and harness for breaking colts or tricky horses, also buffalo, fur, lap and other robes, etc. The assortment of horses kept on sale can always be relied upon as represented by Mr. Derby, and his opinion is relative to equine matters, are considered as final by the horse dealing fraternity, while his stock of carriages embraces coaches, clarences, coupes, landaus, surries, carriages, top and open buggies, road wagons, light express wagons, etc. His stables are kept in the neat and elegant order, being well lighted, ventilated and properly drained, and he has accommodations for thirty-three head of horses. Animals are taken on board, and their contents to the care of Mr. Derby will receive the best attention at the hands of experienced and faithful grooms, while the proprietor supplied is of the very best quality and plenty of it. Here will also be found at all hours of the day or night, fine, stylish turnouts for business or pleasure purposes.

P. H. SHEEHAN, Provisions, Fish, Game, etc., Corner of Harvard and Tyler Streets.—Mr. P. H. Sheehan, dealer in choice provisions, fish, game, etc., has since he was eight years old been a resident of Boston, and is a graduate of the Quincy School. He began business as a junior clerk, and by his keen and industry soon acquired an expert knowledge of the provision trade and was with the old house of W. C. Coolidge for over seven years. In 1888, he began business for himself at the corner of Harvard and Tyler Streets. The store although small was so if placed and well kept, and it speedily became a favorite purchasing depot for the surrounding residents. In February, 1889, Mr. Sheehan fitted up and opened the fine establishment upon the corner, opposite the original site; and has since conducted both establishments with marked effect. The new store is a spacious corner apartment with plate-glass show windows, hard wood fixtures, marble slabs, and in short all the modern adjuncts to convenience, utility and attractiveness. Here as in the old store can at all times be found a large, carefully selected and complete stock of meats, vegetables, fish, game, and in short everything pertaining to the family provision trade. In the old store, Mr. Sheehan carries on a full line of staple and fancy groceries. The extensive general business gives employment to a good number of experienced assistants; the general trade in both large and lucrative.

CHAS. H. COTTON, Beef, Pork, Lard, Hams, Tripe, Tongues, etc., Stall No. 9 Central Market, Nos. 46 and 48 North Street.—Mr. Chas. H. Cotton, who is an old time resident of Boston, is one of the most successful business men in Central Market, where he has occupied stall No. 9 for the past thirteen years. He is well known to the citizens, and as a dealer in dressed beef, pork, lard, hams, tripe, tongues, etc., enjoys an enviable reputation and always has the finest and best, which he is enabled to sell at the lowest prices. The stall is kept neat, clean and every convenience is at hand for supplying all demands. He has the best possible facilities for securing all the various articles of food supply he deals in and has established a large, wide-spread appreciative custom. Mr. Cotton was born in Centre Harbor, N. H., and came to Boston about twenty years ago, and as one of the leading representative dealers in his line of business in Central Market is very popular.

JAMES H. RYAN, Auctioneer, Real Estate and Insurance Broker, No. 42 Broadway, South Boston.

SLATTERY BROTHERS, Merchant Tailors, No. 410 Washington Street.

DANIEL J. CROSS, Grocer, and Dealer in Provisions, Flour, Teas, Butter, etc., Nos. 332 and 334 Dorchester Street, South Boston.

C. H. PACKARD, Pharmacist, No. 65 Hanover Square and No. 112 Chelsea Street, East Boston.

G. W. FREEMAN, Photographer, No. 92 Main Street, Charlestown.

FRANK H. BLACKINTON & CO., Grocers, No. 635 Tremont Street.

G. A. BURLEIGH, Boots, Shoes and Rubbers, No. 96 Essex Street, and No. 36 Beach Street.

GEORGE JAMES & CO., Sole-cutters, No. 16 South Street.—As a dealer in leather and every description of cut stock, and as cut-setters,—being the pioneer in this line of trade, and the first man that ever cut tops and top pieces for the finding and shoemaking,—the firm of George James & Co. are well known, and their enterprise has assumed a magnitude of great importance. Founded in 1871 on High Street, the business was removed in 1880 to the commodious premises now occupied, which have an area of 25,000 feet. Three floors are used by the firm, which are thoroughly fitted up and provided with every facility, including special machinery and appliances, and from 15 to 15 practical workmen are kept constantly engaged. The firm supplies a large demand from the boot and shoe manufacturers, and have a patent process for cutting top pieces and lifting, whereby a clean saving of 7½ per cent is made. Mr. George James, who has full charge of the management of the house, has had many years' practical experience in the boot and shoe business. He is a native of Vermont, and for some years was engaged in the trade in Montreal, Canada. His name to Boston in 1868, and during his business career in the city, he has become widely known, and has built up a business in his special line second to no other in the city.

THOS. R DAVIS, Diamonds, Watches, and Jewelry, No 583 Washington Street.—This well-known and deservedly popular jewelry store was established in 1870 by the present proprietor, and, during the nearly nineteen years since interverting, has been conducted with uniform success, the patronage growing steadily from the start until it has attained highly gratifying proportions. The business premises are commodious and handsomely fitted up, and a large and splendid stock is kept constantly on hand, embracing fine gold and silver watches, superb diamonds, rubies, pearls, and kindred gems, novelties in rings, pins, chains, charms, bracelets, and elegant jewelry in great variety; also solid silver and plated ware, art novelties, clocks in unique and artistic designs, opera-glasses, spectacles, eyeglasses, and everything in the line of optical goods. Watches, jewelry, etc., are repaired likewise in the most prompt and excellent manner, at reasonable rates, two competent assistants being employed; and all work executed here is fully warranted to render satisfaction, special attention being given to fine watch-repairing and diamond-cutting. Mr. Davis, who is a gentleman of middle age and a native of Boston, is a practical and expert watchmaker and jeweler of many years' experience, and is a thorough master of his art in all its branches.

BRIDGHAM & CO., Importers of Fine Woolens, No. 87 Chauncy Street.—An old-established and widely known Boston business-house is that of Bridgham & Co., importers of fine woolens, which is one of the oldest and leading firms engaged in this branch of mercantile activity in the city. The house was founded in 1848 by P. C. Bridgham, who conducted it alone up to 1878, when he admitted into partnership his son, R. C. Bridgham. The business was formerly carried on at No. 104 Summer Street, where the firm were burned out in the great fire of 1872, subsequently moving to No. 40 Bedford Street, where they continued for thirteen years; removing to the commodious quarters now occupied in 1881. The ware-room, which occupies the whole of a 80×85-foot floor, is finely appointed and well ordered in every respect, while eight or ten courteous salesmen are in attendance. A very large and superb stock is constantly carried on hand, embracing everything in the line of fine imported woolens, in correct designs, styles, and patterns, and the trade of the firm, which is of a wholesale character exclusively, extends to all parts of the United States. Mr. Bridgham the elder is a gentleman of about sixty-five, but active and energetic, was born in Maine; and Mr. Bridgham the younger, who is a comparatively young man, is a Bostonian by birth.

JOHN WALER & CO., Manufacturers' Agents; New England Agents for Cleveland Rolling Mill Co., the Falls River Co., Union Steel Screw Co., Chisholm Steel Shovel Works, H. P. Nail Co., Nails & Co. etc.: Nos. 5 Winthrop Square and 273 Devonshire Street.—The business of this widely-known concern was founded twenty-five years ago by Mr John Waler, under whose energetic management the house rapidly grew in strength and volume of trade, and soon acquired an enviable reputation in its special line

of industry. Twelve years since his son, Mr George R. Waler, a young man of excellent business capacity, was admitted to partnership, and the enterprise has been conducted under their joint control. The firm carry on general operations as New England agents for the following prominent manufacturers: Cleveland Rolling Mill Company, Union Steel Screw Company, H. P. Nail Company, Chisholm Steel Shovel Works, and Nails & Co., all of Cleveland, Ohio; the Falls River Company, of Cuyahoga Falls, O., and the Bridgeport Brass Company, of Bridgeport, Ct. The productions of these responsible houses have won a national reputation. The premises occupied by Messrs Waler & Co. comprise a micro and basement 82×110 feet in dimensions. The sale-rooms and offices are handsomely appointed. A heavy stock is at all times carried, and orders from any part of New England are filled promptly and accurately. The Messrs. Waler, who are natives of this state, reside in Brookline.

S. F. DAWSON, Manufacturer "Knox Mills" Leather Board. Nos. 27 High Street and 120 Purchase Street.—A flourishing house engaged in the manufacture of this useful article is that of Mr. S. F. Dawson. Mr. Dawson founded his enterprise eight years ago, and bring fully versed in every branch of the business, he has since built up a large and most desirable trade, having for its tributary area Massachusetts, New York State, and Pennsylvania. The factory is located at Lawrence, is equipped in the most complete manner, and affords employment to about twenty-five skilled workmen, while every facility is possessed to insure a perfect production. A large stock is carried at the factory and also in this city, and all orders meet with close attention and are shipped without delay. Mr. Dawson is a native of England, but has made his home in the United States since 1847, and has become a widely known and respected merchant and citizen.

F. J. WILSON, Manufacturer of Sashes, Doors, and Window Frames, Nos. 99 and 101 Lancaster Street. During the past fourteen or fifteen years Mr. F. J. Wilson, manufacturer of sashes, doors, and window frames, has conducted business with uniform success. The factory, which is situated on the fourth floor, is spacious and commodious, while ample steam power, all necessary machinery, and complete facilities are at hand, and an efficient force of workmen are regularly employed. Mr Wilson is prepared to manufacture to order, at short notice, and in the most superior manner, sashes, doors, and window frames in every size, design, and variety, and all orders for anything in this line are promptly executed under his immediate supervision. Mr. Wilson, who is a native of Maine, is a thoroughly practical and experienced workman.

M. C. KIMBALL, Manufacturer of Finished Leather, No 195 Summer Street.—This business was established seven years ago by the present proprietor, who has since built up a liberal and influential patronage in all sections of New England, New York, and Pennsylvania. He manufactures largely flexible innersoling, grain and split leather. His goods are unrivalled for quality and uniform excellence, and have no superiors in this or any other market. All orders are promptly filled from the Boston office at the lowest possible prices, and all goods are fully guaranteed to be exactly as represented. Mr. Kimball was born in Maine, but at the present time is a resident of Malden. He is a popular member of the New England Shoe and Leather Association, and fully merits the large measure of success secured in this valuable industry.

C. J. SOUTHWICK, Broker in Western Hides and Skins, No. 91 High Street.—Among the leading and responsible wholesale brokers in western hides and skins is Mr. C. J. Southwick. Mr Southwick was born in Massachusetts, and early in life became identified with the trade in which he has achieved such deserved prominence. In 1879 he established in business as a western hide broker, and has the most perfect facilities of any one in the east for meeting the wants of tanners and manufacturers, without largely on account of leading western shippers, and delivering a class of stock that has no superior for quality. Mr Southwick is prepared to promptly fill all and the largest orders, is a popular and respected member of commercial circles, and worthy of the large measure of success and influential connections he has developed.

D. B. BLANEY, Real Estate Agent, No. 3 Winthrop Block, East Boston. —The name of Mr. D. B. Blaney, the popular and respected real estate agent, is a very familiar one in East Boston. Mr. Blaney is to-day the oldest combination business man in the real estate line in this section of the city. It is now forty-eight years since he first embarked in his present branch of enterprise, and he well recollects when what is now the choicest and most valuable section of East Boston was nothing but pasture ands and gardens. He has in the course of business along in the future bought and sold for his customers, land at a few dollars per acre which is now covered with buildings, each one representing a fortune. Mr. Blaney is a recognized authority on the values of realty not only in East Boston but all over the city of Boston and its parlous surroundings. He deals generally in residential and business property, buying, selling, letting and leasing, and has very superior connections, numbering among his customers many of our leading business men. Special attention is given to the management of estates and to the collection of rents. Loans are also negotiated at reasonable rates on bonds and mortgages. Mr. Blaney has always on hand desirable properties for sale that merit the examination of persons seeking profitable investments. Mr. Blaney is a native of Marblehead, Mass., and is an honored and upright representative of the greatest interests of the city. In the same office with him is his son, Mr. F. H. Blaney.

P. H. SMITH, New England Agent for the New Howe Mfg. Co., Wood Sewing Machines, McKay Double Needle Machines, Tailors Press Machines and Crandall Type Writer Co., No. 81 Hayward Place. —An enterprising and well-known gentleman is Mr. P. H. Smith, who is the New England agent for the Crandall type writer, the New Howe sewing machines and the Wood sewing machines, the McKay double needle machine, Tailors press machines and a number of other machines and devices. His store is 35 x 40 feet in area, with a large repair shop attached in which sewing machines are repaired. He sells sewing machines lower than any one in the city, and does not employ any agents and is pushing the sale of the Crandall type-writer, which has recently been very much improved, and is now better in the mechanism than any other type-writer manufactured, having twenty-eight keys, which combine a beginner to learn the machine much easier than any other, and has the advantage of price, being far below that of any other first-class type-writer, and which takes the award of merit wherever exhibited in competition with other type-writers. Mr. Smith is a native of New York and is familiar with all the different machines and type-writers in the country, and is always introducing the best novelties into the New England market, and has built up a large trade by his energy.

J. H. HOWARD, Manufacturer of Mirrors, Counters, Mantels, Office, No. 10 Pitts Street. —The manufacture of ornamental woodwork is a business in which Mr. J. H. Howard has been engaged the past twenty years, and in that time he has won an enviable reputation for the high standard class of his work. He commenced his operations in Chickering Place where he remained until six years ago, when he removed to the location now occupied. The premises are very spacious and commodious and well equipped throughout, and every convenience is provided for the manufacture of plain and ornamental mirror frames and counters and wood mantels and doing all trade of woodwork for stores and fitting up offices and counting-houses. Mr. Howard gets out many new, novel and unique designs and furnishes estimates and makes contracts for all work in his line of business. He also attends to repairing and general jobbing and keeps in stock a great variety of fancy hardwoods of every kind. He has built to order many of the fittings to be seen in some of the leading business houses, hotels, banks, etc. Mr. Howard, who was born in Ireland, came to this country when a boy. He has done a great amount of fine work for the Chickering Piano Co. in the most skillful and artistic manner.

F. J. BALDWIN & CO., Machinists, No. 18 Chelsea Street, Charlestown. —This popular and prosperous firm was established some two and a half years ago, and from the start has enjoyed an excellent patronage. They occupy commodious quarters on the third floor, with a carpenter shop on the second floor, and have ample and complete facilities, including steam-power and all necessary appliances, while several expert mechanics are employed. All kinds of machinery, light and heavy, are built in the most expeditious and excellent manner, special attention also being given to repairing and jobbing of every description, while mechanics' tools of every variety are made to order likewise at short notice, cutting, making and thread dies being specialties, and all work executed here is warranted to render satisfaction. Mr. Baldwin is the inventor and patentee of The "Comfort" Blind Fastener, which is intended to simplify the opening and closing of blinds, by the use of this fastener, the necessity of leaning out of window is dispensed with, which of itself is a very great advantage, especially in stormy weather. There is, also, no possibility of the blinds being lifted from their hangings where the "Comfort" fastener is used. It can be readily attached to any blind at an expense very trifling. Mr. Baldwin, who is the sole member, is a practical and experienced shipwright and has carried on business in this line for over two years.

RICHARD SULLIVAN, Boat Builder, Boats of all Kinds, Built and Repaired, No. 533 Commercial Street. —As a practical boat builder, no one is better known or more appreciated in Boston than Mr. Richard Sullivan, No. 533 Commercial Street, head of Union Wharf. Mr. Sullivan is a native of St. Johns, N. B., and is now in his fifty-first year. He came to Boston twenty-two years ago with a practical knowledge of the boat builders' trade, which he put to good use when he established his present business in 1872. Mr. Sullivan occupies one floor of commodious dimensions, 30 x 75 feet, at No. 533 Commercial Street, where he has been located for the past nine years. He builds boats of all kinds, rowboats, sailboats, skiffs, sculls, etc., and has obtained the highest reputation for the solid character of his work and the graceful proportions of the build. He makes a leading specialty of Whitehall boats and pilots' canoes which are unexcelled anywhere. He also does an extensive business in repairing, which he does in a prompt and satisfactory way, charging only the most moderate prices for work of this kind. Mr. Sullivan's attention to business, particular skill in his trade and general intelligence have won for him the highest respect among all who know him.

DAVID SMITH, Carpenter and Builder, No. 111 Harrison Avenue. —A well-known carpenter and builder in this city is Mr. David Smith, who has for more than thirty years been identified with the improvements that have been going on in that time. He is a native of New Hampshire, and was brought up to the trade and for a number of years carried it on elsewhere. In 1858 he came to Boston and at once attracted attention by the successful manner he accomplished the remodeling of the United States Court House. He is a successful master of his trade and furnishes estimates and plans and specifications for buildings and dwellings and makes alterations, and makes contracts and supplies material. He also fits up stores and offices and attends to making repairs and doing all kinds of jobbing in his line of business. Mr. Smith employs a large force of skilled practical mechanics. He occupies a commodious workshop, which is well fitted up for the requirements of the carpenter, and builder.

FRANK O. GUILD, Apothecary, No. 193 Pleasant Street. —Prominent among those well known in this community as dispensers of medicines is Mr. Frank O. Guild, No. 193 Pleasant Street, who has been identified with the business of the apothecary for some years, and was brought up in it under the careful tuition of his father, Mr. C. K. Guild, who established the business in 1865 and continued it till 1879. The premises occupied, which have an area of 20 x 85 feet, are perfectly equipped, and made attractive by handsome show-cases and ornamental counters and fixtures of modern design. The feature of the business is the prescription department, which is under the personal direction of Mr. Guild, who is assisted by a competent clerk, and every care and attention is given to preparing medicines on physicians' order and also to filling difficult formulas. All the various kinds of drugs are kept on sale and only those of the highest standard character. Chemicals and proprietary preparations and toilet articles and all those requisites used by physicians are also kept on sale. Born in Uxbridge, Mr. Guild has lived in Boston many years.

MRS. C. L. FRASER & SONS, Prescription Druggists, Fraser Square, East Boston.—There are few drug stores in East Boston more widely known and deservedly popular than that of Mrs. C. L. Fraser & Sons. The business of this flourishing concern was organized in [illegible] by the late Mr. Charles L. Fraser, who, on his death in [illegible], was succeeded by his widow and his two sons, Messrs. D. A. and J. J. Fraser, who are natives and residents of East Boston. The store has a frontage of [illegible] feet, with a depth of [illegible] feet, is superbly fitted up, and is one of the handsomest establishments of its kind to be found in the city. The counters bear elegant plate-glass show cases, the shelf-ware is of the most tasteful order, and altogether the arrangements and conveniences are such as to call forth the admiration of the visitor, while they reflect much credit upon the taste of the management. The extensive stock carried embraces a complete assortment of fresh pure drugs and chemicals, family and proprietary remedies, toilet goods, fancy articles, surgical appliances, physicians' supplies and druggists' sundries in general, all derived from the most reliable sources of production. The firm have a number of special preparations of their own manufacture, which are of special merit, among them being: C. L. Fraser's anti-bilious pills, worm powders, comp. mustard liniment, children's diarrhœa and dysentery cordial, hair oil, toothache drops, cough syrup, diarrhœa and dysentery cordial for adults, tonic sedative, anti-rheumatic elixir, blood purifier, pints and half pints, sachet odors, petrola, etc. A large wholesale as well as a brisk retail trade is done in these specialties. Particular attention is given to the compounding of physicians' prescriptions and family recipes, the purest materials only being used, and every care being taken to preclude the possibility of error.

CHARLES H. PAINE, Machine Carpet Cleaning Works, No. [illegible] Medford Street, Charlestown.—There is no house in Charlestown more capable and competent to do such work than that of Mr. Charles H. Paine, whose machine carpet cleaning works has obtained an excellent reputation and is highly endorsed by large numbers of our most refined and distinguished families. Mr. Paine was born in Centre Harbor, New Hampshire, but has been a resident of Charlestown for a number of years. Fully appreciating the wants of the public he founded this establishment April 1, [illegible], and since that date has developed a business of superior character. The premises utilized for the business are spacious and commodious, occupying the entire second floor of a two-story building, [illegible] x [illegible] feet in dimensions, which is fully equipped with the latest improved carpet-cleaning machines, which are driven by steam-power, and a number of hands are given constant employment. Carpets are taken up and cleaned by these machines, which remove thoroughly all dust, moths, etc., without any injury whatever, and are returned and relaid at most reasonable prices, the following being the rates charged: four cents per running yard for wool, Brussels or tapestry, five cents for Wilton, velvet or Axminster; four cents for laying rooms and halls; two cents for taking up carpets, while special prices as agreed upon for laying stair carpets. Mr. Paine makes a specialty of making over and renovating hair mattresses, which is done in the very best manner known to the trade. For the benefit of his patrons order boxes for work can be found at Reed's book store, No. [illegible] Main Street; Allen's printing office, No. [illegible] Main Street; Wiley's stable, Hancock Square; Willard's Pharmacy, Sullivan Square; Pillsbury's grocery, corner Bunker Hill and Elm streets; No. 1 Trenton Street, Charlestown; also C. H. Crago's pharmacy, corner Perkins and Franklin streets, East Somerville, and all orders addressed to works No. [illegible] Medford Street, will receive prompt attention. Goods are taken from and delivered at residences throughout the city free of charge.

A. DA PRATO & CO., Manufacturers and Wholesale and Retail Dealers in Florentine Statuary, and Plaster Center Pieces, Nos. [illegible] and [illegible] Waverly House, Charlestown District.—This concern is the most popular and extensive one in its line in this section of the city. The copartners in the firm are Messrs. A. Da Prato and L. Mariki, both of whom are natives of Italy, and both of whom came to the United States five years ago. As manufacturers of statuary they learned their trade in their own sunny country, and in [illegible] established themselves in business here. They occupy two connecting stores, each [illegible] x [illegible] feet in dimensions, and one of these is utilized as a workroom and the other as salesroom. The latter is finely fitted up and contains an almost endless assortment of beautiful statuary of the Florentine order, and the equal to any imported. The advantages afforded by this house lie in its ability to offer to purchasers statuary as fine in execution as any made at about one-half or less the price charged for imported goods. Five hands are kept busy, and the trade, which now extends throughout New England and the states of New York and Michigan, is rapidly increasing. The firm are always in a position to fill wholesale as well as retail orders.

ANTOINE VINCENT, Carriage Manufacturing, Nos. [illegible], [illegible], [illegible] Dorchester Avenue, South Boston.—A leading and reputable South Boston establishment is that of Antoine Vincent, carriage manufacturer, which, for over twenty-one years has maintained an excellent reputation for fine work, promptness and reliability. This well and favorably known concern was established in [illegible] by the firm of Mitchell & Vincent, who conducted it up to [illegible], when the business passed into sole control of Mr. Vincent who has since continued it alone with unbroken success. The factory is a three story brick structure, [illegible] x [illegible] feet in dimensions, and is completely equipped with all necessary facilities, while a dozen or more skilled mechanics are employed. Carriages, buggies and light wagons of every description are made to order in the highest style of the art and in the most expeditious manner at reasonable rates, the vehicles turned out here being first class in every particular—in beauty of design, ease of motion, construction and elegance of finish. Repairing likewise in all its branches is promptly and reliably attended to, all work executed in this concern being fully warranted to render satisfaction, and, altogether, Mr. Vincent, who is himself a thoroughly practical and expert workman, has a large and growing trade.

A. W. BAILEY, Groceries and Provisions, No. [illegible] Meridian Street, East Boston.—This popular grocery and provision house was inaugurated in [illegible] by Mr. A. W. Bailey. The premises occupied for the business are conveniently located and comprise a salesroom, [illegible] x [illegible] feet in dimensions. This is fitted up with special reference to the business, and presents at all times a very neat, attractive appearance. The stock embraces a general line of groceries, both staple and fancy, such as teas, coffees and spices, sugars, syrups, molasses, canned goods in great variety, table delicacies, condiments, flour, butter, fresh eggs, cheese, cigars and tobacco and ship supplies of every description. The great specialties of this responsible house, however, are the best brands of teas and coffees, which are highly appreciated for their superior qualities. In fact the goods handled here are renowned for their quality, purity and freshness and moderate prices. Particular attention is given to the trade in ship stores, the stock of which is of a most extensive and comprehensive character. The facilities possessed by Mr. Bailey, who draws his supplies from first hands, are such as to enable him to compete successfully with any house in the trade, and to fill all orders with the utmost promptitude. Four assistants and a delivery wagon are in permanent service. Mr. Bailey was born in Maine, and for a score of years has resided in East Boston.

THE MASSACHUSETTS DEPARTMENT STORE, House Furnishing Goods, China, Crockery, Glassware and Notions, W. E. Whipple, Proprietor, No. [illegible] Broadway, South Boston.—This business was founded in October, [illegible], by Messrs. Dawes & Nelson, and has been under the present able proprietorship since September, [illegible]. The store, [illegible] x [illegible] feet in dimensions, is a model of systematic and convenient arrangement, and the general appointment is a happy combination of modern convenience and attractiveness. Upon its shelves and counters is displayed a large and varied stock embracing house furnishing goods, china, crockery, glassware and a thousand and one useful and ornamental articles generalized as notions. Three assistants and an automatic cash system aid the proprietor in supplying the wants of the numerous patronage, and the general business is both large and prosperous. Mr. Whipple is a native of New Hampshire, but has long been located in this city, where through the medium of an extensive clerkship he acquired a comprehensive knowledge of the business in hand.

J. A. O. CURRIER, Successor to Littlefield & Currier, Steam Printer, No. 31 Hawley Street.—The well ordered and reliable establishment of Mr. J. A. O. Currier, steam printer, bears a very reputable name among its contemporaries and the public in consequence of the excellence of its productions and the liberal manner in which its business affairs are conducted. This establishment was founded originally by Messrs. Littlefield and Currier in 1855, and was conducted under that firm name with more than usual success until January 1, 1880, when upon the withdrawal of Mr. Littlefield from the firm Mr. Currier became sole proprietor. Mr. Currier is a Bostonian by birth, and is a thorough exponent of the printing art in all its branches, having acquired his knowledge by close application and several years of experience in all its branches. The premises utilized for the business are of ample dimensions, easy of access by elevator, and embrace a fine business office, press and composing room. The latter is fully equipped with all the necessary machinery, type and appliances of the very latest and most improved styles required in the execution of first-class work, and employment is furnished to a sufficient force of reliable and skilled workmen to meet promptly all the demands of his trade. Its presses and machinery are driven by steam-power, and the range of work includes commercial job printing of every description, such as business, visiting and invitation cards, bill, letter and note heads, envelope and postal card printing, wedding invitations, funeral notices, hotel bills of fare, ball, society, festival, picnic announcement posters, dodgers, circulars, pamphlets, lawyers' briefs, titles of all kinds, catalogues, price lists, etc.

C. H. BUCK & Co.. The Leading Sign Painters, No. 888 Harrison Avenue.—An old established and representative enterprise in its particular field of skilled industry is that of C. H. Buck & Co., sign painters and manufacturers of and dealers in all kinds of advertising signs, also enameled glass and metal letters. This business was founded in 1878, and from its inception has maintained a trade supremacy which fully demonstrates the energy and executive ability brought to bear in its conduct. The present premises, which have been occupied since 1884, consists of an entire first floor, 25 x 80 feet in dimensions, the fore part devoted to an office and supply room while in the rear is a commodious and conveniently arranged workroom. A competent corps of experienced hands is employed and the work turned out is invariably of the highest artistic and mechanical excellence. The house has built up an enviable reputation for superior work, and prompt and satisfactory execution of jobs and its extensive patronage is drawn from the high class city and suburban custom. Mr. Buck is a practical and skilful exponent of the trade with which he has been so long and prominently identified.

GEORGE M. STETSON, Apothecary, Gray's Block, No. 617 East Broadway, South Boston.—A well appointed and well conducted pharmacy is that of Mr. George M. Stetson, located in Gray's Block. The spacious store is fitted up in accord with the best ideas of modern convenience and elegance; the laboratory is supplied with all requisite facilities for compounding the most difficult prescriptions, and the stock of drugs, medicines, toilet and fancy articles, etc., embraces all to be found at a first-class metropolitan pharmacy. Two experienced drug clerks are employed, and the large and liberal patronage received is drawn from the best medical and family custom of the vicinity. Mr. Stetson is a native of South Boston and a graduate of the Massachusetts College of Pharmacy, and has been established here since 1874.

M. F. FARRELL, Sanitary Plumbing and Gas Fixing, No. 123 Summer Street, East Boston.—Mr. M. F. Farrell has been in business in East Boston for the past eight years, and has developed a trade connection of considerable importance. He occupies an eligibly located store and workshop at No. 710 Summer Street, near to Lyceum Hall. A large stock of plumbers' and gas fitters' supplies is at all times carried, including plain, galvanized and brass pipe and fittings of all kinds, sheet lead and lead pipe, water closets and wash bowls and urinals, copper baths and sinks, brass works, plated faucets, in short, everything that a plumber, gas or steam fitter could possibly need in the prosecution of his business. Mr. Farrell is prepared at all times to make estimates and enter into contracts for furnishing buildings of any kind with their water, gas, steam or sewerage connections, and has the facilities for executing the same promptly, however large they may be. In sanitary plumbing, the specialty of the house, and on the proper performance of which so much of the health and comfort of the community depends, an experience of almost a lifetime should certainly be an element to inspire confidence. Such an experience has Mr. Farrell, who was brought up to the business and thoroughly understands it in all its branches. A competent staff of workmen are employed. Mr. Farrell is a native of Massachusetts, and a thorough mechanic.

ALONZO RAND, Merchant Tailor, No. 50 Main Street, Charlestown.—A prominent and reliable headquarters in Charlestown District for fine merchant tailoring is at the establishment of Mr. Alonzo Rand. He is a native of this district, also a resident, and having acquired a thorough and practical knowledge of this business in all its branches, by years of practical experience, he established this house on his own responsibility at the same location in 1878. His patronage is large and permanent, and is derived principally from among our most distinguished and professional classes. His store is spacious and commodious, handsomely furnished, and is equipped with every convenience for the display of his fine assortment of piece goods, and the comfort of patrons. He keeps always on hand a full and complete stock of all kinds of French, English and German broadcloths, cassimeres, worsteds, tweeds, cheviots, melton diagonals, in all the latest desirable and seasonable styles, which have been selected with the greatest care, and cannot fail to satisfy every want, not even the most fastidious, and are offered at the lowest possible prices. Being a practical tailor and cutter, fully up to the times and constant changes in fashions, he knows exactly how to meet the wants of his patrons. Besides keeping a constant supervision of all work done in this establishment nothing is permitted to leave it that does not come up to the highest standard of excellence in style, fit and exquisite workmanship, and none but the best and most reliable workmen are employed and a perfect system of order is observed. Mr. Rand makes a specialty of naval uniforms, which are made up in true republican style and of the best materials, while the workmanship, trimmings, etc., are of the highest character. He is also prepared to do all kinds of repairing, cleansing and pressing at short notice in the most satisfactory manner. Mr. Rand is a skilful cutter and tailor.

GEORGE H. GRIGSON, Ladies' and Gents' Cafe, No. 449 Tremont Street.—One of the most popular resorts in this city by those in quest of a regular meal or luncheon is the ladies' and gentlemen's cafe at No. 449 Tremont Street, of which Mr. George H. Grigson is proprietor. It has been established since 1881 and under able, efficient management it has become widely known and liberally patronized. It is complete in all its appointments, handsomely furnished with neatness in excellent good taste and has dimensions of 80 x 40 feet. The service is of the best, and everything that is furnished is cooked in the best style and first class in every respect. Everything else in season will be found on the bill of fare, and oysters and coffee and lunches may be had at all times. Mr. Grigson, who has lived in Boston many years, is from Cape Cod.

W. L. BARRETT, Butter, Cheese and Eggs, No. 910 South Street.—Mr. Barrett has long been identified with this branch of trade, and his large experience and superior knowledge of the business have obtained for him an ever increasing patronage, while his excellent stock and facilities have secured for him the custom of the leading hotels and restaurants. Mr. Barrett occupies a commodious store, 20 x 40 feet, centrally located and admirably equipped. A fine stock of fresh butter, cheese and eggs is constantly on hand, and competent assistants, under the personal supervision of the proprietor, give prompt and accurate attention to the many orders received. Mr. Barrett is a native of the state of New York, started early in life in his present line of business, and though but recently located in Boston, his natural business ability, and his prompt and satisfactory fulfilment of his customers' wants, have secured for him a large and increasing trade.

E. T. COWDREY CO., Preservers and Importers of Table Delicacies, Nos. 78, 80, and 82 Broad Street.—An important adjunct to the canned-goods trade of New England is the old-established and representative house of E. T. Cowdrey Co., whose office and warehouse in Boston are located at Nos. 78–82 Broad Street. This widely-known and reliable house was established in 1855 by Mr. E. T. Cowdrey, who continued the canning and preserving business and importation of foreign table delicacies till within a few years, when he retired from active life, after a successful and honorable career. In 1888 the business was duly incorporated, under the laws of Massachusetts, under the style and title of the E. T. Cowdrey Co., the general manager and treasurer being Mr. Cromwell T. Schulmerth, who for several years had been the managing partner of the old firm. The company's manufactories and canneries—admirably equipped with the latest improved apparatus and appliances—are situated at Boston, Littleton, and Dighton, Mass., and North Wayne, Me. Here 250 operatives are constantly employed, and the trade of the company now extends not only throughout the entire United States and Canada, but also abroad. The E. T. Cowdrey Co. preserve and can fruits, vegetables, meats, fish, poultry, soups, preserves, jellies, jams, pickles, etc. All of their food products are prepared with scrupulous care and neatness, and are warranted to be exactly as represented ; while the prices quoted for all goods are as low as those of any other first-class house in the trade. Their factories are eligibly located at the best centres of supply, and are furnished with every facility for preserving the freshly-gathered products of the farm. All the goods of the E. T. Cowdrey Co. are unsurpassed for quality and uniform excellence, and are everywhere recognized and appreciated by the trade as standard productions ; the brands being general favorites with the trade and a critical public, always commanding a rapid sale. In conclusion, we would observe that the affairs of the E. T. Cowdrey Co. are placed in able and energetic hands, and it worthily maintains a leading position in this useful and valuable industry, reflecting the greatest credit upon all concerned.

E. T. COWDREY CO. (See descriptive article, opp. page.)

"The Citadel of Hope for Earth, is Home."

THIS place is a charming home. It is situated on high land, in a neighborhood unexcelled by any other. It is, in fact,

" A bower of ease, in which
The past may be forgot."

Neither money or labor was spared in making this house as thorough as brains and talent could devise. It is situated on the corner of two streets; the architectural effect on each is equally pleasing; and is so arranged that every room is very sunny and pleasant.

On the first floor are five rooms, besides a large hall and back room, with large and numerous closets. The smallest room on this floor is 12x13 feet, and all are finished in hard woods, rubbed down and polished to a mirror surface. The floors are inlaid, polished hard woods. There are eight open grates, with mantels and tiled hearths.

Four large chambers and the bath-room open from the front hall up stairs, and one from the back hall; several of the chambers have large dressing-rooms connected with them, set bowls, hot and cold water, etc. The closets are all very large and well fitted up. The back staircase is in quartered oak, and is continued up into the third story, which contains four large, airy, pleasant chambers, finished in pine in the natural color, with large closets and ample store-rooms.

The house is heated throughout with the most recently improved steam apparatus, by indirect radiation. The lawn is large and beautifully laid out. This is a genuine HOME!

This estate is located in Ward 7, city of Newton, and is only twelve minutes' walk from the railroad station, public library, churches, and schools. The estate cost nearly $30,000, was built for ready cash, and is free and clear. It has never before been offered for sale; but owing to changed circumstances, it will now be disposed of at a bargain, on easy terms.

For further particulars inquire of

CHARLES F. RAND,

417 CENTRE STREET, NEWTON.

M. BOLLES & CO.,

No. 70 State Street,

Do a regular banking and brokerage business. The senior is one of the founders of the Stock Exchange, and the house is the oldest one in the business in Boston.

FRANCIS C. STANWOOD,

Cotton Broker,

No. 4 POST-OFFICE SQUARE.

The following pages are devoted to the environs,—Chelsea, Cambridge, Waltham, Hyde Park, Newton, and Somerville.

THE CITY OF CHELSEA.

HE city of Chelsea is one of the most populous and flourishing suburbs of the city of Boston, and is situated from three to four miles northeast of Boston Common. It is separated from Charlestown by the Mystic River, which is crossed by the Mystic Bridge. It is bounded on the south and southeast by an inlet of the sea called Chelsea Creek, which separates it from East Boston.

Chelsea, which is to-day a progressive city of about thirty thousand inhabitants, was in 1739, by direction of the State Legislature, erected a town, which was formed out of what up to that date had been known as Winnisimmet Village, Rumney Marsh, and Pullin Point, and this was ordered " in consideration of the fact that they had long since built a meeting-house and supported the same." The town district then embraced what is now known as Chelsea, Revere, Winthrop, and part of Saugus. This domain, however, underwent at different periods considerable abridgment by the creation of new towns and districts, but since March 19, 1846, Chelsea has retained its present size. It seems that in the early days the present city of Chelsea was in that portion now known as Winthrop and Revere, and in 1731 the population of Chelsea was only thirty persons, while the whole town of which it formed a part contained only about 775 persons. To-day, Chelsea has about 4450 houses, and there are nearly 8000 polls assessed. She has thirty-seven and a quarter miles of streets, well laid out and in good condition ; and she has also twenty-six miles of sewers, making three of the most complete systems of sewerage to be found in any city outside of Boston in the State. The city has not been neglectful in providing " breathing-places," so essential to the health and enjoyment of large communities, for Chelsea has two public parks. The largest is Union Park, which contains 122,000 square feet. The other is Washington Park, which contains 73,000 square feet of land. Both are very tastefully laid out, and are highly prized by the citizens.

The first road into Chelsea was what was known as the "County Road," which started at the old ferry slip and wended its course through part of Broadway, Park, and Hawthorne Streets, and up Washington Avenue. The first steam ferry-boats between Boston and Chelsea began to run in 1832. Taft, who is remembered by old Bostonians as a famous caterer, then kept a noted hostelry in Chelsea, near the ferry landing. Here, on Sundays, the citizens of Boston were wont to resort, and children found fun and delight in a menagerie kept in the back yard. This place answered the same purpose that Nantasket, Chelsea Beach, and other noted watering-places do now.

On May 27, 1857, the first horse-car line was chartered, and ran through Broadway to Boston, and on April 6, 1859, the present Lynn and Boston horse railroad was chartered. The Meridian Street bridge was built in 1854, and connected Chelsea with East Boston.

The first dwelling-house erected within the present city limits was built in 1731, at the corner of what is now Winnisimmet and Williams Streets, by Joseph S. Edwards, and the first store was built by John Low, in 1736, on the corner of Broadway and Everett Avenue, and was a low one-story edifice, about 20x30 feet in dimensions. Mr. Low was chaffed by his friends for " building so far out of the way ;" but his venture was a successful one, for other buildings arose around his. His business prospered, and he waxed rich.

In 1853 the Chelsea Gas Light Company was chartered ; and then the streets were for the first time illuminated by gas. The first sewer was built in 1846, and the first edge stones were set by the town in 1850, on Winnisimmet Street. The largest sewer in Chelsea is in Broadway, from Bellingham to Third Street, thence through Pearl Street to the harbor. It is 1100 feet long and 6 feet in diameter. The first fire recorded occurred in what was then Bascom's wheelwright shop, and was situated on land now facing Chelsea Square. This fire so alarmed the citizens that they at once purchased a fire-engine, and in 1835 the original "Chelsea" was purchased, and in 1837 a second one, named the "Volunteer," was bought second-hand for the small amount of $150. To-day the city has a splendid fire-department, equipped with steam fire-engines, electric fire-alarms, etc. Among the notable events treasured in the memories of old Chelseans is what is known as the "Chelsea Riot," which occurred on Monday, May 7, 1854. A large mob, headed by a man known as "Angel Gabriel," attempted to tear down the Catholic Church, then being located on Cottage Street. The militia was called out and "Gabriel" retreated, while the howling mob dispersed.

In 1856 the "town of Chelsea" had grown to have a population of between 12,000 and 13,000 inhabitants, and a city charter was proposed. A committee composed of Erastus Rugg, Stephen D. Massey, Melin Chamberlain, Samuel Orcutt, and Hosea Ilsley presented to the general court a petition for a city charter on February 11, 1857, and on March 13 of the same year the pleasing news was heralded on the streets of Chelsea that a charter had been granted, which was submitted to the voters on March 22d, and adopted by a vote of 733 to 107. The first mayor elected was Honorable Francis D. Fay, who was elected by a vote of 668 to 27, and he took the oath of office on the evening of April 13, 1857. Chelsea now enjoys the distinction of having one of the youngest mayors ever seated in the executive chair. This is Arthur B. Champlin, who was born in this city and has resided here all his life. He has always followed the profession of a journalist, and is now editor and proprietor of the Gazette, which he established nearly four years ago. He was at one time connected with the Boston Globe, and was for years editor of the Chelsea Record. He was a member of the Common Council for three years, and for two years was its president. He has also been a member of the Massachusetts Legislature for two years.

The members of the Board of Aldermen are: George E. Dyke, Alfred C. Converse, Benjamin T. Martin, Martin V. B. Flanders, W. Frederick Kimball, Henry D. Swasey, John C. Load, and Thomas M. Elwell.

The members of the Council are: Ward One—Charles H. Holmes, Timothy J. Keefe, William H. Farnham, R. Edward Butler, and Albert L. Morse. Ward Two—James Gould, John M. Mason, Fred M. Whiting, George B. Barrett, and Philip H. McLaughlin. Ward Three—Alfred W. Brown, Isaac W. Loring, George H. Carter, Frank E. Winslow, and Melvin L. Breath. Ward Four—Herbert L. Slade, E. Shirley Lombard, Fll C. W. Hiss, Alfred W. Fitz, and John F. Low.

At the beginning of the municipal year of 1889 the city had a net permanent debt of $1,313,259. The tax valuation of the city for 1888 was: Real estate, $17,428,900; personal estate and bank tax, $2,358,190; total, $19,787,090. The State and city tax in 1888 was $364,082; rate per $1000 in 1888, $18.40. Chelsea has one burden less than any other city in the commonwealth—she has no county tax to raise. By an act passed on June 23, 1831, Boston was given exclusive control of all county buildings, and Chelsea was relieved of any expense in that way,

The city owns the waterworks, and the streets are wide, paved, and well kept, and the health of the community is excellent, the death-rate being unusually low.

Chelsea has thirteen churches, and for a city of her age and also vies with any other in the commonwealth in this respect. Many of the church buildings are splendid specimens of modern architecture, and are well attended. The people of Chelsea take pride, as well they may, in the public schools, which are under the direction of a board that is an independent body, elected by the citizens. There are twelve schools, namely, one high school, four grammar schools, and seven primary schools. Among other educational facilities the city has a fine public library, contained in a splendid building, and the large patronage given it proves how much it is appreciated by the citizens. Another valuable educational agency is the press. There are four admirably conducted weekly papers published in the city. The Leader is issued by Mr. W. P. Nickerson, and the Gazette by Mayor Arthur B. Champlin, to both of whom we are indebted for many of the foregoing historical facts. The other newspapers are the Record and Pioneer.

In Chelsea the first marine hospital in this part of the country was built in 1826 and 1827, but was abandoned, and sold to the city on May 18, 1857. The present marine hospital was built at that time, the land on which it is situated being ceded to the Federal Government on February 28, 1828. Efforts have since been made by the municipal government of Chelsea to induce the United States Government to relinquish to Chelsea the lands upon which are located the Marine and Naval Hospitals, and several committees have been appointed to consider the matter, but have reported adversely; and it now seems that the institutions are here to stay for an indefinite time. Congress is, however, to be petitioned to construct a public avenue, wholly on the government lands along the line where the present division fence stands, from Broadway, opposite Medford Street, to Spruce Street. Such a street will be of public benefit.

To-day Chelsea looms up in all the power of a city, has everything pertaining to a great and independent people. She has a fine city hall and many splendid public and private buildings. She has lawyers, doctors, orators, politicians, editors, and professors; and is rich in all that it is necessary for any city to possess.

The city has many large manufacturing establishments within its limits, and these consist of an elastic rubber factory, chemical works, and factories for the manufacture of sewing machinery, brassware, linseed-oil, iron safes, woollens, brushes, machinery, tools, etc. The manufactories and other trade establishments of this city are, as a rule, intelligently and successfully directed and admirably equipped, a fact that will be fully shown in the sketches of individual houses at the end of this chapter. The manufacturing facilities are as complete and perfect as they can be made, the custom being to employ the finest machinery, the most skilful artisans, and all accessories calculated to improve production and economize cost. Thus it has come to pass that the goods made here are in wide demand, and are considered as standard in all markets. The shops and factories of the city give employment to a large number of skilled laborers, receiving good wages; indeed, the people are, as a rule, of the better class to be found in the cities of New England, being composed largely of industrious artisans, while the business men and capitalists are enterprising and large-spirited in contributing to the already phenomenal growth and prosperity of the city. Chelsea has many attractions from a manufacturing and commercial point of view, and also as a place of residence. The land of the district is undulating, and there are many charming natural resorts in and about and within easy reach of the city; Chelsea Beach, with its magnificent family hotels, its bathing-houses, wayside hostelries, pleasure-gardens, restaurants, photographic booths, show-tents, and its long, wide-stretching sandy shore, being one of the famous "watering-places" of New England that attract thousands of visitors in the hot months. The location of the city is everything that can be desired, and its eligibility as a place of residence has exerted a powerful influence in the development of its natural resources. Its broad streets and wide business thoroughfares are well cared for, its fine roads afford fine opportunities for driving, while its numerous elegant private residences and fine public buildings combine to make it an attractive place in which to live. The rents are remarkably reasonable, cost of building low, and the expenses of living as small as those of any other part of the State, while there are always opportunities offered for those to labor who wish to work. The people generally are occupied in some useful sphere of labor, and the homes of all classes have an air of comfort and respectability about them. There are many fine mansions with beautifully laid out grounds, and the flourishing condition of the city finds apt illustration in the constant building of business structures and private residences.

Chelsea has ever been closely connected with Boston in all its literary, intellectual, and political relations, and, were it not for municipal distinctions, might be considered as virtually an integral part of the metropolis.

W. M. GOULD, Groceries, Meats, Vegetables, etc. Cor. Congress Avenue, and Park Street. — One of the most popular establishments devoted to the sale of family groceries, meats, and vegetables in this city, is the well and favorably known stand of W. M. Gould. The store is commodious, neat, and very complete as to stock and fixtures, while an efficient staff of help is employed, with three teams in regular service supplying customers. A large and first class assortment is always kept on hand, including fine teas, coffees, and spices, sugars, syrups, baking-powder, condiments, delicacies, and canned goods of all kinds, best brands of western corn, meal, rice, beans, peas, prime butter, cheese, eggs, smoked and salt fish, crackers, soda, salt, and general groceries, while in the provision department may be found all these choice fresh beef, pork, mutton, lamb, poultry, lard, hams, bacon, etc. The stock also embraces a full and fine line of vegetables, fruits, and table luxuries. This deservedly popular store was formerly conducted by the firm of Gould & Dinsmore, who had succeeded D. S. Plummer, who carried on business here about two years, the present proprietor assuming sole control in 1897. Mr. Gould is a native of Britain, Maine, but a resident of this city quite some time.

WALTER SEARLE & CO., Wholesale and Retail Dealers in Groceries, Flour, Grain and Provisions, Nos. 110 and 112 Park Street. — The popular house of Messrs. Walter Searle & Co., wholesale and retail grocers, so well known for its excellent reputation, has been established for some years and was formerly carried on by a co-operative association, of which Mr. Searle was manager and afterwards became owner and proprietor by purchase. This was some time in 1876. He was soon after joined by his son, and under the present firm-name a good substantial business, which has steadily grown and developed, has been built up. The store has a double front and is quite capacious. The stock embraces everything in the line of staple and fancy foreign and domestic groceries, and flour and provisions, and including canned goods, table delicacies, condiments, etc. Mr. Walter Searle, who is a native of Townsend, Mass., was for many years known as one of the most popular blacksmiths in this vicinity, and for a period covering twenty seven years carried on the business in Ashburnham, and for seven years in Hewes, N. H. He has lived in Chelsea since 1884. Mr. Walter C. Searle is an active, enterprising business man.

GEO. D. EMERY, Mahogany and Cedar Lumber; Office, Mills and Wharves, Nos. 1 to 15 Broadway.

MARTIN & BRO., Manufacturers of the Celebrated "Crown Brand" Loom and Garter Webs, Braid, Frills, etc.

MERRILL & MORRISON, Furniture, Carpenings, Wall-paper, etc., Nos. 34-36 Third Street.

WILLIAM M. JEWETT, Real estate Agent and Auctioneer, Room 2, Granite Block, No. 308 Broadway.

H. A. FOSTER. Groceries, No. 174 Broadway.—To conduct a strictly first-class, general fancy and staple grocery establishment successfully, requires not only ability and energy to a marked degree, and a knowledge of the various influences that affect the trade, but also the faculty of anticipating the constantly varying tastes of the community. A leading and popular house engaged in this line of industry in Chelsea, and deserving of special mention, is that of Mr. H. A. Foster, dealer in fancy and staple groceries, which is centrally located at No. 174 Broadway, and during its entire existence has always maintained a most excellent reputation for the reliability and absolute purity of goods and liberal management of its business affairs. Mr. Foster is a native of Lowell, this state, but has been a resident of this city for a quarter of a century, and prior to engaging in business on his own account was in the employ of Mr. C. Newhall, also a dealer in groceries. Mr. Foster founded this establishment originally in 1890, and from the start he has met with the most gratifying success, which aptly illustrates what may be accomplished by close attention to the wants of customers, dealing in first-class goods only, and adhering to fair, square, honorable methods. The premises utilized for the business are of spacious dimensions, admirably appointed and fully equipped with every facility for the transaction of the already large and rapidly increasing trade, and the comfort of customers. The stock carried is full and complete, and embraces everything in the line of fancy and staple groceries, a specialty being made of absolutely pure and fresh teas from China and Japan, fragrant coffees from Java, Mocha, and South America ground and whole spices, canned goods from the most celebrated establishments, table delicacies, sauces, condiments, foreign and domestic fruits, bakers' and laundry supplies, choice family flour, farinaceous and cereal foods, sugars, syrups, molasses, salt and cured meats and fish, choice dairy and fancy creamery butter, cheese, fresh laid eggs, vegetables, and other farm and dairy products, in fact, all articles usually found in a well regulated house of this character. The goods of this house are noted for their purity and reliability, and are sold at lowest ruling prices. The store is a model of neatness and cleanliness, polite and courteous assistants attend promptly to the wants of customers, and orders are delivered at residences in the city free of charge.

MARTIN'S DRUG STORE AND FLOWER MART, No. 1 Grand Block.—A reference to the pharmacies of Chelsea at once suggests the popular establishment of Mr. A. C. Martin. The business had its commencement in 1885, and five years later was removed to the premises now occupied. It has always been under the control of Mr. Martin, who was educated to the profession. He is cautious and exact, and compounds and prepares and dispenses medicine with that degree of accuracy only attained by long, practical experience. His knowledge of materia medica is comprehensive and thorough. The store, which is tastefully fitted up with ornamental fixtures and plate-glass cases, is 50x10 feet in size, and the store of drugs and medicines it contains is complete and perfect in every detail, including in its assortment only the best, purest, and freshest. There is also a variety of all the different kinds of pharmaceutical preparations and all the standard medicines and toilet-goods, specialties, etc. Mr. Martin is also devoting much attention to supplying the citizens with cut-flowers and rare exotics and growing plants and bulbs, and presents many beautiful specimens of all kinds that are fashionable and desirable. He furnishes bouquets and designs for the table and parlor and also funeral emblems, wreaths, anchors, crosses, etc., and gives his particular attention to arranging flowers for weddings and entertainments, and to decorating halls and churches. He is a great lover of flowers, and an expert floriculturist. A native of Nova Scotia, Mr. Martin came to this country when twelve years of age, and has ever since been a resident of Chelsea.

HARRY W. JEFFERS. Grocer, and Dealer in Flour and Teas, No. 77 Winnisimmet Street.—This well and favorably known store was originally established in 1885 and had passed through several hands up to 1876, and was bought at that period by the present proprietor, by whom the business has since been continued with uninterrupted prosperity. Handling a very fine line of goods, courteous and affable to customers, and withal a young man of strict integrity in his dealings, Mr. Jeffers has been enabled by untiring energy to build up the substantial patronage he deservedly enjoys. The premises occupied are commodious and neatly appointed, and a heavy, first-class stock is constantly carried on hand comprising fresh, pure, and choice teas, coffees, and spices, foreign and domestic fruits, canned goods, prepared cereals, dried fruits, sauces, crackers, confections, fine creamery butter, including the famous "H A" brand which is always uniform fresh made cheese and eggs, prime lard, smoked meats and fish, sugars, syrups, and molasses, best brands of family flour, meal, rice, peas, beans, soda, oatmeal, baking-powder, starch, soap, household specialties, oils, vinegar, and everything in the line of staple and fancy groceries. Four assistants are employed, while two teams are in regular service supplying customers, all orders being promptly and reliably delivered throughout the city and environs; and patrons can rely upon getting an excellent article and full weight, as well as prompt and polite attention at all times. Mr. Jeffers, who is a native of this city, is a gentleman of thorough reliability in his dealings, and fully merits the success that has attended his efforts.

CASWELL BROTHERS. Sanitary Plumbers, Manufacturers and Dealers in Stoves, Furnaces and Ranges, No. 167 Winnisimmet Street.—The work of the plumber is one requiring a peculiar knowledge in its scientific application, a full measure of which is possessed by the Caswell Brothers, who have established a well earned reputation for skill and thorough workmanship. They are prompt in their attention to orders, and furnish plans and specifications for making sewer connections and regulating underground drainage and to ventilation, and introducing water into buildings and dwellings, and setting bath tubs, sinks, etc. Much time and attention has been devoted by the firm to sanitary work appertaining to plumbing, and being familiar with all the details connected with it, do all work in a most complete and satisfactory manner. The Messrs. Caswell Brothers also carry on an extensive business as manufacturers and dealers in stoves, furnaces and ranges, and tinware, and carry a full stock of goods in the well appointed store which has a front of 25 with a depth of 110 feet. In the manufacturing department every convenience is provided, and only the best class of work is turned out. On an average from eight to ten workmen, who are skilled in their respective branches, are kept constantly employed, and a widespread city and a good substantial business derived from all the adjacent sections is carried on. Tin and sheet iron work is done to order, and a special business is made of repairing stoves and ranges, and setting and cleaning furnaces and jobbing generally. The assortment of goods to be found in the store is one of the largest and most complete to be found in the city. Mr. James and Mr. George Caswell, the copartners, are both natives of Amherst, and old residents of Chelsea. The business they are now conducting with much marked ability and success, dates its foundation from 1840, when it was established by Luther Newhall, and has been under the control of the present firm since 1879.

CHELSEA SUSPENDER-MANUFACTURING COMPANY, Manufacturer of Suspenders, Shoulder-braces, Suspender-trimmings, etc. Office and Factory, No. 888 Broadway.—In sketching the notable industrial enterprises that have had inception in this city within recent years, more than passing mention ought to be made of the Chelsea Manufacturing Company, manufacturers of suspenders, shoulder braces, etc., whose office and factory are situated at No. 888 Broadway. The productions of this concern are goods of a very superior character, being noted for their general excellence, and as a consequence, they are in extensive and steadily growing demand in the trade. The Chelsea Manufacturing Company, of which F. S. Wright is sole proprietor, was established in April, 1890; and the circumstances that has attended this enterprise from the first abundantly attests the wisdom that inspired the venture, to say nothing of the unquestionable merit of the articles produced. The factory occupies the third story, 25x80 feet in size, supplied with ample steam-power and the latest improved appliances, while employment is here furnished to from forty to fifty expert hands. The productions include suspenders, shoulder braces, and suspender trimmings in every size, design, shape and pattern, some three hundred different styles being turned out, while as extensive, varied, and elegant assortment being kept in stock always, upwards of 4000 pairs per week being manufactured, and, altogether, a flourishing business is done. Mr. Wright, the proprietor, who is a native of England, but a resident of Chelsea quite a long time, is a man of energy, enterprise, and practical experience in this line, and is thoroughly conversant with the business in all its details.

C. F. PRUDEN, Optician, No. 448 Broadway.—During the past half-century steady advance has been made in the interesting and important branch of activity devoted to the construction of devices for aiding and extending the power of vision, optical instruments, and kindred philosophical and scientific apparatus. The leading sources of supply for this class of goods in Chelsea is the establishment of Mr. C. F. Pruden, the well known manufacturing optician, at No. 448 Broadway, opposite Bellingham car station. This gentleman is recognized as one of the leading exponents of the business in this section of the country, and has been established in trade here since 1891. He has devoted many years to the study and practical work of adjusting glasses to all classes of "eye invalids," and carries in stock the very best quality of pebbles and crystals, in gold, silver, nickel, shell, and rubber frames, at less than Boston prices. He is prepared to repair spectacles and eyeglasses in the most skillful manner, and to carefully set oculists' prescriptions. After long and patient study on this subject, Mr. Pruden is able to offer superior instruments of his own construction. His latest and greatest triumph is option in the production of Pruden's "ophthalmoscopic test lenses," an instrument conceived, manufactured, and adjusted by Mr. Pruden himself, which preserves the merit of perfect accuracy in determining just what kind of a glass will best fit the patient, and supply the deficiency, from whatever cause it may exist. This instrument is most ingenious in design and wonderful in construction, and never fails to indicate the right glass to adopt. Mr. Pruden looks carefully after blurred, weak, and imperfect eyesight, and most perfectly fits and adjusts crystals. Pruden's perfection crystals are the very best glass in the market, and all goods manufactured or sold by him are not surpassed, if equalled, in any feature of merit, in effectiveness, design, finish, or durability, by the products of any cost-experience establishment. Mr. Pruden has resided in Chelsea since 1861, was for forty years employed as an engraver with Reed & Barton and the Whiting Manufacturing Company in Boston, and for three years prosecuted his business as an optician in Cleveland. He is a thorough master of the art in all its branches, experienced as well as scientific, and a reliable and responsible business man of constant popularity in this community.

C. HAYDEN, Photographic Artist, No. 198 Broadway.—This establishment was inaugurated originally in 1869 by Mr. O. W. Baxter, who conducted it with more than ordinary success until 1878, when Mr. Hayden, who is a native of Derby, Vt., long a resident here, and a thoroughly skilled artist, purchased it from Mr. Baxter, and continued the business on his account ever since, and by keeping pace with the advance of science, close study, and devotion to his art, he has made it one of the leading concerns in the state, and enjoys an unusually large patronage, while specimens of his skill are to be found in all sections of country, and he is acknowledged as one of the leading and most progressive exponents of the profession. His premises comprise several apartments, adapted with special reference to the business. The office and reception parlor are elegantly furnished, great taste being observed in the arrangement of all decorations, while the light accessories, landscape, and other backgrounds, together with all the latest improved implements and devices, are as perfect as science and skill has yet produced. Photography in all its branches is produced here, and the best and finest class of work executed, by the aid of the instantaneous, flash, and dry-plate processes, thus enabling patrons to secure accurate and perfect semblances of themselves, friends, and especially of the little folks, and in any desirable style or size, from the miniature for the locket to life-size; old pictures are copied, either reduced or enlarged in size, and preserving at the same time all the effects of the original. He also executes portraits in oils, watercolors, crayon, pastel and India-ink in the highest style of art, satisfaction being guaranteed in all cases.

I. W. EMERSON, Gents' Furnishings, Dry Goods and Small Wares, No. 263 Broadway.—This gentleman is an extensive dealer in gents' furnishings, dry-goods, and small wares, succeeding to the proprietorship of the house in May, 1888. His premises facilities enjoyed by no other merchant in the business, while his aim and policy has ever been to attain a still higher standard of perfection to every article which he offers to the public, and to render stock absolutely comprehensive of everything desirable both in foreign and domestic products, making good his claim as a leader in men's outfittings and ladies' fine furnishings. He brings to bear large and valuable experience in catering to the wants of the fashionable public, and when with his experience are coupled ample resources, judicious facilities, and unrivalled connections, it is readily realized how he has achieved the position he occupies in the business world. The store is a model of elegance and taste in its interior arrangements and appointments, and the stock is a magnificent exhibit of modern achievement in this line. The stock is displayed to the best advantage from the windows, dressed as no others are, to the lengthy array of shelving and show-cases, and includes stores that are marvels of perfection, all grades of underwear in new and correct patterns, scarfs, cravats, and ties, hosiery, gloves, and underwear, handkerchiefs, collars and cuffs, umbrellas, canes, and parasols, toilet articles in great variety, white and colored blankets, ladies' waterproofs, and small wares in endless profusion. The rarest bargains are constantly offered in these goods, and the trade is brisk and lively at all seasons. Mr. Emerson is a native of Vermont, N. H., and was for fourteen years connected with one of the largest dry goods houses in the city, previous to embarking in his present enterprise. He is thoroughly enterprising, progressive, and painstaking in all his business methods, entirely reliable and responsible in all his dealings, and has won the large measure of success he now enjoys by honestly deserving it.

CITY HOTEL, R. C. Morley, Proprietor, Nos. 187 and 189 Broadway.—The City Hotel is the oldest, as well as largest and leading hostelry in Chelsea. It was first opened to the public in 1866, and has been under the management of Mr. R. C. Morley, the present proprietor, since 1874. The structure is five stories in height, 150x100 feet in dimensions, and possesses first class accommodations for one hundred and twenty-five guests. No hotel affords in situation, surroundings, modern conveniences, or experienced management in any hotel is lacking in the city. It is located opposite Everett Avenue, in the business heart of the city, within easy reach of depots and way of access from all points, horse-cars for Boston passing the door every seven minutes, and is convenient alike to the permanent patron, the commercial tourist, and the transient guest. Spacious reading and writing rooms, a fine billiard hall and a well-conducted bar are among the necessities of modern hotel life, which are provided for the use of guests. The cuisine of the City Hotel is worthy of special commendation, being under the most experienced management and kept up to the highest standard of excellence. Everything of the best that the market can furnish is to be found in the menu, private suppers are furnished on a scale of magnificence seldom equalled, parties are catered to with the utmost skill, while the house is conducted on both the American and European plan. In the management of the house every detail has been reduced to a complete and perfect system, having for its aim the convenience and comfort of guests. Special rates are given to permanent guests, and the theatre and travelling patronage is large, first class, and influential at all seasons of the year.

JAMES LYNDE & CO., Funeral Directors, Warerooms, No. 677 Broadway.—The undertaking establishment of James Lynde & Co. is one of the oldest in Chelsea, and has been carried on for more than twenty years. Mr. Lynde has had an experience in the calling extending over forty years, and was for some time previous to his locating in this city foreman and manager for Lewis Jones & Co., undertakers, of Boston. His son, J. B. Lynde, has full charge of the business, his father having retired, and under the present firm name they have become widely known throughout this section as gentlemen well fitted for the delicate and responsible duties of the funeral furnisher and director, and may always be relied upon in the fullest confidence in the discharge of them. Their personal supervision is given to the management of funerals, and they furnish such caskets, coffins, and requirements that are needed. In the prosecution of the calling Mr. Lynde and his son are careful and considerate and have a natural adaptation to it. The office and warerooms are tastefully fitted up, and contain a general assortment of funeral-furnishings of every kind and description. Mr. Lynde is one of the old-esteemed, popular residents of Chelsea. His son, J. B. Lynde, was born here. He is thoroughly familiar with all the duties of his calling, and like his father will be found faithful, obliging, and courteous. Calls at all hours receive the immediate attention of the firm.

McCANN & CO., Real Estate and Insurance, No. ... Broadway, Chelsea; No. ... Washington Street, Boston. — None in the real-estate business in this city has promoted and advanced the interests of the city more than Mr. J. A. McCann, the head and founder of the firm of McCann & Co., real estate operators and insurance agents. He is largely interested in real-estate operations on his own account and for others, and is the owner of much valuable property and building sites in the city and throughout Suffolk County. He has a wide acquaintance among capitalists, and is an authority upon real-estate matters, and is always on the market to buy or sell on his own account or on commission to order. ...

HERBERT H. CARTER, Funeral Director, Office and Residence, No. ... Broadway. — A prominent house in Chelsea, and well deserving of more than passing comment, is that of Mr. Herbert H. Carter, which was established originally in 1885 by Mr. Henry Noyes, who, in order to enjoy better facilities for the prosecution of the business, removed to this location in 1875 ... Mr. Carter is a native of this state and has been a resident of Chelsea ever since 1873.

E. C. SPARROW, Stationery, Toys, Periodicals, and Fancy Articles No. ... Broadway. — The popular concern of Mr. E. C. Sparrow, dealer in stationery, toys, periodicals, and fancy articles, has become the popular resort for those desiring any articles in his line of trade ...

P. J. THOMAS, Merchant Tailor, No. ... Broadway. — Among the custom artistic tailors in this community there are none more prominent or more thoroughly capable of cutting and fitting wearing apparel than Mr. P. J. Thomas, who has been engaged in the business in this city since 1882. ...

GEORGE DYER, Hack, Boarding, Livery and Sales Stable, No. 97 Second Street. — George Dyer has become very popular in catering to the wants of the public in the livery business. His establishment is in every respect a most important and essential convenience to the people of this community. ... Mr. Dyer is from Maine and was formerly in the livery business in Gorham, in that state. He has been established in this city since 1890.

W. L. DRAKE, Surgeon Dentist, No. ... Broadway. — Among the eminent professional gentlemen in this city there are none so well known and popular as Dr. W. L. Drake, who has for many years given his attention to all branches connected with it, and won an enviable reputation and gained distinction for the care and skill he exercises in all operations. ...

ANDREW J. BACON & CO., Groceries and Provisions, Poultry and Game, Yacht Supplies, etc., Corner Broadway, Tremont, and Williams Street.—This time-honored and deserved popular store was originally established in 1650 by the firm of Wentworth & Bacon, and in 1875 the style changed to Wentworth & Bacon, the present senior member some few years subsequently assuming sole control, and under the firm name of Andrew J. Bacon & Co., the business has since been conducted with uninterrupted success. William A. Bacon (son of Andrew J.,) being admitted into partnership in 1883, and, since the retirement of his father to his farm at Pembroke some four years ago, has had entire charge. The store, which has a frontage of 100 feet on Broadway, with equal dimensions on Tremont Street, occupies the whole of a three-story building, and is neatly fitted up and excellently arranged throughout. The stock, which is something immense and finely assorted, comprises choicest teas and coffees, fresh and pure spices, condiments, baking powder, sugars, syrups, canned goods in great variety, dried fruit, prepared cereals, sauces, preserves, pickles, olives, and other palatable relishes, prime quality dairy butter, cheese, and eggs, fine stall-fed beef, Vermont pork, choice hams, bacon, lard, sausages, smoked meats, poultry and game in season; also best brands of family flour, rice, meal, beans, peas, salt, oatmeal, etc., molasses, vinegar, oils, etc., also a fine line of fruits, vegetables, yacht supplies and ship stores. Four courteous clerks and bookkeeper attend to the wants of customers, while three teams are in steady service; all orders by telephone (858) or mail receiving immediate attention. Mr. Bacon the elder is one of Chelsea's staunchest and most respected citizens, serving in the Common Council from 1873 to 1876, and in the Board of Aldermen for two years subsequently, and was the efficient mayor of the city in 1877–1878.

LOUD & STONE, Bread, Cake and Pastry Bakers, No. 87 Broadway.—Special attention is directed to the establishment of Messrs. Loud & Stone, the well-known bread, cake and pastry bakers. The proprietors, are Messrs. John C. Loud and Arthur C. Stone, the former having been identified with this branch of industry for many years, and combined their resources and abilities to form the present firm in August, 1875, purchasing the stand of L. E. Curtis & Co., which was formerly known as the Excelsior Bakery. Thus they have fitted up in a thoroughly first class and elegant manner, and have already built up a trade that is at once extensive, permanent and prosperous. Making and handling a very superior class of goods, and devoting untiring attention to the wants of customers, the result could hardly have been otherwise than the success that has attended their efforts. Wedding-cake is made to order of the shortest notice. They make a specialty of fine bread, which is acknowledged by the general public to be the best made in Chelsea. They also pride themselves on their pastry which they claim to be second to none made in the city. Hot-baked beans are prepared and ready every Saturday at five o'clock, while the prices which prevail are uniformly fair and equitable. Mr. Loud is a native of the state of Maine, and for over 18 years was a member of the firm of J. C. & E. A. Loud, bakers, on Prince Street, Boston. Mr. Stone was born in New Hampshire, and was formerly a member of the wholesale flour and provision firm of Wright Bros., Stone & Co., of Boston.

C. H. FAUNCE, Undertaker and Embalmer, No. 86 Broadway.—In all that appertains to obsequies and interments the United States is immeasurably in advance of any country in the world. And here the calling of the undertaker has developed to the plane of a veritable profession, steps been for of the business, actably embalming, being conducted upon exact scientific principles. Among the leading representatives of this useful and indispensable profession in Chelsea, may be mentioned the name of C. H. Faunce, whose well-ordered office and warerooms are centrally located at No. 86 Broadway, and thus whom none engaged in this line in the city maintains a better reputation, as few enjoy a larger measure of popular favor. Mr. Faunce, who is a comparatively young man, and a native of Oxford, Me., is a gentleman of courteous manners and the highest personal integrity as well as of skill and thorough experience, having formerly been associated in business with his father for ten years at Great Falls, N. H. In May, 1886, he bought out George Bradley (who had been established here some twenty years), and has since conducted the business with uninterrupted success. Mr. Faunce occupies commodious and well equipped quarters at No. 86 Broadway, and keeps on hand always a complete and fine assortment of everything in the line of funeral requisites, including superb caskets, coffins, robes, shrouds, trimmings, etc., while an efficient assistant is in attendance likewise. Undertaking in all its branches is attended to in the most expeditious and superior manner, at the most moderate rates, no pains being spared to render the fullest satisfaction in every instance. Remains are prepared for burial, and embalmed when desired, interments are procured in any of the surrounding cemeteries, while funerals are personally conducted in first-class style, and, altogether, Mr. Faunce receives a highly gratifying patronage.

E. T. CUNNINGHAM & SON, Plain and Artistic Paper-Hangings and Window-Shades, No. 660 Broadway.—Among the old popular representative business men in this city, there are probably none more favorably known than Mr. E. T. Cunningham, who is from the state of Maine originally and has lived in this community nearly half a century. From 1860 to 1882 he was in business with his son Mr. C. C. Cunningham, the accomplished musician, and carried on quite an extensive trade as dealer in musical merchandise and paper-hangings. In the latter year the partnership was dissolved and the business divided, Mr. Cunningham giving his attention to the wall-paper departments, and his son to that devoted to music and musical merchandise. The stock in its assortment is one of the largest and most complete in the city, and embraces paper hangings of every kind and description, from the plainest to the richest and most beautiful and fashionable in handsome designs and patterns in figure and flowers, in gold and harmoniously blended colors and tints, and also handsome centre pieces and high-art artistic decoration. There is also displayed here a general line of window-shades of all kinds and textures. Paper-hanging and the decoration of interiors is a feature of the business.

W. A. NICKERSON, Plumbist in all its branches, Manufacturer and Dealer in Stoves, Ranges, Furnaces, and Kitchen-Furnishing Goods, No. 359 Broadway.—This gentleman is an extensive dealer in stoves, ranges, furnaces, and kitchen furnishing goods, and is also prepared to execute plumbing in all its branches. He originally started in business in 1860, in Boston, as a dealer in paper-stock, and as a member of the firm of Illig & Nickerson. In 1865 he embarked in the present business as a member of the firm of Chic & Nickerson, continuing it until the great fire of '72, in which he suffered a loss of $40,000. In '73 he came to Chelsea, and has since conducted a flourishing and steadily increasing business. At the spacious store is to be found a complete stock of stoves, ranges, tin-ware, and plumbers' goods, all of which are procured direct from the most famous manufacturers in the country. In tin, sheet-iron and copper ware and in every description of kitchen-furnishing goods, the stock recommends its own merits to the patronage of buyers. Employment is given to a large force of skilled workmen in the line of plumbing, tin-smithing, gas-fitting, roofing and spouting, and all kinds of jobbing and repairing, and every facility is at hand for guaranteeing the prompt and perfect fulfillment of all orders and commissions. Mr. Nickerson is a Vermonter by birth, an experienced merchant and successful business man.

S. B. TUKEY, Hardware, Cutlery, and Tools, No. 191 Winnisimmet Street.—The house of Mr. S. B. Tukey is the largest in the hardware trade in Chelsea. The spacious salesrooms are eligibly located for trade purposes, and perfect in conveniences of arrangement for inspection and sale. The several departments are filled with an elaborate and diversified stock, embracing builders' and general hardware, shelf goods and cabinet hardware, carpenters', mechanics' and machinists' tools, table and pocket cutlery, paints, oils and varnishes, plumbers' materials, all sizes of Akron drain pipe, and kitchen-furnishing goods in great variety and profusion. These supplies are purchased in vast quantities direct from the manufacturers, and special attention is given to the character and quality of the productions. Significant advantages are extended to customers in the matter of prices, and all the resources of the house are used to promote the best interests of its patrons. A heavy demand is ministered to in this city and throughout the surrounding country, and the business is continually growing. Mr. Tukey has resided in Chelsea for the past twenty years, and was formerly a large manufacturer of fire brick near Chelsea bridge. He is ably assisted in his present business by his two sons.

ASHER F. BLACK'S HOUSE FURNISHING WAREROOMS. No. 874 Broadway.—This extensive and justly popular establishment is the headquarters for furniture and carpets, stoves and ranges, refrigerators and kitchen furnishing goods of every description, also, for baby-carriages, and pianos and organs of the best makes. The proprietor is thoroughly experienced, gives close and careful study to the changing demands of public taste, and cultivates the resources of his establishment with sound judgment and liberal enterprise. Previous to 1872 he was for some years engaged in the manufacture of furniture in the city of Boston, and in the year named he removed his business to Chelsea, continuing the manufacture till 1875, when he opened extensive furniture warerooms in the old Pythian Hall. Here he occupies over 10,000 square feet of floor space, and possesses unequalled facilities for conducting all branches of the business under the most favorable auspices and upon the largest scale. A branch store is also operated at Malden, which was opened in 1888, and at each place a stock of goods is carried valued at $10,000. The Pythian warerooms in this city are recognized as forming the finest furniture establishment in Massachusetts. The furniture, which is carried in magnificent assortment, ranges in quality from the plainest to the most elaborate, while many beautiful specimens of mechanical skill and excellence are shown in parlor and bedroom suites, and chairs, sofas and sideboards, which arrest the attention and win the admiration of critical and discriminating buyers. In the carpet department a fine display is made, representing the products of most of the American and European manufacturers, and including all the latest patterns and freshest novelties. The stock of stoves and ranges embodies all the recent improvements made in both heating and cooking, and includes a full supply of the celebrated Ware Stove Company's goods, of Taunton, Mass. All other goods are kept in the same variety and abundance. Prices are placed at the lowest point of moderation, and a specialty is made of the popular instalment plan, which enables people of the most moderate means to secure the choicest goods with ease and economy.

GEORGE T. OAKES & CO., Coal, Wood, and Masons' Stock, Hay and Grain; Office and Wharf, No. 89 Marginal Street.—This popular and prosperous concern was established in 1888 by Perkins & Oakes, and under this style the business was carried on for about nine years, when Mr. Oakes assumed sole control and under the firm name that heads the sketch, has since been conducted with uninterrupted success. The wharf and premises are 555 feet deep, with 105 feet water frontage, and have ample and complete facilities including telephone connection (17-5); all orders receiving immediate attention, and customers are assured of getting an excellent article, full weight, and satisfactory service in every instance. A very heavy and first class stock is constantly carried on hand, comprising best quality Delaware & Hudson Canal Co.'s genuine Lackawanna coal, carefully screened, and making a specialty in Blacksmith coal, also soft coal. They carry also a large stock of lime, cement, plaster, sand, brick, hair, drain pipe, hay and grain, while quite a large force are employed, and a number of teams are in steady service supplying customers throughout the city and surrounding towns. Mr. Oakes is a gentleman of entire reliability in his business relations, as well as a man of energy and enterprise.

C. E. BROWN, Photographer, No. 90 Broadway.—Mr. C. E. Brown has always held a most enviable reputation for his artistic productions and superior business management. He is a native of New Hampshire, but has been a resident of this state for many years, and prior to his becoming a resident of this city, was engaged in the same line of industry in Boston for a period of fifteen years. Seeing an advantageous opening for a first-class photographic artist here, he removed in 1884, fitted up his present gallery, and has success he has achieved since that date has been of the most flattering character. His reception-parlor and office are elegantly furnished, while in his operating rooms will be found all the latest appliances and devices known to the art, including the light accessories, plain and landscape and other properties for backgrounds and effects. Mr. Brown is prepared to execute photography in all its branches, and produces in all his work the best and most beautiful effects. Pictures are taken by the new instantaneous and flash processes, and sitters are thus enabled to obtain accurate and perfect

pictures. Photographs of all sizes from the smallest miniature for lockets life-size are taken, also old pictures are recopied and enlarged, etc. Portraits are likewise made in oils, water-colors, pastelle, crayon, and India ink. The great secret of success in this art is the natural, easy, and life-like pose given to the subject, and as these qualifications are possessed by Mr. Brown, his pictures present a true and correct presentment of the original. He is ably assisted by first class and skilful artists.

BROADWAY HOUSE, Broadway Square, N. A. Gustavus, Manager.—One of the most popular cuisines of Chelsea is without doubt, Mr. H. A. Gustavus, the well-known restaurant and manager of the Broadway House adjoining the Academy of Music. The house is very commodious, and presents a front of 50 feet on Broadway Square, and extends through to Park Street a distance of 150 feet. It is a three story structure, and besides the restaurant café and dining-room and parlors has 50 neatly furnished sleeping-rooms all well ventilated and lighted. Mr. Gustavus, who is from Sweden, has been in this country over 20 years, and was for a long time connected with Young's and the United States Hotels in Boston. He is a practical caterer and cook, and furnishes the very best meals and all the substantials and dainties in an unusually good style, served by attendants more than ordinarily prompt and obliging. The restaurant and café are open from 6 a.m. to midnight, and on Sundays from 9 a.m. to 10 p.m. Dinner is served daily at twenty five cents, and special dishes are cooked to order and hot and cold lunches are served in the café at reasonable prices. Permanent boarders are accommodated at from $5.00 per week and upwards, and rooms are to let by the day or week. Special rates are given theatrical people, and meal checks are sold at a discount. A gong connected with the Academy stage is in the café which announces the rising of the curtain to those who came out between the acts.

JOHN N. AMES, Apothecary, Corner of Broadway and William Streets.—Among the best informed and most reliable houses engaged in this industry in Chelsea, is that of Mr. John N. Ames, apothecary, which has always been distinguished for the excellence of its goods, and high order of management. Mr. Ames is a native of this state and has been a resident of this city ever since 1874. Thoroughly learned and practical in all branches of his profession, he founded this establishment on his own responsibility originally in 1874, and by the superior quality of his goods, and the eminent satisfaction rendered to compounding physicians' prescriptions and family recipes, he rapidly attracted a large and first class patronage. His store occupies a corner position and is very neatly arranged, the importance of the dispensing department being recognized and provided with a separate department and provided with every appliance and device known for securing accuracy and safety, in which none but the most reliable assistants are employed, and orders for this branch of the trade are filled promptly at all hours of the day or night. His stock is large and complete, embracing only pure and fresh drugs, chemicals and pharmaceutical preparations, all proprietary medicines of well known merit and efficiency, toilet and fancy articles, perfumery, stationery, physicians' and surgeons' requisites, druggists' sundries—in fact, everything pertaining to a first-class and well regulated pharmacy.

W. F. BAKER, Dry and Fancy Goods, No. 884 Broadway.—The reputation of the popular dry and fancy goods house of Mr. W. F. Baker bears with the establishment in 1876 and from that date it has never waned, but has been steadily growing and the trade constantly expanding. The store which presents a front of 20 with a depth of 60 feet, is a model of convenience, and in its arrangement admirably adapted in every particular for the purposes of the business, and contains an uncommonly fine line of staple and fancy dry goods of every description, embracing in the assortment here beautiful styles and patterns in dress fabrics and silks, and also notions, trimmings, gloves, hosiery, laces white goods, small wares and woollens, and all kinds of domestics. Mr. Baker, who is widely known and popular in this community, was born in Mass., and for a period of 15 years was with this great jobbing house of Ordway, Hodgett & Hidden of Boston, and is familiar with all the details of the dry-goods trade, and is always on the alert looking up rare bargains to offer his customers.

WILLIAM H. NORRIS, Soap Manufacturer, and Renderer of Grease and Tallow, Corner Second and Spruce Streets.—Mr. Wm. H. Norris, soap manufacturer and renderer of grease and tallow, has secured an enduring hold on popular favor, owing to the uniform high standard of excellence at which the products are maintained. The soaps produced in this concern are of a very superior quality, the specialty "Faultless," a laundry soap being an article of exceptional merit, and has an extensive and increasing sale. The factory is a two-story and basement structure, with a 100 feet front on Second Street and [illegible] feet on Spruce Street, and is supplied with ample steam-power and completely equipped with the most improved appliances and general apparatus, while a number of hands are employed. The productions include, besides the "Faultless," also other fine grades of laundry soaps, jelly-soap, soap shavings and old fashioned potash soap; a large, first-class stock being always kept on hand, while an active business is carried on likewise in rendering grease and tallow for the trade, Mr. Norris producing an excellent brand of tallow used extensively in the south. This prosperous enterprise was established in [illegible] by the present proprietor in Charlestown, and there the business was conducted up to 18 years ago, when in order to obtain more ample facilities to meet the requirements of the large and growing demand, it was removed to the present commodious quarters. Mr. Norris, who has for years been ably seconded in the management of the concern by his sons Charles A. and Harry W., is a gentleman in the full prime of life, and has resided in Chelsea some thirty odd years.

THE CITY OF CAMBRIDGE.

OLD CAMBRIDGE, East Cambridge, North Cambridge, and Cambridgeport form the important and growing city of Cambridge, which is a semi-capital of Middlesex County, and lies on the northwest bank of the Charles River, opposite Boston, with which it is connected by two bridges with long causeways, and by a third bridge, now nearing completion. It is the seat of Harvard University, the oldest, richest, and most thoroughly equipped literary institution in the United States.

OLD CAMBRIDGE

About ten years after the landing of the Plymouth Pilgrims, and about three years after the settlement of Boston, Governor John Winthrop and Deputy-governor Thomas Dudley, with the advice of a board of assistants, thought it advisable to establish in the vicinity of the settlement a "fortified place." Charlestown, Roxbury, and Watertown had been already settled. In the early part of December, 1630, a site was selected upon the "Neck," between Boston and Roxbury. But this plan was deemed unsuitable and was abandoned. Accordingly one day later, in the same year, Governor Winthrop and Lieutenant-governor Dudley jumped on horseback and explored the plains and swamps and forests to the westward in search of a capital. The spot they finally picked out, with the help of some assistant magnates, was that of the present Cambridge, and this was held to be "a fit place for a beautiful town." So, on the 29th day of December, a goodly number of persons bound themselves to build houses there early in the spring of the following year. The village they named Newtown, and laid out regularly in squares, the streets bearing such simple names as Creek, Wood, and Water; while there were, as lesser ways, Marsh Lane, Back Lane, and Crooked Lane. That was before the days of aristocratic thoroughfares like Brattle, and Craigie, and Elery, and Fayerweather streets.

Early in 1631 the houses began to rise, and Governor Winthrop set up the frame of his dwelling on the very spot where he first pitched his tent. But the people of Boston reminded him that he had promised previously that he would never move away anywhere unless they accompanied him; and so, in the fall of 1631, he disappointed his Newtown friends by taking down the frame of his unfinished dwelling and setting it up in Boston. Lieutenant-governor Dudley's house was completed meanwhile, and his family installed therein; and he and the rest frigidly let Winthrop go to Boston without offering to accompany him. This affair, as was natural, caused a coolness between Winthrop and Dudley, which was not removed for several years. Dudley assumed the leadership of the "newe towne," that being the only designation given to it. Making the best of their opportunities, the remaining settlers proved so thrifty, and courtly too, that they soon began to deserve the praise accorded them by Wood, the English tourist, some years afterward, who warmly described the place as "one of the neatest and best-compacted towns in New England, having many fair structures, with many handsome-contrived streets. The inhabitants," added this complimentary tourist, "are most of them very rich." In 1632, a number of settlers from Braintree, England, came to Newtown. There is no list of inhabitants extant until after this period, except this memorandum on the title page of the records: "The towne book of Newtowne: The inhabitants there—Mr. Thomas Dudley, Esquire, Mr. Symon Bradstreet, Mr. Edmond Lockwood, Mr. Daniell Patrike, John Poole, William Spencer, John Kirman, Symon Sackett."

The first settlers, soon after their arrival, began works of public improvement. In June, 1631, John Maisters or Masters, having undertaken "to make a passage from Charles Ryver to the new towne, twelve foote broad and seven foot deep," was promised satisfaction by the authorities of Boston, according to expenses incurred; and in the following July the sum of £30 ($150) was levied upon the surrounding towns, the "newe towne" being exempt from the taxation. This canal was constructed by the enlargement of a natural creek, traces of which still exist on the easterly side of the College Wharf, from the Charles River north to South Street. From this point it extended along the edge of South and Eliot streets to Brattle Street, where a footbridge and causeway were made. In February, 1632, the sum of £70 was levied upon the surrounding towns for the building of a "pallysadoe" round the "newe towne." The palisade was built. It commenced at Brick Wharf (generally called Windmill Hill), and it ran alongside the present Common, in Ward 1, and through what was then a thicket, being now Jarvis Field and lands adjacent. It cannot be traced now. In March, the bounds of the "newe towne," between Charlestown and Watertown, were defined by order of the Court of Assistants, and later, in the same month, the town took action requiring that every one who owned any part in the paled land should keep the palm in good and sufficient repair; "and if it happened to have any defect, he should mend the same within three days, or pay a fine of ten shillings." The course of this pale or fence was from the college, extending easterly to the junction of Ellsworth Avenue with Cambridge Street, to the line between Cambridge and Charlestown (now Somerville), at its angle on Line Street with Cambridge Street; thence following that line to the creek, a few rods easterly from the track of the railroad. Beginning again at the point first mentioned, the palisade extended southerly to the marsh near the junction of Holyoke Place with Mount Auburn Street. In the following August, there was an accession to the "newe towne" from England by Rev. Mr. Hooker, who brought with him a considerable number of people, and a meeting-house was erected on what is now Dunster Street. That part of the eastward now known as East Cambridge and Cambridgeport were then called under the general name of the "Neck," and consisted of an upland pasture, swamp, and marsh. The upland and marsh at East Cambridge was known by the name of "Graves, his Neck."

The new town was composed of a dozen streets in the space that is now bounded by Harvard, Brattle, Eliot, South Holyoke, and Bow Streets, this space being inclosed in the paling. Along the river southerly was a succession of marshes, the tract now bounded by North Avenue, Garden, and Linnaean streets being set apart as a "cow common," this being the present Common, in which the Soldiers' Monument stands to-day.

In 1634, the Newtown people began to complain of being overcrowded, and loudly talked, some of them, of moving to Connecticut. To that region the original Braintree settlers, to the number of one hundred, accordingly departed two years later, headed by their minister, the Rev. Thomas Hooker, and driving with them 180 cattle. The same year, 1636, this migratory church was replaced in Newtown by a permanent organization, under the Rev. Thomas Shepard, a recent arrival from England; and the fortunes of the town were also bettered by the establishment in it of the Colony's first school, endowed by the General Court with £400. Nearly all the ministers of the Colony happened to be from the University of Cambridge, in England, and most of them, too, from a single one of its colleges, Emanuel. The neighboring Charlestown clergyman, the Rev. John Harvard, a scholarly and gentle graduate of Emanuel, took from the first a hearty interest in the Newtown school; and, dying in 1638, he left to it his well-selected library of three hundred volumes and half his fortune. This bequest amounted, it is supposed, to nearly £800, or twice as much as the original gift of the General Court; and such was the effect of so magnificent a gift that the colonists determined to raise the school to the grade of a college, and to give to it the name of its benefactor. Thus was founded

THE FAMOUS HARVARD COLLEGE.

In the same year, too, the Cambridge graduates concluded to express their esteem for their own university by changing the name of the village from Newtown to Cambridge. The scholarly fortunes of the town were also aided by the establishment in it of the first printing-office in America north of Mexico, which was set up

276

CITY OF CAMBRIDGE.

in Cambridge in 1639, and the place soon began to be quite a centre of influence both in theology and religion. In 1640, Charlestown Ferry was given to the college, which held it for a hundred and fifty years; in 1650, an act of incorporation was granted the president and fellows; in 1652, the first inn was established, one Andrew Belcher being granted liberty " to sell beare and bread ;" in 1660, a bridge was built over Charles River, making the distance to Boston eight miles; and in 1732 a portion of the territory of Cambridge, on the northwest, was set off into a separate town, Newtown—a process repeated in subsequent years. The rest of the civic history of Cambridge is dull. It became a city in 1846; and early in the present century its trivial commerce induced the Government to make it a port of entry, whence Lechmere's Point, one of the settlements within the town limits, became Cambridgeport.

The history of Harvard College is so closely connected with the literary and architectural annals of Cambridge that it is not worth while to try to dissever them. The Rev. Mr. Harvard, as we have seen, died in 1638, little is known about his personal history. He graduated at Emmanuel College in 1631, and came to Charlestown only a year before his death. The graduates of the College built him a plain monument in Charlestown in 1828. Erected by a Legislature, the new College was almost inevitably a State institution. At its foundation and for many years afterward it was a Government school, established for the education of candidates for the ministry, and with the avowed purpose of maintaining and propagating a religious creed. In 1640 Rev. Henry Dunster was made president of the College, which from that time onward may be regarded as a literary institution, organized and conducted with the purpose of meeting the reasonable demands of the age and the community. The early presidents of the College were men of superior learning for their time; the range of studies was limited, the number of students small (for the first fifty years seldom exceeding twenty), and though there may have been occasional assistant teachers, there was no permanent professor or tutor till the close of the century. During the greater portion of the last century the College was identified with the liberal party in church and state, and could not but bear a prominent part in the movements preceding and accompanying the Revolution, in which the country declared and achieved its independence. In 1775 the library and classes were removed to Concord, the College halls given up to the use of the provincial army, and the president's house offered, and for a short time occupied, as headquarters for General Washington, the commander-in-chief, while the president himself—an ardent patriot—served as chaplain to the troops on numerous occasions, and notably on the eve of the battle of Bunker Hill. After the evacuation of Boston by the British the College resumed its sessions in Cambridge, and maintained for the ensuing thirty years or more a high but hardly growing reputation as a seat of learning. Its era of active and incessant progress may be said to have begun with the presidency of Dr. Kirkland in 1810.

During its history Harvard University has had twenty-two presidents, the present incumbent being Charles William Eliot, who was elected in 1869. Under his administration the university has made wonderful strides, and in every department it stands at the head. Many thousands of students have graduated, and had degrees conferred upon them here. The collection of buildings is remarkable, embracing nearly all kinds of architecture, and many of them the gift of the wealthy alumnæ of the university. The grounds and buildings, which are twenty in number, are rich with interest, and hours can be profitably employed in studying the various collections that have been gathered from all parts of the world.

Among other schools of Cambridge is the Episcopal Theological School of Massachusetts, which was founded in 1867, upon an endowment given by Benjamin T. Reed, of Boston. Although it possesses many advantages from its proximity to Harvard, it is not connected with the latter. The buildings comprise St. John's Memorial Chapel, Reed Hall, Lawrence Hall, and Burnham Hall. The outlay for buildings and land thus far amounts to $225,000.

The centre of Cambridge is Harvard Square, around which the College buildings cluster so closely that the student as he takes some country friend into the " yard " finds it hard to divest his descriptions of the guide-book manner. This so-called square is a somnolent triangle, three miles from Boston, whose natural state of calm is vexed only by the bells of the horse-cars that trundle through it, or by the scream of their wheels as they round the curve. Once in a while, too, its dust is stirred by some mortuary procession of cattle on their way to the neighboring abattoirs. At the eastern end of the triangle, just where the street begins to widen, stands a generous old gambrel-roofed wooden building, now known as Wadsworth House, which was built in 1726 for the official residence of the presidents of the College. Wadsworth was the first to occupy it, the house having been completed the year after his inauguration. For a hundred and twenty years the dwelling was occupied by the successive presidents, Wadsworth, Holyoke, Locke, Langdon, Willard, Webber, Kirkland, Quincy, and Everett having dwelt in it. Presidents Sparks and Walker lived in their own houses, and Felton was the first to occupy the new president's house on Quincy Street, at the eastern end of the yard—a modest brick edifice erected over a score of years ago by Peter C. Brooks, of Boston. No building in Cambridge has sheltered so many people of eminence, probably, as Wadsworth House. Washington slept there several times before taking the Vassall House as his permanent headquarters in 1775; and here he was received when he visited Cambridge in 1789. In good preservation, the ancient edifice is now used as a dormitory, while the office of the College bursar is in a little brick addition.

Between Christ Church and the Unitarian Church lies the old village cemetery, celebrated in the verse of Longfellow and Holmes, in which are buried Presidents Dunster, Chauncy, Leverett, Wadsworth, Holyoke, Willard, and Weber; Andrew Belcher, Cambridge's first innkeeper; Stephen Day and Samuel Green, the first printers; Thomas Shepard, the first minister; and many another man of the elder day. The first rector of Christ Church was the Rev. East Apthorp, a native of Boston, who wanted, the Congregationalists thought, to be appointed Bishop of New England. Apthorp built a large and beautiful house on Main Street, just opposite the present Gore Hall, which is still called the Bishop's Palace. He was disappointed in his aspirations for the rochet, and was so sensitive to the coldness and the somewhat persecuting antagonism of his theological opponents that he resigned and moved to England in 1764. In his house General Burgoyne was imprisoned after his capture. Subsequently, a new proprietor built a third story, for the accommodation, it is supposed, of his household slaves.

Christ Church presents its ancient shapely front toward Cambridge Common, over which a chime of bells, placed in the tower in 1860, pleasantly rings every Sunday. The Common contains some twenty acres, and will always be remembered as the place where the American troops mustered and encamped in 1775. Every morning there started from this now peaceful enclosure the guards for Lechmere's Point, Winter Hill, and the other posts, and here the roughly-equipped and poorly-drilled provincial troops prepared to lay siege to Boston, held by ten thousand experienced and well-prepared soldiers. At the western end stands the elm under which Washington, on July 3, 1775, formally assumed his position as general-in-chief of the Continental army. This venerable tree is of great age. It is surrounded by a simple iron fence, and a plain granite slab tersely records the fact that "Under this tree Washington first took command of the American army, July 3, 1775." Just behind stands the granite edifice of the Shepard Congregational Church, the pulpit in whose chapel is partly made of wood from a branch of the elm necessarily removed. In the middle of the Common, facing the College buildings, is a costly but very ugly monument erected to commemorate the men of Cambridge who fell in the Rebellion. North of the Common stands a gambrel-roofed old house, which was the home of Abiel Holmes, the annalist of New England, and the birth-place of his more famous son, Dr. Oliver Wendell Holmes. About a hundred and sixty odd years old, it had among its proprietors before Dr. Abiel Holmes, Jabez Fox, tailor, of Boston, Jonathan his son, College steward. During the ownership of the latter the building was occupied by the Committee of Safety, who established themselves in it in 1775, and formed plans for the collection and management of the provincial forces. In one of the ground rooms Benedict Arnold received his commission as colonel; and here, probably, were the headquarters of General Ward. Washington dwelt in it for three days. It is now owned by the College. Although the eminent author of the *Autocrat of the Breakfast Table* has always lived in Boston, he has never lost patriotism for his birthplace, in which he seems to consider himself fortunate to have been born. The foundations of his literary reputation were laid here.

Outside of the very many handsome buildings belonging to Harvard University, Cambridge contains many very imposing edifices and points of great interest. The new city building is a brick structure erected in 1876, at a cost of about $75,000, and standing on the south side of Mount Auburn Street. The building is used as a police station, a police court, engine-house, ward meeting-house, several city offices, etc. The interior is well finished. It is, however, inadequate for the purposes for which it was erected, and a new and more magnificent structure is talked of.

NORTH CAMBRIDGE

comprises that section of the city lying beyond the College in a northerly direction, toward the town of Arlington. It was formerly called Porter's, and is a busy section of the town, possessing facilities for manufacturing that are well improved in various lines of enterprises. It is also a commercial point of considerable importance, bordered by Charles River, which affords convenient facilities for navigation to each section of the town. There are numerous churches and public schools, and all the evidences of thrift, culture, and refinement. There are many fine mansions in this section, and new buildings are springing up rapidly. This section was once noted for is cattle fair.

CAMBRIDGEPORT

is that section of the city embraced between the end of West Boston Bridge and Old Cambridge. It is a noted manufacturing point, possessing several industries that have a national reputation. It is a busy bustling mart of trade, and has all the appearances of a city itself. It has a large number of churches and public schools, and an Atheneum, while the residences are noted for their beauty and good taste. Before the West Boston Bridge was built, in 1793, the only means of conveyance between Cambridge and Boston was by a row-boat across the Charles River, and, by land, Boston could only be reached by way of Roxbury and the " Neck" (Washington Street), a distance of eight miles. After the bridge was built public omnibuses came into use, and then the horse railroad and the iron horse. This horse railroad was the first in New England. A new bridge, connecting Cambridgeport with Beacon Street, Boston, and to be known as Harvard Bridge, is now nearly completed, the cost being half a million dollars.

EAST CAMBRIDGE

which is the most recently settled part of the city, was formerly known as Lechmere's Point, and is opposite the northwest portion of Boston, with which it is connected by Craige's Bridge over Charles River, and also with Charlestown by a bridge. It contains the Court-house, Jail, House of Correction, and other county buildings. Here are the extensive glass-works of the New England Glass Company ; also soap, candle, and brush manufactories ; numerous churches, schools, banks, and other industries of interest and value to the community.

MANUFACTURES.

Among the other important manufacturing industries carried on in different parts of the city may be mentioned the production of Britannia ware, chair and cabinet ware, pianos and organs, railroad cars, pianoforte actions, starch, hats and caps, tinware, linseed-oil, leather currying, boots and shoes, bricks, snuff, cigars, building stone, gas, bread, type, l'earbyn marble, confectionery, iron railing, chemical preparations, cordage, pumps, etc.

The manufacturing interests of Cambridge are among its leading attractions. Despite the fact of the age of the town, the manufacturing interest is a growing one, imparting to the city a more permanent and solid character, and placing it among the most prosperous cities of the State. The progress made in this direction has been much more rapid during the past decade than ever before. Old industries have been enlarged, and new ones added, which bid fair to become large and prosperous enterprises. Every manufacturing enterprise here established, when managed with careful, practical, and energetic hands, has proved a success. The natural facilities possessed by Cambridge as a manufacturing point are almost unlimited. Its facilities for transportation are superior to any city in this section, save Boston. It has an abundance of water-power, and all the raw materials at hand—in fact, in every item to be taken into account in the make-up of a manufacturing city comparison is challenged. In accessibility, healthy location, cheapness of living, educational facilities, and social and religious advantages, each of which is important, essential, and of the highest significance, Cambridge is favored in a pre-eminent degree.

RELIGIOUS AND EDUCATIONAL FACILITIES.

Every denomination is represented in Cambridge, and in every portion of the city numerous spires attest the people's hearty acceptance of the benign influences of church organization, and their liberality in providing handsome and substantial edifices. The public schools of the city are of a high standard, and managed for the best interests of its youthful population. The city has a splendid public library, and there are several local weekly newspapers, that fully chronicle local events, and keep the citizens informed of what is going on in the world.

THE CITY GOVERNMENT

for 1889 consists of Henry II. Gilmore, Mayor; Board of Aldermen, representing the five wards of the city: James F. Aylward, John II. Corcoran, Charles L. Fuller, Daniel E. Frasier, Gustavus Goepper, Alexander Millan, William T. Nallon, John E. Parry, Alvin F. Sortwell, and Frank II. Teele; Members of the Common Council: Edward A. Bingham, Elmer II. Bright, Patrick J. Callahan, George E. Carter, John S. Clary, Edward A. Couni-han, John R. Fairbairn, J. Frank Facey, James Grant, Thomas Houlihan, Daniel F. Kennedy, Patrick J. Lam-bert, Walter II. Murdock, John M. Patriquin, John T. Phelan, William T. Piper, Andrew J. Rady, Charles F. Sanborn, Charles B. Seagrave, Edward C. Wheeler. Francis L. Pratt, Messenger to the City Council. The city finances are in excellent shape, and many valuable public improvements are being carried out that will bring what were waste lands into demand for building upon, and thus increase the material wealth and prosperity of the city. Immense sums have been spent in securing additional water supply, and in this respect the city is provided for for a long time to come.

The fire department is a well-disciplined body, and there is an efficient police service.

Persons who have once visited Cambridge need not to be told of its many charms as a place of residence and culture; and those who have not visited it must needs see it to realize its beauties and attractions. The city is growing rapidly. It is so closely allied with Boston, that were it not for the pride the citizens have in the college town, and the common desire to retain the name, it would some time ago have been incorporated with its great neighbor. The time is coming when it will be absorbed by the greater city.

MOUNT AUBURN CEMETERY

is within the district of Old Cambridge, to which we have chiefly devoted our observations as yet. Mt. Auburn, as a beautiful home of the dead, elicits the admiration of all who visit it. It was dedicated Septem-ber 24, 1831. It contains one hundred and thirty-five acres of land, covered with a natural growth of trees, the highest part of which is one hundred and twenty-five feet above the river, laid out with winding gravelled walks, and embellished with every variety of shrub and flower. It is surrounded by an iron fence, with an imposing granite gateway in the Egyptian style, and not far from the entrance is a chapel of granite for the celebration of burial services. Monuments of costly material and exquisite workmanship are erected in all parts of the cemetery.

CITY OF CAMBRIDGE.

J. F. OLSSON, Successor to C. A. Jameson, Manufacturer of Mirror and Picture Frames, No. 8 Harvard Row.—A department of industry which has been developed to a high plane of excellence in Cambridge is the production of artistic picture and mirror frames, for encasing the works of the painter and other artists. A thoroughly representative house engaged in this line of business is that of Mr. J. F. Olsson, successor to C. A. Jameson, manufacturer of mirror and picture frames. The proprietor, Mr. Olsson, is a native of Sweden, but has been a resident of Boston and vicinity ever since 1857, and first established himself in this industry in Boston in [illegible], which he conducted with unvarying success until 1885, when he purchased the present business from Mr. C. A. Jameson, and removed to this location. The premises occupied comprise an elegantly fitted up store, with workshop attached, which is fully equipped with all the necessary tools and appliances required in manufacturing his products, and a number of skilled and proficient workmen are given constant employment. Mr. Olsson prides himself on the superior quality, fine workmanship and general artistic excellence of the work done by him. He is prepared to manufacture to order all kinds of frames for the encasing of mirrors and all art productions in all the latest styles and materials desired. He keeps constantly on hand a fine stock of mouldings, braiding, mats, and other necessary articles from which patrons can make their selections. In his store will be found also a fine collection of oil and water color paintings, etchings, engravings, pastels, crayons, plain and colored photographs, all of the highest artistic merit, which are offered to the public at very low prices. Mr. Olsson makes a specialty of cleaning, regilding and rebronzing of old frames, making them equal to new; also the hanging of pictures and other works of art in the best artistic manner, and the packing of all such articles for shipment or removal.

CHARLES MOORE & CO., Hardware, Kitchen Furnishing Goods, Furnaces, Ranges, Cooking and Parlor Stoves; All Kinds of Tin and Sheet-Iron Work Made to Order, and Roofs Tinned, No. 8 Brattle Street, Corner of Palmer Street.—Commercial enterprises of modern times embrace many features of practical utility, but none which deserve higher consideration than those which relate to the home, its comforts and conveniences. Among such enterprises in Cambridge, prominent mention should be made of that conducted by Charles Moore & Co., at No. 8 Brattle Street, corner of Palmer. This firm are extensive dealers in hardware, kitchen furnishing goods, furnaces, ranges and stoves, and the house is recognized as the oldest and leading exponent of the trade in this city. The business was originally established in 1856 by Messrs. Dennett & Moore, and in 1861 the firm of Chas. Moore & Co. was organized. The business premises comprise two floors and a basement, 30 x 100 feet each, divided into manufacturing and sales departments and giving ample accommodation for supplying the most extensive demand. The stock is the largest and finest in the city of its kind, embracing a full and complete line of kitchen furnishing goods, while the assortment of stoves embodies all the latest and most improved styles for both heating and cooking, whose superior qualities are familiar to every housekeeper. In tin, sheet-iron and copper work this house occupies an unquestioned position at the head of the trade, from which it is abundantly able to make good its claim for accomplishing as thorough work as can be found in any locality, while in the line of roof tinning and general jobbing, every facility is at hand for the prompt and perfect fulfillment of all orders. Steady employment is given to a force of eighteen hands, and business is brisk and lively at all times, forming an important and still growing factor in the mercantile activity of this city. Mr. Charles Moore is a native of the state of Maine, and came to Cambridge thirty-five years ago. He has ever been prominently identified with the business growth and public welfare of the community, serving as a member of the city council, and promoting the prosperity and material interests of the city with energy, discrimination and sound judgment.

J. D. NORRIS, Dealer in Fine Groceries, No. 10 Brattle Street.—Among the old established and most popular business men in Cambridge, must be classed Mr. J. D. Norris, who has been prominently identified with the grocery trade here for about a third of a century. Mr. Norris first established himself in business in 1855 on Harvard Square, where he remained until 1867, when he removed to his present premises at No. 10 Brattle Street. Mr. Norris' business career has been as successful as it has been long, and his customers followed him from the old to the new store, which is commodious, having an area of 20 x 100 feet, and is fitted up in a very attractive and appropriate manner. It contains a full and carefully selected assortment of fancy and staple groceries, etc., such as fresh, new crop teas from Japan and China, fragrant coffees from Java, Mocha and South America, hermetically sealed goods in glass and tin from the most celebrated establishments in Europe and America, spices, condiments, table delicacies, the most select brands of flour, pure and fresh creamery butter, eggs, cheese and other farm and dairy products direct from the producers; also every kind of goods known as grocers' sundries. The goods of this establishment are highly esteemed throughout the city and vicinity for their freshness, absolute purity and low prices, while the services of three courteous and polite assistants and a delivery team are in constant demand. This enterprise is one of the oldest in its line in the city. Mr. Norris was born in Vermont fifty-one years ago, and no resident in Cambridge is better known or more highly respected than he.

REYCROFT & LORD, Druggists, Cambridge Street, Corner Fourth, East Cambridge.—One of the handsomest as well as best conducted drug stores in East Cambridge is that of Messrs. Reycroft & Lord. The commodious and well arranged salesroom, 20 x 35 feet in dimensions, is fitted up in a style which represents a happy combination of modern elegance and convenience, and with its plate-glass front, polished hardwood fixtures, fine soda fountain and well displayed stock constitutes one of the attractive features of this busy avenue. The assortment of drugs, chemicals, medicines, toilet and fancy articles, etc., etc., embraces all to be found at a first-class family drug store. Prescriptions and family recipes of all kinds are skillfully compounded and the large and liberal patronage received is drawn from the most desirable town custom. Messrs. L. W. Reycroft and T. H. Lord, Jr., are experienced and skillful pharmacists, and young men of more than ordinary business tact and ability. After serving as clerks for some years they concluded to embark in the business for themselves and accordingly in December, [illegible], they fitted up and opened the fine store with which they have since been popularly identified.

JAMES C. DAVIS & SON, Manufacturers of Standard Soaps, Factory Nos. 204, 206 and 208 Broadway, Cambridgeport, Office No. 8 Chatham Street, Boston.—It is a cold fact that soap-using is a sign of civilization, just as, in the words of the inspired writer, "cleanliness is next to godliness." Yet there are many soaps which, while nominally the emblems of civilization, are actually vile compounds, made of impure and adulterated materials, their impurities being disguised and their origin concealed by some strong scent. The consumer, therefore, has but one safeguard—to buy no soaps unless they bear the name of some manufacturer recognized as a synonym for excellence and purity of product, whose sole object is not the realization of large profits without regard to consequences as they affect customers. There are such manufacturers—none too many, but they can be found—and in the roll of honor which contains their names, we find none more deserving of praise than Messrs. James C. Davis & Son, the well-known manufacturers of standard soaps, whose factory is located at Nos. 204, 206 and 208 Broadway, Cambridgeport, with main offices at No. 8 Chatham Street, Boston. This house has long enjoyed a national reputation, and a trade coextensive with the limits of the country. It was founded in 1840 by Mr. Davis, who was succeeded by his son and grandson, Messrs. James C. and James H. Davis, under the firm name of James C. Davis & Son, in 1874. Under their enterprising and well directed efforts, the business was placed upon a sound and permanent foundation, and the rapid increase in the demand for their products quickly indicated how perfectly they met the demands of the public. In 1882, Mr. James H. Spaulding, who had been connected with the house as traveling salesman for a period of twelve years, was admitted to partnership. The senior member of the firm, Mr. James C. Davis, died in March, 1889, after an honorable and successful business career, and the enterprise has since been conducted by the surviving partners without change of firm name. The factory is a three-story frame structure, 150 x 150 feet in dimensions, and is perfectly equipped in every way, including the latest improved appliances and ample steam-power, while the work is supervised under the close personal management of the proprietors, whose long practical experience and thorough progressive enterprise are evidenced in the superior qualities of the soap bearing the imprint of this reliable house. Forty expert hands are employed. This firm make a specialty of the "J. C. Davis' Old Soap," the name of which on the wrapper guarantees the quality and merit of a first-class article, which has stood the test of years against all competition. This house has also recently introduced the "Hahne" washing compound, which is emphatically the best and cheapest article of the kind yet manufactured, and in fact taking the place of more expensive products. It now stands without a rival, as perfectly harmless to the skin, death to dirt in any and every form, and creating for itself a permanent future demand. The manufacture of a variety of laundry soaps is also here carried on. Orders of any magnitude are promptly filled, and terms and prices are invariably placed at the lowest point of moderation. The proprietors are natives of Cambridge, thoroughly practical and accomplished manufacturers, and solid and successful business men.

HENRY THAYER & CO., Manufacturing Chemists, Cambridgeport.—The firm of Henry Thayer & Co., manufacturers of medicinal extracts and other pharmaceutical preparations, so well and favorably known to the physician and the druggist for the past forty years, was commenced in a small way by the late Dr. Henry Thayer in 1847, and was the first establishment of the kind in this country to make a specialty of this line of manufacture. The marvelous growth of this industry and the constantly increasing demand for these goods from all quarters of the globe, attest the universal appreciation of all those engaged in selling or dispensing these goods. Uniformity of quality, accuracy in preparation, and an undeviating rule of never handling anything but the purest and best of material, has secured the approval of all who may have had occasion to order from their list. Their present laboratory, which is a large, five-story brick building, with several detached buildings for milling and storehouse purposes, is situated on Broadway, Cambridgeport, and contains every modern appliance in machinery, that skill and science have invented for the turning out of first-class goods at the lowest possible cost of production. The heads of the various departments are thoroughly equipped for service in their different branches, and have allowed no real improvement in any direction to escape their notice, thus enabling them to produce the best goods that it is possible to make. Since the death of Dr. Thayer in 1876, the surviving members of the firm, Messrs. J. P. Putnam and F. D. Hardy, continue to maintain the high reputation which has always been accorded to the house. Their present fine enterprise fluid and solid extracts, elixirs, tinctures, wines, pills, concentrations, resinoids, preparations of malt, pepsin, and a long list of specialties, a catalogue of which will be promptly forwarded to an applicant.

H. M. BIRD, Broadway Iron Foundry, Manufacturer of Iron Castings, Cambridgeport.—This business was established in 1865 by Mr. Bird, who is a thoroughly practical man, fully conversant with every detail of iron founding in all its branches. The premises occupied comprise a superior foundry and commodious pattern and fitting shops. The mechanical equipment embraces a powerful steam-engine, and all the latest improved tools, appliances and machinery known to the trade, and the policy of the proprietor has ever been to adopt every invention and improvement that give promise of perfecting the product. Mr. Bird employs constantly forty skilled workmen, and is prepared with all necessary facilities for the production of machinery castings, which are unrivalled by any other first-class house in the state for smoothness, softness, finish and quality of metal. He likewise cheerfully furnishes estimates for any description of castings, and attends carefully to designing and pattern making. All orders are promptly filled at the lowest possible prices consistent with the best materials and superior workmanship. The trade of this responsible house is by no means confined to Cambridgeport, but extends throughout all sections of New England.

WM. H. WOOD & CO., Lumber, Nos. 12 to 78 Broadway, Corner Third Street, Cambridgeport.—The leading exponent of the lumber trade is the house of Messrs. Wm. H. Wood & Co. This firm is widely prominent as lumber merchants, and the business transacted by them forms one of the largest industries carried on in this community. The house so successfully conducted by them was originally established in 1867 by Mr. Burrage, the present firm succeeding to the control in 1880. The business premises cover an area of 600 x 800 feet, with a fine wharf, and comprising a spacious yard and a series of buildings suitable for the accommodation of the immense and valuable stock that is constantly carried. The yard affords ample space for handling and piling, and always contains some two million feet of the choicest lumber expressly adapted to the wants of builders, manufacturers and other consumers. This house has secured connections with producers and shippers that enable them to offer lumber of a quality and at terms and prices that have given it the very highest reputation. From thirty to forty men are employed, and orders by telephone or otherwise are given immediate and careful attention.

CHARLES S. DARLING, Manufacturer and Importer of Fine Whips and Canes, also Jobber in Whips and Lashes, Nos. 110 and 112 Main Street, Cambridgeport.—A way back in the year 1858 the prosperous business now conducted by Charles S. Darling, manufacturer and importer of fine whips and canes, and also jobber in whips and lashes, was established by this gentleman's father, William Darling, at Brighton, and by him was carried on there for many years. Subsequently, Mr. Darling, the elder, retired, and lived at his farm at Hartford up to 1865, when he resumed business in Cambridgeport, and continued the same until 1872, when his son, the present proprietor, assumed control. The establishment here occupied, which includes store and shop, is commodious and well equipped, all necessary facilities being at hand, and several expert workmen are employed. The productions include fine whips and canes of every description, the manufacture of high-grade carriage whips, however, being a leading specialty, while repairing also is promptly and neatly done. Mr. Darling also imports and deals in whips, canes and lashes, keeping constantly on hand an extensive first-class assortment, and his trade, which is large and steadily growing, extends all over the United States.

GEORGE B. KETCHUM, Pharmacist, Cor. Broadway and Columbia Street, Cambridgeport.—No member of this profession in Cambridgeport bears a higher or more enviable reputation for skill and reliability than Mr. George B. Ketchum. Mr. Ketchum is a native of New Brunswick, about thirty-eight years of age, and has been a resident of this place for many years. He is thoroughly familiar with every department of his business, having acquired his knowledge by long years of close application and practical experience, and is registered under the laws of this state governing the rules of the practice of this profession. He founded this establishment in 1882, and its continued success from that date is evidence of what may be accomplished by close attention to the wants of customers, and handling only the best of goods. He occupies an elegant corner store, which is handsomely fitted up, including display windows, show cases, beautiful counters and an elaborately constructed soda-water fountain and telephone. Recognizing the great importance and heavy responsibility attending the compounding of physicians' prescriptions and family recipes, he has provided a separate department, devoted entirely to this branch of the business, in which will be found all the latest improved appliances and devices to ensure proper accuracy in their dispensation. His stock embraces a full and comprehensive line of pure and fresh drugs, chemicals and pharmaceutical preparations, all of which are up to the highest standard as required by the United States Pharmacopœia, also all proprietary remedies of well-known merit and efficacy, toilet and fancy articles, perfumery, fine stationery, foreign and domestic medicinal waters on draught or in cases, druggists' sundries, physicians' and surgeons' emergency supplies, and in fact everything usually found in a well-regulated first-class pharmacy, while prescriptions and medicines are compounded promptly and accurately at all hours of the day or night. The telephone connection is 719.

CITY MARKET, J. P. McSorley, Proprietor, No. 638 Cambridge Street, Cambridgeport.—Prominent among the well-known business men of Cambridgeport is Mr. J. P. McSorley, of the City Market. Mr. McSorley is a native of the city, and has resided here all his life and been long identified with the meat and provision trade. Since 1878 he has been in business on his own account and been located in his present premises since 1888. The store, which has an area of 20 x 40 feet, is a model of cleanliness and order, is well-lighted and provided with all the necessary conveniences to the successful carrying on of the business. The store is made additionally attractive and inviting by the excellent manner everything in the line of choice cuts of beef, veal, lamb, mutton, pork, etc., is displayed. Poultry and game form a special feature of the business, the better having always the finest and freshest to be found in the city. There is at all times an ample stock of salted and smoked meats, sausages, bologna, fresh luscious fruits and vegetables of every kind in season. In the excellence of its fresh meats this establishment cannot be surpassed, as supplies of the best cuts of well-fed cattle are received daily. Mr. McSorley is one of the best judges of meat in the city. Three assistants are kept constantly busy in filling orders, and goods are delivered free of charge.

JAMES C. NOOR, Family Groceries, etc., No. 191 Cambridge Street, East Cambridge.—The popular house of Mr. James C. Noor dates its foundation from 1880. The business has always been successful and prosperous under Mr. Noor's management, and in 1892 in order to meet the demands of the growing patronage it was removed to the desirable location now occupied. The premises present a front of 25 feet with a depth of 50 feet, and are well lighted and managed for all business purposes. The stock, which is large and of the highest standard quality goods, includes everything in the line of family supplies coming under the head of staple and fancy groceries, and embraces teas and coffees and pure spices and family flour, canned fruits and vegetables, milk, meats and table delicacies, creamery and dairy butter, cheese and eggs and country produce. Three clerks assist Mr. Noor in the conduct of the business. Orders are promptly delivered in any part of the city free of expense. Mr. Noor is always in a position to offer his patrons and the public the best goods at the very lowest prices. He is a native of Maine and is an old esteemed popular merchant.

GREAT AMERICAN UNION TEA COMPANY, T. J. Stevenson & Co., Proprietors, No. 193 Cambridge Street, East Cambridge.—In East Cambridge the best known among those engaged in the business is the Great American Union Tea Co. This concern has been in successful operation since 1887, and under able management, and keeping in stock only the very best and choicest goods, a large permanent business has been established. The store has a double front of plate glass show windows and an area 20 x 50 feet. It is admirably adapted to the purposes of the business, and the stock which embraces the very finest new crop teas from China, Japan, and coffees from Java, Mocha and South America, is one of the largest, most complete, and in greater variety than has ever before been brought together in this section. The goods are all carefully selected and as to quality cannot be surpassed. Low prices prevail and Messrs. T. J. Stevenson & Co., the proprietors, are always in a position to secure the best goods that are brought into the country and can always suit the tastes of the public in teas and coffees and please all in prices. Mr. T. J. Stevenson has the general management of the business and although a young man he has had quite an extended experience in the tea and coffee trade and is an expert judge.

CHARLES E. COMBS, Pharmacist, No. 417 Cambridge Street, Cambridgeport.—Mr. Charles E. Combs has been engaged in this profession for many years, and after serving a period of ten years in the store, he purchased it in 1886, and has since continued to enjoy an uninterrupted career of prosperity. Mr. Combs devotes his personal attention to compounding physicians' prescriptions, which he prepares with skill and exactitude from pure drugs and medicines with promptness and dispatch. The store is very neat and attractive with its marble tile flooring and ornamental show-cases and counters. Everything in the line of drugs, medicines, pharmaceutical and toilet articles and also chemicals, extracts and perfumes is always to be obtained here of the very best quality, and also, all the various requisites needed by physicians in their practice. A native of the state of Massachusetts, Mr. Combs, who is a popular member of the fraternity of pharmacists, is familiar with all the details of the business, and has a thorough, comprehensive knowledge of drugs, their values and properties.

JOHN H. SULLIVAN, Apothecary, Cor. Gore and Third Streets, East Cambridge.—A well conducted pharmacy is that of Mr. John H. Sullivan. The commodious store, 20 x 30 feet in dimensions, is fitted up in a style which combines the best modern ideas of convenience and attractiveness, and upon the shelves and counters and in the large show windows is tastefully displayed a carefully selected stock of drugs, chemicals, surgical appliances, proprietary medicines, toilet and fancy articles and in short everything pertaining to a first-class family drug store. Prescriptions of all kinds are compounded with the utmost skill and care and the general popularity of the establishment is shown in its large and liberal patronage. Mr. Sullivan is a practical and skillful pharmacist. He was hospital steward at Natick, Alabama, for a length of time, and having served his apprenticeship with R. D. McArthur at St. John's, N. B., he succeeded McCormack Bros. at the present site.

E. C. ANDERSON, Pharmacist, No. 369 Broadway, Cambridgeport.—The pharmacy establishment of Mr. E. C. Anderson occupies a very prominent position. Its reputation is of the highest character, and the careful regard of the people's interests, which distinguishes its operations, has gained for it a measure of popularity shared by but few similar concerns in this city. The establishment had been in successful operation for a number of years, and the present proprietor, Mr. Anderson, who is a native of this state, about thirty-five years of age and a graduate of the Massachusetts College of Pharmacy, succeeded to its business in March, 1888. The store is neat and compact, modern in all its appointments and replete with everything that constitutes a thoroughly first-class pharmacy. A very large stock is carried of pure drugs, chemicals, pharmaceutical preparations, essences and extracts, proprietary remedies, toilet and fancy articles, druggists' sundries of all kinds and all other articles usually kept in a concern of this kind. The prescription and family recipe department is carefully and efficiently directed.

H. N. HOVEY & CO., Choice Family Groceries, Paints, Oils, etc., No. 70 Cambridge Street, East Cambridge.—The old reliable business house of H. N. Hovey & Co., is the pioneer in the grocery trade in this community. It was established by Mr. H. N. Hovey in 1855 and continued by him until 1870, when he took in as copartners Mr. George Dearborn and Mr. Henry Connell, who had been clerks in the house, the former for a period of ten years and the latter for thirty-eight years. In 1895 Mr. Hovey retired from the active duties of business, and since that date the operations have been under the sole control and management of Messrs. Dearborn and Connell, who continue the house under the old firm name. The premises are large and consist of a store 25 x 100 feet in dimensions, and a commodious basement. This responsible house has always been conducted upon the highest standard of commercial integrity, and is liberally patronized by a large, first-class custom. The aim has always been to supply the very choicest and best class of goods at fair, reasonable prices, and the success is owing to this method of doing business which is still kept up by the members of the firm, who are only retain the old patrons, but are steadily drawing to the house many new ones who find that everything needed in choice family groceries can always be obtained here, pure, fresh and of the highest standard quality at the lowest prices. Four efficient clerks are employed. In the assortment of goods will be found the very finest new crop China and Japan teas, and Mocha, Java and South American coffees, pure spices and sugars, and the popular brands of family flour, and also canned goods in great variety, and condiments and family supplies generally. There is also a special department for the sale of painters' supplies and materials, in which will be found paints, dry, ready mixed and in oil; also putty, varnishes, oils, and window and picture glass. Both members of the firm are natives of New England. Mr. Dearborn is from New Hampshire and Mr. Connell is a Bostonian by birth.

A. P. SEARS, Merchant Tailor, No. 100 Cambridge Street, East Cambridge.—A leading and popular East Cambridge representative of the merchant tailoring trade is Mr. A. P. Sears. Mr. Sears early learned and became an expert of the tailors' trade and for a number of years subsequently filled a responsible position in leading Boston houses in this line. In 1871 he began business for himself in Somerville, where he conducted a prosperous enterprise for two years. In 1873 he came to East Cambridge and established the firm business with which he has since been both prominently and prosperously identified. Mr. Sears moved to this eligible location this year, and will be pleased to see his patrons at his elegant and commodious store, which is fitted up in the most attractive and convenient modern style, and in the store windows and by reason of various ingenious, interior devices is attractively displayed a large, carefully selected and constantly desirable stock of suitings, trouserings, vestings and overcoatings, representing the best foreign and domestic productions in this line. The work of the house invariably embodies the highest degree of artistic and mechanical excellence, and among his many and desirable patrons drawn from the best local custom, Mr. Sears is regarded as without a superior as an artist tailor.

N. PELOSKKY, Manufacturer of Shirts, Overalls, etc., and Dealer in Dry and Fancy Goods, etc., Nos. 410 and 411 Cambridge Street, Cambridgeport.—Mr. Pelosky has been in business since 1889, and during his career has met with a most pronounced success, and always has something new and beautiful to place before his customers in fashionable, seasonable and desirable dress goods, in ladies' and gentlemen's furnishings and fancy goods of every description, together with a full line of gentlemen's, youths', boys' and children's clothing in new, beautiful fabrics, in styles in perfect accord with the fashionable ideas of the day. Mr. Pelosky commenced the manufacture of overalls and shirts this year at No. 411 Cambridge Street, where he employs eighty hands. He was born in Russia, came to the United States in 1881, and ten years later established the business he is now so successfully conducting. He will be found straightforward and reliable in all transactions. The dimensions of his store are 20 x 50 feet. It is fitted up in a neat, tasteful manner, reflecting the highest credit upon the good taste of Mr. Pelosky.

FRANK H. WILLARD, Prescription Druggist, No. 101 Cambridge Street, East Cambridge.—Among the representative East Cambridge establishments in the important branch of professional industry will be found that of Mr. Frank Willard, who succeeded the firm of Willard & Talbot, January 1, 1893, and of which he was one of the partners. Mr. F. H. Willard is a native of this city and an experienced and skillful pharmacist, practicing under the certificate of registry issued by the State Pharmaceutical Board. After serving a greatly clerkship he bought out an old established business at the present site in 1893. The commodious and elegantly fitted up salesroom is fully stocked with pure drugs, chemicals, proprietary medicines, toilet and fancy articles, and in short everything pertaining to a first-class metropolitan pharmacy, and prescriptions of all kinds are compounded with the utmost skill and care. The house is liberally patronized by the best medical and family custom of the vicinity.

C. H. MILLARD & CO., Cigars, Tobacco, Snuff and Smokers' Articles, and Manufacturers of the La La's Institute, First Choice, and Royal Champions, No. 118 Cambridge Street.—One of the most popular resorts in this vicinity is that of C. H. Millard & Co., which is an old established stand and was purchased by the firm in 1890. In size it is 20 x 55 feet, and is neatly and tastefully fitted up and is very complete in its arrangement. Mr. C. H. Millard is an experienced, practical business man, and is rapidly building up a first-class, substantial custom. The scope of the business embraces the manufacture of high grade cigars, and dealing in all kinds both imported and domestic, and also fine cut plug and smoking tobacco and cigarettes, snuff, pipes and all the various articles required by those who use tobacco in its many forms. Several expert workmen are kept employed, who are engaged in the manufacture of a number of popular brands of cigars, among which are the "La La's" and the "Institute," very choice articles retailing for a dime, and the First Choice and "Royal Champions," very highly prized nickel cigars. These goods are always in demand. In the rear of the store is a handsome pool table which serves to afford amusement to the patrons. Mr. Millard is a Massachusetts man by birth, and for many years was identified with the best and most manufacturing industry in Boston.

A. J. APPLEDATE, Wholesale and Retail Dealer in Watches, Clocks, Jewelry, Silverware, Spectacles and Eye-glasses, No. 571 Main Street, Cambridgeport.—A leading headquarters in Cambridgeport for both watches, clocks and jewelry is the establishment of Mr. A. J. Appledate. The business of this house was originally organized in 1886 by Messrs. Pratt & Co. Mr. Appledate being a member of the firm. The latter, in 1877, purchased his partner's interest in the business, and in 1893, removed to his present location. In watches, clocks, jewelry, silverware and optical goods the display is very attractive and the assortments are not surpassed anywhere. The goods have all been selected with care and judgment, exhibiting a wide range in value, and are calculated to meet the wants of the greatest possible number of buyers. Special attention is given to the repairing of watches, French clocks and jewelry, and satisfaction is guaranteed in every instance. Mr. Appledate is a native of New Jersey.

F. H. MEGGETT, Boots, Shoes and Rubbers, No. 441 Cambridge Street, Cambridgeport.—Among these popular houses is the boot and shoe trade there are probably none better known than that of Mr. F. H. Meggett. It has only been established about two years, but in that time, under the able management and direction of the proprietor, a large, flourishing business has been built up. Possessing unusual advantages for making selections from the stocks of the best known manufacturers, Mr. Meggett is always prepared to offer the newest styles and most fashionable goods at fair, reasonable prices, and guarantees full satisfaction to make, fit and comfort in foot wear. In the store, which is 20 x 50 feet in area and handsomely and tastefully fitted up, a large and varied assortment of all kinds of boots and shoes are displayed for gentlemen's, youths' and boys' wear, and also desirable, seasonable goods for ladies, misses and children, and also slippers and rubbers. These goods are in both fine and medium grades, and all sizes and widths. Mr. Meggett is a native of Worcester.

M. K. KANALY & CO., Manufacturing Confectioners, Nos. ... and ... Hampshire Street, Cambridgeport — Mr. Kanaly has been in this line of trade for a long period, and six years ago embarked in business on his own account. He met with success at the outset, and four years ago his trade had there grown to such dimensions as to necessitate the occupation of more commodious premises. Accordingly, a removal was made to the present location, and the business has been prosecuted here with great vigor and success. The premises occupied comprise two floors, each ... by ... feet in dimensions. The mechanical equipments of the establishment are of the newest and best for securing the most satisfactory results, while about twenty skilled and experienced hands are in service. The manufactures of the establishment consist chiefly of "penny specialties" in choice confectionery, and these have gained a standard reputation, and are considered among the best goods made in the country. They are strictly free from deleterious substances, are pure and wholesome, and find a ready sale not only in the city and neighborhood, but throughout the New England States. The firm manufacture caramels extensively, making a specialty of Kanaly's original caramels and Adams' caramels. The products of the concern aggregate about two hundred tons per year, and annually an increase is experienced. The telephone call is "118-5." Mr. Kanaly was born in New Hampshire and has resided in Cambridgeport for twenty years or more.

M. J. O'KEEFE, Choice Provisions, Fruits and Vegetables, also Fish and Oysters, No. ... Cambridge Street, Cambridgeport — A representative and responsible house is this line in that of Mr. M. J. O'Keefe. Mr. O'Keefe was for twelve years engaged in the same line of business in Lowell, Mass., before coming to Cambridgeport. In 1885, and opening his present establishment. His store has a frontage of ... feet, and is a model of cleanliness and order. It is fitted up with marble counters, refrigerator and all modern conveniences and accessories for carrying on the extensive business, and supplying the demands of the large trade the house enjoys. A heavy stock is carried at all times of smoked hams, shoulders, beef, lard, mess pork, fresh fish, fresh choice cuts of beef, lamb, mutton, veal, etc. A specialty is made of fish and oysters, which are always in plenty and wholesome in quality. Fruits and vegetables in season are alike kept on hand. Mr. O'Keefe is familiar with every branch of the industry in which he is engaged, and which, under his care and management, is being largely increased.

D. N. DESMOND, Registered Pharmacist, No. ... Cambridge Street, East Cambridge — One of the best conducted local establishments in its important branch of professional industry is that of Mr. D. N. Desmond, druggist and apothecary, at No. ... Cambridge Street, corner of Fifth. The commodious and attractively fitted up store is stocked with pure drugs, chemicals, proprietary medicines, toilet and fancy articles, etc., the laboratory is supplied with all requisite facilities for compounding the most difficult prescriptions, and everything about the place is typical of the modern first-class metropolitan pharmacy. Mr. Desmond is a practical and skillful pharmacist, practicing under a certificate from the Massachusetts Registry. He began as clerk in the present store, and in 1887 succeeded to the proprietorship of the business, which under his able and popular management has developed into proportions which place him among the representative local pharmacists.

JOHN A. HEDIN & CO., Furniture, Carpets, Stoves, Ranges, Crockery, etc., Nos. ... and ... Cambridge Street, East Cambridge — Among those establishments deserving of special recognition we desire to call attention to that of John A. Hedin & Co., which was founded in 1881 and from that time under the able direction and management of Mr. Hedin, the head of the firm, it has enjoyed a career of uninterrupted success. The premises present a double front of plate-glass show windows and have dimensions of ... x ... feet, and afford ample facilities for making a fine display of the goods, which embrace a full and general line of parlor and bedroom furniture, richly upholstered in the highest style of the art in all the new, popular, fashionable styles, and all kinds of household furniture generally and bulky Brussels, Axminsters, ingrain, Wilton, Moquette and other carpets in beautiful styles and patterns, and parlor, heating and cooking stoves in handsome designs containing the modern improvements, and also crockery, glass and earthenware and house-furnishing goods of every description. The goods are attractively arranged and popular prices prevail. Three skilled practical workmen are employed. Mr. Hedin worked for a long time at the business in which he is now engaged and has met with a well deserved success.

J. J. COLMAN, The Bazar, Cambridge Street, Cambridgeport — A very prominent house engaged in this line of trade is The Bazar, conducted by Mr. J. J. Colman. This gentleman was born in England fifty-five years ago and in 1881 came to Boston, where, in the following year, he engaged in the grocery trade. In 1873 he abandoned his grocery enterprise and founded The Bazar, which has proved a great success, enjoying as it does, a very liberal and substantial patronage from all classes in the community. The premises devoted to the business comprise an entire building, three stories high, with a frontage of ... feet and a depth of ... feet. This is very finely fitted up throughout, and admirably arranged for securing the comfort of patrons and the effective display of the large, miscellaneous stock carried. The first floor is devoted to toys, notions, china, glassware, etc.; the second to carpets, mattings, wall-papers, etc.; and the third to general house-furnishing goods. Mr. Colman is highly respected by the community as a business man of rare energy.

CHARLES W. BAILEY, Hack, Boarding and Livery Stable, No. ... Cambridge Street, East Cambridge. — One of the oldest concerns of its kind in this section, which was founded away back in 1848 by the present proprietor's father, the late Mr. William Bailey, is that of Mr. Charles W. Bailey at No. ... Cambridge Street. In 1871, the founder took his son into partnership under the style of William Bailey & Son, and on the former's death in 1878, the latter succeeded to the control of the business, which has grown to large dimensions. The stables comprise a series of frame buildings, and these are well ventilated, drained and lighted, and are in charge of careful grooms and stablemen. Particular attention is given to boarding horses by the day, week or month, and the rate taken in such as to afford the most complete satisfaction. Mr. Bailey has fifty stalls and ample accommodations for both horses and carriages. He has, too, some of the finest and most stylish equipages to be found in this section of the country, and a stock of superior horses, which can be hired for business or pleasure, night or day, on moderate business terms. Among the carriages are some elegant coaches, broughams, landaus, landaulettes, cabriolets, buggies, hacks, etc. In the stock of horses will be found those suitable for ladies to ride or drive, and also some splendid steers. A specialty is made of saddle horses and military equipments. Mr. Bailey has spent the whole of his life in the business, and is considered an authority upon the noble animal. In his stables will be found some of the crack horses belonging to gentlemen residing in this vicinity. The telephone call is 157-8. Mr. Bailey is a native of Cambridge.

GEO. F. DICKSON, Steam, Gas and Water Pipes, Chandeliers, Brackets, etc., Douglass Block, No. ... Main Street, Cambridgeport — Mr. George F. Dickson is reportably deserving of mention as conducting an old established, leading and prosperous house. Mr. Dickson's father, Mr. R. W. Dickson, founded this business in 1856, and he conducted it with marked success until retiring in 1879. Then the present proprietor took control of the enterprise, and has since developed a trade commensurate of large proportions, and placed his establishment in the lead in his line of business. He occupies a neat, commodious, well-appointed salesroom and basement, which are filled with an extensive assortment of chandeliers, brackets and other gas fixtures from the plainest to the most elaborately ornamented and costly, steam, gas and water pipes in all sizes and metals, and a full line of plumbers', steam and gas fitters' supplies. The trade is of both a wholesale and retail character, and the patronage substantial and industrial. Mr. Dickson is a native of the town, and is alike popular as a merchant and citizen.

CITY OF CAMBRIDGE.

GEORGE A. DAVIS, Choice Groceries, Crockery, Glass, Wooden Ware and Country Produce, Cigars, Pipes, Snuff and Tobacco, No. 515 Main Street, Cambridgeport.

EDWIN F. BLAKE, Real Estate and Insurance, No. 56 Fifth Street, East Cambridge.

FRANK A. SCHWARZ, Steam Printer, No. 26 Cambridge Street, East Cambridge.

HENRY S. ANDROS, Registered Pharmacist, No. 841 Main Street, Cambridgeport.

BURDITT & WHITE, Hardware, Cutlery, Paints, Oil and Glass, No. 681 Main Street, Cambridgeport.

I. FRANKENSTEIN, Dealer in Dry and Fancy Goods and Ready Made Clothing, etc., No. 388 Cambridge Street, Cambridgeport.

S. C. HIGGINS, Manufacturer of and Dealer in Steam and Hot Water Heating Apparatus, Stoves, Furnaces and Ranges, No. 61 Central Square, Cambridgeport. — A very large and important industrial establishment, and a credit to its enterprising proprietor, and in the city of Cambridgeport, is that which forms the subject of this voluntary tribute to business success. The proprietor, Mr. S. C. Higgins, was born in Maine, forty-five years ago, and for the past eighteen years has resided in Cambridgeport. He was for a long period engaged as a practical workman in the making of steam and hot water heating apparatus, stoves, ranges, etc., and in 1882 he embarked in business on his own account. His enterprise underwent a great development rapidly, and in 1887 it had obtained such dimensions that more commodious premises were needed to cope with the demands upon it. A removal was thus made to the premises now occupied at No. 61 Central Square. These premises comprise an entire building of two floors and basement. The first floor and basement have each an area of 40 by 80 feet, and the capacity of the second floor is 30 by 100 feet. The first floor is utilized as the salesroom and office, and here is displayed a magnificent assortment of steam and hot water heating apparatus, stoves, furnaces, ranges, and a full line of house-furnishing goods. On the second floor is the tin shop, which is equipped with the most efficient mechanical appliances and tools, while ten skilled and experienced assistants are employed in manufacturing all kinds of steam and hot water heating apparatus, repairing and fixing stoves, furnaces and ranges, and in executing all kinds of tin, copper and sheet metal work. A special feature is made of the ventilation of public buildings, and all work undertaken is guaranteed to afford the most complete satisfaction, while the charges will at all times be found fair and equitable. With large experience, a thorough knowledge of the trade and its wants, and every facility for the satisfactory filling of orders, the outlook for a steady and healthy increase of business for Mr. Higgins is excellent. The management is characterized by energy, enterprise and public spirit of the highest order, and Mr. Higgins is, personally, a favorite in trade circles.

E. H. LYKE & SON, Grain and Meal, also, Hay and Straw, Nos. 71 and 73 Main Street, Near the West End of West Boston Bridge, Cambridgeport. — Far away back in the year 1840, when Cambridgeport was a much smaller place than it is to-day, the business of this firm was founded by its senior member, Mr. E. H. Lyke, who has seen the place thrive and expand and attain the dignity of a city. He is familiar with the history and up-growth of the city, for here he was born and spent all the years of his long life. He knows all about the improvements that have been made from one end of the city to the other, has noted all the advances that have been made in the value of real estate until he has become an authority on all questions of realty, and there is no citizen more widely known or more deservedly esteemed than Mr. E. H. Lyke. For nearly forty-nine years he has been in the grain, hay and straw business, and since 1866 has had a partner in the person of his son, Mr. E. H. Lyke, who is also a native of Cambridgeport. Like his father, who is an ex-member of the City Council, the latter is widely known and enjoys the good-will of his fellow citizens. The firm occupy a two-story building, covering an area of 45 by 100 feet. This is provided with all necessary appliances and conveniences, and contains a very heavy stock of grain, meal, feed, hay, straw, etc., in which the firm do a very extensive trade, necessitating the permanent employment of several teams and a number of workmen.

J. J. HORGAN, Marble and Granite Monuments, Headstones, Statues, Urns, etc., Nos. 45 to 53 Main Street, Cambridgeport. — This establishment has a history no less interesting from a personal, than from a business standpoint. Mr. Horgan founded it in 1867, and has by unremitting industry and natural skill acquired a thoroughly artistic and practical knowledge of the business in all its details. He started business in a small, unpretentious way, and by degrees his establishment has grown until it is now in point of extent and in comprising exhibitions of marble and granite monuments second to no other in the city. The premises occupied for the business are commodious and well equipped. They have a frontage of 130 feet on Main Street at the end of West Boston Bridge, and extend back for a depth of 160 feet to a large wharf, with a 110 foot frontage on the Charles River. Derricks and all other mechan-

HORACE D. LITCHFIELD, Funeral and Furnishing Undertaker, No. 473 Main Street, Cambridgeport. — Among those who devote their attention to the calling of the undertaker there are none more prominent in this community than Mr. Horace D. Litchfield, whose office and furnishing warerooms are at No. 473 Main Street. The business, the oldest of the kind in this vicinity, was established in 1862 by Mr. Roland Litchfield, who continued it until 1886, when he was succeeded by his son, Mr. Horace D. Litchfield, who was brought up in the calling and is familiar with all that pertains thereto, and conducts it in the same careful manner which made his father so popular during his long, successful career. The private office is very neatly fitted up in the rear of his store in the front of which is the warerooms, wherein is kept everything requisite for his business. Mr. Litchfield is very considerate in the performance of his duties and furnishes all the requirements for funerals, and takes full charge and directs affairs in a satisfactory manner from the house to the cemetery. He was born in this community and is about thirty-one years of age, and is thoroughly practical and proficient in his calling and sustains a high social status as a business man and citizen, and maintains an excellent reputation as a furnishing undertaker and funeral director, and is the leading representative in the vocation in this vicinity.

JOHN J. McDONALD, Carriage Manufacturer and Painter, etc., No. 4 Cambridge Street, East Cambridge. — Among the well-conducted and prosperous industrial enterprises which form this busy trade district will be found that of Mr. John J. McDonald, carriage maker and painter. Mr. McDonald began business as a carriage painter in 1876, and meeting with good success in this undertaking he increased the compass of his enterprise in 1886 by adding carriage making and repairing. The premises consist of a two-story frame building, 30 x 115 feet in dimensions, and the general equipment of the establishment embraces all requisite tools and appliances for the advantageous prosecution of the business. A corps of ten to twelve experienced and skilful workmen is employed and everything in this line of carriage, wagon and truck making and repairing is executed in the best and most skilful manner. Carriage painting still forms an important feature of the business, to which careful attention is given and the work turned out has a standard reputation for the highest degree of artistic and workmanlike excellence. Mr. McDonald is a practical and skilful exponent of his own trade.

WILLIAM MITCHELL, Manufacturer of Fine and Heavy Harnesses, No. 9 Cambridge Street, East Cambridge. — The business conducted under the above heading was established by Mr. Mitchell upwards of thirty years ago, and has from the start maintained a representative status in the local trade. The premises consist of a two-story frame building at No. 9 Cambridge Street, and the general appointments of the establishment is both systematic and convenient. The product of the establishment comprises fine and heavy harness, also repairing of all kinds, a specialty being made of custom or ordered work. A corps of experienced harness makers is kept busy in the production of the superior work for which the house has long been noted, and the large and liberal patronage received is drawn from the best town and suburban custom. Mr. Mitchell was born in Scotland, where he learned and became an expert at his trade, and does the finest custom work in New England. His success is a direct tribute to his native, able and popular management.

J. A. HOLMES & CO., Best Family Groceries, No. 811 Main Street and No. 1 Central Square, Cambridgeport. The oldest and most widely known house in Cambridgeport in the grocery trade is that of Messrs. J. A. Holmes & Co., which occupies the corner of Main Street and Central Square. Mr. Holmes, the head of the house, who is about seventy-two years of age, was born and brought up in this community and established the business in 1891 on the opposite side of the square, and in 1892 removed to the premises now occupied, which he remodelled in 1895 and fitted up in modern style. The store has a double front of 40 feet and a depth of 75 feet, and in all its arrangements is neatly and perfectly appointed, and bring commodities affords ample facilities for display and business purposes. It is without exception, one of the largest and best conducted business establishments of the kind in the city, and the stock, which includes everything in the line of family groceries, is not excelled in quality or quantity by any other in this vicinity. Unusual care is displayed in selecting the goods and special attention is always given to purity and the best offerings in the market are always secured. In the assortment will be found China and Japan teas of a superior quality, and also Mocha and Java coffees and rich spices, pure sugars, and all the leading brands of extra family and pantry flour and farinaceous goods generally, together with hermetically sealed fruits and vegetables in tin and glass, table delicacies and condiments, and everything belonging to the business both staple and fancy and imported and domestic. Eight competent and efficient clerks are kept employed in the store and customers receive prompt attention, and orders are filled and delivered without delay. This house is well known and popular, and in every respect a useful and progressive factor in its special line of business, and its reputation for honorable, fair and upright dealing is and always has been of the highest standard character.

ANSEL F. XAVIER & CO., Carriage Manufacturers, No. 416 Main Street, East Cambridge.—This house was organized in April, 1888, and has since met with the most substantial and encouraging patronage. The premises occupied comprise a fine two-story frame building, 60 x 90 feet in dimensions, and this is equipped with all the latest improved machinery and tools pertaining to the business, while constant employment is afforded to six skilled and experienced hands, whose operations are all conducted under the personal supervision of the proprietor, Mr. Xavier, who is a practical expert in the trade. The products of the establishment include all kinds of light and heavy fine carriages, which are of superior workmanship and fine finish, as well as original and artistic in design. Special attention is given to the neat and prompt execution of repairs. A large stock of new and second-hand buggies, wagons, sleighs and pungs is always kept on hand for sale at low prices.

G. B. LENFEST, Job Printer, No. 69 Cambridge Street, East Cambridge.—Among those who give their attention to the printing business in this community is Mr. G. B. Lenfest who, in 1874, succeeded to an old stand which had previously been established so long ago as 1839. Mr. Lenfest has made many improvements in the establishment and thoroughly equipped it throughout with the latest improved appliances, including four modern style presses which are operated by steam-power. He also has new type and is well provided with every convenience for doing all kinds of plain and fancy general job and mercantile printing in the very highest style of the art with neatness, elegance and promptness. The dimensions of the premises are 25 x 50 feet. Four expert practical workmen are employed. Mr. Lenfest is not only at the head of the oldest printing house in this vicinity, but is also one of the most accomplished exponents of the "art preservative." He is very moderate in his prices and always guarantees the best satisfaction.

I. L. POLACK, Manufacturer of the J. L. P. Cigar, No. 125 Pleasant Street, Cambridgeport.—Among the enterprising business men of this prosperous town should be mentioned Mr. I. L. Polack, manufacturer of fine cigars. The commodious and well ordered premises are fitted up in a manner appropriate to the purpose and all the modern conveniences are supplied for the advantageous prosecution of the business. Mr. Polack makes a specialty of the justly popular "J. L. P." cigar of which he is the sole manufacturer. This cigar is made from selected tobacco by skilled and experienced workmen, and is especially designed for the best trade. Mr. Polack has driven from the start to make this cigar "second to none" in point of general excellence, and that he has succeeded and met with a popular appreciation of his efforts is clearly shown in the ever-increasing and continually increasing popularity of the "J. L. P." brand. Mr. Polack has had a wide experience in the manufacture of cigars. He was born in New York City, where he early learned and became an expert at cigar packing—a branch of the business which calls for natural as well as acquired ability. For a number of years he was employed in this capacity in leading New York manufactories, and for two years prior to embarking in the present enterprise was engaged in packing high class goods for a leading Boston house. In September, 1897, he established for himself at the present site.

J. F. NEWMAN, Dry, Fancy and Worsted Goods, No. 105 Cambridge Street, East Cambridge.—Among the leading mercantile establishments which line this busy thoroughfare should be mentioned the dry and fancy goods emporium of Mr. J. F. Newman. The spacious salesroom, 20 x 80 feet in size, is fitted up in accord with the best modern ideas of combined elegance and convenience, and the stock of dry goods, fancy goods, ladies' and children's furnishings, embroideries, laces, worsted goods, notions, etc. is attractively displayed, also a fine line of gents' furnishing goods, including hats, caps, neckwear, etc. Mr. Newman in addition to a wide experience in the business on hand possesses also the happy faculty of selecting his goods to conform to the current want and fancy. Here are to be found the newest novelties and most popular styles in the several departments above mentioned. Three experienced and courteous clerks are in attendance. Mr. Newman was born in Germany, but came to Boston at an early age, and after an extensive clerkship embarked for himself in 1876 in the enterprise with which he has since been most popularly and successfully identified.

S. ROSENBERG, Boots, Shoes and Rubbers, No. 250 Cambridge Street, East Cambridge.—The shoe emporium par excellence is the handsome store of S. Rosenberg. This deservedly popular and excellent store was established in 1891, and from its inception has steadily grown in public favor and patronage. The premises occupied are commodious and very tastefully fitted up, and a large, admirably selected stock is constantly carried, embracing ladies', misses', gentlemen's, youths', boys, and children's boots and shoes in all sizes, widths, styles and varieties, both in finest and medium grades; also rubbers and slippers of every description, while fine courteous salesmen attend to the wants of customers, no pains being spared to render the utmost satisfaction to every purchaser. Mr. Rosenberg is a native of Boston, and prior to establishing this flourishing store had been a clerk in the same line for years.

DREHAN'S DRUG STORE, No. 561 Main Street, Cambridgeport.—Drehan's drug store was opened in February, 1896, and at once attracted attention and drew to itself a patronage both substantial and influential, and it has been surroundingly increasing its custom since. The proprietor, Mr. P. E. Drehan, is a pharmaceutical graduate and a practicing pharmacist, whose experience covers a period of twenty years or more. His store is 20 x 50 feet in dimensions, neatly and admirably arranged, fitted up with elaborate show-cases and counters, soda water fountain, etc., and made attractive by the elegant manner in which the fine stock is displayed. The stock is very complete, and includes a general assortment of pure, fresh drugs, chemicals and all other requisites to the line of perfumery and novelties in toilet articles, all the leading proprietary medicines of known merit and reputation, fancy goods and druggists' sundries of all descriptions. Mr. Drehan, who is aided by two competent and courteous assistants, makes a specialty of compounding physicians' prescriptions and family recipes with the strictest care and accuracy from pure drugs, according to the rules of the American Pharmacopœia. Mr. Drehan is a native of Maine, and justly merits the success which he has obtained by his perseverance, energy and ability.

C. **HERBERT McCLARK,** Architect. Office, No. 615 Main Street, Room 10, Cambridgeport.— In the growth and development of every community it is a marked feature that as wealth, refinement, and education increase, a demand arises for splendid public and private dwellings, which embellish and beautify our land. In connection with these remarks the attention of our readers is directed to the architectural works of Mr. C. Herbert McClare, whose office is located in room 10, No. 615 Main Street, and whose residence is at No. 5 Columbia Street. This gentleman, though only established in business here since 1887, has already obtained a substantial patronage, in consequence of his previous extensive experience elsewhere and his ability. Mr. McClare was born some thirty years ago in Nova Scotia, and had a good careful and effective training for his profession, which requires an immense amount of study, a thorough mechanical education, and a practical application of the knowledge as acquired. Mr. McClare has passed through his probation long ago, and his proficiency is established. He is fully prepared with all the necessary facilities to execute or carry out any architectural undertaking, not only promptly but with that intelligent appreciation of design which makes his efforts so highly appreciated. He makes a specialty of designing fine dwellings, and since beginning business here twenty-five dwellings and a church have been erected from his designs and under his superintendence.

C. **B. MOLLER,** Parlor and Chamber Furniture, No. 910 Washington Street, Cambridgeport.— Engaged in the furniture business in Cambridgeport, there are a number of enterprising men of undoubted ability and integrity, among whom we find Mr. C. B. Moller, whose commodious store and warehouse is at No. 910 Main Street. The building is a three-story structure, having dimensions of 30 x 80 feet, and is very conveniently arranged and perfectly equipped in all departments. Mr. Moller is a thorough practical man, reliable and responsible. He makes a fine display of richly upholstered parlor and bedroom furniture in all the new, beautiful, popular styles, and also bed and dining room and general household furniture, and also heating and cooking stoves and ranges, grates, tin and hollow ware, wooden, crockery and glass ware and housekeeping goods. Upholstering and repairing furniture is a special department of the business, all orders receiving the prompt personal attention of Mr. Moller himself and the work is fully guaranteed to be executed in the very best manner. Born in Norway, where he learned the trade of the harness and saddle maker, Mr. Moller came to the United States in 1869 and directed some years to making himself practically proficient as an upholsterer, and in 1880 established the business which now engages his attention, and in which he has been very successful and won an enviable reputation. He is very popular in this community among his fellow citizens and is quite a talented musician.

CITY OF WALTHAM.

WALTHAM, known all over the world for the superiority of the watches manufactured here, is a flourishing city of more than twenty thousand inhabitants, with a steadily increasing population, and is located in Middlesex County, about ten miles from the "Hub." It is one of the most important and prosperous cities in the environs of Boston, and, unless all signs fail, has a bright future. The location is more than favorable, alike as a place for a home, industrial enterprise and mercantile activity; the soil is rich and fertile, and the climate remarkably salubrious, while the natural scenery, tasteful surroundings and attractive improvements render this place an especially desirable residential suburb. It is, in fact, one of the most delightful and healthful of Boston's suburbs, and contains many handsome country seats and beautiful villas, with charming lawns, well cultivated gardens and serpentine drives; and the avenues on the outskirts are spacious and lined with fine shade trees.

There are various reasons too, why this should be so. The locality gets refreshing breezes, yet has the dry air of the foot-hill region, while the adjacent hills shut off the north and east winds, and catch and hold the balmy breezes from the south.

Although watch manufacturing constitutes the chief industry of the city, Waltham has extensive and varied business interests, besides this, many large works, mills, shops, foundries, bleacheries and other manufacturing plants of a diversified character being in operation within the corporate limits; while the trade and commerce of the place have attained very substantial proportions likewise. The Charles River furnishes motive power to a number of factories of various kinds situated on its banks, and new enterprises are continually coming into existence, some of them noteworthy concerns. Notwithstanding that what is now known as Waltham is one of the oldest settlements of the Massachusetts Bay Colony, it is only within a comparatively recent period that the place has assumed importance as an industrial center, and this is directly traceable to the advent of the great watch manufacturing corporations here.

Waltham originally formed an integral portion of Watertown, and in 1738 was incorporated as a town by the general court, Lieutenant Thomas Bigelow being the first town representative. In 1764 the number of houses in Waltham was ninety-four, the number of families one hundred and seven, with thirteen negroes and mulattoes, the entire population being six hundred and sixty-three. The negroes and mulattoes referred to were, it is needless to state, slaves.

The growth of the town from this period to the close of the Revolution was slow, the number of dwellings in 1797 being only one hundred and eleven. In 1840, the population had increased to two thousand five hundred, and ten years later reached four thousand four hundred and sixty-four, and in 1875, had grown to nearly ten thousand, a steady ratio of increase being since maintained.

Waltham was incorporated as a city in 1885, and presently took on all the aspects and dignity as well as the importance of a thriving municipality. The city embraces a superficial area of nine thousand acres, and contains close upon three thousand dwellings. Although not mapped out on exactly rectangular squares or parallel streets, being delightfully irregular in these respects, the city is, nevertheless, very compactly built, and the public buildings, institutions, schools, churches, and places of business are within convenient distance of the whole community.

The Charles River divides the city into two distinct sections, the "North Side" and "South Side;" the former being the older and in all respects the more important section. The principal mercantile thoroughfares are Main Street and Moody Street, and these are broad, well paved and excellently lighted, presenting a scene of bustle, life and activity during shopping hours. In the highly important matter of water supply, sanitary arrangements, artificial illuminating facilities and all the other features of progress, the city is fully abreast with the times. There are many fine public buildings, a spacious common and several excellent educational and eleemosynary institutions. The Public Library which has been in existence a quarter of a century, is one of the notable features. It contains some fourteen thousand volumes, which comprehend every branch of literature, including a liberal supply of periodicals, magazines, reviews and papers, and is in charge of a competent librarian and assistant. The places of worship, too, are numerous and of various styles of architecture, among them some, imposing structures, and nearly all denominations are represented; while two neatly laid out cemeteries—Grove Hill and Mount Feake—are eligibly located on the outskirts.

The city is exceptionally favored in its fire department, which is very complete, ample and thoroughly disciplined, and also maintains a large, well organized police force, in command of an efficient chief. Indeed, the city compares very favorably in all its municipal departments with any of the municipalities in Middlesex or adjoining counties. The local government consists of mayor, board of aldermen and common council, with a city clerk, city treasurer, and other officials, and executive heads of departments.

As has already been mentioned, the manufacture of watches forms the all important branch of industry in Waltham, the Waltham Watch Company and the Boston Manufacturing Company furnishing employment in their factories to a little army of workers, both male and female, while there are also kindred industries of extensive proportions. In addition to these, there are factories devoted to the production of cotton fabrics, emery cloth, emery wheels, carriages, weather vanes, crayons, lock-boxes and tools, also, machine shops, foundries, iron works, bleacheries, grist mills, etc.

In number, variety and elegance of its mercantile establishments Waltham will compare favorably with its more pretentious neighboring cities, Main Street and Moody Street being lined with a class of wholesale and retail stores devoted to the sale of dry goods, millinery, fancy articles, clothing, hats and caps, hardware and cutlery, stoves and house furnishings, groceries, crockery, confectionery, boots and shoes, provisions, fish, fruits, and merchandise generally of a truly metropolitan character, besides first-class hostelries, restaurants, livery stables, express, offices, newspaper and printing offices, photographic studios, art emporiums, news depots, and, in short, every feature of progress to be met with in a progressive and flourishing city. And in this connection the following descriptive and historical sketches of Waltham's leading commercial, industrial and general business enterprises will be found of interest.

ROLAND W. MACURDY, Millinery, Ladies' Gloves and Furnishings, etc., J. W. Parmenter Block, No. 28 Moody Street. — This business is an old established one and it was originally founded in 1851 by Mr. J. W. Macurdy who continued it until that, when he was succeeded by his son, Mr. Roland W. Macurdy, who October 4th of last year moved to the very desirable premises now occupied. Mr. Macurdy, who was brought up to the business, is young and active, and is always introducing all the latest novelties in his line of both European and home production. The house has always been known as the leading representative one in the millinery and fancy goods trade. The premises comprise a store and basement each 25 x 75 feet in dimensions. The store is tastefully and attractively fitted up and the stock, which is extensive, fresh and choice, embraces everything in the line of rich, handsome millinery in the newest and most fashionable styles, including hats and bonnets and ribbons, laces, flowers, feathers, etc., and a general assortment of ladies' gloves and furnishings and all the various materials for art embroidery. Mr. Macurdy is a native of Waltham where he has always resided, and is well known as one of the prosperous young business men of the city.

D. O. WATTS, Baxter, Choice Groceries, etc., No. 10 Lexington Street. — One of the very best among the many well-ordered general grocery stores in Waltham is the popular and excellent stand of D. O. Watts. For quality and variety of goods, or for straightforward dealing, no establishment of the kind in town maintains a better reputation. A strictly cash trade is done, while the very lowest prices consistent with first-class goods and honest weight prevail, quality and quantity being warranted. The store is compact, ample and neatly kept, and a large stock is always carried, comprising choice Vermont dairy butter, fresh country eggs, fine cheese, canned goods, dried fruits, prepared cereals, table luxuries, sauces, preserves, pickles, olives, jellies and fancy groceries in great variety; pure fresh teas, coffees and spices; sugars, maple syrup, fruits, nuts, crackers, confectionery and kindred delicacies. The assortment also includes prime lard, hams, smoked and salt fish, rice, beans, peas, salt, flour, soda, saleratus, baking powder and general family groceries; the leading specialties being Vermont butter, eggs, cheese, maple syrup and delicacies, while several polite clerks attend to the wants of customers, with two teams delivering orders, goods being delivered free throughout Waltham and environs. Mr. Watts is a native of Waterbury, Vt., but a resident of this city a number of years. He commenced business here in 1882, in the butter, cheese and eggs line, to which he devoted himself exclusively up to a few years ago, when owing to his largely increased and rapidly growing patronage, he added a complete line of groceries.

DAILY FREE PRESS, Somers & Starbuck, Publishers, A. Starbuck, Editor, R. B. Somers, Manager, No. 79 Moody Street. — The Daily Free Press, published at No. 79 Moody Street by Somers & Starbuck, A. Starbuck editor; R. B. Somers, manager, as an advertising medium and a newspaper is the most prominent in the community. It is easily gotten up typographically, is newsy, bright, clean and independent, and under the present management its circulation and influence have steadily increased, the daily circulation now exceeding 3600 copies, with a weekly edition of above 1,200. The Free Press has the largest circulation of any paper published in this city. On a competitive trial on the merits of the local dailies as advertising mediums the Free Press proved superior to its contemporary at the rate of fifteen to one, so the written statement in possession of the publisher attests. The Free Press made its initial appearance November 16, 1882, as a weekly with then Phinney as editor and proprietor. It purchased the subscription list and good-will of the Waltham Sentinel in 1876 and in 1884 came into control of Mr. R. B. Somers, who subsequently associated with him in partnership Mr. A. Starbuck. The first daily issue made its

appearance on March 14, 1888. The premises occupied as publication office, composing and press rooms are well equipped with all necessary facilities, including a large cylinder press, one Gordon, one universal and one Prouty press, while eighteen to twenty expert printers, pressmen, etc., are employed. Job printing of every description from a business card or circular to a pamphlet or magazine is executed in the most expeditious and excellent manner, also at reasonable rates, fine commercial work being a specialty.

KNAPP & KIRWIN, Stoves, Furnaces and Ranges, Practical Plumbing and Gas Fitting, No. 376 Main Street. — A leading house in Waltham occupying an honorable place in the trade is that of Messrs. Knapp & Kirwin, which was founded in 1886, and has been uniformly successful from the outset. The enterprise was inaugurated in the year named by Mr. W. E. Knapp, and in 1894, Mr. F. H. Kirwin became his partner. The spacious premises occupied cover an area of 40 x 100 feet, and are equipped in the most thorough manner. Making a leading specialty of plumbing, Messrs. Knapp & Kirwin carry on general operations as practical plumbers and gas fitters, employ a force of skilled workmen and are prepared to fill all orders in a prompt and thoroughly satisfactory manner. They also deal in and carry a large superior stock of stoves, furnaces and ranges, copper wash boilers, tanks, tea kettles, farmers' boilers, ash barrels, and a complete assortment of kitchen furnishing goods, all of which are offered at the lowest prices for cash. Jobbing of all kinds is given careful attention. The members of the firm are both natives of this state, Mr. Knapp having been born at Winchendon and Mr. Kirwin in Cambridge.

C. O. MORRILL, Family Groceries, No. 618 Main Street. — The foundation of the house dates from 1870, and about five years ago it came under the control of Messrs. McWain & Morrill, who continued it until November last, when Mr. Morrill succeeded to it by purchasing the interest of his partner. The premises, which have an average of 25 x 100 feet, are very perfect and complete, and are well arranged throughout for both convenience and display of the large, comprehensive stock, which embraces a choice, well selected assortment of teas, coffees, sugars, spices, canned goods, flour, and the many other articles that belong to the trade which Mr. Morrill's extensive business enables him to turn over rapidly, thus affording his patrons a continual supply of fresh goods, which are constantly being received direct from the leading importers and manufacturers. Besides a book-keeper, several clerks, who are courteous, polite, and attentive, are employed, and two wagons call for and deliver orders without extra charge to any part of the city. Mr. Morrill, who has lived many years in Waltham, is a native of Springfield. He is largely identified with the prosperity of this city.

MR. LEONARD, Choice Family Groceries, Corner Main and Prospect Streets. — The well-appointed and deservedly popular establishment of M. R. Leonard is in all respects a first-class stand, centrally located, commodious and neatly fitted up. The stock, which is large and family assorted, comprises choice teas and coffees, pure and fresh spices, condiments, relishes, preserves and table delicacies, canned goods in great variety, dried fruits, prepared cereals, sugars, syrups, molasses, best brands of family flour, oatmeal, corn meal, rye meal, beans, peas, rice, lard, smoked meats and fish, prime butter, cheese and fresh eggs; also foreign and domestic fruits, nuts, crackers, confectionery, cigars, etc., while several efficient clerks are in attendance, and two teams in regular service, supplying customers throughout the city and environs. Mr. Leonard is a gentleman in the prime of life, and a native of St. Lawrence County, New York. He is a man of ample experience as well as of energy and good business qualities, and prior to establishing this flourishing store in June, 1894, had been for some years in the wholesale grocery trade in Boston.

RUFUS WARREN & SONS, Fine Boots and Shoes, No. 9 Moody Street.—Messrs. Rufus Warren & Sons have one of the finest and best equipped stores in this line of business in the city. The foundation of the house dates from 1847, when it was established by Mr. Rufus Warren on Main Street. In 1887 he took his sons, Mr. C. H. and Mr. C. R. Warren, into partnership, and came three years ago secured and moved to the premises now occupied. The premises comprise first floor and basement, each 25 x 100 feet in area. The store is a model of neatness, elegance and good taste, and is well lighted by two splendid show windows of plate glass, and in its fittings and appointments is not excelled by any other establishment in the city or vicinity. The assortment of goods, which includes in its variety all kinds of foot wear, is always kept up to a full standard and embraces the finest and best goods of the most distinguished manufacturers, particularly those of New York and also those of Douglass and Tracy. The goods are all perfect in fit, style and workmanship and material, and will be found in all widths and sizes for men, women, boys, misses and children, and fully guaranteed in every respect. Rubbers and slippers are also displayed in profusion, and it would indeed be difficult to find any one in the trade in this vicinity who can show a better class of fine goods or goods prices that can compete with this firm, which is liberally patronized by the very best class of customers. Mr. Warren, the founder of the house, is a native of Weston in this state but has been identified with the business and local affairs of Waltham nearly all his life. He is one of the oldest men in the boot and shoe trade and one of the most prominent. Under the old town government some years ago he was a selectman and afterwards a member of the State Legislature, and is now director of the National Bank and a trustee of the Savings Bank and one of the investing committee. His sons, C. H. and C. R., were both born in this city. Mr. Warren, Sr., is a member of high degree in the Society of Good Fellows.

FOSSETT & ATWOOD, Men's, Youths' and Children's Clothing and Furnishing Goods, W. P. Atwood, Manager, A. O. U. W. Building, Moody Street.—A position of recognized importance is that held by the establishment of Messrs Fossett & Atwood. The senior member of the firm, Mr. W. G. Fossett, is a well-known Boston merchant, having been established for over twenty years in that city, at No. 740 Washington Street, in a similar line of business he is conducting here. The store in this city was opened in September, 1896, by Messrs. W. G. Fossett and W. P. Atwood, and has been successfully carried on from the outset. The premises occupied, 25 x 80 feet in dimensions, are handsomely furnished, and are appointed in the most convenient and tasteful manner, being furnished with everything necessary for the rapid manipulation of an extensive trade. The heavy stock carried embraces a complete assortment of the finest class of ready-made clothing for men's, boys' and youths' wear, made in the latest and most fashionable styles, and gentlemen's furnishings in profuse variety. The house is entirely reliable, shares its advantages freely with its patrons, and the prices are always most reasonable. Mr. Fossett devotes his attention to the management of his Boston establishment, while Mr. Atwood directs the affairs of their house in this city. Both gentlemen reside in Waltham.

E. M. RICHARDSON, Hardware, Paints and Oils, Door and Window Frames.—This is decidedly the largest and best-equipped establishment of the kind in this section of the state. The enterprise dates its inception from 1871, when it was founded by the Messrs. Richardson Brothers, continuing under their joint control for five years, when the firm changed to Richardson & Bond, and in 1891 Mr. E. M. Richardson became the sole proprietor. The extent of the business demands the occupancy of three large buildings, and the best of facilities are enjoyed for the systematic manipulation of trade. And the prompt meeting of the requirements of customers. The immense stock constantly carried embraces every description of hardware, paints, oils, varnishes, agricultural implements, windows, blinds, door and window frames, cutlery, tools, builders' hardware, etc. Mr. Richardson secures his goods direct from manufacturers, and is holding out very superior inducements to the public in the matter of prices. Both a wholesale and retail trade is carried on.

GEORGE W. ADAMS, Watchmaker and Jeweler, Dealer in Watches, Clocks, Jewelry, Silverware and Optical Goods, No. 180 Moody Street.—Although this house has been established but little over four years, having been opened in 1894, yet under Mr. Adams, vigorous and energetic management a large and active trade has been acquired, and the firm is one of the leading ones in the city. The store occupied has dimensions of 25 x 70 feet, and is appointed in handsome, tasteful and attractive style. The superior stock carried embraces a very elegant assortment of fine gold and silver watches in all the leading makes, ornamental parlor and hall clocks, silver and plated ware, jewelry in chaste and artistic designs, and a reliable assortment of optical goods. Nothing but strictly reliable merchandise is handled, and all goods purchased here may be fully relied upon to be as represented.

WALTHAM EMERY WHEEL CO., Felton Street.—The emery of commerce is chiefly obtained from the island of Smyrna. The maximum annual product, and the total consumption of crude emery for all purposes, does not exceed five thousand tons and often falls below that quantity. Among the large consumers of this product is the Waltham Emery Wheel Company, of this city. This industry was inaugurated in 1900 by Mr. H. Richardson, by whom it was conducted until 1901, when the Waltham Emery Wheel Company succeeded to the control. The business is now conducted by Mr. Richardson, who has charge of the manufacturing, and Mr. E. P. Hyde, who has charge of the business department, under the above firm name. These gentlemen have had mature experience in all the departments of their business, and are enabled to secure a perfect production. The plant is complete in every respect, the machinery being of the most approved character, and ample steam-power is provided. Employment is afforded some thirty-five expert operatives in the various departments. The company manufacture the celebrated Waltham emery and corundum wheels, the Richardson emery wheels, and deal in emery and corundum and all kinds of emery grinding and polishing machinery, etc., making a leading specialty of their solid emery and corundum wheels. These goods are without a peer, being unrivalled by any similar productions in the world, and they are in extensive use in all parts of the United States and foreign countries.

TOWN OF HYDE PARK.

FOR a place that had no official existence a generation ago, the growth, progress and development of Hyde Park are worthy of note. It is scarcely thirty years old as a district community, and now ranks among the most substantial, prosperous and progressive towns of Norfolk County, and bids fair to outstrip most of the others in importance within a decade or two. From comparatively insignificant proportions Hyde Park has grown during a quarter of a century to be a flourishing town of upward of ten thousand inhabitants, with a steadily increasing ratio in population and constantly developing industrial, commercial and financial interests; and, unless all signs fail, its prospects for the future are even brighter than the past. Although the center of no one special industry that fills the eye, and, therefore, not so widely known as other towns of far less importance in this section of the state, Hyde Park has within its limits a number of extensive manufacturing plants devoted to the production of a great variety of articles, among others boots and shoes, furniture, carriages, machinery, iron, woodwork, etc., while in the purely mercantile lines this town presents all the aspects of a bustling city, containing many notably fine retail stores, with several large wholesale houses also. New enterprises of an industrial and commercial nature are constantly springing up, while many of the older concerns have been enlarging their facilities. Add to this the normal increase of business in all the branches of trade, and it requires no prophetic ken to predict for Hyde Park an enduring era of prosperity into the twentieth century. With two railroads converging here, and, as a consequence low freight rates; rents, taxes and assessments reduced to a minimum, and all the other items of expense to be taken into account in a business venture exceptionally favorable, it is not to be wondered at that the storekeepers in this progressive town are enabled to offer their wares at "Boston prices." Indeed, the figures quoted on such commodities as groceries, dry goods, hardware, house-furnishing articles and staple goods generally by Hyde Park's leading merchants are rather lower, if anything, than those prevailing for the same class of goods in the "Hub"; and thus it is that the prudent housewife and the veritable bargain hunter in this thriving bailiwick do their shopping at home.

The town site, too, has been selected with foresight and excellent judgment with a view to health and comfort, as well as to transportation facilities, natural resources and the advantages the locality affords for manufacturing and mercantile activity, the situation being slightly elevated, the soil fertile, the surroundings pleasing to the eye and the climate healthful, while the supply of pure water is abundant. That the features here roughly sketched, and they are

TOWN OF HYDE PARK.

but a few of the many attractions that render the place desirable alike as a business and residential location, should have induced capital, energy, wealth and culture to find an abiding place hereabouts is in the very nature of things; and it is the sagacity to perceive and utilize such advantages, and the capacity to develop to the fullest such resources more than any other quality, that gives the Yankee first place in the march of progress.

Hyde Park is distant from Boston something over seven miles, and is connected with the latter city by the Boston and Providence railroad, and the New York and New England railroad, the depots of which lines here are ample and conveniently located both for passage and freight traffic, while the service afforded by each is everything that could be reasonably expected. The town has been mapped on an original plan, with spacious squares, delightful resting places and beautiful circular driveways. The streets are broad and well paved, and the wide avenues on the outskirts are lined with handsome shade trees, while on all sides throughout the environs are to be seen superb villas and elegant residences, the homes of wealth, taste and culture. Luxuriant gardens, lovely lawns and charming groves attract the eye on every hand, and flowers, plants and ornamental trees in great profusion border the drives; luscious fruits, nuts and berries in season also growing here in abundance.

Hyde Park proper is compactly built, and is excellently lighted, gas and electric light both furnishing illumination, and has several imposing public buildings, her citizens being liberal and progressive in matters pertaining to the public weal, while the administration of affairs is in the hands of capable and judicious officers. The local government is vested in a board of selectmen, with executive heads of departments and other officials, including town clerk, chief of police and the various officers exercising public functions in a well ordered town. An efficient police force is maintained, also a thoroughly equipped and effective fire service; and in the matter of health and sanitary regulations, street cleaning, educational facilities and eleemosynary institutions, the town is equally well off. The schools are commodious, completely ventilated and admirably conducted, with competent principals and teachers, both in the primary and higher departments, and in their way are models. Hyde Park maintains a well-appointed Public Library, also, which serves as a valuable and indispensable factor in promoting intelligence in the community, and which receives a patronage of a highly gratifying character.

In respect of houses of worship this town is not behind its more pretentious neighboring communities, all denominations being represented, and some of the church edifices are especially fine pieces of architecture. With the vast, varied and growing industries located here, all branches of trade and commerce giving evidence of healthy activity, and the arts and sciences generally cultivated, it is needless to remark that this town contains some solid and judiciously managed banks and fiduciary institutions, officered and directed by some of Hyde Park's staunchest and foremost citizens, whose influence has been no small factor in the rise, progress and material development of the community. The real estate interests of the town, too, are of surpassing importance, the aggregate transactions in realty representing a handsome sum in the course of a year, investments in building lots for fine dwellings being noticeably on the increase; and indications are not wanting that Hyde Park, owing to its beauty of surroundings and natural advantages, is destined to eclipse most of the suburban villa resorts in the vicinity of Boston. While particularly favored in this respect the town in its business section presents something of a metropolitan appearance, its principal thoroughfares being lined with handsome and substantial business blocks, many of which are really noteworthy.

Along the streets are attractive and flourishing establishments, both wholesale and retail, devoted to the sale of dry goods, millinery, clothing, hardware, furniture, stoves and house-furnishing goods, groceries, crockery and glassware, jewelry, fancy wares, hats and caps, boots and shoes, gents' furnishings, confectionery, etc., etc.; also well ordered meat and provision markets, bakeries, photographic studios, art warerooms, music emporiums, dental parlors, tailoring shops, restaurants and, in short, every feature of progress to be found in any of the more pretentious towns or cities in this part of the state.

As fitting addenda to the foregoing review, a series of sketches of Hyde Park's representative merchants, manufacturers and business men is presented herewith in a succinct form, and the attention of our readers is directed thereto.

H. MARKS, Merchant Tailor, Fine Suitings Constantly on Hand, No. 65 Fairmount Avenue.—Among those who are well qualified to produce a fine grade of stylish and fashionable garments, and who have achieved a justly earned reputation for first-class garments and honorable business methods is Mr. H. Marks, merchant tailor and dealer in fine suitings. Mr. Marks is a German by birth, but came to this United States in 1876, and has been a resident of this state the greater portion of the time since. Being a thoroughly practical and skilled tailor and cutter, he followed his trade in Boston for a few years, and subsequently established himself in business there on his own account in 1888, and five years afterwards removed it to Hyde Park, and from the start here he has met with the most gratifying success. The premises occupied comprise a very neatly and tastefully arranged store with workshop attached. The store contains a most carefully selected assortment of French, German, English and domestic cloths cassimeres, meltons, tweeds, diagonals, suitings and trouserings in all the latest and most desirable styles, also, fine trimmings, etc., which are freely utilized in the production of stylish, elegant fitting and fashionable garments. All articles are made to order exclusively and are characterized by artistic cut and most careful workmanship. Mr. Marks keeps fully abreast of the times and is in possession of the very latest styles as soon as placed in the market, and devotes his entire attention to the wants of his patrons while his prices are always extremely reasonable. He is a reliable business man, and is prepared to offer inducements in his line of trade not easily obtained elsewhere.

S. ONES' SHOE STORE, No. 16 Fairmount Avenue.—This is one of the oldest, and, in all respects, one of the most reliable boot and shoe houses in Hyde Park. For a score of years, or more, it has been a noted shoe establishment and for the past two years has been under the energetic management of Mr. B. E. Sones. Since he took control of the business he has greatly popularized the house, and he is regarded as one of the jolliest and most wide-awake business men on the avenue. He aims at securing the best foot wear that is manufactured, and to sell it at such prices as will insure quick and brisk sales. His premises consist of store and basement, each 22 x 80 feet in dimensions. The salesroom is elegant and attractive in its fittings and arrangement. Customers have a fine, varied, fashionable stock to select from, and they find it difficult to refrain from buying on seeing the prices, even when they do not actually stand in need of the goods. Mr. Sones handles among others, J. N. Smith's (Lynn) ladies' fine foot wear, F. A. Parker's misses' goods, and W. L. Douglas' and E. A. Perkins' boots and shoes. The connections of Mr. Sones with manufacturers are of the most favorable character, and thus he is enabled to offer to his customers the rarest inducements as regards excellence of goods and economy of prices. He has resided in Hyde Park also for years.

G. EORGE MILES, West India Goods and Choice Family Groceries, Tucker's Block, Gordon Avenue.—At the commodious and well ordered store of George Miles can always be found an unusually fine line of everything comprehended in "West India Goods" and family groceries at remarkably low figures.—Boston prices prevailing and where patrons are assured of honorable dealing at all times. Only first-class goods are handled, quality and quantity being guaranteed in every instance, while orders are delivered free to any part of Hyde Park and vicinity in the most prompt and satisfactory manner. The store, which is centrally located, is 20 x 70 feet in dimensions, and neatly fitted up, and a very large stock is constantly carried, comprising choice teas, and coffees, fresh pure spices, sugars, syrups, canned goods in great variety, dried fruit, prepared cereals, sauces, preserves, olives, relishes and table luxuries, prime butter, cheese and eggs, smoked meats and fish, best brands of family flour, oatmeal, corn and rye meal, rice, bran, peas, salt, saleratus, soda, soap, starch, baking powder, oriolamos, oils, vinegar, foreign and domestic fruits, nuts,

etc., etc.; also a full line of crockery, glassware, kitchen utensils, brushes, brooms, wooden-ware and housekeeping articles. Five polite clerks attend to the wants of purchasers, while three teams are in regular service. This popular and prosperous store was established in 1871 by the firm of Miles & Slisbury, which continued in prominence up to 1877, when the present proprietor assumed sole control, and has since conducted the business alone with uninterrupted success. Mr. Miles is a native of Roxbury, and stands high in the community both in business and social life. He is a Knight Templar and belongs to most of the benevolent associations.

S. A. COFFIN, Cigars, Tobacco, Pipes, etc., Confectionery, Fruits, etc., Nos 4 and 6 Everett Square.—The headquarters for smokers' supplies in Hyde Park is the well-ordered and excellent store of S. A. Coffin, wholesale and retail dealer in cigars, tobacco, pipes, etc. For variety, completeness and excellence of stock no establishment of the kind in town compares with this, while a neat confectionery and well-appointed diningrooms are maintained in connection also, several polite assistants being in attendance. This popular and prosperous stand was established by the present proprietor about ten years ago. The premises occupied are spacious, ample and tastefully arranged, and a large, first-class assortment is always kept on hand, including besides imported and domestic cigars, in fine and medium grades all the favorite brands of cigarettes, smoking and chewing tobaccos in great variety, snuff, pipes, and everything in the line of smokers' articles; also foreign and domestic fruits, nuts, etc., choice confections, delicious chocolates, caramels, bonbons, pure candies of every description, wholesome and wholesome cakes, all flavors soda water etc., a handsome soda fountain being in service, while refreshments and lunch are served likewise in the most superior manner at very reasonable rates. Mr. Coffin is a native of Hampton, N. H. and a resident of Hyde Park since 1872.

E. H. GOOLD, Bakery, No. 104 Fairmount Avenue.—The bakery par excellence in Hyde Park is unquestionably the well-appointed establishment of E. H. Goold. The goods produced here are maintained at a uniformly high standard of excellence, being absolutely pure, wholesome and toothsome. The very lowest prices consistent with fine goods and upright dealing prevail also—quality and quantity being guaranteed and all orders receive immediate attention. The business premises include a neat, compact store, with well-appointed bake-house in the rear, three expert bakers being employed, while two wagons are in regular service supplying customers throughout the town and vicinity. A large and choice assortment is carried fresh daily, comprising delicious home-made, cottage and family bread; graham, milk, rye and cream breads; rolls, buns, cookies, doughnuts, crackers, cakes, pies, pastry and confectionery in quite a variety; while brown bread and beans are baked every Sunday morning, and ice-cream in any quantity is furnished to order in season, at short notice.

B. OSTON CASH MARKET, Messrs. Holtham & Wetherbee, Proprietors, No. 8 Bank Building.—A leading house engaged in this line in Hyde Park, and one that enjoys the fullest favor and confidence of the public, is that of the Boston Cash Market. This is a young firm, the business having been founded on December 17, 1890, but the unbounded energy brought to bear in the management of the enterprise, quickly won the approval and patronage of the public. The spacious premises occupied consist of a store and basement 160 x 100 feet in dimensions. The salesroom is appointed in the most tasteful and convenient manner, and presents at all times a most inviting appearance. A large stock is in all seasons carried, embracing the choicest meats of all kinds, including the primest cuts of beef, veal, lamb, mutton, pork, etc., and a full supply of poultry, vegetables, and provisions in general. These are sold at the lowest cash prices, and customers have their orders filled promptly and accurately.

A. P. HAMMETT, Locksmith and Bell Hanger, Lawn Mowers Sharpened, Skates Ground, Scissors Sharpened, No. 67 West River Street.—An enterprising house engaged in this line of business and well worthy of mention is that of Mr. A. P. Hammett, locksmith, bell hanger, etc., who has acquired a wide reputation for skill and reliability. Mr. Hammett is a native of Portland, Maine, but has been a resident of this state for a number of years, his principal establishment being on the corner of Dearborn and Dudley Streets in Boston Highlands, where he carries on a very large and prosperous concern in the same line of business. The present enterprise in Hyde Park was founded originally in 1884, and was conducted by the original proprietor until October, 1893, when he disposed of it to the present proprietor. Since Mr. Hammett has taken it in charge he has increased the trade very perceptibly and enlarged its scope of labor and business very much. The premises occupied comprise a business department with workshop attached. The latter is fully equipped with all the latest improved machinery and devices required for turning out first-class work, and a force of skilled workmen are given constant employment. Mr. Hammett is a thoroughly skilled and experienced locksmith, bell hanger and worker in intricate machinery and devices; and is prepared to execute all commissions pertaining to these branches of mechanical art. Intricate locks are out of order and requiring repairs are overhauled and made good as new. Keys for all kinds of locks are fitted and made, wire and electric bells are hung properly in public buildings, hotels, business houses, factories and residences, watchmens' detectors repaired and set up, hotel communicators put in order. In fact all kinds of house outfitting is performed. He also does a very extensive business in sharpening lawn mowers, scissors, razors, mechanics', household and pocket cutlery, and a specialty is made of grinding skates.

E. J. JOHNSON & CO., Proprietor, Everett House Market, Hyde Park; and High Street Market, Dedham.—The leading houses of this kind in this section of the state is that conducted by E. J. Johnson & Co., proprietors of the High Street Market, Dedham; and Everett House Market, in this town. The active proprietor of this progressive concern is Mr. E. J. Johnson, who established his enterprise in 1893, and augmented his operations by opening, in November last, his Hyde Park market. Owing to the energy, perseverance, progressive methods and honorable policy which he has brought to bear in the management of his affairs, his inviolable rule of handling none but strictly reliable merchandise, and of supplying the same at rates as low as those charged for similar goods in Boston, he has developed an extensive, active, influential, most desirable, and increasing patronage. His stores are of spacious proportions, are kept in scrupulously clean condition, and at all times are filled with heavy stocks of prime Chicago dressed beef, lamb, veal, mutton, pork, hams, tripe, sausage, butter, eggs, lard, foreign and domestic fruits, vegetables, and canned goods of all kinds. A full staff of clerks and assistants are employed, polite attention is assured all customers, and orders are promptly filled and delivered. Mr. Johnson is a native of Charlestown, Mass., and resides in Dedham, where he owns considerable real estate. He is a gentleman thoroughly popular in the community, takes an active interest in advancing the public interests, and his thorough success is due entirely to his business ability and his sterling integrity.

C. S. DAVIS & CO., Dry Goods, Small Wares and Gents' Furnishings.—Among the leading establishments of Hyde Park, in the well-known popular dry goods house of Messrs. C. S. Davis & Co. The business was established some time ago by H. C. Chamberlin and succeeded by R. W. Karnan & Co., at No. 11 East River Street, of which firm the present owners were partners, and afterwards removed to the premises now occupied. Last year Messrs. C. S. Davis & Co. succeeded to it by purchase and since that time it has been prosecuted vigorously, the stock increased and the operation greatly extended. The premises, first floor and basement, are each 25 x 60 feet in extent, the store presenting an attractive appearance. The stock, which is unusually large, embraces in its variety a choice, well-selected line of imported and domestic dry goods of every description, and includes besides splendid dress goods in all new styles and velvets and laces and linens and fine woolens, an extensive assortment of hosiery, gloves,

notions and ladies' and gentlemen's furnishings and small wares. The stock in all new and has been carefully chosen expressly for a first-class, fastidious custom and is character and extent is not excelled by that of any other house in the trade in this vicinity. The necessities of the business require the attendance of six clerks. The firm is always on the alert to introduce the new goods as soon as brought out and the patronage is steadily and rapidly growing. Mr. C. S. Davis, the head of the house, is an experienced practical business man, a native of Leominster, and is very popular as a merchant and citizen.

R. E. CHERRINGTON, Upholsterer, and Window Shade Manufacturer, No. 108 Fairmount Avenue.—One of the prominent business houses in the line of specialties on Fairmount Avenue is that conducted by Mr. R. E. Cherrington, who is an upholsterer, window shade manufacturer and a dealer in new and second-hand furniture. This enterprise was founded May, 1897. The premises comprise a salesroom and a basement, each measuring 25 x 100 feet, and appropriately fitted up. The salesroom is well stocked with a splendid assortment of window shades of new patterns and designs, upholstery goods, and new and second-hand furniture of every description, including elegant parlor and chamber suits in plain and artistic designs, superb cabinet ware, handsome mirrors, elegant upholstered goods, and everything in the line of furniture. Mr. Cherrington devotes particular attention to the buying and selling of second-hand furniture, and to the execution of all kinds of upholstery work; but the leading specialty of the business is the manufacture to order of all kinds of window shades. Mr. Cherrington has in stock every kind of window shade materials, opaque and transparent, furniture fringe of all kinds, drapery poles, brass and wood, cords, tassels, spring rollers, and a full line of window fixtures and upholsterers' goods. He makes a leading specialty of "Mourngren polish," which is a fine furniture polish, and is indispensable to manufacturers of furniture and to the household. Mr. Cherrington is a native of Boston.

FRANK W. GLEASON & CO., Dealer in Stoves, Furnaces and Ranges, etc., No. 7 East River Street, Bech Building.—A leading house engaged in steam heating and gas fitting is that of Messrs. Frank W. Gleason & Co. The business of this concern was founded five years ago by the present firm, and owing to the practical knowledge brought to bear in the direction of the enterprise, a success was scored from the outset, and a large influential patronage has been developed. The salesroom has the spacious dimensions of 25 x 70 feet, and contains a large stock of parlor and cooking stoves, furnaces and ranges, tinware, hardware and kitchen furnishing goods of every description, and also a full supply of plumbing materials. The basement is used for the pipe work, steam and gas fitting department, and the firm have a large two-and-a-half story building where their tin work is done. Employment is afforded to none but highly skilled workmen, and special attention is given to the execution of plumbing, steam and hot water heating and gas fitting in all their branches. All orders are performed in a thoroughly finished and workmanlike manner, and the charges made are eminently reasonable and satisfactory. Mr. Gleason is a native of this state, having been born in Bedford, and he is familiarly known to the residents of Hyde Park and vicinity for his enterprise and reliability.

C. L. FARNSWORTH, Baker, No. 8 Central Avenue.—Mr. Farnsworth has had quite an extended and valuable experience in this business and has been established since 1893, occupying commodious premises well equipped in every particular. He has provided all the latest improved ovens and other necessary adjuncts. His establishment is the largest and most important of this kind in the vicinity, and his business operations are wide-spread and extensive and include beside Hyde Park, Milton and Readville, all the neighboring towns. Five teams are kept constantly engaged, and from nine to twelve practical workmen are employed in the bakery. All kinds of family bread and plain and fancy cakes and pastry are made fresh every day, and such is their quality and superior excellence that there is always a brisk demand from the public. The best brands of flour and other carefully selected materials only are used in this establishment. Mr. Farnsworth is a native of this state and an old resident of Hyde Park.

F. R. PERRY, Butter, Eggs, Teas, Coffees, Spices, etc. No 68 Fairmount Avenue.—A highly honorable and prosperous house engaged in this business in Hyde Park is that of Mr. F. R. Perry, successor to Messrs. Howes and Holbrook, dealer in butter, eggs, coffees, spices, teas, etc. This establishment was inaugurated originally in 1887 by Messrs. Howes and Holbrook as a butter and egg house, who conducted it with fair success until November, 1896, when they disposed of it to the present proprietor, Mr. Perry is a native of this state and has been a resident here for some years. Possessing excellent business qualifications, he added to the former stock a well and carefully selected stock of groceries, and has met with the most gratifying encouragement. His store is of ample dimensions, very neatly and tastefully arranged, and supplied with every facility for the transaction of business. The stock embraces a choice line of absolutely pure and fresh teas from China and Japan, coffees from Java, Mocha and South America, pure spices, select brands of hermetically sealed goods in glass and tin, table delicacies, condiments, relishes, select family flour, farinaceous and cereal foods. Mr. Perry makes a specialty of select dairy and fancy creamery butter, and handles only the very best brands from Vermont and other celebrated regions, also cheese, fresh laid eggs and other dairy goods. The goods of this concern have an already established reputation, and customers dealing with this house can always have the complete satisfaction of knowing that they are buying the very best and purest at the lowest prices. Mr. Perry spares no efforts to make his establishment the most popular and cheapest house of its kind in the city.

JOHN CAMERON, Manufacturer of Fine Custom Made Boots and Shoes, West River Street.—Mr. Cameron is a native of Scotland, but came to the United States many years ago, having been a resident of this state since 1888. Having learned this trade, which was supplemented by years of practical experience in all its various branches, he founded this establishment originally in 1891, and from the date of its inception has from the recipient of a very liberal and influential patronage, derived principally from among our leading business men and citizens. The premises utilized for store and shop purposes are of ample dimensions, suitably arranged and fitted up in a very neat and tasteful manner, the workshop being fully equipped with all appliances for the turning out of first-class work, in which a force of workmen sufficient to meet the requirements of the trade are given employment, while in his store will be found a fine assortment of boots and shoes, all of his own superior manufacture, and made of the very best quality of materials and in the best style of workmanship. Being a practical man, Mr. Cameron selects all of his own materials in person and makes a specialty of fine custom work to order. Experienced in taking measures of the foot and a full knowledge of its anatomy, he fits up his lasts for customers so as to insure a comfortable and easy fit, at the same time giving the boot or shoe a stylish appearance. He makes a specialty of unequally sized feet, also, of those having bunions and other troubles, while the construction of his goods is such that they combine pliability with durability.

B. CONNOR, Grain, Meal, Flour and Groceries, Opposite New York and New England Depot.—Mr. B. Connor, the well-known and popular dealer in groceries, grain, meal, flour, etc., is one of the pioneer merchants in this section. Born in Ireland, he moved to Hyde Park in 1889, and settled permanently in the town, and with all the energy for which he is famed, plenty of pluck, industry and youth, but small cash capital, he started in the grocery business. After developing a large, brisk trade he disposed of this business in 1895, and built an extensive grain mill, which he successfully operated for some years, and then disposed of this. He again turned his attention to the grocery trade, and for the past two years has occupied his present store, which has a capacity of 20 x 40 feet, and is appropriately fitted up and appointed. A full and complete stock of choice and new teas and coffees, pure spices, canned goods in great variety, jams, jellies, sauces, pickles, best dairy butter, prime cheese, fresh eggs, molasses, sugars, table delicacies of all kinds, and grocers' sundries of every description is constantly kept on hand. A special feature is made of the handling of the finest brands of family flour, meal, grain and feed of all kinds. The stock is selected from the most reliable sources, and patrons of the house have learned by experience that nothing of an inferior quality or that is adulterated will be sold to them. The prices are placed at the lowest point for first-class goods. Two clerks and a delivery wagon are in regular service, orders are promptly filled, and the fullest satisfaction guaranteed.

CITY OF NEWTON.

NEWTON, the most favored and delightful among the many attractive suburbs of Boston, is distinctly a city of beautiful homes. It has been appropriately designated the "City of Villas." Everything bespeaks material wealth, comfort, taste and refinement, science, art and culture having manifestly worked in harmony with nature in the achievement. The climate, for Massachusetts, is remarkably salubrious, and the topography varied and lovely, gently sloping hills environing the town, while the attractions along the Charles River as this noble stream skirts the city add materially to the natural beauties of the place. Newton is noted for its magnificent country seats and luxurious dwellings, its superb drives, exquisite scenery and elegant surroundings, its beautiful lawns, gardens and conservatories, and is the home of many of the foremost and wealthiest of Boston's merchants, manufacturers, scientists, artists, literary and professional men, who after the hours of active pursuits, retire hither to their palatial residences to enjoy the health imparting air amid the luxuriant surroundings of fruit, flowers and foliage. This is, in short, an ideal American community, and represents the highest development of New England civilization—the very apex of our social structure, so to speak. The town appears to have been mapped out on the progressive ideas that characterize all its other features, the severity of rectangular streets, except in the business section of the city, being softened by the beauty lines of gracefully curving avenues and winding driveways, while spacious parks, handsome fountains and all the other appurtenances of use and ornament that art and wealth could suggest greet the eye on every hand. The soil hereabouts, too, is rich and generous, and yields bountifully of fruits, vegetables and kindred products, the gardens and fields in and around Newton being in a high state of cultivation, and in the summer time afford delight to the eye as well as to the tooth.

Being distant but seven miles from Boston, and being afforded ample and excellent service by the Boston & Albany Railroad, with a line of horse cars, also, between the two cities, Newton becomes as far as time and space are concerned, practically a portion of the metropolis of New England, while maintaining its distinct municipality and enjoying the advantages naturally attaching to a suburban commuity.

Although not immediately associated with any notable historic incidents of colonial days, Newton is one of the oldest settlements of the original Massachusetts Colony, dating its inception back to the early part of the seventeenth century. Soon after the settlement of Charlestown, or, to be exact, in the year 1630, a party of colonists located here and founded a village which in 1688 assumed the dignity and aspects of a town, and as such it remained up to 1873, when it was duly incorporated as a city, the population having attained sufficient proportions at this period to warrant the departure. The present population is upward of 20,000, with a steady ratio of increase, which with annexation of outlying towns and villages, which in the nature of things are bound to take place in the near future, will materially augment the number quoted. The city is divided into seven wards, and contains within its corporate limits something like four thousand dwellings, with a real estate and personal property value aggregating more than $30,000,000.

The municipal government consists of a mayor, board of aldermen and common council, with a city clerk, city treasurer and collector of taxes, deputy collector of taxes, auditor, city engineer, chairman of assessors, water register, city almoner, city messenger, city marshal, chief of fire department, superintendent of streets and superintendent of water works.

From the description of the city, roughly sketched in this review, and the character of its residents, it is easy to infer that Newton has not been lacking in wisdom and judgment in the conservative administration of public affairs in the past no less than the present, the various departments pertaining to the city government being characterized by sagacity, ability and economy. In the matter of police and fire department, Newton is exceptionally favored, both being thoroughly disciplined, well equipped and efficient, and are in all respects fully adequate in their respective functions to the requirements of the city, which for a place of its size and importance, is notably free from the occasions that call for the active services of either. In making provision for the education of the youth and the diffusion of knowledge, the city has been generous to an ample degree, as it is scarcely necessary to observe, her schools and educational institutions being models in their way, while those entrusted with the highly responsible charge of "teaching the young idea" are selected with discrimination and a view to special fitness. The public library is an institution worthy of more than passing notice, being eligibly located, excellently appointed and admirably conducted. The books to be found here run the entire gamut of literature, embracing historical, biographical, mathematical, scientific, poetical and other useful works, with all the standard works of fiction, travel and romance; while the reading-room is supplied with the leading periodicals, magazines, reviews, illustrated journals and newspapers.

In variety and beauty of church architecture, likewise, Newton is well abreast with the times, containing as the city does, many imposing and artistic structures devoted to religious worship, and all the principal denominations are represented here. The system for the protection of public health and the general sanitary arrangements are of a most superior character, having abundant and excellent drainage facilities by the Charles River and its affluents, and the death rate of the city is normally low, while the supply of pure water also is abundant.

The city is equally well cared for in all the other departments pertaining to the public welfare and the streets and squares, which are broad, smooth and well kept, present an attractive appearance. The town is excellently lighted also, and Newton itself supports a well equipped local street car system, besides the line of horse cars connecting the city with Boston. Although Newton proper has never been, strictly speaking, an industrial center like most Massachusetts communities, there are to be found in and around the town several extensive manufacturing plants and important works of various kinds, while in the matter of large mercantile establishments, financial institutions and commercial interests generally the business portion of the city presents substantial indications of progress, activity and permanent prosperity. Newton's business men, merchants, bankers, brokers, real estate dealers and traders being of the class known as "solid citizens."

Spacious and handsome stores of every description, both wholesale and retail, with extensive stocks of goods attractively displayed, at Boston prices, meet the eye on all sides along the leading business thoroughfares which are wide, regular and relieved of monotony by blocks and squares at the intersection of the principal streets, while courtesy and honorable dealing in- the emporiums of trade here are prevailing features. The erection of buildings both for business and residential purposes is constantly going on,—unusual activity being noticeable in this direction during the present year,—and the demand for desirable building lots affords evidence of steady increase. Except about the business quarter of the city, the pieces of realty offered for sale are large, varying from one-eighth of an acre to five or more acres, and the object of this is in order to give purchasers an opportunity to exercise taste in beautifying their grounds by planting flowers, fruit and ornamental trees, etc. There is no such thing, however, as a "real estate boom" here, permanent investments being the order of the day in this fashionable suburb, while the steadily increasing wealthy population of Newton is only to be considered to show the stability of transactions in realty in a locality like this. Notwithstanding its suburban location, Newton presents a thoroughly-metropolitan aspect with its broad, perfectly paved streets lined with imposing and expensive business blocks in brick, stone, iron and wood; the numbers to be seen on the sidewalks; the superb equipage and vehicles of every variety, and the bustle and activity pervading its depots, markets, stores and mercantile emporiums. Here can be found well ordered and flourishing establishments devoted to almost every branch of trade, business, science and art, all which are conducted by men of energy and enterprise closely associated with the material and moral advancement of the community and the progress and development of the city industrially, commercially, financially and socially. And right here attention is directed to the subjoined series of brief sketches of Newton's leading business men, including merchants, manufacturers and traders and the foremost representatives of the arts and professions in the city. These accompanying pages will be found of interest, presenting as they do the instructive and noteworthy fact that almost invariably those who have succeeded in reaching the fore front in the various walks of life here sketched have been the architects of their own fortunes, carving their way up from the lowest rung of the ladder, as the saying is, by the exercise of energy, sagacity and skill in their respective lines, while it is confidently hoped that the perusal thereof may serve to cause others, and especially the younger business men in the community, to emulate those here selected for special mention in the qualities to which their success is manifestly due.

J. B. STODDARD, Hack, Livery and Boarding Stable, Chestnut Street, near Railroad Station, West Newton, Auburn Street, near Railroad Station, Auburndale.—An admirably conducted and deservedly popular hack, livery and boarding stable in West Newton is that of Mr. J. B. Stoddard. Mr. Stoddard has had ten years experience in his vocation, having been engaged in the stable business at South Carolina for many years. The business which he now controls was inaugurated in 1879 by Mr. W. H. Magill, and on January 18, 1889, Mr. Stoddard succeeded to the ownership. He has thoroughly refitted and renovated the premises, and the stable is now exactly what is claimed for it, namely, the best this side of Boston. The building has three floors, each 50 x 140 feet in dimensions, and the place is equipped and appointed throughout with all modern improvements. There are ample accommodations for forty horses and the same number of carriages, and a large number of first-class turnouts are kept for hire. There are also two large barges for picnic and pleasure parties. Stylish and comfortable hacks, coupés, carriages, buggies, carryalls and beach wagons are furnished at the shortest notice. Mr. Stoddard is about adding an undertaking department to his establishment, and will assume full charge of funerals, furnishing coffins or caskets, all requisite funeral furnishings, carriages, etc. A native of Upton, Mass., Mr. Stoddard is familiarly known in this state and elsewhere.

CITY MARKET, Wellington Howes, Proprietor, No. 413 Centre Street.—The business of this concern was founded in 1878 by Mr. George H. Dupee, and in 1890 the present proprietor, Mr. Wellington Howes, succeeded to the control of affairs. Under his energetic and progressive management the patronage of the establishment has become greatly augmented, and it has attained to a leading position in the food-supply trade. The store occupied is of ample proportions, and is fitted up in all its departments in a systematic, convenient style, for the display, handling and keeping of goods. A large stock of superior goods is at all times carried, embracing the choicest beef, lamb, veal, mutton, pork, hams, lard, tripe, sausage, eggs, butter, fruit and vegetables in response to the repeated solicitation of his many patrons. Mr. Howes recently introduced a fish and oyster departments into his establishment, and is now prepared to furnish the best of everything in the sea-food line. A working force of six clerks and five delivery teams are constantly employed, and the active trade furnished never flags, but shows signs of steady increase. Mr. Howes is a native of Newtonville, is an active member of the Odd Fellows, the Order of the Red Men and the Pilgrim Fathers, and he enjoys the popular good-will in both the business and social world.

C. PHILLIPS, Practical Plumber and Sanitary Engineer, Howes' Block, Centre Street.—Among the practical sanitary engineers and plumbers in Newton there are none more thoroughly practical and proficient than Mr. C. Phillips, who has devoted most of his life to the business and is particularly expert in arranging underground drainage and ventilation and in fitting up buildings and dwellings with piping and introducing water and gas, and setting bath tubs, sinks, etc., and making repairs and attending to general jobbing. The premises have dimensions of 20 x 65 feet, and are well fitted up and perfectly equipped with all the necessary appliances for doing work in the best manner. From six to ten practical plumbers and gas fitters are kept continually engaged, and the trade is large and he may be said to receive a great portion of the orders for plumbing and gas fitting and making sewer connections and attending to drainage and ventilation in Newton and vicinity. This business is one requiring a peculiar knowledge in its scientific application, and is by no others so well represented as by Mr. Phillips. He is a native of Newton and a young man of energy, enterprise and ambition.

HOWARD B. COFFIN, Fine Teas and Groceries, Cole's Block.—The reliable establishment of Mr. Howard B. Coffin is the largest grocery in Newton. The business was founded in 1845 and passed into the present proprietor's hands twelve years ago, and under his management the trade has become greatly augmented. The fine store occupied has a frontage of 40 feet and a depth of 70 feet and is admirably appointed in all its departments with every appliance, convenience, and apportioned requisite for the systematic conduct of the business. The working force includes six clerks and six delivery teams. The heavy stock carried embraces choice teas, coffees and spices, foreign and domestic fruits and vegetables, and superior staple and fancy groceries of every description. Mr. Coffin owns a large flour mill in Minneapolis, and makes a leading specialty of handling flour, the brand "Howard's Fancy Roller," his leading one, being accompanied by any other flour in the market. It is made from the best fancy Minnesota spring wheat, and will make the whitest, sweetest and most delicious bread. Both a wholesale and retail trade is supplied.

ELLIOT W. KEYES, Apothecary, Hashim' Block, Auburn Street, Auburndale.—Mr. Elliot W. Keyes for a long time was the trusted clerk of Mr. C. B. Bird, whom he succeeded in 1892, and is well qualified both by experience and training to conduct this business. It is an old established one and since it came under the control of Mr. Keyes, he has entirely remodelled and refitted it and put in a new stock of fresh drugs and medicines and is conducting the business according to modern ideas with marked skill and ability. Since the improvements have been made his above premises a very handsome and attractive appearance and forms one of the features of the town. In dimensions, it is 20 x 35 feet, and contains a valuable assortment of goods, embracing everything belonging to the business in the way of drugs and medicines

of standard strength and purity, also, fresh chemicals, toilet articles and all the various special pharmaceuticals. The prescription counter is ably presided over by Mr. Keyes, who fully appreciates the responsibility resting upon him in this connection and has accordingly provided every convenience and facility for compounding physicians' prescriptions and dispensing medicines with accuracy. A native of Foxboro, Mr. Keyes has lived in Auburndale a long time. In the store he also has a line of choice, well selected imported and domestic cigars of popular brands and also delicious wholesome candies and confectionery made from pure cane sugar.

L. H. CRANTICH, House, Sign and Ornamental Painting, Newtonville.—Mr. L. H. Crantich is one of the best known and most popular house, sign and ornamental painters in this section. He is a native of St. John's, N. B., and has resided in Newtonville for the past twenty-two years. In 1878, he formed a partnership with Mr. Horrigan, under the style of Crantich & Horrigan, and the firm founded the business which Mr. Crantich has been sole proprietor of since 1885, and which has been developed to large proportions. Mr. Crantich occupies commodious premises for his business, and hires but occasionally on hand a very extensive stock of paints, oils, glass, brushes, wall-paper, varnishes, colors and painters' and decorators' supplies of every description. He is a most skillful and practically experienced painter. His services are in constant demand, and during the busy season he employs on an average about twenty journeymen. He executes work all over the district, and never fails to give entire satisfaction. Mr. Crantich performs all work in the same perfect manner, and spares no pains or trouble to give entire satisfaction. Reputable and enterprising, is predict for him a still greater measure of success.

J. CARROLL, Manufacturer of Every Description of Double and Single Harnesses, Washington Street, near City Hall, West Newton.—The harness and saddlery establishment of J. Carroll, located on Washington Street, near City Hall, has been a noted and largely patronized one for the past fourteen years, having been established in 1878 by Mr. Carroll, who conducted the business with marked success until his death in January, 1892. Since then the enterprise has been continued by his widow, who has retained in service the efficient workmen employed by her late husband. The premises occupied for manufacturing and sale purposes are commodious and well equipped for carrying on the business successfully and satisfactorily. The stock of goods consists of all kinds of styles of harness, saddles, bridles, horse-boots and every description of horse-furnishing goods, from a bit to a blanket, also a full assortment of carriage trimmings, and a general assortment of driving gloves. The harness, saddles and collars displayed have been manufactured on the premises, and in them only the very best materials, trimmings, and mountings have been used. A very large custom trade is done in making harness, saddles and collars and a special feature is made of repairing this class of goods and also of carriage trimming. A competent staff of experienced workmen are employed.

ALBERT BRACKETT & SON, Dealers in Wood, Coal, Grain, Meal, etc., Brackett's Block, No. 411 Centre Street.—One of the oldest and most prominent houses engaged in this line in this section of the state is that of Messrs. Albert Brackett & Son, in the block which they are owners of, and which bears their name, and their coal and wood yard, grain mill and elevator are located on Washington Street. The business was founded in 1850 by the senior member of the firm, and in 1885, his son, Mr. A. L. Brackett, was admitted to partnership. The grain mill is equipped with the most improved machinery, operated by a thirty horse-power engine, and fifty horse-power boiler, and the grinding capacity amounts to 150 bushels per day. The firm carry a heavy stock in all seasons, and are general wholesale and retail dealers in grain, meal, bundle hay and straw, sawed and split wood, and the best qualities of furnace and stove coals. Nothing but the best quality in each line is handled, the lowest prices are quoted, and all orders meet with prompt and satisfactory fulfilment. Mr. Albert Brackett is a native of Brighton, Mass., and a gentleman widely known for his business capacity and honorable methods. His son, Mr. A. L. Brackett, was born in Newton and is popularly esteemed.

ARTHUR HUDSON, Pharmacist, Corner Elmwood and Centre Streets.—Mr. Arthur Hudson is Newton's leading and senior representative of the pharmaceutical profession. Physicians' prescriptions and family recipes are here prepared in the most careful and trustworthy manner in every instance, from absolutely pure and fresh ingredients, at all hours, by thoroughly competent pharmacists, while business prizes also prevail. Mr. Hudson was born in England, but has been in this country many years, residing in Newton since 1887. He is a thoroughly practical and expert analytical and pharmaceutical chemist and apothecary, with twenty-eight years' experience in the exercise of his profession in all its branches, and is prepared to conduct investigation as to the composition of matter by analysis or synthesis according to the most approved methods. He has been established in business here since 1878, and from the first he steadily won his way to popular favor and confidence. Some of his own proprietary remedies—notably "Hudson's Dyspepsia Compound," "Hudson's Emollient Embrocation" for chapped hands and Hudson's "Pectoral Cough Syrups"—being preparations of exceptional merit. The premises occupied, including commodious drug store and well appointed laboratory, are fitted up in an especially attractive manner, a magnificent soda fountain costing $1300, handsome plate glass windows, elegant show cases and tasteful arrangement of stock, imparting to the place a superb appearance, while the establishment is also connected by telephone (694). A very large and carefully selected stock is constantly carried, comprising everything in the line of high grade drugs and medicines, chemicals of standard purity, acids, extracts, spirits, alcohol, etc., herbs, barks and botanic medicines, all the standard proprietary remedies, sanitary specialties and druggists' sundries in great variety, while several experienced assistants are in attendance. Mr. Hudson exercising close personal supervision over the prescription department. Mr. Hudson is a well-known member of the Massachusetts and the American Pharmaceutical Associations, and is also an active member of the I. O. O. F., the Royal Arcanum, the Pilgrim Fathers and the Sons of St. George.

DANIELS' NONAUTUM STABLES, Henry C. Daniels, Proprietor.—These stables were erected about half a century ago, near what was formerly the old Nonantum House, and they have been under the management of Mr. Daniels for the past seven years. The building is a commodious structure, covering an area of 200 x 75 feet, and to the front is a neatly furnished office. The interior of the stable is well lighted, thoroughly ventilated and drained, and provided with all the latest improvements and modern conveniences. Mr. Daniels does a general livery business, buys and sells the best class of horses for all kinds of work, and takes horses to board by the day, week or month, and his facilities are not surpassed by any establishment of the kind in the city. Mr. Daniels has about twenty-five horses in the boarders' department, and he keeps on hand about a similar number of horses for hire, together with a splendid line of buggies, hacks, carriages, and vehicles of every description. The turnouts cannot be excelled for elegance and style, and the terms are fair and equitable. Funerals, weddings, parties, festivals, etc., are punctually supplied with carriages in charge of careful and steady drivers, and all orders by telephone meet with prompt attention. Mr. Daniels is a Massachusetts man by birth.

U. R. DYER, Fresh Fish, Oysters, Fruit, Vegetables, Pork, etc., Corner Washington and Walnut Streets, Newtonville.—The leading retail fish, fruit and produce market in this city is the popular stand conducted by U. H. Dyer, where may be found always a thoroughly first-class assortment of sea foods, dairy products and garden produce fresh daily, at the very lowest prices. Only A 1 stock is handled, and all orders are promptly and reliably attended to, three efficient assistants being in attendance, while three delivery wagons are in service, supplying customers throughout Newtonville and vicinity. The store, which is desirably located, is 20 x 70 feet in size, and is neatly fitted up and well equipped in every department, while a large stock is kept constantly on hand comprising fresh fish of every variety in season, pickled, dried and smoked fish, oysters, lobsters and clams, fresh pork, prime lard, choice creamery butter, fresh eggs and a full and fine line of fruits, vegetable and table delicacies, and altogether Mr.

Dyer has a flourishing patronage.—Mr. Dyer, who is a native of Cape Cod, is a man of ample experience in this line, and prior to opening this prosperous market in November, 1887, had been a member of the firm of Dyer & Bean, doing business across the way for about four years. He is an active member of the West Newton Lodge of the I. O. O. F.

FERGUSON & DECKER, Custom Tailors, French's Block, No. 265 Centre Street.—Mr. Neil Ferguson and Mr. Charles S. Decker are both skilled, practical, scientific cutters and merchant tailors and have won an excellent reputation for the handsome manner they design and make to order dress and business suits, overcoats and trousers, etc., which are unsurpassed in quality of goods, style and fashion, cut, fit, workmanship and finish and price. An elegant assortment of choice goods is the place is displayed in the store in beautiful fabrics in fine woolens and suitings and trouserings, broadcloth, vestings, etc., of both home and European manufacture from which to make selections. The assortment is not excelled by that of any other in Newton, and full satisfaction is always guaranteed and given to all customers. Mr. Ferguson is from Nova Scotia and Mr. Decker is a native of this state. They have for some time been residents of Newton. Since 1893 they have been associated as copartners and have built up a flourishing business.

C. E. SCANNAN, Provisions, Waltham Street, West Newton.—The popular establishment of Mr. C. E. Scannan was originally established in 1866 by Messrs. Barlow & Trowbridge, and in 1871 they were succeeded by Mr. Charles Eaton, who, in 1890, disposed of the enterprise to Mr. Scannan. This gentleman is a native of Portland, Me., and has resided in Newton for the past eighteen years. By wise and able management he has developed a very large and rapidly increasing business, and numbers among his patrons the leading citizens. The store occupied has a capacity of 20 x 60 feet, is fitted up with special reference to the trade and thoroughly supplied with cold storage for the preservation of perishable articles in hot weather, which enables Mr. Scannan to supply his patrons with the freshest and best of everything at the most reasonable prices. Three assistants and two teams are in service. Everything classed under the comprehensive term provisions is to be found in this large and superior stock.

BARBER BROTHERS, Builders' and Fancy Hardware, Cutlery, etc. No. 419 Centre Street.—This pushing and popular firm was established in 1888, and from its inception the Messrs. Barber have steadily been winning their way to public favor and prosperity, acquiring in a short time a flourishing trade. The store which is centrally situated, is 25 x 90 feet in dimensions with commodious basement and is neatly fitted up, and connected by telephone. An attentive and excellently selected stock is constantly carried, and comprises everything in the line of builders', shelf and fancy hardware, table and pocket cutlery of all kinds, mechanics' tools in great variety, agricultural implements, machinists' supplies and nails, garden tools, rubber, hose, cordage, household specialties and, in short, everything to be found in a leading, well-ordered establishment of the kind, while three efficient and polite clerks are in attendance with the proprietors.

J. W. CONROY & SON, House and Sign Painters, Chestnut Street, near Depot, West Newton.—This business was started under this style a dozen years ago, but on Feb. 15, 1890, the senior partner, who was a native of Ireland, died, and since then the business has been conducted by his son, Mr. E. F. Conroy, who was born in Boston and reared and trained in the painters' trade. The premises occupied consist of a shop 25 x 50 feet in dimensions, and this is thoroughly and suitably fitted up for facilitating business. A large stock of all materials necessary for ornamentation and painting, comprising paper hangings in all the newest styles and designs in rich, bright shades and tints of imported and the best American goods, a full assortment of mixed and dry paints, etc., is kept on hand. Painting and decoration in all their branches are extended promptly, and estimates are given for all classes of work. From fifteen to twenty workmen are in steady service, and a special feature is made of glazier work.

F. E. HUMPHREY, Agt., Manufacturer and Dealer in Stoves, Furnaces, Ranges and Tinware, Plumbing and Gas Fitting, Chestnut Street, West Newton.

A. WILLIAMS, Apothecary, Newtonville.

A. LLEN & BARRY, House and Sign Painters, Washington Street, West Newton.

J. OHN FLOOD, Second-hand Furniture, Kitchen Goods, etc., No. 347 Nonantum Block.

H. ENRY H. HUNT, Carpenter, Builder and General Jobber, Shop near Railroad Crossing, West Newton.

E. VICKERS, Choice Family Groceries, Flour, etc., Auburn Street, Auburndale.

V. A. PLUTA, Provisions, Corner of Auburn and Lexington Streets, Auburndale.

CITY OF SOMERVILLE.

APART from the manifest advantages enjoyed by the enterprising and progressive community that forms the subject of this necessarily brief sketch, by reason of its close proximity to the metropolis of New England, of which it now virtually constitutes an integral portion, Somerville possesses many other features of attraction that render it desirable, alike as a place of residence and business.

It is, in fact, one of the most healthful, delightful and flourishing of Boston's many charming suburbs, and presents all the outward indications of being the home of comfort, material, wealth, and solid citizens, many of the leading merchants, manufacturers, bankers and business men of the "Hub" residing within its environs. The community is especially favored, both from a geographical and topographical point of view, and is very pleasantly located, the principal section being considerably elevated above the surrounding country, while a magnificent of Boston, the Bay and other points of interest may be had from the top of Win Prospect Hill and adjacent coigns of vantage. The old town is closely associated stirring scenes and historic incidents of revolutionary days, when what is now known ville was part of Charlestown, and traces of the earthworks and embankments const heights just mentioned by the patriotic army for defensive purposes, after the battle of Bunker Hill and during the siege of Boston, are still pointed out as interesting landmarks.

Somerville became an independent township in 1842, and its history since the period to the present day has been marked by steady and gratifying progress, the town increasing in population, area, industry, commerce and trade until the place assumed all the aspects of a busy and prosperous city of upward of thirty thousand inhabitants, and finally was incorporated with Boston, of which as far as time and space are concerned it had always practically formed a part, the State House on Beacon Hill being less than two miles distant from Somerville's business center. Several lines of railroad converge here, and an excellent horse car system connects the place with the principal squares and streets of Boston, the facilities for travel being exceptionally good.

The sanitary arrangements, too, are of a very superior character; the water service is first class, and the streets are well lighted and excellently kept, while in the important matters pertaining to police and fire service Somerville is unsurpassed by any suburban section of the metropolitan district. In respect of schools, public buildings and institutions devoted to the advancement of knowledge, charity and morals, this town is also fully abreast with the times, some notable educational and philanthropic establishments being located hereabouts, among others Tufts College (Universalist) and the McLean Asylum for the insane, while the churches are numerous, various and beautiful in architecture, nearly all religious denominations having places of worship here. The mercantile and manufacturing interests of Somerville are extensive, varied, and constantly developing, the city containing many substantial business houses and noteworthy stores devoted to every branch of trade, while scattered throughout this section are a number of large shops, factories, foundries, bleacheries, dye works, tanneries, brick yards, planing mills and other manufacturing concerns, the most important productions being brass tubes, print goods, leather, boots and shoes, engines and boilers, spikes, iron, bricks, building stone, glass, clapboards, sash and blinds.

S. K. LIBBY, Auctioneer and Real Estate Agent, Appraiser, and Insurance Broker, Union Square, West Somerville. — A representative and reliable West Somerville business man in his important field of commercial activity is Mr. S. K. Libby, whose extensive interests embrace real estate and insurance brokerage and appraising, also auctioneering and all duties therewith connected. Mr. Libby occupies commodious and well appointed offices on Union Square, where he is prepared to transact promptly and satisfactorily all matters pertaining to his extensive business. Possessing a thorough and comprehensive knowledge of realty values his services are duly appreciated among the capitalists, property holders, et al, from whom he has long received a liberal patronage. Mr. Libby transacts a general brokerage business in city and suburban property, purchasing and selling for patrons, houses, lands, building sites, factories, etc. He also negotiates loans on bond and mortgage and is prepared to place insurable risks in the best companies at the lowest rates commensurate with reliable security, and is local agent for several of the best insurance companies. Private and public sales at auction are given every attention, and his fame in this connection extends over a wide territory. Mr. Libby is a native of Maine, but has resided in Somerville for a number of years. For several years Mr. Libby was a member of the city government, and was elected by his townsmen as president of the common council, was a member of the board of assessors for nine years, most of which time he was chairman of that body and is prominent in the political, financial and social circles of this town.

HOTEL WARREN, Silas D. Carter, Proprietor, Union Square. — A well-conducted and deservedly popular hostelry is that commonly known as the Hotel Warren. Mr. Silas D. Carter, medicines etc. ... Proprietor, located on Union Square. The hotel was first opened ... Mr. Carter assuming the proprietorship two years ... since its inception a large and liberal patronage has been ... is a fine, three story brick, surmounted by a ... front, giving ... on the front door, and the general appointments and arrangements are in accord with the best modern ideas of convenience and comfort combined. There are fifty finely furnished sleeping rooms, bath, parlors dining-room, office, etc. The table is supplied with all seasonable viands, cooked and served in the best manner, and every attention is paid to the comfort of guests. The Hotel Warren is especially adapted for family residence and much of the large patronage it enjoys is drawn from this class of custom. Mr. Carter, the genial and courteous proprietor, is a native of New Brunswick, and as experienced and capable hotel man. By his well directed management he has secured for the hotel a well merited popularity, and won for himself the reputation of a first-class landlord.

DUPONT & COTE, Hardware, Stoves, Ranges and Furnaces, Sanitary Plumbing and Heating Engineers, No. 1 Studio Building, Davis Square, West Somerville. — A representative local establishment in its important branch of commercial activity is that of Messrs. Dupont & Cote, dealers in hardware, stoves, ranges, furnaces, paints, oils, glass, putty, lime, cement, etc., at No. 1 Studio Building. This business was originally established in 1885, under the firm name and style of Folger & Dupont. In the summer of 1897, Mr. Dupont withdrew from the firm and with Mr. L. P. Cote formed the copartnership which has since continued. The premises consist of a first floor and basement, 20 x 75 feet each in dimensions, the first fitted up in an attractive and convenient style and occupied as a general salesroom, while the basement is equipped with all the modern tools and appliances requisite for a first-class plumbing shop. The firm carries a remarkably fine general stock of the staple goods and utilities above enumerated, representing all the best improved makes and several designs in cooking and heating apparatus, shelf and heavy hardware of all kinds, and in short everything to be found at a first-class metropolitan establishment. A corps of skilled and experienced mechanics is employed, and all work incident to sanitary plumbing, heating, etc., is executed in the best manner and at the lowest rates compatible with first-class service. Messrs. J. B. Dupont and L. P. Cote compose the firm. Both are practical and experienced business men, who by their well directed management have reared an enterprise which places them among the leading merchants of this their native town.

WM. E. DRAKE, Restaurant and Confectionery, No 1 Medina Block, West Somerville. — One of the best conducted restaurants to be met with in this section is that of Mr. Wm. E. Drake. The commodious apartment, 20 x 20 feet in dimensions, is fitted up in a style which is a happy combination of modern convenience and attractiveness, the cuisine in the rear is supplied with the best improved culinary apparatus, and these particulars the establishment a general neatness which conduces greatly to the popularity which it justly enjoys as a place of entertainment. The bill of fare includes all seasonable delicacies and meats and lunches can be obtained at all hours, cooked and served in the best manner. An attractive feature of the establishment is the confectionery department. On one side of the apartment, Mr. Drake has fitted up a neat candy store where he carries a carefully selected and complete line of choice foreign and domestic confectionery. He manufactures all kinds of the most delicious ice-cream in every flavor, which is sold at wholesale and retail. Parties, weddings, receptions, etc., are supplied at short notice with both cake and ice-cream. Mr. Drake is a native of the Provinces and a wood carver by trade. He came here eighteen years ago and followed his trade until the early part of the present year, when he embarked in the firm enterprise with which he has since been both popularly and prosperously identified.

HW. RAYMOND, Wholesale and Retail Dealer in Wooden, Glass, Crockery Ware, Hardware, Painters' Supplies, Nos. 34 and 36 Union Square. — This business was founded as far back as 1869, by Geo. Meyers, Esq., who was succeeded in 1878 by the present proprietor, under whose well directed and popular management the old time prosperity and existence of the house have been materially augmented. The large double salesroom, 40 x 80 feet in dimensions, is fitted up with all the modern adjuncts to convenience and attractiveness, and a basement beneath of equal size offers every facility for surplus storage. The stock of shelf and heavy hardware, wooden-ware, glass and crockery, painters' supplies, plaster, lime, hair, cement, etc., is one of the largest, most comprehensive and complete to be found outside of Boston, and specialties are made of Russell & Erwin Mfg. Co.'s builders' hardware, Beymer, Bauman & Co.'s white lead, Harrison Bros. & Co.'s pure colors in oil and Japan, and " Town and Country," ready mixed paints, the best in the market, of all of which famous goods complete lines are carried. The house is a recognized headquarters for the goods above enumerated, and a goodly force of clerks and salesmen are kept busy in supplying the wants of the trade, the patronage being drawn from the best town and county centres. Mr. Raymond is a native of this state and a vigorous young business man of wide experience in and possessing a thorough knowledge of the business in which he is engaged.

www.ingramcontent.com/pod-product-compliance
Lightning Source LLC
Chambersburg PA
CBHW030342270326
41926CB00009B/933

* 9 7 8 3 7 4 1 1 6 6 6 0 0 *